THE POLITICS OF MUSICAL IDENTITY

The essays selected for this volume – three of which are presented for the first time in English translation – reflect the work, in both musical and cultural studies, of a distinguished scholar whose international career spans the Atlantic and beyond. The articles explore how composers, performers and critics shaped individual and collective identities in music from Europe and the United States from the 1860s to the 1950s and focus on how music permits new ways of considering issues of nationality, class, race, and gender.

ASHGATE CONTEMPORARY THINKERS ON CRITICAL MUSICOLOGY

The titles in this series bring together a selection of previously published and some unpublished essays by leading authorities in the field of critical musicology. The essays are chosen from a wide range of publications and so make key works available in a more accessible form. The authors have all made a selection of their own work in one volume with an introduction which discusses the essays chosen and puts them into context. A full bibliography points the reader to other publications which might not be included in the volume for reasons of space. The previously published essays are published using the facsimile method of reproduction to retain their original pagination, so that students and scholars can easily reference the essays in their original form.

Titles published in the series
Taking Popular Music Seriously
Simon Frith

Music, Performance, Meaning
Nicholas Cook

Reading Music
Susan McClary

Sound Judgment
Richard Leppert

Music, Structure, Thought
James Hepokoski

Musical Belongings
Richard Middleton

Sounding Values
Scott Burnham

Musical Style and Social Meaning
Derek B. Scott

Music-in-Action
Tia DeNora

Music Education as Critical Theory and Practice
Lucy Green

The Work of Music Theory
Thomas Christensen

The Politics of Musical Identity

Selected Essays

ANNEGRET FAUSER
University of North Carolina at Chapel Hill, USA

ASHGATE CONTEMPORARY THINKERS
ON CRITICAL MUSICOLOGY

ASHGATE

© Annegret Fauser 2015

All rights reserved. No part of this publication may be reproduced, stored in a retrieval system or transmitted in any form or by any means, electronic, mechanical, photocopying, recording or otherwise without the prior permission of the publisher.

Annegret Fauser has asserted her moral right under the Copyright, Designs and Patents Act, 1988, to be identified as the author of this work.

Published by
Ashgate Publishing Limited
Wey Court East
Union Road
Farnham
Surrey GU9 7PT
England

Ashgate Publishing Company
110 Cherry Street
Suite 3-1
Burlington, VT 05401-3818
USA

www.ashgate.com

ISBN 9781472425782

British Library Cataloguing in Publication Data
A catalogue record for this book is available from the British Library

Library of Congress Control Number: 2014949764

Printed in the United Kingdom by Henry Ling Limited,
at the Dorset Press, Dorchester, DT1 1HD

For Tim: the first twenty years

Contents

Acknowledgements ix

Introduction xi

List of Publications xix

PART ONE MUSIC AND POLITICS IN LATE NINETEENTH-CENTURY FRANCE

1. 'Cette musique sans tradition': Wagner's *Tannhäuser* and its French Critics (2009)   3

2. Visual Pleasures – Musical Signs: Dance at the Paris Opéra (2005)   31

3. Oscarine and Réginette: A Comic Interlude in the French Reception of Wagner (2007)   55

4. Gendering the Nations: The Ideologies of French Discourse on Music (1870–1914) (2001)   71

5. Disruptive Histories: Telling the Story of Modern Music in France (2006)   103

PART TWO MUSICAL IDENTITIES IN THE UNITED STATES IN THE 1930s AND '40s

6. Aaron Copland, Nadia Boulanger, and the Making of an 'American' Composer (2006)   121

7. 'Presenting a Great Truth': William Grant Still's *Afro-American Symphony* (1930) (2011)   153

8. 'Dixie *Carmen*': War, Race, and Identity in Oscar Hammerstein's *Carmen Jones* (1943) (2010)   163

PART THREE   GENDER POLITICS IN MUSIC

  9. Rheinsirenen: Loreley and Other Rhine Maidens (2006)   213

10. Creating Madame Landowska (2006)   237

11. *La Guerre en dentelles*: Women and the *Prix de Rome* in French Cultural Politics (1998)   261

12. Composing as a Catholic: Rereading Lili Boulanger's Vocal Music (2006)   309

13. Lili Boulanger's *La Princesse Maleine*: A Composer and her Heroine as Literary Icons (1997)   317

Index   359

Acknowledgements

The chapters in this volume are taken from the sources listed below. The editor and publisher wish to thank the original publishers and copyright holders for permission to use their material as follows:

'"Cette musique sans tradition": Wagner's *Tannhäuser* and its French Critics' (2009), in Annegret Fauser and Mark Everist (eds), *Music, Theater, and Cultural Transfer: Paris, 1830–1914*. Chicago: University of Chicago Press, pp. 228–55. Copyright © 2009 by the University of Chicago. All rights reserved.

'Visual Pleasures – Musical Signs: Dance at the Paris Opéra' (2005), *South Atlantic Quarterly*, **104**, pp. 99–121. Copyright © 2005 Duke University Press. All rights reserved. Reprinted by permission of the present publisher, Duke University Press.

'Oscarine und Réginette: ein komisches Zwischenspiel in der französischen Wagnerrezeption' (2007), in Michelle Biget-Mainfroy and Rainer Schmusch (eds), *'L'Esprit français' und die Musik Europas: Entstehung, Einfluß und Grenzen einer ästhetischen Doktrin. Festschrift für Herbert Schneider zum 65. Geburtstag*, vol. 40: Studien und Materialien zur Musikwissenschaft, Hildesheim, Zürich, New York: Georg Olms Verlag, pp. 575–90.

'Gendering the Nations: The Ideologies of French Discourse on Music (1870–1914)' (2001), in Michael Murphy and Harry White (eds), *Musical Constructions of Nationalism: Essays on the History and Ideology of European Musical Culture, 1800–1945*, Cork: Cork University Press, pp. 72–103.

'Histoires interrompues: raconter l'histoire de la musique en France' (2006), in Sylvain Caron, Michel Duchesneau and François de Médicis (eds), *Musique et modernité en France 1900–1950*, Montréal: Presses de l'Université de Montréal, pp. 19–50. French translation by Hélène Panneton.

'Aaron Copland, Nadia Boulanger, and the Making of an "American" Composer' (2006), *The Musical Quarterly*, **89**, pp. 524–54.

'"Presenting a Great Truth": William Grant Still's *Afro-American Symphony* (1930)' (2011), in Camilla Bork, Tobias Klein, Burkhard Meischein, Andreas Meyer and Tobias Plebuch, *Ereignis und Exegese – Musikinterpretation und Interpretation der Musik. Festschrift für Hermann Danuser zum 65. Geburtstag*, Schliengen: Edition Argus, pp. 644–53.

'"Dixie *Carmen*": War, Race, and Identity in Oscar Hammerstein's *Carmen Jones* (1943)' (2010), *Journal of the Society for American Music*, **4**, pp. 127–74. Copyright © 2010 The Society for American Music. By permission of Cambridge University Press.

'Rheinsirenen: Loreley and Other Rhine Maidens' (2006), in Linda Austern and Inna Naroditskaya (eds), *Music of the Sirens*, Bloomington: Indiana University Press, pp. 250–72. Courtesy of Indiana University Press. All rights reserved.

'Creating Madame Landowska' (2006), *Women & Music: A Journal of Gender and Culture*, **10**, pp. 1–23. Courtesy of the University of Nebraska Press.

'*La Guerre en dentelles*: Women and the *Prix de Rome* in French Cultural Politics' (1998), *Journal of the American Musicological Society*, **51**, pp. 83–129. Copyright © 1998 the American Musicological Society. All rights reserved.

'Composer en tant que catholique: Une relecture de la musique vocale de Lili Boulanger' (2006), *Intersections: Canadian Journal of Music*, **26**, pp. 114–23. French translation by Marie-Hélène Benoit-Otis.

'Lili Boulanger's *La Princesse Maleine*: A Composer and Her Heroine as Literary Icons' (1997), *Journal of the Royal Musical Association*, **122**, pp. 68–108. Reprinted with permission from the *Journal of the Royal Musical Association*.

Introduction

That identities—musical and otherwise—are political is an epistemological truism. Fashioned and absorbed, imposed and rejected, twisted and streamlined, they are malleable and powerful instruments of negotiating social and artistic life. For musicologists, reflecting on the politics of musical identity thus offers a fascinating way into any subject of study, and also into our scholarship as a whole. Indeed, such reflection stands at the heart of what the present Ashgate series calls "critical musicology." It is also one of the key issues that has shaped my own scholarly career from my training at the Rheinische Friedrich-Wilhelms Universität in Bonn and the Ecole Normale Supérieure in Paris through my academic positions in France (Université de Tours François Rabelais), Germany (Humboldt Universität zu Berlin), England (City University, London), and now the United States (the University of North Carolina at Chapel Hill).

As a feminist musicologist whose work has been molded from its beginnings by such transnational experiences in terms of research and teaching, I engaged from the outset of my career with the intersections of music and identity, and their political ramifications, starting with a short article that I published as a graduate student in 1990. This was about Lili Boulanger's song cycle, *Clairières dans le ciel*, a work imbued with signifiers of French artistic identity, but one that brought other identity markers into play, not least the composer's gender. I have not included this very early publication here, but when I pulled together the present selection of writings from two decades of scholarship, I was struck by the fact that deconstructing musical identities—the approach seen already in this first publication—might well be called one *idée fixe* of my work. It also appears in various forms in my three books—on French orchestral song between 1870 and 1920 (my doctoral dissertation), on the 1889 World's Fair in Paris, and on music in the United States during World War II—as well as in other of my writings omitted from the present volume because they did not suit its purpose.

The essays assembled here engage with these issues through a number of lenses, each political (and politicized) in its own way. The first two parts of this volume contain texts that foreground discussions of national identity, whether for France at the turn of the nineteenth century or for the United States in the 1930s and '40s. The third emphasizes gender politics in music. But things are not quite as clear-cut as this division might suggest. My essay on "Rheinsirenen: Loreley and Other Rhine Maidens" also deals with constructions of national identities; "Gendering the Nations: The Ideologies of French Discourse on Music (1870–1914)" presents a feminist discourse-analysis of musical nationalism; and racial stereotyping becomes an issue discussed in "'Dixie *Carmen*': War, Race, and Identity in Oscar Hammerstein's *Carmen Jones* (1943)." These multiple markers of identity point to the concept's slipperiness, complexities, and multivalence. Indeed, it poses significant epistemological challenges, not least because the use of the term "identity" has grown so commonplace that one might be tempted to dismiss it as having become trivial or empty of meaning through unqualified overuse, as sociologists Rogers Brubaker and Frederick Cooper have pointed out (in "Beyond Identity," *Theory and Society* 29 [2000]: 1–47). Yet as I show in a brief theoretical discussion in "Aaron Copland, Nadia Boulanger, and the Making of an 'American' Composer," deconstructing the politics of musical identity remains a valuable and even essential approach in musical scholarship despite the current proliferation of the term and also its inherent problems.

All the essays in this volume have in common a consistent attempt to capture some of the complexities of musical identity through historical analysis, whether of a single work or event or over some longer span. Where they differ, besides in their topics, is in the range of methodological frameworks through which I have been engaging with the issue, from the study of cultural transfer to the discussion of musical genre. I rarely foreground my methodologies explicitly, though occasionally—as a trained philosopher—I cannot resist the siren song of theoretical discourse. Most of the time, however, the reader will find my methodological approaches flagged through the use of key terms, a reference to an author, or a citation in the footnotes. This is a deliberate strategy. My somewhat understated web of references makes the theoretical touchstones transparent, while it avoids turning theory into a gateway only for the initiated and an obstacle for those who are not.

Five of these thirteen essays focus on a single composition or one of its performances, providing thick description that ranges from genesis to reception: of Wagner's Parisian *Tannhäuser*, the now forgotten operetta *Oscarine* by Victor Roger, Lili Boulanger's unfinished opera, *La Princesse Maleine*, William Grant Still's *Afro-American Symphony*, and *Carmen Jones* by Oscar Hammerstein II. The advantage of so in-depth an engagement lies in the opportunity to capture the richness and complexities of music in its cultural, social, and political contexts, be those contexts of French musical culture at a point of crisis (Wagner and Roger), of the construction of gender in composition and reception related to the issue of (auto)biography and music (Boulanger), or of African American identities in a segregated society, calling for an engagement with race as a means of entrance into broader issues of cultural and artistic identities (Still and Hammerstein). But if the case-study approach also characterizes my engagement with such individuals as Wanda Landowska and her early career, other essays focus on broader cultural phenomena: whether the politics of music and national identities in the aftermath of the Franco-Prussian War of 1870 or questions of genre in relation to Parisian cultural practice by way of ballets in nineteenth-century *grand opéra*. The politics of identity is often played out in conversation with an Other, imaginary or real. Many of these texts deal with cultural Others: within U.S. society, for example, in the case of *Carmen Jones*, or on one or other side of the Rhine when writing about French Wagnerism. Sometimes, however, these conversations involve individuals who are themselves immersed in a verbal or even musical dialogue about artistic and other identities, as is the case with Nadia Boulanger and her student, Aaron Copland.

Music and Politics in Late Nineteenth-Century France

The first part of this collection opens with a close reading of the 1861 reception in Paris of Wagner's *Tannhäuser*. When I started work on this essay, I was in the thick of reception- and transfer-studies, but I was also engaging with the history of ethnomusicology as I worked on non-Western music at the 1889 Exposition Universelle. Out of this theoretical constellation developed what would become the key question of this text: what if we changed perspective and took the Parisian critics seriously instead of dismissing them as prejudiced philistines? So much of the literature on the *Tannhäuser* scandal—especially in Wagner scholarship—had created a dichotomy between the few enlightened supporters of the progressive composer and the majority of hidebound Frenchmen excessively devoted to grand opéra and its ballets. My immersion into the contemporary discourse, by contrast, yielded new insight into Parisian perspectives on music and its role in the theater, and also offered fascinating glimpses on the structure of critical debate in a culture that prized public engagement with the arts. Indeed, no other environment at that time provided such a rich forum for exchange as Paris, given the role that the press played in nineteenth-century France, a point currently being reinforced by significant new research initiatives. Thus my essay on the Parisian *Tannhäuser* is closely aligned with the interests of the network of scholars working on "Francophone Music Criticism, 1789–1914" that grew out of a project funded by the U.K. Arts and Humanities Research Council and directed by Katharine Ellis and Mark Everist (see http://music.sas.ac.uk/fmc).

Shifting epistemological perspectives also inspired my article, "Visual Pleasures—Musical Signs: Dance at the Paris Opéra". This text starts with the habitual Wagnerian prejudices against ballet—echoes of the 1861 *Tannhäuser* again—and continues reflecting on ballet's role as a dramatic element in opera, on the one hand, and its use as a window on nineteenth-century musical meaning for modern scholarship, on the other. How vital dance and mime were to the plot of French opera is shown through three examples: Daniel-François-Esprit Auber's *La Muette de Portici* (1828), Hector Berlioz's *Les Troyens* (1863), and Jules Massenet's *Thaïs* (1894). I have included this article not only for its scholarly reflection on nineteenth-century opera (the segment on *Thaïs* in particular offers new insight in understanding dance in late nineteenth-century France), but also because it is itself a document of scholarly change: my impassioned conclusion that "by acknowledging and exploring the nexus of image, gesture, and music in nineteenth-century French spectacle, we might appreciate with greater sophistication not only a historical phenomenon, but also the roots of our own cultural practice" would today be considered a commonplace, well supported by a "Music and Dance" study group of the American Musicological Society. However, it was not so commonly heard when I wrote it in 2004.

If my text on the Parisian *Tannhäuser* engages with French responses to Wagner and his music during his life time, the essay on Roger's operetta *Oscarine* (which is presented here in a new English translation) looks at a range of issues faced by French musicians and audiences when Wagnerism took off after the composer's death. By the late 1880s, Wagnerian compositional techniques had started to become a widespread and much debated issue, especially in the context of opera. Yet because of its pervasiveness, Wagnerism also raised anxieties of influence to new levels, not only where national musical identities were concerned but also with respect to the location of cultural authority and its gendering. What is fascinating when juxtaposing the 1861 *Tannhäuser* scandal and the creation (and reception) of *Oscarine* over a quarter of a century later, in 1888, is the hardening of discursive tropes into stereotypes that could be deployed to critique autochthonous cultural practice whether or not it was directly influenced by Wagner, his music, or his theories. That the protagonist of

Oscarine is a composing spinster thus serves a dual function: not only can it mark Wagnerian music as "sterile" (a trope introduced by François-Joseph Fétis already in 1852) but it can also tarnish composing women with the same brush.

How important gender was in the configuration of national musical identity in France in the wake of the Franco-Prussian War of 1870 forms the topic of "Gendering the Nations: The Ideologies of French Discourse on Music (1870–1914)." In a postwar world that was configured increasingly along the lines of gender binaries, masculinity had become invested with renewed cultural capital, especially in an artistic field such as music that was defined by its competitive relationship with the enemy in that war. If France was to maintain its status as the capital of world culture, it needed to assert the superior and hence masculine quality of its national artistic output. Discursive strategies ranged widely in this ideological enterprise, from calls for a masculinizing of *opéra comique* and for a healthier musical education of the nation's citizens to a reinterpretation along gendered lines both of French folk music and of the nation's music history. They all shared, however, their blatant value judgments when it came to gendering art: that which was considered feminine carried the stigma of triviality and superficiality.

Putting this essay side by side with the English translation of "Histoires interrompues: raconter l'histoire de la musique en France" (as "Disruptive Histories: Telling the Story of Modern Music in France") also unveils the longevity of these kinds of discursive strategies all the way to recent musicological scholarship: while the sonic objects and aesthetic parameters shift over time, the need for historiographical valorization remains constant. Reflecting on some epistemological principles as they pertain to musical historiography, I question one particularly obstinate tenet of musical modernism—the ideology of rupture—and explore what is at stake in our engagement with French musical modernism.

Musical Identities in the United States in the 1930s and '40s

The three essays grouped in this part share not only their geographical ties to the United States but also some central questions about national identity and modernism as they pertain to the country where I now live and work. "Aaron Copland, Nadia Boulanger, and the Making of an 'American' Composer" takes us into the 1920s and addresses the issue of national identity from a transatlantic perspective. For Copland, it was the encounter with French stereotypes about Americans and their culture that contributed to his construction of musical Americanism. The positive French response to jazz—a genre far more contested and racialized in the segregated United States—served as a musical catalyst in this process. Furthermore, the theoretical configuration of musical identity in the circle around Nadia Boulanger gave the American composer a toolkit through which to configure the multiplicity of U.S. aesthetic and stylistic positions into a coherent view of musical Americanism as defined by individuality.

Just as jazz played a role in Copland's construction of American musical identity in the 1920s, so did the blues in the case of William Grant Still's engagement with the symphony in terms of both racial and national identities in music. In his *Afro-American Symphony* of 1930–31, the composer sought to rejuvenate and assimilate the European genre of the symphony into, and through, African American music. He identified motivic development as a compositional technique characterizing both the blues and the symphony. In blending the two genres, Still aimed not only at "elevating" the blues into the concert hall—drawing on the familiar rhetoric of uplift—but also at Americanizing the symphony through its very musical structure.

How to Americanize European art was one of the numerous issues that Oscar Hammerstein II, and his collaborators tried to work out in their adaptation of Georges Bizet's opera *Carmen* as the musical play *Carmen Jones*, premiered at the Broadway Theatre, New York, on 2 December 1943. Set in the American South and then Chicago, the work engaged with race in U.S. culture and society both on-stage and off at a time when World War II brought new challenges to the politics of musical identity. Based on numerous documents that I uncovered in libraries and archives, I offer a close reading of the work's production and its reception, focusing on race and class, gender and nationalism, as well as the role of cultural hierarchies in a democratic and yet deeply segregated society at war.

Gender Politics in Music

As the essays discussed so far also reveal, gender politics has played itself out in musical production, reception, and historiography, whether in nineteenth-century France or twentieth-century America. But gender crosses from cultural identity politics into actual body politics where women musicians are concerned. Deeply interrelated, the ensounding of gender in music and the policing of gender in cultural, social, and political life defined and limited the worlds of musical women throughout history. My own slice of research has focused predominantly on a number of Parisian women, from the Boulanger sisters to Wanda Landowska. However, my third part starts out with a mythological figure: Loreley, the siren whose dangerous music could lure sailors into a watery grave. In "Rheinsirenen: Loreley and Other Rhine Maidens," I follow the fictional seductress through a number of incarnations in the nineteenth and twentieth centuries in order to ask about gendered representations of women, music, and sexuality in music, on the stage, and in film. What I found particularly fascinating was the challenge that Loreley posed to composers of Western classical music: how to distinguish between the two voices of Loreley, her everyday voice and her siren song.

The remaining four essays in this part take us to Paris into the company of historical women and their musical lives around 1900. The article on Wanda Landowska's early career as a harpsichordist draws on numerous newly uncovered manuscript and printed sources to show how the Polish artist forged a brilliant career in the French capital. Landowska, with the assistance of her husband Henri Lew and her manager Gabriel Astruc, carefully crafted an image that would enable her to become a star not only in Paris but also across Europe (and beyond). The ingredients for this recipe were assembled through trial and error. Two of the key elements were the development of Landowska's signature performance style and the fashioning of a musical persona modeled on the operatic divas that Parisian audiences associated with stardom on the stage. What is fascinating is her appropriation of Johann Sebastian Bach as the French-at-heart, aristocratic patron saint of the harpsichord, as she wrested the composer not only from the musical authority of her rival, Blanche Selva, but also from that of numerous male concert pianists.

How important the shaping of an appropriate public persona could be for a musical career in *fin de siècle* France is one of the topics that pervade "*La Guerre en dentelles*: Women and the *Prix de Rome* in French Cultural Politics." Four women—Juliette Toutain, Hélène Fleury, Nadia Boulanger, and Lili Boulanger—tried their hand at winning the coveted Prix de Rome between 1903, the first year a women was admitted to the prestigious competition, and 1913, when Lili Boulanger's *Faust et Hélène* was awarded first prize. Their closely intertwined stories speak not only about music and gender but also about cultural identity politics in France. Archival research often is in itself a detective story, but in this case it was a veritable hunt for clues in dossiers and newspapers, with numerous false trails laid down by bureaucratic administrators to cover up their misdeeds and intrigues. I will never forget the afternoon when I burst into tears in the Archives Nationales (which netted me some strange looks) over a set of letters that uncovered the collusion of Juliette Toutain's father in her exclusion from the competition in 1903. Her betrayal had become mine. Despite the necessary and deliberate distance of scholarly interpretation and reflection as I was writing the article, an attentive reader might still detect some of my original dismay.

The last two texts focus on Lili Boulanger and her music. "Composing as a Catholic: Rereading Lili Boulanger's Vocal Music" centers on the role that Catholicism played in her life and works. In contrasts to earlier texts I had written on Boulanger that avoided, and even outright rejected, the incense with which numerous scholars had enveloped the composer, this short article reflects on Catholicism in the composer's artistic biography, addressing her faith as a marker of cultural as well as religious identity in the context of modern Paris.

Just as my first German scholarly publication dealt with a work by Lili Boulanger, *Clairières dans le ciel*, so did my first English-language one as well. *La Princesse Maleine*, Boulanger's lost (and unfinished) opera based on Maurice Maeterlinck's iconic symbolist play, has intrigued scholars ever since it was known that she had worked on it. Maleine, the heroine of the play, was a Mélisande-like *femme fragile* who bore striking similarity to the image of Lili Boulanger as she was portrayed in the French media at the time. The temptation to collapse the composer and her musical heroine has seduced more than one scholar into rather fanciful prose which did the composer more harm than good. What I set out to do in this article was to sort out these issues by engaging with Boulanger's own play on identity, her activities as a composer, the imposed identities on her and her work, and the issue of a "lost work" in as complex a context as this. It became a study which explored the entanglements of biography in music in a case where a composer, her entourage, her immediate biographers, and subsequent scholars succumbed to literary tropes to shape their own interpretation of an exceptional woman's artistic achievements. My point was not so much to deplore these tropes—deplorable though they might be—as to submit them to an analysis as rigorous as one might apply to any other historical documents given my belief that critical and scholarly reflection is itself, inevitably, a political act.

***

The musical identities addressed in this volume are wide ranging: whether based on nationalism, religion, race, class, or gender. Yet besides engaging with the politics of identity in Western music history in the nineteenth and twentieth centuries, these texts also mirror my own scholarly identities. While all of the present essays—even those originally published in

French and German—stem from my years working in Anglophone worlds, they reflect an intellectual framework the foundation of which was laid during my studies and early career in Continental Europe. As anyone who has moved across cultures can testify, scholarship, too, is an activity that is affected by translation in the cultural sense as well as the literal one. To draw on Edward Said's powerful metaphor developed in his work on Joseph Conrad, an "accent" is more than a linguistic signifier: it affects frameworks of reference, structures of argument, and engagement with methodologies. An article composed in English differs significantly from one written in German or French, and in terms not just of language but also of orientation. Moving into new discourse networks meant that I had to learn how to write "English scholarship" of both the British and the American kinds. It involved a conscious process of acculturation, and were I to analyze things more closely, I might be tempted to draw on Homi K. Bhabha's concepts of mimicry and hybridity in order to theorize my own subject position. But writing with an accent can also be liberating because it frees one's words, sentence construction, argument formation, and intellectual frameworks from the unquestioned structures instilled from childhood, and instead gives room for playing with difference. So despite my conscious adoption of the models of Anglo-American scholarship, the texts in this volume retain their Franco-German accent, as, for example, in my consistent interest in the concept and key issues of cultural transfer as formulated in a number of seminal texts by Michel Espagne and Michael Werner, whose work I encountered for the first time as a graduate student in Paris in the 1980s (see, for example, the theoretical introduction to their edited collection *Transferts: Les Relations interculturelles dans l'espace franco-allemand (XVIIIe et XIXe siècle)* [Paris: Editions Recherche sur les Civilisations, 1988], 11–34).

My move into Anglo-American scholarship happened for biographical reasons: I married a British scholar and moved to London. This transition could have been hard for a writer who until then had only published in German and French, but I was welcomed by an unstintingly generous scholarly community who shared their time, editorial expertise, and intellectual sophistication with me while I developed my first forays into a new medium. I owe them a debt of gratitude that cannot be repaid. Two among them played a particularly central role. My then new husband, Tim Carter, managed the remarkable feat of safeguarding my voice as an author while lending his hand as the exquisite editor and writer he is. He still reads, with unconditional generosity, everything I publish. And without the significant input of Katharine Ellis—scholar extraordinaire and friend—many a text would have been far less elegant in prose and poorer in substance. Thank you for this precious gift. Over the years, the support of friends and colleagues on both sides of the Atlantic has moved in ever-increasing circles: many are mentioned in the first foot- or endnotes in these essays. Names missing from these notes, however, are those vital collaborators whose copy-editing skills benefit all authors, and not just those like me writing in a second or third language. I do not know the names of all my copy-editors—often editors served as intermediaries—but I want to take the opportunity here to thank especially Catherine Gjerdingen, Louise Goldberg, Barbara Norton, and Ian Rumbold for their wonderfully elegant work.

If my own identities are mirrored in these essays, then so is critical musicology as a field and my interactions with it. While the essays in the volume are organized thematically, they also reflect shifting emphases and new questions as they developed over the past two decades, and each should be read with its original date of publication in mind. What might have seemed new in the 1990s became more familiar, and even commonplace, a decade later. This has played itself out in particular with respect to the so-called "new musicology," of which I saw myself a part—and still do—but also in terms of, say, the developing rapprochement of musicology and ethnomusicology on the one hand, and broader cultural studies on the other, both of which might now prompt me to think about my topics in different ways. None of this is to recant what I have previously written over the past two decades. Rather, it is to point out that the texts assembled in this volume are intimately intertwined with broader intellectual shifts and developments both in my own work and in the discipline at large. In their reprinted form, organized in thematic parts rather than chronologically, their own identities now keep shifting between synchronic discourse and diachronic process in ways not dissimilar to the historical and other phenomena they seek to document and analyze. As a historian, I have always been fascinated by such transfers and transformations; as an author, I now see them at work in other, intriguing ways.

Annegret Fauser
Chapel Hill
4 July 2014

List of Publications

Books, Journal Issues, and Editions

Der Orchestergesang in Frankreich zwischen 1879 und 1920. Vol. 2: *Freiburger Beiträge zur Musikwissenschaft*. Laaber: Laaber-Verlag, 1994.
Von Wagner zum Wagnérisme: Musik-Literatur-Kunst-Politik. Edited by Annegret Fauser and Manuela Schwartz. Vol. 12: *Transfer: Die deutsch-französische Kulturbibliothek*. Leipzig: Leipziger Universitäts-Verlag, 1999.
Dossier de presse parisienne: Jules Massenet, "Esclarmonde" (1889). Edited by Annegret Fauser. Heilbronn: Edition Lucie Galland, 2001.
Musical Encounters at the 1889 Paris World's Fair. Rochester: University of Rochester Press, 2005.
"Music & Identity." *The Musical Quarterly* 89 (2006). Special Issue edited by Annegret Fauser and Tamara Levitz.
Music, Theater, and Cultural Transfer: Paris, 1830–1914. Edited by Annegret Fauser and Mark Everist. Chicago: University of Chicago Press, 2009.
Dossier de presse: The Parisian Tannhäuser (1861). Edited by Annegret Fauser, with the assistance of William Gibbons. In *Francophone Music Criticism 1789–1914*, School of Advanced Studies, London, 2009. <http://music.sas.ac.uk/fmc>
Sounds of War: Music in the United States during World War II. New York and Oxford: Oxford University Press, 2013.

Journal Articles and Book Chapters

"Die Musik hinter der Legende. Lili Boulangers Liederzyklus *Clairières dans le Ciel*." *Neue Zeitschrift für Musik* 151/11 (1990): 9–14.
"Frankreich, Paris und die Provinz." *Neue Zeitschrift für Musik* 152/1 (1991): 32–36.
"Die Sehnsucht nach dem Mittelalter. Ernest Chausson und Richard Wagner." In *Les Symbolistes et Richard Wagner—Die Symbolisten und Richard Wagner*. Edited by Wolfgang Storch, 115–20. Berlin: Edition Hentrich, 1991.
"La mélodie avec accompagnement d'orchestre en France." In *150 Ans de Musique Française 1789–1939*. Edited by François Lesure and Benoît Duteurtre, 161–71. Lyon: Actes Sud, 1991.
"*Esclarmonde*. Un opéra wagnérien?" *L'Avant–Scène Opéra* 148 (September–October 1992): 68–73.
"Femme fragile: Zu Lili Boulangers Opernfragment *La Princesse Maleine*." In *Vom Schweigen befreit (3. Internationales Komponistinnen-Festival Kassel): Lili Boulanger, 1893–1918*. Edited by Roswitha Aulenkamp-Moeller and Christel Nies, 72–76. Kassel: Internationales Forum "Vom Schweigen befreit", 1993.

"L'art de l'allusion musicale." *L'Avant-Scène Opéra* 161 (September–October 1994): 126–29.

"Andromède: 'non pas une cantate de concours, mais une œuvre d'art'?" In *Guillaume Lekeu & son temps: Actes du colloque de l'Université de Liège*. Edited by Philippe Vendrix, 85–102. Liège: Société Liégeoise de Musicologie, 1995.

"Lili Boulanger's *La Princesse Maleine*: A Composer and Her Heroine as Literary Icons." *Journal of the Royal Musical Association* 122 (1997): 68–108.

"*La Guerre en dentelles*: Women and the *Prix de Rome* in French Cultural Politics." *Journal of the American Musicological Society* 51 (1998): 83–129. Anthologized as "Fighting in Frills: Women and the *Prix de Rome* in French Cultural Politics." In *Women's Voices Across Musical Worlds*. Edited by Jane Bernstein, 60–86. Boston: Northeastern University Press, 2003.

"Zwischen Professionalismus und Salon: Französische Musikerinnen des *Fin de siècle*." In *Professionalismus in der Musik*. Edited by Christian Kaden and Volker Kalisch, 261–74. Essen: Blaue Eule, 1998.

With Tobias Plebuch. "Gender Studies: Ein Streitgespräch." In *Gender Studies & Musik*. Edited by Stefan Fragner, Jan Hemming and Beate Kutschke, 19–40. Regensburg: ConBrio Verlagsgesellschaft, 1998.

"'L'orchestre dans les sons brave l'honnêteté...': Le rôle de l'élément érotique dans l'œuvre de Massenet." In *Massenet en son temps*. Edited by Patrick Gillis and Gérard Condé, 156–79. St. Etienne: Association du Festival Massenet, 1999.

"Musik als 'Lesehilfe': Zur Rolle der Allusion in den Opern von Jules Massenet." In *Musik als Text: Bericht über den Internationalen Kongreß der Gesellschaft für Musikforschung Freiburg im Breisgau 1993*. Edited by Hermann Danuser and Tobias Plebuch, 462–64. Kassel: Bärenreiter-Verlag, 1999.

"Response: Directions in Musicology." In *Musicology and its Sister Disciplines*. Edited by David Greer, 205–9. Oxford: Oxford University Press, 2000.

"The Songs." In *The Cambridge Companion to Berlioz*. Edited by Peter Bloom, 109–24. Cambridge: Cambridge University Press, 2000.

"'...den muss aus Liebe Schönheit töten': Klang—Körper—Frau." In *Die Worte vergrößern: Bericht über das zweite Internationale Symposium Othmar Schoeck, Luzern, 13. und 14. August 1999*. Edited by Beat A. Föllmi, 51–73. Vol. 3: *Schriftenreihe der Othmar-Schoeck-Gesellschaft*. Zürich: Othmar-Schoeck-Gesellschaft, 2000.

"Alterity, Nation and Identity: Some Musicological Paradoxes." *Context: A Journal of Music Research* 21 (Spring 2001): 1–18.

"Phantasmagorie im deutschen Wald? Zur *Freischütz*-Rezeption in London und Paris 1824." In *Deutsche Meister—Böse Geister? Nationale Selbstfindung in der Musik*. Edited by Hermann Danuser and Herfried Münkler, 245–73. Schliengen: Edition Argus, 2001.

"Gendering the Nations: The Ideologies of French Discourse on Music (1870–1914)." In *Musical Constructions of Nationalism: Essays on the History and Ideology of European Musical Culture, 1800–1945*. Edited by Michael Murphy and Harry White, 72–103. Cork: Cork University Press, 2001.

"World Fair—World Music: Musical Politics in 1889 Paris." In *Nineteenth-Century Music Studies*. Edited by Jim Samson and Bennett Zon, 179–225. London & Aldershot: Ashgate, 2002.

"Die Welt als Stadt: Weltausstellungen in Paris als Spiegel urbanen Musiklebens." In *Musik und Urbanität*. Edited by Christian Kaden and Volker Kalisch, 139–48. Essen: Blaue Eule, 2002.

"De arqueología musical. La música barroca y la Exposición Universal de 1889." Translated by Luis Gago. In *Concierto barroco. Estudios sobre música, dramaturgia e historia cultural*. Edited by Juan José Carreras and Miguel Ángel Marín, 289–307. Logroño: Universidad de La Rioja, 2004.

"Visual Pleasures—Musical Signs: Dance at the Paris Opéra." *South Atlantic Quarterly*, 104 (2005): 99–121.

"Creating Madame Landowska," *Women & Music: A Journal of Gender and Culture* 10 (2006): 1–23.

"Composer en tant que catholique: Une relecture de la musique vocale de Lili Boulanger." Translated by Marie-Hélène Benoit-Otis. *Intersections: Canadian Journal of Music* 26/1 (2006): 114–23.

"Histoires interrompues: raconter l'histoire de la musique en France." Translated by Hélène Panneton. In *Musique et modernité en France 1900-1950*. Edited by Sylvain Caron, Michel Duchesneau, and François de Médicis, 19–50. Montréal: Presses de l'Université de Montréal, 2006.

"Rheinsirenen: Loreley and Other Rhine Maidens." In *Music of the Sirens*. Edited by Linda Austern and Inna Naroditskaya, 250–72. Bloomington: Indiana University Press, 2006.

"Archéologue malgré lui: Vincent d'Indy et les usages de l'histoire." In *Vincent d'Indy et son temps*. Edited by Manuela Schwartz, 123–33. Liège: Mardaga, 2006.

"Aaron Copland, Nadia Boulanger, and the Making of an 'American' Composer." *The Musical Quarterly* 89 (2006) 524–55. Special Issue on "Music & Identity." Edited by Annegret Fauser and Tamara Levitz.

"Comment devenir compositeur: Les stratégies de Lili Boulanger et ses contemporaines." In *Nadia Boulanger et Lili Boulanger. Témoignages et études*. Edited by Alexandra Laederich, 273–88. Lyon: Editions Symétrie, 2007.

"Oscarine und Reginette: ein komisches Zwischenspiel in der französischen Wagnerrezeption." In *"L'Esprit français" und die Musik Europas: Entstehung, Einfluß und Grenzen einer ästhetischen Doktrin. Festschrift für Herbert Schneider zum 65. Geburtstag*. Edited by Michelle Biget-Mainfroy and Rainer Schmusch, 575–90. Vol. 40: *Studien und Materialien zur Musikwissenschaft*. Hildesheim: Georg Olms Verlag, 2007.

"Wagnerism: Responses to Wagner in Music and the Arts." In *The Cambridge Companion to Wagner*. Edited by Thomas S. Grey, 221–34. Cambridge: Cambridge University Press, 2008.

"New Media, Source-Bonding, and Alienation: Listening at the 1889 *Exposition Universelle*." In *French Music, Culture, and National Identity, 1870–1939*. Edited by Barbara Kelly, 40–57. Rochester: University of Rochester Press, 2008.

"Encuentros con lo desconocido: música exótica en las Exposiciones Universales." Translated by Luis Gago. In *Mirada a Oriente*. Edited by Luis Gago, 43–63. Madrid: OCNE, 2008.

"'Cette musique sans tradition': Wagner's *Tannhäuser* and its French Critics." In *Music, Theater, and Cultural Transfer: Paris, 1830-1914*. Edited by Annegret Fauser and Mark Everist, 228–55. Chicago: University of Chicago Press, 2009.

"Debacle at the Paris Opéra: *Tannhäuser* and the French Critics, 1861." In *Wagner and His World*. Edited by Thomas S. Grey, 231–34. Princeton: Princeton University Press, 2009.

"'Hymns of the Future': Reading Félicien David's *Christophe Colomb* as a Saint-Simonian Symphony." *Journal of Musicological Research* 28 (2009): 1–29.

"'Dixie *Carmen*': War, Race, and Identity in Oscar Hammerstein's *Carmen Jones* (1943)." *Journal of the Society for American Music* 4 (2010): 127–74.

"*Carmen in Khaki*: Europäische Oper in den Vereinigten Staaten während des Zweiten Weltkrieges." In *Oper im Wandel der Gesellschaft. Kulturtransfers und Netzwerke des Musiktheaters im modernen Europa*. Edited by Sven Oliver Müller, Philipp Ther, Jutta Toelle, and Gesa zur Nieden, 303–29. Vienna: Oldenbourg and Böhlau, 2010.

"'Presenting a Great Truth': William Grant Still's *Afro-American Symphony* (1930)." In *Ereignis und Exegese. Musikalische Interpretation – Interpretation der Musik. Festschrift für Hermann Danuser zum 65. Geburtstag*. Edited by Camilla Bork, Tobias Robert Klein, Burkhard Meischein, Andreas Meyer, and Tobias Plebuch, 644–53. Schliengen: Edition Argus, 2011.

"Cultural Musicology: New Perspectives on World War II," *Zeithistorische Forschungen/ Studies in Contemporary History* 8 (2011): 282–86. See also on-line edition on http://www.zeithistorische-forschungen.de/16126041-Fauser-2-2011

"Berlioz' Divenmord." In *Diva: Die Inszenierung der übermenschlichen Frau. Interdisziplinäre Untersuchungen zu einem kulturellen Phänomen des 19. und 20. Jahrhunderts*. Edited by Rebecca Grotjahn, Dörte Schmidt, and Thomas Seedorf, 138–46. Schliengen: Edition Argus, 2011.

"What's in a Song? Camille Saint-Saëns's *Mélodies*." In *Saint-Saëns and his World*. Edited by Jann Pasler, 210–31. Princeton: Princeton University Press, 2012.

"Wording Notes: Musical Marginalia in the Guise of an Afterword." In *Words and Notes in the Long Nineteenth Century*. Edited by Phyllis Weliver and Katharine Ellis, 223–27. Woodbridge, U.K.: Boydell and Brewer, 2013.

"Music for the Allies: Representations of Nationhood during World War II." In *Crosscurrents: American and European Music in Interaction, 1900–2000*. Edited by Felix Meyer, Carol J. Oja, Wolfgang Rathert, and Anne C. Shreffler, 247–58. Woodbridge, U.K.: Boydell and Brewer, 2014.

"The Scholar behind the Medal: Edward J. Dent (1876–1957) and the Politics of Music History." *Journal of the Royal Musical Association* 139 (2014): 235–60.

Short texts, editorials, reviews, dictionary articles, and program notes are not included in this list.

Part One

Music and Politics in Late Nineteenth-Century France

CHAPTER 1

Cette musique sans tradition

WAGNER'S *TANNHÄUSER* AND ITS FRENCH CRITICS

> Strangely enough, Paris has become the only city, for which I hold a certain interest of curious sympathy . . . and even today, I prefer it to all other places in the world . . . I could bring myself, as a cultural-historical study, to go to a new opera by Meyerbeer or Gounod in a Parisian theater, for whose circumstances, abilities, and audience it is calculated; in Berlin, Vienna and Munich I would find this impossible.
>
> RICHARD WAGNER, LETTER
> TO KING LUDWIG II OF BAVARIA, 18 JULY 1867

"If God would only bestow such a flop upon me!" According to Richard Wagner, these words were uttered by Charles Gounod soon after the scandalous fiasco of the Parisian premiere of *Tannhäuser* in March 1861 (see fig. 10.1).[1] In February, a

---

I am grateful to M. Elizabeth C. Bartlet, Mark Evan Bonds, and Tim Carter for their helpful and insightful comments on earlier versions of this essay, and to my research assistant, Alicia C. Levin, for her indefatigable help in locating and providing copies of contemporary reviews in French newspapers and periodicals. The epigraph is from *König Ludwig II. und Richard Wagner: Briefwechsel,* ed. Otto Strobel (Karlsruhe: G. Braun, 1936), letter no. 337, 2:185–86, 189: Sonderbarer Weise ist dieses Paris zu der einzigen Stadt geworden, für welche ich eine gewisses Interesse neugieriger Teilnahme hege . . . und noch heute ziehe ich es allen Orten der Welt vor. . . . Ich könnte mich überwinden, eine neue Meyerbeer'sche oder Gounod'sche Oper in einem der Pariser Theater, für dessen Verhältnisse, Leistungen und Publikum sie berechnet ist, als culturhistorische Studie noch mit durchzumachen; in Berlin, Wien und München wäre mir diess durchaus unmöglich. I am grateful to Peter Jost for locating this letter and sharing a copy with me.

1. "Mir wurde von [Gounod] berichtet, daß er in der Gesellschaft überall mit Enthusiasmus für

Tannhäuser *and Its French Critics*

FIGURE 10.1. "Exposition des Baux-Arts appliqués à l'industrie." Caricature by Cham [Amédée de Noé]. The caption reads: "Sir, this is a musical bed: nothing but *Tannhäuser*; one sleeps perfectly in it." *L'illustration*, 21 November 1863. Courtesy of Duke University Library.

month before that fateful event at the Opéra, the chronicler of the Belgian periodical *Le guide musical* wished for a dispute similar to the scandal surrounding the 1830 premiere of Victor Hugo's play *Hernani*, if only to shake the Parisians out of their current complacency and indifference toward the arts. "At least," he wrote, "it would be life."[2] And the event was lively indeed. Few incidents in music history created such waves—politically, culturally, aesthetically, and biographically—as the three performances of Wagner's *Tannhäuser* at the Académie Impériale de la Musique in Paris on 13, 18, and 24 March 1861. Within a couple of days, Wagner's unsuccessful revi-

---

mich eingetreten sei; er solle ausgerufen haben: 'Que Dieu me donne une pareille chûte!'" Richard Wagner, *Mein Leben: 1813–1868*, ed. Martin Gregor-Dellin (Munich: List Verlag, 1994), 653–54.

2. "Tout ce bruit autour du *Tannhaüser* [sic] ne doit point déplaire aux personnes qui s'affligent de l'indifférence qui règne à Paris en matière d'art et de littérature. Plût au ciel, qu'à l'occasion du nouvel opéra de Wagner, on vit se renouveler les luttes des Gluckistes et des Piccinistes, ou les querelles plus récentes des classiques et des romantiques! Au moins ce serait de la vie. Est-ce vivre que nous faisons?" "France," *Le guide musical*, 14 February 1861. The anonymous correspondent for *L'indépendance belge* (17 March 1861) used the same analogy: "C'est le champ de bataille des classiques et des romantiques transporté du Théâtre-Français à l'Opéra." In *Le Figaro*'s "Petite chronique des théâtres" (28 March 1861), we read: "Depuis les orages soulevés par *Hernani* . . . jamais, dans une salle de spectacle parisienne, pareil charivari ne s'était produit."

sions of his opera for Paris became the subject of legend, and they have remained so ever since.

The plot of this tale is all too familiar to music lovers past and present: In the standard telling of the story, Wagner, the greatest German composer since Beethoven, came to Paris to have his *Tannhäuser* performed on the stage of the Opéra, then the most important music theater in Europe. Unfortunately, the administration of the house asked for revisions, in particular the addition of a ballet in act 2, in order to accommodate the taste of its spoiled audience. Aristocrats habitually attended the opera after dinner in time to see their favorite ballerinas perform onstage before the subsequent, more private entertainment in bed. Wagner, however, steadfastly refused to compromise his artistic integrity on the altar of convention. Nevertheless, as a concession to Parisian taste, he used the presence of a well-trained corps de ballet to revise the Venusberg scene in act 1, significantly enlarging the scope of the bacchanal. Alas: Parisian prejudice prevailed when the members of the Jockey Club were prevented by Wagner's artistic vision in act 2 from ogling their favorite ballerinas. They took their revenge, whistling and shouting throughout the reminder of the opera, drowning out Wagner's music with their racket. This scandalous behavior only escalated during the next two performances. A cruel cabal in the French press further encouraged the opera's rejection by Parisian audiences, and so, after the third evening of the battle, Wagner capitulated in the face of overwhelming hostility. In an open letter to Alphonse Royer, the director of the Opéra, he wrote:

> The opposition which has manifested itself against *Tannhäuser* proves to me how right your observations were, at the beginning of this undertaking, about the absence of a ballet and of other conventions of the stage to which the regular subscribers of the Opéra are accustomed. I regret that the nature of my work has prevented me from conforming to these requirements. Now that the vigor of the opposition against it does not even allow those in the audience who want to hear it to give it the attention necessary for its appreciation, I have no other honorable recourse than to withdraw it.[3]

A few weeks after the withdrawal of his *Tannhäuser* from the stage of the Opéra, Wagner left Paris in disgust, never to return to the French capital again. Soon, with

---

3. "L'opposition qui s'est manifestée contre le *Tannhäuser* me prouve combien vous aviez raison quand, au début de cette affaire, vous me faisiez des observations sur l'absence du ballet et des autres conventions scéniques auxquelles les abonnés de l'Opéra sont habitués. Je regrette que la nature de mon ouvrage m'ait empêché de le conformer à ces exigences. Maintenant que la vivacité de l'opposition qui lui est faite ne permet même pas à ceux des spectateurs qui voudraient l'entendre d'y donner l'attention nécessaire pour l'apprécier, je n'ai d'autre ressource honorable que de le retirer." "Nouvelles diverses," *Le ménestrel*, 31 March 1861.

Tannhäuser *and Its French Critics*

the help of King Ludwig II of Bavaria, he established himself first in Munich and then in Bayreuth. In the end, history would prove Wagner right and show the Parisians for what they were: superficial pleasure seekers mired in operatic conventionality who were unable to recognize true art.

My rendering of this tale may seem like a caricature, but for over a century it remained the dominant version circulating in German and Anglo-Saxon literature after it was cemented in Wagner's own words, first in his report about the premiere for the *Deutsche Allgemeine Zeitung* in April 1861 and later in his autobiography.[4] The Wagnerian master narrative was only slightly revised in France through the documents presented by Georges Servières in his 1895 monograph on the Parisian *Tannhäuser*.[5] This changed, however, when in the 1980s musicologists began to develop two new areas of interest: on the one hand, led by the Berlioz renaissance, scholars began to focus on French nineteenth-century music as an area of research and performance, whether for the music of Gounod, Massenet, or Méhul; and on the other, sketch studies grew into one of the main scholarly projects of the period, expanding traditional work on Beethoven to the examination of sketches by Schumann, Wagner, and Rossini. Thus the iconic Parisian opera scandal of the nineteenth century received fresh attention. In the early 1980s Carolyn Abbate went into the Parisian archives and explored many of the materials relating to the Parisian *Tannhäuser*. She presented them in two carefully documented source studies that showed for the first time in detail the literary and musical changes Wagner made for the Paris premiere.[6] In the mid-1980s Gerald Turbow and Jane Fulcher revised the political aspects of the narrative and revealed that the Jockey Club's attack in fact served as a pretext for political protest against the patron of the performance, the French emperor Napoléon III.[7] Yet even in opening up new alleys of inquiry as regards sources and political reinterpretation,

---

4. For bibliographical references, see Carolyn Abbate, "The 'Parisian' *Tannhäuser*" (Ph.D. diss., Princeton University, 1985), 315.

5. Georges Servières, *Tannhœuser à l'Opéra en 1861* (Paris: Librairie Fischbacher, 1895). Although Servières attempts a more nuanced and complete rendering of the events, drawing on a rich fund of primary documents, his story—especially when examining the Parisian press—remains close to the Wagnerian master narrative.

6. Carolyn Abbate, "The Parisian 'Vénus' and the 'Paris' *Tannhäuser*," *Journal of the American Musicological Society* 36 (1983): 73–123; Abbate., "The 'Parisian' *Tannhäuser*." Ulrich Drüner's interpretation of the Parisian *Tannhäuser* offers an alternative reading of the Parisian "Vénus" in his "La version parisienne du *Tannhäuser* de Richard Wagner ou l'introduction du psychologique dans le grand opéra," in *Le théâtre lyrique en France au XIXe siècle,* ed. Paul Prévost (Metz: Éditions Serpenoise, 1995), 163–80.

7. Gerald D. Turbow, "Art and Politics: Wagnerism in France," in *Wagnerism in European Culture and Politics,* ed. David C. Large and William Weber (Ithaca, NY: Cornell University Press, 1984), 134–66; Jane F. Fulcher, *The Nation's Image: French Grand Opera as Politics and Politicized Art* (Cambridge: Cambridge University Press, 1987), 189–98.

ANNEGRET FAUSER

much of the recent scholarly work in effect maintained and even strengthened the century-old Wagnerian master narrative, explaining the reasons for the Parisian rejection of Wagner in political rather than the aesthetic terms of the 1850s, celebrating Wagner the progressive—if not in his own political attitude, then at least in his impact on republican and socialist writers such as Jules Champfleury or avant-garde artists such as Charles Baudelaire—while condemning Wagner's adversaries and ridiculing his critics with choice quotations and summary dismissal.

In contrast, Manuela Schwartz, in her 1999 study on French reception of Wagner, pointed out that the scandal served to politicize the composer himself, turning him from a cosmopolitan with ambivalent political alliances into a German nationalist.[8] In addition, Katharine Ellis's careful reading of French music criticism illuminates the complexities of the aesthetic debate that has surrounded Wagner's music since the 1850s.[9]

Thus, changing the traditional perspective and challenging the Wagnerian master narrative—by taking Wagner's critics seriously instead of disregarding them as incompetent, spiteful, or reactionary—may well reveal that theirs was not simply an unreflecting hostility toward Wagner and his new musical language, but, rather, a mirror of their deep concerns about the future of opera, the primary genre of French cultural life, its institutional context, and its musical and poetic language.[10] Many of the critics went to great lengths to explain to their readers why Wagner's *Tannhäuser* represented a wrong turn in opera. A careful and close reading of Parisian criticism surrounding Wagner's second Parisian sojourn shows in fact that the notorious nature of Wagner's own theories and music served as a prism that turned a spotlight onto a deep-seated polemical undercurrent about the nature of French opera, especially because Wagner was not French. Therefore any perceived danger to the genre could be discussed in time-tested terms of national difference rather than internal artistic conflict.

---

8. Manuela Schwartz, *Wagner-Rezeption und französische Oper des Fin de siècle*, Berliner Musik Studien 18 (Sinzig: Studio Verlag Schewe, 1999), 2–7. Schwartz also points out that the French press was by no means as monolithic in its rejection of Wagner's opera as has been assumed. She cites the case of Ursula Eckart-Bäcker who, in her study of nineteenth-century French music criticism, focused only on the negative reviews (Schwartz, *Wagner-Rezeption*, 5). See Ursula Eckart-Bäcker, *Frankreichs Musik zwischen Romantik und Moderne* (Regensburg: Bosse, 1965), 77–100.

9. Katharine Ellis, "Wagnerism and Anti-Wagnerism in the Paris Periodical Press," in *Von Wagner zum Wagnérisme: Musik, Literatur, Kunst, Politik*, ed. Annegret Fauser and Manuela Schwartz, Transfer: Deutsch-Französische Kulturbibliothek 12 (Leipzig: Leipziger Universitätsverlag, 1999), 51–83.

10. James Ross raises this point in his discussion of the reception of Debussy's *Pelléas et Mélisande*. See Ross, "Crisis and Transformation: French Opera, Politics and the Press, 1897–1903" (D.Phil. diss., Oxford University, 1998), 187.

Tannhäuser *and Its French Critics*

Wagner in Paris

The story of Wagner's Parisian *Tannhäuser* began long before the ill-fated premiere in March 1861. It goes back to the young Richard Wagner's first visit to Paris, between 1839 and 1842, when he tried to establish himself as an opera composer in the musical capital of the nineteenth century. Cherubini, Meyerbeer, Spontini, and Rossini had shown that foreign composers could impose themselves on the French musical stage. In 1840 Wagner came close to placing his *Liebesverbot* with the Théâtre de la Renaissance, but he lost out to Donizetti's *L'ange de Nisida*.[11] That same year, inspired by a short story by Heinrich Heine, Wagner sketched the outline for a one-act opera on the topic of the Flying Dutchman that was intended as a one-act curtain-raiser for a ballet at the Opéra such as *Giselle*.[12] Although the Opéra's administration was interested in the subject, it had other artists in mind to create the work, and 9 November 1842 saw the premiere of Pierre-Louis Dietsch's fantastic opera in two acts, *Le vaisseau fantôme, ou Le maudit des mers*.[13]

When Wagner returned to Paris twenty years later, in September 1859, he was no longer an unknown hopeful from Germany, but a controversial *chef d'école*. In particular, after the publication around 1850 of the so-called Züricher Kunstschriften—*Art and Revolution* (1849), *The Artwork of the Future* (1850), and *Opera and Drama* (1851)—he had become one of the most discussed composers alive. In 1852 François-Joseph Fétis dedicated a series of articles to Wagner's theoretical "system," whose terms would shape the discussion in France for several decades.[14] But although the debate about Wagner's ideas was lively, his music remained virtually unknown in Paris. Thus one of his first acts of self-promotion in Paris was to remedy this lack of musical awareness with three concerts of his own music, which he conducted in January and February 1860. Except for the *Tristan* Prelude, Wagner played it safe: he selected those extracts from his operas that were the closest to the style of French *grand opéra* (see table 10.1). His medley from *Tannhäuser* opened with the march from act 2, the arrival of the guests at the Wartburg, which was modeled on similar marches composed by Meyerbeer and Halévy. After the first concert he added to his program another piece attractive to French tastes that was to become known as the *Romance de l'étoile* ("O du mein holder Abendstern"). The poetic images, the elegiac tone, the regular

---

11. Mark Everist, *Giacomo Meyerbeer and Music Drama in Nineteenth-Century France* (Aldershot: Ashgate, 2005), 309–41.

12. Martine Kahane and Nicole Wild, eds., *Wagner et la France* (Paris: Editions Herscher, 1983), 21.

13. Dietsch, of course, was one of the players in the Paris *Tannhäuser*, twenty years later, for he became the musical director of the Opéra. Not only Dietsch, but also various other players of the 1840s reappeared in the *Tannhäuser* scandal, whether composers such as Berlioz and Rossini or Édouard Monnais, who—under the pen name of Paul Smith—wrote a harsh review in *La revue et gazette musicale de Paris*.

14. On Fétis's Wagner reception and its fallout, see Ellis, "Wagnerism and Anti-Wagnerism."

ANNEGRET FAUSER

TABLE 10.1. Program for the concerts organized and conducted by Richard Wagner at the Théâtre-Italien, 25 January 1860, 1 February 1860, and 8 February 1860

Der fliegende Holländer:
    Ouverture
Tannhäuser:
    March and Chorus
    Introduction to act 3 and Pilgrims' Chorus
    Romance de l'étoile (Jules Lefort) [1 and 8 February only]
    Ouverture
Tristan und Isolde:
    Prelude
Lohengrin:
    Introduction and Bridal Chorus
    Wedding Celebration

phrase structure, and the harp accompaniment of this *romance* were all musical signifiers familiar to his Parisian audience from countless operas of the past decades.[15]

But even though the concert featured the more traditional elements of his music, its reception took place in the context of what was perceived as Wagner's "system" for the "music of the future." Thus, Léon Escudier's review of the concerts carried the title "La musique de l'avenir à Paris," and Paul Scudo declared that Wagner's sobriquet "musicien de l'avenir" had now become an "indelible epithet."[16] Through his negative concert review for the *Journal des débats,* the French "musician of the future," Hector Berlioz, became embroiled in the fight, attacking Wagner's system on the grounds of its lack of tradition and beauty.[17] Parisian audiences quickly became divided into

---

15. On the musical structure and subject matter of operatic *romance*, see David Charlton, "The *romance* and Its Cognates: Narrative, Irony and *vraisemblance* in Early Opéra Comique," in *Die Opéra Comique und ihr Einfluß auf das europäische Musiktheater im 19. Jahrhundert,* ed. Herbert Schneider and Nicole Wild, Musikwissenschaftliche Publikationen der Hochschule für Musik und Darstellende Kunst Frankfurt/Main 3 (Hildesheim: Georg Olms Verlag, 1997), 43–92. That local taste was one of Wagner's main selection criteria when he put together his concert programs becomes obvious in his *Lettre sur la musique,* which he published later that year together with prose translations of his four operatic texts: *The Flying Dutchman, Tannhäuser, Lohengrin,* and *Tristan and Isolde.* See Richard Wagner, *Quatre poèmes d'opéras: Le vaisseau fantôme—Tannhœuser—Lohengrin—Tristan, précédés d'une "Lettre sur la musique,"* new ed. with a preface by Gustave Samazeuilh (Paris: Mercure de France, 1941).

16. Léon Escudier, "La musique de l'avenir à Paris," *La France musicale,* 29 January 1860. "Le titre de *musicien de l'avenir* lui reste acquis comme une qualification indélébile": Paul Scudo, "Revue musicale," *La revue des deux mondes,* 1 March 1860.

17. David Cairns, *Berlioz,* vol. 2, *Servitude and Greatness, 1832–1869* (London: Penguin, 1999), 654–60.

Tannhäuser *and Its French Critics*

Wagnerians and anti-Wagnerians, with polemic reviews and pamphlets published by Wagner himself as much as by his supporters—especially Champfleury—and detractors.[18] Reported the young Georges Bizet to his publisher, Choudens: "Berlioz finds the music of Wagner abominable, Reyer finds it splendid—it is clear that one of them has it completely wrong."[19]

Such was the notorious pervasiveness of the *Zukunftsmusik* epithet that it quickly found entrance into the rich culture of Parisian parodies in the form of a short number composed by Jacques Offenbach for his *Le carnaval des revues*, which premiered on 10 February 1860, just two days after Wagner's last concert.[20] The piece in question is a melodrama, *Le musicien de l'avenir*, in which Wagner meets Grétry, Weber, Mozart, and Gluck in Elysium. After explaining his revolutionary theories to his august predecessors, the musician of the future offers a glimpse of what such music might sound like with a *Symphony of the Future*.[21] Offenbach based his proto-Stravinskyan score of that "symphony" on the "Quadrille des lanciers," one of the best-known dances of the nineteenth century. Offenbach's satire was so successful that it was included in a gala performance at the Théâtre-Italien in April that year at the request of the emperor and was still played at the time of the *Tannhäuser* premiere.[22] Other comic attempts at the sounds of the future followed suit, with works such as H. Thiéry's revue *Il pleut, il pleut, bergère*, with a "great symphony" by the composer Tanne-tout-le-monde in "scie majeur."[23] Both the composer's name, which translates roughly as "getting on everybody's nerves," and the key of the symphony (here spelled *scie*, i.e., a saw, rather than *si*—a comment on the ugliness of the sound) played with perceptions of the music of the future as dissonant and enervating. Caricaturists also had their fun. One of Cham's caricatures in *Le charivari* shows, for example, a mother crying over the fact that her child was to hear naught but such music in the future (see fig. 10.2).[24] Indeed, before Wagner's operas ever reached the Parisian stage, his *musique de l'avenir* was performed as an ongoing saga onstage as well as off.

---

18. Ellis, "Wagnerism and Anti-Wagnerism," 59–62.

19. "Berlioz trouve la musique de Wagner abominable, Reyer la trouve splendide—il est bien évident que l'un des deux se trompe complètement." Hervé Lacombe, *Georges Bizet* (Paris: Fayard, 2000), 269.

20. Jean-Claude Yon, *Jacques Offenbach* (Paris: Éditions Gallimard, 2000), 228. The *Carnaval des revues* was the first piece of Offenbach's to be staged after he became a French citizen.

21. Siegfried Kracauer, *Jacques Offenbach und das Paris seiner Zeit* (Frankfurt am Main: Suhrkamp, 1994), 199.

22. Kracauer, *Jacques Offenbach*, 200. Servières (*Tannhœuser*, 111) offers 27 April 1860 as the date of the gala performance.

23. Servières, *Tannhœuser*, 111.

24. Cham was the pseudonym of the caricaturist Amédée de Noé (1818–79). He published his caricatures in *Le charivari*, *L'illustration*, and *Le journal amusant*, among other periodicals. See John Grand-Carteret, *Les mœurs et la caricature en France* (Paris: À la Librairie Illustrée, 1888), 628.

ANNEGRET FAUSER

— Chère amie, tu pleures sur le berceau de ton enfant ?
— Hi ! hi ! je crois bien !... hi ! hi ! je suis allée hier au soir entendre M. Wagner. Si vous croyez que c'est pas triste de savoir la musique que l'avenir réserve aux oreilles de ce pauvre petit.

FIGURE 10.2. A mother weeping at the cradle of her infant at the prospect of the music of the future. Caricature by Cham [Amédée de Noé]. *Le charivari*, 4 March 1860. Reproduced in John Grand-Carteret, *Richard Wagner en caricatures* (Paris: Librairie Larousse, [1892]), 223. Courtesy of Duke University Library.

By the spring of 1860 Wagner had thus established himself as the latest celebrity in the musical world of Paris, if not quite in the way he desired. As Gerald Turbow has pointed out, Wagner was "the darling of the progressives."[25] But he also moved in more conservative circles, which included the wife of the Austrian ambassador, Pauline von Metternich, who became his principal patron in Paris during these months. During a reception at the imperial court, she suggested to Napoléon III that he support her protégé's thus far fruitless attempts to have an opera performed in Paris. The emperor reacted quickly and on 12 March ordered the performance of *Tannhäuser* at the Opéra.[26] This imperial decree secured Wagner a lavish production on the first national stage, but it also linked him inextricably with the authoritarian and widely despised figure of the emperor, an association that laid the foundation for the *Tannhäuser* scandal a full year before the premiere. Nor did it help that Wagner's opera was the

---

25. Turbow, "Art and Politics," 147.
26. Schwartz, *Wagner-Rezeption*, 4.

Tannhäuser *and Its French Critics*

FIGURE 10.3. M. Despléchin, stage design for *Tannhäuser*, act 1, scene 2. Engraving by Auguste-Paul-Charles Anastasi and Jules Worms. *L'illustration*, 16 March 1861. Courtesy of Duke University Library.

publicly cited reason for the Opéra's refusal to put on Berlioz's still unperformed *Les Troyens* and for the delay of the premiere of Gounod's *La reine de Saba*.

Nevertheless, imperial patronage secured for Wagner all that the Opéra could muster in resources and support. Stars such as Fortunata Tedesco, Marie Sass, and Antonio Morelli were cast for the roles of Venus, Elisabeth, and Wolfram, and on Wagner's request, the Opéra hired the German tenor Albert Niemann to sing the title role. The stage design by Édouard Despléchin was sumptuous and the costumes lavish (see fig. 10.3). Lucien Petipa was to serve as the ballet's choreographer and Eugène Cormon as stage director. The production was overseen by Alphonse Royer, who had a good deal of experience with the adaptation of foreign works for the French opera stage, including Verdi's *I Lombardi* in 1847. It was as close to a dream team as Paris had to offer at that time, and everybody expected a major success if only because of the splendid quality of the production.[27]

The adaptation of foreign-language works for the stage of the Opéra was not unusual. Only four years prior to *Tannhäuser*, in 1857, the Opéra had produced the

27. Servières (*Tannhœuser*, 26) mentions that Wagner would have preferred Jean-Baptiste Faure for the role of Wolfram, but Faure had gone to Britain to spend the season at Covent Garden.

ANNEGRET FAUSER

French version of *Il trovatore*. But whether the composer was Verdi or Weber, Mozart or Donizetti, when a foreign work was performed on France's premier opera stage, it was translated not only in terms of language, but also in terms of theatrical convention.[28] This process of cultural transfer was part and parcel of these productions, to the point that in 1834 the Opéra could advertise Mozart's *Don Juan* as a version in which "Mozart's text has undergone no changes," even though the work was extended to five acts with significant transformations, including the reworking of the title role for the tenor Adolphe Nourrit; the insertion into act 1 of a ballet based on medleys of Mozart's themes; and Donna Anna's falling in love with Don Giovanni, her subsequent suicide, and a danced epilogue portraying Anna's funeral.[29] Such extensive reworking to suit the conventions of the Paris Opéra may seem extreme from today's perspective, but it needs to be understood in the frame of a cultural practice that conceived of opera as a theatrical event tailored toward a specific audience at a specific moment in time; this was not the Wagnerian concept of music drama as an autonomous work of art, a fixed text to be performed according to the author's intentions.[30] Although works of dead composers were arranged by French producers, librettists, and composers to fit their latest home in Paris, living composers such as Verdi often used the opportunity to revise their works for the new context, seeking and often following the advice of the Opéra's creative team. In 1847 Verdi completely reworked his *I Lombardi alla prima crociata* as *Jérusalem*, a four-act opera with ballets included.

Wagner's concept of music drama as a work created solely by the musician-poet proved a serious obstacle to the process of adapting *Tannhäuser* for the Parisian stage. But his reluctance to conform to institutional convention was less pronounced than legend would have it. As Carolyn Abbate has shown, Wagner was delighted to use the opportunity to make changes to the Venusberg scene, and he was far more amenable to the question of the act 2 ballet than later events might imply. Early on Royer had suggested that the finale of act 2—after the arrival of the guests at the Wartburg and before the song contest—would be an ideal place for the traditional act 2 ballet. Al-

---

28. On the adaptation of Weber's *Freischütz* for the Odéon, see Annegret Fauser, "Phantasmagorie im deutschen Wald? Zur *Freischütz*-Rezeption in London und Paris 1824," in *Deutsche Meister—Böse Geister? Nationale Selbstfindung in der Musik*, ed. Hermann Danuser and Herfried Münkler (Schliengen: Edition Argus, 2001), 245–73. For Berlioz's 1841 adaptation of *Freischütz*, see Frank Heidlberger, *Carl Maria von Weber und Hector Berlioz*, Würzburger Musikhistorische Beiträge 14 (Tutzing: Hans Schneider, 1994).

29. Katharine Ellis, "Rewriting *Don Giovanni*, or 'The Thieving Magpies,'" *Journal of the Royal Musical Association* 119 (1994): 214.

30. Hervé Lacombe discusses the more fluid work concept as collaborative performance, which prevailed in nineteenth-century France, in his *The Keys to French Opera*, trans. Edward Schneider (Berkeley and Los Angeles: University of California Press, 2001). See also Mark Everist, "Lindoro in Lyon: Rossini's *Le barbier de Séville*," *Acta Musicologica* 63 (1992): 50–85; and Everist, *Music Drama at the Paris Odéon, 1824–1828* (Berkeley and Los Angeles: University of California Press, 2002), 218–26.

Tannhäuser *and Its French Critics*

though Wagner refused categorically to include a ballet within the opera, he agreed to the intercalation of a newly composed ballet divertissement by Théodore Labarre, *Graziosa,* after act 2.[31] Wagner could have avoided a great deal of controversy had he not made his disdain for the local custom known in an article about the ballet question published in the *Journal des débats* in July 1860, and had he not demanded that the first few performances of *Tannhäuser* be given without the intercalation of *Graziosa*.[32]

From a Parisian standpoint, Wagner made one tactical mistake after another during the lead-up to the premiere, gambling away any general goodwill toward the controversial musician of the future. He demanded to conduct the first three performances of his opera in lieu of Louis Dietsch, the house conductor, whom he found wanting. Rehearsal time was excessive by any contemporary standards. He was rude to the musicians and singers and was perceived as arrogant by the Parisian press because he refused to pay the traditional visits to important journalists.[33] He snubbed the professional claqueurs, depriving them of their income, then hastily brought some of them in at the last minute. His negative views of French composers such as Auber, Halévy, and Berlioz were widely circulated and found offensive. The court case about the rights to the work's translation into French a week before the premiere only added to the general uproar. The press followed the events closely, reporting that opera, "this week, was not in the house at the rue le Pelletier [sic], but at the Palais de Justice."[34] As one journalist observed, "One speaks so much about *Tannhäuser* that its first performance is expected with the liveliest curiosity."[35] Into all of this commotion were mixed "the three magic words"—*musique de l'avenir*—which, according to Charles de Lorbac, served only to divide the French press and public into two camps even before the premiere.[36]

Wagner's Critics: Rereading the Parisian Reception of *Tannhäuser*

This volatile mix exploded at the tumultuous premiere on 13 March, when *Tannhäuser* was greeted by laughter, shouts, noise, and loud abuse. The subsequent two perfor-

31. Servières, *Tannhœuser,* 94, 107.

32. Abbate, "The 'Parisian'" Tannhäuser," 270.

33. He also refused to offer complementary tickets to the press for his 1860 concerts, as Paul Scudo pointed out: "M. Wagner n'a pas daigné, comme c'est l'usage, nous convier à la fête de son esprit." "Revue musicale," *La revue des deux mondes,* 1 February 1860.

34. "L'Opéra, cette semaine, n'était pas dans la salle de la rue le Pelletier [sic], mais bien au Palais de justice." "Actualités," *La France musicale,* 10 March 1861.

35. "En somme, on parle tant du *Tannhäuser,* que la première représentation est attendue avec la plus vive curiosité." *Journal de débats,* 13 March 1861.

36. "Grâce à trois mots magiques, et dont M. Wagner décline pourtant la responsabilité, *Musique de l'avenir,* l'auteur du *Tannhaüser* [sic] a eu le rare bonheur de partager la critique française en deux camps, avant la représentation de son œuvre, et d'appeler sur sa personne la curiosité, l'intérêt même d'un public qui le connaît à peine de nom." Charles de Lorbac, "Richard Wagner," *Le Figaro,* 21 February 1861.

ANNEGRET FAUSER

mances were even more turbulent. Journalists from newspapers and music periodical alike reflected both on the riotous events of the evenings and on their meaning for French opera. Although Wagner's ideas elicited intense debate in the French press in the decade before this performance, these discussions came into sharp focus over *Tannhäuser*, possibly the most important Parisian premiere at the Opéra between Verdi's *Les vêpres siciliennes* in 1855 and his *Don Carlos* in 1867.[37] Given that the soubriquet of the "music of the future" dominated the entire discourse leading up to the *Tannhäuser* premiere, from Offenbach's *Symphony of the Future* and Cham's caricatures to Wagner's own *Lettre sur la musique*, it is no surprise that it became a central issue in the reviews. By asking whether Wagner's *Tannhäuser* was indeed the music of the future, critics could examine a notorious case to analyze how invention and convention related to new styles in music and, more specifically, opera.[38] Through the lens of this controversy, reviewers revisited questions of opera's aesthetic foundation, musical form and style, institutional framework, and modes of reception. Because of the prominence of the scandal and the preceding and consequent exposure of music criticism in the national press, the debate about *Tannhäuser* became itself a performance, self-consciously styled as a key debate similar to the famous eighteenth-century *querelles*. Not only did Wagner's *Tannhäuser* and its reception provide the press with newsworthy tidbits to report, it also served to validate music criticism as a vital arbiter of national culture.

Wittiness became one of the hallmarks of the press reception, contrasting French *esprit* with the Germanic dullness ascribed to Wagner's writings and music. Once more, Wagner and his opera were the subject of caricatures in *Le charivari*, where we find, for example, Venus sobbing about her depressing fate as the only person in Paris who loves Tannhäuser (see fig. 10.4). But wit was also displayed in the feuilletons of the daily press. Whether it was Pier Angelo Fiorentino comparing the song competition in act 2 to the end-of-year competition at the Conservatoire "where one hears the same piano piece twenty-seven times in a row," Léon Gatayes predicting a duel between Wagnerians and anti-Wagnerians where opponents "will cross their scores

---

37. The fact that I am citing two works written by Verdi rather than Gounod, Thomas, or Auber points toward the crisis of French opera in the middle of the nineteenth century. When *L'Africaine* was premiered in 1865 it was as a posthumous work, presented a year after Meyerbeer's death and four years after Scribe's; Gounod's *La reine de Saba* (1862), the work premiered at the Opéra immediately after *Tannhäuser* and *Graziosa*, did not come even close to Gounod's success with *Faust* (1859) at the Théâtre-Lyrique. Indeed, many of the key premieres of French music-theater during those years took place at the Théâtre-Lyrique and the Opéra-Comique. See Lacombe, *Keys to French Opera*; Anselm Gerhard, *The Urbanization of Opera: Music Theater in Paris in the Nineteenth Century*, trans. Mary Whittall (Chicago: University of Chicago Press, 1998), especially 345–87. For Wagner criticism prior to the *Tannhäuser* premiere, see Ellis, "Wagnerism and Anti-Wagnerism." See also Katharine Ellis, *Music Criticism in Nineteenth-Century France: "La revue et gazette musicale de Paris," 1834–1880* (Cambridge: Cambridge University Press, 1995), 206–18.

38. On convention in French opera, see Gerhard, *Urbanization of Opera*, 8–12; Lacombe, *Keys to French Opera*, 252–301.

Tannhäuser *and Its French Critics*

FIGURE 10.4. Venus weeping because of *Tannhäuser*. Caricature by Cham [Amédée de Noé]. *Le charivari*, 17 March 1861. Reproduced in John Grand-Carteret, *Richard Wagner en caricatures* (Paris: Librarie Larousse, [1892]), 227. Courtesy of Duke University Library.

and ram them through their bodies," or Arthur Pougin characterizing Wagner's apparently nebulous writing style as "reflecting the sunshine of his country," reviewers sharpened their pens and used the occasion to perform deliberately their role as *French* writers and critics.[39] To be sure, if national culture was defined above all by *esprit*, which the critic Gaston de Saint-Valry in his review explicitly linked to Voltaire, then the critics' strategy of peppering their reviews with sarcasms and witticisms could be read as a performative act in a contest not over French opera versus Wagner's, but over critics' skill with the pen.[40]

Even in the battle between Wagnerians and anti-Wagnerians, the successful use

39. "Ces concours du Conservatoire où l'on entend vingt-sept fois de suite le même morceau de piano": Pier Angelo Fiorentino, "Théâtres," *Le constitutionnel*, 18 March 1861. "On croisera les partitions et on se les passera au travers du corps": Léon Gatayes, *L'univers musical*, 14 March 1861. "Le style rappelle le soleil de son pays": Arthur Pougin, "M. Richard Wagner," *La jeune France*, 3 March 1861.

40. Gaston de Saint-Valry, "Revue dramatique," *Le pays*, 19 March 1861.

of wit became a yardstick for critics' powers of persuasion. The assiduous Wagnerian Auguste de Gasperini saw Parisian wit as the signal flaw that precluded any serious discussion of music and aesthetics in the French press: "To be amusing, witty, this is the first condition required of today's critic; and whichever the journal in which he reigns—whether *Le moniteur* or *Le constitutionnel*, *La presse* or *L'opinion*—he must, under threat of immediate devaluation, primarily search for merriment and the mocking word, with the rest coming as an extra."[41] Léon Leroy, for his part, sarcastically characterized one fellow writer's feuilleton as empty pyrotechnics before revealing Benoît Jouvin's famous malapropism in his review in *Le Figaro*, where he had confused the auditory with the olfactory nerves.[42]

Journalists also evoked Parisian wit as one reason behind the inevitability of Wagner's failure, for the German composer had committed the cardinal sin of boring his French audience with his theories, his plot, his poetry, and his music while alienating his French hosts with his boorish behavior. By blatantly and openly disregarding the tastes of his audience and the conventions of French *grand opéra*, according to his critics, Wagner had made himself a target of both the audience's disapproval and the journalists' attack; therefore, the reviews turned to lessons on the institution of French *grand opéra* and its audience. Much was at stake, because if Wagner was successful in his critique of convention, then the central position of Paris as a musical capital was in jeopardy. Thus Paris as a cultural center played a big role in these reviews. Albert Wolff reminded his readers that "Paris is not only the capital of France, but the center of the artistic world."[43] Instead of adopting an appropriate humility in the face of such an august performance context, Wagner showed hubris:

> No, Wagner is not one of those foreign composers who—like Rossini, Meyerbeer, Donizetti, and Verdi, paying homage to our tastes, our enlightenment, our impartiality—has come loyally and without flattery to present to us his views about

---

41. "Être plaisant, spirituel, telle est la première condition exigée du critique de nos jours; et quel que soit le journal où il règne, au *Moniteur*, ou au *Constitutionnel*, à la *Presse* ou à l'*Opinion*, il doit sous peine de démonétisation immédiate, chercher d'abord la gaîté et le mot pour rire, le reste venant de surcroît." Auguste de Gasperini, "Courrier musical," *Le journal de Francfort*, 4 April 1861.

42. "Le compte-rendu pyrotechnique de M. de Saint Victor est sans doute fort brillant, comme de coutume, mais ne contient pas un mot de critique raisonnée, au point de vue de la musique—si ce n'est que le feuilletoniste déclare préférer le chœur de pèlerins de *Jérusalem* à celui de *Tannhauser*.... Nous demandions tout à l'heure ce que M. de Saint-Victor entendait par 'une voix bien modulée' nous demanderons maintenant ce que signifie cette autre phrase de M. Jouvin, toujours à propos du *Tannhauser:* 'La musique brutale et banale est celle qui ébranle seulement le nerf OLFACTIF.' Auditif, M. Jouvin, auditif, s'il vous plait!—à moins que par un autre phénomène de votre organisation, vous ne perceviez les sons musicaux par le nez." Léon Leroy, "La cabale et les critiques," *La causerie*, 31 March 1861.

43. "Paris n'est pas seulement la capitale de la France, c'est le centre du monde artiste." Albert Wolff, "Le courrier de Paris," *Le Figaro*, 24 March 1861.

Tannhäuser *and Its French Critics*

the future of art and to submit to our judgment original compositions written under the inspiration of a new ideal. . . . But no, for the year that he has spent among us, the author of *Tannhäuser* plays with intolerable grandiloquence the role of the misunderstood man, of the messiah of a new art, of the pathbreaking genius. He pours contempt on works that form the object of our admiration; he writes books in which the name of Rossini is omitted with an affectation that would be impertinent if it were not so entirely puerile.[44]

At least on the surface of the negative reviews, Wagner's offense was therefore not the simple fact that he was trying to be innovative as a composer or that he was a foreigner, but that he so openly disdained that what his audience and critics enjoyed seeing and hearing in their theaters. "Richard Wagner's greatest mistake," Édouard Monnais observed, "was to ignore what might please or displease the French public."[45] Such pride deserved punishment in many eyes. Some were up front about their intent, especially Oscar Comettant, who spelled out Wagner's crime and punishment *expressis verbis:*

Of course, if Mr. Wagner had not shown, in his numerous writings published in Germany and in France, his disdain for the works of the great masters past and present, and if he had not sustained with such incredible pride his system of opera composition as the *nec plus ultra* of the beautiful, and if he had not made his operas out to be the only ones worthy to be listened to by serious minds, the Parisian public—naturally benevolent and polite—would have been content to remain silent before the misshapen, dull, and wrongheaded work of the unfortunate composer. But to a pretension without limits and which nothing justifies, an exemplary lesson needs to be taught.[46]

---

44. "Non, Wagner n'est pas un de ces compositeurs étrangers qui, comme Rossini, Meyerbeer, Donizetti, Verdi, rendant hommage à nos goûts, à nos lumières, à notre impartialité, est venu loyalement et sans flatterie nous exposer ses vues sur l'avenir de l'art, et soumettre à notre jugement des compositions originales, écrites sous l'inspiration d'un nouvel idéal. . . . Main non, l'auteur du *Tannhauser* [sic], depuis un an qu'il est parmi nous, joue avec une jactance intolérable le rôle d'homme incompris, de messie d'art nouveau, de génie initiateur; il déverse le mépris sur les œuvres qui font l'objet de notre admiration; il écrit des livres où le nom de Rossini est omis avec une affectation impertinente, si elle n'était avant tout puéril." "Feuilleton," *L'ami de la religion,* 21 March 1861.

45. "Le plus grand tort de Richard Wagner, c'est, à nos yeux, d'ignorer ce qui peut plaire ou déplaire à un public français." Paul Smith [Édouard Monnais], "Théâtre impérial de l'Opéra: *Tannhœuser,*" *La revue et gazette musicale de Paris,* 17 March 1861.

46. "Certes, si M. Wagner n'avait pas manifesté, dans de nombreux écrits publiés en Allemagne et en France, son mépris pour les œuvres des grands maîtres passés et présents, et s'il n'avait pas soutenu avec un incroyable orgueil son système de composition lyrique comme le *nec plus ultra* du beau, et posé ses opéras comme les seuls dignes d'être écoutés par les esprits sérieux, le public parisien, naturellement bienveillant et courtois, se fût contenté de rester silencieux devant l'ouvrage informe, terne et faux du compositeur malheureux. Mais à une prétention sans limites et que rien

ANNEGRET FAUSER

The Parisian journalists responded in this strong and concerted fashion not only because Wagner had offended French taste, but because his competing aesthetics called into question everything they prized. The aesthetic position of Wagner's opponents was strongly influenced by the eclectic philosopher Victor Cousin, whose 1853 tract *Du vrai, du beau et du bien*, was cited by Scudo in his 1860 review of the Wagner concerts.[47] If Comettant worried about Wagner's claim to the "*nec plus ultra* of the beautiful," then a key concept of French aesthetics was indeed under attack. This probably seemed to justify the critics' concerted action, often described as a cabal.[48]

Whether the French reviewers simply picked up on current debates or had agreed upon certain critical tactics for their feuilletons, a significant number of reviews share common topics, discursive strategies, and even formulations—not only those written by the ringleaders of anti-Wagnerian invective such as Alexis Azevedo, Oscar Comettant, Pier Angelo Fiorentino, Benoît Jouvin, and Paul Scudo, and but also those of the more equanimous albeit equally negative critics such as Paul Bernard, Franck-Marie (Franco Maria Pedorlini), Stéphen de la Madeleine, Joseph d'Ortigue, and Arthur Pougin (table 10.2). Wagner himself had provided the starting point for a significant number of these topics and strategies: he published his *Lettre sur la musique* in late 1860, three months before the premiere, enough time for it to be circulated among and discussed by Parisian critics. Not only did this text synthesize Wagner's most provocative ideas about opera and drama; it also contained, thanks to the translator, Paul Challemel-Lacour, some mistranslations that made matters worse by insulting Italian music.[49] Three issues in particular served to provoke the *Tannhäuser* reviewers: Wagner's discussion of melody and the introduction of his metaphor of the *mélodie de la forêt* for his *unendliche Melodie;* his open disdain for current opera, its conventions, and its traditions (including his disavowal of his earlier compositions as pandering to public taste); and his discussion of the symphony as dramatic music.[50] These three themes, which intersected with Fétis's criticism (by then a commonplace) that Wagner lacked form, melody, and rhythm, became key issues in the press reception, in which Wagner's own writing was used against him.

Among the critics who referred to and often cited Wagner's *Lettre sur la musique*

---

ne justifie, il fallait une leçon exemplaire." Oscar Comettant, "Académie Impériale de Musique: Tannhauser," *L'art musical*, 21 March 1861.

47. Ellis, "Wagnerism and Anti-Wagnerism," 59. Gasperini ("Courrier musical," *Le journal de Francfort*, 4 April 1861) sarcastically refers to Cousin's omnipresence in French criticism when he concludes that "M. Cousin's eclecticism ran all through it" (l'éclectisme de M. Cousin a passé par là).

48. Servières (*Tannhœuser*, 60–63) identified Scudo as the ringleader.

49. See Peter Jost, "Zu den französischen Übersetzungen von Wagners Schriften zu Lebzeiten," in *"Schlagen Sie die Kraft der Reflexion nicht zu gering an": Beiträge zu Richard Wagners Denken, Werk und Wirken*, ed. Klaus Döge, Christa Jost, and Peter Jost (Mainz: Schott, 2002), 32–47, especially 38.

50. Wagner, *Quatre poèmes d'opéras*, 13–110.

TABLE 10.2. Selected reviews of *Tannhäuser* from Parisian periodicals

Critic	Journal	Comment
Charles Baudelaire	*Revue européenne* (1 April 1860)	Favorable review praising Wagner as the founder of a new art
Paul Bernard	*Le ménestrel* (24 March 1861)	Negative review of poem and music
Gustave Chadeuil	*Le siècle* (26 March 1861)	Negative review of poem and music
Pier Angelo Fiorentino	*Le constitutionnel* (18 March 1861)	Criticizes unsuccessful music and plot; labels Wagner a "symphonist"
M. Franck-Marie [Pedorlini]	*La patrie* (24 March 1861)	Mixed review; critical of poem and musical structure, but celebrates Wagner as a "great musician" following in steps of Bach and Beethoven
Adolphe Giacomelli	*La presse théâtrale et musicale* (17–21 March 1861)	Claims critics mounted a cabal and did not understand Wagner's music
J.-L. Heugel	*Le ménestrel* (17 March 1861)	Criticizes music as formulaic and without beauty
Benoît Jouvin	*Le Figaro* (18 March 1861)	Criticizes music as unnatural and unintelligible, music insulting to its audience
Léon Leroy	*La causerie* (31 March 1861)	Mostly positive review; attacks the "cabal"
Paul de Saint-Victor	*La presse* (18 March 1861)	Criticizes Wagner's music as mainly monotonous; calls to rally under the "classical flag of the Latin genius"
Paul Scudo	*La revue des deux mondes* (1 April 1861)	Author is leader of anti-Wagner cabal and follower of Victor Cousin; review attacks Wagner's music, poem, system, and behavior

ANNEGRET FAUSER

were both his more passionate critics such as Azevedo, Comettant, Scudo, and Wilhelm, and those—such as de la Madeleine, d'Ortigue, and Pougin—whose responses seem more balanced in their rejection.[51] Wagner was taken to task first and foremost over the "melody of the forest," which was then applied to reading the score. Thus Scudo's attack on the Venusberg scene used Wagner's own terminology, including the contrast between the *unendliche Melodie* (to which he aspired) and the (wrongly translated) "Italian melody," for it seems that Challemel-Lacour translated *welche Melodie* as "Italian melody," probably confusing *welch* and *welsch,* an old German term for Italian:[52] "This first scene of *Tannhäuser,* which was written in Paris and reveals the maestro's latest manner, cannot be compared to anything that exists in music. It is chaos, it is nothingness, but scientific chaos and nothingness; it is the great *melody of the forest* that has nothing in common with the Italian melody."[53] The "scientific" quality of Wagner's music was not a new charge, and metaphors were often industrial, in a manner already familiar from Berlioz criticism: this became a way of disputing any natural beauty of Wagner's "new manner," mocking his own reference to nature in the *Lettre sur la musique.* Paul Scudo described the *Tannhäuser* overture as a "vast music machine," while J.-L. Heugel likened Wagner's tendency toward extended use of formulaic accompaniment patterns to the transatlantic telegraph cable.[54] Jouvin, in his review for *Le Figaro,* compared Wagner's vocal lines to a bobbin that never empties itself of its endless thread, and he concluded that it was "music against nature."[55] And any music that was not based on the "charm and the sentiment of the melody"—so wrote Heugel, playing on the familiar trope—would lead to a path *"without future for music."*[56]

---

51. Paul Scudo, "Revue musicale," *La revue des deux mondes,* 1 April 1861; Joseph d'Ortigue, "Théâtre de l'Opéra," *Journal des débats,* 23 March 1861; Arthur Pougin, "M. Richard Wagner," *La jeune France,* 3 March 1861; Wilhelm [Édouard Monnais], "Revue musicale," *Revue contemporaine,* 31 March 1861; Stéphen de la Madeleine, "Revue des Théâtres Lyriques," *L'univers musical,* 31 March 1861; Alexis Azevedo, "Musique," *L'opinion nationale,* 19 March 1861; and Oscar Comettant, "Académie Impériale de Musique: *Tannhauser,*" *L'art musical,* 21 March 1861.
52. Jost, "Zu den französischen Übersetzungen," 38.
53. "Cette première scène du *Tannhäuser,* qui a été écrite à Paris et qui révèle la dernière manière du maître, ne peut se comparer à rien qui existe en musique. C'est le chaos, c'est le néant, mais le chaos et le néant scientifiques; c'est cette grande *mélodie de la forêt* qui n'a rien de commun avec la mélodie italienne." Scudo, "Revue musicale," *La revue des deux mondes,* 1 April 1861.
54. "Une vaste machine de musique": Scudo, quoted in Ellis, "Wagnerism and Anti-Wagnerism," 60. "Une formule d'accompagnement . . . se prolonge indéfiniment, à l'instar du câble transatlantique": J.-L. Heugel, "Académie Impériale de la Musique: *Tannhauser,*" *Le ménestrel,* 17 March 1861.
55. "La phrase de M. Wagner . . . est un fil sans fin . . . Figurez-vous une bobine qu'on déviderait toute une soirée, une *bobine inépuisable*"; "la musique de l'avenir, cette musique contre nature." Benoît Jouvin, "Théâtre: *Le Tannhauser,*" *Le Figaro,* 21 March 1861.
56. "Le charme et le sentiment de la mélodie"; "sans avenir pour la musique." J.-L. Heugel, "Académie Impériale de la Musique: *Tannhauser,*" *Le ménestrel,* 17 March 1861.

Tannhäuser *and Its French Critics*

If nature served as the foundation to true beauty—an idealist claim shared by both Wagner and his detractors—the classical qualities of proportion, clarity, and variety were conjured in these reviews as the pillars of genuine art against which Wagner's *Tannhäuser* was to be judged, for nature alone was not enough for the French critics: "Who among us would accept this so-called *melody of nature* which nobody could repeat? Nature has only noises, and art alone gives them sense. The melodic idea is for noise and notes what the plan of a palace is for marble and stones, what a painting's design is for its colors."[57] The critics homed in on form as a marker of successful operatic music. Their critical approach thus became threefold: they denounced most of Wagner's music as formless and monotonous, they contrasted it with form as an essential element of music, and they used traditional form—when it could be identified in *Tannhäuser*—as surefire proof of form's irrepressibly musical quality.

The charges of monotony and formlessness were closely linked. Monotony was seen as the direct result of any deviation from good operatic practice; thus, for Sylvain Saint-Étienne, it was the consequence of Wagner's Germanic poetic procedures, while most other critics blamed the abandoning of distinct forms, the disproportionate length of pieces such as Tannhäuser's Rome narration, and the recitative-like style of the vocal lines for the impression of the "great ocean of monotony."[58] Fiorentino saw the Rome narration as a twenty-page travelogue, monotonous and declamatory, "aggravated by all the incidents, all the encounters and all the emotions of a trip to Rome, there and back."[59] Another scene that allowed Wagner's reviewers to criticize such "monotony" was the song contest in act 2, which, according to Bernard, was an "eminently musical subject" that Wagner treated without inspiration.[60] Saint-Valry compared it to an endless disputation between philosophers at the Sorbonne. What is the point, Saint-Valry asked his reader, of having Tannhäuser interrupt Wolfram in the song contest if it is only to interject more of the same? One would have hoped rather that Tannhäuser would "sing some honest-to-goodness Italian melody, bursting with tenderness and voluptuousness."[61]

Saint-Valry's demand for contrast harks back to the notion of *varietas*, an aesthetic

---

57. "Qui de nous accepterait cette prétendue *mélodie de la nature*, que personne ne pourrait redire! La nature n'a que des bruits, et l'art seul leur donne un sens. L'idée mélodique est aux bruits et aux notes ce que le plan d'un palais est au marbre et aux pierres, ce que le dessin d'un tableau est aux couleurs." Wilhelm [Édouard Monnais], "Revue musicale," *Revue contemporaine*, 31 March 1861.

58. "Océan de la monotonie." Benoît Jouvin, "Théâtres," *Le Figaro*, 21 March 1861.

59. "Vingt pages d'une narration monotone et déclamatoire, aggravé de tous les incidens, toutes les rencontres, et toutes les émotions d'un voyage à Rome, aller et retour." Pier Angelo Fiorentino, "Théâtres," *Le constitutionnel*, 18 March 1861.

60. "Sujet éminemment musical." Paul Bernard, "*Tannhaüser*," *Le ménestrel*, 24 March 1861.

61. "[On croit que Tannhæuser] va chanter quelque franche mélodie italienne, frémissante de tendresse et de volupté. C'était bien la peine d'interrompre Wolfram pour continuer exactement dans le même style; la mélopée, le plein-chant l'emportent, l'amour sensuel est célébré d'une façon aussi accablante que l'autre." Gaston de Saint Valry, "Revue dramatique," *Le pays*, 19 March 1861.

ANNEGRET FAUSER

key concept in French music, which had found its way into the aesthetics of *grand opéra*.[62] Critics linked variety to character development on the one hand, and to musical form and structure on the other. D'Ortigue deplored the absence of "a form, a frame, a melody, a rhythm, a syntax that are distinguishable, perceptible."[63] Without form—so Scudo reminded his readers—there was no beauty, which was, after all, "the first aim of art."[64] Similarly, Franck-Marie argued that because of the lack of clear-cut form, Wagner's music was naught but a "long psalmody," in which "nothing remains graven on memory."[65] For Franck-Marie, Wagner's resistance to form was the result of his enmity toward operatic convention; he maintained that all opera was, by definition, naught but convention:

> The form that Wagner gives to his airs only serves to increase the tedium that results from the absence of any dramatic element in his subject. Enemy of all convention, the master does not want that singers set themselves apart to perform a cavatina, an aria, a duet. The action stops during that time, he thinks, and it is not at all natural that a person should step aside in that manner from those who surround her in order to repeat a long *a parte*. . . . Opera is founded solely on conventions of all kinds; why not admit, among so many others, one more when it can offer so much variety and interest to singing?[66]

Oscar Comettant similarly reflected on the needs of the musical stage, defining its essence as riveting drama based on variety and contrast and invoking Aristotelian rules of dramatic structure:

---

62. Herbert Schneider, "Scribe and Auber: Constructing Grand Opera," in *The Cambridge Companion to Grand Opera*, ed. David Charlton (Cambridge: Cambridge University Press, 2003), 168–88. Schneider cites both a letter by Scribe and a passage from Auber's memoirs that emphasize the importance of "variety" for an opera (168, 170). See also Lacombe, *Keys to French Opera*, 87–143, on the construction of mid-century French opera.

63. "Une forme, un cadre, une mélodie, un rythme, une syntaxe saisissables, perceptibles." Joseph d'Ortigue, "Théâtre de l'Opéra," *Journal des débats*, 23 March 1861.

64. "La beauté, premier but de tous les arts"; "la forme, sans laquelle l'esprit humain ne peut rien comprendre." Paul Scudo, "Revue musicale," *La revue des deux mondes*, 1 April 1861.

65. "Wagner ne déterminant jamais ses mélodies d'une manière précise, par des formes bien arrêtés, sa partie chantée n'est plus qu'une longue psalmodie se déroulant à satiété. Rien ne se grave dans l'esprit, car rien ne se détache sur ce fond d'harmonie uniforme par trop de continuité." Franck-Marie [Perdolini], "Revue musicale," *La patrie*, 24 March 1861.

66. "La coupe que Wagner donne à ses airs ne fait qu'accroître l'ennui qui résulte de l'absence tout élément dramatique dans le sujet. Ennemi de toute convention, le maître ne veut pas que les chanteurs s'isolent pour exécuter une cavatine, un air, un duo. L'action s'arrête pendant ce temps, pense-t-il, et il n'est point naturel qu'un personnage s'écarte ainsi de ceux qui l'entourent pour répéter un long *à parte*. . . . L'opéra n'est fondé que sur les conventions de toutes sortes; pourquoi dès lors, au milieu de tant d'autres, n'en pas admettre une de plus lorsqu'elle peut donner tant de variété et d'intérêt au chant?" Franck-Marie [Perdolini], "Revue musicale," *La patrie*, 24 March 1861.

Tannhäuser *and Its French Critics*

What one wants from theater is a gripping drama, clearly set up, well developed, with a strong dénouement, and which permits a musician to give full scope not to his own sentimental dreams that affect none but himself, but to the well-characterized emotions of the heart. And because variety is one of the key elements of musical theater, one needs, next to the grand manifestations of passion, graceful pieces of various characters that charm the ear and hold the attention.[67]

In the journalists' view, Wagner's music itself served as the ultimate proof of their aesthetic position. Even his harshest critics heaped lavish praise (albeit sometimes grudgingly) on those segments of *Tannhäuser* that conformed to the conventions of French *grand opéra*. These reviewers did not use their praise as a means to soften the blow they were dealing Wagner, but rather to strengthen it. For Heugel, the traditional pieces served as a "condemnation of the culprit by the culprit himself," and Saint-Valry asked whether they were "not the most significant condemnation of his unhappy inventions."[68] The march in act 2 was compared to similar compositions by Auber, Meyerbeer, and Halévy, to whom Wagner was sometimes judged a close second and at other times an equal. For the septet at the end of act 1, scene 4, comparisons were drawn to the music of Bellini, Donizetti, and Verdi, with Wagner's music emerging not unfavorably. Thus Heugel considered the "andante of the septet a fragment that Bellini and Donizetti would have signed with both hands, entrusting the voices with [the melodic lines] that Wagner gave to the violins."[69] And Bernard characterized the same extract ("à l'italienne") as an ensemble "in which the voices were married with a rare success. The musician of the future arrives, in this respect, at effects that Verdi, the *sound-colorist*, could rightfully envy."[70] By thus homing in on the traditional aspect of the score—whether in terms of form or musical texture—these

---

67. "Ce qu'on veut au théâtre, c'est un drame saisissant, clairement exposé, bien conduit, dénoué avec force, et qui permette au musicien de donner un libre essor, non à ses rêveries sentimentales et dont personne autre que lui n'est affecté, mais aux émotions bien caractérisées du cœur. Et comme la variété est un des éléments par excellence de la musique théâtrale, il faut, à côté des grandes manifestations de la passion, des morceaux gracieux de différents caractères qui charment l'oreille et tiennent l'attention en éveil." Oscar Comettant, "Académie Impériale de la Musique: *Tannhauser*," *L'art musical*, 21 March 1861.

68. "La condamnation du coupable par le coupable lui-même": J.-L. Heugel, "Académie Impériale de la Musique: *Tannhæuser*," *Le ménestrel*, 17 March 1861. "Les quelques morceaux réussis de *Tannhæuser* qui semblent procéder de l'éducation première du compositeur ne sont-ils pas la condamnation la plus caractéristique de ses malheureuses inventions?": Gaston de Saint-Valry, "Revue dramatique," *Le pays*, 19 March 1861.

69. "L'andante du septuor, un fragment que Bellini et Donizetti auraient signé des deux mains, en confiant aux voix ce que M. Wagner fait chanter aux violons." J.-L. Heugel, "Académie Impériale de la Musique: *Tannhauser*," *Le ménestrel*, 17 March 1861.

70. "Les voix se marient, alors avec un rare bonheur. Le musicien de l'avenir arrive, sous ce rapport, à des effets que Verdi, le *sonoriste coloré*, pourrait à bon droit lui envier." Paul Bernard, "*Tannhauser*," *Le ménestrel*, 24 March 1861.

ANNEGRET FAUSER

critics responded to Wagner's own declaration in the *Lettre sur la musique*, where he claimed that he no longer made concessions to the frivolous tastes of the audience.[71] Jouvin explicitly referred to this attitude in his review, in which his praise of the act 2 march was framed with a scathing assessment of Wagner's condescension: "The musician has such contempt for anything that resembles a melody even from afar, for the periodic and rhythmic phrase, that he considers the march in question as a sin of his youth, as a cowardly concession to the routine taste of an irreverent public."[72]

French opera, for Wagner, was indeed "an institution whose particular purpose is almost exclusively to offer a distraction and an amusement to a population that is as bored as it is pleasure-seeking."[73] By attacking the institution of French opera and its audience, Wagner raised hackles. How much so becomes clear in the almost ubiquitous reference in the reviews to French audiences as arbiters of taste. Descriptions of the audience as "impartial" (Monnais), "competent" (Fiorentino), "benevolent, welcoming, and courteous" (Comettant), and "intelligent and generous" (Wolff) are liberally strewn across the negative reviews, defending audiences' taste against Wagner's charge by highlighting their "generous" and "enthusiastic" applause for the right kind of music.[74]

But these operatic numbers in *Tannhäuser* could also be used to broaden the critical discussion to questions about genre by setting French definitions of opera against Wagner's evocation of the symphony in his *Lettre sur la musique*. For Wagner's adversaries, opera and symphony were mutually exclusive genres, and to introduce symphonic procedures into opera went against its dramatic essence. Franck-Marie called the traditional numbers "sublime pages, written with all the inspiration and skill of the genius." He continued by identifying them as "pieces which by their nature detach themselves from the action and only enter the general framework of the drama in the guise of symphonic hors-d'œuvre."[75] Comettant used a long segment of his review to contrast the theater's need for "gripping drama"—created by musical numbers of great variety—with the opposing aesthetic aim of symphonic unity:

---

71. "Ces concessions que mon premier modèle, mon vénéré maître, Weber, se croyait encore obligé de faire au public d'opéra, vous ne les rencontrez plus, je puis, je pense, m'en flatter, dans mon *Tannhœuser*." Wagner, *Quatre poèmes d'opéras*, 106.

72. "Le musicien a un mépris tel pour tout ce qui ressemble de près ou de loin à de la mélodie, pour la phrase périodique et rythmée, qu'il considère la marche en question comme un péché de jeunesse, comme une concession sans courage faite à l'esprit routinier du public profane." Benoît Jouvin, "Théâtres," *Le Figaro*, 21 March 1861.

73. "Je voyais dans l'opéra une institution dont la destination spéciale est presque exclusivement d'offrir une distraction et un amusement à une population aussi ennuyée qu'avide de plaisir." Wagner, *Quatre poèmes d'opéras*, 34.

74. See, for example, Scudo, "Revue musicale," *La revue des deux mondes*, 1 April 1861.

75. "Des pages sublimes écrites avec toute l'inspiration et la science du génie. Qu'on remarque que nous citons justement des morceaux qui, par leur nature, se détachent de l'action et ne rentrent dans le cadre général du drame qu'en guise de hors-d'œuvre symphoniques." Franck-Marie [Perdolini], "Revue musicale," *La patrie*, 24 March 1861.

Tannhäuser *and Its French Critics*

Now, the invention of Mr. Wagner consists of turning opera into an instrumental symphony with the obbligato accompaniment of singers.... How can a musician of the worth of Mr. Wagner (because, after all, Mr. Wagner is a man of infinite talent) hold to such terms? Has Mr. Wagner forgotten that the great interest—so to speak, the only interest—of the symphony resides in the developments of a given theme that serves, so to speak, as the thesis for the comments of the composer[?] Can one imagine a symphony without unity of thought, and without this ingenious treatment of the parts that establishes itself as a piquant and often witty conversation between the various instruments on the given subject of the conversation, on the theme[?] Of course not, and nobody doubts it. However, these ingenious developments of a main theme are simply impossible once the music is required to follow dramatic and scenic action. In fact, as the action proceeds little by little, the characters necessarily express different feelings, and the music that expresses them is obliged to change character; consequently, no more unity of sentiment, and no more possible developments of a gestational musical idea.[76]

Not only Wagner's music but also the characters of his dramas were judged in this generic binary between symphony and opera. By using legends instead of the more traditional historic plots of French *grand opéra*—another controversial change Wager advocated in the *Lettre sur la musique*—Wagner was seen as eliminating human interest from his dramas. Instead he replaced them with "abstractions" (according to Azevedo, Comettant, and Wilhelm) without flesh and blood. When de la Madeleine compared *Tannhäuser* to the librettos of *La juive* (Scribe), *La reine de Chypre* (Saint-Georges), and *Les huguenots* (Scribe and Deschamps), Wagner's poem seemed "primitive" and "naive."[77] De la Madeleine and other critics thus contrasted Wagner's sup-

---

76. "Or l'invention de M. Wagner consiste à faire de l'opéra une symphonie instrumentale, avec accompagnement obligé de chanteurs.... Comment un musicien de la valeur de M. Wagner (car, après tout, M. Wagner est un homme d'infiniment de talent) peut-il tenir un langage pareil? M. Wagner a-t-il oublié que le grand intérêt, pour ainsi dire l'unique intérêt de la symphonie, réside dans les développements d'un thème donné qui sert, pour ainsi dire, de thèse aux commentaires du compositeur. Peut-on imaginer une symphonie sans unité de pensée, et sans ce travail ingénieux des parties qui s'établit comme une conversation piquante et souvent spirituelle entre les divers instruments, sur le sujet donné de la conversation, sur le thème? Non, certes, et cela n'est douteux pour personne. Eh bien, ces développements ingénieux d'un motif principal sont tout simplement impossibles dès que la musique doit suivre d'action dramatique et scénique. En effet, au fur et à mesure que l'action s'avance, les personnages expriment nécessairement des sentiments différents et la musique qui les exprime est obligée de changer de caractère; par conséquent, plus d'unité de sentiment et plus de développements possibles d'une idée musicale mère." Oscar Comettant, "Académie Impériale de la Musique," *L'art musical*, 21 March 1861.

77. "Examinons donc tout d'abord son libretto; jugeons-le en lui-même, puis comparons-le à tous ces pauvres poëmes dont on a fait la pauvre musique de *la Juive*, de *la Reine de Chypre*, des *Huguenots* et de *la Muette*.... On voit que M. Wagner n'aime pas les imbroglios trop compliqués; ce deuxième acte est d'une simplicité primitive. Le troisième est encore plus naïf." Stéphen de la Madeleine, "Revue des Théâtres Lyriques," *L'univers musical*, 21 March 1861.

posed naiveté with the professionalism of the librettists of French *grand opéra*. Gustave Chadeuil similarly looked to successful models of the past when judging Wagner's proposed changes to the genre, mocking his attempts to replace "prosaic" historical persons with "poetic" legendary figures: "Mr. Wagner does not want to represent just any ordinary lover, whether Arnold in *Guillaume Tell* or Raoul in *Les huguenots*. He wants to represent love."[78] By creating "allegorical characters" that inhabit "an imaginary world," wrote Franck-Marie, Wagner did not relate "the rigorous conditions of human truth; and opera must be human before anything else, because it is drama, that is, life, true reality, and not a dream."[79] Contrasting Wagner's libretto and genre theory with classic Aristotelian theories of drama, the critics pulled the rug out from under Wagner's own reference to Greek tragedy in his *Lettre sur la musique* as validation for his dramatic theories. Classic French tragedy—whether theatrical or operatic—was held up as a mirror to the arrogant German upstart who sought to supplant appropriate historic subjects with legends of a "German simplicity that falls into puerility."[80]

By casting the debate over *Tannhäuser* in nationalist terms that had been familiar for over a century, the journalists could defend the honor of French art without engaging in the question of musical progress in France itself. For conservative critics, Wagner's work—dangerous as it was—also proved a boon. As the often long theoretical elaborations of the nature of French opera show, Wagner's opera served as a substitute for French works, where attacks on musical and dramatic change might be more problematic. If the traditional mold of the number opera, with its clear-cut melodic phrases and ensembles, were reworked by a French composer, then such complete rejection could be more problematic. But by identifying these characteristics as either German or idiosyncratically Wagnerian, French (and Italian) music could be defined by its past masterworks and timeless rules of clarity, elegance, and form. Furthermore, *Tannhäuser* provided a weapon for future criticism, for now any deviation from the French tradition could either be celebrated as a French (and therefore elegant) form of progress or criticized as foreign infiltration. The latter was the focus of the hostile reviews of Charles Gounod's *La reine de Saba* (1862).[81] But when Reyer's new opera *La statue* was given at the Théâtre-Lyrique on 11 April, a few weeks after the *Tannhäuser* debacle, de la Madeleine recontextualized Reyer's style in a modern, French school that developed melody without falling into the excesses of Wagner:

---

78. "M. Wagner ne veut pas représenter un amoureux quelconque, soit l'Arnold de *Guillaume Tell*, soit le Raoul des *Huguenots*. Il veut représenter l'amour." Gustave Chadeuil, "Revue musicale," *Le siècle*, 26 March 1861.

79. "Tous ces personnages allégoriques, ces fictions plus ou moins brillantes puisées dans un monde imaginaire, ne sauraient convenir aux conditions rigoureuses d'une vérité humaine, et l'opéra doit être humain avant tout, parce qu'il est le drame, c'est-à-dire la vie, la réalité vraie et non le rêve." Franck-Marie [Perdolini], "Revue musicale," *La patrie*, 24 March 1861.

80. "Une simplicité allemande qui tombe dans la puérilité." Benoît Jouvin, "Théâtres," *Le Figaro*, 21 March 1861.

81. Steven Huebner, *The Operas of Charles Gounod* (Oxford: Clarendon Press, 1990), 64–65.

Tannhäuser *and Its French Critics*

Today we have the researchers about whom I spoke last Thursday—the likes of Félicien David, Gounod, Berlioz, Reyer, and even Mr. Wagner himself—who present their melodic thought in a more complicated guise, more closely linked on the one hand to the harmony, which defines its tessitura, and, on the other, to the words of which it is the most complete and most passionate expression. It is these qualities, whose excess has been blamed so strongly on Mr. Wagner, which today make the fortunes of *La statue* at the Théâtre-Lyrique.[82]

These brief glimpses into the passionate debate over the Parisian *Tannhäuser* show that much was at stake for the institution of the Paris Opéra and its guardians. By all accounts, Wagner was the first musician in the history of the Opéra who refused so blatantly to bend to the dictates of the genre as determined by the French. Not only did he resist actively the translation of *Tannhäuser* into the generic framework of *grand opéra*, but his theoretical writings had also challenged the genre and its music famously as "effect without cause." For Wagner's critics, the missing ballet—the pretext for the Jockey Club's protest—was inconsequential and rarely mentioned. What was essential, however, was to demonstrate that Wagner's music of the future had no such future in Paris, not only because he failed to consider his audience, but also because his music lacked beauty. Although the political circumstances and Wagner's own refusal to compromise certainly contributed to the rejection of *Tannhäuser*, its core challenge to the Opéra rested in the work itself. Critics whose aesthetic position held up the tradition of French and Italian opera had no choice but to condemn this kind of music of the future lest they jeopardize the true future of a genre which was the nation's image.

For the critics, both in the theater and in the press, this end justified the means. Two intertwined themes dominated the post-mortem debate: was the French public right to react so violently to Wagner's opera, and was Wagner victim of a cabal? The first was more disturbing for the critics than the second. Rumors of a cabal were dismissed as musings of disgruntled Germans.[83] Moreover, three of his fiercer detractors—Bernard, Heugel, and Jouvin—accused Wagner and his acolytes of turn-

---

82. "Nous avons aujourd'hui ces chercheurs dont je parlais jeudi dernier, les Félicien David, les Gounod, les Berlioz, les Reyer, et M. Wagner lui-même, qui présentent leur pensée mélodique sous un aspect plus compliqué, plus étroitement lié, d'une part à l'harmonie qui lui sert de tessiture, et, de l'autre, à la parole, dont elle est l'expression plus complète et plus passionnée. Ce sont ces qualités, dont l'excès a été si vertement blâmé chez M. Wagner, qui font aujourd'hui la fortune de *la Statue* au Théâtre-Lyrique." Stéphen de la Madeleine, "Six nouveaux morceaux de chant par M. Edmond Michotte," *L'univers musical*, 2 May 1861.

83. See, for example, Albert Wolff, "Courrier de Paris," *Le Figaro*, 24 March 1861: "Dans les salons et dans les cafés, on n'a cessé depuis huit jours de discuter la musique de l'avenir. Les Allemands étaient généralement d'avis que la cabale française avait fait tomber l'œuvre de leur compatriote. Je

ing the *Tannhäuser* debacle into a martyr's trial. What seemed more problematic to Parisian critics was the continued and increasing misbehavior of the audience in the opera house during the three performances of *Tannhäuser*. Although some defended the mischief-makers as truly French—because they could not stand to be bored and insulted by Wagner—many others, including d'Ortigue, Pougin, and Francis Sept-Fontaines, saw this as inappropriate for French dignity. In particular, Pougin—who was otherwise highly critical of Wagner's ideas and score—was horrified by such improper behavior from a people at the zenith of cultural sophistication:

> And so! In our France, in this hospitable land to which all the foreign geniuses come in order to ask for the supreme consecration of their renown, it is here that a conscientious artist, full of faith, convinced—rightly or wrongly—of the worth of his doctrines, an artist who for close to twenty years has impassioned an entire people, comes to invite us to pronounce ourselves openly, with frankness, on the merit of his works, and in order to welcome him, we the royal people, we the elegant people, we the enlightened people, we the polite people, we the witty people, can only offer insult, disdain, sarcasm, and irony. Truth be told, I would have believed my compatriots to be more just, more benevolent, and more sensible.[84]

For Pougin, the Parisians had missed an opportunity not only to show themselves as cultivated, but also to judge the work in a calm and sophisticated manner for what it was worth. Instead, because of the unmeasured reaction of the audience and critics, Wagner's star remained high in the firmament of the operatic sky, and the threat he posed was, in fact, far from neutralized. The critics' own betrayal of the ideals of *justesse* and moderation in their reviews jeopardized their otherwise legitimate criticism of a perceived incompatible dramatic system, proposed by an artist who openly showed his disdain for native French culture. Because of their extremeness, the reactions of Scudo, Heugel, Azevedo, d'Ortigue, Fiorentino, and others were dismissed as reactionary and incompetent by their contemporaries Baudelaire, Champfleury, Gasperini, and Léon Leroy, whose ideology of musical progress meshed seamlessly with the Wagnerian master narrative. Instead of protecting the institutionalized opera they fought so hard to defend against the threat of Wagner, the critics discredited

---

considère comme un devoir de protester contre ces accusations injustes. La question de nationalité n'a rien à voir dans le *Tannhäuser*, qui n'est qu'une question de plus ou moins de trombones."

84. "Eh quoi! en notre pays de France, en cette terre hospitalière à laquelle tous les génies étrangers viennent demander la consécration suprême de leur renommée, voici qu'un artiste consciencieux, plein de foi, convaincu—à tort ou à raison—de la valeur de ses doctrines; un artiste qui pendant près de vingt ans a passionné tout un peuple, vient nous inviter à nous prononcer ouvertement, franchement sur le mérite de ses œuvres, et nous ne trouvons pour l'accueillir, nous le peuple roi, nous le peuple élégant, nous le peuple éclairé, nous le peuple poli, nous le peuple spirituel, que l'injure, le dédain, le sarcasme et l'ironie! En vérité, je croyais mes compatriotes plus justes, plus bienveillants et plus sensés." Arthur Pougin, "Chronologie musicale," *La jeune France*, 31 March 1861.

their own aesthetic position and opened the door to precisely the "music without tradition" (in Saint-Valry's words) that they feared.

The 1861 *Tannhäuser* scandal had disastrous consequences for the institution of French *grand opéra*. Once the Wagnerian ideology of musical progress began to dominate aesthetic and musicological discourses not only in the nineteenth century but also in the twentieth, the tables were turned. Instead of judging music drama by the tenets of French classicist aesthetics, music critics and musicologists dismissed the operas of Auber, Meyerbeer, and Halévy—so beloved by Wagner's critics—as overly determined by the very convention and the very institution that Wagner attacked in his *Lettre sur la musique*. Wagner's Parisian critics were far more astute than posterity ever gave them credit for: their attack on *Tannhäuser* was indeed a cabal, because only a concerted, last-ditch effort could help preserve an operatic tradition that had become obsolete by the late 1850s. The price for their rather spectacular failure was high: ridiculed themselves, they were left behind in the dust of history, for it was Wagner's music—not that of Auber, Rossini, Meyerbeer, and Halévy—that dominated the artistic future they helped to shape in this March of 1861.

CHAPTER 2

Visual Pleasures—Musical Signs:
Dance at the Paris Opéra

Among the more familiar images associated with the Paris Opéra are the ballet dancers that Edgar Dégas portrayed in his paintings, where he offered to the gaze of observers, whether inside or outside his pictures, young female bodies in white-tulle tutus, often bent in graceful or provocative poses.[1] The flesh market of young ballerinas, so keenly exploited within the institution of *grand opéra* in the French capital and explored by writers such as Balzac and Zola, still seems the predominant picture of the world of French nineteenth-century ballet. Moreover, in musical circles this impression is reinforced by the best-known musical scandal of the nineteenth century, the débâcle of the Paris performance of Wagner's *Tannhäuser* in 1861, in which the young aristocrats of the Jockey Club noisily disturbed each of the three performances because the ballet of the *Venusberg* in act 1 came too early in the evening, at a time when fashionable Parisians would still be having dinner.[2] For Wagnerian performers and scholars, on the other hand, ballet and its frivolous dancers had no place in serious art, and they have tried to expunge a genre that seemed to have one purpose only—entertainment—and thus, most would feel that it has no place in the hallowed genre of music-drama.[3]

Even today, musicological research on ballet focuses mainly on the modernist reinvention of the genre through the Ballets Russes and modern dance. The works that Debussy, Ravel, Satie, and Stravinsky wrote for Diaghilev's company—in particular *The Rite of Spring*—have become staples of the repertory (albeit, and significantly, as much in the concert hall as on the stage) and of scholarly inquiry. Over the last decade, however, musicologists have begun to discover that French ballet has much to offer as a key to the world of nineteenth-century Parisian music-theater.[4] The paradigms of our discipline have changed enough to warrant research on works and performers outside the canon of "great" art, and although nineteenth-century ballet lacks the widespread academic appeal of genres such as film music, it nevertheless allows for new approaches to Parisian cultural life. Ballet has always had its marginal devotees, but now the medium is coming into the scholarly mainstream.

Ballet in nineteenth-century Paris also provides new insights to questions that have become central to musicology, in particular issues of musical "meaning" and representation.[5] The musical and gestural space between the often diegetic, patterned dance (which has become the predominant mode of classical ballet in the twentieth century) on the one hand, and the narrative impetus of nineteenth-century ballet-pantomime on the other, points toward a sophisticated semiotic field. From a musicological point of view, dance can offer a window onto the meaning of otherwise inaccessible codes. The journey of uncovering some of those codes will lead us through French ballet and opera, where works by Daniel-François-Esprit Auber, Hector Berlioz, and Jules Massenet will provide crucial snapshots of the use of dance in opera in order to explore the complex interrelationship of music, image, and gesture on the nineteenth-century French stage.

Opera and Dance in Nineteenth-Century Paris

In the historiography of Western music, seeking origins often becomes an ideologically inflected search for some kind of essence of the object under consideration. For example, accounts of the genesis of opera differ along national fault lines. The very earliest historical accounts of Italian opera, which were written shortly after its birth (Marco da Gagliano was writing about opera as early as 1608), associate the genre primarily with musical and dramatic expressivity, gained chiefly by way of the new musical recitative. Only much more recently has the central role of danced *balli* and splendid *intermedio*-like musical and scenic effects been acknowledged.[6] Conversely, the beginnings of French opera have commonly been located in dance, with Baltasar de Beaujoyeulx's *Balet comique de la Royne* (1581). Typically, both the Italians and the French (in the seventeenth century and later) sought to claim Humanist sanction for their brand of opera: the Italians focusing on the role of music in Greek tragedy, and the French on that of dance therein.[7] But dance as a characteristically French operatic trait has remained the common thread running through all historical accounts of the genre, with the danced splendor of the Louis XIV–era *tragédie en musique* leading almost seamlessly to the visual opulence of nineteenth-century *grand opéra*.[8] The differences between the Italian and French positions became famously articulated in a late-seventeenth-century disaster that created no less a scandal than that roused two centuries later by the Paris *Tannhäuser*. The Italian Francesco Cavalli was commissioned to write an opera for the marriage of Louis XIV in 1660, but his *Ercole amante* was performed in Paris only two years later and rendered acceptable only by the addition of extended ballets by Jean-Baptiste Lully. Proponents of seventeenth-century Italian opera decried the intrusion (and still do); those of French opera proclaimed it an inevitability.

Indeed, dance was an integral part of French music-theater from the late sixteenth to the early twentieth centuries. While, during the seventeenth century, only men performed in the *ballets du roi*, female dancers such as Marie Sallé quickly became the stars of the public stage in eighteenth-century Paris. In the bourgeois opera of the July Monarchy, dancers took on an even more prominent and overtly sexual role after Louis Véron had become the Opéra's director in 1831.[9] That he himself was very much aware of the female dancers' attractions to a male audience becomes clear from his *Memoirs*, in which he dedicated an entire chapter to ballet dancers and their role in the institution of opera both onstage and off.[10] Indeed, Véron was the first to grant select male patrons access to the ballerinas in the *foyer de la danse*, calculatingly catering to their "erotic daydreaming" in a fantasy world created by men for men.[11] Véron also cut the salaries of the *corps de ballet* so drastically that "without outside income, many of [the dancers] were too destitute to pay for food, fuel and lodging."[12] In order to support and nourish herself, many a dancer had to resort to virtual or actual prostitution within the framework of the *foyer de la danse*. The dancers of the *corps de ballet* were at the beck and call of their male protectors, and, as Marian Smith has observed, the plots of ballets "tended to mirror this backstage relationship by promoting in no uncertain terms a particular set of values that upheld the notions of masculine power and feminine submissiveness."[13] With this feminization of the ballet came the progressive marginalization of male ballet dancers who, by the 1840s, "fidgeted on the margins of the stage."[14] By that time, the notion from the era of Louis XIV that male dancing had connotations of control, virtuosity, strength, discipline, and even militarism as a counterpart to fencing or horse riding, had disappeared completely.

By turning his dancers into erotic commodities, Véron affected not only ballets, their plots, and their reception, but also the role of dance within *grand opéra*. This genre had developed in the late 1820s with works such as Daniel-François-Esprit Auber's *La Muette de Portici* (1828) and Gioacchino Rossini's *Guillaume Tell* (1829), and its characteristic elements remained stable until the end of the nineteenth century with such operas as Camille Saint-Saëns's *Henry VIII* (1884) and Jules Massenet's *Le Cid* (1885). Among its main traits were the massive scale of performance forces and scenery, the absence of spoken dialogue, the (usually) five-act structure, the organization of the acts in tableaux, and the obligatory ballet divertissements that typically were located in acts 2, 3, and/or 4. These characteristics had become institutionalized not only through cultural practice but also through state legislation. Only the Paris Opéra had the right to perform (and, more important, premiere) full-length operas with substantial ballet divertissements and without spoken dialogue.[15]

Grand opéra was geared toward visual splendor, and dance contributed significantly to the brilliance of the spectacle, as Charles Soullier had already remarked in 1855.[16] Indeed, almost all major operatic premières in Paris contained ballets with important solos for the prima ballerina, most famously in the notorious ballet (featuring the disrobing ghosts of corrupted nuns in a ruined, moonlit cloister) in act 3 of Giacomo Meyerbeer's *Robert le Diable* (1831), which served as a vehicle for Marie Taglioni's dancing and miming skills. This ballet quickly became a model for the integration of dance into the plot of *grand opéra*, and it has also served as an exemplar for discussions of ballet in nineteenth-century French opera. Rather than simply imparting local color through national or exotic dance, or representing danced moments within the plot—as in the *bal masqué* in Auber's *Gustave III* (1833)—the nuns' ballet in *Robert le Diable* became, according to two recent scholars, the "true dramatic center of the work."[17] It represented both the culmination and the turning point of the drama, as the devilish Bertram summons the ghosts of the sinful nuns in order to seduce his son Robert into his satanic ways. Like the Wolf's Glen scene in Carl Maria von Weber's *Der Freischütz* (1821), with its mysterious music and gruesome monsters, the amalgamation of fantastic image and colorful music in Meyerbeer's ballet fascinated Parisian audiences and proved to be one of the enduring aspects of ballet in opera, whether in the ghost scene in Ambroise Thomas's opera *Hamlet* (1868) or the fantastic hunt in Jules Massenet's *Esclarmonde* (1889), where dance was replaced by projected images in the manner of the illuminated advertisements on the boulevards.[18]

Even more ambitious was the fusion of ballet and opera in Auber's *La Muette de Portici*, in which the protagonist is a mute. Indeed, few other operas responded so extensively to the challenge of interlinking music and gesture. A particularly striking moment is the entrance in act 1 of the two female characters, the Spanish princess Elvire, and the Neapolitan girl Fenella (the mute). These scenes clearly contrast dance, mime, and voice. After Elvire's virtuosic entrance-aria, her entourage performs two "Spanish" dances, a *guarache* and a *bolero*, as signifiers for her national origins.[19] The *musique dansante* accompanying these performances followed the nineteenth-century formula of national dance music, with characteristic melodies, distinctive rhythms, and regular eight-bar phrases. Auber found a different kind of music, however, for when the mute Fenella runs on stage, hiding from her pursuers and seeking shelter with the princess. The only means she has to explain her story are gestures, both physical and musical. In a fast-moving dialogue, Fenella's mime, accompanied by brief musical interjections, is contrasted with Elvire's mostly unaccompanied voice asking questions and commenting on Fenella's story. For a short time, voice and gesture (musical and physical) become separate as means of expression. Indeed, this entire sequence, from aria to mime, makes both visible and audible various possible forms of communication, representation, and expression in the musical theater.[20]

Although *La Muette de Portici* remained a more or less isolated case in its blend of mute character and singers—we know only two other works using this strategy from the 1830s[21]—mimed scenes remained a powerful tool for composers and librettists of *grand opéra*. Indeed, formal ballet was just one facet of the use of movement and gesture in a genre that, given its massive proportions, often had to rely on visual elements over verbal communication in transmitting the plot. Tableaux with large choruses, processions, and other public scenes formed the backbone of these spectacles, where the drama of private lives was but a by-product of the great political conflicts of history.[22] The visual impact of these tableaux on Parisian audiences was so powerful that this "operatic" organization of space was soon reflected in the historical paintings of Géricault and Delacroix.[23] In addition, the dimensions of the Opéra, and the large performance forces, were diametrically opposed to an intimate chamber play where each word might be heard. Thus in *grand opéra* both dance and expressive gestures became essential elements in order to convey the drama.

While some ballet divertissements, as in *Robert le Diable*, represented key moments in plot development, more often in opera, dance served as entertainment, distraction, and contrast. The gypsy dances in Fromental Halévy's *La Juive*, for example, granted a moment of erotic abandon to the otherwise tense drama unfolding between medieval knights and Jews. Increasingly throughout the nineteenth century, exotic locations and the customs of distant lands served as prompts for ballets, as, for example, in Charles Gounod's *La Reine de Saba* (1862) or Massenet's *Hérodiade* (1881). Given that the erotic equation of dancer and dance remained the most persistent quality of operatic ballet throughout the nineteenth century, foreign realms allowed for more lascivious ballets than Breton meadows. As in the 1830s, "ogling the ballerinas" continued to be a powerful draw for the male public.[24] By the last decades of the century, however, ballet was also becoming a symbol of what musicians and critics objected to in *grand opéra* as empty spectacle or, in the words of Richard Wagner, "effect without cause."[25] Yet so powerful were the institutions and conventions of *grand opéra* that ballet remained a major element of French opera until the early twentieth century. Even in operas such as Augusta Holmès's *La Montagne noire* (1895) or in *Messidor*, a work created in a collaboration between Alfred Bruneau and Emile Zola in 1897, ballet had its place.[26] The fight over the staging of the ballet in *Messidor* between the directors of the Opéra and the two authors shows just how ingrained the convention of the ballet had become: "[The directors] had an unshakable belief in the use of the 'tutu' ... We considered, on the contrary, that it was essential that our ballerinas should wear costumes."[27] But neither Holmès nor Bruneau and Zola ever considered avoiding dance altogether.

Countering the notion that ballet was redundant, some extolled its virtues, and its potential, as a powerful means of conveying elements of the unfolding plots in ways not available to song and instrumental music.[28] During the 1890s, a new approach to the role of dance in French opera also led to the introduction of allegorical ballets, not only in *La Montagne noire* and *Messidor*, but also in other operas such as Massenet's *Thaïs* (1894), probably the first to have recourse to this kind of mimed ballet in the 1890s.[29] I would argue that rather than characterizing these and similar fin de siècle ballets as "some sort of compromise between the ideational demands of *drame lyrique* and the convention of the ballet" engendered by the institutional framework of the Opéra,[30] this use of dance may also have served a different purpose. Precisely in this period, French opera was undergoing a period of crisis and renewal under the (positive or negative, depending on the point of view) influence of Wagnerism. Repositioning the role of dance in French opera was a way of renewing the genre from the inside out, by maintaining one of the key features of French opera in a way that linked it back to its origins in the seventeenth and eighteenth centuries, where allegorical figures populated the ballets of Lully, Destouches, and Rameau, and where dream sequences figured among the more familiar balletic tropes.[31]

Thaïs was written at a key juncture between Wagnerian and French opera, and Massenet amalgamated various strands of music-theater from the "French" operatic ballet to the Wagnerian orchestral melody in a search to create a new music-dramatic medium for contemporary opera. However, this was not the first attempt to reintegrate ballet and mime into *grand opéra* at a point when the genre was thought to need renewal. Hector Berlioz, for example, used pantomime effectively in dramatic key moments in his operas, following the lead of his teacher, Jean-François Le Sueur. Thus in Berlioz's *Benvenuto Cellini*, premièred at the Opéra in 1838, the pantomime of King Midas in act 2 becomes the catalyst for the dramatic turn toward murder and redemption. But the pantomime here is justified as a diegetic moment of theater-within-theater. Almost twenty years later, however, Berlioz refined the use of mime during the composition of his magnum opus, *Les Troyens*, which he wrote mostly between 1856 and 1858. Here the dramatic means are much more integrated and provided a model for later composers such as Saint-Saëns and Massenet.

Ballet and Pantomime in Hector Berlioz's *Les Troyens*

Hector Berlioz's *Les Troyens* (1863) contained both pantomime (especially in the Royal Hunt) and dance (at the court of Dido). Indeed, Berlioz's self-imposed task for *Les Troyens* was the creation of an exemplary opera (rather than the run-of-the-mill variety performed at the Opéra in the 1850s), including exemplary ballets and pantomimes.[32] While Berlioz's criticisms of ballets and operas are numerous and acerbic, it would be a misconception to assume that he disavowed the (self-consciously) French tradition of dance and pantomime as musico-dramatic devices. In his *Memoirs*, written in part at the time of the composition of *Les Troyens*, Berlioz recalled an 1822 performance of the ballet-pantomime *Nina*, "devised and composed" by Louis-Luc Persuis and based on Nicolas Dalayrac's *opéra comique* with the same title:

> The ballet . . . delighted me and I was profoundly moved to hear, played by Vogt on the cor anglais during a heart-rending mime scene by Mlle Bigottini, the tune of the hymn which my sister's companions had sung at the Ursuline convent on the day of my first communion. It was the romance "Quand le bien-aimé reviendra." A man sitting near me, who was murmuring the words to himself, told me the name of the composer and the opera from which Persuis had taken it. I learnt that it was from Dalayrac's *Nina*. However remarkable the singer who created the role of Nina, I find it hard to believe she can ever have made it sound as natural [*vrai*] and touching as it did on Vogt's instrument, heightened as it was by the acting of the famous mime.[33]

Mime and instrumental melody thus gel into dramatic expression that is more natural (or true, depending how one translates Berlioz's *vrai*) and touching than any singer might produce, more immediate in its impact than the aria on which it is based. Accordingly, in *Les Troyens* mime differs from the use of dance, which, in act 4, becomes a locus of exoticism and gender stereotyping, reflecting the feminizing of the genre in the mid-nineteenth century.[34] Here, the three dances could serve as a *locus classicus* of musical representations of race and gender in nineteenth-century French opera.[35] In the lascivious dance of the Egyptian slave girls, descending chromatic lines embroider a static harmony of G major in an orchestration dominated by strings, while the rhythmically energetic and mainly diatonic dance (also in G major) of the male slaves with its woodwind and brass, modulates assertively at a fast pace. The third dance for Nubian slave girls is set in the relative minor, and reproduces one feature that Berlioz associated with oriental dance: the dancers sing—in a fantasy "Nubian"—accompanied by an orientalizing ensemble of high woodwind, low strings, and monotonous percussion instruments.[36] We see and hear an exotic African world that, for Berlioz, was both the origin of his revered Rome and a modern-day French colony.[37] The Egyptian women's lasciviousness, the Near-Eastern men's virility and the Nubians's exotic difference correspond to tropes of musical and visual Orientalism and gender stereotypes that were rampant in Second-Empire Paris.[38] The customary place for such representation within opera was, indeed, dance, for it offered the eroticized bodies of the dancers unmediated by speech directly to the dominant gaze (whether defined as male or colonial). In this context, the arrival of the African queen Dido in a wordless procession immediately before the Oriental ballet associates her with the body politic of the Orient rather than with Aeneas's Rome.

This contrasts with Berlioz's use of mimed sections at expressive and dramatic key moments in *Les Troyens*, in particular the appearance of the mourning Andromache in act 1, the Royal Hunt at the beginning of act 4, and the various mimed scenes surrounding Dido's death in act 5. Andromache's mime was accompanied, in Berlioz's words, by an "instrumental piece with chorus," and for him it was one of the most important scenes of the entire opera.[39] In a letter to Caroline Princess Sayn-Wittgenstein, Berlioz made it clear that he perceived a difference between "the sounds of mime music, desolate, haunting, (if possible) heartbreaking" and the other music of the opera, whether sung or danced. In the same scene, the chorus comments on Andromache's mourning for Hector in lines that "will be sung or rather chanted in an aside during the playing of the mime music."[40] Thus the layer of music that Berlioz identifies as "mime music" is inseparably associated with the expression and gestures of Andromache and her son, just as mime and the *cor anglais* melody coalesced into one experience during his youthful visit to the ballet. When composing the scene, Berlioz "wept buckets over it."[41]

But if the mime music for Andromache was expressive, the interlude for the Royal Hunt was pictorial:

> The day before yesterday I finished the devilish scene of the storm during the Royal Hunt, where there are many different stage pictures that the music absolutely must render: naiads bathing amid the calm of the forest, distant fanfares, huntsmen alarmed at the approach of the storm, streams transformed into torrents, cries of ill omen from the rampaging nymphs at the moment when Dido follows Aeneas into the cave, grotesque dances by the satyrs and fauns brandishing, like torches, the branches of a tree struck by lightening, etc., etc.[42]

Mimed scenes were musically either representational or mimetic, and in both cases music contributed significantly to the communicative immediacy that Berlioz had experienced as a listener in the mimed air of *Nina*. In the case of these scenes in *Les Troyens*, Berlioz also provided explicit descriptions and staging instructions for actions and gestures in very specific terms. Thus the spectacular reality of Berlioz's *grand opéra* celebrated the visual through dance and mime music that can lead us from erotic flights of fantasy to the poignant and haunting melody of Andromache's mourning.

Berlioz's restoration of French *grand opéra* in his *Les Troyens* remained marginal to the cultural practice of the mid- and late-nineteenth-century France, for the opera's first performances (in a truncated version) were limited to a brief run at the Théâtre Lyrique instead of the Opéra, for which the work was conceived.[43] Instead, the impulse to address the musical and dramaturgic structure of French opera entered the mainstream only with the challenge of Wagner whose claim to the "music of the future" threatened to leave French operatic traditions behind in the dust. French composers now faced a mighty task, and whether in adaptation or in rejection of Wagnerian aesthetics and techniques, they still needed to engage with the key elements of the French tradition. In particular Jules Massenet's balancing act between French tradition and Wagnerian influence shows how the nexus of image, gesture, and music remained a preoccupation of the French stage.[44]

Massenet's *Thaïs*: A Wagnerian Approach to French Ballet

Massenet's opera, based on the eponymous novel by Anatole France, tells the story of the conversion of the Alexandrian courtesan Thaïs by way of the monk Athanaël. While Thaïs attains sainthood through Christian martyrdom, Athanaël becomes obsessed with his carnal desire for her and ends his life as a condemned soul. The moment of his downfall is reflected in the "Ballet de la Tentation" ("Ballet of Temptation") when the soul of Athanaël leaves his body during slumber and encounters temptation in the form of the allegorical figure of Perdition (first danced by Rosita Mauri, then the *étoile* of the Paris Opéra) and a gaggle of phantasmagorical apparitions. Given Massenet's proclivity for intertextual references, the allusions in the "Ballet de la Tentation" to eighteenth-century *Sommeil* scenes and to the fantastic *Ur*-ballet of the nuns from Meyerbeer's *Robert le Diable* were probably neither accidental nor unreflected.[45] Rather, the composer seems to explore ways in which dance and mime could indeed contribute to a renewed French spectacle.

However, his path was not smooth. Massenet's *Thaïs* had started out in 1892 as an *opéra comique* in three acts without ballet, before it was subsequently adapted to the mold of *grand opéra* when the work followed its diva, Sybil Sanderson, to the stage of the Opéra.⁴⁶ One salient aspect of the transformation from one genre to another was chronicled for the public as, on July 23, 1893, *Le Ménestrel* published a notice that informed its readers: "Last Monday at the Opéra, M. Massenet played the ballet that he has just composed for *Thaïs*. Being entirely part of the action, this ballet—which lasts for at least twenty minutes—is of an entirely new and original kind and allows for very beautiful stage effects."⁴⁷ The announcement that the ballet would be something "entirely new and original" was (and is) part of customary advertising strategies. What is more important in this notice, however, is the statement that the ballet formed an integral part of the action, and in a later announcement, published shortly before the première, this crucial claim of the complete integration of ballet and plot was repeated.⁴⁸ Indeed, in *Thaïs* not only the ballet but also several vision scenes and symphonic interludes contributed to this complex operatic narrative of voice, image, gesture and music.⁴⁹ The mimed and the purely instrumental key scenes in the 1894 première are given in table 1.⁵⁰

The "Ballet de la Tentation" and the mimed visions contrasted markedly with the ballets of *grands opéras* such as Camille Saint-Saëns's *Henry VIII* or Massenet's own *Hérodiade* from the 1880s, where they generally represented actual (diegetic) dance within the plot, whether in the form of peasant dances in a *fête populaire* or that of the titillating dances of Babylonian and Egyptian slave girls. Massenet was much more aware than his librettist Louis Gallet of the differences in music and staging between mere seductive dance and the more complex pantomime of the "Ballet de la Tentation." In a letter that referred to an earlier section of the opera, Athanaël's vision of Thaïs in act 1—a key scene because it sets the opera's action in motion—Massenet asked Gallet to inquire with Anatole France and find out "exactly whether, in the theater of Alexandria (of *this period*, the fourth century), Thaïs *danced* or *mimed*" (Massenet's emphases).⁵¹ As we have seen, mime enabled the conveying of dramatic content through gesture, and another letter from Massenet to Gallet suggests that the composer saw it as a music-dramatic tool with even more impact than text. Here Massenet refers to the "Apparition de Thaïs" in act 3. Concerned that the staging would visually

Table 1: Nonvocal Episodes in Massenet's *Thaïs*

Act	Title	Description
Act 1	*Vision d' Athanaël*	In his sleep, the monk Athanaël sees Thaïs in the theater of Alexandria, miming the loves of Aphrodite, including a striptease performed with her back to the Parisian theater audience.
Act 2, tableau 1	Symphonie: *Les Amours d'Aphrodite*	In Alexandria, Thaïs performs the beginnings of her mime of the loves of Aphrodite. The curtain closes, and the Parisian audience listens (in the dark) to the symphonic interlude that accompanies the (imagined) continuation.
Act 2, end of tableau 2	*Méditation*	Instrumental interlude between tableaux 2 and 3, representing the conversion of Thaïs
Act 3, tableau 2	*Ballet de la Tentation*	The temptation of Athanaël in his sleep by the seven spirits of temptation, Perdition, sirens, gnomes, and other figures. He succumbs to temptation.
Act 3, tableau 2	*L'Apparition de Thaïs*	Thaïs appears to the sleeping Athanaël and tries to seduce him in a brief duet.
Act 3, tableau 2	*Vision d'Athanaël*	Athanaël sees Thaïs surrounded by saints and seraphim.
Act 3, tableau 2	Symphonie: *La Course dans la nuit*	Orchestral interlude. Amid thunder and lightning, Athanaël runs off the stage; the stage becomes completely darkened and enveloped with clouds. The interlude continues after the curtain falls.

convey Thaïs's seduction of Athanaël, Massenet writes in his "Notes pour l'Opéra," "This is not a calm, statue-like appearance—it is Thaïs appearing close to Athanaël's bed and tempting him with words and even more with *the gestures* that accompany and underline the performed scene" (Massenet's emphasis).[52]

Both of the mimed scenes to which Massenet referred in these letters were part of the earliest layer of the opera, already intended for the Opéra Comique. Hence from the outset, the opera's authors had integrated mime into the narrative strategy of the plot. This approach contrasts with earlier works of Massenet, especially *Hérodiade*, in which Herod's vision of a sexually appealing Salome during his aria "Vision fugitive" remains entirely imagined.[53] In *Hérodiade*, we envision what Herod tells us; in *Thaïs*, we see exactly what Athanaël sees when he sees it. The integration of the "Ballet de la Tentation" into the subsequent version of *Thaïs* for the Opéra was thus chiefly a consequence of the opera's dramaturgic concept of making visual a sequence of male erotic fantasies. Indeed, all we see mimed in this opera are Athanaël's visions; we are mostly left to imagine Thaïs's actual striptease in the first tableau of act 2 to the music of the symphonic interlude, "Les Amours d'Aphrodite," and the curtain falls before the courtesan's conversion during the purely instrumental *Méditation* at the end of the second act.

Gesture, Image, and Music

The "Ballet de la Tentation" contains both dance and mime, thus resembling not so much its immediate forbears of the 1880s as the earlier pantomime-ballets of the July Monarchy such as Théophile Gautier's and Adolphe Adam's *Giselle* (1841), in which narrative and danced sections alternated. Indeed, pantomime made up a large part not only of *Giselle* but also of most other ballets of that period, including that of the nuns in *Robert le Diable*.[54] As Marian Smith has shown, this was reflected also in different musical languages: while the "musique dansante" in ballets adopted formal, regular structures resembling the dance tunes known from ballrooms and other entertainments, and also the piano literature, music accompanying pantomime provided a continuous musical flow that fluctuated with the action, imitated speech patterns, reflected physical gestures, and represented emotional responses.[55] Although Massenet's toolbox contained other compositional resources, in particular the musical prose gleaned from Wagner's music-dramas and the model of the "Venusberg" from *Tannhäuser*, his "Ballet de la Tentation" pays homage first and foremost to the genre of *grand opéra* at the time of Meyerbeer and Halévy. In Massenet's ballet, dance music, such as the seductive waltz performed by Perdition (the "female demon"), is followed by instrumental recitative in the short evocation of the seven spirits, before moving into a lilting instrumental song of green-haired sirens.[56] The ballet contains music for an instant of religious reflection as well as for the cataclysmic "Sabbath" with its *ronde infernale*, and crowds of fantastic creatures have their music just as Athanaël has his.

The rich tapestry of music in the "Ballet de la Tentation" invites some further reflection on the issue of musical representation. Just like the piano-vocal scores of the 1830s, the 1894 score for *Thaïs* had a condensed description of the ballet's action printed above its musical staves. The piano-vocal score was the medium through which musically literate amateurs could get to know new theatrical pieces, and in the case of the ballet in *Thaïs*, the description offers an immediate interpretation of the music by its composer, with signified and signifier coming together in intriguing ways. In this and other representations of operatic ballets, physical and musical gestures are conflated in both text and performance, offering a hermeneutic window into nineteenth-century music that is all too often neglected or denounced as trivial. If we take seriously Carl Dahlhaus's assertion that European musical culture of the early nineteenth century was characterized by a literary understanding of music, these ballets shed new light on the complex issue of musical meaning and representation.[57]

What distinguishes this mimetic music from other genres that lay claim to conveying meaning through sonic narration, in particular nineteenth-century program music, is its specific and simultaneous embodiment in dance: the audience can see, and the reader can understand, what these sounds mean. As Carolyn Abbate has pointed out, narrative gestures in music involve a distance between "the musical fabric and the phenomenal objects it is said to express (a funeral, a battle, interactions of tonal characters, a conflict between musical forms)."[58] In the mimed sections of nineteenth-century ballet, however, such distance seems to disappear entirely, with musical and physical gestures illuminating each other reciprocally and instantaneously even while their phenomenological difference remains intact.[59] But here the process is not so straightforward as "mickey-mousing," save in a few instances. The pantomime music in the "Ballet de la Tentation" falls mainly into the stylistic context of the instrumental interludes of late-nineteenth-century French opera, its discursive character based on its proselike enchaining of musical topoi in quick succession.[60] Thus the visualization through dance—or "imagetext" in Kramer's recent discussion of musical meaning—can be understood as acting as an interpretant for the complex musical symbols both within and outside of the ballet, at least within the context of late-nineteenth-century Parisian music-theater.[61]

How analogically gesture and language were understood as specific interpretants of musical signs, or vice versa, can be detected in the stage directions for *Thaïs*, which were published at the time of the first performance: after the Star of Redemption appears (to the sound of an organ) in the middle of the temptation scene, the stage directions instruct the soul of Athanaël to kneel "in the center of the stage and *say through gestures*: 'This is the awakening, this is salvation!'" (my emphasis). The pantomime then is to convey that "he understands . . . he understands! . . . But where was he? Explosion of joy and recognition: He is saved! saved!"[62] Thus gestures were purportedly a silent language able to convey the meaning, while music offered the sonic element of the text. As Marian Smith has shown, however, the practice of communication through gesture and sound was less immediate than the stage directions might lead us to believe.[63] The written word of the libretto—including its condensed version in the piano-vocal score—was needed to clarify the meaning both of gestures and of their associated music, at least for those who could not see the dancers on the stage.

If image, gesture, and music are explicit in their interrelationship within Athanaël's visions and the "Ballet de la Tentation," they prove more elusive, if no less intriguing in the symphonic interludes. The first interlude, "Les Amours d'Aphrodite," plays out musically what the audience glimpses in the first pantomime, Athanaël's vision of Thaïs's striptease. The music is based on a syncopated motif, urging itself forward to an extended *fortissimo* climax before relaxing into a soft and melodious episode that is quite literally postclimactic. By this period, musical representations of sexual climax were not unheard of in French opera, and only five years earlier, in 1889, Massenet had famously rendered sexual intercourse audible in the act 2 interlude of his opera *Esclarmonde*.[64] Neither piece leaves much to the listener's imagination, but in both *Esclarmonde* and *Thaïs* the imagination is the only place where musical gestures could find their visual or physical counterpart. The incongruence between the (non-)image on the stage (the closed curtain) and the music's evocative development creates a carefully calculated discrepancy opening an interpretative space for the listener's directed associations.[65]

Thus prepared, the audience confronts the second interlude, again in front of closed curtains, with the *Méditation*, an *Andante religioso* whose passionate violin part seems to give voice to the heroine in a sensual moment of spiritual *jouissance* that is underscored by the timbre of the wordless chorus (often omitted in twentieth-century performances and recordings).[66] Like the first, erotic interlude, the timbral dramaturgy of the *Méditation* and its musical topoi create a field of significance that invites imagination as the adequate mode of reception, echoing notions that music was the perfect translator of the ineffable and the unmentionable.[67] The third interlude, representing both Athanaël's disturbed state of mind and his race through the night is as mimetic as the first interlude, representing the movement through the predominant iambic rhythm, the swelling of the storm and Athanaël's anxiety in a massive crescendo, and its calming down on his arrival at Thaïs's deathbed.

All three interludes are played in front of the closed curtain—this is acousmatic music in terms of the unfolding drama, even if the audience can identify (although not necessarily see) the source of the music as emanating from the orchestra pit. In terms of the opera, the absence of the imagetext creates a dramatic void that calls for the listener's imagination, seeking the truth behind the curtain by listening.[68] As Clair Rowden has shown, these interludes reflect new cognitive ideas of a pre-Freudian, symbolist environment that experimented with hypnosis, diagnosed hysteria, and began to explore dreams.[69] In *Thaïs*, dreams and reality inhabit different phenomenological realms: the ballet and vision scenes—in the wordless mime to music—allow us to share Athanaël's dreams and visions, while the unfolding musical drama of sung dialogue belongs to the story. Finally, music by itself enters into a dialogue with the audience to convey what words and images are not permitted to illustrate.[70] In *Thaïs*, image and gesture thus inhabit both the real world and the subconscious, while words remain firmly on the side of the rational and music points toward the inexpressible.

In terms of the use of dramatic media, Massenet's eclectic approach to French tradition and Wagnerian music-drama in *Thaïs* leads to a musicodramatic hybridity that may well show that by virtue of their long experience of ballet and pantomime, nineteenth-century French audiences developed a musical sophistication in terms of matching music to meaning without the aid of text that, in turn, enabled composers such as Massenet to load their operatic instrumental music with greater semiotic burdens. At that point, the text becomes an unnecessary interference, and instead, the more immediate reciprocal relationship between physical and musical gesture seems to come into its own, regardless of whether the physical gestures are performed or merely imagined.

Dance and mime formed a continuous presence in French ballet and opera. Contrary to the modernist enterprise of the twentieth century, for which music became the embodiment of abstract art, music in nineteenth-century France relied on shared horizons of expectation and reception that bestowed music with meanings far more specific than a modernist aesthetic of absolute music might prefer. Pantomime music in nineteenth-century French opera has a twentieth-century parallel in both film music and MTV, not only in phenomenological terms but also with respect to its presumed triviality. But after more than a century of reading music in absolute terms, the pastness of operatic artifacts makes approaches that seek to understand musical codes still necessary, however uncomfortably so. By acknowledging and exploring the nexus of image, gesture, and music in nineteenth-century French spectacle, we might appreciate with greater sophistication not only a historical phenomenon, but also the roots of our own cultural practice.

Notes

This essay is indebted to the lively discussions in my graduate seminar on French opera and ballet in the nineteenth century at the University of North Carolina at Chapel Hill, and I am grateful to Virginia Christy Lamothe, Zarah Ersoff, Jason Gersh, Peter Lamothe, Ethan Lechner, and Ben Lee for their stimulating contributions to the seminar. I would also like to thank Tim Carter and Katharine Ellis for their helpful, informative, and challenging comments on earlier versions of the text.

1. Jill De Vonyar and Richard Kendall, *Degas and the Dance* (New York: Harry N. Abrams, 2002).
2. While the reasons for the repeated disturbances are far more complex, including the club members' intense dislike of Princess Metternich, one of Wagner's patrons in Paris, the most widely told part of the story is the one concerned the wrong positioning of the ballet. See Hervé Lacombe, *The Keys to French Opera in the Nineteenth Century*, trans. by Edward Schneider (Berkeley: University of California Press, 2001), 39–40. On Wagner's adaptation of *Tannhäuser* for Paris, see Carolyn Abbate, "The Parisian 'Vénus' and the 'Paris' Tannhäuser," *Journal of the American Musicological Society* 36.1 (Spring 1983): 73–123.
3. Charles Rosen's account of French *grand opéra* as "junk" and "trash" culminates in his judgment that these works were "cheap melodrama dressed up as aristocratic tragedy" (Rosen, *The Romantic Generation* [Cambridge: Harvard University Press, 1995], 604–7). On the issue of voyeurism, see Anselm Gerhard, *The Urbanization of Opera: Music Theater in Paris in the Nineteenth Century*, trans. by Mary Whittall (Chicago: University of Chicago Press, 1992), 232–37.
4. French ballet of the nineteenth century has been the focus of two recent studies: Marian Smith, *Ballet and Opera in the Age of Giselle* (Princeton: Princeton University Press, 2000), and Maribeth Clark, *Understanding French Grand Opera through Dance* (PhD diss., University of Pennsylvania, 1998). See also Gudrun Oberzaucher-Schüller and Hans Moeller, eds., *Meyerbeer und der Tanz (Meyerbeer and Dance)* (Feldkirchen: Ricordi and Paderborn University Press, 1998). Music, voice, and gesture are also addressed in Mary Ann Smart, *Mimomania: Music and Gesture in Nineteenth-Century Opera* (Berkeley: University of California Press, 2004). In her preface, Marian Smith denounces traditional musicology's "streak of distaste for dance" (xv).
5. A key text in bringing the issue of musical meaning back on the musicological agenda was

Susan McClary, *Feminine Endings: Music, Gender, and Sexuality* (Minnesota: University of Minnesota Press, 1991), esp. 3–34.

6 Tim Carter, *Monteverdi's Musical Theatre* (New Haven: Yale University Press, 2002), 1–46; Silke Leopold, "Die Anfänge von Oper und die Probleme der Gattung" ("The Beginnings of Opera and the Problems of Genre"), *Journal of Seventeenth-Century Music* 9.1 (2003), http://sscm-jscm.press.uiuc.edu/jscm/v9/no1/Leopold.html (accessed May 27, 2004).

7 The issue of dance has yet to be explored properly, but see the preliminary remarks in Irene Alm, "Humanism and Theatrical Dance in Early Opera," *Musica disciplina* 49 (1995): 79–93.

8 James R. Anthony, *French Baroque Music from Beaujoyeulx to Rameau*, rev. ed. (Portland, OR: Amadeus Press, 1997), 41–63. Baltasar de Beaujoyeulx was part of Jean-Antoine de Baïf's Académie de Poésie et de Musique. The preface to the print of the *Balet comique de la Royne* indicates that Beaujoyeulx was aware of having created an "invention moderne" with this *ballet de cour*, which was probably the first major work of its kind containing dramatic unity. Throughout the eighteenth century, the *Balet comique de la Royne* remained unchallenged as the first French work to encapsulate the ideas of music-theater, for example in the writings of Germain Boffrand (1715) and Pierre-Louis d'Aquin de Château-Lyon (1753); see Anthony, *French Baroque Opera*, 42.

9 According to Ralph P. Locke, the "obvious emphasis on display, on conspicuous consumption, on the coordination of high individual achievement into a greater enterprise—or at least a more impressive 'product'—clearly marks French grand opera as a prime cultural expression of the entrepreneurial and professional classes that profited so much from the July Monarchy" (Locke, "Paris: Centre of Intellectual Ferment," in *Music and Society: The Early Romantic Era between Revolutions: 1789 and 1848*, ed. Alexander Ringer [Englewood Cliffs, NJ: Prentice Hall, 1990], 32–83, quotation at 54).

10 Louis Véron, *Mémoires d'un bourgeois de Paris, comprenant la fin de l'Empire, la Restauration, la Monarchie de Juillet, la République jusqu'au rétablissement de l'Empire* (*Memoirs of a Bourgeois from Paris, Including the End of the Empire, the Restoration, the July Monarchy, the Republic until the Re-establishment of the Empire*), 5 vols. (Paris: Librairie nouvelle, 1857), 4:196–231. The chapter carries the title "Les demoiselles de l'Opéra."

11 Smith, *Ballet and Opera*, 68. According to Smith, "The *foyer de la danse* had been opened to male patrons in the eighteenth century ... but ... the practice was expressly forbidden by the early nineteenth century" (265).

12 Smith, *Ballet and Opera*, 70.

13 Smith, *Ballet and Opera*, 70.

14 Maribeth Clark, "Bodies at the Opéra: Art and the Hermaphrodite in the Dance Criticism of Théophile Gautier," in Roger Parker and Mary Ann Smart, eds., *Reading Critics Reading: Opera and Ballet Criticism in France from the Revolution to 1848* (Oxford: Oxford University Press, 2001), 237–53, quotation on 243.

15 For more information on *grand opéra* as genre, see Jane Fulcher, *The Nation's Image: French Grand Opera as Politics and Politicized Art* (Cambridge: Cambridge University Press, 1987); Gerhard, *The Urbanization of Opera*; Patrick Barbier, *Opera in Paris, 1800–1850: A Lively History*, trans. by Robert Luoma (Portland, OR: Amadeus Press, 1995); Lacombe, *Keys to French Opera*.

16 Charles Soullier, "Académie de Musique," in *Nouveau dictionnaire de musique illustré*

(Paris: E. Bazault, 1855), vol. 1, 128, given in Hervé Lacombe, "Définitions des genres lyriques dans les dictionnaires du XIXe siècle" ("Definitions of Lyric Genres in Nineteenth-Century Dictionaries"), in Paul Prévost, ed., *Le théâtre lyrique en France au XIXe siècle* (Metz: Edition Serpenoise, 1995), 297–334, quotation at 305: "Le ballet tient une grande place dans l'histoire de l'Opéra. La danse a contribué pour sa part à l'éclat du spectacle" ("Ballet holds a large place in the history of the Opéra. The dance has contributed to the splendor of the spectacle").

17 Sieghart Döhring and Sabine Henze-Döhring, *Oper und Musikdrama im 19. Jahrhundert (Opera and Music-Drama in the Nineteenth Century)*, Handbuch der musikalischen Gattungen, vol. 13 (Laaber: Laaber Verlag, 1997), 150.

18 Weber's opera (premièred in 1821 in Berlin) was first performed in Paris at the Théâtre de l'Odéon as *Robin des bois* in 1824. On the Paris reception of Weber's *Der Freischütz*, see Annegret Fauser, "Phantasmagorie im deutschen Wald? Zur *Freischütz*-Rezeption in London und Paris 1824" ("Phantasmagory in the German Forest? The Reception of *Freischütz* in 1824 London and Paris"), in Hermann Danuser and Herfried Münkler, eds., *Deutsche Meister — Böse Geister? Nationale Selbstfindung in der Musik (German Masters — Bad Spirits? The Development of National Identity in Music)* (Schliengen: Edition Argus, 2001), 245–73; Mark Everist, *Music Drama at the Paris Odéon, 1824–28* (Berkeley: University of California Press, 2002), 258–69.

19 On the role of national dances in French nineteenth-century ballets, see Lisa C. Arkin and Marian Smith, "National Dance in the Romantic Ballet," in Lynn Garafola, ed., *Rethinking the Sylph: New Perspectives on the Romantic Ballet* (Hanover: University Press of New England, 1997), 11–68. Antoine Reicha, in his *L'art du compositeur dramatique* (1833), introduced this concept of using national airs as signifiers of local color into his advice to aspiring opera composers; see Gerhard, *The Urbanization of Opera*, 164.

20 For a concise analysis of these musical and gestural means, see Smith, *Ballet and Opera in the Age of Giselle*, 125–38. See also Fulcher, *The Nation's Image*, 11–46, Gerhard, *The Urbanization of Opera*, 122–57, and Smart, *Mimomania*.

21 Daniel-François-Esprit Auber and Eugène Scribe, *Le Dieu et la Bayadère* (1830); Fromental Halévy, Edmond Duponchel, and Casimir Gide, *La Tentation* (1832).

22 Isabelle Moindrot, "Le geste et l'idéologie dans le 'grand opéra': *La Juive* de Fromental Halévy," ("Gesture and Ideology in 'grand opéra': Fromental Halévy's *La Juive*"), *Romantisme: Revue de la Société des Etudes Romantiques*, no. 102 (1998): 63–79.

23 Jürgen Maehder, "Historienmalerei und Grand Opéra: Zur Raumvorstellung in den Bildern Géricaults und Delacroix' und auf der Bühne der Académie Royale de Musique" ("Historic Painting and *grand opéra*: The Concept of Space in the Paintings of Géricault and Delacroix"), in Sieghart Döhring and Arnold Jacobshagen, eds., *Meyerbeer und das europäische Musiktheater (Meyerbeer and European Musical Theater)* (Laaber: Laaber Verlag, 1998), 258–87; Thomas Steier, "'Bewegte' und 'bewegende' Musik: Zur Intermedialität von Bühne und Malerei" ("'Moved' and 'Moving' Music: Intermediality of Stage and Painting"), in Sibylle Dahms, Manuela Jahrmärker, and Gunhild Oberzaucher-Schüller, eds., *Meyerbeers Bühne im Gefüge der Künste (Meyerbeer's Stage in the Network of the Arts)* (Feldkirchen: Ricordi, 2002), 170–89.

24 Lacombe, *The Keys to French Opera*, 49. The quotation stems from Pier Angelo Fiorentino, a critic for the daily newspaper *La France*.

25 Carl Dahlhaus, *Die Musik des 19. Jahrhunderts (Nineteenth-Century Music)*, vol. 6, *Neues Handbuch der Musikwissenschaft* (Laaber: Laaber Verlag, 1980), 101.

26 In his thoughtful *French Opera at the Fin de Siècle: Wagnerism, Nationalism, and Style* (Oxford: Oxford University Press, 1999), Steven Huebner shows how complex the developments of opera were in the tension field of *grand opéra* and Wagnerian music-drama.

27 Alfred Bruneau, *A l'ombre d'un grand cœur: Souvenirs d'une collaboration* (Paris: [n.p.], 1931; reprint Geneva: Slatkine, 1980), 89–90, given in Lacombe, *The Keys to French Opera*, 24.

28 In his 1884 pamphlet *In Teatro*, the Italian librettist and critic Ferdinando Fontana envisages mimed scenes (termed *poemi sinfonico scenici*) as a progressive, Wagnerian alternative to the aria-based form of Italian opera, without tracing their ancestry to French *grand opéra*, even though the genre had strongly influenced the operas by not only Wagner but also Verdi, Boito, and Puccini. He put his theory into practice in his libretto for Giacomo Puccini's early opera *Le Villi* (1884). See Ferdinando Fontana, *In Teatro* (Rome: Sommaruga, 1884).

29 Huebner, *French Opera*, 109–10, 409–10. On *Thaïs* and the "Ballet de la Tentation," see Clair Rowden, *Jules Massenet:* Thaïs, *Dossier de presse parisienne (1894)* (Heilbronn: Musik-Edition Lucie Galland, 2000), xxi–xxxiii. The content of the "Ballet de la Tentation" is reproduced in Patrick Gillis, "Thaïs dans tous ses états: genèse et remaniements" ("Thaïs in All Her States: Genesis and Revisions"), *Avant-Scène Opéra*: Thaïs, no. 109 (May 1988): 66–74, quotation at 73–74.

30 Huebner, *French Opera*, 410. Huebner here follows the librettist rather than the composer, for Gallet himself referred to the "Ballet de la Tentation" as a compromise (Rowden, *Jules Massenet*, xxiii n70).

31 The justification of ballet's extravaganza through dream sequences remained intact even in twentieth-century Broadway musicals such as Rodger's and Hammerstein's *Oklahoma!*

32 See Ian Kemp, *Hector Berlioz: Les Troyens*, Cambridge Opera Handbooks (Cambridge: Cambridge University Press, 1988); *Avant-Scène Opéra: Les Troyens*, no. 128–29 (February–March 1990); David Cairns, *Servitude and Greatness*, vol. 2, *Berlioz* (London: Allen Lane, 1999), esp. 591–627.

33 *The Memoirs of Hector Berlioz*, trans. by David Cairns (London: Panther Books, 1970), 55.

34 Marian Smith, "About the House," in Parker and Smart, *Reading Critics Reading*, 217–36, quotation at 235.

35 For the impact of gender issues on Berlioz's aesthetics, see Katharine Ellis, "Berlioz, the Sublime, and the *Broderie* Problem," *Ad Parnassum* 1.1 (2004).

36 In a letter to his sister Adèle dated February 25, 1857, Berlioz announced, "I'm going to work on the ballet. I want to do an almehs' dance, just like the music and dancing of the Indians I saw here sixteen or seventeen years ago. My colleague at the *Débats*, Casimirski, is going to give me a verse from the Persian poet Hafiz which I shall have sung in Persian by the singing almehs, as the Indian girls did. There's nothing anachronistic about that. I've gone into the question. Dido could easily have had Egyptian dancers at her court who'd come earlier from India" (given in Cairns, *Berlioz*, 618).

37 Early plans for the opera included in lieu of a projection of Rome "the dying Dido's allusion to French domination of Africa" (see Berlioz's letter to Caroline Princess Sayn-Wittgenstein, December 25–26, 1856, given in Cairns, *Berlioz*, 614).

38 The literature on Orientalism and Exoticism has proliferated in the last decade. The musicological key essay is Ralph P. Locke, "Constructing the Oriental 'Other': Saint-Saëns's *Samson et Dalila*," *Cambridge Opera Journal* 3.3 (November 1991): 261–302.
39 Cairns, *Berlioz*, 616.
40 Letter from Hector Berlioz to Caroline Princess Sayn-Wittgenstein, November 14, 1856, given in Cairns, *Berlioz*, 612–13.
41 Letter from Hector Berlioz to Toussaint Bennet, February 5–6, 1857, given in Cairns, *Berlioz*, 616.
42 Letter from Hector Berlioz to his sister Adèle, April 9, 1857, given in Cairns, *Berlioz*, 620.
43 In 1868, Ludovic Celler published a study, *Les Origines de l'opéra et le Ballet de la Reine (1581)*, which opens with the following praise to dance: "Ballet is probably the oldest entertainment that man has invented; I understand by the word *Ballet* a recreation of dance and song, a kind of mimed scene accompanied by music" (*"Le ballet est peut-être le plus ancien des divertissements que l'homme ait inventés; j'entends par ce mot ballet, une récréation de danse et de chant, une sorte de scène mimée avec accompagnement de musique"*). The subsequent 364 pages of the volume focus mainly on the French beginnings of opera in the *Balet comique de la Royne*. The book was published at a politically highly charged time. The Second Empire of Napoléon III was in deep crisis, and Germany had become a threat. In reiterating the shopworn claim that France, not Italy, was the cradle of music drama, and that the path of opera led (with a short detour via Monteverdi and Cavalli) directly from the *ballet de cour* to Meyerbeer, by way of Rameau and Gluck, Celler's patriotic intentions are clear. See Ludovic Celler [pseud. Louis Leclercq], *Les Origines de l'opéra et le Ballet de la Reine (1581). Etude sur les Danses, la Musique, les Orchestres et la Mise en scène au XVIe siècle* (Paris: Librairie Académique, 1868), 1. I am grateful to James Haar for his reference to this book.
44 On Massenet and Wagner, see Annegret Fauser, *"Esclarmonde. Un opéra wagnérien?"* (*"Esclarmonde:* A Wagnerian Opera?"), *L'Avant-Scène Opéra: Esclarmonde*, no. 148 (September–October 1992): 68–73; Huebner, *French Opera*, 25–166.
45 According to Huebner, Massenet's friend and disciple Raymond de Rigné called such allusions to other works *"petites malices*, or little tricks" (*French Opera*, 89). See also Annegret Fauser, "L'art de l'allusion musicale" ("The Art of Musical Allusion"), *Avant-Scène Opéra: Panurge et Le Cid*, no. 161 (September–October 1994): 126–29. The allusion to *Robert le Diable* was picked up by the critics of the première and discussed in their reviews of the opera (Rowden, *Jules Massenet*, xxiv–xxv).
46 Gillis, "Thaïs dans tous ses états," 68. Sanderson, for whom the opera was written, left the Opéra Comique in Summer 1893 and moved to a better paid contract at the Opéra.
47 Patrick Gillis, "*Thaïs* à l'Opéra: du roman à la comédie lyrique, pertes et profits" ("*Thaïs* at the Opéra: From the Novel to the *comédie lyrique*: Losses and Gains"), in Marie-Claire Brancquart and Jean Dérens, eds., *Anatole France: Humanisme et Actualité* (Paris: Agence culturelle de Paris, 1994), 107–34, quotation at 117: "A l'Opéra, lundi dernier, M. Massenet a lu le ballet qu'il vient d'écrire pour *Thaïs*. Faisant corps absolument avec l'action, ce ballet, qui durera au moins vingt minutes, est d'un genre absolument nouveau et original et prête à de très beaux effets de mise en scène."
48 Gillis, "*Thaïs* à l'Opéra," 118.

49 Rowden, *Jules Massenet*, xxi–xlv.
50 The opera underwent several changes, both immediately following the first performance and then before its 1898 revival; see Gillis, "Thaïs dans tous ses états."
51 Letter from Jules Massenet to Louis Gallet, spring 1892: "Pouvez-vous voir Anatole France & savoir exactement par lui si au théâtre d'Alexandrie (à *cette époque*: IVe siècle) Thaïs a *dansé* ou *mimé*?" (cited in Rowden, *Jules Massenet*, xxvi).
52 "Notes pour l'Opéra," a letter from Jules Massenet to Louis Gallet, July 28, 1893: "Il ne s'agit pas d'une apparition calme—il s'agit de Thaïs paraissant près de la couche d'Athanaël et le tentant par des paroles et encore plus par *les gestes* qui accompagnent et soulignent cette scène jouée" (cited in Gillis, "*Thaïs* à l'Opéra," 131–34, quotation at 133).
53 For an interpretation of this scene and its solipsistic character, see Clair Rowden, *Massenet, Marianne, and Mary: Republican Morality and Catholic Tradition at the Opera* (PhD diss., City University, London, 2001), 162–69.
54 On *Giselle*, see Smith, *Ballet and Opera*, 167–200.
55 Smith, *Ballet and Opera*, 6–18 and 101–14. On the fluid interchange between stage and ballroom in the 1830s, see also Maribeth Clark, "The Quadrille as Embodied Musical Experience in 19th-Century Paris," *The Journal of Musicology* 19.3 (Summer 2002): 503–26.
56 Jules Massenet and Louis Gallet, *Thaïs*, piano-vocal score (Paris: Heugel, 1894), 192–96.
57 Dahlhaus, *Die Musik des 19. Jahrhunderts*, 5–6. See also Carolyn Abbate, *Unsung Voices: Opera and Musical Narrative in the Nineteenth Century* (Princeton: Princeton University Press, 1991), 19–27. Both Smith in her analysis of *Giselle* and its transformation (*Opera and Dance*, 177–86) and Stephanie Jordan in her account of changing relationships between dance and music in the twentieth century point toward the modernist project of divorcing music as an absolute art from the literary and concrete understanding of music through much of the nineteenth century; see Stephanie Jordan, *Moving Music: Dialogues with Music in Twentieth-Century Ballet* (London: Cecil Court, 2000), 3–21. But Jordan's section (65–73) on "Music as Meaning" is problematic inasmuch as her framework of reference is limited to music from the late nineteenth and twentieth centuries (save for a brief and superficial reference to earlier music and its theory on page 66).
58 Abbate, *Unsung Voices*, 26.
59 Lawrence Kramer suggests that "music–imagetext combinations may occur both aesthetically, via mixed-media forms, and performatively, via social ritual, festivity, and other 'musicalized' events" (Kramer, *Musical Meaning: Towards a Critical History* [Berkeley: University of California Press, 2002], 177–78).
60 Kofi Agawu's observation that semiotics in music are intrinsically bound to style analysis has significant implications for the issue of its contextualization within its historic framework of creation and reception; see Agawu, "The Challenge of Semiotics," Nicholas Cook and Mark Everist, eds., *Rethinking Music* (Oxford: Oxford University Press, 1999), 138–60.
61 Kramer, *Musical Meaning*, 152–53.
62 "Mise en scène" for Jules Massenet and Louis Gallet, *Thaïs* (Paris: Au Ménestrel, [1894]), 44: "*Athanaël*, à la vue de l'Etoile, s'agenouille au milieu de la scène et dit par gestes: 'C'est le réveil, c'est le salut! Il comprend . . . il comprend! . . . Mais où donc était-il? Explosion de joie et de reconnaissance: Il est sauvé! sauvé!'"

63 The term *silent language* stems from Smith, *Opera and Dance*, 97. On nineteenth-century criticism of gestures as language, see Smith, *Opera and Dance*, 116–23.
64 Annegret Fauser, "'L'orchestre dans les sons brave l'honnêteté . . .': Le rôle de l'élément érotique dans l'œuvre de Massenet" ("'The Orchestra with Its Sounds Challenges Decorum . . .': The Role of Eroticism in Massenet's Work"), in Patrick Gillis and Gérard Condé, eds., *Massenet en son temps*, Actes du colloque organisé en 1992 à l'occasion du deuxième Festival Massenet (St. Etienne: Association du Festival Massenet, 1999), 156–79; Huebner, *French Opera*, 84–85.
65 The reviews for *Esclarmonde* in particular explore the meaning of the "nuptial" interlude in great detail; a selection of the criticism is reproduced in Annegret Fauser, ed., *Dossier de Presse parisienne: Jules Massenet, "Esclarmonde" (1889)* (Heilbronn: Edition Lucie Galland, 2001).
66 For a nuanced interpretation of the *Méditation* as musical *extase*, see Rowden, *Massenet, Marianne and Mary*, 215–26.
67 Kendall Walton, "Listening with Imagination: Is Music Representational?" in Jenefer Robinson, ed., *Music and Meaning* (Ithaca: Cornell University Press, 1997), 57–82.
68 Denis Smalley, "The Listening Imagination: Listening in the Electroacoustic Era," in John Paynter et al., eds., *Companion to Contemporary Musical Thought*, vol. 1 (New York: Routledge, 1992), 514–54.
69 Rowden, *Massenet, Marianne and Mary*, 153–97.
70 Ironically, the first interlude ("Les Amours d'Aphrodite") and the "Ballet de la Tentation" were among the first pieces cut in the long revision process. The replacement ballet in act 2 offers conventional dance numbers during the feast at Nicias's house. Together with the new Oasis Tableau, these changes tone down the erotic edge of the opera.

CHAPTER 3

Oscarine and Réginette: a Comic Interlude in the French Reception of Wagner[*]

Just as self-reflection was inextricably associated with the creation and reception of opera from its earliest days—and, in a sense, even preceded it—so has comedy, parody, and travesty played an important role since the seventeenth century in the arsenal of such reflexive engagement within the genre.[1] Parodies of successful operas tended to reflect the original work's main plot lines, whether in the distorting mirror of boulevard theater in Vienna, London, and Paris, or in the marionette theaters of Lyons.[2] On the other hand, such musical comedies as Favard's *Le Procès des ariettes et des vaudevilles* (1760) or Mozart's *Der Schauspieldirektor* (1786) targeted contemporary operatic practice and genre theory. Already during Lully's time, the *tragédie lyrique*—which, as the premier genre of French theater, stood consistently in the spotlight of debate—had become the object of parody in the Ancien Théâtre Italien.[3] In eighteenth-century Paris, such parodies and comedies usually reflected heated operatic conflicts, whether during the *querelle des bouffons* or the Gluck–Piccinni controversy. For its part, the genre of *opéra comique* at that time seemed to possess *sui generis* "a specifically genre-reflective character."[4]

The role of musical comedy as a distorting mirror of aesthetic conflicts and artistic idiosyncrasies remained important in Paris also during the nineteenth century, especially in

---

[*] This is my translation of "Oscarine und Réginette: ein komisches Zwischenspiel in der französischen Wagnerrezeption," in *"L'Esprit français" und die Musik Europas: Entstehung, Einfluß und Grenzen einer ästhetischen Doktrin. Festschrift für Herbert Schneider zum 65. Geburtstag*, edited by Michelle Biget-Mainfroy and Rainer Schmusch, Studien und Materialien zur Musikwissenschaft, 40 (Hildesheim, Zürich, New York: Georg Olms Verlag, 2007), 575–90. In order to preserve the integrity of the text, I have not updated any of the footnotes or added further references, even though some of the issues have been addressed in more recent scholarship.

[1] This theory-based approach to opera is already evident in Rinuccini's and Peri's preface to their *L'Euridice*, the work which is generally cited as marking the beginning of opera. The text of the preface is reproduced in Italian and English translation in *Composing Opera: From "Dafne" to "Ulisse Errante,"* edited by Tim Carter and Zygmunt M. Szweykowski (Krakow: Musica Iagellonica, 1994), 15–33.

[2] On the parody of operas in Lyonnais marionette theater, in particular the parody of Ernest Reyer's *Salammbô*, see Herbert Schneider, "Die kompositionsgeschichtliche Stellung der *Salammbô* (1890) von Ernest Reyer," in *Flauberts "Salammbô" in Musik, Malerei, Literatur und Film*, edited by Klaus Ley (Tübingen: Gunter Narr Verlag, 1998), 51–89, esp. 84–89.

[3] See François Moreau, "Lully en visite chez Arlequin: parodies italiennes avant 1697," in *Jean Baptiste Lully: Kongressbericht*, edited by Jérôme de la Gorce and Herbert Schneider, Neue Heidelberger Studien zur Musikwissenschaft, 18 (Laaber: Laaber Verlag, 1990), 235–50.

[4] Thomas Betzwieser, "'Si tu veux faire un opéra comique…': Stil- und Gattungsreflexionen in der Opéra Comique zwischen 1800 und 1820," in *Die Opéra Comique und ihr Einfluß auf das europäische Musiktheater im 19. Jahrhundert*, edited by Herbert Schneider and Nicole Wild (Hildesheim: Georg Olms Verlag, 1997), 121–50; quotation on p. 122: "einen spezifisch gattungsreflexiven Charakter."

response to key works of the repertoire such as Rossini's *Guillaume Tell* (1829) or important adaptations of such foreign operas as Carl Maria von Weber's *Der Freischütz* as *Robin des bois* in 1824.⁵ It comes therefore as no surprise that the sharp wit of Parisian parodies would also await Richard Wagner when he came to the French capital in 1860 to establish himself at the Opéra as an internationally successful opera composer with *Tannhäuser*. Wagner's music of the future is satirized in the "Symphonie de l'avenir"—a scene in Jacques Offenbach's *Le Carnaval des revues* (1860)—through a dissonant and noisy fantasy over the well-known *Quadrille des Lanciers*, while H. Thiéry's revue *Il pleut, il pleut, bergère* (1860) contains a grand symphony in "scie majeur" by a composer aptly named Tanne-tout-le monde.⁶ Wagner's response ten years later in *Eine Kapitulation*—ostensibly cast as a satire which lacked, however, any form of Parisian *esprit* and was hence nothing but insulting—is one of the best known episodes of the complicated interrelationship between Wagner and the music milieu of Paris after the *Tannhäuser* debacle. Less well known, however, is the fact that the Parisian reception of Wagner in the later nineteenth century also found its echo in parody and comedy. French Wagnerism received both a reflection and a response not only in such avant-garde works as Alfred Jarry and Claude Terrasse's satirical *Ubu Roi* (1896) but also in the musical comedies of the commercial boulevard theater. One of these latter works, the operetta *Oscarine*, is particularly remarkable in this context, not just because it addresses a number of burning issues in French Wagnerism, but also because it is fully enshrined within the tradition of French operetta, without even a hint of challenging the genre and its context. The fact that aesthetic and political problems of Wagnerism were worked out in this kind of conventional operetta shows perhaps more clearly than such exceptional avant-garde pieces as *Ubu Roi* which aspects of Wagnerism were considered by French librettists and composers to be particularly explosive and in need of creative engagement.

Oscarine was premiered on 15 October 1888 at the newly renovated Théâtre des Bouffes-Parisiens in front of a distinguished Parisian audience. The theater had become famous in the 1860s by way of Offenbach's operettas, and it was still the foremost stage in Paris for the performance of light musical entertainment. In the 1888–89 season it had a new director, Charles Chizzola, replacing the previous one, the singer and composer Delphine Ugalde. The text of *Oscarine* was written by the experienced team of Charles Nuitter and Albert Guinon; the composer was the successful young musician, Victor Roger; and such stars of the operetta stage as Montrouge and his wife, and the soprano Madame Thuillier-Leloir played the main characters. The evening was a commercial success, and the newspapers reported on it extensively. However, the work and its reception fit squarely into the continuous flow of operetta premieres in the French capital in the 1880s, and so it did not merit any special attention.

---

⁵ Weber's *Robin des bois* was parodied in 1825 at the Théâtre du Vaudeville as *Le Chasseur rouge*. See Annegret Fauser, "Phantasmagorie im deutschen Wald? Zur *Freischütz*-Rezeption in London und Paris 1824," in *Deutsche Meister—Böse Geister? Nationale Selbstfindung in der Musik*, edited by Hermann Danuser and Herfried Münkler (Schliengen: Edition Argus, 2001), 245–73, at 270–71.

⁶ Georges Servières, *Tannhæuser à l'Opéra en 1861* (Paris: Librairie Fischbacher, 1895), 111. Jean-Claude Yon, *Jacques Offenbach* (Paris: Editions Gallimard, 2000), 228; Jean-Christophe Keck, "The Art of Offenbach: An Adroit Alchemical Fusion of Romanticism and Foolishness," in *Anne Sofie von Otter Sings Offenbach* (Hamburg: Deutsche Grammophon, 2002), 8–13, at 9.

But there was a twist: the operetta's chief character was a wealthy, unmarried, older Wagnerian woman composer who sought to have her masterpiece *Thusnelda*—a music drama in five acts—performed, even though every single theater director in Paris had refused to stage it. By chance, she hears the painter Philibert Doudouille sing as he paints her house. She engages him for 2,000 francs to take on the heroic role of Ambrionx in her opera, and she arranges a self-financed performance in the newly founded Théâtre des Fantaisies Électriques, run by the impresario Tamponnet de la Pétandière. Philibert's fiancée, the washerwoman Réginette, has little enthusiasm for this new arrangement and instigates a hilarious incident at the opera's première (located at the end of Act II): not only does she win against the Wagnerian piece in a rowdy musical battle, singing her popular chanson: "Lavez votr' ling' sal' en famill'" (Wash your dirty laundry in private), but she is also discovered to be a singer herself. In the third and final act, Réginette—now a famous diva—stars in the fictitious casino of Saint-Galmier (alias Dieppe). Philibert has renounced his career as an operatic baritone and asks Réginette for forgiveness. But she leaves him hanging, prompting him to seek death as a jockey in a horse race which, however, he wins. While the two lovers reconcile, Tamponnet de la Pétandière commits to performing *Thusnelda* with Philibert as Ambrionx, though this is set to take place only after the end of the operetta.

Critics and audiences were well aware that *Oscarine* was a thinly veiled adaptation of Adolphe Adam's *Le Postillon de Lonjumeau* (1836). This intertextual reference to one of the best known *opéras comiques* of the nineteenth century was as programmatic in terms of positioning *Oscarine* as a self-consciously French comedy as was the exploration of the conflict between Wagnerian and autochthonous musics in the new operetta itself. Indeed, if we read *Oscarine* and its reception carefully, three central aspects of French musical culture fall under the spotlight. Act 1 introduces Oscarine as a dilettante composer, whose Wagnerism reveals itself to be highly problematic, and whose authority—based solely on her affluence—derails Philibert's natural talent from the true path of national art. This act addresses in one fell swoop questions of gender-specific creativity, of artistic authority, and of the dangers of foreign art. Act II explores the confrontation between French and German-inspired art in the conflict played out between Oscarine and Réginette, while finally, in Act III, true French womanhood and true French art triumph in the happy ending. Both the art and the morality of the Third Republic are thus preserved, and from so secure a position, even a (planned) performance of *Thusnelda* is a possibility.

Act I: "Moi, j'ai du génie" (Oscarine)

Save for the unusual heroine, the plot of *Oscarine* is not particularly ingenious. Rather, it follows a well-tested mold of the intertextual references which firmly situate the piece aesthetically and ideologically within the tradition of French *opéra comique* and operetta. But from this straightforward starting point, the authors engage with gender, genius, national music, and genre, tackling some thorny issues in nineteenth-century aesthetic debate. This starts already with title role, Oscarine, who represents everything a composer should not be: a woman, unmarried, a dilettante, and a Wagnerian. The positive counter-image would be a Conservatory-trained male composer firmly grounded in the profession and in French aesthetics: someone like Ambroise Thomas or Jules Massenet.

Example 1: Nº 1bis, **Musique de Scène. Roger, *Oscarine* (piano–vocal score), 16**

The creators of the operetta came up with a clever strategy to introduce the protagonist. The opening scene shows the Pavillons, a nouveau-riche couple who have rented a house in the country. Instead of finding peace and quiet in the new surroundings, however, they hear the loud cries of a female voice ("En chasse"—"To the hunt!") to a piano accompaniment, finishing on a dissonant chord (Example 1).[7]

The couple wonders what they might have heard:

HERNANCE, *effarée*:
Qu'est-ce que c'est que ça?

HERNANCE, *alarmed*:
What's that?

PAVILLON:
Ça vient d'en face!

PAVILLON:
It comes from opposite us.

HERNANCE:
C'est peut-être quelqu'un qui a une
attaque de nerfs!

HERNANCE:
Maybe someone has an attack of
hysteria!

PAVILLON:
Ça expliquerait les cris, mais ça
n'expliquerait pas la musique.[8]

PAVILLON:
That would explain the screams, but it
would not explain the music.

---

[7] This and the following music examples are transcribed from the piano–vocal score. See Victor Roger, *Oscarine* (Paris: Choudens, 1888).

[8] Printed Libretto: *Oscarine: Operette en trois actes, paroles de MM. Charles Nuitter et Albert Guinon, musique de M. Victor Roger* (Paris: Tresse & Stock, 1888), 2–3.

Example 2:   N° 1ᵗᵉʳ, Musique de Scène. Roger, *Oscarine* (piano–vocal score), 16

As the angry couple is about to close the window, the music starts anew. This time we hear a wordless, chromatic cantilena accompanied rather inappropriately by a harmonium (Example 2).

A while later, the couple ask their landlady (alias Oscarine) whence this noise had come:

PAVILLON:
Voilà de quoi il s'agit, Madame ... ce ne sera pas long! Ce matin [...] nous avons été surpris par un vacarme effroyable!

OSCARINE, *ne comprenant pas*:
C'est bizarre! je n'ai rien entendu!

PAVILLON:
Vous n'auriez pas dans le voisinage un asile d'aliénés?

OSCARINE, *même jeu*:
Non, monsieur. ... mais enfin, qu'est-ce que c'était ce vacarme?

PAVILLON:
Here is what this is about, Madame ... I will be short! This morning [...] we were surprised by a terrifying racket!

OSCARINE, *who does not understand*:
That's strange! I didn't hear a thing!

PAVILLON:
There wouldn't be a lunatic asylum in the neighborhood, would there?

OSCARINE, *in the same manner*:
No, sir. ... But tell me, what kind of noise are you talking about?

HERMIONE:
Nous avons cru distinguer un piano avec une orgue de barbarie.

OSCARINE, *se redressant*:
Hein?

PAVILLON:
Il y avait aussi des cris d'animaux! Ça devait faire aboyer un chien!

OSCARINE:
Pas un mot de plus, Monsieur, j'ai compris! C'était moi qui chantais un fragment de mon opéra inédit en cinq actes![9]

HERMIONE:
We thought we could recognize a piano with a hurdy-gurdy.

ORCARINE, *straightening*:
What?

PAVILLON:
There were also animal cries! It could have made a dog bark!

OSCARINE:
Not another word, sir, I understand now! It was me singing a fragment of my unpublished five-act opera!

Figure 1: Henriot [Henry Maigrot], "Aux Bouffes-Parisiens" (detail), *Le Journal amusant* 41 (1888): 7

---

[9] *Oscarine* (libretto), 9.

The dialogue ends with the dissolution of the rental agreement, not only because Oscarine feels insulted by the Pavillons, but also because the couple dreads having to listen to this kind of music day in, day out. In the course of the conversation, the audience learns that the country house is Oscarine's eighteenth domicile after having been evicted from seventeen other residences on account of her music.

As the act unfolds, we encounter the painter Philbert singing the *romance* "Quand ta lèvre, ô Ninon" while he is painting the house. Oscarine engages this natural talent for her new opera's leading role (Figure 1), having in the meantime found in Tamponnet de la Pétandière a producer for "*Thusnelda*, opéra en cinq actes, sujet Gaulois" (opera in five acts, Gallic subject).[10]

Example 3: N° 5, Trio bouffe (extract). Roger, *Oscarine* (piano–vocal score), 34–35

---

[10] *Oscarine* (libretto), 31.

Example 3 *Concluded*

In the final comic trio (with Philibert and Tamponnet), Oscarine declares that she is not only the author of text and music—signifier of a true Wagnerian—but also a composer of genius (Example 3).

After having been given a taste of her music at the beginning of the act, the audience knows, of course, that Oscarine is anything but a misunderstood genius. The Parisian press used this set-up in Act I to point out that women composers were a strange and ridiculous brand of musicians. For example, we read in the conservative weekly, *L'Illustration*:

> Do you know the woman composer? Not she who contents herself with some pleasant *romance* or a pretty salon waltz, skillfully retouched by an indulgent master, but she who aims at great art, at the art consecrated by the gods? Barely has she finished with the requisite lessons than she rushes straight to the composition of a five-act opera, all but searching in the Edda or the Nibelungen for some Scandinavian or German Childebrand. She decks him out with melodies even more barbaric than her hero, she puts him into an opera, a musical drama, or whatever; she then drags him from one opera administration to the next, from singer to singer, until the day when—forever rejected and misunderstood—she decides to produce the masterpiece at her own expense. This is what happens to Oscarine as Messrs. Nuitter and Guinon present her. Oscarine has written—words and music—a grand opera, *Thusnelda*.[11]

A woman composer transgressing what was perceived as compatible with women's limited ability to contribute to the "art d'agréments" could only be a figure of fun. Henry Bauer made this explicit in his review for *L'Echo de Paris*: "Oscarine is the name of a ridiculous woman musician who has composed a grand music drama in five acts."[12] Other

---

[11] *L'Illustration* 46 (1888): 306: "Connaissez-vous la femme compositeur? non pas celle qui se contente de quelque agréable romance, ou de quelque jolie valse de salon, adroitement retouchée par un maître indulgent, mais celle qui vise au grand art, à l'art sacré des dieux? A peine a-t-elle fini les études indispensables, que la voilà courant droit à l'opéra en cinq actes, allant chercher presque dans l'Edda, ou les Niebelungen [*sic*], quelque Childebrand scandinave ou germain; elle l'affuble de mélodies plus barbares encore que son héros, le met en opéra, en drame lyrique, que sais-je? puis le traîne de direction en direction, de chanteur en chanteur, jusqu'au jour où, toujours repoussée et incomprise, elle se décide à monter à ses frais le chef-d'œuvre. Telle est Oscarine que nous présentent MM. Nuitter et Guinon. Oscarine a écrit, paroles et musique, un grand opéra, *Thusnelda*[.]"

[12] "Oscarine est le nom d'une femme musicienne ridicule, laquelle a composé un grand drame lyrique en cinq actes." H[enry] B[auer], "Les premières représentations," *L'Echo de Paris*, 17 October 1888.

critics described Oscarine as a musician bitten by the "lyrico-dramatic tarantula" and suffering from "the mania of musical composition."[13] Indeed, as Charles Rousseau explained, "as one sees it, this satire about women composers . . . presents an interesting subject."[14] In contrast to most of his colleagues, the first of our critics—writing for *L'Illustration*— allowed for women's contribution to musical composition, provided that she limited herself to innocuous salon genres. Such works, which were at the bottom of the generic hierarchy in nineteenth-century music, could be subsumed under the bourgeois women's contribution to the cultural life of the home, the socially acceptable "arts d'agrément."[15] But too much serious music, and too many hours of practicing, were seen as detrimental to the goal of such activities, aimed at creating a harmonious home wherein the wife or daughter of the house contributed with no apparent effort pleasantly sounding trifles for the entertainment of family and guests.

However, women composers whose professionalism exceeded such pretty dilettantism of the private domain stepped into a cultural field marked specifically as masculine, crossing the borders framing what was acceptable for a middle-class woman. Yet in late nineteenth-century Paris, a number of composers had successfully entered the public sphere, including Cécile Chaminade, Louise Farrenc, Marie Clémence Vicomtesse de Grandval, and the Wagnerian Augusta Holmès. Among them, the latter two in particular seem to be the target of this particular satire about women composers: Marie de Grandval had just completed the opera *Atala* (to a libretto by Louis Gallet), while Augusta Holmès—the author of *Lutèce*, *Les Argonautes*, and *Ludus pro patria*—was a well-known admirer of Wagner and, in the words of the critic Chamillac, an "extraordinary musician–poet."[16] Grandval, financially independent like Oscarine, was able to underwrite performances of her works; for her part, Holmès's Wagnerian music figured among the exacting compositions of the Parisian avant-garde. Both composers sought the respect afforded to professional musicians. Grandval no longer counted as one of the "aristocratic dilettantes who make music by virtue of their station and engage with it for lack of anything better to do,"[17] and she signed her letters as "Compositeur de Musique."[18] And although Holmès also composed songs, she wrote symphonic works and participated in such official competitions as the Prix de Composition de la Ville de Paris which netted her a second prize in 1880 and consequently her nomination as Officier de la Légion d'honneur. Holmès passed for a "new woman" in the fine arts, whose "virile chic that

---

[13] "elle est en outre piquée de la tarantule lyrico-dramatique." A. Biguet. "Premières représentations," *Le Radical*, 17 October 1888 / 26 Vendémaire an 97 (see also " Oscarine est une vieille folle piquée de la tarantule musicale." Victor Wilder, "Premières représentations," *Gil Blas*, 17 October 1888); "la manie de la composition musicale." Fauchery, "Premières représentations," *L'Intransigeant*, 17 October 1888.

[14] "Comme on le voit, cette satire à l'adresse des femmes compositeurs-auteurs . . . fournit un sujet intéressant." Charles Rousseau, "Chronique musicale," *Le Voltaire*, 17 October 1888.

[15] On the construction of the bourgeois woman of the late nineteenth century, see Anne Martin-Fugier, *La bourgeoise: Femme au temps de Paul Bourget* (Paris: Grasset, 1983), and Annegret Fauser, "Zwischen Professionalismus und Salon: Französische Musikerinnen des *Fin de siècle*," in *Professionalismus in der Musik*, edited by Christian Kaden and Volker Kalisch (Essen: Blaue Eule, 1998), 261–74.

[16] Chamillac, "L'Ode triomphale d'Augusta Holmès," *La Revue illustrée* 4 (1889): 203–6.

[17] "aristocratiques dilettanti, qui font de la musique par genre et en entendent par désœuvrement." Eugène de Solenière, *La Femme compositeur* (Paris: La Critique, 1895), 12.

[18] Letter from Marie Clémence de Grandval to an unidentified correspondent, dated "Samedi—1879," Bibliothèque Nationale de France, Département de Musique, l.a.Grandval, 2.

is so fashionable among certain women artists" presented a danger, so it was perceived in the nineteenth century, not only to true art but also to true femininity.[19]

Act I therefore defined in both musical and scenic terms what bad music is—ambitious works by unmarried women composers who, moreover, were inspired by Wagner—and so what constitutes good music. The latter is shown by negative example to be works by professional male composers, and also—by the favorable comparison with Philibert's *romance*—music in the style of French *opéra comique*. This dual conflict of art and femininity is further sharpened and played out in Act II.

Act II: "Je suis l'amour—Je suis la gloire" (Réginette versus Oscarine)

Act II spans the rehearsals for, and premiere of, Oscarine's opera *Thusnelda*. Philibert's fiancée Réginette becomes increasingly jealous and finally has enough of Philibert's newly found self-importance as a Wagnerian opera hero and his financial dependence on Oscarine, who has amorous intentions towards him. In a trio with Philibert, both Oscarine and Réginette tempt him with their respective attractions: love from Réginette, and fame from Oscarine (Example 4).

Philibert choses the treacherous fame offered by Oscarine, at which point the opera's premiere takes place (Figure 2). However, we hear very little of the music of the opera, for Réginette and her followers—comprising a group of gymnasts—gatecrash the performance. The musical difference between Wagnerism and autochthonous French music is composed out within an ensemble-piece in which Réginette and the chorus of gymnasts sing over Thusnelda (alias Oscarine) and Ambrionx (alias Philibert). Finally, when Oscarine tries to rescue the performance of *Thusnelda* from the intrusion, even her opera director consoles her with a short promise that it would be heard later. To the chorus's question who might be this crazy woman insulting the newly crowned diva Réginette, Oscarine replies "Qui je suis? Je suis Thusnelda!" (Who am I? I am Thusnelda.) The chorus retorts "Thusnelda? Connaissons pas ça" (Thusnelda? Never heard of it).

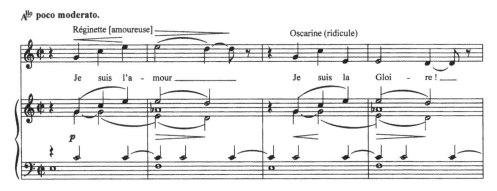

Example 4: Nº 11, Couplets et Terzetto (extract). Roger, *Oscarine* (piano–vocal score), 94

---

[19] "chic de virilité si fort à la mode chez certaines femmes artistes." "L'Ode triomphale," *L'Eclair*, 12 September 1889.

Oscarine et son ténor rappellent dans l'exécution de *Thusnelda* les beaux jours de la *Walkyrie*... Vous devinez, n'est-ce pas? que le peintre Philibert (M. Piccaluga), renoncera au théâtre et retrouvera sa Réginette.

Figure 2: Henriot [Henry Maigrot], "Aux Bouffes-Parisiens" (detail), *Le Journal amusant* 41 (1888): 7

Here, too, the critics picked up on the critique of Parisian cultural life thinly disguised in this satire. Act II emphasized that Wagner-influenced opera was nothing but boring, while French music was entertaining and bound to generate enthusiasm. Oscarine's music drama was described as "a Gallic opera, *Thusnelda*, which is nothing but a long cacophony," the melodies of which were even more "barbaric" than those of her hero, Richard Wagner.[20] Fauchery (Henri de Gramont) wondered whether the operetta might have been intended as a satire on Wagner and his Parisian reception so as "to poke fun at modern music, Wagner, *Sigurd* [by Ernest Reyer], and the idea, charitably presented to Charles Lamoureux by his enemies, to found an opera house in the outskirts of Paris."[21]

Indeed, when *Oscarine* was premiered, Richard Wagner's music and ideas were still hotly contested in Paris. Already in 1852, François-Joseph Fétis laid the foundation for French

---

[20] "un opéra gaulois, *Thusnelda*, qui n'est qu'une longue cacophonie." P.G., "Les Premières Représentations," *Le Petit Parisien*, 17 October 1888. Other critics used similar terms to describe and discuss Act II.

[21] "l'intention de 'blaguer' la musique moderne, Wagner, *Sigurd*, et la pensée, charitablement présentée à M. Lamoureux par ses ennemis, de fonder un théâtre lyrique aux environs de Paris." Fauchery (Henri de Gramont), "Premières représentations," *L'Intransigeant*, 17 October 1888.

Wagner criticism with a series of articles published in the *Revue et Gazette musicale de Paris*, where he denounced Wagner's ideas as a sterile system of compositional rules which did not leave any room for inspiration or imagination.[22] Following the *Tannhäuser* scandal in March 1861, the Parisian musical world remained strongly divided between Wagnerians and Anti-Wagnerians, especially after the Franco-Prussian War of 1870. Wagner was declared by one French critic to be "the Bismarck of music" and therefore a symbol of German musical hegemony; both his own compositions and those in a Wagnerian vein were treated as suspect in the nationalist discourse of the postwar years. It was not until seventeen years after the Franco-Prussian War, in 1887, that the first staged performance of a Wagner opera was possible in Paris. This was Charles Lamoureux's production of *Lohengrin*. Rehearsals were accompanied by bomb threats and demonstrations; Lamoureux conducted the opera with a pistol on his podium; while outside, the event needed massive police presence to keep in check protesters who had had threatened to disrupt the performance.[23] In 1888, the year of *Oscarine*, memories of the *Lohengrin* scandal were still fresh and might have found an echo in the performance of *Thusnelda* interrupted by Réginette and her followers.

But *Oscarine* offers a far more acute engagement with Wagner than it seems at first glance. While *Thusnelda* was portrayed as a typical Wagnerian opera—boring, long, and complex— it was also the product of a woman composer. What made the character of Oscarine such a perfect figure through which to criticize Wagnerian concepts of music drama and composition is the fact that she was an elderly spinster. Thus she was alienated from true womanhood which was defined, in the later nineteenth century, though marriage and motherhood; while as a composer she followed Wagner's "system" rather than true inspiration. In both cases, she is proven sterile.[24] Indeed, ever since Fétis's review of 1852, the "sterility" of Wagner as the leader of a "school" formed a trope in Wagner criticism, and a composer who followed such a system as Wagner's blindly could neither escape convention nor offer a pathbreaking contribution to French music theater. From the perspective of French criticism, theories of female physiology and musical aesthetics could be blended, in the figure of Oscarine, to represent a powerful allegory of the German system of opera, and one that even echoed Wagner's own rhetoric. In a much cited passage in *Oper und Drama* (1851), Wagner tried his hand at describing the relationship of music, language, and drama in gendered terms reverberating with contemporary theories of femininity and masculinity:[25]

---

[22] On Fétis's critique of Wagner, see Katharine Ellis, "Wagnerism and Anti-Wagnerism in the Paris Periodical Press," in *Von Wagner zum Wagnérisme: Musik, Literatur, Kunst, Politik*, edited by Annegret Fauser and Manuela Schwartz, Transfer: Die deutsch-französische Kulturbibliothek, 12 (Leipzig: Leipziger Universitäts-Verlag, 1999), 51–83.

[23] On the Parisian *Lohengrin* premiere, see Manuela Schwartz, "'La question de Lohengrin' zwischen 1869 und 1891," in *Von Wagner zum Wagnérisme*, edited by Fauser and Schwartz, 107–36.

[24] Issues of female fertility and reproduction were one of the key topics of public discourse in late nineteenth-century France, when birth rates fell in comparison with those of neighboring states, most prominently that of Germany. Among the best known works addressing this issue is the opera *Messidor* by Alfred Bruneau and Emile Zola. See Karen Offen, "Depopulation, Nationalism and Feminism in Fin-de-Siècle France," *American Historical Review* 89 (1984): 648–76.

[25] Silke Leopold, "Von der Allgewalt vollsten Hingebungseifers: Weibs-Bilder in Wagners 'Ring,'" in *Richard Wagner "Der Ring des Nibelungen": Ansichten des Mythos*, edited by Udo Bermbach and Dieter Borchmeyer (Stuttgart: Metzler, 1995), 59–74.

Music is the child bearer, the poet the procreator. ... *Music is a woman*. Her nature is love: but this *love* is the *conceiving* kind, which in conceiving *gives itself* without restraint. Woman only receives full individuality at the moment of self-abandonment. She is the mermaid who swims, soulless, through the waves of her element, until she receives her soul through the love of a man.[26]

Wagner's metaphor stands for the relationship of text and music in generating the drama. But while Wagner himself referred here to notions of genius—rooted in the eighteenth century and widespread in the nineteenth—with a masculine-defined author blending both genders in the act of creation, the Parisian audiences of *Oscarine* saw and heard an incarnation of Wagner in the form an incompetent and sterile old maid who can neither bring her opera to performance nor conquer her singer for herself. By feminizing Wagner in the role of Oscarine, the Wagnerian threat to French culture could be countered powerfully through laughter.

One twist to the story, however, lies in the persona of Charles Nuitter, one of the librettists of *Oscarine*. He had translated Wagner's *Lohengrin* the previous year for the première by Charles Lamoureux. He was a passionate Wagnerian, but also a fervent patriot. It is difficult to tell whether his satire was aimed at Wagner himself or, rather, at the threat that Wagner posed to French culture through the inept appropriation of his music and ideas. The Parisian press, however, reduced a plot that might even have been intended as an amiable parody of Wagnerism to a direct attack on Wagner and his imitators.

Act III: "J'aimais, j'étais aimé" (to Réginette)

The final act of the operetta brings the triumph of Réginette, the new French diva (Figure 3). After a series of comic imbroglios, she shows herself as generous, forgiving a repentant Philibert and becoming a happily married woman. The equally repentant Oscarine is promised a performance of her opera as a consolation prize. In this third act, Réginette's French music and true womanhood thus triumph over Oscarine's sterile artistic ambition and spinsterhood. It concludes with the ultimate victory of French music over Wagner's.

In contrast to a feminized German music, French music in *Oscarine* has two faces: one is male, that of Philibert, and one female, that of Réginette. Neither character pretends to be a composer, but both sing French music. Like any stereotypical operatic hero, Philibert has to live through temptation and crisis until he finds the proper way. What is less usual, however, is that his heroic journey is musical. A natural musician, he sings at first unconsciously and without any artifice, in particular in his *romance* "Quand ta lèvre, Ninon." From that state of musical innocence he is then corrupted by money, German-style music, and singing exercises, until he experiences the lowest point of his alienation and also emasculation during the catastrophe of the *Thusnelda* performance. Following this crisis, he returns to true French music and finds his true (French) voice in the nostalgic *romance* "J'aimais, j'étais aimé." He attains a more mature and self-confident place within the tradition of French music,

---

[26] Richard Wagner, *Oper und Drama*, edited by Klaus Kropfinger (Stuttgart: Reclam, 1984), 118: "Die Musik ist die Gebärerin, der Dichter der Erzeuger. ... *Die Musik ist ein Weib*. Die Natur des Weibes ist die *Liebe*: aber diese Liebe ist die *empfangende* und in der Empfängnis rückhaltlos *sich hingebende*. Das Weib erhält volle Individualität erst im Moment der Hingebung. Es ist das Wellenmädchen, das seelenlos durch die Wogen seines Elementes dahinrauscht, bis es durch die Liebe eines Mannes erst die Seele empfängt." (Wagner's emphasis.)

Figure 3: Henriot [Henry Maigrot], "Aux Bouffes-Parisiens" (detail), *Le Journal amusant* 41 (1888): 7

which may possibly include a career in Paris at the Opéra or the Opéra Comique. It is no accident that Philibert's "truly" French music consists of two *romances*, for in the nineteenth century no other vocal genre signified Frenchness so unequivocally as this.[27] Not only the two *romances* but also the intertextual reference to Adam's *Le Postillon de Lonjumeau* mentioned above point further to another national genre: the *opéra comique*. Indeed, following the Franco-Prussian war, the discourse celebrating *opéra comique* as an eminently French genre had been moved back to the front burner. It described the genre as tracing its origins to the "first opera," Adam de la Halle's *Jeu de Robin et Marion*, and incorporating such core French genres as the *chanson populaire* and the vaudeville.[28] In Camille Bellaigue's words: "Through the *opéra comique*, we can reattach modern times to

---

[27] On the romance and its national signification, see David Charlton, "The *Romance* and its Cognates: Narrative, Irony and *Vraisemblance* in Early Opéra Comiques," in *Die Opéra Comique und ihr Einfluß*, edited by Schneider and Wild, 43–92; Annegret Fauser, "The Songs," in *Cambridge Companion to Berlioz*, edited by Peter Bloom (Cambridge: Cambridge University Press, 2000), 109–24.

[28] The discourse in the 1880s on *opéra comique* as a historically grounded genre is addressed in Annegret Fauser, *Musical Encounters at the 1889 Paris World's Fair* (Rochester, NY: University of Rochester Press, 2005), 79–91. On the reception of *Jeu de Robin et de Marion*, see Katharine Ellis, *Interpreting the Musical Past: Early Music in Nineteenth-Century France* (Oxford and New York: Oxford University Press, 2005), 164–73.

the old ones."[29] How commonplace this notion of *opéra comique* as a truly French genre had become can be seen a year after the première of *Oscarine*, when the critic Georges Lefèvre commented on the occasion of a concert with extracts from famous *opéras comiques*: "Accordingly it is a well-known and settled issue to which we do not need to return. *Opéra comique* is a French genre."[30] Both *romances* and the *opéra comique* were thus considered as French answers to the challenge of Wagnerism.

While Philibert develops into an accomplished French musician through musical crisis and transformation, Réginette follows her instincts and never alienates herself from either true French music or true womanhood. Her music carries different signifiers from those of Philibert, however. Réginette sings chansons which, in the ideology of post-1870 Paris, had come to signify the true voice of a nation. Two major studies exploring the musical vitality and richness of French folk music were published in the 1880s: Jean-Baptiste Weckerlin's *La Chanson populaire* (1886) and Julien Tiersot's *Histoire de la chanson populaire en France* (1889).[31] Seen in this context, Réginette's music is the unadulterated voice of the people and therefore represents an unmediated form of Frenchness. Consequently, the victory of Réginette over Oscarine and her German-style opera was no mere routine plot; it was a thinly veiled challenge in terms of musical politics. In the third act of *Oscarine*, sterile Wagnerian opera was thus doubly defeated: by the genre of French *opéra comique*, represented by the *romances*, and by the fertile ground of French popular music.[32]

The cultural work of *Oscarine* consisted in dramatizing satirically the debate on genre, gender, and nationhood. That the operetta's heroine was a woman composer might well have been aimed at particular professional musicians such as Holmès and Grandval, and the link—rarely disputed in public—between sex and genius was one of the points picked up with relish by the press. But what incited the sharpest comments, both within the fictional stage action and in reviews of the production, was the Germanic tastelessness of Oscarine's opera, *Thusnelda*. The ingenuity of the creators of *Oscarine* was to show and musically represent Wagnerian music drama as emasculated and sterile, a travesty of true opera, both in terms of genre and of gender-specific composition. What the Parisian audience witnessed during this comic interlude in the French reception of Wagner on 15 October 1888 was not only the battle of Réginette and Oscarine for Philibert, but also the opposition between French and German music in the fight for the future of opera. That France was victorious

---

[29] "Nous pouvons, par l'opéra comique, rattacher aux temps anciens les temps modernes." Camille Bellaigue, *Un siècle de musique française* (Paris: Librairie Ch. Delagrave, 1887), 6.

[30] "Donc, c'est une chose entendue, convenue, sur laquelle il n'y a point à revenir. L'opéra-comique est un genre français." Georges Lefèvre, "Hommes et choses: opéra-comique," *Le Rappel*, 12 September 1889.

[31] Jean-Baptiste Weckerlin, *La Chanson populaire* (Paris: Librairie de Firmin-Didot et Cie, 1886); Julien Tiersot, *Histoire de la chanson populaire en France* (Paris: Librairie Plon/Au Ménestrel, 1889). During the time, in which the two books were written, Weckerlin and Tiersot were both employed as librarians of the Bibliothèque du Conservatoire; Tiersot was Weckerlin's assistant from 1883 to 1909 when he succeeded him as head librarian.

[32] On the nationalist discourse on popular music and genre, see Annegret Fauser, "Gendering the Nations: the Ideologies of French Discourse on Music (1870–1914)," in *Music and Nationalism: Re-evaluations of the History and Ideology of European Musical Culture, 1830–1945*, edited by Michael Murphy and Harry White (Cork: Cork University Press, 2000).

in both cases was part of the happy ending of a comic interlude and presented a moment of triumph for both audiences and critics. That women were judged by their proper place as spouse and mother, however, made the moral of the operetta all the more appropriate for the Third Republic which was continually in a political and cultural competition with its neighbor across the Rhine.

CHAPTER 4

Gendering the Nations: The Ideologies of French Discourse on Music (1870–1914)[1]

When, on 7 December 1871, Ferdinand Hérold and Eugène de Planard's *opéra comique*, *Le Pré aux Clercs*, was performed for the thousandth time,[2] Gustave Bertrand, one of the music critics for *Le Ménestrel*, took advantage of this celebration – so close to the French defeat in the Franco-Prussian war – to make the following remarks:

> Finally we claim, and this is what we want to insist on most, that the thousandth performance of *Le Pré aux Clercs* is a celebration for the French school. At this moment more than ever we need French art to affirm strongly all its legitimate glories in order first to console and brace us, and then to encourage itself to seek other [glories] ... However, what marks out, in our eyes, the importance of this thousandth performance of so completely a French masterwork is the fact that it sets everything back in place and that it appears to me as a milestone destined to stand out in the history of public taste, indeed of *opéra comique*.[3]

Opéra comique, Bertrand pledged, should become 'something more masculine and sinewy (because comedy does not exclusively mean feminine smiles, superficial gaiety [or], even less, trivial merriness)'.[4] Performing French music and masculinising French art would thus constitute patriotic acts, bestowing cultural identity on and power to the defeated France. The newly founded Société Nationale de Musique's motto 'Ars Gallica' became the all-embracing battle-cry for the next decades, and protectionist legislation not only ensured that institutions such as the Opéra, the Concerts Colonne and Concerts Lamoureux employed French musicians but also made certain that they performed new French music for at least a specified amount of time each season.[5] French discourse on music contributed to and reflected these nationalist undertakings to redefine French music as an inherently national art through essentialising 'Frenchness' in music and masculinising both France's musical heritage and her overcoming of Germanic influences. Independent of a given writer's aesthetic or political allegiances, such discourse proclaimed the new French music as the most vital art in Europe.

The French defeat in 1871 was a pivotal event in the forging of cultural identity in nineteenth-century France. Perceived as the victory of a Prussia that 'founds its force on the development of primary education and on the identity of army and nation',[6] the débâcle challenged France's identity as a nation-state.[7] Finding a French 'collective identity' became a central preoccupation for the Third Republic,[8] especially given that, as Ernest Renan put it in 1870, 'once one has rejected the principle of dynastic legitimisation, there is nothing but the right of nationalities, that is, natural groups determined through race, history and the will of the people, to give a basis to the territorial limits of states'.[9] Symbols referring to the 'heroic past' and 'glory' represent the 'social capital' on which such Republican national identity could be established after the humiliating defeat of the corrupt Second Empire with its cosmopolitanism, *grandes cocottes* and operettas,[10] thus creating a link with the purer and glorious days of the earlier periods of the *Ancien Régime* and the French Revolution.

This process of forging a national identity after the Franco-Prussian war was, however, characterised by an antagonistic debate between two theoretical positions: one (appropriated by the Republican left) based on Sieyès's revolutionary concept of a free association of like-minded individuals, sharing similar concepts under the same law; the other (defended by the right) referring to Joseph de Maistre's traditionalist concept of nationality as a common destiny into which one is born.[11] The two positions on defining nationality – in Finkielkraut's terms, 'nation-contrat' (contractual nationality) versus 'nation-génie' (spiritual nationality)[12] – led to sharp conflicts over the question of who and what is French, culminating in the 'war of the two Frances' during the Dreyfus affair.[13] The debate started out as a reaction to the defeat by a nation whose identity, in France, had been defined in cultural instead of political terms ever since Madame de Staël's *De l'Allemagne* (1810).[14] Therefore the issue of cultural legitimisation became an important topic in the debate. Whereas Republicans such as Renan and Fustel de Coulanges refuted the notion of race, language and birth as the decisive elements of creating nationhood, they defended a 'community of ideas, interest, affections, memories and hopes' as its foundation.[15] Thus, soon after its election in 1879, the new left-wing government of Grévy and Ferry appealed to the Republican memory in installing the 'Marseillaise' as the national anthem (1879) and 14 July as the national holiday (1880).[16] Here, cultural symbols and historical events were appropriated for political ends and inscribed with meaning, but they were not – as in the case of the right – perceived as concretising of the French national soul as such. This is where a 'patriotic' left-wing Republican approach towards building nationhood differs fundamentally from the 'nationalist' right, which continued to refer to blood, soil and Catholicism as the foundation of national identity. Catholicism – in Maurice Barrès's words – was 'the expression of our blood',[17] and nationhood represented the mystical rooting of all members in the essence of its historical and racial selfness; thus the collision course between the nationalist movement of the right and the laicist Republican government (from 1879) was inevitable.[18]

Whether to create cultural symbols or to identify a genuinely French inheritance, references to the past became an important element in the discourse of both left and right throughout the Third Republic. Whereas the interpretations of such references could take on a wide range of political, social and cultural meanings, some strategies of approaching these issues were very similar. One of those discursive strategies consisted of the attempt to 'masculinise' French culture, either implicitly or explicitly – as in Bertrand's assessment of *opéra comique* above. 'Masculine' and 'feminine' were loaded terms when used in political and aesthetic discourse of the late nineteenth century, but they were particularly meaningful in France after the 1871 defeat, for the reciprocal connection made between women's emancipation and the loss of the war called into question the virility both of France and of Frenchmen.[19] As for aesthetic discourse, 'masculine' and 'feminine' transcended the specific human body and became signifiers that used sexual difference as a powerful metaphor to categorise political and cultural manifestations in accordance with a value system embodied in late nineteenth-century French society. In order to be successful, metaphors need to refer to concepts on which a relatively clear consensus exists within a shared cultural context. Such concepts offer a system of signs that abbreviate the world with its infinite complexity and variation.[20] These abbreviations – which, according to Nietzsche, can be described as 'solidified metaphors'[21] – allow for individual interpretations without the necessity of explication.[22] This is the epistemological context in which the terms 'masculine' and 'feminine' operated at the time.[23]

The terms 'masculine' and 'feminine' constituted a referential system which could be used either in direct reference or in allusion. Thus the novelist Joséphin Péladin was able to describe Chopin and Brahms[24] as 'feminine', but Beethoven and Wagner, on the other hand, as 'masculine'.[25] The two terms could also be evoked through substitution ('virile' for 'masculine') or allusion (thus the reference to the 'lovely flowers' of French folk-song in a German publication points towards its 'feminine', even 'effeminate', character).[26] But 'masculine' and 'feminine' were not only categorising and describing terms, they also implied a value judgement. Masculine qualities such as virility, strength, structure, logic, concision and coherence were character traits celebrated in popular, philosophical and educational literature in nineteenth-century France, whereas softness, confusion, decadence, weakness and sweetness were deemed less positive attributes, not only with respect to life in general but also as manifestations of culture.[27] The undertaking of restoring pride in France and her culture, shared by both right and left with similar fervour, thus needed to emphasise their 'masculine' qualities. With respect to music, several topics became particularly important after 1870: the representation of patriotic subjects; the acknowledgement of music's role in education as a valuable tool for instilling a sense of national conscience in French citizens; the heritage of popular music and French art music (whether as common memories or expression of the national soul); and the writing of (music) history. Although all of these issues were addressed soon after the end of the war, the exploitation of patriotic subjects presented the most immediate form of response.

Defending 'la patrie': patriotism through music

The musical world in France responded to the Franco-Prussian war through militaristic rhetoric in its journals, the composition of numerous patriotic songs such as 'La Française'[28] and a patriotic choice of subjects for vocal music. Thus the return of Pauline Viardot from her adopted Baden-Baden to Paris was celebrated as a 'true conquest by France over the German musical world',[29] and Henri Heugel found it necessary to incite his compatriots to a more nationalist support of French music as a patriotic act.[30] Patriotism was clearly the motive behind the choice of text for the 1871 *Prix de Rome* competition: an adapted fragment of Jules Barbier's play *Jeanne d'Arc* containing the scene of Jeanne's call to save France. The choice takes up Jules Michelet's earlier interpretation of Jeanne d'Arc as the incarnation of 'the French collectivity and the French soul', 'transforming her into a Republican heroine and symbol of a non-monarchical nation'.[31] The Republican Jeanne is not the devout virgin of pro-royalist interpretations of the legend, but the masculinised embodiment of the French people:

> And one should not be surprised if the people appear here in the guise of a woman, if a woman passes from patience and sweet virtues to virile ones, those of war, if a saint becomes a soldier.[32]

This masculinised reading of the heroine is reflected in the edition of selected pieces from the prize-winning cantata by Gaston Serpette. The cover represents Jeanne d'Arc as an androgynous figure in full armour, wearing the beret well known from portraits of great Renaissance kings such as François I (see Figure 1).[33] Indeed, this engraving could be seen as an example of drawing together various cultural references in a way that Renan had argued would help forge a Republican national identity.

Two years later, on 8 November 1873, Barbier's complete *Jeanne d'Arc* was staged with music by Charles Gounod at the Théâtre de la Gaité, and its patriotic appeal was evident, especially with respect to Jeanne's martyrdom, underlined by Gounod's poignant Marche Funèbre:

> Under the transfigured form of Jeanne d'Arc, it was our country itself that appeared to all; from the orchestra stalls and the boxes, there was an outburst of ardent enthusiasm; it was France, loved even more in her disasters, that was acclaimed; and in this explosion of all that which these Parisian hearts, boasters of scepticism, had confined until now, suddenly the national sentiment of our glories and our misfortunes was awakened.[34]

Figure 4.1

Gounod's music, in particular the Marche Funèbre and the chorus *Nous fuyons la patrie* – 'the *Super flumina Babylonis* of the invaded and repressed France'[35] – was perceived as strengthening the emotional impact of the play's patriotic message. Although the role of Gounod's music was rather secondary in this context, his contribution was received not just as a major new work by one of France's leading composers but as a patriotic act.

Three years later, the newly built Palais Garnier gave as its first new opera the première of Mermet's *Jeanne d'Arc*. Again this was clearly a patriotic choice, but the subject alone was no longer enough to guarantee the work's success. And by the end of the decade, Jeanne d'Arc had become too controversial a figure to be used for Republican ends without ambiguity. Maurice Agulhon identifies 'un contre-culte nationaliste autour de Jeanne d'Arc' as one of the means of the nationalist right to fight the Republic with its own symbolic impersonation in 'Marianne'.[36] Although the history of Jeanne d'Arc remained one of the most popular topics in French music,[37] patriotic criteria for the choice of subject were slowly superseded by more nationalist considerations of developing a French music of the avant-garde, especially in the context of the reception of Wagner,[38] who had soon been assigned the role of a cultural giant within the camp of the enemy against whom developments in French art were measured. As in the case of other issues such as schooling, the German comparison never disappeared, and, although the selection of operatic subjects was still linked to political factors, the arguments about such topics and their sources became more and more focused on aesthetic and cultural issues.[39]

Educating healthy 'French' citizens

However, patriotic concerns were still present in other parts of French cultural life. Renan claims that widespread popular education as a decisive element in Germany's victory became a national obsession in Third-Republic France, and French educational reforms after 1871 emphasised patriotic issues in their teaching programmes.[40] Although music had already been introduced into primary education towards the end of the Second Empire in 1865, it received a new Republican function of developing a national conscience in the school system after 1870, justified not only by educational ideals derived from Plato's *Republic* and Aristotle's *Politics* but even more through its ability to forge a sense of collectivity by way of choral singing.[41] The German educational system provided both a model and a measuring stick, and justification for French educational practice was often sought by comparison with it.[42] Thus, when Louis-Albert Bourcault-Ducoudray[43] was asked to report on choral singing in French secondary schools, he came to the conclusion that Germany had its vibrant musical and artistic culture because of the ideas of Luther and their reception:

> Luther thus created, with unprecedented success, opportunities for his fellow believers to express collective religious feeling; at the same time as he made evident the usefulness of music in applying it to an elevated and civilising aim, he taught Germany, once and for all, the function and virtue of 'great art', inculating therein a love and respect for it forever.[44]

Music, Bourcault-Ducoudray asserted, had an educating mission, creating '"unity" in the heart of a nation',[45] and, properly applied, choral singing would produce a 'sacred trembling in young hearts' with reference to the heroic past of France.[46] Bourcault-Ducoudray not only provided a theoretical justification for the educational value of music but also composed 'patriotic' songs specifically for schools. His 'chant scholaire,' 'Esprit de la France!' offers a perfect example of the nationalist if not revanchist spirit of some such pieces, emphasising heroism, patriotism and male qualities in general. The diatonic setting in march rhythm underlines the text's message:

> Esprit de la France, Nous sommes toujours
> Inspire à nos cœurs La race fidèle
> Les saintes ardeurs, A l'être si belle
> La mâle espérance! De paix et d'amour.
> Afin qu'on proclame Mais si l'on outrage
> Nos rudes travaux, Le sol des aïeux,
> Allume en notre âme, Aux champs du carnage
> La généreuse flamme Nous courons comme eux![47]
> Des héros!

This educational role of music was by no means trivial: it was the key to nationalising French art and to creating both a healthy musical taste and healthy French citizens. As early as 1872, *L'Art musical* published a defence of music as part of higher education, stressing these aspects of mental and physical health.[48] In 1910, Jules Combarieu went much further, writing that: music is a 'school of solidarity', even a 'school of attention and discipline,' for pupils who need to give the same attention to their conductor 'as soldiers to their colonels on a field of manoeuvre'.[49] In the practice of choral singing, melody and rhythm intensify all feelings expressed in the text, which is why music is an ideal tool in patriotic education:

> The verbal phrase fades; the melody engraves. For example, you may give a lesson to the children on patriotism, on military courage, on the necessity of believing in victory when one has to pay with one's own life: you will find it easy to move and to interest them. But make them then sing the *Chant du départ*: 'La victoire en chantant nous ouvre la barrière . . .' Which of these two lessons will provide the deepest and most long-lasting effects? It will certainly be the second.[50]

But choral singing achieved even more for the French Republic: 'music educating both ear and voice, so important in a democracy; music teaching to speak clearly – and to listen'.[51]

Although such discourse refers to earlier concepts, as, for example, the emphasis on developing physical and spiritual health – to which reference is often made with respect to the Orphéon movement – it takes on a different and much more Republican slant here. Plato's ideal republic, Aristotle's ideas of music's 'ethos', the glorious memory of the 'chants révolutionnaires' in the first revolution[52] and the perceived success of choral training in Germany formed the mainstays of the argument to give vocal music a new weight in French public education. Choral singing is the form of musical practice which is the chief object of such masculinising rhetoric: virtue, power and glory are recurring terms.[53] However, so invigorating a musical education is useful not only for boys, but also for girls. The ideology of 'Republican motherhood' – the exaltation of 'the crucial part [women] would play in nurturing and educating the Republic's new-born citizens'[54] – had lost nothing of its attraction since the early nineteenth century, in particular because 'the decline of the old gender order accelerated in the aftermath of the revolutionary Commune and France's humiliating defeat in the Franco-Prussian war (1870–71).'[55] One major French concern thereafter was that France's birth-rate was the lowest in Europe.[56] Campaign followed campaign to fight against this form of decay; the question of national health developed into a public neurosis. Not only was motherhood understood as the 'patriotism of women' (Dumas) through repopulating the nation, but women's health and education were perceived as essential to the breeding of a strong and healthy race:

> The mother makes the race. It is she who gives vigour, intelligence and the foundations of education; the stronger and more intelligent she is and the more noble her character, the more powerful will be the race.[57]

Thus, in the project of educating 'Republican' mothers, choral singing again held a central place. Not only would it provide 'localised gymnastics' to prevent sore throats and respiratory problems[58] – an important factor in a period of rampant tuberculosis – but it would form women spiritually and intellectually. Furthermore, such choral singing would prevent them from preferring vulgar music-hall songs and their environment over the 'pure and sublime joys of ensemble music'.[59]

Cultural migrations I: 'la bonne et saine chanson française . . .'

It was not only choral singing in schools that was used to instil patriotism and health in future French citizens and their mothers, keeping them from the temptations of the café-concert. The same function was fulfilled by the newly founded co-educational 'universités populaires' and choral societies for working-class women, such as Ernest Chebroux's L'Œuvre de la Chanson Française.⁶⁰ As Mary Ellen Poole has shown, one of the central musical focuses of these institutions was 'la bonne et saine chanson française', rallying socialist, Republican and right-wing forces in the shared undertaking of revitalising 'true' French musical culture after 1870. These practical projects relied heavily on an industry of collecting, editing and researching French folk-songs headed most prominently by Julien Tiersot, who played a central role in the theoretical and practical mediation of the *chanson populaire*.⁶¹

As with the introduction of music into primary education, French interest in national folk music pre-dates the beginning of the Third Republic. It was mainly a literary movement, fuelled not only by contact with German literature and philology⁶² but also by the French encounter with the English folksong movement and historical novels.⁶³ Thus from the 1830s to the 1860s the collecting of French folksongs concentrated on the presentation of poetic anthologies either by collectors such as Charles Nisard or by poets inspired by the German and English Romantic movements. One well-known example of such poets is Gérard de Nerval with his *Chansons et légendes du Valois*, published as part of his *Les filles du feu*,⁶⁴ which he presented as a response to the cultural challenges posed by France's two powerful neighbours whose creative artists had apparently not been alienated from the inspirational source of a national folk culture.⁶⁵ During the 1850s, a government-sponsored collection primarily of folksong texts led to an increase in the number of poetic anthologies before 1870.⁶⁶ However, the two most influential studies of the musical aspects of French *chansons* appeared in the late 1880s within the space of three years, during a crucial moment for the survival of the Third Republic. Both Weckerlin's *La Chanson populaire* (1886) and Tiersot's *Histoire de la chanson populaire en France* (1889)⁶⁷ can be interpreted as attempts to grasp and define an essentially French national heritage in the face of both external and internal threats, from Bismarck's Germany on the one hand, and General Boulanger's right-wing attack on the Republican government on the other. Both books offer almost perfect examples of the process of masculinising popular music in an act of nationalist appropriation, not only through their descriptive vocabulary but also by their authors' scholarly way of taking intellectual control over this repertoire.

Weckerlin and Tiersot presented French folksong as an answer both to external challenges against France's music – particularly Wagner – and to scepticism among the French themselves regarding the possibility of a specifically French national tradition of (vocal) music. Rousseau's classic verdict that the French language was – as Daniel Heartz has put it – 'expressive only of ideas, not sentiments; [that] it had no marked accent'⁶⁸ had been perpetuated throughout French music criticism of the nineteenth century, beginning with Julien-Louis Geoffroy, the influential opera critic of the *Journal des débats* from 1800 to 1814.[69] It surfaced periodically to discursive prominence as a 'topos obligée', for example in Stendhal's widely read *Vie de Rossini* (1824). Weckerlin's argument is based on his division between on the one hand, 'le peuple', close to their roots, and on the other the aristocracy with its universalist art music, a division that he dates back to the Middle Ages with its troubadours.[70] For Weckerlin, following a line of argument reminiscent of Hippolyte Taine, it is folksong that truly expresses 'the type, specific physiognomy and characteristic rhythms' of a people.[71] Because of her specific location and history, France proves to be 'the kingdom of song, for the French are born singers'.[72] Superior in her natural musical skills to any other nation, France's popular culture proves to be vibrant, vital and masculine in its strength, a direct expression of the 'génie français'. Weckerlin carried forward these arguments from Gaston Paris's preface to his *Chansons du XVe siècle*, published in 1875 (by the same publisher as Weckerlin's), and unequivocally undertaken as a patriotic act by one of France's leading philologists.[73] Both Paris and Weckerlin attributed Rousseau's essential musical quality of 'true sentiment' to France's folksongs (whereas they decry its loss in French art music, which is alienated from its source),[74] and at the same time they inscribed the aesthetic principles of classic *tragédie* such as *clarté* and *simplicité* as national characteristics presenting direct artistic articulation of the French people through the *chanson populaire*. Both Paris and Weckerlin are careful in expressing their claim for French superiority within the European context, even with respect to Germany. Thus Gaston Paris hid his claim in a footnote spreading over four pages, and limited his comments in the text to the following:

> Another interest attached to the old *chansons* is their importance for comparative literature. Whatever will be the final word in a just born science on the date, origin and relationships of the popular poetry of Roman and Germanic nations, it is already certain that the [poetry] from France will have to hold a significant place in the depicting of these relationships and in the study of these origins.[75]

Julien Tiersot's book, written at almost exactly the same time as Weckerlin's (when Tiersot began to work as Weckerlin's assistant at the Bibliothèque du Conservatoire), took all these points one step further. His foreword spelled out what the other two texts only implied, referring not only to Rousseau but to an even older concept which by then had acquired the status of an important topos in French culture, the notion of the 'translatio studii'. This concept, which originated in the idea of philosophic progression 'through time and space until it reaches France'[76] in the sixteenth century, was based on the belief that cultures followed a necessary trajectory from primitive beginnings to a period of splendour, followed by decline. In the Paris of François I, the 'home of the greatest cultural achievements was thought to have shifted from its origins in the East to Greece, Rome, modern Italy and finally France as each old civilisation became exhausted and corrupt'.⁷⁷ By the eighteenth century, this concept of cultural progression in the direction of France had become a widely used topos underpinned by new theories of environmental influence, especially through the climate. Writers such as d'Espiard in his *Essais sur le génie et le caractère des nations* (1743) based their defence of France's cultural superiority on an amalgam of the new 'scientific' ideas on climate with the older notion of the 'translatio studii'.⁷⁸ During the nineteenth century, these notions retained an important place in aesthetic discussions and were developed still further, fuelled by the Republican metaphor of France as the 'new Rome'.⁷⁹ Tiersot clearly referred to the concept of the 'translatio studii' in his attempt both to justify the superiority of a French national culture and to attribute cultural value to the *chanson populaire*. He says at the very outset of the book:

> Greece had exerted her sovereign influence over the entire civilisation of antiquity. Creator and then disseminator of all the arts, she had brought them to the highest perfection that the ancient world had known, and had spread amongst all civilised peoples the accomplished types of serene maturity and sober elegance that she had produced. In music, her influence was considerable ... Through Rome, who had become the pupil and imitator of Greece, the influence of Greek art was exerted on the greater part of the Roman empire ... This rich Greco-Latin culture flourished to the highest degree in Roman Gaul.⁸⁰

Thus, within a few sentences, Tiersot introduced the foundation of French culture through Greece and Rome and set France at the head of this 'Greco-Latin' cultural field. France, he continued, was unique because it not only assimilated the two different genres of Greco-Roman music (theatre and religious music) and the truly Latin form of North Italian popular music ('une troisième forme lyrique, cette fois purement latine'),⁸¹ but also because the French were able to amalgamate these influences with their 'celtic' heritage and its 'particular artistic instincts'.⁸² The superiority of this sophisticated French form of cultural eclecticism becomes immediately obvious when compared with the neighbouring Germanic tribes whose music Tiersot characterised through the following tale, loosely based on Tacitus' *Annals*:⁸³

> Tacitus mentions the savage war-songs through which the Germans excited each other in the battles. Around King Chlodevech, the Frank warriors sang epic songs which consecrated the memory of their national hero Siegfried during meals and in war council. At the occasion of the first battle in Gallia between the [invading] Franks of [Chlodevech] and the legionnaires of Aétius, the Franks were camping on a

> hillside and celebrated the marriage of one of their leaders to the sound of songs and dances sung in chorus; these noises revealed their presence to the Romans; they were taken by surprise: their taste for resounding music was the reason for their first defeat.[84]

Indeed, Tiersot used here the authority of an author well known to every French *bourgeois*, given that Tacitus was a staple in French secondary education.[85] In the context of the late 1880s in Paris, the political undertones of Tiersot's rendering of the tale are obvious: Wagnerian noise could well be the reason for Germany's cultural – at least – defeat when faced with a nation whose cultural values were based on the assimilation of the most noble and vibrant cultures in human history.

Victor Cousin's influential theory of eclecticism had not only become the 'official philosophy of Louis-Philippe's reign' during the July monarchy[86] but also persisted during the Third Republic as the Republican model for artistic progress in France.[87] In an interesting rhetorical strategy, Tiersot turned this to his advantage. Like Paris and Weckerlin, he saw a split between an art music becoming more and more decadent and subject to foreign influence and a folk music that remained virile and truly French and which possibly represented the seed of a renewed French cultural identity. The *chanson populaire* is the only cultural remnant of the ideal world of the Middle Ages, embodying the virtues of the France of Jeanne d'Arc, to whom both Paris and Tiersot refer.[88] The notion of a medieval 'golden age' was not new in the 1880s – Romantic fascination in the earlier nineteenth century with champions such as Viollet-le-Duc had paved the way – but by then the concept had become a powerful image as the counter-world to a materialistic, decadent and corrupt present. At this central point in his argument Tiersot uses the full register of masculinising rhetoric, insisting on the non-flowery, concise, logical, profound and vital qualities of the *chanson populaire*:

> We find again this same *chanson* [of the times of Jeanne d'Arc] still alive at the end of our nineteenth century ... Rhyme is unknown in it; at most, it is replaced by assonance, the last remnant of the versification traditions of the Middle Ages.[89] ... Its phrase is short and clear; the right word leaps from it with a splendour that even the most erudite verse would envy; and always an admirable concision, no superfluous development: the narration aims straight for its goal with logical and natural deductions, without lingering on anything useless; or else, the sentiment is expressed in simple but profound and penetrating words. And on this verse are admirable melodies, short and concise like them, but of intense appeal and inexhaustible vitality.[90]

In Tiersot's concept of the *chanson populaire* and its history, French folk music stands at the beginning of all Western art music, its genres as well as its harmonic language.[91] His quest for 'historical truth' enables him to re-read music history, presenting the musical language of the French people, and thus an inherently national music, as art music's true basis:

> One has to go back to the Middle Ages, and one will see these two arts [Gregorian chant and *chanson populaire*], the first and primitive forms of French music, play in concert with respect to the creation of opera, a role exactly similar to the one which we have seen them play in studying the creation of harmony.[92]

This statement is part of a substantial chapter on the *mélodie populaire* on stage, in which Tiersot traces the role of folksong in the creation and development of music theatre. It begins with a lengthy quotation from the third book of Wagner's *Oper und Drama* that immediately marks this chapter as a response to the impact of Wagner's theories and music. Thus Tiersot traces music theatre back to one major French work, Adam de la Halle's *Le Jeu de Robin et Marion*,[93] which he would later edit and write about.[94] Throughout the rest of the book, he judges music, especially French opera, with respect to its relationship with folksong. *Opéra comique*, for example, is hailed as a truly French genre because it grew out of the French people's musical language, and a successful *opéra comique* will always show this affinity with French popular music, as for example François-Adrien Boieldieu in *La Dame blanche*.[95] When in 1894 the thousandth performance of Ambroise Thomas's *opéra comique, Mignon,* was celebrated as a major event in French music, Tiersot praised its popular elements in an article entitled '*Mignon* et la chanson française'. Here Tiersot claims that Thomas's music corresponded so well to the language of the *chanson populaire* that two of his *romances* had become part of that tradition. Tiersot describes them being orally transmitted and sung on the streets and in villages by 'the people' without knowledge of their origin as works of a specific composer. This process of popular appropriation had proven their quality as true folk-songs.[96]

With this book, Tiersot offered a powerful philosophy of French music and its history that would find a nationalist and right-wing reception in the circles of the Schola Cantorum. Although Tiersot was later to align himself with the Schola and its ideals, the present book stands in the context both of patriotic and Republican attempts to define French music[97] and of French Wagnerism. Tiersot never denied his fascination with Wagner and saw the composer's strength in his ability to draw on his national popular culture. But Tiersot's book proposed a French model as an answer to this challenge, suggesting a genuinely French identity for musical language. He was able not only to assimilate the 'Wagnerian' references to the Middle Ages into his theory but also the 'Latin' qualities of *clarté* and *simplicité*, redefining these as characteristics embodied in French cultural expression *sui generis* instead of the 'aristocratic' and universalist context of the *Pléiade*, the poetic circle of the Renaissance that is usually perceived as the historical foundation of France's artistic glory.

Tiersot's study marks the beginning of what might be called the French 'folksong consensus'.[98] Like the reception of Wagner, the reference to popular music as an inspirational source for a truly French music became a shared topos of French aesthetic discussions.[99] It found its way in the writings of a wide variety of authors, ranging from Wagnerian and anthroposophist Edouard Schuré to the biographer of Massenet, Louis Schneider.[100] When in 1906 the Schola Cantorum began the publication of *Les Chansons de France*, a trimestrial journal dedicated to folksong research, the first issue contained supporting letters not only from Frédéric Mistral, Vincent d'Indy and Pierre Lalo but also from the director of the Conservatoire, Gabriel Fauré.[101]

Musical heritage and the 'new' French music

The vibrant, masculine and truly French *chanson populaire* was not the only foundation on which a renewed French music would be based. Fiamma Nicolodi has recently demonstrated the powerful nationalist potential of the myth of 'early music'.[102] Whereas before 1870 any reference to earlier music had often been part of either universalist scholarly projects, such as Farrenc's *Le Trésor des pianistes*, or movements for the renewal of religious music as in the case of Choron, the overwhelmingly nationalist appropriation of past French music began to flourish mainly in the aftermath of the Franco-Prussian war. This was directed in two ways: on the one hand, the publication, study and performance of French (and other 'Latin'; i.e. Italian) early music not only in order to create a 'canon' of French musical masterpieces but also to provide models of a truly French musical language; on the other, the (re-)evaluation and aesthetic defence of traditional genres such as *opéra comique* and new genres such as French orchestral song.

This interest in early music reflects similar concerns to those of the folksong revival. In fact, the main champions of the regeneration of popular music – for example, Tiersot, Weckerlin, Bourcault-Ducoudray, Bordes and d'Indy – were also key figures in the early-music movement. The division between popular and 'high' art with respect to *chansons françaises* was perceived as only liminal, and their use for patriotic and nationalist definitions of French art through both left and right was almost identical, as were the rhetorical strategies ascribing masculinity to this repertoire. An interesting example for this *modus operandi* is Henry Expert's preface to the first volume of his series *Les Maîtres musiciens de la Renaissance française* (1894),[103] where he explicitly refers to the virile qualities of French Renaissance music:

> However, from the first hours of the sixteenth century, in the vigour of a male and fruitful youth, music rejected the rigid formalism of the primitives [i.e. the music of the Ars Nova]; linked to an erudite technique,

> conscious of her expressive energies, [music] could attempt the interpretation of feelings; she possessed from now on this *secret and almost unbelievable virtue of moving the hearts in one way or another* (Calvin). And to begin with, the secular spirit, this powerful Gallic foundation nurtured by the Renaissance, appears fully in secular music ... And while the poetic school of Marot and the Pléïade gave music its most beautiful jewels, fervent Humanism tried, under the pen of erudite musicians, to revive the likes of Horace and Virgil, Ovid, Catullus and Martial.[104]

Again, the virility of the French musical heritage is linked to the powerful symbolic imagery of France as the 'new Rome', with the concept of the 'translatio studii' serving as justification. In an interesting twist, Expert also ascribes this masculine musical quality to both Catholic and Protestant sacred music of the French Renaissance, given that the churches had no choice but to respond to this 'triumphant spirit' of the sixteenth century.[105] Furthermore, the expressive qualities of Renaissance music make it an ideal point of historical reference if Rousseau's verdict on French music's lack of expression and Wagnerian demands on the expressive role of music are kept in mind.[106] As with the *chanson populaire*, these early works provided models of a French music which satisfied the requirements of an inherently French musical language.[107] Eventually such collections would constitute a 'canon' of French musical heritage – whether of the 'race' or of a cultural association – and create a French tradition of referential masterpieces.[108] In his *La Musique et les musiciens français*, Albert Lavignac makes it clear to young composers that traditional French qualities were always part of past artistic achievements, whereas their negation would necessarily lead to awkward and thus ridiculous works:

> It is impossible to finish this chapter [on the national French style] without urging young French composers to concern themselves before anything else with conserving the characteristic qualities of our national art, which have always been its glory, which one finds in all great eras and which are *clarity, elegance* and *sincerity of expression*. It is the only way for them to be natural and to succeed in creating a proper style, a personality; because every time that they stray from these traditions inherent to the race, to the genius of [French] language as to the French spirit, they will only be awkward imitators and plagiarists; they will remind us of people who speak a foreign language badly with a ridiculous accent.[109]

Thus it is not necessary to look across the Rhine for musical guidance because France's own glorious past provides rich inspiration and shining examples. Lavignac's nationalist approach is deeply rooted in the proclamation of a racial heritage as expressed in the idea of the 'nation-génie', but similar forms of argument – now referring to a common cultural past in the wake of Renan's ideas – can be found in writings of declared Republicans such as Camille Saint-Saëns.

This attitude becomes particularly evident with respect to *opéra comique*, a genre much discussed in the early Third Republic. More than any other form of musical drama, *opéra comique* could be re-appropriated as a national operatic genre in the ambivalent context of French Wagner reception, whereas *grand opéra* was much more problematic because of its more cosmopolitan history and appeal. However, *opéra comique* had carried the stigma of being judged a feminine genre since the eighteenth century. Both plot and music were often judged as facile, naïve, charming, *à la mode* and cloying.[110] It was not only described in these feminised terms, but was also a genre which was thought to be suited to women composers such as Sophie Gail, Lucile Grétry, Caroline Wuiet, to name just a few from the eighteenth century. Bertrand's already cited demand that *opéra comique* needed to become more masculine was echoed in writings such as Camille Bellaigue's extensive discussion of *opéra comique* in his study *Un siècle de musique française*[111] and in reviews of opéra-comique performances. An interesting case is the first performance of Camille Saint-Saëns's *Phryné* in 1893, which was clearly conceived as a work reviving traditional characteristics of earlier *opéra comique*.[112] For Saint-Saëns, one of the ways to 'masculinise' *opéra comique* was to use alexandrine verse, the 'noble' metre of classical French tragedy, for both sung and spoken text. This corresponds to his earlier theories that the renewal of French opera was to be found in, amongst other things, a return to classical rhythm in both text and music.[113] Saint-Saëns not only attempted to include elements of the *tragédie* but also the modes of ancient Greek music. These modes had not been tainted by Wagnerian chromaticism and were thus 'pure' and promising for musical progress.[114] The première of *Phryné* was celebrated as a significantly French event after the first Parisian performance of Wagner's *Die Walküre* just two weeks earlier at the Opéra, and critics did not miss the opportunity to emphasise once more the traditional French (i.e. Latin) qualities of *clarté, esprit* and *justesse* in comparison to Wagner's ungainly Germanic noise.[115]

But it was not only in the revival of traditional French genres such as *opéra comique* that the French attempted to represent inherently French musical characteristics. Avant-garde forms such as French orchestral song were discussed in similar terms. In the case of this genre, the notion of intrinsic French musical qualities was reflected in the lively discussions about its merits; and although the answers were slightly different in their orientation, some issues such as the specific aesthetic value of French prosody were linked to the glorious tradition of French vocal music. But orchestral song – as opposed to orchestrated song – also had an innovative aspect: France appeared as the creator of a new, advanced genre of symphonic vocal music.[116] These 'poèmes pour chant et orchestre' began their life in the context of *Weltanschauungsmusik* and musical experiments in the 1870s and 1880s in Paris, when composers such as César Franck, Henri Duparc and Camille Saint-Saëns tried to revive French music outside the opera house. Orchestral songs were symphonic music in the strong sense of the term, with its aesthetic meaning being seen in the same manner as that of symphonies and symphonic poems. The boundaries were fluid, and structures such as sonata form (e.g. in Saint-Saëns's *La fiancée du timbalier*) or cyclic musical organisation of several movements (as in Ropartz's *Quatre poèmes d'aprés l'"Intermezzo' d'Henri Heine* or Ernest Chausson's *Poème de l'amour et de la mer* – reflected these aesthetic claims in musical terms. French absolute music (in particular symphonies) demanded a model of explication which would take German achievements into account. Thus French symphonic music of the *fin de siècle* was represented in the writings of musicians as different as d'Indy and Saint-Saëns as flourishing, inventive and taking on the baton in the relay race of nineteenth-century Beethoven reception.[117] Yet works of a genre such as orchestral song could be easily defended as genuinely French, given the clearly established link to the past.

Cultural migrations II: Reading national music history

This reading is congruent with contemporary notions of music history. The writing of music history reaches back to the encyclopaedic eighteenth century with works such as De la Borde's *Essai sur la musique ancienne et moderne* (1780). As for the nineteenth century, during the decades before 1870 some major historical surveys reflected the growing interest in founding, justifying and integrating French and others' music and aesthetic judgement in a historical lineage.[118] In particular François-Joseph Fétis, influenced by Victor Cousin's synthetic concept of eclecticism and Auguste Comte's evolutionary model of linear progress, proved to be one of the most powerful writers of music history before 1870.[119] After the Franco-Prussian war, a panoply of music histories swept France, and 1879 saw the introduction of a new class in music history at the Conservatoire.[120] Books on music history had many purposes, serving for example as textbooks for classes at the Conservatoire and, later, in secondary schools. In the field of music journalism, historical accounts – usually of a specific topic such as the history of harpsichord music – became an essential branch of the trade, published mainly in the specialist musical press, from *Le Ménestrel* to *Musica*. However, the notion of linear artistic 'progress', which Fétis had already perceived as full of problems[121] – even if it still represented the aesthetic mainstay of the early Third Republic[122] – gave way to a wide variety of approaches to the construction of music history that echoed the different aesthetic and political currents outlined above.

All these French music histories were faced with the difficulty of assessing and evaluating French music, both in a historical and a contemporary context, particularly with repect to the overwhelming aesthetic and musical presence of German music. Thus these historical constructions had to create readings that would represent France in a central position within European music and its history. The now familiar model of the 'translatio studii', strengthened by its 'scientific' support through recent Darwinian and Taineian philosophies, proved particularly useful in this endeavour, for it allowed French writers to achieve two goals: on the one hand, they could ascribe to France a key role as 'enabler' of the development of German music in the late eighteenth and the nineteenth centuries, thus continuing the path of cultural migration from France to Germany; on the other, the model provided a helpful tool to redirect this migration to contemporary France by representing German culture as reaching a period of decadence after the death of Beethoven or Wagner – paradigmatically formulated in Debussy's famous *bon mot* on Wagner as a glorious sunset erroneously mistaken for a sunrise.[123]

Thus, for example, Albert Soubies, a declared adherent of the philosophical concept of eclecticism, places the influence of Rousseau at the beginning of Germany's national artistic awakening. Indeed, 'the influence of Rousseau on the other side of the Rhine was considerable',[124] and it was Rousseau's ideas that allowed the Germans to find their own national voice, completely developed for the first time in the towering *œuvre* of Beethoven that epitomised the virile traits of this new, powerful German music whose influence would be predominant in nineteenth-century Europe, particularly with respect to symphonic music.[125] Soubies's masculinisation of Beethoven's music was typical for the period, not only in the composer's French reception but also in Germany and England.[126] For the eclectic Soubies, German achievements held a positive place, even with respect to contemporary French music:

> As for France, finally, whose characteristics in art have always been a clear-sighted and delicate eclecticism, intelligent and fine combination, [and] the skilful adaptation of very diverse elements, one knows with what brilliance, with what abundance of resources we have, in what M. Lavoix has called 'the century of Beethoven', received and put in its true light the German tradition.[127]

Soubies's reference to German achievements implied a demand for their acculturation, their transfer back to France. His rhetoric stands in the context of a post-war relationship between France and Germany which was determined by cultural competition. Through cultural imports, new ideas could be infused into French music, offering a catalyst to its further development.[128]

Other writers such as Vincent d'Indy who opposed such an eclectic theory gallicised the lineage from Beethoven. Instead of assimilating Germanic concepts in an eclectic manner, d'Indy's hero, César Franck, developed – in ways similar to those outlined by Tiersot for the Latinising of folksong – what he encountered in Beethoven's music into an essentially French composition technique:

> With Franck, the inspired French continuer of the immortal German symphonist, begins a new and so far *exclusively French* period. The value and power of the best works belonging to this period rely on all the innovations of Beethoven and on the *cyclic* construction finally understood and realised. Under this benign influence, the traditional sonata form has already recovered, at least in our country, a vitality and youth that are truly surprising after half a century of decadence and oblivion ... It falls to France to continue and to realise the transformation of sonata form, clearly indicated by Beethoven: not one of his German successors, in fact, knew how to or seriously wanted to attempt this truly *cyclic* renovation, the sole means of giving life to this beautiful form which was atrophying and seemed close to disappearing, at least in Germany, despite the timid endeavours of Schumann and Brahms. Thus the *cyclic* tradition can be considered as transmitted *directly* from Beethoven to César Franck.[129]

D'Indy clearly uses this masculinising rhetoric with respect both to the old and now surpassed German style (i.e. Beethoven) and to the new French sonata form in order to emphasise the vitality and youth of a triumphant new French school. Like Debussy with Wagner, d'Indy identifies the moment of decline with the death of a key Germanic figure, spelling out what Debussy implied: that the new way forward in music was to be found in France.

The concept of the decadence of German music, either after Beethoven (with respect to absolute music) or after Wagner (with respect to opera) and culture's new dynamic haven in the France of the Third Republic, pervades all levels of music history right through to educational literature such as Laure Collin's highly popular *Histoire abrégée de la musique et des musiciens* or Elise Vigoureux's *Manuel d'histoire générale de la musique à l'usage des classes de solfège*.[130] These authors implicitly (and sometimes explicitly, like d'Indy) used the gender metaphor to feminise current developments in Germany and to masculinise the French future. Authors might choose the eclectic model, like Soubies, or a more nationalist model emphasising the 'national soul' expressed through music, like Lavoix in his *La Musique française*;[131] however, they all rose to the challenge to find and apply an explicatory model for the ambivalent cultural migration between France and Germany. As Werner and Espagne have shown, the issue of cultural relationship in this case has been determined by competition particularly after 1870–71, given that the French defeat has been ascribed not only to military reasons but also as a 'result of a cultural inferiority'.[132] The arts of other countries such as Italy – a major reference point in Stendhal's time – became less important in discourse after 1870. Whereas music journalism had to react to new 'others' such as music from Russia, adapting models and metaphors to new situations,[133] music histories from 1870 to 1914 were fixated on a bilateral relationship between France and Germany.

Discourses on a national music in France after 1870 reveal similar masculinising tendencies, as can be observed in Imperial Britain, the Germany of the Weimar Republic – with its discussion of 'Neue Sachlichkeit' and 'Moderne' – or the United States immediately after the Second Word War.[134] It appears as if these cultures needed to redefine and consolidate their aesthetic values in times of political instability (either in defeat or expansion) by emphasising accepted cultural values that met a need for reassurance in threatening times. Given that the shared notion of 'masculinity' represented the highest and healthiest concept in the cultural and social hierarchy of Republican France, its constant presence in the cultural discourses of the *fin de siècle* is anything but unexpected. It played an important role in redefining and appropriating French music past and present for the endeavour of patriotic and nationalist self-definition of both the French right and left in all their different shades. In the same way that right and left colluded during the period between 1870 and 1914 to keep women in the home – to produce either healthy young republicans or good French subjects – they perpetuated masculine ideals in their aesthetic and historical discourses on music. To develop a healthy, vibrant and truly French art had become a major concern in a culture that could see the threat of decadence and effeminacy not only in the world of their enemies but also at home.[135]

Notes and References

1   I wish to thank the British Academy for a research grant enabling me to spend the necessary time in Paris in order to conduct my research for this chapter. I am grateful to Linda Phyllis Austern, Tim Carter, Katharine Ellis, Andrea Musk and Steve Stanton for their most helpful comments on earlier versions of this chapter. Such versions were also presented as papers at the University of Southampton, City University, London, and King's College, London; I am indebted for the insightful and challenging comments and questions by staff and students.
2   Stéphane Wolff, *Un demi-siècle d'opéra-comique* (Paris, 1953).
3   Gustave Bertrand,'Opéra-Comique/Hérold/1000e représentation du *Pré aux Clercs* – Rentrée de Mme Carvalho', *Le Ménestrel*, 37, 1870–71, pp. 361–2:'Disons enfin, et c'est là-dessus que nous aimons le plus à insister que la millième représentation du *Pré aux Clercs* est une fête pour l'école française. Nous avons besoin, en ce moment plus que jamais, que l'art français nous affirme hautement toutes ses gloires légitimes, pour nous consoler d'abord et nous réconforter, et puis pour s'encourager lui-même à en chercher d'autres. . . . Or, ce qui fait avant tout, à nos yeux, l'importance de cette millième représentation d'un chef-d'œuvre si absolument français, c'est qu'elle remet toutes choses en leur rang, et qu'elle m'apparaît comme une borne milliaire destinée à marquer dans l'histoire du goût public, en fait d'opéra-comique'.

4 Gustave Bertrand,'Opéra-Comique/Hérold/1000e représentation du *Pré aux Clercs*', p. 362: 'quelque chose de plus mâle et de plus nerveux dans le comique (car enfin qui dit comédie, ne dit pas exclusivement jolis sourires féminins, gaieté superficielle [ou] encore moins joyeusetés triviales)'.
5 On the conditions of subsidy for the concert societies, see Annegret Fauser, *Der Orchestergesang in Frankreich zwischen 1870 und 1920*, Freiburger Beiträge zur Musikwissenschaft, Vol. 2 (Laaber, 1994), pp. 141–54. For documents relating to state subsidies for the concert societies, see Archives Nationales, Paris, $F^{21}4626$. For the Opéra, see Frédérique Patureau, *Le Palais Garnier dans la société parisienne, 1875–1914* (Liège, 1991), with a list of archival sources on pp. 471–6.
6 Ernest Renan,'La Guerre entre la France et l'Allemagne' (1870), *'Qu'est-ce qu'une nation?' et autres essais politiques*, ed. by Joël Roman (Paris, 1992), p. 104: 'La Prusse fonde sa force sur le développement de l'instruction primaire et sur l'identité de l'armée et de la nation'.
7 On the question of nationalism and nation-state in more general terms, see Heinrich August Winkler (ed.), *Nationalismus*, 2nd edn. (Königstein/Taunus, 1985); Eric J. Hobsbawm, *Nations and Nationalism since 1870: Programme, Myth, Reality* (Cambridge, 1990); Gil Delannoi and Pierre-André Taguieff (eds.), *Théories du nationalisme: Nation, nationalité, ethnicité* (Paris, 1991).
8 Joëlle Caullier, *La Belle et la Bête: L'Allemagne des Kapellmeister dans l'imaginaire Français (1890–1914)* (Tusson/Charente, 1993), p. 60.
9 Ernest Renan,'Lettre à M. Strauss' (1870), *'Qu'est-ce qu'une nation?'* , p. 120: 'Il est clair que, dès que l'on a rejeté le principe de la légitimié dynastique, il n'a y plus, pour donner une base aux délimitations territoriales des Etats, que le droit des nationalités, c'est-à-dire des groupes naturels déterminés par la race, l'histoire et la volonté des populations'.
10 Ernest Renan,'Qu'est-ce qu'une nation?' (1882), *'Qu'est-ce qu'une nation?'*, p. 54: 'Un passé héroïque, des grands hommes, de la gloire (j'entends de la véritable), voilà le capital social sur lequel on assied une idée nationale'.
11 See Alain Renaut,'Logiques de la nation', in Gil Delannoi and Pierre-André Taguieff (eds.), *Théories du nationalisme*, pp. 33–8; Alain Finkielkraut, *La défaite de la pensée* (Paris, 1987), pp. 22–69. Finkielkraut quotes de Maistre's famous observation:'Il n'y a point d'homme dans le monde. J'ai vu dans ma vie des Français, des Italiens, des Russes. Je sais même grâce a Montesquieu qu'on peut être persan; mais quant à l'homme, je déclare ne l'avoir rencontré dans ma vie; s'il existe, c'est bien à mon insu' (p. 28).
12 Alain Finkielkraut, *La défaite de la pensée*, p. 44.
13 Pierre Birnbaum,'Nationalisme à la française', in Gil Delannoi and Pierre-André Taguieff (eds.), *Théories du nationalisme*, pp. 125–38; Danny Trom,'Frankreich: Die gespaltene Erinnerung', in Monika Flacke, *Mythen der Nationen: Ein europäisches Panorama*, exhibition catalogue (Berlin, 1998), pp. 129–51.
14 See Wolfgang Leiner, *Das Deutschlandbild in der französischen Literatur*, 2nd edn. (Darmstadt, 1991), pp. 79–95 and 154–80.
15 Fustel de Coulanges,'L'Alsace est-elle allemande ou française?' (1870), in Ernest Renan, *'Qu'est-ce qu'une nation?'*, p. 260: 'Ce qui distingue les nations, ce n'est ni la race, ni la langue. Les hommes sentent dans leur cœur qu'ils sont un même peuple lorsqu'ils ont une communauté d'idées, d'intérêts, d'affections, de souvenirs et d'espérances. Voilà ce qui fait la patrie'.
16 Maurice Agulhon, *La République de Jules Ferry à François Mitterand, 1880 à nos jours* (Paris, 1990), p. 24.
17 Given in Pierre Birnbaum,'Nationalisme à la française', p. 134:'l'expression de notre sang'.

18 Geneviève Bernard-Krauß ('Nationalismus und Internationalismus in Frankreich von 1870 bis zum zweiten Weltkrieg', Proceedings of the Quinquennial Conference of the International Musicological Society, Madrid 1992, *Revista de Musicologia*, 16 (1993), at pp. 658–60) attempts to distinguish between three phases of nationalist musical awakening in France between 1870 and 1914. However, her linear and chronological model reflects neither political differentiations nor the complex intertwinings and parallel developments of the various positions in French musical life after 1870.
19 Edward Berenson, *The Trial of Madame Caillaux* (Berkeley, 1992), pp. 114 and 116–17.
20 See Werner Stegmaier, 'Weltabkürzungskunst: Orientierung durch Zeichen', in Josef Simon (ed.), *Zeichen und Interpretation* (Frankfurt am Main, 1994), pp. 119–41.
21 Josef Simon, *Philosophie des Zeichens* (Berlin and New York, 1989), p. 263.
22 Paul Ricoeur, 'Die Metapher und das Hauptproblem der Hermeneutik', in Anselm Haverkamp (ed.), *Theorie der Metapher*, 2nd edn. (Darmstadt, 1996), pp. 356–75.
23 On the use and meaning of these terms in nineteenth-century France, see Marcia J. Citron, *Gender and the Musical Canon* (Cambridge, 1993), pp. 120–44; Katharine Ellis, 'Female Pianists and Their Male Critics in Nineteenth-Century Paris', *Journal of the American Musicological Society*, 50 (1997), pp. 353–85; Annegret Fauser, 'Lili Boulanger's *La princesse Maleine*: A Composer and her Heroine as Literary Icons', *Journal of the Royal Musical Association*, 122 (1997), pp. 100–6; Annegret Fauser, '*La Guerre en dentelles*: Women and the Prix de Rome in French Cultural Politics', *Journal of the American Musicological Society*, 51 (1998), pp. 83–129; Jeffrey Kallberg, 'The Harmony of the Tea Table: Gender and Ideology in the Piano Nocturne', *Representations*, 39 (1992), pp. 102–33; Jann Pasler, 'The Ironies of Gender, or Virility in the Music of Augusta Holmès', *Women and Music: A Journal of Gender and Culture*, 2 (1998), pp. 1–25; Deborah L. Silverman, *Art Nouveau in Fin-de-Siècle France: Politics, Psychology and Style* (Berkeley, 1989), pp. 63–106; Tamar Garb, *Sisters of the Brush: Women's Artistic Culture in Late Nineteenth-Century France* (New Haven and London, 1994), pp. 105–52; Tamar Garb, *Bodies of Modernity: Figure and Flesh in Fin-de-Siècle France* (London, 1998), pp. 25–53.
24 The French reception of Brahms reveals some specific traits. He was not at first perceived as a symphonist in the tradition of Beethoven (the German reception model) but the composer of small-scale pieces in the wake of Schumann. See Edouard Lalo, *Correspondance*, ed. Joël-Marie Fauquet (Paris, 1989), pp. 14 and 123–4.
25 Joséphin Péladin, *Istar* (1888), quoted in Michel Cadot, 'Un ardent wagnérien: Joséphin Péladin (1858–1918)'; Annegret Fauser and Manuela Schwartz (eds.), *Von Wagner zum Wagnérisme: Musik, Literatur, Kunst, Politik* (Leipzig, 1999), p. 478.
26 Karl Bartsch, *Alte französische Volkslieder* (Heidelberg, 1882), p. iii: 'diese liebliche Blüten des französischen Volksgeistes'.
27 The connotations of such gendered value judgements are discussed in the works cited in note 22. A blatant example of the use of the gender metaphor in Vincent d'Indy's aesthetics is given in Marcia J. Citron, *Gender and the Musical Canon*, p. 136.
28 Gustave Nadaud's 'La Française' shared with Rouget de Lisle's 'Marseillaise' and Alfred de Musset's '*Le Rhin allemand*' the favour of the Parisian public in 1870–71.
29 'Nouvelles diverses', *Le Ménestrel*, 37, 1870/71, p. 374: 'Mme Pauline Viardot est de retour à Paris, avec l'intention formelle d'y résider désormais. Voilà une bonne fortune pour l'art du chant français. Mme Viardot, abandonnant sa villa de Bade pour reprendre possession de son ancienne habitation de la rue Douai, n'est-ce pas là une vraie conquête faite par la France sur l'Allemagne musicale?'
30 H. Moreno (i.e. Henri Heugel), 'Semaine théâtrale', *Le Ménestrel*, 38, 1872, p. 91.

31 Susan Dunn, 'Michelet and Lamartine: Making and Unmaking the Nationalist Myth of Jeanne d'Arc', *Romanic Review*, 80 (1989), pp. 404 and 407.
32 Jules Michelet, *Histoire du Moyen-Age*, Vol. 5 (Paris, n.d.), pp. 15–16, quoted in Susan Dunn, 'Michelet and Lamartine', p. 408.
33 For a short survey on the different appropriations of Jeanne d'Arc, see Danny Trom, 'Frankreich: Die gespaltene Erinnerung', pp. 136–40. He shows there how the 'militaristic' Jeanne was used in Republican iconography, whereas the young devout country girl figures mainly in the Catholic and nationalist representations of the myth.
34 Marc Gérard, 'Un peu de patriotisme', *Le Gaulois*, 11 November 1873, p. 1: 'Sous la forme transfigurée de Jeanne d'Arc, c'était la patrie même qui apparaissait à tous; des fauteuils d'orchestre et des loges, un ardent enthousiasme éclatait; c'était la France, plus aimée encore dans ses désastres, qu'on acclamait; et dans cette explosion de tout ce que ces cœurs parisiens, fanfarons de scepticisme, avaient contenu jusqu'alors, s'est réveillé tout à coup le sentiment national de nos gloires et de nos revers'.
35 Benedict, 'Chronique musicale', *Le Figaro*, 11 November 1873, p. 3: 'C'est le *Super flumina Babylonis* de la France envahie et refoulée'. Benedict refers here to Psalm 137, an interesting reference insofar as the psalm not only laments Jewish captivity but also incites revenge.
36 See Maurice Agulhon, *Marianne au pouvoir: L'imagerie et la symbolique républicaines de 1880 à 1914* (Paris, 1989), p. 326.
37 Composers who took up the subject between 1870 and 1894 include Alfred Bruneau, Théodore Dubois, Benjamin Godard, Charles Lenepveu and Charles Marie Widor. Emile Huet offers a bibliographical survey of more than 90 pages in his *Jeanne d'Arc et la musique: Essai de bibliographie musicale* (Orléans, 1894).
38 On Wagnerism, see Sieghart Döhring and Sabine Henze-Döhring, *Oper und Musikdrama im 19. Jahrhundert*, Handbuch der musikalischen Gattingen, 13 (Laaber, 1997), pp. 282–96; Annegret Fauser and Manuela Schwartz (eds.), *Von Wagner zum Wagnérisme*; Manuela Schwartz, *Wagner-Rezeption und französische Oper des Fin de Siècle: Untersuchungen zu Vincent d'Indy's 'Fervaal'*, Berliner Musik Studien, 18, (Sinzig, 1999).
39 The relationship between opera and political context was not only crucial with respect to France but also other countries such as *fin de siècle* Italy. See for example Jürgen Maehder, 'Die italienische Oper de Fin de siècle als Spiegel politischer Strömungen im umbertinischen Italien', in Udo Bermbach and Wulf Konolf (eds.), *Der schöne Abglanz: Stationen der Operngeschichte. Oper als Spiegel gesellschaftlicher Veränderung* (Berlin and Hamburg, 1992), pp. 181–210.
40 Alexander Schmidt, 'Deutschland als Modell? Bürgerlichkeit und gesellschaftliche Modernisierung im deutschen Kaiserreich (1871–1914) aus der Sicht der französischen Zeitgenossen', *Jahrbuch für Wirtschaftsgeschichte* (Berlin, 1992), p. 234.
41 For an attempt to understand the music of his time in terms of Aristotle, see Camille Bellaigue, 'Les idées musicales d'Aristote', *Etudes musicales*, troisième série (Paris, 1907), pp. 1–28.
42 The German system of education with its inclusion of music was also cited by English reformers of the late nineteenth century. See Vic Gammon, 'Folk Song Collecting in Sussex and Surrey 1843–1914', *History Workshop: A Journal of Social Historians*, 10 (1980), p. 78.
43 Already in 1869, Louis-Albert Bourcault-Ducoudray (1840–1910) had founded a choral society with the explicit aim 'to encourage people to sing choral music', and over the years music education developed into a 'patriotic obsession' for him; see Jann Pasler, 'Paris: Conflicting Notions of Progress', in Jim Samson (ed.), *Man and Music: The Late Romantic Era from the Mid-19th Century to World War I* (London, 1991), p. 394.

44 Louis-Albert Bourcault-Ducoudray, 'L'Enseignement du chant dans les lycées', *La Revue musicale*, 3 (1903), p. 725: 'Luther a donc créé, avec un succès inouï, des occasions pour ses coreligionnaires d'exprimer le sentiment collectif religieux; en même temps qu'il rendait l'utilité de la musique évidente en l'appliquant à un but élevé et civilisateur, il renseignait l'Allemagne, une fois pour toutes, sur la fonction et la vertu du "grand art", et lui en inculquait à jamais l'amour et le respect'.
45 Ibid., p. 727: 'faire "l'unité" dans le cœur d'une nation'.
46 Ibid., p. 728.
47 Louis-Albert Bourcault-Ducoudray, *Esprit de la France!* (Paris, 1901). Another example for such a piece is Camille Saint-Saëns' 'Hymne à la France', specifically written for secondary schools.
48 Mark de Thémines, 'La Musique dans les lycées', *L'Art musical*, 11 (1872), pp. 177–8.
49 Jules Combarieu, 'L'Etude du chant à l'école primaire', *La Revue musicale*, 10 (1910), pp. 314–17 and 339–43, at p. 315: 'elle est une école de solidarité'; 'elle est une école d'attention et de discipline . . . [car l'attention] doit être entière, absolue, comme celle des soldats devant leur colonel sur un champ de manœuvre' (p. 315).
50 Ibid., p. 316: 'La phrase verbale estompe; la mélodie engrave. Par exemple, faites à des enfants une leçon sur le patriotisme, sur le courage militaire, sur la nécessité d'avoir foi dans la victoire quand il faut payer de sa personne: il vous sera facile de les toucher et de les intéresser. Mais faites-les chanter ensuite le *Chant du départ*: "La victoire en chantant nous ouvre la barrière . . ." De ces deux leçons, quelle est celle qui produira les effets les plus profondes et les plus durables? Ce sera certainement la seconde'.
51 Ibid., p. 316: 'la musique [chorale] faisant l'éducation de l'oreille et celle de la voix, si importante dans une démocratie; la musique apprenant à parler nettement – et à écouter!' Katherine Bergeron refers to a similar concept with respect to French art song in her current research on the *mélodie française*.
52 Bourcault-Ducoudray unequivocally refers to both in his report 'L'Enseignement du chant dans les lycées', p. 725: 'Il lui faut, pour vivre, des sentiments réels, vivants, palpitants, qui aient besoin de se formuler et de s'épancher en un flot musical. En France, ces occasions n'ont jamais existé, ou du moins, si elles ont existé, c'est à une seule époque, pendant la première Révolution. En 1792, l'Etat voulut employer les arts et surtout la musique à exalter des sentiments "réels", comme le fit l'antiquité grecque.'
53 This form of masculinising rhetoric could include militaristic vocabulary, in particular with respect to German choral practice. See, for example, the short notice on a choral meeting in Vienna in 1888, published under 'Nouvelles Diverses: Etranger' in *Le Mnestrel*, 54 (1888), p. 70: 'L'Alliance chorale allemande, connue sous le nom de Sngerbund, et qui ne compte pas moins de 63,512 chanteurs – une arme – donnera son prochain grand festival, qui sera le quatrime, Vienne, en 1889.'
54 Edward Berenson, *The Trial of Madame Caillaux*, p. 106.
55 Ibid., p. 103.
56 A short survey of the statistics appears in Jann Pasler, 'Paris: Conflicting Notions of Progress', p. 395. A more detailed analysis is quoted in Karen Offen, 'Depopulation, Nationalism, and Feminism in Fin-de-Siècle France', *American Historical Review*, 89 (1984), pp. 648–76, and Hartmut Kaelble, *Nachbarn am Rhein: Entfremdung und Annäherung der französischen und deutschen Gesellschaft seit 1880* (Munich, 1991) (esp. chapter 2).
57 Dr H. Thulié, 'Variétés. La Femme. Fonctions sociales', *L'Harmonie sociale*, 8 April 1893, quoted in Anne Cova, *Maternité et droits des femmes en France (XIXe–XXe siècles)* (Paris, 1997), p. 36: 'La mère fait la race. C'est elle qui donne la vigueur, l'intelligence et la base de l'instruction; plus elle sera forte et intelligente, plus son caractère sera noble, plus la race sera puissante'.

58 Jules Combarieu, 'L'Etude du chant à l'école primaire', p. 316: 'La musique enfin considérée comme une gymnastique locale; il est reconnu que les personnes ayant l'habitude de chanter sont beaucoup moins sujettes que les autres aux maux de gorge et aux accidents des voies respiratoires'. Katharine Ellis has discovered similar justifications in the context of an earlier experiment by Adolphe Sax promoting wind-playing for women; see Katharine Ellis, 'The Fair Sax: Women, Brass-Playing and the Instrument Trade in 1860s Paris', *Journal of the Royal Musical Association*, 124 (1999), pp. 221–54.

59 Camille Saint-Saëns, 'L'Enseignement du chant dans les lycées', *La Revue musicale* 4 (1904), p. 11.

60 On the musical education of working-class women, see Mary Ellen Poole, 'Gustave Charpentier and the Conservatoire Populaire de Mimi Pinson', *19th-Century Music*, 20 (1997), p. 234.

61 I borrow the term 'mediation' (as a form of transmitting cultural artefacts and concepts mediated through the collector's or writer's political, social and aesthetic ideas) from Dave Harker, *Fakesong: The Manufacture of British 'Folksong' 1711 to the Present Day* (Milton Keynes and Philadelphia, 1985). I am grateful to Steve Stanton for drawing my attention to this book.

62 Reinhart Meyer-Kalkus, *Die akademische Mobilität zwischen Deutschland und Frankreich (1925–1992)*, DAAD-Forum: Studien, Berichte, Materialien, 16 (Bonn, 1994), p. 22. See also Michael Werner, 'Le Prisme franco-allemand: à propos d'une histoire croisée des disciplines littéraires', in Hans Manfred Bock, Reinhart Meyer-Kalkus and Michel Trebitsch (eds.), *Entre Locarno et Vichy: Les relations culturelles franco-allemandes dans les années 1930*, 2 vols. (Paris, 1993), pp. 305–6. See also Michael Werner and Michel Espagne (eds.), *Transferts. Les Relations interculturelles dans l'espace franco-allemand (XVIIIe et XIXe siècle)* (Paris, 1988).

63 For example, James Macpherson's *Fragments of Ancient Poetry* (1760–63), which contained the Ossian poems, and the novels and poetry of Walter Scott. For a Marxist interpretation of the folksong movement in Britain since 1700, see Dave Harker, *Fakesong*.

64 Gérard de Nerval, *Les filles du feu*, ed. Béatrice Didier (Paris, 1972), pp. 166–78; on Nerval's interest in popular culture, see Paul Bénichou, *Nerval et la chanson folklorique* (Paris, 1970), esp. pp. 177–84.

65 Gérard de Nerval, *Les filles du feu*, pp. 168–9: 'Est-ce dont [sic] la vraie poésie, est-ce la soif mélancolique de l'idéal qui manque à ce peuple pour comprendre et produire des chants dignes d'être comparés à ceux de l'Allemagne et de l'Angleterre? Non, certes; mais il est arrivé qu'en France la littérature n'est jamais descendue au niveau de la grande foule; les poètes académiques du dix-septième et du dix-huitième siècle n'auraient pas plus compris de telles inspirations, que les paysans n'eussent admiré leurs odes, leurs épîtres et leurs poésies fugitives, si incolores, si gourmées'.

66 On these earlier collections and their political meaning, see Jane F. Fulcher, 'The Popular Chanson of the Second Empire: "Music of the Peasants" in France', *Acta musicologica*, 52 (1981), pp. 27–37.

67 Jean-Baptiste Weckerlin, *La Chanson populaire* (Paris, 1886); Julien Tiersot, *Histoire de la chanson populaire en France* (Paris, 1889). During the time in which both books were written, Weckerlin and Tiersot were employed as librarians in the Bibliothèque du Conservatoire: in fact, Tiersot was Weckerlin's assistant from 1883 to 1909, when he succeeded him as head librarian.

68 Daniel Heartz, 'Jean-Jacques Rousseau', in Stanley Sadie (ed.), *The New Grove Dictionary of Music and Musicians*, 20 vols. (London, 1980), 16, p. 272. The most influential passage stems from Rousseau's *Lettre sur la musique française* (1753), in

which he describes a hypothetical language, easily recognisable as French, and its effects on music: 'une [langue] qui ne serait composée que de sons mixtes, des syllabes muettes, sourdes ou nasales, peu de voyelles sonores, beaucoup de consonnes et d'articulations, et qui manquerait encore d'autres conditions essentielles dont je parlerai dans l'article de la mesure. Cherchons, par curiosité, ce qui résulterait de la musique appliquée à une telle langue. Premièrement, le défaut d'éclat dans les sons des voyelles obligerait d'en donner beaucoup à celui des notes; et, parce que la langue serait sourde, la musique serait criarde. En second lieu, la dureté et la fréquence des consonnes forceraient à exclure beaucoup de mots, à ne procéder sur les autres que par des intonations élémentaires; et la musique serait insipide et monotone: sa marche serait encore lente et ennuyeuse par la même raison; et quand on voudrait presser un peu le mouvement, sa vitesse ressemblerait à celle d'un corps dur et anguleux qui roule sur le pavé'. Quoted in Catherine Kintzler, *Poétique de l'opéra français de Corneille à Rousseau* (Paris, 1991), pp. 459–60. Catherine Kintzler gives an excellent overview of Rousseau's aesthetic concepts and their immediate influence on pp. 333–514. On Rousseau's ideas on music in general, see also Peter Gülke, *Rousseau und die Musik* (Wilhelmshaven, 1984). With respect to his reception in France in the eighteenth and early nineteenth centuries, see Jane F. Fulcher, 'Melody and Morality: Rousseau's Influence on French Music Criticism', *International Review of the Aesthetics and Sociology of Music*, 2 (1980), pp. 45–56.

69 See Katharine Ellis, 'A Dilettante at the Opera: Issues in the Criticism of Julien-Louis Geoffroy, 1800–1814', in Roger Parker and Mary Ann Smart (eds.), *Opera and Ballet: Criticism from the Revolution to 1848* (Oxford, 2000).

70 Jean-Baptiste Weckerlin, *La Chanson populaire*, pp. iii–iv: 'Les troubadours se trouvant sous notre plume, nous en profitons pour dire que leur répertoire aristocratique n'ayant rien de commun avec la chanson du peuple, nous n'avons pas à en parler. On n'a qu'à examiner les œuvres de Thibaut de Champagne ou de Charles d'Orléans . . ., et l'on verra bien qu'aucune de leurs chansons n'a passé dans le répertoire populaire, que ces deux littératures étaient scindées, aussi différentes l'une de l'autre que l'étaient les grandes classes de la population française, l'aristocratie et le peuple'.

71 Ibid., p. 3: 'Les chansons populaires d'un pays expriment mieux son type, sa physionomie spéciale, ses rythmes particuliers, caractéristiques, que la musique des compositeurs de ce même pays, parce que l'art étant universel, ne peut avoir comme type tel ou tel pays, tandis que la chanson du peuple reste circonscrite dans un rayon, déterminé généralement par la même langue ou le même dialecte'.

72 Ibid., p. 3: 'La France est le royaume de la chanson, car le Français naît chansonnier'.

73 Gaston Paris, *Chansons du XVe siècle, publiées d'après le manuscrit de la Bibliothèque nationale de Paris par Gaston Paris et accompagnées de la musique transcrite en notation moderne par Auguste Gevaert* (Paris,1875).

74 Ibid., p. ix: 'Par une réaction remarquable, elle [la poésie populaire] s'est dégagée à l'époque où la littérature proprement dite est le plus éloigné de la nature, de la simplicité et du sentiment vrai'.

75 Ibid., p. vi: 'Un autre intérêt s'attache aux vieilles chansons, c'est leur importance pour la littérature comparée. Quel que soit un jour le dernier mot d'une science qui naît à peine sur la date, l'origine et les rapports de la poésie populaire des nations romanes et germaniques, il est sûr dès aujourd'hui que celle de la France doit occuper dans le tableau de ces rapports et dans l'étude de ces origines une place prépondérante'.

76 Margaret W. Ferguson, 'The Exile's Defense: Du Bellay's *La deffence et illustration de la langue françoyse*', *Publications of the Modern Language Association of America*, 93

(1978), pp. 280–1, quoted in Jeanice Brooks, 'Italy, the Ancient World and the French Musical Inheritance in the Sixteenth Century: Arcadelt and Clereau in the Service of the Guises', *Journal of the Royal Musical Association*, 121 (1996), p. 148. The notion of the 'translatio studii' – which refers to cultural transfer – needs to be understood in the context of the political concept of 'translatio imperii': 'Dieser Theorie liegen antike Konzepte einer Nationalcharakterlehre zugrunde, die im Mittelalter unter eschatologischen Vorzeichen zu Transfertheorien der Weltherrschaft ausgebaut wurden (translatio-imperii-Theorien), die in der Neuzeit aus ihrem heilsgeschichtlichen Kontext herausgelöst wurden und nunmehr in Gestalt transnationaler Geschichtsphilosophien entfaltet werden . . . Es gibt Leitnationen der Menschheitsgeschichte, deren Bewegungsverlauf zeitweilig identisch ist mit dem weltgeschichtlichen Entwicklungsstruktur. Dies bedeutet, daß sich die Menschheitsgeschichte realisiert über die Teilgeschichte von Kulturräumen, von Nationen und Epochenumschwüngen'. Thus, for example, the French Revolution could be understood as the revolution of humanity. See Jörn Garber, 'Peripherie oder Zentrum? Die "europäische Triarchie" (Deutschland, Frankreich, England) als transnationales Deutungsmodell der Nationalgeschichte', in Michel Espagne and Michael Werner, *Transferts*, pp. 98–9.

77 Jeanice Brooks, 'Italy, the Ancient World and the French Musical Inheritance', p. 148.
78 See Werner Oechslin, 'Le goût et les nations: débats, polémiques et jalousies au moment de la création des musées au XVIIIe siècle', Edouard Pommier (ed.), *Les Musées en Europe à la veille de l'ouverture du Louvre* (Paris, 1995), pp. 367–414, esp. pp. 381–385. I wish to thank Matthias Waschek for bringing this article to my attention.
79 See Edward Berenson, *The Trial of Madame Caillaux*, pp. 103–17.
80 Julien Tiersot, *Histoire de la chanson populaire en France*, p. i: 'La Grèce avait exercé son influence souveraine sur la civilisation de l'antiquité tout entière. Créatrice, puis vulgarisatrice de tous les arts, elle les avait portés au plus haut point de perfection que le monde ancien ait connu, et avait répandu parmi tous les peuples civilisés les types accomplis de maturité sereine et de sobre élégance qu'elle avait produits. En musique, son influence fut considérable . . . Par Rome, devenue l'élève et l'imitatrice de la Grèce, l'influence de l'art grec s'exerça sur la plus grande partie de l'Empire romain . . . Cette riche culture gréco-latine était au plus haut point florissante dans la Gaule romaine'.
81 Ibid., p. ii.
82 Ibid., p. iii.
83 Cf. Tacitus, *The Annals of Imperial Rome*, trans. by Michael Grant (1956) (Harmondsworth, rev. edn. 1971), pp. 61–2. The episode related by Tacitus in *Annals* 50–51 has little bearing on Tiersot's tale which freely adds names to the Roman description, especially the one of Siegfried, for Tiersot most probably Wagner's hero, given the musical reference. I wish to thank Tim Carter for providing the Tacitus reference.
84 Julien Tiersot, *Histoire de la chanson populaire en France*, pp. iii–iv: 'Tacite fait mention des sauvages chants de guerre dont les Germains s'excitaient les uns les autres dans les combats. Autour du roi Chlodevech, les guerriers franks chantaient, aux repas et dans les assemblées guerrières, les chants épiques qui consacraient la mémoire de leur héros national Siegfried. Lors de la première bataille qui fut livrée en Gaule entre les Franks de Chlodion et les légionnaires d'Aétius, les Franks, campés sur une colline, célébraient les noces d'un de leurs chefs au son des chansons et danses chantées en chœur: ces bruits relevèrent leur présence aux Romains; ils furent surpris: leur goût pour une musique éclatante fut cause de leur première défaite'.

85 Wolfgang Leiner, *Das Deutschlandbild in der französischen Literatur*, p. 17.
86 Katharine Ellis, *Music Criticism in Nineteenth-Century France: 'La Revue et Gazette musicale de Paris', 1834–1880* (Cambridge, 1995), p. 35.
87 Jann Pasler, 'Paris: Conflicting Notions of Progress', p. 398. See also Annegret Fauser, 'L'art de l'allusion musicale', *L'Avant-Scène Opéra*, 161 (September-October 1994), pp. 126–9.
88 On the ideal world of the Middle Ages in French *fin-de-siècle* imagery, see Annegret Fauser, 'Die Sehnsucht nach dem Mittelalter: Ernest Chausson und Richard Wagner', in Wolfgang Storch and Josef Mackert (eds.), *Les Symbolistes et Richard Wagner: Die Symbolisten und Richard Wagner* (Berlin, 1991), pp. 115–20.
89 With this sentence, Tiersot reinstalls France's own medieval poetic traditions, offering an essentially French alternative to the Wagnerian theories of versification which were much discussed during the 1880s and 1890s in Paris. On the reception of Wagner's poetic ideas through translations, see Jean Louis Jam and Gérard Loubinoux, 'D'une *Walkyrie* à l'autre: Les adaptations françaises de Wagner', *in* Annegret Fauser and Manuela Schwartz (eds.), *Von Wagner zum Wagnérisme*, pp. 401–30. On Wagner's concept of versification, see Reinhart Meyer-Kalkus, 'Richard Wagners Theorie der Wort-Tonsprache in "Oper und Drama" und "Der Ring des Nibelungen"', *Athenäum: Jahrbuch für Romantik*, 6, 1996, pp. 153–195.
90 Julien Tiersot, *Histoire de la chanson populaire en France*, pp. vi–vii: 'Nous retrouvons cette même chanson encore vivante à la fin de notre dix-neuvième siècle ... La rime y est inconnue: tout au plus est-elle remplacée par l'assonance, dernier reste des traditions de la versification du moyen âge ... Sa phrase est courte et nette; le mot juste y ressort avec un éclat qu'envierait le vers le plus savant; et toujours une concision admirable, point de développement superflu: le récit va droit au but, par déductions logiques et naturelles, sans s'attarder à rien d'inutile; ou bien le sentiment s'exprime en des mots simples, mais profonds et pénétrants. Et sur ces vers sont d'admirable mélodies, comme eux simples et concises, mais d'une saveur intense et d'une inépuisable vitalité.'
91 Such appropriations can be found in other countries as well, as for example in England. See Robert Stradling and Meirion Hughes, *The English Musical Renaissance, 1860–1940: Construction and Deconstruction* (London, 1993), p. 23.
92 Julien Tiersot, *Histoire de la chanson populaire en France*, p. 489: '[I]l faut aller jusqu'au moyen âge, et l'on verra ces deux arts, formes premières et primitives de la musique française, jouer de concert, dans la création du théâtre lyrique, un rôle exactement semblable à celui que nous leur avons vu en étudiant le création de l'harmonie'.
93 Ibid., p. 495.
94 See Julien Tiersot, *Sur le Jeu de Robin et Marion d'Adam de la Halle* (Paris, 1897). This perception of Adam de la Halle's *Jeu de Robin et Marion* goes back to Fétis in his article 'Adam de la Halle,' in Franois-Joseph Fétis, *Biographie universelle des musiciens et Bibliographie générale de la musique* (Paris, 2nd edn., 1860), 1, pp. 12–13. I wish to thank Katharine Ellis for this reference.
95 Julien Tiersot, *Histoire de la chanson populaire en France*, p. 529.
96 Julien Tiersot, '*Mignon* et la chanson française', *Le Ménestrel*, 60 (1894), pp. 155–6.
97 The book celebrates, for example, the Republic and the French Revolution in an entire chapter on the patriotic strength of folk music as expressed in the 'Marseillaise'. See Julien Tiersot, *Histoire de la chanson populaire en France*, pp. 275–86. Tiersot concludes this passage with the following judgement: '[œuvre] où n'en revit pas moins avec une rare intensité l'esprit de la race française, et même, fait curieux à signaler au sujet d'un chant révolutionnaire, sa tendance à rester constamment fidèle à ses plus anciennes traditions' (p. 286).

100 *Annegret Fauser*

98 I borrow the term from Dave Harker, *Fakesong*. The rhetorical strategies employed in the research and mediation of English folksong rely on similar concepts to the French, drawing on nationalist and essentialist interpretations. The central text in this respect is Cecil Sharp, *English Folk-Song: Some Conclusions* (London, 1907).
99 See Jane F. Fulcher, 'Wagner in the Cultural Politics of the French Right and Left before World War I', in Annegret Fauser and Manuela Schwartz (eds.), *Von Wagner zum Wagnérisme*, pp. 137–54.
100 See Edouard Schuré's foreword to the 1902 edition of his *Histoire du Lied ou la chansons populaire en Allemagne* (Paris, 1902), and Louis Schneider, *Das französische Volkslied* (*Die Music*, ed. by Richard Strauss, 28/29) (Berlin, 1908).
101 *Les Chansons de France: Revue trimestrielle de musique populaire*, 1, 1906, pp. 4–6.
102 Fiamma Nicolodi, 'Nationalistische Aspekte im Mythos von der "alten Musik" in Italien und Frankreich', in Helga de la Motte-Haber, *Nationaler Stil und europäische Dimension in der Musik der Jahrhundertwende* (Darmstadt, 1991), pp. 102–21. Katharine Ellis is currently researching a book on the reception of early music in nineteenth-century France which will give more detailed insights into this very complex reception history. The political implications of the early-music revival form an important part of Jane F. Fulcher's study, *French Cultural Politics and Musical Aesthetics from the Dreyfus Affair to the First World War* (Oxford, 1998).
103 Henry Expert, *Les Maîtres musiciens de la Renaissance française*, 1: Orlande de Lassus, *Premier Fascicule des Mélanges* (Paris, 1894), pp. i–vi.
104 Ibid., pp. i–ii: 'Toutefois, dès les premières heures du XVIe siècle, dans la vigueur d'une mâle et féconde jeunesse, la musique a rejeté le formalisme rigide des primitifs; rompue à une technique savante, consciente de ses énergies expressive, elle peut tenter l'interprétation des sentiments: elle possède désormais cette *virtu secrette et quasi incredible à esmouvoir les cueurs en une sorte ou en l'autre* (Calvin). Et d'abord, l'esprit laïque, ce puissant fonds gaulois fécondé par la Renaissance, apparaît pleinement dans les musiques profanes ... Et tandis que l'école poétique de Marot et la Pleiade donnent à la musique leurs plus beaux joyaux, l'Humanisme fervent s'essaie, sous la plume de savants musiciens, à faire revivre les nombres d'Horace et de Virigile, d'Ovide, de Catulle et de Martial'.
105 Henry Expert, *Les Maîtres musiciens de la Renaissance française*, p. ii: 'A ces chants où éclate et triomphe l'esprit de la Renaissance, l'Eglise répond par les chef-d'œuvres de son art sacré'.
106 On the 'metaphysical' qualities of music in the context of Wagner reception, see Katharine Ellis, 'Wagnerism and Anti-Wagnerism in the Paris Periodical Press, 1852–70', in Annegret Fauser and Manuela Schwartz, *Von Wagner zum Wagnérisme*, pp. 51–83; Annegret Fauser, 'Die Sehnsucht nach dem Mittelalter'; Manuela Schwartz, *Wagner-Rezeption und französische Oper*.
107 Similar phenomena can be observed in other art forms. Debora Silverman shows, for example, how the rococo revival of the 1890s in the *art-nouveau* movement became politicised within a 'profoundly nationalist discourse'. See Debora L. Silverman, *Art Nouveau in Fin-de-Siècle France*, pp. 8–9 and 142–58.
108 A similar form of canon creation through the publication of editions took place in Germany during the nineteenth century. See Philip Brett, 'Text, Context, and the Early Music Editor', in Nicholas Kenyon (ed.), *Authenticity and Early Music: A Symposium* (Oxford and NewYork, 1988), pp. 85–6.
109 Albert Lavignac, *La Musique et les musiciens français* (Paris, 1895), p. 431–2: 'Il est impossible de terminer ce chapitre sans exhorter les jeunes compositeurs français à s'attacher avant tout à conserver à notre art national les qualités caractéristiques qui en ont toujours fait la gloire, qu'on y retrouve à toutes les grandes époques, et qui sont: *la clarté, l'élégance* et *la sincérité d'expression*. C'est pour eux la seule manière

d'être naturels et d'arriver à se créer un style propre, une personnalité; car toutes les fois qu'ils voudront s'écarter de ces traditions inhérentes à la race, au génie de la langue comme à l'esprit français, ils ne seront jamais que des imitateurs maladroits et des plagiaires; ils feront penser à des gens qui parlent péniblement une langue étrangère avec un accent ridicule'.

110 These terms recur in countless criticisms and other writings on *opéra comique*. Marie-Claire Mussat quotes some of these remarks in her 'Diffusion et réception de l'*opéra comique*', in Herbert Schneider and Nicole Wild (eds.), *Die Opéra Comique und ihr Einfluß auf das europäische Musiktheater im 19. Jahrhundert* (Hildesheim, 1997), pp. 283–96.

111 Camille Bellaigue, *Un siècle de musique française* (Paris, 1887), pp. 1–141.

112 For a brief discussion of this subject, see Annegret Fauser, 'Saint-Saëns: *Phryné*', in Sieghart Döhring (ed.), *Piper Enzyklopädie des Musik-theaters*, Vol. 5 (Munich, 1994), pp. 521–2.

113 Camille Saint-Saëns, 'La poésie et la musique' (1881), *Harmonie et mélodie* (Paris, 1885), pp. 257–66.

114 In a late letter to his friend Camille Bellaigue, he claims that his chorus 'C'est Phryné, quand elle passe' is 'en pure mode grec, le 2e ton du plain chant.' Letter from 27 February 1919, F-Pn, l.a. Saint-Saëns 116.

115 This essentialist opposition of Latin qualities and Germanic metaphysical bombast has its roots in the eighteenth century, with texts by writers such as the Marquis d'Argens (see Werner Oechslin, 'Le goût et les nations') and aesthetic debates as expressed by the 'querelles des Gluckistes et Piccinistes'. Through Fétis it became part of the French Wagner reception as early as 1852. See Katharine Ellis, *Music Criticism in Nineteenth-Century France*, pp. 206–18, and Katharine Ellis, 'Wagnerism and Anti-Wagnerism in the Paris Periodical Press, 1852–70'. A comprehensive collection of press reviews of the first performance of *Phryné* is kept in the 'Dossier d'œuvre: *Phryné*', Bibliothèque de l'Opéra, Paris.

116 On French orchestral song, see Annegret Fauser, *Der Orchestergesang in Frankreich zwischen 1870 und 1920* (Laaber, 1994), esp. pp. 59–139.

117 See the brief discussion in Annegret Fauser, *Der Orchestergesang in Frankreich*, pp. 11–15. Brian Hart has examined the aesthetics of the symphony in his 'The Symphony in Theory and Practice in France, 1900–1914' (PhD diss., Indiana University, 1994), esp. chapter one. See also Brian Hart, 'Wagner and the *Franckiste* "Message-Symphony" in Early Twentieth-Century France', in Annegret Fauser and Manuela Schwartz (eds.), *Von Wagner zum Wagnérisme*, pp. 315–37.

118 For a still fascinating discussion on the foundation, historic dimensions and implications of music history, see Carl Dahlhaus, *Grundlagen der Musikgeschichte* (Köln, 1977), esp. his chapters 'Historismus und Tradition' (pp. 91–117) and 'Historische Hermeneutik' (pp. 120–38). In the latter, Dahlhaus discusses the implications of 'the theory of historic understanding', developed in the nineteenth century (p. 121). On the philosophical context of German nineteenth-century music criticism and history, see Carl Dahlhaus, *Klassische und romantische Musikästhetik* (Laaber, 1988), pp. 219–90.

119 On Fétis's role in the development of music history, see Katharine Ellis, *Music Criticism in Nineteenth-Century France*, pp. 33–45.

120 See Rémy Campos, '"Mens sana in corpore sano": l'introduction de l'histoire de la musique au Conservatoire', in Emmanuel Hondré, *Le Conservatoire de Musique de Paris: Regards sur une institution et son histoire* (Paris, 1995), pp. 145–71. The first holder of the chair of the *Classe d'histoire générale de la musique* was Louis-Albert Bourcault-Ducoudray (p. 146).

121 Katharine Ellis, *Music Criticism in Nineteenth-Century France*, pp. 44–5.

122 See Jann Pasler,'Paris: Conflicting Notions of Progress'.
123 Claude Debussy,'L'Influence allemande sur la musique française' (1903), in François Lesure (ed.), *Claude Debussy: Monsieur Croche et autres écrits* (Paris, 2nd edn. 1987), p. 67: 'Wagner, si l'on peut s'exprimer avec un peu de la grandiloquence qui lui convient, fut un beau coucher de soleil que l'on a pris pour une aurore...' Decadence and decline were detected not only in Germany's music but also in her musical life. See, for example, the gleeful note in 'Nouvelles Diverses: Etranger', *Le Ménestrel*, 54 (1888), p. 70: 'Un signe de la décadence du thâtre lyrique en Allemagne. L'Opra grand-ducal de Darmstadt, qui, il ya quelques années, était au premier rang des scénes allemandes, a été obligé pour relever l'état de ses finances, de faire appel au genre de l'opérette. *Le Baron des Tziganes*, de Johann Strauss, y a été représenté, pour la premiére fois, le 5 février dernier'.
124 Albert Soubies, *Histoire de la musique allemande* (Paris, 1897), p. 194: 'L'influence de Rousseau fut considérable au delà du Rhin'.
125 Ibid., p. 290.
126 On the gendered British Beethoven-reception, see Maria McHale, 'The Discourse on Gender in British Writings on Music 1880–1914' (MA diss., City University, London, 1997).
127 Albert Soubies, *Histoire de la musique allemande*, p. 291: 'Pour la France, enfin, dont la caractéristique, en art, a toujours été l'éclectisme clairvoyant et délicat, la combinaison intelligente et fine, l'habile adaptation d'éléments très divers, on sait avec quel éclat, quelle abondance de ressources a été, chez nous, dans ce que M. Lavoix a nommé "le siècle de Beethoven", recueillie et mise en valeur la tradition allemande'.
128 For an excellent discussion of the implications of cultural transfer, see Michel Espagne and Michael Werner, 'Deutsch-französischer Kulturtransfer als Forschungsgegenstand: Eine Problemskizze', *Transferts*, pp. 11–34.
129 Vincent d'Indy, *Cours de Composition musicale* (deuxième livre, première partie), rédigé avec la collaboration de Auguste Sérieyx d'après les notes prises aux Classes de Composition de la Schola Cantorum (Paris, 1919), pp. 391 and 421–2: 'Avec Franck, génial continuateur français de l'immortel symphoniste allemand, commence une période nouvelle et *exclusivement française* jusqu'à présent. La valeur et la force des meilleurs œuvres appartenant à cette période reposent sur toutes les innovations beethovéniennes et sur la construction *cyclique* enfin comprise et réalisée. Sous cette influence bienfaisante, la traditionnelle forme Sonate a déjà reconquis, dans notre pays tout au moins, une vitalité et une jeunesse vraiment surprenantes après un demi-siècle de décadence et d'oubli. [...] C'est à la France qu'il devait appartenir de poursuivre et de réaliser la transformation de la Sonate, clairement indiquée par Beethoven: nul de ses successeurs allemands, en effet, n'avait su ou voulu tenter sérieusement cette véritable rénovation *cyclique*, seule capable de rendre la vie à cette belle forme qui s'étiolait et semblait près de disparaître, en Allemagne tout au moins, malgré les timides essais de Schumann et de Brahms. La tradition *cyclique* peut donc être considérée comme transmise *directement* de Beethoven à César Franck.'
130 Laure Collin, *Histoire abrégée de la musique et des musiciens*, 7th edn. (Paris, 1891); Elise Vigoureux, *Manuel d'histoire générale de la musique à l'usage des classes de solfège* (Marseilles, 1904).
131 H. Lavoix fils, *La Musique française* (Paris, 1891), p. 6.
132 Michel Espagne and Michael Werner, 'Deutsch-französischer Kulturtransfer als Forschungsgegenstand', p. 15.
133 Jann Pasler showed this in her paper 'Making Alliances through Music: Russia as Embraced by the French', read at the International Conference on Nineteenth-Century Music, Surrey, 14–17 July 1994 (to be published).

134 For a feminist re-reading of American canon formation after the Second World War see Nina Baym, 'Melodramas of Beset Manhood: How Theories of American Fiction Excluded Women Authors' (1981), in Elaine Showalter (ed.), *The New Feminist Criticism: Essays on Women, Literature and Theory* (London, 1986), pp. 63–81. On the implications of masculinised music theory and history for historical and current judgement and canon formation, see Marcia J. Citron, *Gender and the Musical Canon*, pp. 15–43 and 120–45.
135 See Eugen Weber, *France: Fin de Siècle* (Cambridge, MA, 1986), pp. 9–26.

CHAPTER 5

Disruptive Histories: Telling the Story of Modern Music in France*

History is a contested field in scholarship, especially in recent years with the debates around new historicism, post colonialism, and postmodernism. Yet it is a discipline that needs addressing when engaging with so historically charged a phenomenon as modernism in France, given the complex intertwinings of theory and history in the debates of modernism and postmodernism. Furthermore, both as an academic and as a popular pursuit, history also held a privileged position in nineteenth- and twentieth-century France.[1] *Whether* history mattered never seemed to be a modern French question, certainly not for Claude Lévi-Strauss, Jacques Derrida, or Jean-François Lyotard. Their debates explored, rather, *which* kind of history mattered *how* and for *whom*.[2] Such centrality of history in French cultural tradition creates complications especially for music historians, for it forces us to engage with a very complex cultural field that is characterized by a range of diachronic and synchronic tensions within specific cultural, political, and historical contexts. At the same time, and as Carl Dahlhaus has observed more than once, we are forced to confront the ephemeral phenomenon of music's sonic presence and the power of music's reception history. Telling the story of music in French modernity thus poses some exciting challenges to today's music historians, and I will be addressing three of them: the challenges of history, of musical modernism in general, and of Paris in particular.

1. The Challenge of History

In a thought-provoking article published in 2001, Jean-Jacques Nattiez posed the question of how to write music history in the postmodern era.[3] He critiqued various authors—both modern and postmodern—before throwing in his lot with the concept of history as a plausible emplotment of local truths. Few scholars today would disagree with Nattiez's conclusions.

---

* I am grateful to Mark Evan Bonds, Tim Carter, and Keith Simmons for their challenging and very helpful comments on earlier drafts of this text. It is a slightly abbreviated and revised version of "Histoires interrompues: raconter l'histoire de la musique en France," translated by Hélène Panneton, in *Musique et modernité en France 1900-1950*, edited by Sylvain Caron, Michel Duchesneau, and François de Médicis (Montréal: Presses de l'Université de Montréal, 2006), 19–50. The particular slant of this text comes from its position as a keynote address to the conference, on which that volume is based; in the present version I have removed its first two pages, which related specifically to the conference, and have made some other minor changes.

[1] Antoine Prost, *Douze leçons sur l'histoire* (Paris: Editions du Seuil, 1996), 14–18.
[2] For an excellent discussion of the role and meaning of history in structuralism, anthropology, and postmodernism, see Kerwin Lee Klein, "In Search of Narrative Mastery: Postmodernism and the People without History," *History and Theory* 34 (1995): 275–98.
[3] Jean-Jacques Nattiez, "Comment écrire l'histoire de la musique à l'âge postmoderne?" *Il saggiatore musicale* 8 (2001): 73–87.

But his opening contains a remark that I find very intriguing and which became the starting point for my own reflections here on the historiography of music. The characteristical throwaway reference to Leopold von Ranke's famous dictum at the beginning of Nattiez's text is worth citing because the formulation has some serious epistemological consequences:

> Today, no-one believes any more in a positivist conception of history that, according to Ranke in the nineteenth century, proposed to describe "wie es eigentlich gewesen," how things really happened.[4]

Nattiez's reference to Ranke's oft-quoted remark deserves further consideration: I am particularly interested in its customary translation from German into French and English, and in its relationship to positivism and dialectics in both past and present.

Ranke's remark was published in 1824 in the introduction to his *Geschichten der romanischen und germanischen Völker von 1494 bis 1514*.[5] It has come to stand for all things wicked or naïve in nineteenth-century historiography, and many of us are guilty of using the epigram in the dismissive tone adopted by Nattiez. Following Nietzsche, the claim that we might ever be able to know "how it really was" has been rejected as a phenomenological impossibility. Instead, the battle cry that all is interpretation—and that all history is fiction—has become a hermeneutic commonplace.[6] Yet rereading Ranke's remark in German and in its context made me wonder whether he did not say something very different, something—ironically—far closer to our own concerns. Indeed, a reinterpretation of the Rankean sentence might help clarify some recent historiographic debates.

I want to draw our attention to Ranke's choice of words both in the famous remark and in the title of the book in which it was published. Ranke proposes that his work would "blos zeigen, wie es eigentlich gewesen." "Blos zeigen" means "merely to show"—but to show what? The usual translation, "how it really was," is, in fact, a distortion, and the nuances of the remark's various meanings have been lost in translation, reduced to a single interpretation of naïve historicism. "Eigentlich" is not the same as "wirklich." "Eigentlich" is a complex word—referring to both the real and the virtual, the actual and the intrinsic, the proper and the true.[7] This allows us to read the remark as a surprisingly nuanced declaration, placing the ownership of historical

---

[4] "Personne ne croit plus aujourd'hui à la conception positiviste de l'histoire qui, selon Ranke au XIXème siècle, proposait de décrire *wie es eigentlich gewesen*, comment les choses se sont réellement produites." Nattiez, "Comment écrire l'histoire de la musique," 73.

[5] Leopold von Ranke, *Geschichten der romanischen und germanischen Völker von 1494 bis 1514*, 2d edition (Leipzig: Verlag von Duncker und Humblot, 1874). The reference to "wie es eigentlich gewesen" is on p. vii: "Man hat der Historie das Amt Vergangenheit zu richten, die Mitwelt zum Nutzen zukünftiger Jahre zu belehren, beigemessen: so hoher Aemter unterwindet sich gegenwärtiger Versuch nicht: er will blos zeigen, wie es eigentlich gewesen."

[6] See in particular the essay collection *Zeichen und Interpretation*, edited by Josef Simon (Frankfurt am Main: Suhrkamp Verlag, 1994).

[7] Theodor W. Adorno used the complexities and ontological overtones of these words in his critique of German ideology, *Jargon der Eigentlichkeit*, published in vol. 6 of *Gesammelte Schriften* (Darmstadt: Wissenschaftliche Buchgesellschaft, 1997), 413–526. *Jargon der Eigentlichkeit* was originally conceived as part of the *Negative Dialektik* (ibid., 524). Its title in English was rendered as *Jargon of Authenticity*, though—given the debates on "authenticity" in musical performance—the term's philosophical complexity might be lost in translation. For present purposes, it might be more fruitful to think about Adorno's title as "jargon of actuality."

events with the subjects of the narrative and not just the historian, and thus ascribing agency to both past and present. Ranke seemed to be very much aware of the act of interpretation in the composing of history when he stated earlier in his text, in a clever play on words, that "Die Absicht eines Historikers hängt von seiner Ansicht ab" (The intention of a historian depends on his opinion).[8] Here Ranke seems to say that a historian's intention depends on her point of view. He then delivers a definition of history. He contrasts "History," which embraces European modern history as a plot of representing human progress towards the universally valid advances of Enlightenment, with histories—local, individual histories of individual peoples, humans, and times, that are excluded from the *grand récit* of universal History. These histories may be interdependent and related, but any unity is achieved only through the voice of the historian by simply showing how things were—intrinsically, or maybe virtually, properly, actually, truly. Not for nothing did Ranke choose to call his book *Histories of the Roman and Germanic Peoples from 1494 to 1514* (again, an incorrect albeit authorized translation has it as *History of the Latin and Germanic Nations...*) so as to draw attention to the fact that he was not writing History.[9] These were the words of a "young turk," not quite thirty years old, rattling the cage of an idealist, post-revolutionary historiography which subsumed its topics under the master narrative of human progress for the benefit of Prussian public education.[10]

As Peter Burke has pointed out, Ranke was a counter-revolutionary, reacting against earlier trends in historiography.[11] But I disagree with Burke's assessment that what Ranke attacked was the liberated "new history" of the eighteenth century as a kind of *Annales* school *avant la lettre*. His objection was against the abstract form of Fichtean and Hegelian History which, in Hegel's words, needed to be "general," "universal," and "abbreviated" in order to show the large expanses of development of "world history."[12] Conversely, Ranke's resistance to universalist abstraction was satirized by Hegel in his lectures when he accused Ranke of collecting colorful details from all kinds of sources, whether political or private, as would a novelist like Sir Walter Scott.[13]

---

[8] Ranke, *Geschichten der romanischen und germanischen Völker von 1494 bis 1514*, v. See Leopold von Ranke, *History of the Latin and Germanic Nations from 1494 to 1514*, translated from the German by Philip A. Ashworth (London: George Bell and Sons, 1887).

[9] Ranke, *Geschichten der romanischen und germanischen Völker von 1494 bis 1514*, vi.

[10] Wolfgang J. Mommsen, "Einleitung," in *Leopold von Ranke und die moderne Geschichtswissenschaft*, edited by id. (Stuttgart: Klett Cotta, 1988), 7–18, at 8–9.

[11] Peter Burke, "Ranke the Reactionary," in *Leopold von Ranke and the Shaping of the Historical Discipline*, edited by Georg G. Iggers and James M. Powell (Syracuse: Syracuse University Press, 1990), 36–44.

[12] Hegel offers definitions for his "history of the world" both in the introduction to the *Vorlesungen über die Philosophie der Geschichte* and, with fascinating asides, in the manuscript of his first introduction to the lectures, where he specifically refers to Ranke. Georg Friedrich Wilhelm Hegel, *Vorlesungen über die Philosophie der Geschichte*, vol. 12 of *Werke in zwanzig Bänden*, edited by Eva Moldenhauer and Karl Markus Michel (Frankfurt/M.: Suhrkamp Verlag, 1970), 11–28 and 543–56. On Ranke and Hegel, see Werner Berthold, "Die Konzeption der Weltgeschichte bei Hegel und Ranke," in *Leopold von Ranke*, ed. Mommsen, 72–90.

[13] Hegel, *Vorlesungen*, 553: "[Sie] lesen diese allenthalben her zusammen (Ranke). Die bunte Menge von Detail, *kleinlichen Interessen*, Handlungen der Soldaten, *Privat*-sachen, die auf die *politischen* Interessen keinen Einfluß haben, – unfähig, ein Ganzes, einen allgemeinen Zweck [zu erkennen]. [Eine] Reihe von Zügen – wie in einem Walter Scott'schen Roman – überall her aufzulesen,

Could one therefore call Ranke a postmodernist *avant la lettre*? At least in 1824 he was someone who certainly fits Lyotard's definition of postmodernism as involving an "incredulity toward master narratives," favoring instead "les petites histoires."[14] Because "master narrative" has become such a shopworn term, we often forget that for Lyotard the great master narrative (or "maître-récit") was the "grand récit marxiste."[15] Thus Lyotard's response to Marxism strikingly resembles the young Ranke's critique of Hegel's philosophical approach. As Georg Iggers pointed out, Ranke perceived the philosopher's view as reducing "reality to a system which sacrificed the unique qualities of the historical world," which in turn led Ranke to opt for a pre-Enlightenment approach of writing histories (plural).[16]

I have spent this much time reinterpreting Ranke's famous remark not to find out whether or not he resisted the universal claim of Hegelian world history—in the end, he did not—but because it leads me to some fundamental questions about our enterprise as music historians in reevaluating the music, art, and intellectual movements of French modernism.[17] To propose a reevaluation of the past means to acknowledge its independence as a historic Other in need of retranslation into our present epistemological horizons, horizons which can no longer accommodate earlier discourses. The enterprise of reevaluation thus posits an Other as a past reality in need of fresh discovery, or to show through our hermeneutic lenses—to quote Ranke once more—how it "eigentlich" was. Reinhart Koselleck examined the complex interrelationship of historic traces and their interpretation in his 1979 study *Vergangene Zukunft*, and he proposed a thought-provoking solution: the sources cannot tell us what to say, for we (in good Collingwoodian fashion) need to make them speak through our interpretative work. But the sources have a right of veto, and thus possess agency in the historical enterprise.[18]

---

fleißig und *mühselig* zusammenzulesen, – dergleichen Züge kommen in den Geschichtsschreibern, Korrespondenzen und Chronikenschreibern vor." Even Ranke's successor, Johann Gustav Droysen, the first major German systematic historian, used the comparison of Ranke's historiography with the novels of Sir Walter Scott as a negative descriptor in his 1892 "Grundriß der Historik." See Eberhart Lämmert, "'Geschichte ist ein Entwurf': Die neue Glaubwürdigkeit des Erzählens in der Geschichtsschreibung und im Roman," *German Quarterly* 63 (1990): 5–18, at 5. Similar reproaches were made against the French historian, Jules Michelet.

[14] Both Lyotard quotations are taken from Klein, "In Search of Narrative Mastery," 280, 282. See also Jean-François Lyotard, *Instructions payënnes* (Paris: Editions Galilée, 1977), 35. That Ranke is not the only historian of the nineteenth century who could be characterized as postmodern *avant la lettre* is shown with respect to the French historian Prosper de Barante (1782–1866) in Frank R. Ankersmit, "Historismus, Postmodene und Historiographie," in *Geschichtsdiskurs*, edited by Wolfgang Küttler, Jörn Rüsen, and Ernst Schulin, 5 vols., vol. 1: *Grundlagen und Methoden der Historiographiegeschichte* (Frankfurt am Main: Fischer Taschenbuch Verlag, 1993), 65–84, at 77.

[15] Klein, "In Search of Narrative Mastery," 280–81; Lyotard, *Instructions payënnes*, 25, 31.

[16] Georg G. Iggers, "Historicism: The History and Meaning of the Term," *Journal of the History of Ideas* 56 (1995): 129–52, at 131. The Enlightenment concept of History as opposed to earlier histories has been discussed in Lionel Gossman, "History as Decipherment: Romantic Historiography and the Discovery of the Other," *New Literary History* 18 (1986): 23–57, at 30–34.

[17] Georg Iggers points out that Ranke was in fact not contradicting Hegel with respect to a Christian, teleological world order; rather, Ranke's approach was simply to reveal the coherence behind the phenomenal world through careful study of detail. See Iggers, "Historicism," 131.

[18] Reinhart Koselleck, *Vergangene Zukunft: Zur Semantik geschichtlicher Zeiten* (Frankfurt am Main: Suhrkamp Verlag, 1979), 206: "Streng genommen kann uns eine Quelle nie sagen, was wir

Koselleck's celebration of historical sources as agents within an interpretative plot is only possible because of what Leo Treitler has shown to be the hard-won gains of positivism.[19] I would push this even further: without positivist historical work, postmodern interpretation—at least in the context of Western art music—will necessarily remain limited to already established dominant cultures. This can be seen in the writings of Susan McClary, Lawrence Kramer, and Edward Said whose cultural critique focused predominantly on the established Western canon. Whatever we may say of musicological positivism, one thing is certain: it does take historical Alterity more seriously than any other disciplinary approach. In fact, the *a priori* acknowledgment of a historic subject is positivism's *raison d'être*. But positivism's powerful epistemological structure leads to a conundrum, for it demands *per se* to be taken as the harbinger of historic truth, an authoritative claim that postmodernism—or rather post-Nietzschean philosophy—has shown as an aporia. The relationship between positivist and postmodern approaches is thus paradoxical. However, as I have written elsewhere, the hermeneutic paradox of postmodern positivism offers a possible interpretative way to acknowledge the competing designs of both the historical Other as truth and historiographical discourse as interpretation.[20] This paradoxical construct hinges on the concept of truth: for positivism, the method— if we adhere to it well—will allow the formulation of "true" statements about the past Other; for postmodernism, truth is a relative value of satisfactory interpretation that absorbs the past into our present discourse. The interdependence of these concepts of truth as, on the one hand, pertaining to an historic Other as absolute and, on the other, to localized present interpretations of an unattainable past, shifts the competition between these epistemological claims into an dynamic albeit paradoxical situation: we cannot avoid viewing the past as an Other and searching for the "truth," despite the simultaneous recognition of the limits of our own epistemic and interpretative situation at any given time.

However, the competing forces of positivism and postmodernism point not only towards my synchronic paradox, but also towards another, diachronic route: that of a dialectical unfolding of historical work in Western discourse. As my earlier play on Ranke has suggested, I consider the past 250 years or so of historiography as the continued contesting of epistemological ground as either locally or universally defined, and as either embracing or unsuccessfully rejecting the transcendental presence of scholarly methodology. That, in Michel Foucault's formulation, is the crisis of History. In this sense, we are today still playing out the same modern–postmodern dialectical play as Hegel and Ranke in the 1820s, and that Foucault performed almost 150 years later in the concluding remarks to his *Archéologie*

---

sagen sollen. Wohl aber hindert sie uns, Aussagen zu machen, die wir nicht machen dürfen. Die Quellen haben ein Vetorecht. [...] Das, was die Geschichte zur Geschichte macht, ist nie allein aus den Quellen abzulesen: es bedarf einer Theorie möglicher Geschichten, um Quellen überhaupt erst zum Sprechen zu bringen."

[19] In his review essay on Joseph Kerman's *Contemplating Music* (1985), "The Power of Positivist Thinking," *Journal of the American Musicological Society* 42 (1989): 399–402.

[20] Annegret Fauser, "Alterity, Nation and Identity: Some Musicological Paradoxes," *Context: A Journal of Music Research* no. 21 (Spring 2001): 1–18. Jann Pasler uses the formulation in her "Material Culture and Postmodern Positivism: 'Popular' in Late-Nineteenth-Century French Music," in *Historical Musicology: Sources, Methods, Interpretations*, edited by Stephen A. Crist and Roberta Montemorra Marvin, Eastman Studies of Music (Rochester, N.Y.: University of Rochester Press, 2004), 356–87.

du savoir.²¹ In another context, Foucault also cautioned that "just when you think you have escaped Hegel, you turn the corner, and suddenly there he is, refiguring the predicament of culture as the cunning of history."²²

My dialectic follows Adorno in that dialectic negation is not seen in the traditional positive light of hermeneutic progress, but as inevitable ruptures in an unfolding paradox of historiographical effort. It is the impossibility of an epistemic resolution that characterizes the diachronic paradox and that refuses itself to be resolved in any "clear" and transcendental realization of history, whether in form of Homi K. Bhabha's "third space," or Francis Fukuyama's concept of liberal universalism.²³ A paradox is no trifle, and at least one paradox, that of the liar, is said to have caused the death of the philosopher, Philetas of Kos.²⁴ But the paradoxical resistance to universal resolutions in historiography does offer a postmodern space to ask the question of historical truth in a paradoxical formulation in order to reevaluate the past in an interpretation satisfactory for the present.

2. The Challenge of Musical Modernism

Many of us probably wish to affirm ourselves as post-"modernist" scholars, emancipated from History, and as cultural critics who "see the world as the product of multiple perspectives all of which have some truth."²⁵ To do so, we need to face the major challenge posed by linear and progressive *avant-garde* interpretations of musical modernism. No other cultural field of the past is so crucial to, and therefore so contested by, post-war and current historiography. But in the process of the recuperation of modernism as postmodernist past, we ourselves repeat the paradigmatic act of modernist rupture in our effort to pry the modernist past away from *avant-garde* discourse. It has often been argued that such a disruptive concept of history is, indeed, one of the key-characteristics of French and possibly Western modernity around 1900.²⁶ But in fashioning our own postmodern modernism, we have a vested interest in emphasizing the plurality, complexity, and discordant sides of modernism, its disparate aspects, and its contradictions. Thus our millennial version of the modernist past appears to be one more sophisticated and more complex than that of History, and yet it still inscribes postmodern approaches into a grand narrative of scholarly progress. Ironically, such

---

²¹ Michel Foucauld, *L'Archéologie du savoir* (Paris: Gallimard, 1969), 259–75. To what extent resistance to Hegel has become a leitmotif in twentieth-century philosophy of history becomes obvious in the contributions to *Emmanuel Lévinas et l'histoire: Actes du Colloque international des facultés universitaires Notre-Dame de la Paix*, edited by Nathalie Frogneux and Françoise Mies (Paris and Namur: Editions du Cerf and Presses Universitaires de Namur, 1998), especially the essay by Guy Petitdemange, "La notion paradoxale d'histoire" (17–44).
²² The wording of Foucault's warning is by Klein, "In Search of Narrative Mastery," 294.
²³ Francis Fukuyama reenforces the liberal normativity of his universalist approach to world history in "Reflections on the End of History, Five Years Later," *History and Theory* 34 (1995): 27–43.
²⁴ Many thanks to my colleague at Department of Philosophy at the University of North Carolina at Chapel Hill, Keith Simmons, for this information.
²⁵ Jann Pasler, "Postmodernism," in *Grove Music Online*, edited by Laura Macy (accessed 22 February 2004), < http://www.grovemusic.com.libproxy.lib.unc.edu >.
²⁶ Jann Pasler, "Deconstructing d'Indy, or the Problem of a Composer's Reputation," *19th-Century Music* 30 (2006): 230–56.

ideologies of progress, so much criticized within historical master-narratives, are still deeply ingrained in the academic scholarly enterprise: even the best-bred postmodernist wishes to uncover ever greater (relative) truths and make hermeneutic progress. After all, who wants to be *passé*? The alignment of modern music of the early twentieth century with our epistemological concerns of the early twenty-first functions thus as a mirror, but we may do well to reverse the warning etched in our cars and remember that objects in the mirror are in fact not closer but further away than they appear.

How much can be at stake, and how strongly the current concerns can inflect scholarly questions, can be shown in my own work on Lili Boulanger. For many decades after her early death, the composer Lili Boulanger was represented as a musical *femme fragile*, whose purity and devoutness sanctified her early death. I started out with both interpretative and positivist work: as I pointed out earlier—positivism takes the Other very seriously, indeed. But as usual, interpretation intervened in the guise of the scholar's point of view (to refer to Ranke again). I am a rather secular feminist, brought up in a musical context that valued Pierre Boulez and György Ligeti over such seemingly reactionary composers as Philip Glass. My sources appeared to underpin my construction of Boulanger as a modernist composer—all the elements fit beautifully, especially when focusing on her secular works such her *Clairières dans le Ciel* and the opera *La Princesse Maleine*. Indeed, I finished my 1997 article on Boulanger's opera with the triumphant conclusion that my reevaluation would allow us to unveil a "potent young composer of the avant-garde, a composer of major modernist works."[27] Today, those final words make me uneasy, for I know full well that I fell squarely into the trap of the rhetoric of musical progress and the concept of modernism as rupture. *My* composer, I emphasized with implied value judgment, was one who was on par with her contemporaries and younger siblings, whether Arthur Honegger, Darius Milhaud, Igor Stravinsky, or Olivier Messiaen. But two things have happened since: on the one hand, my own horizon as a scholar has changed in the context of the historiographical debates of the last ten years, when "modernism" as a concept became problematized anew, and, on the other hand, the sources started to veto some of my work. In my zeal to free Boulanger from the shackles of religious oppression through her environment and a masculinist historiography, I reduced my composer into a secularized modernist when some sources point towards a far more complex personality, and I cannot silence those sources any longer. After all, Boulanger was a Catholic, and over half of her works were setting some kind of religious text. For the occasion of a study day dedicated to the Boulanger sisters in October 2003 in London, I decided to listen to my sources and focus on Boulanger's composing as a Catholic which offered some fascinating perspectives on the complex interrelationship of modernism, Catholicism, and music in France in the 1910s. But imagine my relief when the sources allowed me to interpret her sacred music as that of a Catholic modernist rather than just a Lourdes pilgrim.[28]

What makes musical modernism so attractive for recontextualization in our postmodern context is not just its being contested referential ground. Rather, it is the fact that our

---

[27] Annegret Fauser, "Lili Boulanger's *La Princesse Maleine*: a Composer and her Heroine as Literary Icons," *Journal of the Royal Musical Association* 122 (1997): 68–108, at 108.

[28] Annegret Fauser, "Composing as a Catholic: Rereading Lili Boulanger's Vocal Music" (see this volume, 309–16).

epistemological mirror reflects something uncannily familiar. Many of the themes that pervade current cultural and political debates are reflected in new questions being asked about earlier musical modernism: technology and nature; Self and Otherness; nationalism and globalization; heritage, progress and identity; nostalgia and mysticism; exploration and war; and, above all, the issue of meaning. Our telling the story of modern music in France, in fact, depends on laying bare the polyphonic voices of the past and on emphasizing multivalence and impurity, rather than striving for the clarity of a linear and exclusionary discourse of musical progress. The image that we search for in the mirror of Herodotus—to use a phrase coined by François Hartog—is a Paris that will reflect back our own "intention" as historians (Ranke again).[29]

3. The Challenge of Parisian Modernism

One story might clarify the issues that I have raised thus far in a more concrete fashion. On 29 May 1913, members of the buzzing audience in the Théâtre des Champs-Elysées in Paris, heard the following sounds from Stravinsky's *Le Sacre du printemps* after the lights dimmed (Example 1).

Example 1: Igor Stravinsky, *Le Sacre du printemps*, mes. 1–4

Eighteen years earlier, in 1895, another iconic piece, Claude Debussy's *Prélude à l'Après-midi d'un faune*, had opened with the following sequence (Example 2).

Example 2: Claude Debussy, *Prélude à l'Après-midi d'un faune*, mes. 1–4

---

[29] For contrasting Herodotus and Thucydides and developing Herodotus as cultural historian, see Carl E. Schorske, "History and the Study of Culture," *New Literary History* 21 (1990): 407–20, esp. 409–12.

Finally, another thirty-five years back leads us to a series of famous concerts in Paris in 1860, so eloquently evoked by Charles Baudelaire and where the prelude to *Tristan and Isolde* was performed (Example 3).

Example 3: Richard Wagner, Prelude to *Tristan and Isolde*, mes. 1–11

Three openings to well-known pieces of musical modernism, sharing some important character-traits, such as the single melodic line emerging out of silence and gradually developing its ambitus and dynamic range, the meandering quality of its melodic shape, its ambivalent relationship to any subsequent harmonic underpinning, an irregular phrase structure, and the prominence in each of one specific woodwind instrument: flute, bassoon, and—still masked in Wagner by oboe and cellos—the English horn. While the iconic English horn of the *Tristan* opening is fleeting at this first melodic statement, it becomes ever more present throughout the opera until it is heard in splendid nudity at the beginning of Act III, in the long-winding solo with its characteristic emphasis of the second note of the melody (Example 4).

Example 4: Richard Wagner, *Tristan und Isolde*, Act III, mes. 52–60

The intertextuality between these three works allows for various interpretations of Stravinsky's referential opening gesture in *Le Sacre du printemps*.[30] First, the gesture posits the work from the outset in a lineage of key modern works whose sound emerges out of silence in a fresh attempt at creating contemporary sonority. In the case of Debussy, the intertextual reference is even closer because Vaslav Nijinsky's choreography for *L'Après-midi d'un faune* was premièred by the Ballets Russes in the year before *Le Sacre du printemps*. But Stravinsky's woodwind solo may signify even more. In 1913, Nijinsky claimed that "Le *Sacre du printemps* ... is really the soul of nature expressed by movement in music. It is the life of the stones and the trees. There are no human beings in it. It is only the incarnation of Nature."[31] If nature was the plot of *Le Sacre du printemps*, it certainly figured prominently in Debussy's and Nijinsky's evocation of a Greece of nymphs and fauns and also, in a more veiled fashion, in Wagner's "alte ernste Weise" performed by the shepherd in Act III. Thus Stravinsky's opening melody could be read as signifying an awareness of and even desire for origins—both music-aesthetical and transcendental—that is embodied in this music.

But the loop of references does not end there. A wonderful musicians' joke (Example 5) captures perfectly the sonic double-entendre of Stravinsky's opening.[32]

---

[30] Peter Burkholder notes a second reference to Debussy in *Le Sacre du printemps*, the evocation of *Nuages* at the beginning of Part II of Stravinsky's ballet. J. Peter Burkholder, "The Uses of Existing Music: Musical Borrowing as a Field," *Notes* 50 (1994): 851–70, at 865.

[31] Interview with the *Pall Mall Gazette* on 15 February 1913, given in Jann Pasler, "Music and Spectacle in *Petrushka* and *The Rite of Spring*," in *Confronting Stravinsky: Man, Musician, and Modernist*, edited by ead. (Berkeley, Los Angeles, and London: University of California Press, 1986), 53–81, at 69–70.

[32] I am grateful to Anne MacNeil for sharing this joke with me.

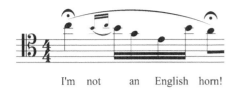

I'm not an English horn!

Example 5

Yet the English Horn that in nineteenth-century France and Germany is so prominently associated with the Wagnerian construction of world as desire in *Tristan and Isolde* carries a different meaning in nineteenth-century Russian music, where it is used to evoke the East when combined with sinuous melodic contour, repetition of melodic cells, excessive ornamentation, and irregular phrase structures.[33] Given that the melodic construction of the beginning of *Le Sacre du printemps* uses the same markers that one could find in melodies such as Alexander Borodin's markedly oriental second theme (for the English Horn) in his short symphonic sketch, *In the Steppes of Central Asia*, Stravinsky's opening points to another form of reflecting nature through musical signifiers, that of Russian Orientalism, even though the fact that it is *not* played by an English Horn, but by a bassoon masquerading as English Horn, creates ironic distance in Stravinsky's critical reconfiguration of the stock-Orientalist markers. Such Russian in-jokes may not have been lost on a Parisian audience, either, given that such works as Maurice Ravel's *A la manière de Borodine* for piano from 1913 (the year of the ballet's première) were written for the French market.[34]

The story of *Le Sacre du printemps* that I have told so far is one of tradition and intertext, focusing on the continuity and complexity of artistic and intellectual networks rather than on the older story-line of rupture as being the distinctive element of Stravinsky's so-called Russian period, a plot still favored by Philippe Albèra recently in his discussion of rupture and tradition in the new *Enciclopedia Einaudi*.[35] This is, of course the more familiar reading, most powerfully encapsulated in the probably most famous moment in *Le Sacre du printemps*, the "Augurs of Spring" (Example 6).

---

[33] I am grateful to Kevin Bartig for this information. On the English Horn as a signifier for orientalism, see Richard Taruskin, "'Entoiling the Falconet': Russian Musical Orientalism in Context," *Cambridge Opera Journal* 4 (1992): 253–80, at 266–69. See also Dorothea Redepenning, *Geschichte der russischen und der sowjetischen Musik* (Laaber: Laaber-Verlag, 1994), 294–302, for a list of Russian Orientalist works.

[34] Taruskin, "'Entoiling the Falconet'," 268.

[35] Philippe Albèra, "Tradizione e rottura della tradizione," in *Enciclopedia della musica*, edited by Jean-Jacques Nattiez, vol. 1: *Il Novecento* (Turin: Einaudi, 2001), 27–47, 27: "D'altra parte Stravinskij, nelle opere del 'periodo russo', ruppo in modo radicale con l'eredità romantica, scegliendo di appogiarsi sulle tradizioni popolari della musica slava [...]."

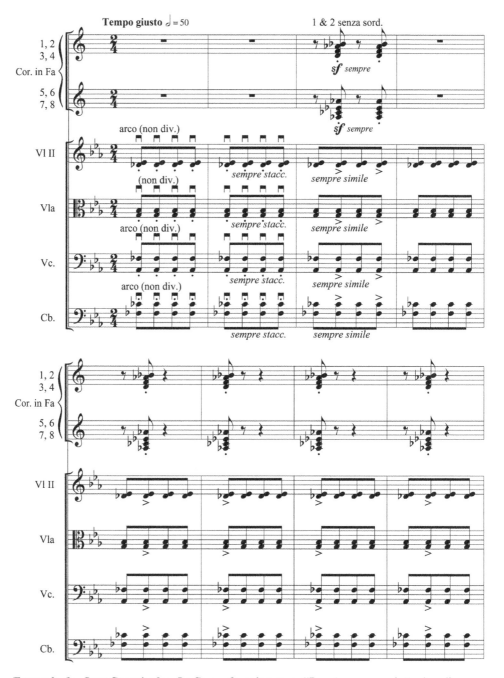

Example 6: Igor Stravinsky, *Le Sacre du printemps*, "Les Augures printaniers," mes. 1–7

More than any other instance of Stravinsky's music, this iconic ostinato section became a sonic marker of modernity that can be traced in works as diverse as Béla Bartók's *The Miraculous Mandarin*, Manuel de Falla's *Il retablo de maese Pedro*, Carlos Chávez's *Sinfonía india*, Henry Cowell's *Antinomies* and his Piano Concerto, or Aaron Copland's *Rodeo*, and these are only a handful of examples taken from a course on musical modernism that I taught in 2004. But the ostinato section itself, with its foregrounding of the rhythmic over the melodic and harmonic, is also embedded within a rich web of traditions: Russian—as Richard Taruskin has demonstrated—and European, especially that of the nineteenth century, as the beginning of the "Danse noubienne" from Hector Berlioz's *Les Troyens* may show (Example 7). Especially in the context of theatrical music, such sonorities signified what was "primitive" and natural, close to the roots. As a musical signifier, it was often—albeit not exclusively—associated with exotic Others. Thus the concept of "rupture" as a hermeneutic tool becomes problematic even in an apparently so clear-cut case as the scandalous *Sacre du printemps*.

Example 7: Hector Berlioz, *Les Toyens*, "Danse noubienne," mes. 1–8

Moreover, Richard Taruskin's well-known uncoupling of Stravinsky from Allen Forte's purist modernist readings has shown in detail that even the famously "primitivist" gesture of the "Augurs of Spring" was a device of Russian folk music.[36] He thus relocated Stravinsky within a long tradition of nineteenth-century Slavic folklorism of works such as Bedřich Smetana's *Ma Vlást* (My Fatherland) or Mily Balakirev's *Second Overture on Russian Themes* (later published as *Russia*).

According to Albèra, for composers such as Debussy, Mahler, and Ives, modernist rupture with tradition means not a rejection of the past as a whole, but an amplification of its meaning by expanding it synchronically to include folk music and exotic markers.[37] But in his story, the Russian-period Stravinsky remains a composer rejecting outright the past of nineteenth-century European music through his realignment with popular and primitivist roots. My brief interpretation of the two passages from *Le Sacre du printemps* has shown that even one of the apparently most disruptive works in the canon of modernism has firm roots in the traditions of nineteenth-century European music and could be read as reinterpreting and appropriating nineteenth-century procedures and models rather than rejecting them. While Taruskin's rooting of Stravinsky in Russian folklore seems driven by the attempt to set the record straight against the post-war Stravinsky himself, I am going further even, by showing that the text is thoroughly entrenched within a turn-of-the-century musical history.

The contrary strands in the scholarly treatment of Stravinsky's *Le Sacre du printemps* thus offer a perfect example for the paradoxical demands of interpretation in the context of postmodern positivism. My reading of it as a work embedded in both Western art-music traditions of the nineteenth-century and kuchkist traditions of Russian folklorism, and those other, more modernist, discourses of rupture—an interpretation funneled by the composer himself—could each be seen as equally valid interpretations of musical texts that depend on the viewpoint of the interpreter: mine is one that recontextualizes the work in these specific musical frameworks, while a different reader may legitimately focus on the modernist shift in Stravinsky's musical language, his relationship to his native Russia, or, as in the case of Allen Forte, the organization of the work's pitch materials.[38] A positivist approach might point out, however, that modernism is not just about the notes on the page such as when I drew on those musical intertexts earlier. Indeed, a broader range of sources would veto so limited a musical interpretation as inadequate because it ignores historical facts, especially those of the modernist discourse and reception at the time of the work's creation. While the musical text may contain ample traces of tradition and point toward continuities, the emphasis on rupture in the rich context of historical sources will tell different and competing stories. Thus what my own interpretation might add is a muddying of the waters by a contrary reading, but unless it acknowledges its place as such while also acknowledging the rights of the sources to qualify it, this emplotment is—in positivist terms—as problematic as my earlier reinterpretation

---

[36] Richard Taruskin, "Russian Folk Melodies in 'The Rite of Spring,'" *Journal of the American Musicological Society* 33 (1980): 501–43.

[37] Albèra, "Tradizione e rottura della tradizione," 44: "Pur sviluppando le scritture molto diverse, Mahler, Ives e Debussy hanno dato vita a una rotture con la tradizione che non mirava a rifiutare il passato nel suo complesso ma ad ampliarne il concetto."

[38] Allen Forte, *The Harmonic Organization of The Rite of Spring* (New York and London: Yale University Press, 1978).

of Lili Boulanger as a pure modernist. Here unfolds the paradox between positivist claims to truth—even if never attained—and postmodern plays of interpretation. This cannot be resolved, but it can caution us against too much glibness in our scholarly enterprise.

The archives—in both the traditional and the Foucauldian sense of the word—of French modern music are waiting for us musical archaeologists to explore, discuss, deconstruct, and hear them in the tension field between postmodern interpretation and positivist work on sources, all so as to find creative answers to Ranke's much maligned question about "wie es eigentlich gewesen." Our enterprise is located in a historiographical space where both our and our subjects' shifting perspectives may prevent clear and final answers, but where we can celebrate difference, complexity, and an open-endedness of discourse, acknowledging postmodernism as aspects of modernism writ large but without the purism of modernist political or ideological agendas. In the context of historiographical debates, it is deeply ironic that we would then be throwing in our lot with Ranke by acknowledging how our viewpoints shape our scholarly intentions.

Part Two

Musical Identities in the United States in the 1930s and '40s

CHAPTER 6

Aaron Copland, Nadia Boulanger, and the Making of an "American" Composer

Aaron Copland identified himself early on as a composer "anxious to write a work that would immediately be recognized as American in character."[1] Indeed, Copland's identity as an "American" composer has long been established as a common, unquestioned trope in both contemporary reception and scholarship. However problematic such a reductive characterization may be, it continues to hold a privileged position within the discourses on his music.[2] On the heels of this representation of Copland as national icon follows the question of its origins. The customary answer—given by Copland himself and repeated in almost all the secondary literature—points to Paris as the source of Copland's nationalism, especially his discovery of jazz as an "American"-sounding musical vernacular in the defamiliarized surroundings of 1920s France.[3] But whereas Copland's own depiction of Paris prominently featured Nadia Boulanger as the pivotal figure of his musical self-discovery, more recent accounts of Copland's Parisian experiences often drastically marginalize her role in favor of, for example, French writers such as André Gide, Copland's friends in Paris (especially Harold Clurman), his encounter with Les Six (most prominently Darius Milhaud) and their music, and Gertrude Stein.[4] Yet even at the age of fifty, Copland described his "introduction to Nadia Boulanger and her acceptance of [him] as a pupil" as the "most important musical event of his life."[5] Indeed—as Minna Lederman speculated—his methods of composing were established by the time he had left Paris: "I don't think anyone since the early student days with Boulanger has had any great effect on him."[6] My concern in this essay, however, is not whether or how Boulanger may have influenced Copland's compositional development (although clearly she did). Rather, I am interested in her role in the shaping and sustaining of Copland's concepts of national identity in music, and, in consequence, how both the musical and the discursive aspects of his self-representation as an "American" composer can be relocated within the broader context of transatlantic cultural politics of the 1920s and 1930s. Such a recontextualization offers perhaps a more nuanced understanding of Copland's self-fashioning as "American" within increasingly globalized cultural and political frameworks.[7]

The question of Copland's national identity as a composer also becomes a test case in exploring the vexed issue of identity in music. Research on the identity politics of national, regional, religious, and other communities has recently taken center stage in the wake of Benedict Anderson's *Imagined Communities*, a study described as "without doubt, one of the most influential books of the late twentieth century."[8] Furthermore, recent work on music in the Diaspora has offered a rich body of transnational perspectives examining the role of music in the formation, preservation, and transformation of national and ethnic identities.[9] As critical discourse in these fields has developed, the concepts of both "identity" and "Diaspora" have became more fluid, encompassing an ever "larger semantic domain that includes words like immigrant, expatriate, refugee, guestworker, exile community, overseas community, ethnic community. This is the vocabulary of transnationalism."[10] But Rogers Brubaker and Frederick Cooper have pointed out that the notion that "identities are fluid, constructed and multiple" also bears dangers, especially when self-understandings "harden, congeal, and crystallize." They raise another problem that is particularly relevant to Copland's European experience, that of being defined as different by the external forces of a majority: "If [identity] is constructed, how can we understand the sometimes coercive force of external identifications?"[11] But while Brubaker and Cooper argue compellingly that the term "identity" has lost some of its usefulness in contemporary social analysis, the concept remains a valuable one in historical analysis, even though it may hover uncomfortably among issues of racial, national, and ethnic stereotyping with all its essentialist pitfalls, and between the dialectics of nationalism and transnationalism, not to mention facing possible charges of the intentional fallacy, even in an analysis of reception. As Aleida Assmann and Heidrun Friese point out in the introduction to their important essay collection, *Identitäten*, "the stagings of identity are understood both as being part of social and political practice and as a cultural text marked by different meanings, coded in historically different ways, and generating and activating different images."[12] Yet the transnational perspective of Copland's identity formation leads me to invoke a third critical category, that of "cultural transfer." Cutting across various fields, from translation study to the history of tourism, the concept of "cultural transfer encompasses the transport of cultural materials from one culture to another. In most contemporary usages, the term 'culture' refers exclusively to national, regional or other ethnographic grouping, but cultural transfer seeks to explain the migration of sets of practices from one geographical position to another."[13]

Drawing on all three concepts—identity politics, the notion of Diaspora (in the sense of an expatriate overseas community), and cultural transfer—I would argue that Copland's European experience should be interpreted as the learning of a set of cultural practices that he appropriated in response to external nationalist identifications of culture. Indeed, Copland's developing identity as an American musician reflects not only his own national self-image but also the transformative effects of the French gaze. Thus Copland's American identity was not immanent but was constructed in dialogue with French culture and its understandings of American cultural practice. I will begin by investigating the external identifications Copland encountered in Paris through the French stereotyping of American culture, especially the representation of the United States as a land of industrialized mass production. These discourses were particularly virulent in the French reception of jazz as a modern artistic medium, and one of some dispute in terms of its suitability for compositional engagement. Jazz also played an important role in the cultural mediation of Copland's teacher, Nadia Boulanger, and influenced her part in the construction of Copland as an "American" composer. This is particularly evident in her incorporation of jazz in an almost abstract compositional manner, much in the vein of her neoclassicist aesthetic. One of the consequences of this appropriation of jazz in the spirit of neoclassicism led both her and her pupils to separate the musical elements of jazz from its racial and historical origins in order to create an abstract component of national identity formation.

External Identifications: An American in Paris

When Copland and Boulanger met at Fontainebleau in the summer of 1921, Americans had become an increasingly familiar sight in Paris. Expatriate American art lovers such as Winnaretta Singer (the Princesse de Polignac) and Natalie Barney already formed an important part of the cultural elite of prewar Paris. During World War I, joint Franco-American relief committees—as, for example, the Franco-American Committee for the War Blind—brought together officials and philanthropists from both countries.[14] Indeed, Boulanger and her sister Lili were driving forces behind the Comité franco-américain du Conservatoire de Paris and—together with the American diplomats Blair Fairchild and Whitney Warren—belonged to its *comité d'action*.[15]

Furthermore, it was through her work on this committee that in 1918 Boulanger would meet Walter Damrosch, the American conductor who was instrumental in the founding of the Conservatoire Américain de Fontainebleau.[16] By the end of 1917, American soldiers were a visible presence in France, and soon after the war, students, artists, tourists, and businessmen traveled to France for study, entertainment, and economic, social, and cultural commerce.[17]

Deeply battered by four years of a war that had decimated her population and destroyed parts of her countryside, cities, and industries, France now had to deal with an America that was emerging as a vigorous, politically assertive, and economically powerful force in global politics. By 1919 France's war debt to the United States amounted to $4.2 billion (or 21 billion francs)—over four times France's national budget in 1913.[18] Repayment of the war debt became a hotly debated issue in a country whose economy was all but destroyed, and within a few years anti-American sentiment ran high, with the French statesman Georges Clemenceau pointedly comparing France's toll of 1,364,000 deaths to that of 56,000 Americans.[19] Not surprisingly, the American insistence on payment brought sharply negative responses that turned "Oncle Sam" into an "Oncle Shylock" demanding money even after France had already provided her "pound of flesh" for the common victory. Some commentators used such blatantly anti-Semitic rhetoric to denigrate American capitalism in general. Others characterized the United States as an imperialist power in "conquest of Europe."[20]

While the American refusal to forgive the war debt turned the French wartime fervor for the United States into postwar animosity, other aspects of Franco-American relations were more ambivalent. The industrialist Ernest Mercier promoted a full-blown reorganization of French industries, invoking Taylorism and Fordism as successful models.[21] These were, however, rejected by the French Left, and attempts at reorganization were met with strikes. Similarly, American society and culture prompted both fascination and revulsion, often being criticized by the French as *mécanique* and anti-individual.[22] In particular, the film industry became targeted as a symbol of mass-produced entertainment, to be contrasted with the true, centuries-old culture of France.[23] Such cultural chauvinism was part of French attempts to reaffirm timeless qualities by promoting France as the cultural center of the world, even in the face of her perceived economic and political postwar weakness. A directive of the Ministry of Foreign Affairs from the 1920s made matters clear: "Our literature, our art, our civilization of the intellect, our ideas have exercised across the ages a powerful attraction on other nations. Our universities and our schools abroad are veritable

Making of an "American" Composer

centers of propaganda for France. [This] intellectual penetration abroad [amounts to] one of the most powerful forms of influence we have worldwide."[24] By referring to the decades-old ideology of the French *mission civilisatrice*, French government policy thus relied on a trusted commonplace that contrasted "benign" Gallic cultural influence in the service of humanity with the menace of Anglo-American economic and military expansionism.[25]

Already on the ocean liner crossing the Atlantic to France, Copland encountered these French prejudices against Americans when he struck up an acquaintance with the painter Marcel Duchamp. While Copland later recounted Duchamp's encouragement to take his "chances in Paris" so as to fully immerse himself into French art, Copland's Parisian roommate and cousin Harold Clurman told a different story "of how Duchamp had tried to discourage him, advising him to forget art and become a businessman like his father, exclaiming 'America is a place of business.'"[26] According to Clurman, Copland was "depressed" about this statement for several months and needed his friend's explanation of French disaffection for him to regain his confidence:

> "It is all very well for a Frenchman to talk that way," I said. I was angry. "The French are surfeited with culture; they are sick of a culture that did nothing to prevent the disastrous war. But we Americans are *new*; we need art, which, to begin with, is simply a self-realization for us as individuals and as a community." Aaron was satisfied, and Duchamp's irony dispelled, by the passionate outburst.[27]

While Duchamp's remark about the futility of art may have expressed Dadaist irony—as Clurman implies here—his comment about America as "a place of business" and therefore unsuited to art reflects French prejudice at its fullest.[28] Meanwhile, Clurman's identification of the American need for art as "self-realization for us as individuals and as a community" introduces a dialectic and, potentially, a paradox that exposes the particular challenges facing artists of the New World.

That Copland discovered himself as an American in Paris is a common trope in the literature. Such remarks as his comment that he could "see America more clearly from across the ocean" are usually read as reflecting Copland's awakening to a national consciousness through experiencing his difference within the context of an unfamiliar cultural environment.[29] In these accounts, Copland has agency, finding his own identity by way of positive acts. But a careful reading of the sources suggests that, to paraphrase Brubaker and Cooper, Copland was also subject to the "coercive force" of nationalist stereotyping in Paris, not only in general terms but also as applied specifically to himself. He recounts how, by the winter of 1922, he began to be known as "that talented American composer," a form of identification by national origin widely used for foreign musicians in Paris.[30] Looking back in 1930 to his years in France, Copland emphasized this aspect: "It is a current European fashion to be conscious of Americans as Americans rather than as men. Particularly with regard to our music they are over anxious to discover the American note."[31] He was also disturbed in other ways by apparent American stereotypes; he was dismayed when his new landlords for 1923, a "mulatto family," inquired "politely if we held any racial prejudices."[32]

In 1926, two years after the end of his studies in Paris, Copland returned to Europe for the summer, highlighted by two concerts in Paris featuring his music. One, organized by Nadia Boulanger for the Société Musicale Indépendante, was dedicated to music by young transatlantic composers, announced as a "Concert hors-série de musique américaine."[33] His music was also programmed on Serge Koussevitzky's 1926 concert series, with Copland playing the piano part of his *Music for the Theatre*. Copland recalled a remark after the concert by French composer Florent Schmitt: "See here, Monsieur Copland, what is the meaning of this? If you Americans begin now to export music instead of merely to import music, where will we poor French composers be?"[34] Harold Clurman's account of the same scene was less lighthearted; he described Schmitt as "a chauvinist and an anti-Semite" who had "lashed out at [Copland] with 'You Americans are geniuses in business, what do you mean by engaging in such foreign pursuits as musical composition?' Aaron took this as a joke and laughed. But Schmitt was not joking."[35] Both accounts reflect the continued French prejudice against Americans as being suited only to business already revealed by Duchamp, but Schmitt's comment also suggests the worry of French music being driven out of the global marketplace of artistic consumption.

Copland's experience of being treated as an "American" national abroad was not unique. Virgil Thomson, who had lived in Paris for almost two decades between 1921 and 1940, read his own rejection by the Parisian establishment in the mid-1920s as motivated by nationalist concerns. His response was to adopt an isolationist position in keeping (we shall see) with one current political trend, while casting it, somewhat self-servingly, in a relatively noble guise:

> I was clearly not grist either for the French immortality-mill or for international snob-bohemia. I am sure that the treatment I began to

> receive at this time from the talent scouts of both machines, a treatment courteous but reserved, was from their point of view wise and in the long run for me beneficial. It kept me an American composer and removed temptation toward trying to be anything else.... And coming to think about it, as I did a great deal in the ensuing weeks during a grippe-cold (probably acquired for that purpose), I considered the creation of an American music by myself and certain contemporaries to be a far worthier aspiration than any effort to construct a wing, a portico, even a single brick that might be fitted on to Europe's historic edifice.[36]

Indeed, in contrast to other foreigners such as Arnold Schoenberg, Igor Stravinsky, or Manuel de Falla, few American composers of what we usually term "art music" found their compositions at the center of Parisian musical life. Among the exceptions was the performance, championed by the American expatriate community of the Left Bank, of George Antheil's *Ballet mécanique* in June 1926 in the Théâtre des Champs-Elysées, "with an audience of more than 2,000 people among whom one can distinguish James Joyce, Serge Koussevitzky, Ezra Pound, Darius Milhaud, Nadia Boulanger, Marcel Duchamp, Alfred Knopf, Boris de Schloezer, etc."[37] More typical were niche events, such as Boulanger's 1926 concert mentioned above or the Copland–Sessions concert on 17 June 1929 at the Salle Chopin, billed as a "Concert d'œuvres de jeunes compositeurs américains."[38] As with the 1926 concert, reviews appeared mainly in U.S. newspapers and periodicals. The French reception was limited mostly to the circle of insiders that had gathered around Boulanger.[39] Instead, what Parisians associated much more commonly with American music was jazz.

Imagined Soundscapes: American Jazz in Parisian Salons and Concert Halls

Copland's encounter with jazz in Europe is surely one of the most discussed aspects of the composer's early career.[40] What seems to dominate the discussion are his rediscovery of jazz as a national, American art form; his response to Milhaud's *La création du monde* as a model for the integration of jazz and art music; and his growing awareness once back in the United States of "authentic," African American jazz as a form of musical recovery.[41] In contrast to New York, for example, where jazz often carried negative racial and class-based connotations, jazz in Paris formed part of a musical and social network that cut across significant segments of French society and was received in multiple ways. As Jeffrey H. Jackson has pointed out, jazz dominated not only the nightlife of Montmartre and Montparnasse but also, and increasingly, more bourgeois locales. Moreover, it interfaced with modernist music more effectively in Europe than it did in the United States.[42] But Copland's encounters with, and responses to, jazz in Paris were also filtered, at least in part, by interactions within his own musical circles, and by Boulanger's responses to the genre. Vivian Perlis has recently asked the question: "Where did Nadia Boulanger get a sense of what was 'American'? She had never been to the States and was hardly the type to hang out in jazz clubs late into the night."[43] We might reasonably try to find an answer, for while nightclubs were indeed the dominant environment for jazz performance in 1920s Paris, other spaces offered performances of a music that may have been less controversial in France than in New York, and that combined the thrill of an (American) urban modernity with the attraction of the (African) exotic in the connotation of a *musique nègre*.[44]

Among the French musicians who promoted jazz was the Conservatoire-trained pianist and composer Jean Wiéner, who moved between jazz performance and classical music with much-admired virtuosity. He was part of the circle of musicians who met at the brasserie named after his friend Darius Milhaud's 1919 ballet, *Le bœuf sur le toit*, where he performed American jazz tunes together with the Belgian pianist Clément Doucet.[45] While a range of musicians visited the brasserie—from the singer Jane Bathori to composers such as Milhaud and Satie—Wiéner also introduced jazz into the environment of the classical concert. Thus, on 6 December 1921, in the inaugural concert of the Concerts Wiéner (his new series of modern music at the venerable Salle des Agriculteurs), he programmed Billy Arnold and his band next to an arrangement of part of Stravinsky's *Rite of Spring* for player piano, and a performance of Milhaud's Sonata for flute, oboe, clarinet, and piano, op. 47. Copland, among many other musicians and socialites, attended the concert and identified it in his list of attended performances specifically as a "jazz concert."[46] Reactions in the audience were mixed. In his autobiography, Wiéner describes Albert Roussel walking out in protest, although Ravel enjoyed the concert tremendously.[47] The reviewer for *Le Ménestrel*—probably André Schaeffner—designated jazz as the "poor relation" of contemporary art music, comparable to the hurdy-gurdy of earlier periods, pointing out that France's musicians now were finding their inspiration in American bars. However, the concert presented "the excellent American orchestra of Mr. Billy Arnold, a correct and almost ceremonial jazz band," playing for about an hour. The transition from their performance to the chamber music later in the program was then achieved quite properly, Schaeffner wrote, by a "mechanical" piano playing excerpts from Stravinsky's almost equally "mechanical" *Rite of Spring*.[48]

Making of an "American" Composer

Wiéner navigated easily between the worlds of the concert hall, the salon, and the nightclubs of Montmartre. He was a favorite of the Princesse de Polignac, who commissioned his *Concerto franco-américain*, premiered in her salon just before having its first public performance at the Concerts Pasdeloup on 31 October 1924.[49] The concerto "juxtaposed neo-Bachian passages (harmonically closer to Gédalge than Stravinsky) with French popular song, music hall styles and jazz (both written and improvised)."[50] Reaction ranged from enthusiasm to ridicule and outrage. Jean Lobrot, the critic for *Le Ménestrel*, played with the culture–business dichotomy of popular French anti-Americanism and declared that the work's apparent failure was a cultural consolation:[51] "Ironically exaggerated applause and some boos taught this young man that if—as some people pretend—the old France has to take lessons from the young America as far as business is concerned, some of her sons are still in great need of the musical teachings of our country. And this offers some comfort about the exchange rate of the dollar!"[52]

Another musician who moved in these same circles was Cole Porter, who already in November 1917 seems to have been performing "jazz" in the salon of the Princesse de Polignac.[53] Milhaud and Porter also met there in 1923, an encounter that soon led to the commissioning of Porter's only ballet, *Within the Quota*, for the Ballets Suédois,[54] which premiered at the Théâtre des Champs-Elysées on 25 October 1923 together with Milhaud's *La création du monde*. Whether on purpose or by serendipity, few theater evenings could have been designed more convincingly to represent the two aspects of Parisian jazz reception in the 1920s, even presenting the works in an order that seems influenced by racialist notions of cultural progression from the "primitive" to a more "developed" urban environment, starting with *La création du monde* (which exploited the *musique nègre* aspect of jazz) and closing with the urban, "American" side of jazz in *Within the Quota*, even though Porter's ballet was originally commissioned as the curtain raiser.[55] It portrays the reactions of a Scandinavian immigrant arriving in America. American critic and jazz aficionado Gilbert Seldes, writing for *Paris-Journal*, introduced it as follows:

> *Within the Quota* is properly speaking an American ballet, the first to be staged by a foreign company and the first in which popular American music is used to illustrate an American theme. It is in the course of the action itself that the most interesting theme evolves: the possibility of reducing this little comedy [of] "how the Scandinavians are integrated" to eighteen minutes. The figures passing before the immigrant's eyes are the mythological heroes of modern American life, in part as the average

European imagines them from the cinema, in part as they really are. The intention is satirical, the method exaggeration. There is nothing more delightful than Cole Porter's talent as a jazz composer.[56]

The ballet was performed in front of a painted drop cloth representing the front page of a mock newspaper, with a man-size headline that read "Unknown Banker Buys Atlantic."[57] The movie industry was also present, with a camera onstage during the finale. Gerald Murphy's scenario outlines the characters whom the immigrant encounters:

A millionairess, bedecked with immense strings of pearls, ensnares him; but a reformer frightens her away. Then a Colored Gentleman appears and does a vaudeville dance. He is driven away by a "dry agent" who immediately thereupon takes a nip from his private flask and disappears to the immigrant's increasing astonishment. The Jazz Baby, who dances a shimmy in an enticing manner, is also quickly torn from him. A magnificent cowboy and a sheriff appear, bringing in the element of Western melodrama. At last the European is greeted and kissed by "America's Sweetheart"; and while this scene is being immortalized by a movie camera, the dancing of the couples present sweeps all the troubles away.[58]

Porter had provided tunes that were orchestrated by Charles Koechlin, and the choreography borrowed heavily from American popular dances, with which Parisian moviegoers had become familiar. As Copland had previously written home in 1921, "in the Paris moving picture houses, I noticed that they advertised only American pictures, with Ray Charles and Norma Talmadge and Charles Chaplin."[59]

The reception of Porter's ballet was generally highly positive, with *Le Figaro* hailing it as a triumph.[60] In his memoirs, Milhaud described the music as "a pure emanation of Manhattan, in which nostalgic blues alternated with throbbing ragtime rhythms."[61] According to the critic for *Le Ménestrel*, Pierre de Lapommeraye, "the Americans, present in great number the other night, gave an enthusiastic welcome to the music of their compatriot, Mr. Cole Porter."[62] He remained silent, however, on the reactions of the French audience members. For their part, Copland and Clurman, who attended the performance and were delighted by *La création du monde*, had nothing good to say about *Within the Quota*. As Clurman noted:

Like the naïve French, who protest that it is unfair to judge them by the Parisian boulevards and their cafés, the Folies Bergères and the yellow-back novels published for foreign exportation, certain Americans believe that our movies together with extravagant newspaper reports, American "dancings" etc., have given Europeans an entirely superficial and caricatural conception of American manners and morals. The present ballet by Messrs. Murphy and Porter is supposedly a satire on this excessively simplified conception of the American scene, though without the preliminary warbling furnished by the program one would be hard put to it to tell precisely whether the satire was directed at the European view of America or whether it was intended as a satire on Americans for the amusement of Europeans.[63]

This view was probably shared by Copland, and their concern over the butt of the joke (Europeans or Americans?) was coupled, it would seem, with an increasing sensitivity to Parisians' stereotyping of American culture as dominated by big business, popular music (vaudeville and jazz), Prohibition, and cowboys. Porter's jazz idiom—so different from Milhaud's more composerly and, in Copland's view, therefore more authentic approach to the style—thus worked to the detriment of the ballet. Jazz became a double-edged sword.

Clurman sharply criticized Porter's music for the ballet as "betraying hardly the glimmer of an idea" and being "entirely destitute of originality," although he did evoke (urban) jazz—without reference to race—as the "true American folk song. It is the chant of the spoiled children of the big cities and America is a country of big cities. Our tiniest 'one-horse town' is a would-be New York."[64] Thus, while jazz "proper" might have made a positive impact on the Clurman–Copland duo, they perceived Porter's version as inferior, in part because the subject pandered to European prejudices and also, one assumes, because his compositional contribution to the ballet consisted of the songs (i.e., the melodies) rather than what both Clurman and Copland believed was the essence of jazz: its rhythm. Here Clurman's assessment of the music may have been shaped by notions of jazz (and American music) as they were developed in these years in the Boulanger circle.[65] He was, after all, a dedicated member of the "Boulangerie," spending many an evening in the company of Boulanger both at her home and in social settings.

Invented Traditions: "American" Music at the Boulangerie

The 1920s brought significant changes for Nadia Boulanger. Before the war, she had developed her career as composer and performer, supporting herself and her family through teaching, mainly in private lessons and at the Conservatoire Femina-Musica (more of a musical finishing school for young women than a professional conservatory). Now in her thirties, she shifted the focus of her professional life toward a career in performance and teaching, with both formal and informal involvements in concert management. Her employment at the newly founded Conservatoire Américain de Fontainebleau brought her into close contact with many young and eager students from the United States who were willing to worship this attractive and brilliant teacher. Some—such as Melville Smith—fell head over heels in love with her.[66] Others—including Copland—were in awe of her knowledge, her musical connections, and her sophistication. Boulanger's Twenties may not have been "roaring," but she epitomized the modern European woman, whether in her professional life or by tearing (at infamously high speed) through the countryside in her own automobile. Her demeanor in those years was more relaxed and cheerful than ever before or after. We know from her diaries that she went not only to concerts but also to the movies with her friends.[67] She was intrigued by what she considered American jazz, which she would have heard performed in Parisian concerts and salons, including her own.[68] "Could it have been the discovery of that free-mannered American Youth at Fontainebleau," asks Jérôme Spycket, that may have contributed to this blossoming?[69] Boulanger's letters over the years certainly reflect a sustained fondness for the New World, and she traveled to the United States whenever possible.

For the increasing number of American students who came to Paris to study with her, Boulanger's role as teacher and cultural mediator was far-reaching. In addition to emphasizing technical skills such as harmony, part-writing, and orchestration, Boulanger's composition teaching in the 1920s offered the excitement of exploring contemporary music together with the study of a wide, if idiosyncratic, range of historical works.[70] In the early 1920s, hers was a place where students could encounter and discuss not only contemporary French compositions such as Arthur Honegger's *Le roi David* (1921), but also such works as Arnold Schoenberg's *Pierrot lunaire* (1912) and Alban Berg's *Wozzeck* (1922/25).[71] When Copland traveled to Germany and Austria for summer study in 1922 and 1923, respectively, he offered to acquire new music for Boulanger's library. In 1922, she asked for a copy of Schoenberg's *Harmonielehre* and the orchestral version of Ernest Bloch's Suite for Viola and Piano, and requested also that he buy "something *new* that you might find interesting."[72] Boulanger's concept of music history was strongly shaped by her own Conservatoire education, but it became inflected by working with students from abroad who were not educated within the French system and who had particular needs. Nor could Boulanger expect a shared cultural background, and her teaching thus gave an increasingly prominent role to the promotion of French and European music.

Boulanger's aesthetic enabled her to tread a fine line between universalism and national specificity. Thus the organic principle of *la grande ligne* became an underlying hermeneutic device that Boulanger applied to the analysis of music from Monteverdi to Fauré, and although she certainly explored national particularities in the discussion of various composers—both past and contemporary—and their works, this was always secondary to issues of individuality on the one hand and universality on the other.[73] In one of the earliest texts he wrote on Boulanger, Copland tried to explain what this approach meant for his own identity as American composer:

> Nadia Boulanger has never singled out an American composer as different, as such, from a French composer or a Spanish composer. She seeks rather the profound personality that can create great music and considers such a personality as beyond a question of territorial boundaries. In doing this she throws each pupil back on the strengths or weaknesses of his own individuality. She makes him the stronger by so doing. At the same time her faith in the future of America is striking. But her faith does not rest on a blind sympathy, but in testimony of the works she already knows.[74]

In an intriguing statement to Barbara Zuck in 1974, Copland rephrased this as "Mlle Boulanger made no particular point about nationalism during my student years or thereafter."[75] Thus Boulanger's underlying theoretical framework became a crucial aspect in her students' development, carefully avoiding the essentializing exteriorities rampant in Paris, while at the same time enabling Copland to explore Americanism as an aspect of his individual musical and cultural makeup.

For Boulanger, compositional maturity meant musical individuation. In 1925 she celebrated her own teacher Fauré's approach as one that helped students "to find their own particular road to self-realization," quoting André Gide: "it is in being the most individual that one is the most universal."[76] In her view, a composer's voice emerged out of the individual realization of universal musical truths that could be analyzed and explored across the repertoire of "great works."[77] These individual voices were, however, part of a tradition, and it therefore behooved her students to become "aware of their musical heritage, and should therefore understand how their own music fitted into that tradition."[78] Interpreted within this framework, a composer's national identity—like any other musical element—emerged in a dialectical relationship between the collective (including its past) and the individual.[79] While Boulanger's approach to national identity in music drew on the republican notions of eclectic appropriation and national style that had dominated her education in fin-de-siècle Paris, it was also inflected by the various discourses on music and national context that circulated in Paris in the early twentieth century.[80] She subscribed to eclecticism as a powerful French character trait, enabling her to recognize "beauty and merit wherever they happened to be found," and while she deferred to the writings of her fellow Conservatoire-trained colleague Charles Koechlin and the Italian neoclassicist Alfredo Casella for a formal history of music,[81] her belief that the essence of beauty transcends centuries—with similar elements audible in music from across the ages—also reflected notions of musical sincerity promoted by Tolstoy and integrated by Vincent d'Indy into his more spiraling concept of music history.[82]

For Boulanger's American students, and especially Copland, an approach that emphasized individual achievement as encapsulating a composer's human essence—national context included—was refreshing and highly promising, for it opened the possibility of American music becoming the precise locus for the flourishing of a fresh national school in dialogue with the rest of the musical world. During a luncheon in New York on 1 January 1925, held in her honor by the American Guild of Organists during her first visit to the United States, Boulanger clarified the roles of individuality and collective identity in an address that was cited in several newspapers. Here, perhaps for the benefit of her American audience, she twisted the dialectical relationship of the individual and historical, national, and other contexts into a tautology by making individuality a collective national character trait:

> American composers and students of composition whom I have known ... show certain characteristics in common. I would say they are distinguished by a very marked feeling for the rhythmic element of composition and for the cultivation of individuality. Their work is very direct and shows power in handling the element of form. These things lead to the creation of a type of composition which will eventually be recognized as distinctly American. I do not believe it will arrive as the result of any external influences but will simply be the expression of the national characteristics in music.
>
> Would jazz be considered a distinctively American musical expression? I am sometimes asked. Yes, of course it would; that is, it expresses a certain part of American feeling. Some of my students have played it for me, and I am anxious to study it here on its native soil. It

Making of an "American" Composer

has interesting possibilities. It will not necessarily be a basis for American music, however.[83]

The tautology was somewhat troublesome—there is no American collective other than its collection of individuals—and would become more so for developing notions of an American national music. But for the moment, Boulanger felt that American music had the potential to grow on its own terms given that, in her opinion, its national cultural makeup contained two key elements of modern music: a sense of rhythm and the cultivation of individuality. In contrast to other musicians such as (famously) Dvořák, Milhaud, and Ravel, she saw jazz as incidental rather than intrinsic to the development of American music; it had some potential—by all accounts because of its rhythmic qualities that could be read as modern in terms of contemporary styles—but not as a wholesale model eo ipso.[84] Her view also conflicted with the widely disseminated French prejudices that portrayed American culture as mass-produced, anti-intellectual, and cliché.[85] Instead, Boulanger emphasized individuality as a powerful national trait, offering her American students a positive counter image to the prejudices they encountered elsewhere in Paris. While, for Boulanger, individuality was the marker of all good music, only Americans (so her argument ran) were also individualists by nationality; here she appropriated tropes of American cultural history in which the individual as questioner of tradition had long been a cherished concept. In his memoirs, Virgil Thomson pointed out the difference between Boulanger and "other French musicians, who, while friendly enough toward Americans (we were popular then), lacked faith in us as artists."[86]

Rereading Copland's experience in Paris through this perspective reveals that Boulanger's teaching enabled him to develop an assertive American identity while at the same time creating his own "usable past," rather than simply accepting either internal or external constructions of American music.[87] Indeed, for Copland, this is what he learned when Boulanger introduced him to the work of Stravinsky, for Copland was "struck by the Russian element in music."[88] As Boulanger pointed out in her 1925 lecture on Stravinsky, his music was characterized by a reliance on Russian folk idioms on the one hand and, on the other, by its use of complex and fluid rhythms.[89] In his 1941 lectures on new music, Copland reshaped the argument, conflating Boulanger's dialectic of collective (i.e., folksong) and individual (rhythm): "This extraordinary rhythmic puissance Stravinsky owes to his Russian heritage—to the folksongs of his country, the music of Mussorgsky and Borodin and of his teacher Rimsky-Korsakov."[90] Again, a dialectic becomes tautologous.

But the parallel that Copland saw between Stravinsky's rhythmic complexities and "our American sense of rhythmic ingenuity" was what led him, in retrospect, to proclaim that the most important aspect of encountering Stravinsky through Boulanger was that his works "proved it was possible for a twentieth-century composer to create his own tradition."[91] For Copland, Stravinsky thus provided an example of a cultural outsider finding success in the synthesis of nationalist elements and rhythmic innovation. Indeed, the "primitivist" associations with jazz and Copland's emphasis on rhythmic interest might well represent an "Americanist" appropriation of Stravinsky's compositional techniques, especially in such works as *The Rite of Spring* and *Petrushka*.[92]

How to create an American tradition was certainly part of the discourse within the Boulangerie. Copland's early letters to Boulanger touch on this: "During my stay in Salzburg I read André Gide's new book on Dostoievsky.... I must tell you one quotation he makes from the German, Rathenau, which I think eminently true. Rathenau says that it is because she has never consented either to sin or to suffering that America has no soul ..."[93] Yet Copland playfully called himself "French" in this letter and complained that—in the first concert of the International Society for Contemporary Music—national affiliation trumped intrinsic musical quality. Copland identified the concert's multinational programming with an "internationalism" that was justified "because the world has so much need of internationalism these days."[94] Here the acknowledgment of national identity in music seems to be discussed as a political necessity in terms of the postwar League of Nations. Yet Copland's own identity as American was never far in his exchanges with Boulanger, and he reaffirmed it a year later, in one of the most personal letters he wrote to his teacher, when he confessed to not being able to express his feelings outright because "This is what being American is like!"[95]

This still leaves open the question of what "being American" could mean in the Boulanger circle. Certainly Copland recalled exploring jazz-derived "polyrhythmic devices together" with Boulanger.[96] But it seems that jazz was examined less for its potential to give American music an impulse toward the development of a musical vernacular than for its elements (in particular, rhythm) that might contribute to a national, or even international, modernism. Thus discourses about musical materiality, national identity, and even universal musical truths were intimately intertwined in the debates on jazz and other music within the Boulanger circle. An American composer could not simply create a national style by adopting jazz idioms; at best, these idioms needed to be assimilated within a composer's individual voice, and they also needed to be transcended for the greater good of musical modernism.

As a performance art, jazz almost by definition resisted such individuation and such an identification with the composer; as an improvisatory art, it also resisted the permanence necessary to achieve transcendence. But the fact that it also harbored other problems is revealed in a hitherto unexamined article that Boulanger's first American student, Marion Bauer, published in April 1924 in *La revue musicale*.[97] The opening of Bauer's text is revealing. Within four sentences, she revisits the issue of jazz as American music, the problem of the external identification of Americans and their culture, the question of national identity, and the problem of foreign influence on American music:

> For the "country mouse," the countryside does not have the same value as for the "city mouse." The same is true with "jazz" in America: one dances, one amuses one-self, one hears it everywhere without realizing that it has become *a* national language, even if it is not *the* national language for us. People always say that we have no folk music, but are we not present at the birth of a folk music? (Save that it is probably not a legitimate child!) America is an amalgamation of all peoples, but Americanism—a psychological factor that is more powerful than inheritance—is a microbe and it is impossible to avoid being infected with it. "Jazz" is the only music from the New World known in Europe; even though one begins to hear, from time to time, "cultivated" music, people repeatedly say, and not without reason, that there is no properly American music apart from "jazz."[98]

Thus, for Bauer, jazz may be an American idiom, but she makes it clear that the idea of jazz as *the* American music is something of a European misconception. While she goes on to acknowledge the African American roots of jazz, she then moves quickly to describe jazz as the musical manifestation of a psychological reality: the experience of "blues" in urban living, in particular as an integral part of the New York experience. From there it is not much of a stretch for her to declare Irving Berlin as the "father of jazz."[99] This sleight of hand allows Bauer to distinguish between jazz as American popular music in more general terms and specific performing practices (e.g., by African American players), thus separating the potential of jazz for musical modernism from its African American components.[100] This carries strong racist undertones, given that Bauer here divorces abstract musical elements suitable for modernist composition from the black history of jazz. However, one aspect of jazz performance by African Americans—their tendency to "bend" notes in performance—placed her in a double dilemma, one caused by her admiration in spite of racial prejudice, and the other—a not unusual consequence—raising the question of nature versus art. Such note bending made jazz "the first occidental music to employ *quarter tones*. Is this then an evolution of harmonic sound or a return to natural sound?"[101] Given that quarter tones were a hot topic of discussion in the Boulanger circle after Copland's encounter with Alois Hába's music in Salzburg in September 1923—which led Copland to use "quarter tones in the viola solo linking the slow movement of *Grohg* to the Finale"—Bauer's claim of primacy for American music may have particular relevance. For if jazz was the first music in the West to employ quarter tones, their use in modernist music could be defined as an Americanist device, carrying with it the claim that Americans deserved the credit for inventing quarter tones and therefore were the *fons et origo* of this aspect of musical modernism.[102] However, Bauer never would, or could, grant this primacy specifically to African Americans.

After explorations of the spiritual and of minstrel shows as sources for American jazz idioms of the past—their very pastness being an important aspect of her argument—Bauer finishes with two observations. She comments rather sarcastically that "it is mainly European composers of today who throw themselves on 'jazz' like hungry dogs on a bone," using the "savage" rhythms as an antidote to Impressionism. Thus she implies that jazz in European music is simply an exoticist means to an end for a musical culture that needs to reconnect with its own origins.[103] Bauer's evaluation of rhythm as the last vestige of savagery is inscribed fully in French nineteenth-century theories of music and race, which attributed harmonic complexity to European art music in contrast with the "primitive" quality of foregrounded rhythms.[104] They are also responsible for her second point, when she emphasizes that—while jazz is "the true child of its time"—it is also dance music from the "rock bottom of the civilized world and stems from inferior social classes."[105] Nevertheless, her final sentence claims that jazz is indeed a music with a future.

Bauer's deeply conflicted text—veering between praise and condemnation of jazz—may indicate some of the issues discussed within the Boulanger circle. Musically, jazz offered a rhythmic complexity that Boulanger herself highlighted as a strong attribute.[106] However, she avoided the taint of primitivism by her emphasis on *la grande ligne*, which led directly to rhythmic counterpoint as a significant device of modern composition. Jazz thus modified made it suitable for musical modernism, although its origins in black music and urban dance halls made it more problematic than the Russian folk songs exploited by Stravinsky. Toward the end of her life, she compared jazz to a compost heap from which American music grew both shoots and roots.[107] But even in January 1925, in her address in New York cited above, she had hedged against jazz as "a basis for American music."

Read in this context, Copland's own remarks about jazz appear similarly ambivalent. After a text published in 1925 on "Jazz as Folk Music," where he claimed that "if we haven't a folk-song foundation we must invent one," he then focused on the purely musical characteristics of jazz in his 1927 article on "Jazz Structure and Influence."[108] Here he opens his argument with the claim that it is jazz's "structure, which interests me most as a musician," neatly sidestepping the problem of jazz's origins by way of an inherently formalist approach. His article then deals almost exclusively with polyrhythm, declaring it "the real contribution of jazz."[109] He subsequently applies one of Boulanger's critical methods to the European appropriation of jazz elements by distinguishing between simple exoticism—which remains external to the music— and what he calls an "authentic" (i.e., musically internalized) use of jazz.[110] The latter he finds only in one piece, Milhaud's *La création du monde*, but it is the path he predicts for modern American composers.[111] Copland thus willfully and revealingly ignored Gershwin and his *Rhapsody in Blue* in order to favor a different, neoclassicist lineage. Like Boulanger, Copland saw in jazz only a possibility for American music, not its salvation. Like Bauer, he needed to deracinate the idiom while remaining ambivalently attached to its origins: not for nothing did Copland write to Leonard Bernstein in 1938, "Don't make the mistake of thinking that *just* because a Gilbert used Negro material, there was therefore nothing American about it. Theres [sic] always the chance it might have an 'American' quality despite its material."[112] And again like Boulanger, he rests his final judgment on a composer's singularity. Writing about "America's Young Men of Promise" in 1926, Copland presented a motley group of seventeen composers—not identified as a single school—where the highest praise was reserved for the achievement of individuality: for example, he lauded G. Herbert Elwell's distinct voice, whereas Virgil Thomson had "not entirely found himself as yet."[113] In that same year, Roger Sessions (who had recently spent a significant amount of time with the Boulanger circle, without ever studying with her) also celebrated the individual nature of American composers when he wrote that "an encouraging number of interesting individualities have begun to emerge, owning the American background as common starting point."[114]

By examining the dynamic and complex relationship between a young American composition student and the environment of 1920s Paris, especially the Boulanger circle, I have shown that Aaron Copland's ideas about national identity in music were shaped within a cultural field where he found himself stereotyped as someone whose culture, and consequently national music, was inferior—and jazz was not necessarily the exception that proved the rule, given racialist discourses on its origins. Instead of the traditional remedies of, for example, a Dvořák, Nadia Boulanger offered a theoretical model of modern music that linked individual achievement to national identity in the service of broader aesthetic goals. Copland's transfer of this model onto American music in the 1920s led not only to a positive configuration of his own identity as an American composer, but also to an open discourse that wove together the individual voice, national identity, and transnationalist notions of musical universalism.

As Elizabeth Crist has recently shown, Copland's notions of American identity shifted notably around 1928, when he became involved with the politics of the Popular Front.[115] Furthermore, his 1926 encounter with Carlos Chávez yielded a productive substitute for jazz as a signifier of Americanism. As we hear in *El salón México* (begun in 1932), the alternative both to the European tradition and to jazz was now a musical pan-Americanism.[116] Copland's public shift away from an international, pro-European attitude in favor of pan-Americanism was very much in alignment with the broader American politics of isolationism, itself in part a consequence of the political debate that was fueled by France's still unpaid war debt. But it also invoked a new (for Copland) debate that tied national identity to blood rather than to culture. In a 1933 letter to Mary Lescaze, Copland described Mexico as "pure and wholesome": "The source of it I believe is the Indian blood which is so prevalent. I sensed the influence of the Indian background everywhere—even in the landscape. And I must be something of an Indian myself or how else explain the sympathetic chord it awakens in me."[117] This is quite a different notion of what might be American, just as Copland's nostalgic desire for blood-based identity is a far cry from his playful reference to being one of "nous autres Français" in his 1923 letter to Boulanger. In 1932 Copland targeted the "importation of foreign artists and foreign music" as detrimental to the "true musical culture" and—in contrast with his earlier, pronounced modernist rhetoric—called for the development of "a school of composers who can speak directly to the American public in musical language which expresses fully the deepest reactions of the American consciousness to the American scene."[118] Yet he still felt the Parisian prejudice against

Making of an "American" Composer

America as an urban landscape constructed wholly in thrall to business. His new "American" music of the 1930s shifted from the skyscrapers of New York to a pastoral fantasy, in which Copland tried to find not only *a* country but also *the* country, whether in the Maya villages of Mexico, or the wide open spaces of Billy the Kid's Midwest and Southwest. Crist has argued convincingly that even Copland's works set in pastoral pasts and exotic locales engaged with contemporary and pressing social issues of the 1930s.[119] But in contrast to the presentism and the so visibly integrated engagement with jazz in 1920s modernism, these rural spaces also served as a utopian pastoral during the Great Depression, when the widespread interest in American folk cultures fostered a perception of them as wholesome, healthy alternatives to modern-day urban life. Copland's shift to this different type of Americanism around 1930 was not only part of the pro- and pan-American folk movements of the 1930s, but it also resembled a conventional retreat into the exotic Other, where the composer from Brooklyn could fantasize, however briefly, that he, too, had Indian blood in his veins.

While Copland's identity in the 1920s was that of someone finding his musical individuality within the context of American music and against external stereotyping, his rhetorical shift to nationalist propaganda in the 1930s was part of a wider discourse on music and national identity that was as prevalent in, say, the Weimar Republic as it was in the United States. Here there is a story waiting to be told. But that story will not be found in Copland's autobiography or his writings. Following his lead, we have tended to conflate Copland's developing discourses on national identity with the benign crusade of a cultural subaltern in the world of Western music, fueled by his experience of musical Diaspora not only as an expatriate in Europe but also as an American composer of art music in New York. A more careful reading that pays attention to the shifts and chronological developments in Copland's notions of what constitutes national identity draws our attention to a more complicated, less linear Copland whose cultural work contributed as significantly to the complex, shifting ideologies of American music as it did to its sonorities.

Notes

Annegret Fauser is Professor of Music at the University of North Carolina at Chapel Hill. She has published on French song and opera, women composers, exoticism, nationalism, reception history, and cultural transfer. Her publications include monographs on French orchestral song (1994) and on *Musical Encounters at the 1889 Paris World's Fair* (2005), and an edition of reviews of the first performance of Jules Massenet's opera *Esclarmonde* (2001); she co-edited, with Manuela Schwartz, a major publication on Wagnerism in France (1999). Currently she is editing the correspondence between Nadia Boulanger and Aaron Copland and writing a monograph on music in the United States during World War II. Email: fauser@email.unc.edu

I am grateful to Kevin Bartig, Tim Carter, Elizabeth B. Crist, Kimberly Francis, and Tamara Levitz for their helpful and stimulating comments in response to earlier drafts of this paper. The text represents a first foray into the complex, rich relationship of Nadia Boulanger and Aaron Copland, which is reflected in a correspondence that spanned more than half a century. This correspondence is forthcoming as *"Mon cher Copland": The Correspondence of Nadia Boulanger and Aaron Copland*, ed. Annegret Fauser (New York: Oxford University Press).

1. Aaron Copland, "Composer from Brooklyn" (1939), quotation given in Elizabeth B. Crist, *Music for the Common Man: Aaron Copland during the Depression and War* (Oxford: Oxford University Press, 2005), 4.

2. In his essay, "Copland Reconfigured," Leon Botstein points to a broader range of identity configurations with respect to Copland, including his individualism, sexuality, political leanings, urbanism, and—most importantly—his Jewish identity. See Leon Botstein, "Copland Reconfigured," in *Aaron Copland and His World*, ed. Carol J. Oja and Judith Tick (Princeton, NJ: Princeton University Press, 2005), 439–83. Recent research concerning Copland as an "American" composer include Crist's *Music for the Common Man*, which analyzes the composer's politics and music as specifically American; Richard Taruskin, *The Oxford History of Western Music* (Oxford: Oxford University Press, 2005), vol. 4, chap. 57, "In Search of the 'Real' America," which presents Copland as a composer corrupting jazz through modernist appropriation and his fostering of "prairie neonationalism" (662); Nadine Hubbs, *The Queer Composition of America's Sound: Gay Modernism, American Music, and National Identity* (Berkeley: University of California Press, 2004), a study deconstructing the "American" sound as (essentially) queer; and Gayle Minetta Murchison, "Nationalism in William Grant Still and Aaron Copland between the Wars: Style and Ideology" (PhD diss., Yale University, 1998).

3. Aaron Copland and Vivien Perlis, *Copland: 1900 through 1942* (New York: St. Martin's, 1984), 90.

4. It is particularly striking that the most recent book on Copland—which sets out to explore "his world"—marginalizes Boulanger to the point of some passing references in the various articles. See *Aaron Copland and His World*, ed. Oja and Tick. Even though Howard Pollack dutifully includes a five-page segment on Boulanger, he generally focuses on the overall context of Parisian (and European) musical life as a decisive influence on Copland's development. See Howard Pollack, *Aaron Copland: The Life and Work of an Uncommon Man* (Urbana: University of Illinois Press, 1999), 45–50. Even Mark DeVoto's essay "Copland and the 'Boulangerie'" focuses more on Copland's encounter with his colleagues than on Boulanger's work as their teacher. See Mark DeVoto, "Copland and the 'Boulangerie,'" in *Copland Connotations: Studies and Interviews*, ed. Peter Dickinson (Woodbridge, UK: Boydell Press, 2002), 3–13.

5. Julia Smith, *Aaron Copland: His Work and Contribution to American Music* (New York: E. P. Dutton, 1955), 45.

6. Copland and Perlis, *Copland* (New York: St. Martin's Press), 114.

Making of an "American" Composer

7. Two notable contributions to understanding Copland through an international perspective on national identity are Alan Howard Levy, *Musical Nationalism: American Composers' Search for Identity* (Westport, CT: Greenwood Press, 1983), 30–61, and Carol J. Oja, *Making Music Modern: New York in the 1920s* (Oxford: Oxford University Press, 2000), 237–51. Murchison provides a useful collection of citations on this issue; see "Nationalism in William Grant Still and Aaron Copland," 189–204.

8. Benedict Anderson, *Imagined Communities: Reflections on the Origin and Spread of Nationalism* (London: Verso, 1983). See Partha Chatterjee, "Anderson's Utopia," in "Grounds of Comparison: Around the Work of Benedict Anderson," special issue, *Diacritics* 29 (1999): 128–34, 128.

9. For a brief survey, see Mark Slobin, "The Destiny of 'Diaspora' in Ethnomusicology," in *The Cultural Study of Music: A Critical Introduction*, ed. Martin Clayton, Trevor Herbert, and Richard Middleton (New York: Routledge, 2003), 284–96.

10. Khachig Tololyan (1991), quotation cited in Slobin, "The Destiny of 'Diaspora' in Ethnomusicology," 284.

11. Rogers Brubaker and Frederick Cooper, "Beyond Identity," *Theory and Society* 29 (2000): 1–47, 1.

12. Aleida Assmann and Heidrun Friese, "Einleitung," in *Identitäten: Erinnerung, Geschichte, Identität 3*, ed. Aleida Assmann and Heidrun Friese (Frankfurt: Suhrkamp, 1998), 11–23, 12: "Die Inszenierungen von Identität werden dann als Teil sozialer und politischer Praktikern sowie als kultureller Text verstanden, der unterschiedliche Signifikate bezeichnet, historisch unterschiedlich kodiert ist und unterschiedliche Bilder hervorbringt und aktiviert."

13. Annegret Fauser and Mark Everist, "Introduction," in *Stage Music and Cultural Transfer: Paris, 1830–1914*, ed. Annegret Fauser and Mark Everist (forthcoming). For an excellent survey of the concept of cultural transfer, see the introduction by the editors, "Deutsch-französischer Kulturtransfer als Forschungsgegenstand: Eine Problemskizze," in *Transferts: Les relations interculturelles dans l'espace franco-allemand (XVIIIe et XIXe siècle)*, ed. Michael Werner and Michel Espagne (Paris: Editions Recherche sur les Civilisations, 1988), 11–34.

14. See Glenn Watkins, *Proof through the Night: Music and the Great War* (Berkeley, CA: University of California Press, 2003), 103–8; Sylvia Kahan, *Music's Modern Muse: A Life of Winnaretta Singer, Princesse de Polignac* (Rochester, NY: University of Rochester Press, 2003), 194.

15. Jérôme Spycket, *Nadia Boulanger* (Paris: Payot Lausanne, 1987), 52.

16. Spycket, *Nadia Boulanger*, 60.

17. By the end of 1917, 200,000 American soldiers had arrived in France, with 100,000 per month following. See Philippe Roger, *L'ennemi américain: Généalogie de l'antiaméricanisme français* (Paris: Editions du Seuil, 2002), 341. On American war propaganda through music, see Watkins, *Proof through the Night*, 251–69.

18. War-debt figures are from Jean-Baptiste Duroselle, *France and the United States: From the Beginnings to the Present*, trans. Derek Coltman (Chicago, IL: University of Chicago Press, 1978), 122.

19. Georges Clemenceau, *Grandeurs et misères d'une victoire* (1930), cited in Roger, *L'ennemi américain*, 344.

20. Roger (in *L'ennemi américain*, 411) cites four titles representative of these sentiments: "*L'Oncle Shylock* de J.-L. Chastanet (1927), *L'Impérialisme américain* d'Octave Homberg (1929), *L'Abomination américaine* de Kadmi-Cohen, *L'Amérique à la conquête de l'Europe* de Charles Pomaret (1931)." See also Benjamin D. Rhodes, "Reassessing 'Uncle Shylock': The United States and French War Debts, 1917–1929," *Journal of American History* 55 (1969): 787–803.

21. Egbert Klautke, "Amerikanismus und Antiamerikanismus im Frankreich der Zwischenkriegszeit," in *Amerikanismus, Americanism, Weill: Die Suche nach kultureller Identität in der Moderne*, ed. Hermann Danuser and Hermann Gottschewski (Schliengen: Edition Argus, 2003), 67–90, esp. 68–78.

22. Klautke, "Amerikanismus," 82.

23. Klautke, "Amerikanismus," 85; Roger, *L'ennemi américain*, 550.

24. Unsigned note, "Action ... dans le domaine de la propagande," written before 1928 (Archives of the Ministère des Affaires Etrangères), quoted in translation in Robert J. Young, *Marketing Marianne: French Propaganda in America, 1900–1940* (New Brunswick, NJ: Rutgers University Press, 2004), 81.

25. On the ideological contexts of the *mission civilisatrice*, see Alice L. Conklin, *A Mission to Civilize: The Republican Idea of Empire in France and West Africa, 1895–1930* (Stanford, CA: Stanford University Press, 1997).

26. Copland dedicated three pages to his encounter with Duchamp in his autobiography (Copland and Perlis, *Copland*, 43–45; quotation, 43). See Gail Levin, "Study Abroad: The Parisian Avant-Garde," in *Aaron Copland's America: A Cultural Perspective*, ed. Gail Levin and Judith Tick (New York: Watson Guptill, 2000), 18–21; citation, 19. Clurman's story is recounted in his *All People Are Famous: Instead of an Autobiography* (New York: Harcourt Brace Jovanovich, 1974), 65–66.

27. Clurman, *All People Are Famous*, 65–66.

28. That Duchamp's remark had affected Copland quite strongly emerges in a letter to Leonard Bernstein, dated 23 March 1938: "At 21, in Paris, with Dada thumbing its nose at art, I had a spell of extreme disgust with all things human." See *The Selected Correspondence of Aaron Copland*, ed. Elizabeth B. Crist and Wayne Shirley (New Haven, NJ: Yale University Press, 2006), 124.

29. Copland and Perlis, *Copland*, 82. Elizabeth Crist has pointed out to me that, even in 1938, during the composition of *Billy the Kid*, Paris served as a catalyst for Copland's use of American folk melodies. Copland noted: "There in a studio on the rue de Rennes next door to David Diamond, I began to compose *Billy the Kid*. Perhaps there is something different about a cowboy song in Paris." Copland and Perlis, *Copland*, 280. See also Pollack, *Aaron Copland*, 320.

30. Copland and Perlis, *Copland*, 77. By the later nineteenth century, Parisian reception of foreign musicians was characterized by national taxonomies. See my account of concerts by foreign orchestras and non-Western musicians in *Musical Encounters at the 1889 Paris World's Fair* (Rochester, NY: University of Rochester Press, 2005), 42–58.

31. Aaron Copland, contribution to the *Fontainebleau Alumni Bulletin* (May 1930), cited in Kendra Preston Leonard, *The Conservatoire Américain: A History* (Lanham, MD: Scarecrow Press, 2007), 22.

32. Copland and Perlis, *Copland*, 91.

33. The program is listed in Michel Duchesneau, *L'avant-garde musicale et ses sociétés à Paris de 1871 à 1939* (Sprimont, Belgium: Mardaga, 1997), 321. Roger Sessions reviewed the concert under the header "An American Evening Abroad," in *Modern Music*, November/December 1926, 33–36.

34. Copland and Perlis, *Copland*, 124.

35. Clurman, *All People Are Famous*, 36.

36. Virgil Thomson, *Virgil Thomson* (New York: Alfred A. Knopf, 1966), 116–17.

37. Aaron Copland to Israel Citkowitz, 12 July 1926, in *Selected Correspondence of Aaron Copland*, ed. Crist and Shirley, 50.

38. Carol J. Oja, "The Copland-Sessions Concerts and Their Reception in the Contemporary Press," *Musical Quarterly* 65 (1979): 220–21.

39. Indeed, Boulanger was instrumental for the programming of American composers, mostly in concerts at Fontainebleau (thus within the context of an American-signifying institution). From time to time, she also succeeded in having a work by a former student performed at the regular concerts of the Société Musicale Indépendante, on whose executive board she served for years. Her fellow composer Charles Koechlin remembered: "Nadia Boulanger (chez qui avaient lieu les comités de lecture), admirable pianiste, possédait l'art de présenter les œuvres de ses élèves américains de si habile façon, qu'elles semblaient excellentes et qu'on les admettait d'emblée, sans les avoir entendu in extenso: aux concerts, on avait parfois des déceptions." Cited in Duchesneau, *L'avant-garde musicale*, 91.

40. On Copland and jazz, see, for example, Murchison, "Nationalism in William Grant Still and Aaron Copland," 201–18 and 259–68; Pollack, *Aaron Copland*, 113–20; David Schiff, "Copland and the 'Jazz Boys,'" in *Copland Connotations*, ed. Dickinson, 14–21; Gail Levin, "The Influence of Jazz," in *Copland's America*, ed. Levin and Tick, 22–28; Judith Tick, "The Origins and Style of Copland's "Mood for Piano' No. 3, 'Jazzy,'" *American Music* 20 (2002): 277–96; and Stanley V. Kleppinger, "On the Influence of Jazz Rhythm in the Music of Aaron Copland," *American Music* 21 (2003): 74–111. The literature on the French reception of jazz in the early twentieth century has grown significantly over the last decade. Three studies in particular should be cited here: William A. Shack, *Harlem in Montmartre: A Paris Jazz Story between the Great Wars* (Berkeley: University of California Press, 2001), a study of African American jazz musicians in Paris; Jeffrey H. Jackson, *Making Jazz Modern: Music and Modern Life in Interwar Paris* (Durham, NC: Duke University Press, 2003), which focuses on the various aspects of French reception and appropriation of jazz; and Colin Nettelbeck, *Dancing with De Beauvoir: Jazz and the French* (Carlton, Australia: Melbourne University Press, 2004).

41. In contrast with most scholars who try to absolve Copland when he redeems himself in their eyes by—finally—discovering "true" and "authentic" jazz, Elizabeth B. Crist rightly points out that the meaning of jazz needs to be understood within the context of the 1920s: "Like the idea of Americanism itself, the characteristics, qualities, and meanings of 'jazz' are rather flexible. To white American and European modernists

in the 1920s, it was a multifarious commercial music that captured the urban experience and epitomized the modern American city." See Elizabeth B. Crist, "Copland and the Politics of Americanism," in *Aaron Copland and His World*, ed. Oja and Tick, 277. For a similar approach, see also Anne C. Shreffler, "Classicizing Jazz: Concert Jazz in Paris and New York in the 1920s," in *Die klassizistische Moderne in der Musik des 20. Jahrhunderts*, ed. Hermann Danuser (Winterthur, Switzerland: Amadeus Verlag, 1997), 55–71, and Barbara A. Zuck, *A History of Musical Americanism* (Ann Arbor, MI: UMI Research Press, 1978), 79–80.

42. Jackson, *Making Jazz Modern*, 52–70.

43. Vivian Perlis and Libby Van Cleve, *Composers' Voices from Ives to Ellington: An Oral History of American Music* (New Haven, NJ: Yale University Press, 2005), 265.

44. Jackson, *Making Jazz Modern*, 97.

45. Kahan, *Music's Modern Muse*, 225. The program is reproduced in Jean Wiéner, *Allegro Appassionato* (Paris: Pierre Belfond, 1978), 50.

46. Concert visit listed as "Jean Wiener—Jazz Concert," in "List of performances attended in Paris during 1921 & 1922 (noted in those years) // A.C. '65," Library of Congress, Aaron Copland Collection, box 243. I could not ascertain whether Boulanger attended this concert (her appointment book for 1921 is missing from the collection of the Bibliothèque nationale de France). She did, however, attend the next concert, which featured the premiere of Schoenberg's *Pierrot lunaire*. See Nadia Boulanger, "Agenda 1922," Bibliothèque nationale de France, Rés.Vmf.ms.90, entry for 16 January 1922: "Concert Wiéner Pierrot Lunaire."

47. Wiéner, *Allegro Appassionato*, 48.

48. A.S., "Concerts Jean Wiéner," *Le Ménestrel* 83 (1921): 502. "Il est entendu maintenant que nos musiciens ne sauraient chercher leurs inspirations ailleurs que dans les bars américains.... D'ailleurs chaque époque littéraire témoigne un engouement particulier pour tel ou tel parent pauvre de la musique; après le cornet à pistons des bals « suburbains » ou de Bullier, après l'orgue de Barbarie de nos cours, après la musique à vapeur de nos foires, voici le jazz-band ... M. Jean Wiéner avait invité à son concert du 6 décembre un orchestre américain—celui, excellent, de M. Billy Arnold: un jazz-band correct, presque cérémonieux. Une heure durant, nous nous adonnâmes aux plaisirs écœurants de la syncopation alors qu'un trombone virtuose vagissait des trémolos et des glissandos plaintifs. La meilleure transition entre le jazz et la musique de chambre ne pouvait être que le piano mécanique. Nous y entendîmes des fragments du *Sacre du Printemps*, rendus ainsi à peu près inexpressifs et dénués—à part la *Danse sacrale*—de puissance même mécanique."

49. Kahan, *Music's Modern Muse*, 246–47.

50. David Drew, "Jean Wiéner," *Grove Music Online*, ed. Laura Macy, http://www.grovemusic.com (accessed 22 March 2007).

51. In the two years between 1922 and 1924, the exchange rate changed from 12.193 francs to 19.096 francs per dollar. See EH.Net, "What Was the Exchange Rate Then?" http://eh.net/hmit/exchangerates (accessed 23 March 2007).

52. Jean Lobrot, "Concerts Pasdeloup," in *Le Ménestrel* 86 (1924): 452. "Des applaudissements ironiquement exagérés et quelques « hou! hou! » vinrent apprendre à ce

Making of an "American" Composer

jeune homme que si, comme certains le prétendent, la vieille France a des leçons à prendre en affaires, de la jeune Amérique, quelques-uns de ses fils ont encore grand besoin de l'enseignement musical de notre pays. Et cela console un peu du cours du dollar!" Compare Boris de Schloezer's review for *La revue musicale*, cited in Kahan, *Music's Modern Muse*, 247.

53. The "jazz concert" in the Rue Contambert took place only twelve days after a concert in which Nadia Boulanger played the organ. Whether or not Boulanger attended the "jazz concert" is unknown, but she definitely moved in the same orbit at that time. See Kahan, *Music's Modern Muse*, 387.

54. William McBrian, *Cole Porter: A Biography* (New York: Alfred A. Knopf, 1998), 89.

55. On the genesis of *Within the Quota*, see Robert M. Murdock, "Gerald Murphy, Cole Porter, and the Ballets Suédois production of *Within the Quota*," in *Paris Modern: The Swedish Ballet, 1920–1925*, ed. Nancy Van Norman Baer (San Francisco, CA: Fine Arts Museum of San Francisco, 1995), 108–17.

56. Gilbert Seldes, review in *Paris-Journal* (1923), cited in Bengt Häger, *Ballets Suédois* [The Swedish Ballet], trans. Ruth Sharman (New York: Harry N. Abrams, 1990), 212. On Seldes, see Judith Tick, "The Music of Aaron Copland," in *Aaron Copland's America*, ed. Levin and Tick, 142.

57. On the drop cloth, see Gail Levin, "The Ballets Suédois and American Culture," in *Paris Modern*, ed. Van Norman Baer, 120.

58. Gerald Murphy, "Scenarios," cited in Levin, "The Ballets Suédois and American Culture," 120.

59. Aaron Copland to his parents, 25 June 1921, in *Selected Correspondence of Aaron Copland*, ed. Crist and Shirley, 11.

60. McBrian, *Cole Porter*, 91.

61. Darius Milhaud, *Ma vie heureuse* (1973), cited in Häger, *Ballets Suédois*, 212.

62. Pierre de Lapommeraye, review, *Le Ménestrel* 85 (1923): 453–54. At p. 454: "Les Américains, fort nombreux l'autre soir, ont fait un accueil enthousiaste à la musique de leur compatriote M. Cole Porter."

63. Harold Clurman, "American Night at the Swedish Ballet (Letter from Abroad)" (November 1923), in *The Collected Works of Harold Clurman: Six Decades of Commentary on Theatre, Dance, Music, Film, Arts and Letters*, ed. Marjorie Loggia and Glenn Young (New York: Applause Books, 1994), 1006. The editors date the text erroneously as "Nov. '22." On Copland's reading of and commenting on Clurman's Parisian writings, see Clurman's account of their student days in Copland and Perlis, *Copland*, 58.

64. Clurman, "American Night at the Swedish Ballet," 1006.

65. Clurman remembered his visits to Boulanger in *All People Are Famous*, 32–33. In a long letter to Boulanger, dated 4 July 1924, Clurman proclaimed himself as her student, since Copland had repeated his lessons to him in great detail after each of his sessions with Boulanger. Bibliothèque nationale de France, Département de la Musique, call no. N.1.a.62 Clurman.

66. Mark DeVoto, "Melville Smith: Organist, Educator, Early Music Pioneer, and American Composer," in *Perspectives on American Music, 1900–1950* (New York: Garland Publishing, 2000), 265–99. See pp. 267–68 for a letter by Smith to Bernard DeVoto, dated 3 January 1922, in which he writes about his feelings for Boulanger: "The incomparable Nadia is as incomparable as ever. One day, about a month ago, when my feelings were again at the zenith, I had the courage to profess the extent of my affection for her. Since then my feelings towards her have lost much of their sexual stimulus and retained a deep love which I hope will endure."

67. Thus, on 2 June 1923, Melville Smith and Annette Dieudonné come to dinner before all three go out to the movies; four days later, on 6 June, Boulanger attends a Société Musicale Indépendante concert with Copland and the Dutch composer Matthys Vermeulen. See Nadia Boulanger, "Agenda 1923," Bibliothèque nationale de France, Rés.Vmf.ms.91, entries for 2 and 6 June 1923.

68. According to Rosenstiel, Mario Braggiotti—an "uncommonly handsome Italian-American jazz pianist" who studied with Boulanger in 1923—played jazz in her salon prior to the Wednesday classes, and "she seemed to approve of his jazz playing." See Léonie Rosenstiel, *Nadia Boulanger: A Life in Music* (New York: W. W. Norton, 1982), 167, 170.

69. Spycket, *Nadia Boulanger*, 68: "N'est-ce pas plus simplement la découverte à Fontainebleau de cette jeunesse aux allures libres, d'autant plus exubérante qu'elle est elle-même hors du carcan puritain de son pays, qui l'a en quelque sorte libérée par contagion?"

70. For recent interpretations of Boulanger's teaching, see Caroline Potter, *Nadia and Lili Boulanger* (Aldershot, UK: Ashgate, 2006), 127–47, and Jeanice Brooks, "Performing Autonomy: Modernist Historiographies and the Concerts of Nadia Boulanger" (paper presented at the annual meeting of the American Musicological Society, Washington, DC, 20 October 2005); abstract available at http://www.ams-net.org/Abstracts/2005-DC.pdf.

71. Pollack, *Aaron Copland*, 47.

72. Nadia Boulanger to Aaron Copland, September 1922, Library of Congress, Aaron Copland Collection, box 248: "Si vous voyez quelque chose de *nouveau* qui vous paraisse intéressant, voulez-vous l'acheter pour moi."

73. See Copland and Perlis, *Copland*, 67: "At the period when I was her student, Boulanger had one all-embracing principle, namely, the desirability of aiming first and foremost at the creation of what she called 'la grande ligne' in music. Much was included in that phrase: the sense of forward motion, of flow and continuity in the musical discourse; the feeling for inevitability, for the creating of an entire piece that could be thought of as a functioning entity."

74. Copland, contribution to the *Fontainebleau Alumni Bulletin* (May 1930), cited in Leonard, *The Conservatoire Américain*, 22.

75. Zuck, *A History of Musical Americanism*, 248.

76. Nadia Boulanger, "Lectures on Modern Music," *Rice Institute Pamphlets* 13 (1926): 124.

77. Potter, *Nadia and Lili Boulanger*, 143–44.

Making of an "American" Composer

78. Potter, *Nadia and Lili Boulanger*, 144.

79. Boulanger, "Lectures on Modern Music," 194.

80. For a summary of these discourses, see Carlo Caballero, "Patriotism or Nationalism? Fauré and the Great War," *Journal of the American Musicological Society* 52 (1999): 593–625. On fin-de-siècle music aesthetics in France, see Jann Pasler, "Paris: Conflicting Notions of Progress," in *Man and Music: The Late Romantic Era from the Mid-19th Century to World War I*, ed. Jim Samson (London: Macmillan, 1991), 389–416.

81. Boulanger, "Lectures on Modern Music," 121.

82. On d'Indy's concepts of history, see Catrina Flint de Médicis, "The Schola Cantorum, Early Music, and French Cultural Politics" (PhD diss., McGill University, 2006). See also the contributions of Katharine Ellis ("En Route to Wagner: Explaining d'Indy's Early Musical Pantheon," 111–22) and Annegret Fauser ("Archéologue malgré lui: Vincent d'Indy et les usages de l'histoire," 123–33) to the essay collection *Vincent d'Indy et son temps*, ed. Manuela Schwartz (Liège, Belgium: Mardaga, 2006).

83. "Predicts National School of Music: Nadia Boulanger, French Teacher, Foresees a Distinctly American Type," *New York Times*, 2 January 1925, 19.

84. It seems that Boulanger's view of jazz had shifted in its emphasis by 1928, probably in response to works by her American students, especially Copland's *Music for the Theatre* and *An Immorality* (a choral work she programmed repeatedly), for she declared about the future of music (according to an unreferenced quotation in Rosenstiel, *Nadia Boulanger*, 222), "I believe in the music born of Jazz, in the music born of New York, in the music born also of the sun, the desert, the immense mountains."

85. This reproach was leveled most persistently with respect to the Hollywood movie industry. See Klautke, "Amerikanismus," 83–86.

86. Thomson, *Virgil Thomson*, 54.

87. On the particular elements of Copland's construction of a "usable past," see Pollack, *Aaron Copland*, 107–20.

88. Copland and Perlis, *Copland*, 73.

89. Boulanger, "Lectures on Modern Music," 183: "For several centuries now, we have lived under the tyranny of the bar-line, of a 'strong' beat which recurs at *regular* intervals with insistent monotony. Consequently, we find ourselves helpless when we are forced, as we are so often in Stravinsky's music, to admit another type of rhythm, a rhythm in which the metre is constantly changing and where we are obliged to feel accents as intervals that are no longer regular."

90. Aaron Copland, "Stravinsky's Dynamism (1941, 1967)," in *Aaron Copland: A Reader: Selected Writings, 1923–1972*, ed. Richard Kostelanetz (New York: Routledge, 2004), 163.

91. Copland and Perlis, *Copland*, 73.

92. I am grateful to Elizabeth Crist for pointing out these parallels.

93. Aaron Copland to Nadia Boulanger, 12 August 1923, Library of Congress, Aaron Copland Collection, box 248. The text in question is Gide's 1923 *Dostoïevski: Articles et causeries*. This volume was not part of Copland's library (see the list in Paul Anderson, "'To Become as Human as Possible': The Influence of André Gide on Aaron Copland," in *Aaron Copland and His World*, ed. Oja and Tick, 68). Walther Rathenau (1867–1922) was a prominent Jewish industrialist and one of the founders of the German Democratic Party (DDP). He became minister of reconstruction in 1921 and was assassinated by two right-wing army officers on 24 June 1922.

94. Copland to Boulanger, 12 August 1923: "Le Ravel et le Stravinsky que vous et moi—je veux dire nous—(nous autres Français!)—connaissons depuis longtemps, ont été acclamés par toute la salle.... Je suis bien sûr qu'on a joué Kilpinen parce qu'il est finlandais et Whithorne parce qu'il est américain et de même pour plusieurs autres. Naturellement, le monde ayant tant besoin d'internationalisme en ces jours-ci, on *peut* le supporter; mais c'est de la mauvaise musique tout de même!"

95. Several of Copland's letters to Boulanger are published in *Selected Correspondence of Aaron Copland*, ed. Crist and Shirley. The quoted letter of 12 June 1924 appears on p. 41.

96. Copland and Perlis, *Copland*, 67.

97. Marion Bauer, "L'influence du 'jazz-band,'" *La revue musicale* 5 (1 April 1924): 31–36.

98. Bauer, "L'influence du 'jazz-band,'" 31: "Pour le 'rat des champs' le paysage n'a pas la même valeur que pour le 'rat de ville.' Il en va de même pour la 'jazz' en Amérique: on danse, on s'amuse, on l'entend partout sans s'apercevoir qu'il est devenu *une* langue nationale, même s'il n'est pas *la* langue nationale de chez nous. On dit toujours que nous n'avons pas de musique populaire, mais n'assistons-nous pas à la naissance même d'une musique populaire? (Seulement ce n'est peut-être pas un enfant légitime!) L'Amérique est un amalgame de tous les peuples, mais l'américanisme, facteur psychologique, plus puissant que l'hérédité, est un microbe dont on ne peut éviter l'inoculation. Le 'jazz' est la seule musique du nouveau monde qu'on connaisse en Europe; bien qu'on commence à y entendre, de temps en temps, la musique 'cultivée,' on répète, et non sans raison qu'il n'y a pas de musique proprement américaine en dehors du 'jazz.'"

99. Bauer, "L'influence du 'jazz-band,'" 32: "Le père du 'jazz' est Irving Berlin ... il est très travailleur—et très riche. Bien qu'il ne soit ni nègre ni même Américain de naissance il a le génie du 'jazz.'"

100. That the concept of jazz as specifically African American, rooted in slavery and essentialized as black music, is itself a racialist construct has been argued in Ronald Radano, *Lying Up a Nation: Race and Black Music* (Chicago: University of Chicago Press, 2003).

101. Bauer, "L'influence du 'jazz-band,'" 33: "Et voici encore une chose intéressante à noter: le 'jazz' est la première musique d'Occident qui emploie le *quart de ton*. Y a-t-il là évolution des sons harmoniques ou un retour aux sons naturels?"

102. Copland and Perlis, *Copland*, 90.

103. Bauer, "L'influence du 'jazz-band,'" 36: "Mais ce sont surtout les compositeurs européens d'aujourd'hui qui se jettent sur le 'jazz' comme chiens affamés sur un os: Stravinsky, Milhaud, Casella, Jean Wiéner dans sa *Sonate Syncopée*; et les résultats sont

assez intéressants. Il est évident que la période de l'impressionnisme est passée, et que nous sommes sous le signe d'un réalisme qui reflète la civilisation contemporaine. Le rythme est une manifestation physiologique et matérielle, ce qui reste du sauvage dans l'homme. Aujourd'hui on constate un retour au rythme, à la brutalité, au bruit, réaction contre une période de préciosité et d'intellectualisme."

104. On nineteenth-century theories of music and race, see Fauser, *Musical Encounters*, 146–58.

105. Bauer, "L'influence du 'jazz-band,'" 36: "Le 'jazz' est le véritable enfant de l'époque; mais il ne faut pas oublier qu'il est aussi l'enfant des bas-fonds du monde civilisé et qu'il provient des couches inférieures de la société."

106. In the 1920s Boulanger repeatedly focused on rhythm as a key ingredient of "great" music and its performance. See, for example, her discussion of Beethoven's Seventh Symphony, where she declared: "Une œuvre comme la VIIe vit d'abord par son rythme, là est son élément primordial." Nadia Boulanger, "Concerts Colonne," *Le Monde Musical* 35 (1923): 326. I am grateful to Alexandra Laederich for sharing a copy of this article.

107. Bruno Monsaingeon, *Mademoiselle: Conversations with Nadia Boulanger*, trans. Robyn Marsack (Manchester: Carcanet, 1985), 72–73.

108. Aaron Copland, "Jazz as Folk Music" (1925), referred to in Pollack, *Aaron Copland*, 113. Aaron Copland, "Jazz Structure and Influence (1927)," in *Aaron Copland: A Reader*, ed. Kostelanetz, 83–87.

109. Copland, "Jazz Structure and Influence," 87.

110. Boulanger discusses the difference between exoticism and authenticity in her analysis of Roussel's *Padmâvatî*. See Boulanger, "Lectures on Modern Music," 143–44.

111. Copland, "Jazz Structure and Influence," 87.

112. Aaron Copland to Leonard Bernstein, 7 December 1938, in *Selected Correspondence of Aaron Copland*, ed. Crist and Shirley, 126.

113. Aaron Copland, "1926: America's Young Men of Promise," in *Aaron Copland: A Reader*, ed. Kostelanetz, 171–76.

114. Sessions, "An American Evening Abroad," 36.

115. Crist, "Copland and the Politics of Americanism," 284–85, and Crist, *Music for the Common Man*, 4–5.

116. Crist, *Music for the Common Man*, 44.

117. Aaron Copland to Mary Lescaze, 13 January 1933, in *Selected Correspondence of Aaron Copland*, ed. Crist and Shirley, 101.

118. Aaron Copland, "The Composer and His Critic" (1932), quoted in Tick, "The Music of Aaron Copland," 147.

119. Crist, *Music for the Common Man*.

CHAPTER 7

"Presenting a Great Truth":
William Grant Still's *Afro-American Symphony* (1930)[1]

Musing from the vantage point of the 1960s, William Grant Still commented on the reasons why he composed his *Afro-American Symphony*: "I knew I wanted to write a symphony; I knew that it had to be an *American* work; and I wanted to demonstrate how the *Blues*, so often considered a lowly expression, could be elevated to the highest musical level."[2] Taken together with another, earlier comment that he had hoped for "presenting a great truth" in his first symphony (of five), Still's retrospective remark situated his perhaps most famous composition in a conceptual framework that drew on several key tenets of both transnational and Americanist discourses about music during the 1930s.[3] Here he addressed not only the work's genre and its nationalist agenda, but also formulated an emphatic claim to sounding *Weltanschauung* at its most categorical. As Hermann Danuser has shown in numerous influential texts, the aesthetic and political categories of genre, musical nationalism, and *Weltanschauung* proffer a referential net whose interwoven strands characterize the cultural field of musical production and reception as they change their patterns in accordance to shifts in specific historical, geographical, and aesthetic conditions.[4] In the case of Still's *Afro-American Symphony*, these categories – as formulated by Danuser – provide a set of markers that allow for reading the work in a transnational horizon of musical modernism instead of focusing primarily on its ethnic and local particularity.[5] In the following remarks, I will focus on two crucial such markers – 1930s musical popu-

---

1 This essay originated in Berlin during my year as a fellow at the Wissenschaftskolleg. It benefited not only from the input of the Wiko Study Group dedicated to "The Fatigue of Avant-garde Movements and the Emergence of New Paradigms in Art and Culture in the 1930s" (lead by Boris Gasparov and Galin Tihanov), but also from renewed musicological conversation with Hermann Danuser on such varied topics as *Weltanschauungsmusik*, musical nationalism, and the symphony as genre. I also owe thanks to Tim Carter and Carol J. Oja for their thoughtful comments on this text.

2 Cited in Paul Harold Slattery, "The Symphonic Works," in *William Grant Still and the Fusion of Cultures in American Music*, second and revised edition, ed. Judith Anne Still and Robert Bartlett Haas (Flagstaff/Az.: The Master-Player Library, 1995), 101.

3 William Grant Still stated this as a key goal for his *Afro-American Symphony* in a set of notes addressed to Harold Bruce Forsythe in 1933, given in Judith Tick, *Music in the USA: A Documentary Companion* (Oxford and New York: Oxford University Press, 2008), 440-42 (quotation at p. 442).

4 Among Hermann Danuser's numerous publications pertinent for this essay are *Die Musik des 20. Jahrhunderts* (Laaber: Laaber Verlag, 1984); "Auf der Suche nach einer nationalen Musikästhetik," in *Amerikanische Musik seit Charles Ives: Interpretationen, Quellentexte, Komponistenmonographien*, ed. Hermann Danuser, Dietrich Kämper, and Paul Terse (Laaber: Laaber Verlag, 1987), 51-59; "Gattung," in *Die Musik in Geschichte und Gegenwart*, ed. Ludwig Finscher, Sachteil, vol. 3 (Kassel: Bärenreiter, 1995), 1042-69; "Rewriting the Past: Classicism of the Inter-War Period," in *The Cambridge History of Twentieth-Century Music*, ed. Nicholas Cook and Anthony Pople (Cambridge: Cambridge University Press, 2004), 260-85; and *Weltanschauungsmusik* (Schliengen: Edition Argus, 2009).

5 Though framing her assessment in an Americanist framework (rather than the transnational one that I am pursuing in this essay), Carol J. Oja similarly emphasizes the work's modernist aspects in her "'New Music' and the 'New Negro': The Background of William Grant Still's 'Afro-American Symphony'," *Black Music Research Journal* 12/2 (Autumn 1992), 145-69. For recent interpretations that privilege local and ethnic particularity, see, for example, Gayle Minetta Murchison, *Nationalism in William Grant Still and Aaron Copland Between the Wars:*

lism on the one hand, and the genre of the symphony, on the other – both of which stand in direct correlation to the *Afro-American Symphony*'s overarching character as *Weltanschauungsmusik*.

When William Grant Still wrote his *Afro-American Symphony* in 1930, he had already gained considerable exposure among the New York set of avant-garde composers. A protégé of his teacher, Edgard Varèse, he was one of the most frequently performed composers in the modernist concert series of the International Composers' Guild, and such well-known conductors as Leopold Stokowski and Howard Hanson started to champion his works.[6] Still had come to New York after studies at Oberlin College and several years of playing in popular-music orchestras conducted by, among others, William C. Handy, Paul Whiteman, and Artie Shaw. In New York, he found himself in the situation of numerous other African American artists who had to straddle the "distinct yet intersecting" worlds of Harlem and Manhattan both musically and professionally.[7] This dual citizenship in an African American orbit, on the one hand, and a mostly white and internationally identified musical modernism, on the other, had a profound impact on Still's musical choices as a composer.[8] He addressed this dualism repeatedly in his writings and integrated it into a dialectical representation of his compositional development.[9] Accordingly, he started out composing in the "ultramodern idiom" of Manhattan, when he sought to combine traditional African American music with the musical modernism advocated by Varèse. This was followed, in the later 1920s and early 1930s, by his "racial idiom," as he returned to a more tonal language and fused it with African American folk forms. The two strands were sublated in his third approach, starting in the mid 1930s and termed his "universal idiom," as a way to integrate specific African American issues with the universal concerns of (contemporary) art. As a work marking simultaneously the culmination of his "race idiom" and pointing self-consciously toward the universalism foregrounded in his more synthetic approach, Still's *Afro-American Symphony* was – in his own judgment – a disappointment: he had tried to create a work "of value to mankind in general," yet "this symphony approaches but does not attain to the profound symphonic work I hope to write."[10]

Still's strategies for creating his *magnum opus* consisted in the fusion of the classical, four-movement symphony with thematic material and formal strategies

---

Style and Ideology, Ph.D. dissertation, Yale University, 1998, 293-334; Jon Michael Spencer, *The New Negroes and Their Music: The Success of the Harlem Renaissance* (Knoxville: University of Tennessee Press, 1997), 72-106; Gayle Murchison, "'Dean of Afro-American Composers' or 'Harlem Renaissance Man': The New Negro and the Musical Poetics of William Grant Still," in *William Grant Still: A Study in Contradictions*, ed. Catherine Parsons Smith (Berkeley: University of California Press, 2000), 39-65; Catherine Parsons Smith, "The *Afro-American Symphony* and Its Scherzo," in ibid., 114-51; Catherine Parsons Smith, *William Grant Still* (Urbana/Chicago: University of Illinois Press, 2008), esp. 48-51.

6 Oja, "'New Music' and the 'New Negro'," 149-50.
7 Ibid., 146.
8 This dual identity is one of the key topics in the secondary literature discussing William Grant Still and his music, in particular the texts cited in footnote 5. In addition, one analysis of the *Afro-American Symphony* uses this dualism as its analytical lens; see Paul-Elliott Cobbs, *William Grant Still's "The Afro-American Symphony": A Culturally Inclusive Perspective*, D.M.A. dissertation, University of Washington, 1990.
9 Murchison (in "'Dean of Afro-American Composers'," 46-60) organizes her discussion of Still's music along these categories.
10 Still (1933), cited in Tick, *Music in the USA*, 442.

signifying African American culture. He started composition on 30 October 1930 and completed the score on 9 January 1931.[11] The economic fall-out from the Great Depression had deprived Still of several of his free-lance jobs, leaving him more than two months of almost uninterrupted time to dedicate himself to this large-scale composition. About twenty-eight minutes long, the work's four movements are: I. Moderato assai (Longing); II. Adagio (Sorrow); III. Animato (Humor); IV. Lento, con risoluzione (Aspiration). Oscillating between A flat major and F minor, the symphony blends tonal and modal (mostly Dorian) harmony and draws on both African American and neoclassical idioms. It was premièred on 29 October 1931 by the Rochester Philharmonic Orchestra, conducted by Howard Hanson, who also directed the work's second performance in March 1932 (again in Rochester) as well as its third performance in January 1933, which took place in Berlin with the Berlin Philharmonic Orchestra.[12] By 1937, it had been performed by the principal orchestras of New York, Philadelphia, and Chicago.

Still's evident problem was how to cement the fusion he obviously sought in his new work. Clearly, he turned to the authority of Europe not only for the work's genre but also in its invocation of the transcendental. Not for nothing did Still refer to Johann Sebastian Bach's well-known gesture when he inscribed his score "With humble thanks to God, the source of inspiration."[13] Furthermore, he decided to accompany each movement with verses by the famed African American poet, Paul Laurence Dunbar, to underpin the Symphony's musical narrative in the mold of the Beethovenian formula *per aspera ad astra*.[14] For the "Afro-American" elements, however, Still faced the difficulty of what might best serve as ethnic underpinning. He considered the music most often identified with African American culture, the Spiritual, as tainted by "the influence of Caucasian music."[15] (It is not clear whether this taint, to Still's mind, was because of the influence of hymnody or of its associations with slavery.) In contrast, Still felt that the Blues was "the secular folk music of the American Negro" and therefore better suited to furnish an authentic African American voice, despite its perceived triviality as a genre. Therefore, underlying his Symphony's cyclical structure and use of developing variation is a twelve-bar theme that evokes in its melodic contour, harmonization, and rhythm the famous *St Louis Blues* composed by Still's former mentor, Handy (Figure 1). With Beethoven on one side, and Handy on the other, Still's Symphony thus carries several emphatic messages, the somewhat heavy-handed ostentation of which puts it at the vanguard of populist composition in the 1930s in the U.S.

One especially striking American development of music at this time, as Hermann Danuser has shown, was the emergence of an aggressively nationalist musical popu-

---

11 For detailed information on the chronology of the work's genesis, see Smith, "The *Afro-American Symphony* and Its Scherzo."
12 Judith Anne Still, Michael J. Dabrishus, and Carolyn L. Quin, *William Grant Still: A Bio-Bibliography* (Westport, Conn.: Greenwood Press, 1996), 50–51.
13 William Grant Still, *Afro-American Symphony* (New York: J. Fischer & Bro., 1935), flyleaf.
14 Danuser discusses the narrative implications of similar compositional strategies in Franz Liszt, especially his *Die Ideale*; see Danuser, *Weltanschauungsmusik*, 121–30. For a detailed analysis of Still's poetry selection, see Smith, "The *Afro-American Symphony* and Its Scherzo," 124–27.
15 Still, draft foreword for the *Afro-American Symphony* (1931), given in Smith, "The *Afro-American Symphony* and Its Scherzo," 121.

Figure 1: William Grant Still, *Afro-American Symphony*, Blues Theme and Harmonic Scheme (mm. 7–8).

lism around 1930.[16] While this populist turn was neither unique nor exclusive to U.S. culture, some of its aspects were nevertheless locally specific, as is borne out in the *Afro-American Symphony*.[17] Among the shared traits of this cultural shift across the Western world were two trends in particular: the turn towards cultural roots, and the appropriation of a classical heritage for the nation. The turning to roots came to prominence during the 1930s in innumerable ways: take, for example, craft revivals (from quilting to ceramics), developments in folklore research (Béla Bartók and John Lomax are well-known cases for music), or the search for embodied history (as in the semantic paleography of Olga Freidenberg in the Soviet Union).[18] But in order to reground art (including music) in each nation's specific identity, it was not enough to simply draw on folk motives or local and national historic markers. Perhaps even more essential for claiming national cultural preeminence was the "great appropriation" of world culture.[19] In the Soviet Union, for example, high-profile edition and translation projects served to frame the heritage of Western literature in the context of the Marxist-Leninist ethos, following the founding, in 1931, of a new scholarly serial, *Literaturnoe Nasledstvo* ("Literary Heritage").[20] Across the Atlantic, also in the 1930s, Mortimer Adler and Robert Hutchins started to push the "great books" program at the University of Chicago as a foundational curriculum of American higher education.[21] Parallel to this appropriation of the world's literary legacy, the large-scale classicism of new representational architecture integrated the stylistic heritage of the past into

---

16 Danuser, "Auf der Suche nach einer nationalen Musikästhetik," 56.

17 For a general discussion of parallel developments in the U.S., Germany, and Italy, see Wolfgang Schivelbusch, *Entfernte Verwandtschaft: Faschismus, Nationalsozialismus, New Deal, 1933–1939* (München and Wien: Hanser, 2005). In *Die Musik des 20. Jahrhunderts* (pp. 166–94), Danuser explores this international shift for music.

18 One example presenting the variety of craft revivals in the U.S. is the exhibition catalogue, *Revivals! Diverse Traditions, 1920–1945: The History of Twentieth-Century American Craft*, ed. Janet Kardon (New York: Harry N. Abrams, 1994).

19 I am borrowing this term from Katerina Clark, "From Production Sketches to 'World Literature/World Culture': The Search for a Grander Narrative," paper presented at the international conference, "From Building the Future to an Evolving Present: The Emergence of New Cultural Paradigms on the Turn of the 1930s," Berlin, Freie Universität and Wissenschaftskolleg, 25–26 June 2010.

20 I am grateful to Galin Tihanov for sharing this information with me.

21 Joan Shelley Rubin, *The Making of Middlebrow Culture* (Chapel Hill and London: University of North Carolina Press. 1992), 188–90.

the grand visual narratives of 1930s projects such as the Palais Chaillot in Paris, the Italian Embassy in Berlin, or the National Archives building in Washington, D.C. Indeed, when President Herbert Hoover laid the foundation stone, in 1933, for the new National Archives, a neo-Palladian "temple" on the capital's mall, it was intended "for one of the most beautiful buildings in America, an expression of the American soul," which was to provide a dignified frame for "the romance of our history."[22] Just like classical architecture and literature, "classical" music played a significant role during that decade in the making of "middlebrow" culture in the U.S. (to use a term popularized in 1933 by Margaret Widdemer).[23] Prepared by countless music appreciation books and radio shows, American audiences consumed Beethoven and Rachmaninov as the well-publicized products of the booming recording industry and the radio.[24]

When Still set out to write his *Afro-American Symphony*, these trends were just starting to emerge, however. His circle of colleagues in New York began to embrace a new, politically motivated simplicity as their populist paradigm, whether Aaron Copland (who would later coin the term "imposed simplicity") or Elie Siegmeister.[25] Yet while Still shared this strategic turn toward "middlebrow" music on the part of his Manhattan colleagues, his motivation lay not in the Popular Front ideals soon to become rampant in post-Depression New York, but, rather, in the ideologies associated with the Harlem Renaissance, whose key intellectuals formed part of the international discourse network on cultural identity formation in the 1920s and '30s.[26] This movement focused on cross-cultural translation of African American culture to and from mainstream modernism in order to "create a cohesive, collective, and modern Black identity."[27] Part of this identity project was the search of "authentic" Black cultural roots, including musical forms not mediated by White America. Here

---

22 Herbert Hoover (22 February 1933). The speech is transcribed at John T. Woolley and Gerhard Peters, eds., *The American Presidency Project* (www.presidency.ucsb.edu/ws/?pid=23434).

23 Rubin, *The Making of Middlebrow Culture*, XII–XIII.

24 On the role of the phonograph in this process, see Mark Katz, "Making America More Musical through the Phonograph, 1900–1930," *American Music* 16 (1998): 448–76. On music appreciation in 1930s America, see Rebecca Meador Bennett, *The Anxiety of Appreciation: Virgil Thomson Wrestles with a "Racket,"* Ph.D. dissertation, Northwestern University, 2009. See also the overview of music criticism's take on music appreciation in Mark N. Grant, *Maestros of the Pen: A History of Classical Music Criticism in America* (Boston: Northeastern University Press, 1998), 195–225.

25 On the concept of "imposed simplicity" in Copland's aesthetic, see Elizabeth B. Crist, *Music for the Common Man: Aaron Copland during the Depression and War* (Oxford and New York: Oxford University Press, 2005), 5; on Siegmeister's populism, see Carol J. Oja, "Composer with a Conscience: Elie Siegmeister in Profile," *American Music* 6 (1988): 158–80. As Giselher Schubert points out, "new simplicity" (Prokofiev's term in a 1930 interview with the *Los Angeles Express*) was one of the key characteristics of the international crop of works commissioned by Serge Koussevitzky for the fiftieth anniversary of the Boston Symphony Orchestra; see Giselher Schubert, "Symphonische Ausdrucksformen um 1930: Das Beispiel der zum 50jährigen Jubiläum des Boston Symphony Orchestra geschriebenen Werke," in *Symphonik, 1930–1950: Gattungsgeschichtliche und analytische Beiträge*, ed. Wolfgang Osthoff and Giselher Schubert (Mainz: Schott, 2003), 12–27.

26 The literature on the intellectual and artistic developments during the Harlem Renaissance is proliferating. For a recent overview, see *The Cambridge Companion to the Harlem Renaissance*, ed. George Hutchinson (Cambridge: Cambridge University Press, 2007). On transatlantic intellectual and artistic exchange, see Paul Gilroy's still foundational *The Black Atlantic: Modernity and Double Consciousness* (Cambridge, Mass.: Harvard University Press, 1993).

27 Daphne Mary Lamothe, *Inventing the New Negro: Narrative, Culture, and Ethnography* (Philadelphia: University of Pennsylvania Press, 2008), 1.

the Blues – with its mystique as a rural genre grounded in the toiling of post-Reconstruction soil – played a particularly important role.[28] Still made this point, when he explained that, in the case of the Blues, "the pathos of their melodic content bespeaks the anguish of human hearts."[29] Even though the Blues was cast here as embodying universal emotion (and hence suitable for cultural translation in the context of the Harlem Renaissance), Still's point of reference was, however, the "authentic" African American life experience of a mythologized South:

> "I seek in the *Afro-American Symphony* to portray not the higher type of colored American, but the sons of the soil, who still retain so many of the traits peculiar to their African forebears; who have not responded completely to the transforming effect of progress. Therefore, the employment of a decidedly characteristic idiom is not only logical but also necessary."[30]

As Still explained in a 1931 letter to the music critic Irving Schwerké (a regular correspondent with many U.S. composers):

> "From the hearts of these people sprang Blues, plaintive songs reminiscent of African tribal chants. I do not hesitate to assert that Blues are more purely Negroid in character than very many spirituals."[31]

These two comments are revealing insofar as they situate Still squarely in the ethnographic project of the Harlem Renaissance, when African American scholars, writers, and artists found themselves "at the borders of American interracial and cross-cultural encounters," speaking simultaneously to both Black and White audiences.[32] These Black translation projects of African and African-derived cultures in the U.S. served both to define historical, cultural, and geographical origins as part of a modern, African American identity, and to address and instrumentalize the Western fascination with the so-called "primitive," while subverting it from a Black perspective in addressing stereotypes and posing the question of legitimacy.

Still had to develop a style that could serve as a medium for his deliberately African American compositions. As he wrote in 1931:

> "I feel it is best for me to confine myself to composition of a racial nature. The music of my people is the music I understand best. It offers the medium through which I can express myself with greater clarity and ease."[33]

The idea of cultural translation can also be seen as the key to his turn to a more accessible compositional idiom. His brand of musical populism was guided by the

---

28 On the perception of the rural Blues as authentic African American expression, see Tammy Kernodle, "Having Her Say: The Blues as the Black Woman's Lament," in *Women's Voices Across Musical Worlds*, ed. Jane Bernstein (Boston: Northeastern University Press, 2003), 213–31.

29 Still, draft foreword for the *Afro-American Symphony* (1931), given in Smith, "The *Afro-American Symphony* and Its Scherzo," 121.

30 Still, undated early commentary on the *Afro-American Symphony*, cited in Smith, "The *Afro-American Symphony* and Its Scherzo," 122.

31 Still, letter to Irving Schwerké, dated 5 October 1931, cited in Wayne Shirley, "William Grant Still and Irving Schwerké: Documents from a Long-Distance Friendship," in *William Grant Still: A Study in Contradictions*, ed. Catherine Parsons Smith (Berkeley: University of California Press, 2000), 238–69, at p. 245.

32 Lamothe, *Inventing the New Negro*, 1.

33 Still, untitled essay (dated by Murchison as 1931), cited in Murchison, *Nationalism in William Grant Still and Aaron Copland Between the Wars*, 297.

need to make audible the African American heritage for the lay listener who might either be repelled by the "ultra-modernistic and too sophisticated" modernist idiom (so Alain Locke characterized it in 1936) or unable to discern the specific African American side of the composition: "Experiments proved to me," as Still explained looking back in 1966, "that the Negroid idiom tends to lose its identity when subjected to such [ultra-modernist] treatment."[34] The difficulty, however, was how to turn musical materials drawn from oral tradition to symphonic ends: in a letter to Schwerké, he declared that "as I see it the music of the American Negro has resulted from the union of the religious songs you mentioned and the primitive songs of Africa."[35] Yet the introduction of such pastoral simplicity into the modern and, to all intent and purposes, urban musical idiom of Manhattan posed new challenges. In another letter to Schwerké, Still pondered on the compositional consequences of using this music as source material:

> "These are an humble people. Their wants are few and are generally childlike. Theirs are lives of utter simplicity. Therefore no complex or elaborate scheme or harmonization would prove benefitting in a musical picture of them. 'Tis only the simpler harmonies, such as those employed, that can accurately portray them."[36]

Soon thereafter, in a short statement published in 1933, Still affirmed that

> "colored people in America have a natural and deep-rooted feeling for music, for melody, harmony, and rhythm. Our music possesses exoticism without straining for strangeness. Our natural practices in this music open up a new field which can be of value in larger musical works when constructed into organized form by a composer who, having the underlying feeling, develops it through his intellect."[37]

What saved Still from mere condescension – in addition to his own ethnic authority – and granted plausibility to his enterprise was the fact that "exoticism" without "strangeness," and "intellect" underpinned by "feeling," represented values in sympathy with emerging anti-modernist tendencies in both the U.S. and Europe ("ultra-modernistic" music being defined as "strange" and overly dominated by "intellect"). Besides the populist claim of broader accessibility to his African American inspired compositions, Still's turn toward traditional harmony and form in these works carried thus a second, ideological justification: the simple harmonies and melodic character that he ascribed to Black folk music – in particular the Blues – were perceived as incompatible with ultra-modernist atonality and therefore required the turn toward a more middlebrow style that ploughed the cultural high-ground yet in a user-friendly way. His argumentation parallels not only similar concerns of, for example, the anti-formalism that gained significant momentum in the U.S.S.R. at around the same time, but also contemporaneous debates in South and Latin America, lead by such composers as Silvestre Rivueltas and Carlos Chavez (both also linked to Varèse's In-

---

34 Still, "American Art and Culture: The Negro's Contribution" (1966), cited in Murchison, "'Dean of Afro-American Composers'," 49. On Still's turn to musical populism, see also Murchison, *Nationalism in William Grant Still and Aaron Copland Between the Wars*, 293–95.

35 Still, letter to Irving Schwerké, dated 29 July 1931, cited in Shirley, "William Grant Still and Irving Schwerké," 243.

36 Still, letter to Irving Schwerké, dated 5 October 1931, cited in Ibid., 245.

37 Still, "An Afro-American Composer's Viewpoint" (1933), reproduced in *William Grant Still and the Fusion of Cultures in American Music*, ed. Still and Haas, 52.

ternational Composers' Guild). Indeed, Still's vision of musical populism shared with these and other groups both the shift to tonal and modal idioms, and the turn toward large-scale traditional concert forms such as the symphonic poem (for example in Still's *Africa*, also 1930) and the symphony.

In the early 1930s in the U.S., the allure of the symphony as a genre was twofold: on the one hand, it was a classical form within which to pour a nationally coded musical "heritage," just as classical architecture could be instrumentalized for the conservation of the nation's greatest treasures in the new National Archives. This jibed with Still's desire to write a specifically "American" work in this particular symphony. One the other side, the genre's exalted status as the culmination of transnational universalism made it particularly suitable for his project of racial uplift by working with thematic material and syntactic procedures marked as African American.[38] The *Afro-American Symphony* can thus be read as a textbook example for the particularly American pathway of symphonic composition of this period, as Hermann Danuser identified it in the transnational framework of his *Die Musik des 20. Jahrhunderts*. Therein he situates the genre in the U.S. as developing in a field shaped simultaneously by reference to folklore and universalist tendencies, appropriating the genre for the artistic validation of nationalist populism.[39] One might add that this dual reference to local particularity and universalist form was a central strategy employed by American critics to cast individual symphonies composed between 1893 and 1950 as the musical equivalent of the "great American novel," a literary genre that had gained new currency in the 1920s and whose conceptual matrix focused on realist story-telling, especially – as Lawrence Buell pointed out – because of "related phenomena of multiple ethno-literary renaissances starting in the 1920s."[40] However, we are also dealing, in Still's case if not elsewhere, with more than just a compiling and combining of references; rather, the question – or the problem – was one of would-be integration in an aesthetic and even perhaps political sense of the term. Indeed, Still's symphony bears the hallmarks of the genre not only in his grounding of the work in the musical realities of the Blues but also through his self-consciousness with respect to the traditional symphonic form including its post-Beethovenian penchant for thematic unity. In a letter to Irving Schwerké in October 1931, Still presented the various derivations of the Blues theme for each of the four movements.[41] Similarly, he stressed thematic unity in his 1931 draft preface for the symphony where he pointed out that the Blues theme

> "is employed originally as the principal theme of the first movement. It appears also in various forms in the succeeding movements, where I have sought to present it in a characteristic (style) manner."[42]

---

38 Oja was the first to emphasize the role of racial "uplift" in Still's symphonic projects. See Carol J. Oja, *Making Music Modern: New York in the 1920s* (Oxford and New York: Oxford University Press, 2000), 456.

39 Danuser, *Die Musik des 20. Jahrhunderts*, 224.

40 See Julie Schnepel, *The Critical Pursuit of the Great American Symphony: 1893-1950*, Ph.D. diss., Indiana University, 1995; Lawrence Buell, "The Unkillable Dream of the Great American Novel: *Moby Dick* as Test Case," *American Literary History* 20 (2008): 132-55, at p. 140.

41 Still, letter to Irving Schwerké, dated 5 October 1931, cited in Shirley, "William Grant Still and Irving Schwerké," 245-46.

42 Still, draft foreword for the *Afro-American Symphony* (1931), given in Smith, "The *Afro-American Symphony* and Its Scherzo," 121.

How self-conscious Still was about the normative concepts of the symphony shines through in the defensive tone of a 1939 comment when he noted:

> "When judged by the laws of musical form the Symphony is somewhat irregular. This irregularity is in my estimation justified since it has no ill effect on the proportional balance of the composition."

After remarking on the freedom afforded by society to architects and other artists, Still claimed that one could "hardly deny a composer the privilege of altering established forms as long as the sense of proportion is justified."[43] The argument was particularly necessary, however, because of Still's ultimate ambition:

> "I wanted to prove conclusively that the negro musical idiom is an important part of the world's musical culture. That was the reason I decided to create a musical theme in the Blues idiom and develop it into the highest of musical forms – the symphony."[44]

Even though this last comment stems from the late 1960s, it offers the final piece of the puzzle of Still's *Afro-American Symphony* as both an American and transnational work in this weighty genre. Contrary to Günter Moseler's claim that U.S. composers sported an "altogether unburdened" approach to the symphony, Still's example shows that American concepts of the genre carried, at least in the 1930s, an ideological burden similar to – and sometimes even heavier than – European ones.[45] If the symphony is cast as "the highest of musical forms" and – to return to the quotation at the beginning of this essay – is presented as the medium that would enable a genuinely African American idiom (in Still's reckoning) to "be elevated to the highest musical level," then it is exactly the universal authority ascribed to the genre and its global historic lineage that served as validation for the *Afro-American Symphony* in terms of inserting an African American musical language into the transnational horizon of concert music, rather than merely aiming to carve out a place for Black music in the limited context of White America.

Over the past twenty years, scholars have acknowledged the purposely transatlantic focus of Harlem Renaissance aesthetics.[46] Inserting Black culture into a transnational discourse network offered a third space that allowed for bypassing some of the fraught bi-racial dichotomies that dominated American culture, especially

---

43 Still, comments (1939) on the *Afro-American Symphony*, given in Tick, *Music in the USA*, 442.

44 Still, untitled speech (1968), cited after Murchison, *Nationalism in William Grant Still and Aaron Copland Between the Wars*, 296. Neither Murchison nor Smith, Slattery, Avery, and Cobbs discuss the genre's ideological power and instead refer to the symphony mostly as a textbook-derived formal concept. For a reflection of genre in the *Afro-American Symphony* that addresses briefly some aspects of the symphony in the U.S., see Orin Moe, "A Question of Value: Concert Music and Criticism," *Black Music Research Journal* 6 (1986): 57–66, esp. pp. 61–64.

45 Günter Moseler, "Die Symphonie in den Vereinigten Staaten," in *Die Symphonie im 19. und 20. Jahrhundert*, ed. Wolfram Steinbeck and Christoph von Blumröder (Laaber: Laaber Verlag, 2002), 176–93, at p. 176. Douglas Shadle demonstrated to what extent the American engagement with the post-Beethovenian symphony was fraught with ideological implications even in the nineteenth century; see his *Music of a More Perfect Union: Symphonic Constructions of American National Identity, 1840–1870*, Ph.D. dissertation, University of North Carolina at Chapel Hill, 2010.

46 See, in particular, Gilroy, *The Black Atlantic*; Michael North, *The Dialect of Modernism: Race, Language and Twentieth-Century Literature* (Oxford and New York: Oxford University Press, 1994).

among the avant-garde, in the interwar years.[47] In the case of Still's *Afro-American Symphony*, this aesthetic context bore fruit not only in his compositional strategies but also in the work's musical and programmatic claim to embody *Weltanschauung* in its very structure. Indeed, musical and ideological goals are tightly intertwined in the symphony. Read in a transnational instead of a simply national horizon, recent analytical observations on Still's formal fusion of Blues transformations with symphonic development throughout the Symphony take on a more powerful meaning.[48] By fusing Blues and Symphony on a structural level rather than simply integrating autochthonous material into a symphonic structure (as one might describe such contemporaneous works as Charles Ives' third and fourth symphonies or Virgil Thomson's *Symphony on a Hymn Tune*), Still's *Afro-American Symphony* adopts a double-voicing of form that inscribes the politics of racial uplift into the musical text itself.

Although Still's Symphony is often considered as epitomizing his return to tradition, it also pushes the boundaries of symphonic composition in the U.S. in intriguing ways. For example, the cherished post-Beethovenian concept of motivic unity is no longer justified by symphonic tradition alone, but by the very essence of the Blues, a genre whose meaning stems from its transformation in performance. This can be used both for understanding motivic and musical development within each movement and for grounding the overarching structure for the symphony as a whole. Read in this way, the Blues becomes the mirror image of the symphony as genre: noble in its own right. Indeed, if we take seriously Still's explicit and also implicit claims to elevating the Blues – and, by extension, African American musical traditions – in the *Afro-American Symphony*, then his compositional double-voicing in this work may well be read as aiming to "presenting a great truth" in the music itself. In effect, *Weltanschauung* remains not simply an extrinsic part of the symphony's program but becomes the *raison d'être* for Still's compositional choices. At that point, his championing of Black musical populism by way of classical forms – and his championing of classical forms by way of Black musical populism – has a subversive inevitability wholly in keeping with the Harlem Renaissance agenda writ large. Still not only seeks to ennoble the Blues through fusion with the universalist genre of the symphony, but lends necessary new life to the venerable genre by grounding it in the soil tended by rural African Americans. The "great American symphony," as it were, must then be, precisely, the *Afro-American*.

---

[47] The attraction of Europe particularly to jazz musicians offers a slightly different pathway to relate to this escape from bi-racial intracultural tension. See, for example, William A. Shack, *Harlem in Montmartre: A Paris Jazz Story between the Great Wars* (Berkeley, Los Angeles, and London: University of California Press, 2001), and Jeffrey H. Jackson, *Making Jazz Modern: Music and Modern Life in Interwar Paris* (Durham and London: Duke University Press, 2003).

[48] The most extensive analytical descriptions can be found in Murchison, *Nationalism in William Grant Still and Aaron Copland Between the Wars*; Smith, "The *Afro-American Symphony* and Its Scherzo"; Cobbs, "William Grant Still's *The Afro-American Symphony*". Orin Moe's comment ("A Question of Value: Concert Music and Criticism," 64) that it is "more fruitful to approach this work as a blues-dominated symphony rather than symphonically dominated blues" hints at the issue in question.

CHAPTER 8

"Dixie *Carmen*": War, Race, and Identity in Oscar Hammerstein's *Carmen Jones* (1943)

Abstract
In December 1943, an all–African American cast starred in the Broadway premiere of Carmen Jones, *Oscar Hammerstein II's adaptation of Georges Bizet's* Carmen. *When Hammerstein began work on* Carmen Jones *a month after Pearl Harbor, in January 1942,* Porgy and Bess *was just being revived. Hammerstein's 1942 version of* Carmen, *set in a Southern town and among African Americans, shows the influence of the revised version of* Porgy and Bess, *with Catfish Row echoed in a cigarette factory in South Carolina and the Hoity Toity night club. It took Hammerstein more than eighteen months to find a producer, and when the show opened by the end of 1943, the setting in a parachute factory and urban Chicago reflected new priorities brought on by wartime changes. Commercially one of the most successful musical plays on Broadway during its run of 503 performances,* Carmen Jones *offers a window on the changing issues of culture, class, and race in the United States during World War II. New archival evidence reveals that these topics were part of the work's genesis and production as much as of its reception. This article contextualizes* Carmen Jones *by focusing on the complex issues of war, race, and identity in the United States in 1942 and 1943.*

On 19 October 1943, *Carmen Jones* opened its tryout in Philadelphia before an enthusiastic audience that included numerous visitors from New York. Among them was the Broadway producer and film publicist A. P. Waxman, who congratulated the show's creator, Oscar Hammerstein II, for having produced "a two-fold contribution to American culture. You are the first one to make Opera in English 100% entertainment for the general public. You have also broadened the horizon for Negro talent, and gained for them the increased recognition they are entitled to."[1] Thus Waxman identified key cultural parameters that shaped the creation and reception of *Carmen Jones* during World War II. If, on the one hand,

---

Earlier versions of this article have been presented as a guest lecture at the Peabody Institute of the Johns Hopkins University, Baltimore, and as a keynote address at the 2009 Conference of the Midwest Graduate Music Consortium at Northwestern University in Evanston. I would not have been able to write this text without the generosity of Bruce Pomahac (Musical Director of the Rodgers & Hammerstein Organization), Mark Eden Horowitz and his colleagues of the Library of Congress, Jonathan Hiam (New York Public Library), and George Ferencz (University of Wisconsin–Whitewater). They granted me access to unpublished and sometimes difficult to locate materials and shared vital information. I also owe thanks to Tim Carter, Brigid Cohen, George Ferencz, David Garcia, Ralph P. Locke, Howard Pollack, and my anonymous readers for their thoughtful and inspiring comments about earlier drafts of this study, and to Alice Hammerstein Mathias for sharing with me memories of the first production in an extensive telephone conversation (on 21 April 2009). Furthermore, I am grateful to the National Endowment for the Humanities for support during the creation of this article. The work is characterized as "Dixie *Carmen*" in an unsigned article published in the *Los Angeles Times*, 11 August 1942 ("'Show Boat,' Dixie 'Carmen' Outlined by Hammerstein").

[1] Abraham P. Waxman, letter to Oscar Hammerstein II, 20 October 1943, Library of Congress, Oscar Hammerstein II Collection (hereafter *Wc* OHC). *Wc* OHC is the source of all letters cited in this text save where otherwise indicated. All materials from this collection are published with the permission of the Rodgers & Hammerstein Organization.

Hammerstein's version of Georges Bizet's *Carmen* counted as an important chapter in the vexed history of European opera in the United States of America, on the other, it played a significant role in the long struggle of African American performers to gain access to, and recognition in, mainstream U.S. theaters.[2] Furthermore, both aspects were inextricably intertwined with debates about class and culture, which had become freshly acute during a global war that pitted (at least so far as American public discourse was concerned) democratic ideals against fascist totalitarianism. In crystallizing several key currents of U.S. wartime culture, the 1943 production of *Carmen Jones* provides a unique window on the changing social and political concerns of a country in search of a modern identity at a particular time of anxiety over the intersection of transnational, national, and local concerns.

Overshadowed since the mid-1950s by its glamorous Hollywood offshoot starring Dorothy Dandridge and Harry Belafonte, the 1943 stage production of *Carmen Jones* has received only scant attention from musicologists and theater historians, even though it was—at least in commercial terms—one of the most successful shows on Broadway for its run from 2 December 1943 to 10 February 1945.[3] Neither an autochthonous "folk opera" like the Gershwins' *Porgy and Bess* nor a modernist work in the vein of Gertrude Stein and Virgil Thomson's *Four Saints in Three Acts*, *Carmen Jones* fits none of the categories developed to discuss opera in the United States. Nor does the work fare any better in histories of the Broadway musical, which focus mainly on the two prevalent models of revue-style shows and the "integrated" musical. As a French opera adapted for the Broadway stage and an all–African American cast, *Carmen Jones* falls between the cracks of music historiography, taxing the categories and narratives of musicological discourse on American music.

However, it is precisely the work's resistance to fitting into established historiographical tropes that makes it so powerful both to gain entrance to a specific historico-cultural context and as a challenge to current methodological practice. As Robert L. A. Clark has pointed out, *Carmen Jones* multiplied cultural identities in its transformation from Bizet's French opera mimicking and appropriating Spanish music into an English-language musical play set in the American South.[4]

---

[2] For an assessment of *Carmen Jones* in the context of African American musical theater, see Allen Woll, *Black Musical Theatre: From* Coontown *to* Dreamgirls (Baton Rouge: Louisiana State University Press, 1989), esp. 184–89.

[3] The regular financial tallies in the *New York Times* reflected and commented on the commercial success of the show. Besides Woll (*Black Musical Theatre*), few other authors discuss the 1943 production in any detail. The most extensive references to the Broadway version of *Carmen Jones* can be found in Hugh Fordin, *Getting to Know Him: A Biography of Oscar Hammerstein II* (New York: Random House, 1977), 179–208; and Robert L. A. Clark, "Local Color: The Representation of Race in *Carmen* and *Carmen Jones*," in *Operatic Migrations: Transforming Works and Crossing Boundaries,* ed. Roberta Montemorra Marvin and Downing A. Thomas (Aldershot, England: Ashgate, 2006), 217–39. Benoît Depardieu offers a brief discussion of the 1943 production based mainly on Hammerstein's preface to the printed libretto in his article "*Carmen Jones:* A Carmen 'à la Afro-America'," *Studies in Musical Theatre* 2/1 (December 2008): 223–34. Most of the secondary literature focuses predominantly on Otto Preminger's 1954 film version.

[4] Clark, "Local Color," 217–18. On the Spanish aspects of Bizet's *Carmen,* see Ralph P. Locke, "Spanish Local Color in Bizet's *Carmen:* Unexplored Borrowings and Transformations," in *Music, Theater, and Cultural Transfer: Paris, 1830–1914,* ed. Annegret Fauser and Mark Everist (Chicago: University of Chicago Press, 2009), 316–60.

Dixie *Carmen*

Hammerstein's multilayered act of textual translation was then further compounded in the stage realization when the creative team of the première inserted their own agencies into the show as producer, arranger, choreographer, stage director, dancers, and singers, with the interplay of reception in performance and criticism further enriching the contrapuntal texture of the work. Crossing these converging, but somewhat diverging, acts of creation and transformation were a number of cultural, social, and political currents relating to issues of race, class, language, identity, and artistic authority that established a force field anchored in the wartime United States but spanning the Atlantic in multiple directions and creating an example of what has been called (by Paul Gilroy) a "webbed network between the local and the global."[5] These crosscurrents and intersections resist any one-dimensional interpretation of *Carmen Jones* by challenging such easily essentialized categories as authenticity, ownership, and ethnic particularity.[6]

Of course, *Carmen Jones* was neither the first American adaptation of a European opera, nor unique in its all–African American cast. In particular, the Negro Units of the Federal Theatre Project had been active in adapting European works for African American performers, as, for example, with *Macbeth* in New York (1936), *Fra Diavolo* in Los Angeles (1937), or the *Swing Mikado* in Chicago, New York, and elsewhere across the country (1938).[7] Broadway, too, had its share of African American musical shows, with several produced in proximity to *Carmen Jones* and—in some cases—involving the same personnel.[8] Some had only short runs, including Roark Bradford's *John Henry* (1940, with Paul Robeson in the lead) and the 1943 revival of Hall Johnson's *Run, Little Chillun* (1933). Others, such as Vernon Duke's *Cabin in the Sky* (1940), producer Cheryl Crawford's revival of *Porgy and Bess* (1942), and Katharine Dunham's celebrated *Tropical Review* (1943) proved to be artistically and commercially successful productions. On the other hand, the early 1940s brought thriving Broadway adaptations of European operas and operettas. Most notably *Rosalinda* (alias *Die Fledermaus*) with its highly Gilbertian flavor was very successful, with a run of 611 performances between its première on 28 October 1942 and its final evening on 22 January 1944. Both these African American–cast productions and Americanized European opera thus provided a framework within which Hammerstein's version of Bizet's *Carmen* came to be.

---

[5] Paul Gilroy, *The Black Atlantic: Modernity and Double Consciousness* (Cambridge, Mass.: Harvard University Press, 1993), 29.

[6] For a critique of these issues, see ibid., esp. 29–31 and 96–99; Ronald Radano, *Lying Up a Nation: Race and Black Music* (Chicago: University of Chicago Press, 2003), 10; Ralph P. Locke, "Doing the Impossible: On the Musically Exotic," *Journal of Musicological Research* 27/4 (2008): 334–58.

[7] On the "Haitian" *Macbeth*, see the extensive collection of materials presented on the Library of Congress Web site at http://memory.loc.gov/ammem/fedtp/ftsmth00.html. On the Los Angeles *Fra Diavolo*, see Tim Carter, "Music and the Federal Theater Project: A View from the West Coast," paper presented at the 35th Annual Conference of the Society for American Music, Denver, 2009. Jennifer Myers at Northwestern University is currently researching a Ph.D. on the Chicago Negro Unit's activities as part of Federal Project One between 1935 and 1939, which will include a chapter on *The Swing Mikado*.

[8] For an overview of African American musical plays on Broadway, see Woll, *Black Musical Theatre*.

By the time *Carmen Jones* had its Broadway première on 2 December 1943, it had gone through almost two years of gestation. A first version, completed in July 1942, failed to be produced on Broadway. It set Bizet's *Carmen* in rural North Carolina and—although shortening some of the original—stayed relatively close to the opera's plot, save for the ending. Hammerstein then rewrote the work for the 1943 production, introducing significant changes (including the complete relocation of the work's second half to Chicago). Three broad cultural issues dominate the reception of *Carmen Jones*. As a so-called musical play that transferred Bizet's opera into a setting in the contemporary United States, Hammerstein's book was scrutinized in the context of operatic translations and recent American drama. As the performance of an African American cast, the production evoked a broad response shaped by U.S. notions of black theatrical expressivity and its African roots. Finally, as an operatic soundscape, *Carmen Jones* relocated, at a critical point in time, a particularly prominent European score on Broadway and challenged (while still perhaps reinforcing) concepts of class and race in United States.

Hammerstein's *Carmen Jones*

The souvenir program for *Carmen Jones* offers a brief explanation for the work's genesis. In 1934 Oscar Hammerstein II (see Figure 1)—a man of the musical theater with opera in his veins—had

> heard a concert performance of the opera at the Hollywood Bowl. "Carmen" was played that night without sets or costumes. The principals just got up and sang when their tune came. "The music came through," Mr. Hammerstein remembers. "And so did the story. It dawned on me then that there was something universal about this opera. It would translate. That is what I tried to accomplish in the new libretto and lyrics. I translated them. I did not adapt them. I did not change an essential note."[9]

As brief as the comment may be, it presents a good tale of a solitary visionary's artistic program for the future of great art, one that was revealed to him at a transformational moment in his past. Although Hammerstein's story follows a standard narrative pattern of artistic revelation, it conveys much about his need, in late 1943, to cast *Carmen Jones* as a path-breaking production without peer or precedent when, in effect, it competed not only with *Oklahoma!* (another Hammerstein production that was presented as revolutionary) and Crawford's revival of *Porgy and Bess*, but also with several concurrent adaptations in New York and Philadelphia of European operas in vernacular English, not least *Rosalinda*. Hammerstein's emphasis on his artistic vision and on the uniqueness of *Carmen Jones*, however, was not simply a clever marketing strategy. Rather, his insistence on his artistic authority and

---

[9] *Carmen Jones*, Souvenir Program for the Broadway production premièred on 2 December 1943, 3 (Wc OHC). Hammerstein's grandfather, Oscar Hammerstein (1847–1919), had established, in 1906, the Manhattan Opera House as a rival company to the Metropolitan Opera House. The concert performance of *Carmen* in the Hollywood Bowl and Hammerstein's fascination with its potential can be corroborated through newspaper reports and letters that put him in Los Angeles when Pietro Cimini conducted Bizet's opera in June 1934 and where the playwright discussed a modern adaptation for the cinema with Sam Katz, an MGM musical supervisor. See "Resident Conductors to Present Nights of Opera," *Los Angeles Times*, 27 May 1934, and Fordin, *Getting to Know Him*, 179–80.

Dixie *Carmen* 131

Figure 1. Portrait of Oscar Hammerstein II, published in the souvenir program (1943). Courtesy of the Rodgers & Hammerstein Organization.

innovative approach points toward a quest to validate the complicated period of the work's gestation, begun—as he later put it—at the "lowest part of my slump."[10] Moreover, *Carmen Jones* was "the first time I ever sat down and wrote a play without first arranging for a production with a manager in advance."[11] A lot of symbolic capital thus rode on the originality of his approach.

If the Hollywood Bowl *Carmen* provided the impetus for the project, however, Hammerstein later acknowledged a second key influence that sets *Carmen Jones* into a longer genealogy of *Carmen* adaptations involving African American performers. As he explained in 1959, "I wanted to do a version of 'Lula Belle' [sic], which was the Carmen story, and I had invited Duke Ellington to do the score with me. He was late for an appointment one day, and since he had a night club life and I like to work at 9 o'clock in the morning, I didn't think it would be a happy collaboration, and I abandoned the idea."[12]

Lulu Belle, a four-act play by Edward Sheldon and Charles MacArthur, was produced in 1926 at New York's Belasco Theatre with a cast of over one hundred African American and fifteen Caucasian actors. This adaptation of the *Carmen* story ran for 461 performances, transporting the plot (but only a very small amount of Bizet's music) into the black New York of San Juan Hill and Harlem, with a final act in Paris (where African American singers such as Josephine Baker had

---

[10] "Oscar Hammerstein—June 1959—Typed and transcribed by the Oral History Research Office, Columbia University, NYC," 29 (*Wc* OHC). Hammerstein refers to the years prior to the premières of *Oklahoma!* and *Carmen Jones* (both in 1943) as "slump" because they were marked by a number of failures.

[11] Oscar Hammerstein II, letter to Bill Hammerstein, 25 October 1943.

[12] "Oscar Hammerstein—June 1959," 29.

become famous in recent years).[13] The production saw the press up in arms and the audiences streaming into the theater to see for themselves a show that was dubbed by one incensed critic "the lowest descent of our stage since 'The God of Vengeance,'" a Yiddish play whose entire cast had been arrested on obscenity charges in 1923.[14] Debates in the press focused on the staging on the one hand, and the subject matter on the other. The African American newspapers, especially, were divided over the issue of whether a *Carmen* transferred to the nightclub scene of Harlem was detrimental to the black cause by featuring a Creole vamp cutting a swath of sexual destruction through Harlem and Paris and thus reinforcing white prejudices about African American morals, specifically the myth of the oversexualized woman of mixed race.[15] Yet a number of black newspapers such as the *Chicago Defender* and the *New York Amsterdam News* supported the play because it featured a significant number of African American performers in a major Broadway show: "For the first time in a decade our dramatic actors will have an opportunity to measure talents with the opposite race, at a distance favorable for fair comparison."[16] The lead roles of Lulu and her lovers, however, were performed by white actors in black makeup, which offended Sylvester Russell of the *Pittsburgh Courier*, who accused the show of discrimination for not casting the leads with African American actors as well.[17] The majority of critics across the spectrum of the press, however, focused on the actors' ability to perform the roles in a dramatically credible fashion, though the difference between white leads and African American supporting cast was emphasized even in otherwise supportive reviews.[18]

Actress Evelyn Mason was enthusiastic over the possibilities: Belasco had

> broken down the barrier that has existed all these years, relegating our best actors to small colored houses.... Watch with me, dear ones, the opportunity that results from this sensational Broadway hit. I prophesy in the very near future colored casts working on Broadway under other white producers that would never have had the courage had not the "Lulu Belle" success inspired them. And many, many more avenues of employment will be opened to the colored actor.[19]

---

[13] *The Stage Works of Charles MacArthur*, ed. Arthur Dorlag and John Irvine (Tallahassee: Florida State University Foundation, 1974), 12; Freda Scott Giles, "Lulu Belle," in *Encyclopedia of the Harlem Renaissance*, ed. Cary D. Wintz and Paul Finkelman (New York: Routledge, 2004), 746.

[14] James Stetson Metcalfe, "Negrofying the Stage," *Wall Street Journal*, 12 February 1926. Even though the Yiddish play continued to be performed, a grand jury indicted two managers and twelve cast members in *The God of Vengeance* for "indecent, immoral and impure theatrical performance." See "'God of Vengeance Cast' Is Indicted," *New York Times*, 7 March 1923.

[15] See in particular John S. Brown's letter to the *New York Amsterdam News*, 24 February 1924, in which he calls for a boycott by African American actors to perform in "plays that degrade us." Brown was president of the Ethiopian Art Theatre.

[16] "William Townsend on Dave, Lulu Belle," *Pittsburgh Courier*, 6 February 1926. See also Alexander Woollcott's comments in "Critic Styles 'Lulu Belle' a 'Carmen' of Harlem," *Chicago Defender*, 20 February 1926: "Mr. Belasco has marshaled a great troupe for 'Lulu Belle.' For the most part, he has turned the Negro roles over to Negro players, and the performance is the better on that account."

[17] Sylvester Russell returned to this issue in several columns in the *Pittsburgh Courier*, published between 23 January and 13 February 1926.

[18] See, for example, "Lulu Belle Sensation," an unattributed article in the *Chicago Defender*, 13 February 1926.

[19] "Mr. Belasco's 'Lulu Belle'," *New York Amsterdam News*, 3 March 1926. Evelyn Mason performed the previous year in Garland Anderson's play *Appearances*, the first full-length play by an African American playwright produced on Broadway.

Dixie *Carmen*

Whether or not *Lulu Belle* was in any way the direct impetus for Broadway producers bringing out more plays with African American performers, it is striking that two major works featuring an African American cast had their premières soon after *Lulu Belle:* Paul Green's Pulitzer Prize–winning play *In Abraham's Bosom*, opening on 30 December 1926, and the Theatre Guild presenting Dorothy and DuBose Hayward's *Porgy* in October 1927. One intriguing possible afterlife of *Lulu Belle* did not materialize, however, for George Gershwin had considered turning the play in an opera before settling, with *Porgy and Bess,* on another *Carmen*-like story.[20]

For Hammerstein in particular, *Lulu Belle* may have been a memorable model because of its historical and thematic proximity to *Show Boat*. Premièred less than two years after *Lulu Belle*, on 27 December 1927, *Show Boat* featured Julie LaVerne, a quite different mixed-race heroine whose desire for quasi-bourgeois normalcy stood in sharp relief from the Carmen figure. Yet in the case of *Carmen Jones,* *Show Boat* remained—on Hammerstein's part—a relatively hidden intertext, even though it continued the earlier show's themes of racial segregation in the United States. The production of *Lulu Belle,* on the other hand, left a number of traces in Hammerstein's adaptation, both where there were similarities—for example, in the eventual rendering of Escamillo as a boxing champion—and in their differences. In particular, *Lulu Belle* and its reception may have influenced Hammerstein's location of his adaptation in wholesome North Carolina instead of Harlem. Even the fleeting involvement of Duke Ellington in the project during the 1930s might have found an echo in *Carmen Jones,* for in the 1942 version, Escamillo was portrayed not as the boxer Husky Miller, but as Hepcat Miller, a successful bandleader. For the time being, however, the *Carmen* project receded under the demands of the movie studios where Hammerstein worked for much of the 1930s.

It is not entirely clear when Hammerstein picked up the *Carmen* project again. After his return to New York, success on Broadway remained elusive for several years, but he followed other productions closely. In October 1941, Cheryl Crawford produced *Porgy and Bess* for the Maplewood Theatre in New Jersey, a revival so successful that it moved to the Majestic Theatre on Broadway on 22 January 1942. Streamlined and without recitatives, Crawford's version of *Porgy and Bess* presented a "musical play" that pleased critics and audiences.[21] Hammerstein had seen the performance at the Majestic, and he wrote to Ira Gershwin, on 2 February 1942, about his joy at the sold-out theater, adding that "the excellence of the performance and the beauty of the opera thrilled me no more than the audience itself."[22] Indeed, seen as an opera with spoken dialogue, the Crawford *Porgy and Bess* carries a strong

---

[20] *Stage Works of Charles MacArthur,* 12. It is not entirely clear how serious Gershwin's request really was; see Ben Hecht, *Charlie: The Improbable Life and Times of Charles MacArthur* (New York: Harper, 1957), 124.

[21] Crawford's production is discussed in Hollis Alpert, *The Life and Times of* Porgy and Bess*: The Story of an American Classic* (New York: Alfred A. Knopf, 1990), 137–39; Howard Pollack, *George Gershwin: His Life and Work* (Berkeley: University of California Press, 2006), 609–12; and John A. Johnson, "Gershwin's 'American Folk Opera': The Genesis, Style, and Reputation of *Porgy and Bess* (1935)," Ph.D. diss., Harvard University, 1996, 606–11 (p. 608 on the work's patriotic appeal during World War II).

[22] Oscar Hammerstein II, letter to Ira Gershwin, 2 February 1942. The continuation of this letter is quoted in Tim Carter, *Oklahoma!: The Making of an American Musical* (New Haven: Yale University Press, 2007), 24.

resemblance to Bizet's *Carmen*, with the heroine as an outsider-temptress against the background of a conservative community. Just over two weeks after Hammerstein attended *Porgy and Bess*, a letter (19 February 1942) by producer Richard Berger to Mrs. Cornelius Vanderbilt Whitney (the opera singer Eleanor Searle) reveals that he and Hammerstein were starting to raise money for a new production scheduled for the fall of 1942, an African American show set in North Carolina and based on Bizet's *Carmen*. This letter refers already to all the key elements of the first version—from Escamillo's portrayal as bandleader to the preservation of the original musical style as operatic instead of swing—and presents it as a logical project in the wake of the *Porgy and Bess* revival:

> Oscar Hammerstein, 2nd, who wrote SHOW BOAT and numerous other tremendous successes, and I have an idea for doing a modern version of CARMEN with an all negro cast. Briefly, our plan is to set the show in North Carolina, where CARMEN JONES, as we are going to call her, works in a cigarette factory; Don José (JOE) will be a soldier at a present day training camp; Escamillo will be a colorful figure such as Cab Calloway is, and the smugglers will be bootleggers of moonshine liquor. We plan to keep Bizet's music intact but hope to delete unnecessary repetitions, and Mr. Hammerstein is going to write modern, earthy lyrics instead of making a literal translation from the French.
>
> We are not going to swing the score in the sense of the words, but we are going to have everything we use reorchestrated in the modern idiom. We think that CARMEN is a basically interesting story and that the already proven melodies will develop into popular hit songs, aided by the Hammerstein lyrics.
>
> It is our desire to produce this in New York in the fall and if you think that Mr. Whitney might be interested in such a venture, I would like to have him meet Mr. Hammerstein. We are really hot about this and have great hopes for its success, particularly on the strength of the fine reception that PORGY AND BESS received on its revival.[23]

Although Hugh Fordin reports that Hammerstein was sitting "alone at the farm one day in January 1942," listening to a recording of Bizet's *Carmen* and setting out "to work modernizing the opera," it was certainly not done without "saying a word about it to anyone outside his family."[24] Indeed, Hammerstein worked toward realizing the production before even the first act of his new musical play was completed.

As he remembered later, Hammerstein took his time with the revisions given that there "was no deadline." Certainly, "I had more pleasure than I've ever had writing anything."[25] It is not clear when the first act was finished, but on 25 June 1942, Hammerstein wrote a letter to Hall Johnson that reveals not only that he had completed the second act and was "hard at work on the third," but also that by then Robert Russell Bennett had become involved in the production as the score's musical arranger: "Mr. Bennett, at this point, feels that he would like to handle the whole musical job which would include the vocal as well as the instrumental arrangements." Hammerstein's letters of late July refer to completing *Carmen Jones*,

---

[23] Berger was production manager for Hammerstein and Romberg's 1935 musical *May Wine* and was involved in the *Show Boat* production in St. Louis in August 1942.
[24] Fordin, *Getting to Know Him*, 179.
[25] "Oscar Hammerstein—June 1959," 29.

Dixie Carmen

which was deposited with the copyright office of the Library of Congress on 31 July 1942.[26] All the while, auditions for the principal roles continued, potential financial backers of the show became involved, a new producer appeared on the scene in the person of Max Gordon, and Hammerstein started to discuss with Hollywood agent Elizabeth A. Shaw the involvement of the African American dance star Katherine Dunham.[27]

At this point, *Carmen Jones* was significantly different from what would be the final 1943 version. A three-act "version of 'Carmen' for colored singers" with spoken dialogue, the work was set near an unidentified town in North Carolina.[28] The first act took place outside a cigarette factory where an Army Corps of Engineers was building a road. Obviously, the location was influenced by the fact that North Carolina was tobacco country. In its structure and themes, this act, perhaps, is closest to Meilhac and Halévy's original libretto, with characters very similar to those in Bizet's opera. In addition to Carmen Jones (Carmen) and Joe (Don José), we encounter Cindy Lou (Micaëla), Morrell (Moralès), and Sergeant Brown (Zuniga). The second act, in Billy Pastor's café, still follows the original libretto in much of its development. Frankie (Frasquita) and Myrt (Mercédès) dally with the whiskey smugglers Rum (El Remendado) and Dink (El Dancaïro); Joe gets roped into smuggling by having Carmen play on his jealousy just as in the original; and the toreador is—if anything—more dazzling than the original bullfighter in his transformation into the bandleader Hepcat Miller, whose "Toréador prends garde" becomes "Open de door," a solo number detailing his successes in cafés playing for "white folks," and whose family resemblance to Sportin' Life points once again to *Porgy and Bess* as a prototype for *Carmen Jones*.[29] The last act merges Bizet's Acts 3 and 4. Scene 1, "In the Hills," is a much shortened version of Act 3; Scenes 2 and 3 contain much of the music of Act 4 and play outside the Hoity Toity Club, a segregated establishment whose members applaud black entertainers but exclude African American patrons. (The echoes of the famous Cotton Club in Harlem are clear.) Scene 2 is the only scene with a white performer, cast as a policeman detailed to keep Hepcat Miller's African American fans in line, quite possibly a self-conscious reference to the white policemen in *Porgy and Bess* and further emphasizing that work's shadow looming heavily over the genesis of *Carmen Jones*.[30]

---

[26] In a letter to Peter Piper of 21 July 1942, Hammerstein wrote that he had been "concentrating on the job of finishing my adaptation of 'Carmen.'" The copyright script of the first version can be found at the Library of Congress, Performing Arts Reading Room, shelf mark ML50 B625C4 1942.

[27] The surviving documents do not indicate when Max Gordon became involved in the show, but an article in the *New York Times* of 13 July 1942 reveals that, with *Carmen Jones*, "Max Gordon announces the addition of a fourth production to his Autumn schedule." See "Gordon to Offer All-Negro Opera," *New York Times*, 13 July 1942. The first references to Gordon's involvement in the correspondence preserved in the Hammerstein Archives dates from two days later, 15 July 1942.

[28] The location is described as "near a southern town," but in Act 2, Hepcat Miller sings of his return to Carolina. Hammerstein, *Carmen Jones* (1942), list of cast, and 2–5. Correspondence and other documents in 1942 specify North Carolina, perhaps in order to emphasize geographical distance from the South Carolina of *Porgy and Bess;* furthermore, North Carolina was home to a number of military bases, including Fort Bragg, to which several reviewers referred.

[29] Ibid., 2–5.

[30] The libretto describes his actions: "A white POLICEMAN paces up and down, keeps the line back and preserves order." Ibid., 3-2-1.

These last scenes of Act 3 reveal much about the politics of this first version of the play in their explicit staging of racial segregation. In Scene 2, African American onlookers observe the guests entering the club (off-stage), commenting on their dress and speculating that Hepcat was going to make at least "a cool twen'y gran'!"[31] But into the banter about the sequins on women's garments and the pleasures of "classy mobsters" creep comments about segregation: a girl's sigh, "Wisht day'd let us go inside an' watch"; the retort by her friend, "Well wish again!"; the chorus's comment, "Oh, boy! Ef we wus inside / We'd show dem dopes how to glide! / We c'd show dem how to glide / Ef we wus ever allowed inside."[32] Scenes 2 and 3 shift seamlessly into each other by the lifting of a scrim that moves the action from the side of the club to its parking lot, where we see Hepcat's shadow conducting his band behind the "big center window with the shade pulled down," the barrier between white and black unmistakably in place. As Hepcat plays, the chorus sings about his music. Then the onlookers "start to dance because they just can't help themselves."[33] In this dance scene, stereotypical concepts of black physicality, primitive authenticity, and mimicry play with notions of authority and identity when three girls peek through the door of the white club and start laughing at the ineptitude of the white dancers. At the crowd's invitation to "give a imitation ob the way dey do what we do," the women start performing white. Hammerstein's stage direction hints at the possible subversiveness of this moment: "The trio of girls and their partners now give an imitation of white folks dancing like colored folks. This is done in an extravagant spirit of travesty, and is a terrific hit with the onlookers, who start to imitate the imitators."[34]

This scene plays with the performativity of racial identity in a complex chain of doublings when African Americans imitate other African Americans imitating Euro-Americans imitating African Americans in the black stage world created by a white playwright whose own identity as a Jewish American was far from fixed in the increasingly binary world of American race relations in the early 1940s.[35] The scene becomes an object lesson in deconstruction, demonstrating Zora Neale Hurston's comment that everyone "seems to think that the Negro is easily imitated when nothing is further from the truth."[36] Its mirroring of games with identity and cultural authority is compounded by the incongruence between sound and movement, for instead of the expected "race" music of Hepcat Miller (or his two models: Duke Ellington and Cab Calloway), the orchestra and on-stage chorus

---

[31] Ibid., 3-2-2. I discuss Hammerstein's use of black dialect further below.

[32] Ibid., 3-2-1 and 3-2-2.

[33] Ibid., 3-3-1.

[34] Ibid., 3-3-2.

[35] In this respect, the scene reflects a very different power dynamic from Bhabha's notion of mimicry as a "strategy of authority in colonial discourse" that allows for the potential of an "insurgent counter-appeal" of the "fetishized colonial culture." See Homi K. Bhabha, *The Location of Culture* (1994), 2nd ed. with a new preface by the author (London: Routledge, 2004), 129–30. On Jewish playwrights on Broadway and their identity politics, see Andrea Most, *Making Americans: Jews and the Broadway Musical* (Cambridge, Mass.: Harvard University Press, 2004).

[36] Zora Neale Hurston, "Characteristics," as cited in Susan Gubar, *Racechanges: White Skin, Black Face in American Culture* (Oxford: Oxford University Press, 1997), 54.

Dixie Carmen

would have performed Bizet.[37] Following Susan Gubar, who explored transracial performativity in her study of "skin trade," the play on imitations in Scene 3 might be termed "racechanges." *Carmen Jones* as a whole, however, can also be interpreted as a challenge to "the color line that W. E. B. Du Bois saw as the central problem of the twentieth century" by following Bizet's opera, to cite Gubar again, "closely enough to suggest that the logic of erotic thralldom will work itself out inexorably in the lives of men and women, regardless of racial, geographic, or historical factors."[38]

Had Hammerstein's 1942 version been staged, the cultural authorities of Bizet's music and African American dance would have fused in this scene into the performance of a powerful critique of identity in the segregated United States. Here *Carmen Jones* touches on issues already put on the stage in *Show Boat*, where Hammerstein and Kern problematized perceptions of "race" and its natural expression in the second-act "In Dahomey" number, in which African Americans from New York perform as "Zulus" during the 1893 World's Fair in Chicago. Once the performers succeed, in this number, in frightening off their white audience, they reveal themselves as well-brought-up New Yorkers who prefer knives and forks to the primitivism of the "Dahomey show." Both the fake Zulus' lines "Let the Africans stay / In Dahomey— / Gimme Avenue A / Back in old New York," and Kern's shift to modern ragtime at the moment when the "Dahomians" reveal themselves as African Americans, break open fixed concepts of identities in a deliberate representation of "ambivalence about the representation of black otherness."[39] Fifteen years later, in *Carmen Jones*, Hammerstein expanded this chain of multiple identities by the insertion of an African American imitation of white renderings of black dance.

A number of political and aesthetic currents intercross in this complicated performance of identities, not the least Hammerstein's own interstitial identity in a culture where he was both insider (as a white man) and outsider (as a Jew). Jewishness as an "ethnoracial" category was in flux at that time as it transferred from one side of the U.S. racial binary to its white opposite.[40] As Andrea Most points out in her study of Jewish creators on Broadway, black and Jewish identity politics remained closely intertwined during the 1930s and 1940s.[41] The advent of Nazi Germany heightened awareness of the diasporic nature of Jewish communities in the United States and reinforced their precariousness. Hammerstein was a founding member, in June 1936, of the Hollywood Anti-Nazi League, which clearly addressed U.S. racial politics as much as German fascism in its revised mission statement of 1937 requiring its members to "combat racial intolerance and thus combat Nazism, which uses

---

[37] David Garcia discusses the conflation between the acoustic and the physical in American notions of "primitive" black dance in "Going Primitive to the Movements and Sounds of Mambo," *Musical Quarterly* 89/4 (Winter 2006): 505–23.

[38] Gubar, *Racechanges*, 31.

[39] Richard Middleton, *Voicing the Popular: On the Subjects of Popular Music* (New York: Routledge, 2006), 66.

[40] Karen Brodkin, *How Jews Became White Folks and What That Says about Race in America* (New Brunswick, N.J.: Rutgers University Press, 1998), 175.

[41] See Most, *Making Americans*, especially in her first chapter, "Acting American" (12–31), which offers an introductory overview before her case studies. *Carmen Jones* is entirely absent from this book.

intolerance as a weapon to attain power."[42] As Hammerstein's biographer, Hugh Fordin, points out, involvement in the League marked the start of the playwright's civil-rights activities. He supported African American causes both financially and in other ways. When he received the National Urban League's call for equal access to defense work for African Americans, around the time he completed the third act of *Carmen Jones* in July 1942, he not only made a financial contribution, but also offered nonmonetary support: "Due to pressure of other causes being made upon me, the enclosed check is all I can afford at the moment. Later in the year, however, I hope I will be able to augment this by a larger one. Meanwhile, I am so interested in the philosophy behind the movement of your League that I would be delighted to help you in other ways, if you can point out to me what I can do."[43]

That Hammerstein was aware of how segregation affected Broadway theater at the time of *Carmen Jones* is also borne out by a clipping in his archives of an article in *Variety* from July 1942 that discusses African American performance and its segregated history in New York. It recounts how the Theatre Guild had "cancelled the booking of Paul Robeson in 'Othello'" the previous year, and predicts that because "it is an election year and feelings about race discrimination are running high, the booking of 'Carmen Jones' would probably create an incident. It would be magnified into national importance and perhaps taken up by both parties, who are struggling to get the Negro vote."[44] For Hammerstein, who had already engaged with segregation in *Show Boat* and who counted African American artists from Hall Johnson and Duke Ellington to Todd Duncan and Paul Robeson among his friends and acquaintances, these local forms of racism seem to have had as much bearing on his treatment of segregation on the stage in *Carmen Jones* as national race politics and global fascism.

Once the book for *Carmen Jones* was completed, Hammerstein redoubled his efforts to cast a show still planned to open in fall 1942, even though he was by then also involved with a new project that would become *Oklahoma!* He tapped into his network of African American colleagues—including Hall Johnson in Hollywood—to find a cast of high-level black opera singer/actors, but with very little success. Despite all of his efforts, by September 1942, Hammerstein had lined up only three of the performers who would eventually appear in *Carmen Jones:* Carlotta Franzell, Muriel Rahn, and Napoleon Reed. Charles Holland, one possible tenor for the role

---

[42] Fordin, *Getting to Know Him*, 141–43; quotation on p. 143.

[43] For the request for support, see Todd Duncan and Anne Brown (National Urban League), letter to Oscar Hammerstein II, 15 July 1942. For the response, see Oscar Hammerstein II, letter to Todd Duncan and Anne Brown (National Urban League), 5 August 1942. The National Urban League pushed toward full implementation of Roosevelt's 1941 Executive Order 8802 that called for "no discrimination in the employment of workers in defense industries or government." See David M. Kennedy, *Freedom from Fear: The American People in Depression and War, 1929–1945* (New York: Oxford University Press, 2005), 767. On the involvement of Jewish Americans in black civil-rights causes, see Nancy J. Weiss, "Long-Distance Runners of the Civil Rights Movement: The Contribution of Jews to the NAACP and the National Urban League in the Early Twentieth Century," in *Struggles in the Promised Land: Toward a History of Black-Jewish Relations in the United States*, ed. Jack Salzman and Cornel West (New York: Oxford University Press, 1997), 123–52.

[44] *Wc* OHC. In the course of my research I have consulted both newspapers and the scrapbooks in *Wc* OHC. Articles preserved in the scrapbooks are cited as such.

Dixie *Carmen*

of Joe, was inducted into the U.S. Army in the summer of 1942; another contender for the role, George Scott, was drafted in October 1942. Hammerstein's casting problems were systemic: Because of segregation, especially in U.S. opera houses, African American artists had little opportunity to hone their skills outside the concert stage and popular entertainment unless they exiled themselves to Europe or South America.[45] To find singers both experienced on the stage and trained as classical performers therefore proved a major obstacle.

Hammerstein had equally bad luck finding his ideal choreographer, which—given the prominence of dance in the 1942 version—was an important aspect of the preparation. After Katherine Dunham had turned him down in July because of scheduling conflicts for the upcoming season, Hammerstein approached another famous proponent of black concert dance, Asadata Dafora. A dancer and choreographer from Sierra Leone, Dafora's American career began in the 1920s with his stylized form of West African folkloric dance. Both Dunham and Dafora were among the leading dancers and choreographers of modern African American dance, grounding their work in a pronounced claim to African authenticity through either birthright or anthropological research.[46] By engaging either of them, Hammerstein would have been able to collaborate with a leading proponent of a dance style that paralleled in movement what he had created in the libretto.[47] The potential collaboration with Dafora started off promisingly in a meeting in mid-August, only to end in a disastrous audition in October: Half of Dafora's troupe did not turn up because of a car accident, and the rest performed in a manner contrary to what Hammerstein had been led to expect.[48] About a week later, Max Gordon pulled out as producer, which left the Hammerstein with barely a cast, few financial backers, and a book for which he cared deeply.

On 19 November, however, the fate of *Carmen Jones* began to change when Hammerstein sent his script to a potential producer who was known for his flamboyant shows—notably *Jumbo* (1935) and the *Aquacade* during the 1939 World's Fair—and his dazzling New York nightclub, the Diamond Horseshoe.[49] William

---

[45] Famously it was not until 1955 that, with Marian Anderson and Robert McFerrin, two African Americans performed on the stage of the Metropolitan Opera in New York. Aside from some all-African American productions of the Federal Theatre Project in the 1930s, few opportunities arose for African Americans to perform opera in the United States, which is why, in 1941, Mary Caldwell Dawson founded the National Negro Opera Company. See Annegret Fauser, "*Carmen in Khaki*: Europäische Oper in den Vereinigten Staaten während des Zweiten Weltkrieges," in *Oper im Wandel der Gesellschaft. Kulturtransfers und Netzwerke des Musiktheaters im modernen Europa*, ed. Sven Oliver Müller, Philipp Ther, Jutta Toelle, and Gesa zur Nieden (Vienna: Oldenbourg and Böhlau, 2010), 303–29.

[46] See John O. Perpener III, *African-American Concert Dance: The Harlem Renaissance and Beyond* (Urbana: University of Illinois Press, 2001), with chapters on Dafora (101–27) and Dunham (128–60). On Dunham's anthropological fieldwork in Jamaica, Martinique, and Haiti from 1935 through 1936, see Joyce Aschenbrenner, *Katherine Dunham: Dancing a Life* (Urbana: University of Illinois Press, 2002), 43–90.

[47] In 1946, Hammerstein engaged Pearl Primus, another proponent of African American concert dance, for the revival of *Show Boat*.

[48] See Asadata Dafora, letter to Oscar Hammerstein II, 1 October 1942.

[49] Oscar Hammerstein II, letter to Billy Rose, 19 November 1942: "Here is my adaptation of CARMEN which I promised to send. It sounds much better with music but I hope you will get

Samuel Rosenberg, known to the world as Billy Rose, was enthralled by the script. Hammerstein, however, was not entirely happy with this outcome, as he confided, on 27 November, in a letter to his son Bill:

> I gave Billy Rose my version of *Carmen* to read over last week-end. He has been chasing me ever since. He wants to produce it. He will put all the money up. He would undoubtedly exploit it to the hilt and might give it a very vital production. It is a big step for me to take, however. He is a very wearing little fellow, I mean wearing down. He is stubborn, self-assertive, and a lot of things I don't like. But he is also a lot of things I do like.

Whatever Hammerstein's misgivings, he entered into an agreement with Billy Rose on 3 January 1943 in which he gave the impresario "the right to produce" *Carmen Jones*, for which the playwright was "to receive a royalty of 5–1/2% based on weekly box office receipts."[50]

Billy Rose's *Carmen Jones*

Billy Rose was a producer "synonymous to all things spectacular in the world of theater."[51] Known to spare no cost, his shows were lavish affairs visually as well as musically. In contrast to other Broadway producers who often created a consortium of investors to finance a show, Rose had developed enough financial resources to back any major enterprise himself, which gave him complete control over the process and—should a show be successful—significant returns.[52] With *Carmen Jones*, Rose's first point of action was to reassess the production needs and to slow things down as Hammerstein turned his full attention to *Oklahoma!* as it went into rehearsal.[53] While in the spring of 1943 *Oklahoma!* wound its way through rehearsals, tryouts, and première, Rose reconsidered Hammerstein's unsuccessful strategy for casting *Carmen Jones*, which had involved drawing on "well-known names and established personalities." Instead, he took a leaf from the Theatre Guild's much publicized tactic with *Oklahoma!* by searching for untried talent, which—in the case of *Carmen Jones*—added a different slant to the casting that was exploited to the hilt in the publicity for the production as a "Cinderella story in multigraph—or the triumph of the obscure."[54] No longer a show characterized by seasoned performers as in the case of Crawford's *Porgy and Bess*, Rose's enterprise

---

some enjoyment out of it just as it is." According to Fording (*Getting to Know Him*, 204), Rose and Hammerstein had discussed *Carmen Jones* first after an ASCAP meeting they both attended the previous day.

[50] Billy Rose, letter to Oscar Hammerstein II and countersigned by him, 3 January 1943, New York Public Library, Billy Rose Collection (hereafter *NYp* BRC). The formal contract, ratified by the Author's League, was not signed until 30 September 1943 (*NYp* BRC). The formal contract splits the royalties between Hammerstein (5%) and Robert Russell Bennett (0.5%).

[51] Billy Rowe, "Billy Rose Takes over 'Carmen Jones,'" *Pittsburgh Courier*, 2 January 1943.

[52] It is not entirely clear whether Hammerstein was able to convince Rose to include the original handful of backers into the deal, although documents show that he tried. See Oscar Hammerstein II, letter to Charles Brackett (Hollywood), 11 January 1943.

[53] Rehearsals for *Oklahoma!* started on 8 February 1943. See Carter, *Oklahoma!*, 138.

[54] "The Triumph of the Obscure," *Carmen Jones*, Souvenir Program, 6. Quotations about the *Oklahoma!* cast "composed of unknowns" (*Daily News*, 7 January 1943) can be found in Carter, *Oklahoma!*, 63–64.

Dixie Carmen

turned the work into an "all-American" operatic success story that challenged the hallowed institution of opera precisely because of its casting strategies, staging decisions, and the location of the performance.[55]

With 115 singers and dancers needed for the production, the casting posed a significant logistic challenge, for which Rose relied on the help of jazz producer John Hammond, Jr., who was well known for organizing the "From Spirituals to Swing" concerts at Carnegie Hall and who had become a board member of the NAACP in the late 1930s.[56] In what was then hyped as "one of the most exhaustive talent hunts in history," Hammond held auditions in Boston, Philadelphia, Chicago, Detroit, Los Angeles, and "twenty-five college campuses, where music departments, choirs, glee clubs, and other singing groups might be expected to have trained voices with stamina. I visited Howard, Spelman, Talladega, Fisk, Tuskagee, and went as far west as Texas."[57] The cast's biographies in the souvenir program focused on the regional origins and nonmusical occupations of the singers, be it Muriel Smith (Carmen) from New York, "who was employed in a camera shop at $15 a week"; Luther Saxon (Joe) from South Carolina, who worked "as a checker at the Philadelphia Navy Yard"; or Glenn Bryant (Husky Miller), who was "a member of the New York Police Department, assigned to juvenile delinquency work in Harlem."[58] Their status as "common folk" and their lack of theater experience were emphasized throughout and picked up by the press, as in Richard Maney's article about the production in the *New York Times* (28 November 1943), where he provided biographical information on the lead performers and then listed other cast members as a "Detroit social worker, a Cleveland housewife, a Los Angeles chauffeur, a Buffalo bellhop." In this story, *Carmen Jones* became an embodiment of the "American dream" through the Pygmalion plot of its cast, awkwardly combining the notion of racial and social uplift and "all-American" inclusiveness with one of white patronage and control.

This emphasis on the cast's inexperience was all the more noticeable as it contrasted sharply with the highlighting of the consummate professional achievement of the show's production team in the souvenir program and in reviews. With Hammerstein's return to the show's preparations after the première of *Oklahoma!* he and Rose started to select the production lineup, which included Charles Friedman as director and Eugene Loring as choreographer. (Loring's *Billy the Kid* with music by Aaron Copland had recently been revived at the National Theatre in 1942.) Hassard Short was responsible for staging and lighting; he was perhaps the best-known figure among the production team, with a long string of successful Broadway shows under his belt. The set designer, Howard Bay, was another well-known player on Broadway, who, in 1943, designed the sets for both *Carmen Jones* and Kurt Weill's *One Touch of Venus*.

---

[55] There was barely any overlap between the cast of *Porgy and Bess* and *Carmen Jones*. Jack Carr (who played Sergeant Brown) had performed Jim in the 1935 production of *Porgy*, whereas June Hawkins (Myrt) was in the chorus for the 1942 revival and Edward Lee Taylor (Rum) had held a bit role in Crawford's 1943 run on Broadway.

[56] John Hammond and Irving Townsend, *On Record: An Autobiography* (New York: Ridge Press, 1977), 241–43.

[57] "The Triumph of the Obscure," 6; Hammond and Townsend, *On Record*, 242–43.

[58] "The Triumph of the Obscure," 10.

With a first-rate production team in place by the middle of July 1943, Hammerstein was hard at work revising his play. He had already announced to his son Bill on 2 May that he would return to *Carmen Jones:* "I am going to do quite an extensive re-write on it. Reading it over after not seeing it for some time I believe I can improve it about 25%." On 14 July, he reported to Bill: "Have finished new first act of C.J.[,] will finish second August 1st." It was not until 30 September, however, that the new version was signed in by the copyright office in the Library of Congress.[59] Hammerstein's revisions were extensive and changed the character of the work significantly. Whereas his first version conceived *Carmen Jones* with *Porgy and Bess* as an intertext and segregation an important theme, the revised play focused on World War II and modern U.S. life as a framework for the *Carmen* story. The new version tightened the work by cutting several musical numbers, changing the dialogue from distant paraphrase to a wholesale new text, and combining the original Acts 1 and 2 into a new first act. Robert Russell Bennett responded to Hammerstein's plans for the revisions in the late spring of 1943: "The changes you write of are most promising. The only argument from me on fidelity to the original *Carmen* will come from the mutilation of music—not from cuts of whole numbers or changes in format. After all, our aim is to cash in on what we know to be a score that has proven its effectiveness and at the same time has only scratched the edge of its possibilities with the American public."[60]

In the new version, the location is transformed into a Southern defense plant producing parachutes for both the army and the navy (see Figure 2), though Joe explains to Brown early on that it used "ter be a cigarette fac'ry before de war" (perhaps an in-joke on Hammerstein's part, and certainly one that emphasizes the wartime shift).[61] Instead of opening with black army engineers engaging in the heavy manual labor of building a road, now soldiers are standing guard at a defense plant with black workers, thus responding, at least on the stage, to the National Urban League's 1942 call for equal access to defense work for African Americans. The opening line of the play has soldiers and workers united in singing "Send along anudder load / An' win dat war, win dat war!" Morrel's explanation that the plant is working for both the army and the navy is echoed by the Foreman, who comments "We got to do de job togedder til de job is through!"—a line that elicits "enthusiastic comments from the others, supporting this statement."[62] Echoing the words of one of Hammerstein's war songs, *Buddy on the Nightshift* (1942, with music by Kurt Weill)—and also reversing the oppressive work song that begins *Show Boat*—this new opening was pure wartime propaganda. When the women come out of the

---

[59] The copyright script of the second version can be found at the Library of Congress, Performing Arts Reading Room, shelf mark ML50 B625C4 1943. It carries a date stamp of 30 September 1943. The gap between the announced completion date (1 August) and the copyright date might be explained either by ongoing revisions (leading to a deposit in late September) or by delays in acknowledging the script due to the war.

[60] Robert Russell Bennett, undated letter to Oscar Hammerstein II. The reminder of the content places the letter in late spring (probably late May) of 1943.

[61] *Carmen Jones* (1943), 1–1–4.

[62] Ibid., 1–1–4. These lines are cut from the printed libretto. See Oscar Hammerstein II, *Carmen Jones* (New York: Alfred Knopf, 1945).

Dixie *Carmen*

Figure 2. *Carmen Jones* (1943), Act I, Scene 1, "Dat's Love"; Muriel Smith (Carmen Jones) and Ensemble. Courtesy of the Rodgers & Hammerstein Organization.

factory to take their break, they relay how "Ain' nuffin' but good luck parachutes made in dis fac'ry." Indeed, "Ev'y parachute we send out got a prayer wrapped up in it."[63] Carmen's and Sally's altercation starts onstage now and centers around women's roles in the war effort, as expressed in Sally's sententious reminder: "How we goin' to help de war effort if we don' git to work on time? / You cain' help de sojers by stayin' home in your bed!"[64] As one critic summed up the play in that respect: "'Carmen Jones' is concerned with United States soldiers and a defense worker."[65] Hammerstein's increased war work might well have been the reason behind this revised treatment of the opening. In April and May, he contributed to a film produced by the Office of War Information, and in June he became involved in another project for the propaganda agency.[66] Furthermore, he presided over the Writers' War Board and was closely involved in the Stage Door Canteen.[67] With his

---

[63] *Carmen Jones* (1943), 1–1–6. These lines are also cut from the 1945 print.
[64] Ibid., 1–1–6.
[65] "Alias 'Jones,' But She's Still Bizet['s] 'Carmen,'" *Christian Science Monitor*, 21 October 1943.
[66] Hammerstein comments on the OWI film in a letter to Bill from 17 May 1943: "Actually that O.W.I. picture has been hanging over my head and blocking out everything else. After I finished it I had an obligation to do an article for the N.Y. Times."
[67] Fordin, *Getting to Know Him*, 183.

Example 1. "Stan' up an' fight" (Husky Miller). Text: Oscar Hammerstein II; music: Georges Bizet ("Toréador, prends garde," mm. 34-39). Based on Georges Bizet, Robert Russell Bennett, and Oscar Hammerstein II, *Carmen Jones,* Restored Edition. New York: Rodgers and Hammerstein Theatricals, 2007, 126–27. Courtesy of the Rodgers & Hammerstein Organization.

son Bill enlisted in the navy and his own sense of civic responsibility, Hammerstein considered the war his most important cause.

Martial sentiment also characterized the change of lyrics as Escamillo was transformed from the bandleader Hepcat Miller into the boxer Husky Miller. The new words for "Toréador, prends garde" now emphasize fighting "like hell," as the maxim the heavyweight champion (and everyone else) "must remember" (see Example 1). This number became possibly the best-known extract of *Carmen Jones,* with numerous requests for performances, as, for example, by the OWI music director, Macklin Marrow, for a radio program that would have the famed baritone Lawrence Tibbett perform the song.[68]

The war as point of reference becomes particularly poignant in the new third scene of Act 1 in which Joe tries to make the defense-plant worker Carmen understand not only that he is in the army but also that he has ambitions of getting into Officers' Flying School.[69] According to the typescript of the new libretto, Joe knocks down Brown (the play's Zuniga figure) in a jealous rage. As he thinks about surrendering himself rather than deserting, Carmen takes the initiative in the cruelest of all deceptions by announcing to the returning crowd that Joe has just gotten news that he has been chosen for flight training and will not return to camp but leave immediately for his new assignment. Despite Joe's dazed protestations, the crowd cheers: One of theirs has been selected into the elite group of African Americans

---

[68] Macklin Marrow, letter to Oscar Hammerstein II, 1 November 1943. It is not clear whether Marrow broadcast the planned radio show on American adaptations of European art works.

[69] *Carmen Jones* (1943), 1–3–20. See also the printed libretto, p. 76.

Dixie Carmen

now training to become pilots. Hammerstein's words for the crowd make Carmen's deception seem increasingly unpatriotic when they exclaim: "Hot diggedy! / Joe's goin' to be an officer! . . . Show dem Japs where dey git off!" A fellow soldier chimes in: "Hey! D'you know what dis means? We got a boy from our outfit goin' to be a officer!"[70] The happy cheering ends in a reprise of "Beat out dat rhythm on a drum," but the punch line of the verse is altered first into "An' show 'em how to win de war!" and, the second time round, into "An' kick ol' Hitler out de door!"[71] It is not clear from the sources whether Hammerstein toned this scene down before the tryouts or only later in the process by replacing the verses referring to the "Japs" and Hitler with the more neutral reprise of "Good Luck, Mr. Flyin' Man" in the printed version of 1945.

The rewritten ending to the scene at Billy Pastor's was, in its own way, as powerful a statement about African Americans and civil rights in the United States as was the first version's segregation finale. The year 1943 was one in which increasing attention was drawn to the abuse of African Americans in the armed forces, which had begun to enlist black soldiers after the collective lobbying of civil-rights organizations and the black press had led to the Burke-Wadsworth Draft Bill's (1940) inclusion of a mandatory 10 percent quota of African American inductees.[72] Whereas that quota was filled overall (and even doubled in service units) by 1943, only 1.1 percent of officer candidates were African American.[73] In the fully segregated armed forces, African Americans were organized in black units but usually commanded by white officers. Combat units, including the Army Air Force and the Marine Corps, were especially slow to accept African Americans, though the 99th Pursuit Squadron, established in 1941, soon became renowned as the Tuskegee Airmen for their outstanding record in the war. Flying their first battle missions in the spring and summer of 1943, the airmen became living proof of African American achievement in combat.[74] The daredevil glamour associated with the Army Air Forces—one of the deadliest combat assignments in World War II—thus contributed to the uphill battle that African Americans were fighting in the armed forces and the United States as a whole.

Hammerstein's Carmen could not have done anything more terrible than use this symbolic achievement of African Americans as airmen in her destruction of Joe. In that sense, Hammerstein's Carmen proved even more dangerous than either Mérimée's or Bizet's: There, she was a powerful woman against whom weak men had little chance; in *Carmen Jones*, she is an actively destructive force. In this portrayal of Carmen as villainess, war propaganda crosses powerfully with melodrama in a figure who owes her character to, among others, the stock seductresses in wartime movies who put selfish desires ahead of the needs of their country. With Cindy Lou

---

[70] *Carmen Jones* (1943), 1-3-25. Hammerstein cut out most of the scene in the published libretto (p. 81), but kept the soldier's line.

[71] *Carmen Jones* (1943), 1-3-26.

[72] Bryan D. Booker, *African Americans in the United States Army in World War II* (Jefferson, N.C.: McFarland, 2008), 53.

[73] Ibid., 68. This number was a marginal improvement over the situation in 1940, when "the regular army had just five black officers, three of them chaplains." Kennedy, *Freedom from Fear*, 765.

[74] Kennedy, *Freedom from Fear*, 773.

as the quintessential and sacrificial "good girl" (with marginally more American spunk than her hapless predecessor), Carmen Jones stands out as the bogeywoman of war propaganda: the enemy within. That Hammerstein's portrayal was successful shines through the unfiltered private commentary of his wife, Dorothy, after she attended a rehearsal in Philadelphia: "Carmen is an awful character really. Oscar claims that her saving grace is her honesty, but this Carmen is even worse than the Spanish Carmen [in] that she makes Jo [sic] desert in war time. Of course you wouldn't hate her if Jo wasn't such a good boy. The cast is swell. Carmen is simply wonderful & every time Cindy Lou sings I cry."[75]

Hammerstein's revisions to Act 2 were even more extensive: No longer in rural and segregated North Carolina, it presents an even tighter plot in its new setting on the South Side of Chicago (perhaps also an echo of *Show Boat*), where, in the Meadow Lawn Country Club, an elegantly dressed Carmen tries to get rid of the unkempt deserter who has followed her. The club presents a modern and glitzy world of African American achievement that Carmen Jones, now turned into a social climber, wants to join. With its relocation to the outside of a baseball park, the finale of Act 2 regained some of its parentage from the opera's bullfight ending, with Carmen throwing her ring away and Joe stabbing her.[76] Despite the setting in a modern urban community in which segregation is no longer overtly represented, Hammerstein may nevertheless have chosen Chicago's South Side also as a reminder that many African Americans still lived (and died) in urban ghettos, a fact that had been driven home in June 1943, just months before the première of *Carmen Jones*, during the race riots in Detroit.

Billy Rose and his production team went all out to create an extravagantly stunning show that had the audiences and critics enthralled by its sheer modernist glamour. In contrast to Crawford's cash-strapped *Porgy and Bess* (which had downsized the work's staging to make it an economically viable enterprise), Billy Rose's *Carmen Jones* was the most expensive production on Broadway of its period. It had cost $176,000 by the time it had completed its tryouts and arrived on Broadway (equivalent to the purchasing power of about $2 million in 2009).[77] In comparison, the cost of *Oklahoma!* was between $82,000 and $84,488.[78] Whether such lavishness was due to Billy Rose's unstinting commitment to the show or whether he did not care because his money would be gone anyway, given the new tax laws during the war, *Carmen Jones* started life—by all accounts—in a breathtaking staging.[79]

---

[75] Dorothy Hammerstein, letter to Bill Hammerstein, 3 October 1943. Original reads "and that" instead of "in that."

[76] *Carmen Jones* (1943), 2-2-11. See also the printed libretto, p. 137.

[77] For a detailed account of the show's costs, see the "Schedule of Production Costs" prepared by Charles Orenstein, a financial auditor for Billy Rose (*NYp* BRC). Current purchasing power calculated with http://www.measuringworth.com/ppowerus (accessed 4 October 2009).

[78] Carter, *Oklahoma!*, 222.

[79] A letter by Hammerstein to Leighton K. Brill (11 January 1943) hints at the financial situation as one motive, even when the projected cost of the show was as low as $75,000: "[Rose's] ability to meet the budget without passing the hat is well known to you. In fact if CARMEN JONES doesn't get his $75,000, Morgenthau will." Henry Morgenthau, Jr., was Secretary of the Treasury in the Roosevelt administration.

Dixie *Carmen*

Hassard Short had developed a color concept in which each location was tinted differently, with costumes, lighting, and sets all in one matching color: yellow for the parachute factory, purple for Billy Pastor's bar, blue for the country club, and red for the sports stadium.[80] Howard Bay's sets presented a streamlined yet playful scenery, whether for the scene in rural North Carolina or the glitzy country club, and the costumes put both protagonists and supporting cast in silk, velvet, and linen (with a few cotton costumes for parachute workers and MPs).[81] Through this symbolic and unrealistic color concept, the exceptionality of the play was thus reinforced by the exceptionality of the staging. Short's concept may have been an attempt to translate on Broadway the new three-strip Technicolor in Hollywood pictures of the 1930s. Yet his use of primary colors in three out of the four sets prompted critics to delve into language that equated the use of strong colors with African American vitality, thus taming the powerful allure of the appealingly "wild" production through stereotyping it as inspired by "the Negro love for primary colors in bold combinations."[82]

With the sets and staging concepts shaping up and the work finally cast, *Carmen Jones* went into rehearsal on 13 September 1943.[83] The tryouts in Philadelphia and Boston were scheduled, but what would happen in New York remained unclear as all the theaters on Broadway were booked. As Hammerstein announced to Bill around 12 September: "Business for legits and movie houses alike is terrific. The streets are jammed at night, London has been the same since the blitzes subsided." When the show opened in Philadelphia on 19 October 1943, it was a huge success. The newspapers fêted the production and its performers, and a large number of New Yorkers made the trip south to see the new hit. Moreover, the tryout version was already in excellent shape.[84] As *Carmen Jones* moved to the Boston Opera House on 9 November (where it gained as much success as in Philadelphia), the New York fate of the production remained uncertain. There was still no house

---

[80] Unfortunately, all surviving photographs of *Carmen Jones* that I could find are in black and white. However, the illustrator, Miguel Covarrubias, created four colored drawings of the show that are reproduced (albeit out of sequence) on http://www.americanartarchives.com/covarrubias.htm (accessed 15 March 2009). I am grateful to Bruce Pomahac for discovering the Web site. A printed set of the drawings can be found in *Wc* OHC. How powerful Short's color scheme was in shaping the theatrical experience is clear from my conversation with Alice Hammerstein Mathias, who evoked it as her first and most striking memory of the production. Mathias became Hammerstein's assistant shortly before *Carmen Jones* went into rehearsal (telephone interview, 21 April 2009).

[81] Only three watercolors of Howard Bay's set designs and several of his technical drawings survive in Box 2 of the Howard Bay Collection at *NYp*. For a detailed list of the costumes, see the inventory drawn up at the end of the show's run, *NYp* BRC.

[82] L. A. Sloper, "'Carmen Jones' Applauded at Opera House," *Christian Science Monitor*, 10 November 1943.

[83] The brief note in the *New York Times* of 8 September 1943, announcing the beginning of rehearsals for "next Monday," corresponds to other documents in the *Wc* OHC that indicate the beginning of rehearsals in mid-September.

[84] See Oscar Hammerstein's letter to Bill Hammerstein, 25 October 1943: "It also is the first time I've opened a play out of town and not had one bit of rewriting to do! It will open on Broadway just as it opened in Philadelphia—except for some polishing in the direction of the scenes and numbers. It is a dream show."

in sight, a situation that was noted especially by the African American press.[85] Finally, Lee Shubert's Broadway Theater became available when the revue-style show *Artists and Models* folded on 27 November after a short, unsuccessful run.[86] *Carmen Jones* opened there on 2 December 1943, and it was a triumph. It played eight times a week to a packed house that seated 1,950 people. Its sheet music sold like hotcakes, and its cast and production team were treated as celebrities in newspapers from the *New York Times* to the *Chicago Defender*. Not only drama and music critics but also reporters from many other departments published their thoughts on *Carmen Jones* in the following months. These texts offer a fascinating window on a number of key issues in the wartime United States of 1943–44. They address in particular Hammerstein's poetic and dramaturgical choices in the text, the performance of the African American cast, and the role of Bizet's music in the show.

American Vernacular: Speaking *Carmen Jones*

With the entry of the United States into World War II, the discourse about the vernacular in the musical theater took on renewed urgency. Opera in English had become once more a hot-button topic that had critics, producers, and audiences alike reassessing current performance practice. Yet Hammerstein's radical adaptation of Bizet's *Carmen* pushed the debate also into the broader contemporary discussions about a national theater, its genres, and its languages. Indeed, in the reception of *Carmen Jones*, these two conversations overlapped, revealing disquiet and self-consciousness in a time of heightened nationalism when a dependence on imported cultural products—whether English theater or European opera—proved to be even more problematic than during the interwar years. With opera in particular, dependence on the canonic European repertoire remained unavoidable. Indeed, although composers such as Deems Taylor and Virgil Thomson had tried their hand composing "American opera," the operatic canon remained almost exclusively European, and worse—with works by such composers as Rossini, Verdi, Puccini, and Wagner—dominated by Axis composers. This situation led to rhetorical contortions in justifying the continued performance of such operas and made the genre's transfer into an American vernacular realm ever more pressing. Moreover, opera could too easily be associated with a small, elite audience: As Marc Blitzstein put it polemically in 1937, in the United States, "opera means only the Met."[87] Given that

---

[85] See, for example, "'Carmen' Has No N.Y. Home," *Pittsburgh Courier*, 13 November 1943; "Carmen Jones the 'Opera' Is an Orphan; Can't Find House," *Chicago Defender*, 27 November 1943.

[86] Richard Maney, "Billy Rose and 'Carmen Jones,'" *New York Times*, 28 November 1943.

[87] Marc Blitzstein, untitled manuscript ("In America..."), given in Michael Denning, *The Cultural Front: The Laboring of American Culture in the Twentieth Century* (London: Verso, 1997), 285. The manuscript probably dates from the 1937 rehearsal period of *The Cradle Will Rock*. The translation and adaptation of European opera for U.S. audiences have a long and complex history that placed the genre in a reception field between minstrel shows (so-called Ethiopian operas), English-language folk theater, and snobbish Europhilia. For a survey of opera in the United States in the nineteenth and early twentieth centuries, see Lawrence W. Levine, *Highbrow/Lowbrow: The Emergence of Cultural Hierarchy in America* (Cambridge, Mass.: Harvard University Press, 1988), 85–104.

Dixie *Carmen*

this country purportedly had joined the global conflict in December 1941 in order to save democracy, that kind of exclusive cultural practice now became tricky at the very least. Access to so-called high-brow culture on the part of the masses could no longer be solely the social concern of such New Deal agencies as the Federal Theatre Project; rather, it quickly turned into a national necessity.[88] Opera in the wartime United States thus had to respond to two interrelated issues: It needed to be both Americanized and democratized.

Advertisements and reviews pointed to fresh translations, U.S. singers, and up-to-date staging as key ingredients in the formula for turning European opera into an American art form. Thus an advertisement for performances of *Il barbiere di Siviglia* and *Carmen* in Pasadena claimed: "Grand opera, Americanized by new English translations and young American singers, will be presented by the American Music Theater of Pasadena at the Civic Auditorium in that city next month."[89] In Washington, newspapers announced a season of "Grand opera produced in the 'American way'" for the winter of 1943.[90] Surprisingly enough, even the Metropolitan Opera joined the trend and presented several productions in English, particularly of operas using spoken dialogue (where the vernacular could more easily be justified), ranging from *The Magic Flute* in 1941 to *Fidelio* in 1945.[91]

In addition to the question of translation, the continuous touting of the successful employment of American singers added an openly chauvinist note to this discourse that could not entirely hide the insecurities about the international competitiveness of home-grown performers. In particular, the Met had been infamous for its preference for European singers, but because of the war, Europeans were no longer in easy supply after the 1941–42 season. Music critics and producers alike turned this absence into a patriotic virtue, echoing a debate favoring native artists over foreign ones that went back at least to the Dickstein "Alien Actors" Bill considered in Congress in early 1935. Sponsored by the chairman of the House Immigration Committee, Samuel Dickstein (D-N.Y.), this protectionist bill aimed at excluding foreign artists from performing in the United States. Olin Downes described the change in November 1942 as being highly beneficial: "Wartime has brought its trials, but also, on the long view, certain blessings in disguise to the Metropolitan and to American opera.... Up to the present time the Metropolitan has imported its principal stars from overseas. This season there has not been a single importation from Europe."[92] This nativist emphasis on U.S. performers

---

[88] For an excellent discussion of the rhetorical emphasis on democratic values in the wartime United States, see Barry Schwartz, "Memory as a Cultural System: Abraham Lincoln in World War II," *American Sociological Review* 61/5 (October 1996): 908–27.

[89] "Music and Musicians," *Los Angeles Times*, 30 May 1943.

[90] "Plans Complete for 'American' Grand Opera," *Washington Post*, 3 January 1943.

[91] According to the *Annals of the Metropolitan Opera: Performances and Artists, 1883–2000*, CD-ROM, ed. Geoffrey R. Peterson (New York: Metropolitan Opera Guild, 2002), the following works were given in English translation during World War II: Johann Sebastian Bach, *Phoebus und Pan* (1941–42); Ludwig van Beethoven, *Fidelio* (1944–45); Wolfgang Amadeus Mozart, *Die Zauberflöte* (1941–45); Nikolai Rimsky Korsakov, *Zolotoy petushok* (1944–45); Bedřich Smetana, *Prodaná nevěsta* (1941–42); and Giuseppe Verdi, *Falstaff* (1943–44).

[92] "Opera Opening," *New York Times*, 22 November 1942. Downes reinforced this point in a *New York Times* column on 21 March 1943 ("Season in Review") with the comment: "For the first time in

was even more prevalent in other companies from Philadelphia to San Francisco: The Philadelphia Opera Company prided itself, for example, on only employing native artists.[93] The advantage of this casting strategy was the creation of productions that—so the press noted—offered well-rehearsed theater by youthful "singing actors."[94]

When *Carmen Jones* opened in the fall of 1943, the show was embedded in a field of cultural production and reception that defined Americanized opera as an English-language work performed by U.S. singer/actors in an accessible and well-staged production. But Hammerstein's translation, with its use of African American dialect, also inscribed the reception of *Carmen Jones* into contemporary debates about a national theater and its use of vernacular speech. As one reviewer stated: "Mr. Hammerstein apparently understands the American idiom, whether he is writing about the West, as in 'Oklahoma,' or the Negro, as in 'Carmen Jones.' His dialogue is excitingly true and sure. His characters speak and sing words that come from the heart."[95] References to *Carmen Jones* as "an American folk drama set to music" and "a folk play with music or a 'Green Pasturized' version of Bizet" thus placed Hammerstein's book in a long tradition of linguistic regionalism in the American theater, in particular those works that used the African American vernacular.[96] The terms "folk play" and "folk drama" also invoked broader nationalist agendas that were now hinging, precisely, on generic labels that were, in turn, strongly coded.

In what can be interpreted as an effort to read *Carmen Jones* as both modern and intrinsically "American," the reviews reveal that the discourse about folk dramas underwent a subtle change in the early 1940s by merging earlier modernist tropes about the vernacular with subsequent debates in the 1930s focusing increasingly on national identity and authenticity. As Gavin Jones has pointed out in his study of dialect literature, American vernacular was a "slippery entity [whose] definition and function shifted considerably as it was made to serve a variety of cultural and ethical agendas. . . . Dialect could entertain a simultaneity of different motivations, a mixture of competing functions." The same work could employ dialect to foster a national literary agenda while stereotyping the linguistic subaltern "along the lines of ethnicity, race, and class."[97] In contrast to the European use of dialect— for example, in the stage works of Karl Kraus and Gerhart Hauptmann in the

---

Metropolitan annals they present more Americans than Europeans, there being forty-six native-born artists to forty aliens in the personnel of the association."

[93] Josephine Ripley, "Philadelphia Opera Company Starts Rehearsals in Boston," *Christian Science Monitor*, 7 January 1942; Olin Downes, "Philadelphia Opera," *New York Times*, 14 February 1943.

[94] S. S., "*Pelléas et Mélisande*," *Christian Science Monitor*, 10 January 1942.

[95] M. L. A., "The Stage: Boston Opera House: 'Carmen Jones,'" *Boston Daily Globe*, undated review, scrapbook for *Carmen Jones*, Wc OHC (hereafter scrapbook).

[96] "Carmen Jones," *Boston Herald*, 15 November 1943; Edwin H. Schloss, "Billy Rose and All-Negro Cast Stage New Version of 'Carmen,'" *Philadelphia Record*, 20 October 1943. Schloss's reference relates *Carmen Jones* to Marc Connelly's play *The Green Pastures* (1930), which included spirituals arranged by Hall Johnson.

[97] Gavin Jones, *Strange Talk: The Politics of Dialect Literature in Gilded Age America* (Berkeley: University of California Press, 1999), 210, 9.

Dixie *Carmen*

German-speaking countries, where its focus was mainly comic relief, idiomatic authenticity, or realist portrayal of (usually lower-class) individuals within the same linguistic orbit—U.S. English usage, especially in the 1920s, had an outspoken nationalist component in its rejection of what was perceived as the "linguistic authoritarianism" of the hegemonic standardization of English.[98] Furthermore, such dialect art often included a form of "racial masquerade" that shifted European social impersonations into ethnic or racial imitations that simultaneously celebrated the heterogeneity of U.S. society and reinforced its internal divisions, most dramatically in the use of stereotyped black speech (including its resonances of minstrelsy).[99] Yet this form of masquerade in turn was also part of an international phenomenon of modernist artistic appropriation of black art in a "cross-cultural, multimedia interchange" that proliferated "connections between Primitivism, beginnings, cultural myth, and ethnic difference" in both Europe and the United States.[100]

Whereas U.S. English dialect literature in the so-called Jazz Age was characterized by the complex crosscurrents between transatlantic modernism and national identity politics, the onset of the Depression turned the focus of cultural politics inward in "a flurry of renewed national interest in indigenous folk culture."[101] Even though dialect theater continued to cut across a wide range of ethnic linguistic origins, especially outside the more homogeneous New York stages and under the auspices of the Federal Theatre Project, the concept of folk drama became increasingly synonymous with African American vernacular speech and topics and took center stage in a larger project of building a "national art on indigenous folk traditions while simultaneously broadening the public's perceptions of America's folk to include and even privilege African Americans."[102] African American writer Richard Wright grudgingly acknowledged this conflation in 1937 when he wrote that "Negro writers must accept the nationalist implications of their lives."[103] This

---

[98] Michael North, *The Dialect of Modernism: Race, Language & Twentieth-Century Literature* (Oxford: Oxford University Press, 1994), 13, 26. As Jones (*Strange Talk*) points out in his second chapter, "The Cult of the Vernacular" (37–63), the use of the vernacular as criticism against social and linguistic bourgeois hegemony can be traced back to the eighteenth century. I am grateful to Reinhart Meyer Kalkus for his reference to the use of dialect German-language theater, not only with respect to parody and theatrical naturalism in German and Austrian plays but also in such operas as Hugo von Hoffmannsthal and Richard Strauss's *Der Rosenkavalier* (1911), which is replete with dialect-infused literary German.

[99] North, *The Dialect of Modernism*, 3–34.

[100] Glenn Watkins, *Pyramids at the Louvre: Music, Culture, and Collage from Stravinsky to the Postmodernists* (Cambridge, Mass.: Belknap Press, 1994), 211. See also Gubar, *Racechanges*, 44–45; North, *The Dialect of Modernism*, 59–64. For a discussion of the modernist agenda in the casting of African Americans in Stein and Thomson's *Four Saints in Three Acts*, see Lisa Barg, "Black Voices/White Sounds: Race and Representation in Virgil Thomson's *Four Saints in Three Acts*," *American Music* 18/2 (Summer 2000): 121–61.

[101] Ray Allen, "An American Folk Opera? Triangulating Folkness, Blackness, and Americaness in Gershwin and Heyward's *Porgy and Bess*," *Journal of American Folklore* 117/465 (Summer 2004): 243–61, quotation on p. 243. Even such nationalist agendas themselves were, in the 1930s, a pronouncedly international phenomenon as nation states from Germany and France to the United States and Stalinist Russia foregrounded national ideologies of art.

[102] Allen, "An American Folk Opera?" 255.

[103] Richard Wright, "Blueprint for Negro Writing" (1937), cited in Denning, *The Cultural Front*, 238. Wright continued his blueprint with a plea to transcend nationalism in African American writing.

slippage between American and African American culture led to a heated debate on cultural authority and ethnic authenticity that had African American authors and journalists in particular query a white writer's ability to represent black culture authentically.[104] The issue came to the fore, for example, when the "American folk opera" *Porgy and Bess* presented African American life as national drama, and the work elicited impassioned comments on its ability (and right) to do so. Celebrated by the majority of critics as a "milestone in the development of a national opera," the work was submitted to intense scrutiny as to how and whether the text and music fulfilled so lofty a goal.[105]

Thus *Carmen Jones* rested on the shoulders of almost two decades of folk plays produced on Broadway and an even longer debate over American folk literature. By the onset of World War II, critics no longer queried either the national credentials of an African American dialect play or its modernist identity, or even, for that matter, a white playwright's justification to appropriate African American models.[106] On the contrary, in the case of *Carmen Jones,* reviewers celebrated Hammerstein's "ultramodern" contribution to "20th-century American theatre" in this "contemporary Negro Fable."[107] The conflation of "American Negro idiom" with "American idiom" *tout court* in the reviewers' descriptions of the libretto indicates to what extent African American dialect had become, at least in some circles, a cipher for a national art. Robert Garland celebrated the work as an "amazing translation of the original French text into the beautiful *American* Negro—Southern Negro— idiom. And if you don't think this dialect is truly beautiful, read 'Uncle Remus' out loud."[108] Still, the question remained whether such an adaptation was suitable for a nineteenth-century opera. The famed music critic Olin Downes, who was otherwise rather critical of *Carmen Jones,* nevertheless proclaimed Hammerstein's translation as the proof "that an opera which reflects some real phase of contemporaneous life, as we know it, and is sung and enunciated in a language the audience can understand, gains greatly in the force of its appeal to the public."[109] Only one reviewer among the dozens who commented on Hammerstein's choice of dialect attacked the translation as ruining the French text of the opera through the

---

As Michael Denning points out (239), ethnicity and race were intimately linked to the working-class experience of each community, and they were mapped in the increasingly popular genre of ghetto-pastorals.

[104] As North (*The Dialect of Modernism*), Gilroy (*The Black Atlantic*), Gubar (*Racechanges*), Radano (*Lying Up a Nation*), and numerous other authors have discussed, African American challenges to white authors' cultural authority began in the second half of the nineteenth century and increased significantly in the 1920s, in particular in the context of the Harlem Renaissance.

[105] Pollack, *George Gershwin,* 604.

[106] For a thoughtful cultural analysis of the shift between 1930s populism and 1940s wartime politics, see Lisa Barg, "Paul Robeson's *Ballad for Americans:* Race and the Cultural Politics of 'People's Music,'" *Journal of the Society for American Music* 2/1 (February 2008): 27–70.

[107] Lewis Nichols, "The Play," *New York Times,* 3 December 1943; Waters, "Play Out of Town: Carmen Jones" (scrapbook); Howard Barnes, "The Theater," *New York Herald Tribune,* undated review (scrapbook).

[108] "The Drama," *New York Journal American,* undated review (scrapbook).

[109] "'Carmen Jones,'" *New York Times,* 19 December 1943.

Dixie *Carmen*   153

"unlovely Negroid idiom, with all of the phonetic vulgarity inherent in this mode of speech."[110]

Most critics spent a significant amount of time discussing the specific literary achievements of *Carmen Jones*, although few went so far as Robert Garland, who compared extracts from Hammerstein's version both with the French original and with what he called "the hideous translation on sale at our local Opera House."[111] African American music critic Nora Holt also dedicated a significant part of her review to the text, inviting her readers to acquire a copy of the libretto given that "the Negro idiom as Hammerstein has caught it, is so quaint and piquant it is a great joy to read it and everyone should have a copy to follow the play." Yet with all the praise, Holt also voiced her sole but serious misgiving about Hammerstein's adaptation with respect to the final lines of *Carmen Jones*:

> I rather take exception to the dramatic last words of Joe, who accepts with fatalistic philosophy the doom that faces him as a murderer. His final words are:
>
>> String me high on a tree.
>> So dat I soon will be
>> Wid my darling! my baby!
>> my Carmen!
>
> The first line is all too reminiscent of atrocities committed in the South when lynching parties occur ever and again to arouse us to shame, hatred and finally acceptance, but never forgetfulness.[112]

Joe's final lines—with their echo of Abel Meeropol's "Strange Fruit," a song made famous by Billie Holiday in 1939—had remained unchanged from Hammerstein's first version that was overtly critical of Southern segregation and may very well have been intended to evoke such atrocities deliberately as a political gesture rather than being the careless reference Holt implies. Yet in the revised version, with its emphasis on modernity and urban life, Joe's final words might indeed seem out of place without the previous social context that could have given them a critical edge.

Beyond the libretto itself, the critics tried to explore the generic implications of the adaptation of this European opera for American musical theater. Hammerstein himself addressed the matter in an interview in which he defined *Carmen Jones* as a "musical play" (the term recently canonized by *Oklahoma!*, although it was not new) as opposed to lighter genres on Broadway:

> The point is that in a musical play you are asking the audience to take the characters seriously. Usually, too, the story includes several serious, or even tragic, events.... In "Show Boat" there was the blood scene, among others; in "Oklahoma!" there is a murder, and "Carmen

---

[110] "Harlem Carmen," *Cue*, 11 December 1943. One reader of the *New York Times* complained in a letter that the "English language, and especially the Negro idiom, does not fit and fill Bizet's melodies properly, as far as I feel it." See Eric Greiffen Hagen, "Drama Mailbag: On 'Carmen Jones,'" *New York Times*, 9 January 1944.

[111] "The Drama," *New York Journal American*, undated review (scrapbook).

[112] "'Carman [sic] Jones' Magnificent with Quips, Says Nora Holt," *New York Amsterdam News*, 8 January 1944. Although Holt criticizes content, she praises Hammerstein's use of dialect. Miles M. Jefferson characterized the lyrics as "ingenious and ingenuous at the same time—quite excellent in their own right" even though he found the production overall not melodramatic enough. See Miles M. Jefferson, "The Negro on Broadway," *Phylon* 6 (1945): 48.

Jones" has a tragic ending. These realistic twists are typical of the musical play; they give a depth and an interest it wouldn't have otherwise.... The blood flows redder in "Carmen" than in "Oklahoma" of course, but essentially they are the same dramatic form.[113]

Instead of following Hammerstein's lead in relating *Carmen Jones* to Broadway musical theater, several reviewers praised the work as a powerful model in fusing folk drama and European opera into a new, hybrid form. Jerry Gahan described the work as "a genuine and successful experiment in the combining of two previously unrelated stage forms," whereas Howard Barnes praised it as a "major theatrical event" that opened "infinite and challenging horizons for the fusion of two art forms."[114] Indeed, Barnes rejoiced in *Carmen Jones* as a work that was "not 'Carmen,' but what 'Carmen' might have been had it achieved a more perfect balance of theater, spectacle, song and dancing in the first place." He thus judged the modern American version as superior to the French original, which he regarded as trapped by nineteenth-century convention. The *Boston Herald*'s music critic, Rudolph Elie, even called upon gendered language when he proclaimed Hammerstein's libretto the redemption of Bizet, who had been forced to content himself with the "emasculated setting" of a conventional libretto. "For the first time, perhaps, the story approached the level of the music."[115]

A single dissenting voice, however, denounced "the Afro-Americanization of Bizet's opera" as not just an expedient political maneuver but one that played into enemy hands. According to the anti-modernist critic Warren Storey Smith, "We do not have in 'Carmen Jones' the first instance of a brand new libretto. It has been done in the case of Weber's 'Euryanthe' because the original text was atrociously bad, and it has been done by both the Soviets and the Nazis for ideological reasons. Mr. Hammerstein's efforts, while transiently productive of good entertainment, filled no crying need."[116] This sharp comment was a slap in the face for the production's creators given their own stated claim to do patriotic work by adapting a well-known "master work" for U.S. audiences in wartime, and also because *Carmen Jones* was no less a war play than Irving Berlin's *This Is the Army* (1942) or Moss Hart's *Winged Victory* (1943) and hence, at least in part, was explicitly ideologically motivated. However, just as the literary critic Eric Bentley accused *Oklahoma!*, or at least those who wrote so favorably about it, of crypto-totalitarianism (whether of the Nazi or the Soviet kind), so too, it seems, did at least one reviewer of *Carmen Jones*, who did not accept the work's Americanized innocence.[117]

---

[113] Otis L. Guernsey, Jr., "The Playbill: Hammerstein, a Broadway Stage Dynasty," *New York Herald Tribune* (?), undated review (scrapbook).

[114] "Billy Rose's 'Carmen Jones'; in premiere at Erlanger," *Philadelphia Daily News*, 27 October 1943; Howard Barnes, "The Theater," *New York Herald Tribune*, undated review (scrapbook).

[115] "'Carmen Jones' Is Real Credit to Rose and Hammerstein," *Boston Herald*, 10 November 1943.

[116] "Of 'Carmen Jones' and 'Carmen'—A Comparison" (scrapbook). Smith, a Boston composer, usually wrote for the *Boston Post*.

[117] Carter, *Oklahoma!*, 209. Both Carl Dahlhaus and Pamela Potter have called for a transnational exploration of music during the 1930s and 1940s that would cut across the ideological division of apparently fascist and democratic musical styles. See Pamela Potter, "What Is 'Nazi Music'?" *Musical Quarterly* 88/4 (Winter 2005): 428–55.

Africa Evoked: Embodying *Carmen Jones*

On the face of it, it would seem absurd to associate *Carmen Jones* with Nazi and Soviet ideologies, not least given its evident ethnic location: Clearly, Warren Storey Smith was seeking to exorcise other demons contained, he must have felt, within the work. Here issues of race, and racism, come to the fore, and although the cast of *Carmen Jones,* and also their envoicing, might have been viewed as benign and even praiseworthy, there was also a darker edge. What if, in the end, *Carmen Jones* was not at all "American," standing outside, rather than within, the famed melting pot of social and cultural assimilations conjured up particularly during World War II as granting the force of right to the side of the United States?

If the wartime United States were the first point of the cultural triangle that shaped the creation and reception of *Carmen Jones,* Africa was the second. In a complex discursive pattern Africa was turned, on the one hand, into a bridge for *Carmen*'s travel to America from Europe—almost tracing the black transatlantic Middle Passage—and on the other, into a mythical, modernist concept of authentic cultural expression that validated the Americanized production of the work. In either case, Africa was constructed as that timeless locus of unadulterated and unmediated human expression that had fascinated modernists since the late nineteenth century.

The power of Africa as a cultural marker emerges in a comment by Hammerstein to his son Bill (19 October 1943), in which he equated the recognition of some African quality in Bizet's *Carmen* with particularly modern insight: "Our publicity man dug up a fascinating story. He found a critique of Carmen by Nietsche [*sic*] who said that the music was neither French nor German—but African! I am not as original as I thought and Nietsche was ahead of his time. Furthermore, I am pretty sure I am misspelling his name."[118] This private remark is revealing both in its reference to Africa and in its equation of this relationship with modernity. Nor is this Hammerstein's only evocation of Africa with respect to *Carmen Jones*. In the 1942 opening of Act 2—the scene at Billy Pastor's—Hammerstein describes the dancers as whirling "in a wild series of varied evolutions combining jive, jitters and African frenzy," a reference deleted in the revised version.[119] What remains of the African allusion, however, are Carmen's lyrics in "Beat out dat rhythm on a drum," which have her "feel it beatin' in my bones, / It feel like twent'y millyun tomtoms. / I know dere's twen'y millyun tomtoms / Beatin' down deep inside my bones!"[120] The musical effect was accentuated by the on-stage presence of renowned drummer Cozy Cole, who turned this sequence into a virtuoso showpiece, and

---

[118] Compare Friedrich Nietzsche, *Der Fall Wagner: Ein Musikantenproblem* (Leipzig: C. G. Naumann, 1892), 4–5: "Diese Musik ist heiter; aber nicht von einer französischen oder deutschen Heiterkeit. Ihre Heiterkeit ist afrikanisch; sie hat das Verhängniss über sich, ihr Glück ist kurz, plötzlich, ohne Pardon. Ich beneide Bizet darum, dass er den Muth zu dieser Sensibilität gehabt hat, die in der gebildeten Musik Europa's bisher noch keine Sprache hatte,—zu dieser südlicheren, bräuneren, verbrannteren Sensibilität.... Il faut méditerraniser la musique."

[119] *Carmen Jones* (1942), 2–3.

[120] Ibid., 2–2. All drafts until the printed 1945 libretto have Carmen perform "Beat out dat rhythm on a drum," and both the program for the Philadelphia performance and the playbill for the Broadway première indicate it as performed by "Carmen, Drummer, Dancers & Ensemble" (*Wc* OHC). In the

whose increasingly dominant use of the bass drum throughout that number—sonically prominent even in the number's truncated version on the original-cast album—mimicked the sonorities of the tom-toms. According to Naomi André, Harlem Renaissance authors in the 1920s and 1930s had coded the sound of the tom-toms as embodying the essence of Africa to the point that William Grant Still opened his composition *Africa* with it.[121] The same would apply, ironically, to countless representations of Africa in the movies of the 1930s on, as, for example, in Johnny Weissmuller's *Tarzan* series (1932–48). Similarly, popular music referred to the tom-tom, famously in Cole Porter's "Night and Day" ("Like the beat, beat, beat of the tom-tom / when the jungle shadows fall"). The tom-tom thus had become a widely used sonic marker of African-ness in the 1930s and 1940s, whether as a means of African American self-fashioning or as a popularized geographic signifier.

By the time of the première, Nietzsche was quoted not only by the show's publicity people but also by Billy Rose, who was not "above citing Friedrich Wilhelm Nietzsche in his critical verdict that 'Carmen's' music is more African than Spanish."[122] L. A. Sloper, the critic of the *Christian Science Monitor,* related African Americans to the Spanish because of their proximity to Africa, referring to Nietzsche as the authority who identified the Mediterranean quality of the music as the opposite of Wagner's broodings. Indeed, Sloper intimated that Nietzsche would have approved of *Carmen Jones,* for "temperamentally the Negroes are closely allied to the Spaniards. They have the capacity for expressing primitive emotion, gay or sinister. Africa borders on the Mediterranean, and this is Mediterranean music, as Nietzsche remarked. I think Nietzsche who (after he quarreled with Wagner) came to hate the Wagnerian ponderosities, would have loved this account of his favorite opera."[123] This slippage from drama to music in the references to Africa (via Nietzsche) became even more pronounced later, in 1945, when Hammerstein justified his adaptation as born out of the music itself in his introduction to the printed libretto, where he explained that the "score of *Carmen* is a Frenchman's version of Spanish music. Do not forget, however, that Spanish music was deeply influenced by the Moors from Africa."[124]

Because of the association with artistic "primitivism," Africa was not an uncontested site of reference in either the creation or the reception of *Carmen Jones.* This issue came to the fore especially in the opera's dances, where a "primitivist" rhetoric prompted some fascinating responses, as, for example, when Nora Holt attacked Olin Downes for his remark that the dancers' performances were not genuine enough and carried "evidence of too much white man's training."[125] Holt

---

original-cast recording (Decca 440 066 780-2), however, the number is sung by June Hawkins, the Frankie of the Broadway production. It is unclear when this shift happened.

[121] Naomi André, "Tom Toms and the New Negro: What Is *Africa* to William Grant Still?" paper presented at the 35th Annual Conference of the Society for American Music, Denver, 2009.
[122] Richard Maney, "Billy Rose and 'Carmen Jones,'" *New York Times,* 28 November 1943.
[123] "'Carmen Jones' Applauded at Opera House," *Christian Science Monitor,* 10 November 1943.
[124] *Carmen Jones* (1945), xviii.
[125] Olin Downes, "'Carmen Jones,'" *New York Times,* 19 December 1943.

Dixie *Carmen* 157

responded that African American dancers and actors were as much embedded in the modern world as any other of its citizens and therefore fully embodied modern culture:

> "Carmen Jones" does not suffer from a dearth of acting, contrary to the review of one critic who thought their acting creditable but flavored too much of the white man's training. Evidently this critic is still tuned to the Negro of the minstrel era and forgets that today he, the Negro, knows, hears and sees all the nuances of the modern passing show and his reactions would obviously be a part of the modern trend.[126]

Dan Burley, who reviewed *Carmen Jones* for the *New York Amsterdam News*, one of the largest African American newspapers of the 1940s, pointed to the difference between still-present minstrel traditions in contemporary theater and the modern dance of *Carmen Jones*: "The things Negroes are 'expected' to do in the theatre are conspicuous by their absence; there is no tap dancing, no crap games, no 'amen, Lawd,' no hand-clapping and shouting, praying and bowing and scraping. Instead there are marvelous ballets danced with precision, grace and dignity, as well as high skill by some of the best colored dancers in the country."[127] Eugene Loring's choreography was danced by a troupe of twenty-six dancers who—so John Hammond recalled—"came from Karamu House in Cleveland, a settlement house with great creative verve."[128] It seems, however, that Hammond's recollections were limited to the dancers he himself signed during his casting trip. Eleven members of the troupe had already performed on Broadway in such productions as *Four Saints in Three Acts* (1934), *Cabin in the Sky* (1940), and the revival of *Run, Little Chillun*, which ended its short run on 26 August 1943, three weeks before rehearsals started for *Carmen Jones*.

The reception of African American concert dance, as Susan Manning has observed, "underwent considerable change, and by the end of the war Negro dance

---

[126] "'Carman [sic] Jones' Magnificent with Quips, Says Nora Holt," *New York Amsterdam News*, 8 January 1944. Holt's use of the strongly coded term "passing" in opposition to minstrelsy identifies contemporary African American performance as an activist strategy. As David Garcia has pointed out to me, the debate between Downes and Holt is part of a broader discourse on black assimilation to white culture and survival of African cultural specificity (in particular with respect to Afro-Caribbean and Afro-Latin cultures) that involved foundational figures in American ethnomusicology and African diasporic studies, including Meville J. Herskovits, Richard A. Waterman, George Herzog, and E. Franklin Frazier.

[127] "All-Negro Opera, 'Carmen Jones,' Scores in Philly Première," *New York Amsterdam News*, 30 October 1943. Burley, who was the managing editor as well as the theater and sports critic of the *New York Amsterdam News*, compiled in these years his *Original Handbook of Harlem Jive* (1944), in which he documented African American speech patterns of the period. One possible target for Burley may have been *Porgy and Bess*, which contains all the elements he listed in his review, save the tap dancing (unless Sportin' Life's moves were seen as such).

[128] Hammond and Townsend, *On Record*, 243. In her article about the dances, Margaret Lloyd reports that the troupe consisted of twenty-six dancers who had not been hired from theatrical agencies but instead found by Hammond in his casting tour through the United States, in a manner similar to the Cinderella story of the singer/actors. See "Co-Incidental Dances," *Christian Science Monitor*, 4 December 1943. On Karamu House, see Reuben Silver, "A History of the Karamu Theatre of Karamu House, 1915–1960," Ph.D. diss., Ohio State University, 1961.

had established its authority on the American stage."[129] For Dan Burley and Nora Holt, at least, *Carmen Jones* was part of this positive change. Alas, Loring's papers contain barely a trace of his *Carmen Jones* choreography, possibly as a result of his contract that transferred sole ownership of the choreography to Billy Rose.[130] This lacuna limits the information about the dances in *Carmen Jones* to a handful of photographs and summary descriptions in the newspapers, although Loring's work for Hollywood immediately after *Carmen Jones* might offer some idea of his choreography in the exotic dances he staged in *Yolanda and the Thief* (1945) and, especially, the final sequence of *The Thrill of Brazil* (1946).[131] However, the most informative text on the choreography comes from an article based on an interview between Loring and Margaret Lloyd of the *Christian Science Monitor* (4 December 1943). Here we learn that Loring insisted that African American performers were individuals in their abilities and tastes and resented especially when they were "told that boogie-woogie is Negro dancing. What the serious artists among them want to develop is a Negro art dance that will be just as fine and rich in its way as ballet is in its." Whether the words were Loring's or his interviewer's, the text makes a difference between "Negro art dance" and "ballet" that echoes other discussions about African American concert dance in the 1940s as a distinct art form on its own. According to this interview, *Carmen Jones* had three main ballets: a "little opening dance in waltz time" (to "Good Luck, Mr. Flyin' Man"); a "big dance number in Billy Pastor's café" (to "Beat out dat rhythm on a drum"); and a "Spanish Dance" in Act 2 (to music drawn from Bizet's *Roma Suite*). As Loring pointed out in the interview, each number fulfilled a different function in the musical play.

The first was a brief number that had dancers intermingled with the chorus, who moved into a dance halfway through. The final ballet, on the other hand, provided entertainment in honor of Poncho the Panther (Husky Miller's Brazilian challenger) and hence offered "something Spanish" by dancers who were presented as performers at the "Cuba Libra Night Club."[132] In contrast, Loring's remarks on the central ballet of *Carmen Jones* at Billy Pastor's café suggest his interest to choreograph a programmatic representation of racial "uplift":

> [The dance] starts with Cozy Cole's drum beats and the pulse is regular, simple, like heart beats. But the rhythms soon arouse deep instincts and emotions, causing one of the girls to come forward and do a primitive dance alone. The feeling spreads as the rhythms become

---

[129] Susan Manning, *Modern Dance, Negro Dance: Race in Motion* (Minneapolis: University of Minnesota Press, 2004), 142.

[130] Contract between Eugene Loring and Billy Rose, 26 July 1943, *NYp* BRC: "All dances staged and all other ideas conceived, created or contributed by you, shall be the sole property of Billy Rose's Diamond Horseshoe, Inc." Neither Loring's papers in *NYp* nor his archives at the University of California at Irvine contain more than scrapbooks and programs with respect to *Carmen Jones*.

[131] I am grateful to one of my anonymous reviewers for pointing me to these numbers and their historic proximity to the staging of *Carmen Jones*.

[132] Music for both ballets, identified as "Parachute Dance" and "Spanish Ballet" respectively, is preserved at *NYp*, shelf mark JPB 82–75 no. 3 (l, t). Lloyd's spelling seems influenced by the popular *Cuba Libra* cocktail.

Dixie *Carmen*

    wilder, and soon all are dancing their individual response to the call of the drums. There are three outstanding types—one represented by the earthy first girl giving free vent to her feelings; a second by a group who try to hide the primitive under a cloak of sophistication; and a third, feeling the urge as strongly as the others, but transmuting it into a sense of aspiration (draw what parallels to racial problems you will). The aspiration culminates in the ascent of one over the bent backs of her companions into an unusual lift. She eventually falls (rolling down over these same backs) and is caught up in the terrific physical and emotional conflict that ends in exhaustion.

Loring's rhetoric of "uplift" fits into broader discussions about representations of racial politics in music and dance in the early 1940s, whether in the performances of the Karamu Dancers at the New York World's Fair (who related African ritual to modern dance in an evolutionary sequence of numbers) or in Duke Ellington's presentation, in January 1943, of *Black, Brown, and Beige* in a concert at Carnegie Hall, a programmatic piece that traced African American experiences from slavery to a Utopian future in modern U.S. society.[133] As Lisa Barg has argued, Ellington's work faced the difficulty of "preserving a discrete racial and cultural identity while at the same time embracing 'European' evolutionist ideology";[134] but whereas the political implications of Ellington's composition and performance shaped the work's reception, the multilayered representation of black cultural identity and its evolution as developed by Loring and his African American dancers in the "Billy Pastor" ballet in *Carmen Jones* remained a hidden program, at least as far as the reaction of the critics was concerned. Instead, the scene at Billy Pastor was fêted as representation of primitive dance to a music "whooped up with added jungle rhythm by Cosy [*sic*] Cole as a demon drummer who cuts loose in pulse-pounding fashion."[135]

A (Universal) European Soundscape: The Music of *Carmen Jones*

If the dancers were caught in the dichotomy between celebrations of modern dance on the one hand and expectations of "primitive" authenticity on the other, the singers found themselves in an even more complex bind, given that the music remained ostensibly European even as everything else was transferred to the United States. Viewed positively, this dialogical multivalence inscribed the singers as an embodiment of cultural hybridity between American modernity, African authenticity, and European culture; viewed negatively, it left them lost in a cultural aporia. For the most part, the positive view prevailed, as perhaps was inevitable given *Carmen Jones*'s evident success and its wartime mission. Critics attributed a "naturalness"

---

    [133] On the performance of the Karamu Dancers in New York, see Silver, "A History of the Karamu Theatre," 327–28. *Black, Brown, and Beige* has been discussed, with respect to its politics of race in the wartime United States in Kevin Gaines, "Duke Ellington, *Black, Brown, and Beige,* and the Cultural Politics of Race," in *Music and the Racial Imagination,* ed. Ronald Radano and Philip V. Bohlman (Chicago: University of Chicago Press, 2000), 585–602.

    [134] Lisa Barg, "National Voices/Modernist Histories: Race, Performance and Remembrance in American Music, 1927–1943," Ph.D. diss., State University of New York at Stony Brook, 2001, 180.

    [135] Linton Martin, "'Carmen Jones' Opens at Erlanger," *Philadelphia Inquirer,* undated review (scrapbook).

to the African American cast, with the result that passages "that sometimes seem out of the grasp of white singers are done effectively."[136] Virgil Thomson declared that the "production has two elements of authenticity. One is Oscar Hammerstein's translation, and the other is the Negro company."[137] By imbuing the African American cast with such authenticity—a wholly positive term for him in this context—Thomson and his fellow critics appropriated the work for the United States through a rhetorical twist that turned the French original into the race-changing copy, as, for example, when John Chapman reported in early 1944 that he had gone "to hear the standard, or whiteface French, version of 'Carmen'."[138] Deems Taylor seems to have been the source for this flipping of standard performances of Bizet's opera (as presented by the Met) into inferior and inauthentic travesties when he wrote to Hammerstein immediately after experiencing *Carmen Jones* for the first time: "Saw the old version of 'Carmen' at the Met, on Monday night. Did you know? They're doing it in *white*-face!"[139] *Carmen Jones* thus stood as a truly American alternative not only to its French original but also to the exclusive pretensions of the Metropolitan Opera House.

For this appropriation to work, however, the music needed to remain Bizet's, given that any obvious tampering with the score would undermine the work's cultural authority in this complicated web of cultural transfer. Indeed, from the very first document—Berger's letter from 19 February 1942 (cited above)—private as much as public conversations about the work emphasized the fact that *Carmen Jones* went against the grain and did not "swing" the score. As Billy Rose put it in an interview: "Naturally we would not dare alter the music."[140] This "naturally" is intriguing, for it proclaims (or at least, pretends) a transcendence that protected the work from wartime anti-European sentiment (a danger even with its French origin) and also granted a U.S. appropriation some sense of universality. Hammerstein, Rose, and their publicity team refer repeatedly to Bizet's "immortal music" from, one might infer, a now-occupied country, the very survival of which was severely in doubt.[141] Hammerstein had already demonstrated his nostalgia for all things French in the lyrics of the Academy Award–winning song "The Last Time I Saw Paris" (1940, with music by Jerome Kern). Now he had gone a definite step

---

[136] Robert Bagar, "Opera Relives in Carmen Jones," *New York Herald Tribune*, undated review (scrapbook).

[137] Virgil Thomson, "Carolina *Carmen*" (5 December 1943), in *The Art of Judging Music* (New York: Alfred Knopf, 1948), 127. Later in the article, however, the oblique reference to *Four Saints in Three Acts* suggests some resentment: "This is not the first Negro opera production Broadway has seen nor the most distinguished" (ibid.). The issue of African American embodiment and notions of "authenticity" in the context of *Four Saints* are discussed in Nadine Hubbs, *The Queer Composition of America's Sound: Gay Modernists, American Music, and National Identity* (Berkeley: University of California Press, 2004), 19–63.

[138] John Chapman, "'Carmen' in Mixed-up French vs. 'Carmen Jones' in Good English," *New York Daily News* (?) (scrapbook).

[139] Deems Taylor, letter to Oscar Hammerstein II, 30 November 1943. John Chapman referred to this letter when he revealed that "Deems Taylor recently wrote Oscar Hammerstein that he'd just been to the Metropolitan to see 'Carmen' in whiteface" (unreferenced article scrapbook).

[140] "Alias 'Jones,' But She Is Still Bizet['s] 'Carmen,'" *Christian Science Monitor*, 21 October 1943; Sam Zolotow, "Opening Tonight of 'Carmen Jones,'" *New York Times*, 2 December 1943.

[141] This quotation is from the program of the Philadelphia première, 19 October 1943.

Dixie *Carmen* 161

further by choosing the most famous French opera and its timeless music for this adaptation.

The press picked up on the (supposed) fidelity to Bizet's score by insisting that save "a few minor rephrasings and a couple of cuts, for purposes of theatrical comfort, the score has been left intact," or, in another critic's words, "the music remains untouched."[142] According to John Chapman, "This production is no hopped-up version of an opera; it's no 'Hot Mikado' or 'Swing Mikado.' It is straight 'Carmen.'"[143] Linton Martin for his part emphasized that Bizet's music had received far better treatment in *Carmen Jones* than Tchaikovsky's at the hand of arrangers: "No Tin Pan Alley twist has been given to any of the arias, dance rhythms or marches, unlike the liberties that have been taken with Tchaikovsky by the unholy hands of tawdry tunesmiths."[144] Such claims may have been unjust: Leta Miller points out that *The Swing Mikado* remained surprisingly faithful to Gilbert and Sullivan save for the altered orchestration and the added swing numbers.[145] Yet the fact that they were made remains significant. In contrast to other shows such as *Oklahoma!* where his skill as orchestrator stood in the foreground, the praise that Robert Russell Bennett received for his arrangement of Bizet's score highlighted the fact that he remained as faithful to the original as was possible with the smaller orchestra of a Broadway show.[146]

Bennett's own comments in interviews and in the souvenir program emphasized his role as a servant to great music. He pointed out that Bizet was "the combination of a great tune-writer and great orchestrator" and that in "adapting the orchestration to Mr. Hammerstein's vivid version of the drama my effort has been to carry out George Bizet's intention of color and balance. . . . Mine has been truly a labor of love."[147] It is striking that Bennett's view of his task as a "labor of love" was so close to Hammerstein's, and in both cases the trope seems to embody claims for authenticity (here for Bizet's score) and even for artistic status. In an undated letter

---

[142] "Escamillo vs. Husky Miller," *Christian Science Monitor*, 4 November 1943; Sam Zolotow, "Opening Tonight of 'Carmen Jones,'" *New York Times*, 2 December 1943.

[143] "New York Has Another Theater Hit: 'Carmen Jones,'" *Chicago Daily Tribune*, 12 December 1943.

[144] "Debut of 'Carmen Jones' Is Provocative Occasion," *Philadelphia Inquirer*, 24 October 1943. In the contemporaneous MGM short *Heavenly Music* (1943), Tchaikovsky complains about his fate at the hands of American arrangers (and the ensuing lack of royalties).

[145] I am grateful to Leta Miller for sharing this information from her article "Elmer Keeton and His 'Bay Area Negro Chorus': Creating an Artistic Identity in Depression-Era San Francisco" (forthcoming, *Black Music Research Journal* 30/2 [Fall 2010]). Recent musicological research has begun to explore the history of "swinging" classical works (including such operettas as Gilbert and Sullivan's *The Mikado*) in the United States during the 1930s and 1940s. See, for example, David W. Stowe, *Swing Changes: Big-Band Jazz in New Deal America* (Cambridge, Mass.: Harvard University Press, 1994).

[146] Originally Bennett was slated not only to arrange Bizet's score but also to conduct the rehearsals and performances of *Carmen Jones*. This arrangement, however, became problematic given Bennett's less than stellar performances as conductor during the Philadelphia tryout. In the end, Bennett had to be replaced by Joseph Littau, a seasoned conductor who was described in the souvenir program fittingly as "one of those rarities in musical America, a native-born conductor, of purely American stock" (*Carmen Jones*, Souvenir Program, 15).

[147] Robert Russell Bennett, "The Music of 'Carmen Jones,'" *Carmen Jones*, Souvenir Program, 5.

to Hammerstein, Bennett agreed to the wholesale cutting of numbers but added "a short list of things I don't believe in doing to Bizet's music:

1. Making jump arrangements out of melodies that will long outlive jump arrangements.
2. Interpolating songs by Jerome Romberg.
3. Building up routines by Bob Alton, with special choruses and fancy exits.
4. 'Saving' numbers by Hartman methods."[148]

For Bennett, his work on *Carmen Jones* was the fulfillment of the dream that had brought the "all-American" farm boy from Kansas to the study of classical music. Both in an interview and in his autobiography, Bennett connected his involvement in this particular project to his youthful musical aspirations and presented it as the fulfillment of his own social and cultural uplift, especially when he contrasted his making a living by working with contemporary Broadway composers such as George Gershwin, Cole Porter, and Jerome Kern with the personal form of inspiration found in studying "the scores of the great masters."[149] Whenever Bennett discussed his work on *Carmen Jones*, he presented himself as a translator of Bizet into the pit of a Broadway theater, not an arranger of his music. Both Bennett and Hammerstein, it seems, felt that musically, at least, *Carmen Jones* remained true to its operatic type and could hence be claimed as a work sui generis that kept it equally distant from the Met's operas and Broadway's musicals.

The musical sources—so far as they survive—support the claim that Bennett's arrangement remained close to Bizet's original. As in *Oklahoma!*, he used a slimmed-down version of a typical symphony orchestra (no saxophones in either score), although the ensemble for *Carmen Jones* was larger than that of usual Broadway productions, starting out with forty musicians.[150] Bennett created his text by re-working a printed orchestral score for the available instruments, referring to it in the manuscript of some of his adaptations, for example, in the finale of Act 2 (Act 4 in Bizet) where he requested first "Copy from page 469 measure 4 to page 470

---

[148] Bennett's reference to Jerome Romberg presents a humorous conflation of two composers' names, Jerome Kern and Sigmund Romberg; Robert Alton was a highly successful Broadway choreographer in the 1930s and 1940s; and the "Hartman method" may refer to Paul and Gracie Hartman, a successful dance team whose numbers, for example in their noted "Hoke Bolero," were interpolated into Broadway shows such as *Keep 'Em Laughing* (1942). I am grateful to Daniel Goldmark and one of my anonymous reviewers for their help identifying these references.

[149] Lucy Greenbaum, "About an Arranger: Mr. Bennett Discusses His Craft and Talks of 'Carmen Jones,'" *New York Times*, 24 October 1943; *"The Broadway Sound": The Autobiography and Selected Essays of Robert Russell Bennett*, ed. George J. Ferencz (Rochester, N.Y.: University of Rochester Press, 1999), 188.

[150] The orchestra got cut, however, to thirty-two in January when the American Federation of Musicians Union Local 802 insisted on reclassifying the work as a "Class B opera" instead of an "operetta." Ironically the public discourse on *Carmen Jones*, with its emphasis on the operatic aspect of the work, made it easier for the union to defend its reclassification, which meant that the players were paid $99 per week instead of $88. See "'Carmen' Band Gets More $$$," *New York Amsterdam News*, 15 January 1944. The same article alleges that the actors' salaries "are some of the lowest on Broadway."

Dixie *Carmen* 163

measure 3," and then, a page later, demanded: "All down 1 ½ tones to E major."[151] Indeed, in those musical numbers that were transferred from the opera into *Carmen Jones* (see Appendix), Bennett used his skill as orchestrator to reproduce the sound of Bizet's full symphony orchestra as closely as possible with the instrumentalists available, and the original-cast album that was recorded in the Broadway Theater on 17–20 September 1944 gives an excellent sense of this musical feat.

Bennett also added several extracts from Bizet's other output to the *Carmen Jones* score: Bizet's *Roma Suite* provided the "Spanish Ballet" in Act 2; an extract from *La Jolie Fille de Perth* seemed to have been planned as an opening to the original Act 2 (Act 1, Scene 3 in the revised version); and part of the *Arlesienne Suite* became Husky Miller's entrance ("new No. 19").[152] Other fragments from *Carmen* were reorchestrated as underlay for melodramas, for example, the reprise of the Habanera as No. 12 after Carmen's ditty "Coupe-moi, brûle-moi" (translated by Hammerstein as "You ain' no police'm"). According to Bennett's autobiography, he reworked the arrangement of "Beat out dat rhythm on a drum" at Billy Rose's request into a more glittering and "modern" orchestration after the Philadelphia tryouts. For Bennett, however, this change proved his point that Bizet's original scoring was more effective than any more jazzy revision, because he felt that the powerful counterpoint between Cozy Cole's "wild and wonderful" drumming and Bizet's score created a more exciting sonic result than the sleeker new version ever could.[153] In the end, Bennett was rewarded for his work on *Carmen Jones* with a Billboard Award for the best score.[154]

The original-cast recording, which was recorded during, and released soon after the end of, the American Federation of Musicians' (AFM) recording ban, offers a fascinating window on the music for *Carmen Jones*.[155] From the overture to the finale, it resembles closely the albums of operatic highlights from *Carmen* that were recorded by the Metropolitan Opera House and contains only numbers that were originally part of the *Carmen* score. The overture, in particular, could have opened a traditional operatic recording such as the one from the Met that Sir Thomas Beecham had conducted in 1943. The main difference between the two overture recordings is the slightly reduced orchestra in *Carmen Jones*, for which the sound engineers clearly tried to compensate to the best of their

---

[151] *NYp*, JPB 82–75 no. 3 (l). I have not been able to ascertain which score Bennett used, but assume it was probably the Choudens score, which he could have acquired during his studies in Paris with Nadia Boulanger.

[152] *NYp*, JPB 82–75 no. 3 (o) names the extract as such. For the original "No. 19," Bennett adapted Carmen's 6/8 "Là-bas, là-bas dans la montagne" as a *Valse vive* in 3/4. I am grateful to Lesley Wright for identifying this fragment. Manuscripts for the *Valse vive* can be found in *NYp*, JPB 82–75 no. 3 (n, v). Whereas several critics picked up on the use of the *Roma Suite* for the Spanish Ballet, only one critic, Robert Bagar in the *New York Herald Tribune*, mentioned the use of "a fragment of the Arlesienne music."

[153] "The Broadway Sound," 190.

[154] "Voice of the Turtle Wins New Award," *New York Times*, 4 July 1944. Other awards that went to *Carmen Jones* were "best musical play," "best musical direction" (Hassard Short), and "best lyrics" (Oscar Hammerstein).

[155] The ban ended on 11 November 1944, when the last of the major record companies signed the contract about performance royalties with the AFM.

ability. The operatic quality of the music is particularly noticeable in the vocal style adopted by Muriel Smith (Carmen Jones), Carlotta Franzell (Cindy Lou), and June Hawkins (Frankie), whose enunciation and vocal production were self-consciously operatic. The odd number out in this recording is "Beat out dat rhythm on a drum," just as it was in the stage production. Here Cozy Cole's drum kit replaces the Spanish-tinted percussion in Bizet's score and brings the world of jazz into counterpoint with Bizet's music, creating an Americanized sonority enveloping the European score. Yet the very next number, Husky Miller's "Stan' up an' fight," restores Bizet's sound world through its orchestral introduction, "Spanish" triangles included.

The orchestra for *Carmen Jones* was integrated, with at least five African American performers, including Cozy Cole, who besides his on-stage solo played percussion in the pit, and Everett Lee, the concertmaster of the production. Apparently Billy Rose forced the hand of the AFM by insisting on their inclusion.[156] Cozy Cole's presence (especially under an on-stage spotlight during the scene in Billy Pastor's café) lent to the production the cachet of a famous jazz drummer: His drum solos during his years (1938–42) with Cab Calloway's nationally known jazz band were widely celebrated. Reviewers and audiences alike applauded him accordingly. For Everett Lee, on the other hand, *Carmen Jones* became a turning point in his career. In a portrait celebrating this "First Negro Concert Meister," Nora Holt claimed that he was thus far "probably the only Negro ever to have held that title."[157] At the suggestion of the show's main conductor, Joseph Littau, Lee also prepared himself to conduct the score should the necessity arise, which indeed came to pass about two months into the Broadway run. As his wife remembers, this "was the first time that an African American had conducted a major Broadway show."[158]

The attention of the critics focused mainly on the singers, and in particular, the principals. The uncontested star of the show was Muriel Smith, a young singer trained at the Curtis Institute, who performed the title role (see Figure 3). For Hammerstein, Smith was "probably the best [Carmen] in several generations."[159] Smith—so one critic said—was "ideal in appearance for the part" and sang "with assurance in a mezzo-voice of agreeable quality and sufficient volume."[160] Others called her "a remarkable combination of actress and vocalist," praised her as "the best acted Carmen I ever saw," and pushed alliteration in describing her as a "sexy,

---

[156] Steven Suskin, *The Sound of Broadway Music: A Book of Orchestrators and Orchestrations* (Oxford: Oxford University Press, 2009), 356.

[157] "Everett Lee, First Negro Concert Meister, Soloist in 'Carmen Jones,'" *New York Amsterdam News*, 29 January 1944. Lee performed two solos throughout the run of *Carmen Jones*. A third, on-stage solo was cut, however, after the tryouts because it slowed down the action in Act 2.

[158] Schiller Institute, "Dialogue with Sylvia Olden Lee, Pianist and Vocal Coach," 7 February 1998, http://www.schillerinstitute.org/fid_97-01/fid_981_lee_interview.html (accessed 1 February 2009). According to the interview, Littau had tried to convince Billy Rose to appoint Lee officially as his assistant but Rose refused, and Lee's opportunity came when Littau did not show up one evening. Given the lack of opportunities for African American conductors in the United States, Lee moved to the Federal Republic of Germany and Sweden after the war.

[159] Letter to Bill Hammerstein, 25 October 1943.

[160] "'Carmen Jones' Opens at Erlanger," *Philadelphia Inquirer*, undated review (scrapbook).

Dixie *Carmen* 165

Figure 3. *Carmen Jones* (1943), Act I, Scene 3, "Dis Flower"; Muriel Smith (Carmen Jones) and Luther Saxton (Joe). Courtesy of the Rodgers & Hammerstein Organization.

sinuous siren—an ideal Carmen."[161] For Muriel Smith and her fellow singers, the point of comparison was not, in the end, a Broadway show such as *Cabin in the Sky* but the concurrent performance of *Carmen* at the Met.[162] Indeed, as Dan Burley reported, there were "veteran critics who said Miss Muriel Smith is almost sure to sing the role in the Metropolitan 'Carmen' next season."[163] Of course, she

---

[161] Waters, "Play Out of Town: Carmen Jones," (scrapbook); John Chapman, "New York Has Another Theater Hit: 'Carmen Jones,'" *Chicago Daily Tribune*, 12 December 1943; Robert Coleman, Rose Does Fine Job in 'Carmen Jones'," *New York Daily Mirror*, undated review (scrapbook).

[162] This point has eluded scholars, who routinely insert *Carmen Jones* solely into the performance tradition of Broadway and film, and therefore miss a significant part of the debate. See Woll, *Black Musical Theatre*, 184–89; Susan McClary, *Georges Bizet: Carmen* (Cambridge: Cambridge University Press, 1993), 131–35; Clark, "Local Color"; Depardieu, "*Carmen Jones*"; and especially Jeff Smith, "Black Faces, White Voices: The Politics of Dubbing in *Carmen Jones*," *The Velvet Light Trap* 51 (Spring 2003): 29–42.

[163] "All-Negro Opera, 'Carmen Jones,' Scores in Philly Première," *New York Amsterdam News*, 30 October 1943. Burley's article was picked up by the Associated Negro Press (ANP) and published, in abbreviated form, in the *Pittsburgh Courier*, also on 30 October 1943.

never did.[164] Other performers—such as Napoleon Reed—were associated with the National Negro Opera Company, founded by Mary Cardwell Dawson in 1941 with the intention to "convince members of our racial group, and our friends among other races, many of whom are already well initiated in operatic culture, of the possibilities of our efforts in this field."[165] For Dawson, the operatic canon was the medium of choice for engendering "racial pride," thus imbuing classical music with the same kind of symbolic capital that W. E. B. Du Bois had ascribed to the great books of Shakespeare, Aristotle, or Dumas in his formulation of a Black University.[166] Likewise, according to Walter White in the *Chicago Defender:* "'Carmen Jones' marks a new round in the upward ladder of Negroes in the theatre. Negro actors and actresses gave new life to Shakespeare in the WPA production of 'Macbeth' in 1936. 'Carmen Jones' does the same for grand opera."[167] Especially during World War II this discourse about racial uplift crossed with a broader, national agenda of cultural uplift through education that transferred New Deal sensibilities into a national agenda of class politics.

By contrasting *Carmen Jones* with *Carmen* at the Met, critics addressed the issue of class and classical music. *Carmen Jones*, so wrote one critic, was "no highfalutin opera."[168] In contrast to the usual fare at the "snooty Metropolitan Opera House," *Carmen Jones* was "the greatest proof the theater has had thus far that opera can be a living art and not a museum of memories."[169] Again, this clearly was overstated. The Met had long attempted—through its decade of broadcasts and, now, its war-generated drop in ticket prices—to contribute to the broader dissemination of opera. However, Hammerstein was glad to point out that "long-haired musicians and even the critics" had been won over by *Carmen Jones*, and Warren Storey Smith applauded, if somewhat backhandedly, the success of "lowbrows" in an arena "where aesthetes would fear to tread."[170] For John Chapman it was precisely the contrast to the Metropolitan Opera stars' vocal prowess that made the performances of Muriel Smith and Luther Saxon (Joe) so appealing, given that "the whole production has been built around this very fact, and the result is a 'Carmen' without heroics in

---

[164] According to the obituary of Muriel Smith published in *The Black Perspective in Music* 13/2 (Autumn 1985), 244–45, Smith left the United States in 1949 and built her career in London, where she performed the title role in *Carmen* at Covent Garden. In our telephone conversation (21 April 2009), Alice Hammerstein Mathias recalled that Muriel Smith later did a significant number of uncredited voice-overs in movies. Among others, Smith lent her voice to Zsa Zsa Gabor in *Moulin Rouge* (1952).

[165] Program book, *Aida*, Pittsburgh, 30 October 1941, p. 2, National Negro Opera Company Collection, Library of Congress, Box 1.

[166] Gilroy, *The Black Atlantic*, 121. For a study emphasizing the intersections of race, class, and gender in the developing discourses of "uplift," see Kevin K. Gaines, *Uplifting the Race: Black Leadership, Politics, and Culture in the Twentieth Century* (Chapel Hill: University of North Carolina Press, 1996). See also Christopher Wells, "Grand Opera as Racial Uplift: The National Negro Opera Company (1941–1962)," M.A. thesis, University of North Carolina at Chapel Hill, 2009.

[167] "People and Places," *Chicago Defender*, 6 November 1943.

[168] "New Musical in Manhattan," *Time*, 13 December 1943.

[169] "New Plays in Review," *Clue*, 11 December 1943; "Carmen Gone Broadway," *Newsweek*, 13 December 1943.

[170] Hammerstein quoted in M. L. A., "'Carmen Jones' Defies All Opera Tradition," *Boston Daily Globe*, undated review (scrapbook); Warren Storey Smith, "Billy Rose Opens New Show Here," *Boston Post*, 10 November 1943.

Dixie *Carmen* 167

which everybody seems like a living, normal person. Of how many operas you have seen can you say that?"[171] Again, an African American cast gave *Carmen Jones* the flavor of the natural, a view whose potential to backfire (in favor of the primitive) was mitigated by wartime inclusiveness. Moreover, *Carmen Jones* was now seen as the ideal opera for everyone, a truly appropriate presentation of European classical music for the needs of contemporary U.S. Americans.[172] As Edwin H. Schloss noted: "Some years ago the late George Gershwin told this reporter that Bizet's 'Carmen' was 'a hit show with a dozen hit tunes—only the public doesn't know it yet.' Now thanks to Billy Rose's cash and intrepidity, Hammerstein's uncommon skill as a librettist, Hassard Short's direction, the costumes of Raoul Pene du Bois and above all, Bizet's music, it appears the public needn't remain in ignorance much longer."[173]

* * *

The public certainly celebrated *Carmen Jones* in 1943 and 1944. Lee Shubert's Broadway Theater remained sold out week after week, and on one evening in January 1944, the audience even became involved in physical altercations because the box office had sold the tickets for a section of the balcony twice.[174] Capitalizing on its successful run in New York, *Carmen Jones* soon opened in Chicago and then went on tour across the country; after the war, the work was performed abroad, and finally, in 1954, transformed into the well-known motion picture. Yet as successful as *Carmen Jones* was as a musical play, it remained its own product. Contrary to Hammerstein's hopes, Americanized operatic adaptations on Broadway in the vein of *Carmen Jones* were the exception rather than the rule. One such work was *My Darlin' Aida* (1952), which set Verdi's opera in the U.S. South during the Civil War and which involved several members of the *Carmen Jones* production team, including Charles Friedman (who wrote the book and directed the show), Hassard Short (as production supervisor), and Robert Shaw (as choral director). After the war, however, opera found different media to reach the masses, and even the mainstream opera houses of the United States started, albeit slowly, to engage African American singers. It is perhaps no coincidence that Hammerstein's version of *Carmen* more or less vanished from the American stage when singers such as Grace Bumbry set new standards for the performance of Bizet's opera. Yet, after decades of relative obscurity, both Hammerstein's concepts of operatic transfer and *Carmen Jones* itself have presently found a new life. Thus recent *Carmen* adaptations—whether Robert Townsend's *Carmen: A Hip Hopera* (2001) or (especially) Mark Dornford-May's South African *U-Carmen e-Khayelitsha* (2005)—use similar dramaturgical strategies to Hammerstein's.

---

[171] "New York Has Another Theater Hit: 'Carmen Jones,'" *Chicago Daily Tribune*, 12 December 1943.

[172] I will address the roles of classical music in the United States during World War II in my forthcoming monograph *Sounds of War: Music in America during World War II*.

[173] "Billy Rose and All-Negro Cast Stage New Version of 'Carmen,'" *Philadelphia Record*, 20 October 1943.

[174] "Twice-Sold Tickets Upset Performance," *New York Times*, 21 January 1944.

As for *Carmen Jones:* When the Royal Festival Hall in London presented its first staged production after its extensive refurbishment, it opened, on 25 July 2007, with Hammerstein's musical play. The coproducer, populist impresario Raymond Gubbay, lauded the adaptation as "accessible and approachable for a huge and a wide public who might not ordinarily go to the opera house."[175] In order to make the production more relevant for today's audience, the director, Jude Kelly, and her designer, Michael Vale, decided to change the setting to twenty-first-century Cuba.[176] According to Vale, adhering to the original setting of *Carmen Jones* in the United States of the 1940s ran "the danger of it becoming a little bit of a museum piece." Furthermore, whereas Vale concurred that "some of the references... were very modern and evocative and contemporary at the time it was written in the 1940s," he felt that they did not have "the same kind of resonance now."[177] The cast, led by the South African soprano Tsakane Valentine Maswanganyi as Carmen, was black (as Hammerstein had stipulated should be the case for the entire cast in every performance of the work), and Jude Kelly explained in an interview with *The Times* that this was "partly why I chose the piece.... I feel strongly that there just aren't enough opportunities for black British or black American musical performers to demonstrate their talents. There aren't enough vehicles, and as a result their voices often don't get trained for demanding work like *Carmen Jones*. It's a circle that needs breaking."[178] Whether in the claim to democratizing opera, in the call for musical theater to be relevant, or in the assertion of offering performance opportunities for black opera singers, the rhetoric swirling around the 2007 production of *Carmen Jones* presents an eerie echo of most of the discourse surrounding the original *Carmen Jones* in wartime New York. It seems as if even in a current production, Hammerstein's work cannot but help to be instrumentalized as a symbol of art's social dimension, just as it was during World War II in the United States.

APPENDIX: Main Musical Numbers in *Carmen* and *Carmen Jones**

This table of the main musical numbers represents the following stages of *Carmen Jones* in comparison to Bizet's and Halévy's *Carmen*:

1. The first version (copyright libretto of 1942)
2. The revised version (copyright and production libretti of 1943). I have noted the two instances where this version differs from the final version (libretto: New York: Alfred Knopf, 1945; score: Rodgers and Hammerstein Theatricals, 2007)

---

[175] Pre-production interview with Raymond Gubbay, podcast at http://www.southbankcentre.co.uk/carmenjones/behindthescenes/podcast.html (accessed 10 December 2008).

[176] Sam Marlow, "Bizet Meets Buena Vista," *The Times,* 9 June 2007. Marlow makes the point that the production echoed the recent fascination with all things Cuban, not least since Wim Wenders' 1999 *Buena Vista Social Club.*

[177] Pre-production interview with Michael Vale, podcast at http://www.southbankcentre.co.uk/carmenjones/behindthescenes/podcast.html (accessed 10 December 2008).

[178] Marlow, "Bizet Meets Buena Vista."

Dixie *Carmen* 169

Carmen (1875)	*Carmen Jones* (1942)	*Carmen Jones* (1943)
Overture	Prelude	Prelude
ACT I *A Square in Seville, outside a Cigarette Factory*	ACT I *Outside a Cigarette Factory, near a Southern Town*	ACT I *Outside a Parachute Factory, near a Southern Town*
1. Chœur (Soldats) Sur la place chacun passe 2. Air et Chœur (Moralès) Attention! chut! attention! 3. Chœur (Gamins) Avec la garde montante 4. Chœur et Scène La cloche a sonné	Chorus (Engineers) Git along, you ingineers Scene (Morrell, Cindy Lou) No. You's in de right place Chorus (Urchins) Lift 'em up an' put 'em down Chorus (Men, Girls) Middle of de day	Chorus (Soldiers) Send along anudder load Scene (Morrell, Cindy Lou) Cain' let you go! Chorus (Urchins) Lift 'em up an' put 'em down Chorus **Men:** Honey gal o' mine **Girls:** Good luck, Mr. Flyin' Man
5. Havanaise (Carmen) L'amour est un oiseau rebelle 6. Scène (Jeunes Gens, Carmen) Carmen! sur tes pas 7. Duo (José, Micaëla) Parle-moi de ma mère! 8. Chœur (Cigarières, Soldats) Au secours! 9. Chanson et Mélodrame (Carmen, Lieutenant) Tra la, la, la, la, la, la, la	Habanera (Carmen) Love's a baby dat grows up wild Scene (Men, Girls) Miss Jones, Is you get a ingagement tonight Duet (Joe, Cindy) I is sure she is wrong Chorus (Girls) Hurry up! Finale of Scene 1 (Carmen, Brown) You ain' a police'm	Habanera (Carmen) Love's a baby dat grows up wild Scene (Men) Hey, Joe! Don't let her git her hooks into you! Duet (Joe, Cindy) I tol' your maw Chorus (Girls) Murder! Finale of Scene One (Carmen, Brown) You ain' a police'm **Entr' Scene (Urchins)** Carmen Jones is goin' to jail
		Scene 2
10. Chanson et Duo (Carmen, José) Près des remparts de Séville 11. Finale	Seguidilla (Carmen, Joe) Dere's a café on de corner Finaletto	Seguidilla (Carmen, Joe) Dere's a café on de corner **Finaletto and Entr' Scene**
ACT II *The Tavern of Lillas Pastia*	ACT II *Billy Pastor's Café*	Scene 3 *Billy Pastor's Café*
12. Chanson Bohémienne (Carmen) Les tringles des sistres tintaient Tra la la la 13. Chœur et Ensemble Vivat! vivat le torero! 14. Couplets (Escamillo) Votre toast Toréador, prends garde 15. Quintette (Dancaïre, Frasquita, Mercédès, Remendado, Carmen) Nous avons en tête une affaire! 16. Chanson (José) Halte-là! 17. Duo (Carmen, José) Je vais danser en votre honneur La fleur que tu m'avais jetée	[Chanson Bohémienne] (Carmen) I'll tell you why I wanna dance Beat out dat rhythm Chorus Git hep, git hep wid de Hepcat [Couplets] (Hepcat Miller) Ain' no state Open de door Quintet (Dinky, Frankie, Myrt, Rum, Carmen) Would you like to make you some do re mi? Song (Joe) Who dat? Duo (Carmen, Joe) I'll do a dance, special fo' you Dis flower	[Chanson Bohémienne] (Carmen) I'll tell you why I wanna dance Beat out dat rhythm [Couplets] (Husky Miller) Thanks a lot! Stan' up an' fight Quintet (Dinky, Frankie, Myrt, Rum, Carmen) Wanna make a trip on de crack Chicago train? Scene (Carmen and Joe) Thinkin' 'bout you all de time Dis flower

18. Finale	Finale Reprise: Quintet "High on a hill"	Finale of Act I Reprise: "Beat out dat rhythm on a drum"[†]
ACT III *In the Mountains*	ACT III, Scene 1 *A Clearing in the Wooded Hills*	ACT II, Scene I *The Meadow Lawn Country Club*
19. Introduction Écoute, écoute, compagnon, écoute!		Solo for Violin based on Entr'Acte music between Acts III and IV of *Carmen*[‡]
20. Trio (Frasquita, Mercédès, Carmen) Mêlons! Coupons! En vain, pour éviter	Trio (Frankie, Myrt, Carmen) Cut 'em? Cut 'em! Dat ol' boy	Trio (Frankie, Myrt, Carmen) Cut 'em? Cut 'em! Dat ol' boy
21. Morceau d'Ensemble Quant au douanier	"Improvised Song" Fall down, you red tuhmayter sun!	Chorus Poncho de Panther **Spanish Ballet** (Roma Suite)
22. Air (Micaëla) Je dis, que rien ne m'épouvante	Aria (Cindy) My Joe	Aria (Cindy) My Joe
23. Duo (Torero, José) Je suis Escamillo	Duet (Hepcat, Joe) I is Hepcat Miller	
24. Finale	Finale	Finale
ACT IV *A Square in Seville*	Act III, Scene 2 *Outside the Hoity Toity Club*	Act II, Scene 2 *Outside a Baseball Park*
25. Chœur À deux cuartos!	Chorus All de swells in town are dere	Chorus Git yer program for de big fight
26. Chœur et Scène (Escamillo, Carmen) Les voici, les voici Si tu m'aimes Carmen	**Chorus and Scene (Hepcat, Carmen)** Wave dat stick Won' you say dat you love me?	Chorus Dat's our man
27. Duo final (Carmen, José) C'est toi!	Duet (Carmen, Joe) All I've wantin' to do	**Scene: Carmen and Joe** All I'm wantin' to do **Finale**

* This comparative table does not list the numerous melodramas and incidental segments that Bennett added (based on Bizet's music from *Carmen*, *L'Arlésienne*, and *La Jolie fille de Perth*) to the *Carmen Jones* score, given that the sources are complete only for the final version (1945), which—in this respect—is clearly different from the earlier ones (1942, 1943) but which cannot be reconstructed based on the limited musical sources.
† In the 1945 version, this number was exchanged with "Good luck, Mr. Flyin' Man."
‡ Cut in 1945 version.

References

Archival Collections:

Library of Congress. National Negro Opera Company Collection.
Library of Congress. Oscar Hammerstein II Collection.
New York Public Library. Musical Arrangements for *Carmen Jones* (Autograph-Score Fragments by Robert Russell Bennett, Manuscript Copies of Parts, Mimeographed Orchestral and Choral Parts, and Annotated Orchestral Parts from Bizet's *La Jolie Fille de Perth* and *Arlésienne Suite*).
New York Public Library. Billy Rose Collection.
New York Public Library. Howard Bay Collection.

Dixie *Carmen* 171

Primary Sources:

Bizet, Georges, Robert Russell Bennett, and Oscar Hammerstein II. *Carmen Jones*. Original-Cast Recording (1944). Decca 440 066 780-2, 2003.

Bizet, Georges, Robert Russell Bennett, and Oscar Hammerstein II. *Carmen Jones*, Restored Edition. New York: Rodgers and Hammerstein Theatricals, 2007.

Covarrubias, Miguel. *Carmen Jones*. Four Colored Drawings (1944). http://www.americanartarchives.com/covarrubias.htm, accessed 15 March 2009.

Hammerstein, Oscar, II. *Carmen Jones*. Typescript. Copyright Deposit 31 July 1942. Library of Congress, Performing Arts Reading Room, shelf mark ML50 B625C4 1942.

Hammerstein, Oscar, II. *Carmen Jones*. Typescript. Copyright Deposit 30 September 1943. Library of Congress, Performing Arts Reading Room, shelf mark ML50 B625C4 1943.

Hammerstein, Oscar, II. *Carmen Jones*. New York: Alfred Knopf, 1945.

Thomson, Virgil. *The Art of Judging Music*. New York: Alfred Knopf, 1948.

U.S. periodicals and newspapers cited in addition to the extensive clippings file in Wc OHC: *Boston Herald, Chicago Daily Tribune, Chicago Defender, Christian Science Monitor, Cue, Los Angeles Times, New York Amsterdam News, New York Times, Newsweek, Philadelphia Record, Phylon, Pittsburgh Courier, Time, Variety, Wall Street Journal, Washington Post*.

Secondary Literature:

Allen, Ray. "An American Folk Opera? Triangulating Folkness, Blackness, and Americaness in Gershwin and Heyward's *Porgy and Bess*." *Journal of American Folklore* 117/465 (Summer 2004): 243–61.

Alpert, Hollis. *The Life and Times of* Porgy and Bess: *The Story of an American Classic*. New York: Alfred A. Knopf, 1990.

André, Naomi. "Tom Toms and the New Negro: What Is *Africa* to William Grant Still?" Paper presented at the 35th Annual Conference of the Society for American Music, Denver, 2009.

Aschenbrenner, Joyce. *Katherine Dunham: Dancing a Life*. Urbana: University of Illinois Press, 2002.

Barg, Lisa. "Black Voices/White Sounds: Race and Representation in Virgil Thomson's *Four Saints in Three Acts*." *American Music* 18/2 (Summer 2000): 121–61.

Barg, Lisa. "National Voices/Modernist Histories: Race, Performance and Remembrance in American Music, 1927–1943." Ph.D. diss., State University of New York at Stony Brook, 2001.

Barg, Lisa. "Paul Robeson's *Ballad for Americans*: Race and the Cultural Politics of 'People's Music'." *Journal of the Society for American Music* 2/1 (February 2008): 27–70.

Bhabha, Homi K. *The Location of Culture*. 2nd ed. London: Routledge, 2004.

Booker, Bryan D. *African Americans in the United States Army in World War II*. Jefferson, N.C.: McFarland, 2008.

Brodkin, Karen. *How Jews Became White Folks and What That Says about Race in America.* New Brunswick, N.J.: Rutgers University Press, 1998.

Carter, Tim. "Music and the Federal Theater Project: A View from the West Coast." Paper presented at the 35th Annual Conference of the Society for American Music, Denver, 2009.

Carter, Tim. *Oklahoma!: The Making of an American Musical.* New Haven: Yale University Press, 2007.

Clark, Robert L. A. "Local Color: The Representation of Race in *Carmen* and *Carmen Jones.*" In *Operatic Migrations: Transforming Works and Crossing Boundaries,* ed. Roberta Montemorra Marvin and Downing A. Thomas, 217–39. Aldershot, England: Ashgate, 2006.

Denning, Michael. *The Cultural Front: The Laboring of American Culture in the Twentieth Century.* London: Verso, 1997.

Depardieu, Benoît. "*Carmen Jones:* A Carmen 'à la Afro-America'." *Studies in Musical Theatre* 2/1 (December 2008): 223–34.

Dorlag, Arthur, and John Irvine, eds. *The Stage Works of Charles MacArthur.* Tallahassee: Florida State University Foundation, 1974.

Fauser, Annegret. "*Carmen in Khaki:* Europäische Oper in den Vereinigten Staaten während des Zweiten Weltkrieges." In *Oper im Wandel der Gesellschaft. Kulturtransfers und Netzwerke des Musiktheaters im modernen Europa,* ed. Sven Oliver Müller, Philipp Ther, Jutta Toelle, and Gesa zur Nieden, 303–29. Vienna: Oldenbourg and Böhlau, 2010.

Ferencz, George J., ed. *"The Broadway Sound": The Autobiography and Selected Essays of Robert Russell Bennett.* Rochester: University of Rochester Press, 1999.

Fordin, Hugh. *Getting to Know Him: A Biography of Oscar Hammerstein II.* New York: Random House, 1977.

Gaines, Kevin. "Duke Ellington, *Black, Brown, and Beige,* and the Cultural Politics of Race." In *Music and the Racial Imagination,* ed. Ronald Radano and Philip V. Bohlman, 585–602. Chicago: University of Chicago Press, 2000.

Gaines, Kevin. *Uplifting the Race: Black Leadership, Politics, and Culture in the Twentieth Century.* Chapel Hill: University of North Carolina Press, 1996.

Garcia, David. "Going Primitive to the Movements and Sounds of Mambo." *Musical Quarterly* 89/4 (Winter 2006): 505–23.

Giles, Freda Scott. "*Lulu Belle.*" In *Encyclopedia of the Harlem Renaissance,* ed. Cary D. Wintz and Paul Finkelman, 746. New York: Routledge, 2004.

Gilroy, Paul. *The Black Atlantic: Modernity and Double Consciousness.* Cambridge, Mass.: Harvard University Press, 1993.

Gubar, Susan. *Racechanges: White Skin, Black Face in American Culture.* Oxford: Oxford University Press, 1997.

Hammond, John, and Irving Townsend. *On Record: An Autobiography.* New York: Ridge Press, 1977.

Hecht, Ben. *Charlie: The Improbable Life and Times of Charles MacArthur.* New York: Harper, 1957.

Hubbs, Nadine. *The Queer Composition of America's Sound: Gay Modernists, American Music, and National Identity.* Berkeley: University of California Press, 2004.

Johnson, John A. "Gershwin's 'American Folk Opera': The Genesis, Style, and Reputation of *Porgy and Bess* (1935)." Ph.D. diss., Harvard University, 1996.

Jones, Gavin. *Strange Talk: The Politics of Dialect Literature in Gilded Age America.* Berkeley: University of California Press, 1999.

Kennedy, David M. *Freedom from Fear: The American People in Depression and War, 1929–1945.* New York: Oxford University Press, 2005.

Levine, Lawrence W. *Highbrow/Lowbrow: The Emergence of Cultural Hierarchy in America.* Cambridge, Mass.: Harvard University Press, 1988.

Library of Congress. American Memory, Federal Theatre Project: *Macbeth.* http://memory.loc.gov/ammem/fedtp/ftsmth00.html., accessed 1 March 2009.

Locke, Ralph P. "Doing the Impossible: On the Musically Exotic." *Journal of Musicological Research* 27/4 (2008): 334–58.

Locke, Ralph, P. "Spanish Local Color in Bizet's *Carmen:* Unexplored Borrowings and Transformations." In *Music, Theater, and Cultural Transfer: Paris, 1830–1914,* ed. Annegret Fauser and Mark Everist, 316–60. Chicago: University of Chicago Press, 2009.

Manning, Susan. *Modern Dance, Negro Dance: Race in Motion.* Minneapolis: University of Minnesota Press, 2004.

Marlow, Sam. "Bizet Meets Buena Vista." *The Times,* 9 June 2007.

McClary, Susan. *Georges Bizet: Carmen.* Cambridge: Cambridge University Press, 1993.

Middleton, Richard. *Voicing the Popular: On the Subjects of Popular Music.* New York: Routledge, 2006.

Miller, Leta E. "Elmer Keeton and His 'Bay Area Negro Chorus': Creating an Artistic Identity in Depression-Era San Francisco." *Black Music Research Journal,* forthcoming, 30/2 (Fall 2010).

Most, Andrea. *Making Americans: Jews and the Broadway Musical.* Cambridge, Mass.: Harvard University Press, 2004.

"Muriel Smith." Obituary in *The Black Perspective in Music* 13/2 (Autumn 1985): 244–45.

Nietzsche, Friedrich. *Der Fall Wagner: Ein Musikantenproblem.* Leipzig: C. G. Naumann, 1892.

North, Michael. *The Dialect of Modernism: Race, Language & Twentieth-Century Literature.* Oxford: Oxford University Press, 1994.

Perpener, John O., III. *African-American Concert Dance: The Harlem Renaissance and Beyond.* Urbana: University of Illinois Press, 2001.

Peterson, Geoffrey R., ed. *Annals of the Metropolitan Opera: Performances and Artists, 1883–2000.* CD-ROM. New York: Metropolitan Opera Guild, 2002.

Pollack, Howard. *George Gershwin: His Life and Work.* Berkeley: University of California Press, 2006.

Potter, Pamela. "What Is 'Nazi Music'?" *Musical Quarterly* 88/4 (Winter 2005): 428–55.

Radano, Ronald. *Lying Up a Nation: Race and Black Music.* Chicago: University of Chicago Press, 2003.

Royal Festival Hall. Promotional Web site for the Performance of *Carmen Jones,* 2007. http://www.southbankcentre.co.uk/carmenjones, accessed 10 December 2008.

Schiller Institute. "Dialogue with Sylvia Olden Lee, Pianist and Vocal Coach." 7 February 1998. http://www.schillerinstitute.org/fid_97-01/fid_981_lee_interview.html, accessed 1 February 2009.

Schwartz, Barry. "Memory as a Cultural System: Abraham Lincoln in World War II." *American Sociological Review* 61/5 (October 1996): 908–27.

Silver, Reuben. "A History of the Karamu Theatre of Karamu House, 1915–1960." Ph.D. diss., Ohio State University, 1961.

Smith, Jeff. "Black Faces, White Voices: The Politics of Dubbing in *Carmen Jones.*" *The Velvet Light Trap* 51 (Spring 2003): 29–42.

Stowe, David W. *Swing Changes: Big-Band Jazz in New Deal America.* Cambridge, Mass.: Harvard University Press, 1994.

Suskin, Steven. *The Sound of Broadway Music: A Book of Orchestrators and Orchestrations.* Oxford: Oxford University Press, 2009.

Watkins, Glenn. *Pyramids at the Louvre: Music, Culture, and Collage from Stravinsky to the Postmodernists.* Cambridge, Mass.: Belknap Press, 1994.

Weiss, Nancy J. "Long-Distance Runners of the Civil Rights Movement: The Contribution of Jews to the NAACP and the National Urban League in the Early Twentieth Century." In *Struggles in the Promised Land: Toward a History of Black-Jewish Relations in the United States,* ed. Jack Salzman and Cornel West, 123–52. New York: Oxford University Press, 1997.

Wells, Christopher. "Grand Opera as Racial Uplift: The National Negro Opera Company (1941–1962)." M.A. thesis, University of North Carolina at Chapel Hill, 2009.

Woll, Allen. *Black Musical Theatre: From* Coontown *to* Dreamgirls. Baton Rouge: Louisiana State University Press, 1989.

Part Three

Gender Politics in Music

CHAPTER 9

Rheinsirenen

Loreley and Other Rhine Maidens

In the film *Gentlemen Prefer Blondes,* young Henry Spofford III spots Lorelei Lee stuck in a porthole as she is trying to escape from private detective Malone's cabin. He explains why he is helping her: "The first reason is, I'm too young to be sent to jail. The second reason is, you've got a lot of animal magnetism."[1] Throughout the film, blonde and beautiful Lorelei Lee (Marilyn Monroe) shows herself in the possession of magic power, turning all men but one into helpless victims. Although her brunette friend Dorothy Shaw (Jane Russell) shares Lorelei's clothes, her music and, in one scene, even her blonde hair, the mysterious charm of Lorelei is never within her reach.[2] Lorelei's inexplicable spell over men becomes most obvious when she is seducing and singing; but even her simple entry into a room can create uncontrolled male responses.

    Lorelei Lee does justice to her first name, which makes us understand where her seductive power comes from. It identifies her as a "siren"—and not just any siren, but as the dangerous Loreley. This beautiful sorceress combs her blonde hair with a golden comb, sitting on a rock high above the Rhine, where she sings her songs, captivating the attention of passing sailors and thus causing their deaths in the swirls of the river. Even our first visual impression of Lorelei Lee in the opening song, "We're Just Two Little Girls from Little Rock," is linked to this siren image through the sparkling, sequined red dress that fits Monroe's body as if she had a fishtail. And as the finishing touch, the number ends in front of a shimmering, dark-blue curtain, which adds to the marine impression. For the robust Dorothy, "a horse used to be my closest pal," while Lorelei's seductive voice tells us about her broken heart; they are different beings, not just different women. This siren image became so strongly identified with the role of Lorelei Lee, that we find it even in a recent collector's "Marilyn Monroe" Barbie doll, while the visual link between Monroe and Loreley as the "American siren" was never stronger than in her famous rendering of "Happy Birthday, Mr. President" a decade later, sparkling sequins included.[3] Lorelei Lee's affinity to music was present already in the literary source for the film. Anita Loos's novel *Gentlemen Prefer Blondes* shows Lorelei Lee as a woman with only two talents, for music and for seduction, but given that music-making demands practice, the heroine—a "professional lady"—decides to rely on her seductive charm alone.[4]

The Siren of the "Lurley Rock"

Sirens feature in many an ancient legend and have repeatedly been "associated with the enchanting, inspirational and prophetic quality of music."[5] Sirens are related also to knowledge, seduction, and danger, most famously in Homer's *Odyssey*. As a result of the nineteenth century's fascination with sexuality, nature, and culture, the siren became a trope for the alluring threat of female seduction, in particular the *femme fatale*. Countless paintings show beautiful women holding a lyre and singing. Their victims either are the spectator or the painter lured into the scene, or are represented as doomed or already dead male bodies. We encounter sirens in operas such as E. T. A. Hoffmann's *Undine* (1816) and Antonín Dvořák's *Rusalka* (1901), and we hear their wordless song in Claude Debussy's nocturne, *Sirènes* (1901). In this context, it is not surprising that the mechanical sound that warns us from danger—the siren—takes the name of its female embodiment.

Loreley, the siren of the Rhine, is rather young for a mythical creature. We even know her year of birth, 1802, and her genealogy as the main character in a long ballad by Clemens Brentano, which was included in his novel *Godwi*. The ballad told of a beautiful young fisherman's daughter, betrayed by love, who was transformed into the sorceress Loreley.[6] Brentano introduced "this magical Rhine seductress as an incarnation of the landscape where her fatal song and body guarded the Nibelung

[Musical notation: Andante, 6/8. Voice: "Ich weiss nicht was soll es be-deu-ten, dass ich so trau-rig bin, Ein Mähr-chen aus al-ten Zei-ten, das geht mir nicht aus dem Sinn"]

Example 8.1. Friedrich Silcher, *Lorelei*, poem by Heinrich Heine, mm. 1–8; transcription of autograph score, Silcher Museum.

treasure for Father Rhine."[7] Loreley was named after the "Lurley" or "Lorle" Mountain, a rock formation above the Rhine near Goarshausen, which had featured in various texts about the Rhine Valley and its geography since the thirteenth century. The presence of a "spirit" in the rock was first mentioned in the early seventeenth century in the *Origines palatinae*, and by the mid-eighteenth century, local folklore started gendering the spirit as female.[8] The first literary text that turned the spirit into a woman and thus fixed the local narratives into a quickly and widely accepted pan-German legend was, however, Brentano's *Lorelei* ballad. Through it, the modern Rhine Siren was born, and the landscape was transformed into its female embodiment by naming the siren after the rock. Within a short span of time, Loreley became a widely appropriated legend, and her transformations—of which Marilyn Monroe's Lorelei Lee is but one of the more recent—provide a fascinating case-study of the cultural tropes involving the alluring but ultimately fatal seduction attributed to sirens in the nineteenth and twentieth centuries.

The Loreley myth played an important role in the forging of German national identity in the nineteenth century, particularly through Friedrich Silcher's 1837 setting of Heinrich Heine's *Loreley* (ex. 8.1). The strophic song in a lilting 6/8 barcarole rhythm was conceived as a folk-like melody, appropriate for a poem that depicted an "old fairy tale."[9] Silcher's version acquired the status of a popular national hymn, which traveled with immigrants to the shores of the United States of America and to the German colonies in South West Africa.[10] The iconic power of the Silcher song becomes evident at the beginning of the 1979 television drama *Holocaust*, when a wedding party, comprising a wide range of the political and religious strands of 1930s Germany, unites in singing "Ich weiß nicht, was soll es bedeuten." Loreley had become the symbol for German "Rheinromantik," invoking patriotic nostalgia and nationalism in all its colors.

While European writers were fascinated with various female spirits in general, the Rhine Siren continued to represent German Romanticism in European literature, from Gérard de Nerval's enraptured evocation in *Loreley, souvenirs d'Allemagne* in 1852 to Maurice Genevoix's ambiguous novel *Lorelei* from 1978,[11] in which Genevoix's hero Julien refers to Romanticism's dark but seductive side: "Romanticism? . . . That is dangerous. More so than the dazzling golden adornment and the song of the Loreley above the crags of the Rhine."[12] English travelers and readers encountered the romantic Loreley as well, as for example in the nineteenth-century compilation *Legends of the Rhine:*

> It is no wonder, that there are so many popular tales about the rock of the 'Lurley' for there is not a mountain so romantically situated and so interesting. In times of yore a charming 'undine' had selected this rock for her abode; every evening she sate [sic] at the top of it, combed her golden hair or accompanied her pathetic and melodious songs on a golden lute. Every one, who saw and heard her, was charmed and felt in his heart a deep and passionate love, so that for the purpose of seeing the lovely enchantress, a great many boats, approaching too near the rock, were dashed on it and hurled into the foaming waves.[13]

The enchantress with her lyre is visible right at the outset of this book, on the engraving opposite the title page.

We also encounter Loreley in engravings that decorate sheet music and vocal scores. Thus even before we hear her music, we see its effect. Hans Pfitzner recalled his first encounter with the Rhine Siren when he opened the vocal score of Max Bruch's 1863 opera *Die Loreley* (fig. 8.1):

> Ich war noch ein Schulbub, höchstens elf bis zwölf Jahre alt . . . da fand ich . . . eines Tages in dem Notenschrank meines Vaters einen großen Klavierauszug. Er war dunkelgrün geheftet, das Titelblatt zeigte folgendes Bild: Ein Strom, von hohen Felsen begrenzt. Im Vordergrunde ein Baum mit breiten Ästen, in deren Schatten ein Liebespaar sich umschlungen hält—ein Jäger, an ihn geschmiegt ein Mädchen. Auf einem der hohen Felsen im Hintergrunde eine Frauengestalt in fliegenden Gewändern, mit der Harfe im Arm, am Fuß des Felsens im Nebel undeutlich ein Geisterreigen. Auf dem Grunde des Stromes die Leiche eines Mannes. Das war die 'Loreley' von Max Bruch.

> (When I was still a schoolboy, no more than eleven or twelve years old . . . I found . . . one day in my father's music library a large vocal score. It was bound in dark green, and the title page showed the following picture: A stream, surrounded by high cliffs. In the foreground a tree with large branches, in the shade of which a couple embraces—a young hunter, a girl nestled against him. On a high rock in the background, a woman in floating dress, with a harp in her arm; at the foot of the rock, blurred in the mist, a round of ghosts. On the bottom of the river the body of a man. This was the *Loreley* by Max Bruch.)[14]

Figure 8.1. Title page of Max Bruch, *Die Loreley,* text by Emanuel Geibel (Breslau: Verlag Leuckart, 1863). By permission of the Staatsbibliothek Berlin Stiftung Preußischer Kulturbesitz.

Indeed, so quickly did the image of the harp- or lyre-playing beauty on the rock become the familiar manner of representing Loreley that it could serve as a clear iconographic reference even in caricatures, as in a title page of *The Wasp* from 1883 that shows the American president Grover Cleveland as "the new Lorelei" whose song caused the shipwreck in the background (fig. 8.2).

The magic power of Loreley's singing is often echoed in the legend's non-German reception, from the British musical play *A Royal Exchange* to George and Ira Gershwin's *Pardon My English* from 1933.[15] In *A Royal Exchange,* one of the hero's refrains begins "Your melody haunts me like a

Figure 8.2. *The New Lorelei*, cartoon, title page of *The Wasp*, August 11, 1883. Hawai'i State Archives, Honolulu. Kahn Collection. Corner note: "We are glad to hear evidences that the monumental fraud called the Kingdom of the Sandwich Islands, which has been maintained for the past twelve years at the expense of the people of the United States, is ready to fall to pieces. We presume that England will then step in and assume a protectorate."

Figure 8.3. Leonard Emil Bach, *Die neue Loreley,* opus 28, text by Siegmey (Berlin: C. A. Challier & Cie, 1878), title page. By permission of the British Library.

Lorelei." In *Pardon My English,* the Gershwins clearly combine the image of both political and sexual danger in the song *Lorelei*: in its refrain, the (German) female character describes herself as treacherous, lecherous, and full of passion, while interpolating this statement with the German "Ja, ja." Her love had overtones of both Wagner's Valkyries and yodeling:

> She used to love in a strange kind of fashion,
> With lots of hey! hodeho! hidehi!
> And I can guarantee I'm full of passion
> Like the Lorelei.

This number continued to refer to the famous Rhine song, for the "satiric tag finish of the printed music . . . echoed Silcher's familiar setting of the Heine poem."[16] Given the political situation, it is not surprising that the song was republished in London in 1944 or that, in a novel set toward the end of World War II, the "mission Loreley" would take the heroes into occupied Lorraine and the Rhine Valley.[17] But Loreley had already served as a German national symbol in the Franco-Prussian War of 1870, where Germans evoked her in a traditional siren's or mermaid's role as guardian of rivers, streams, wells, and oceans.[18] A striking example of this chauvinist literature is Siegmey's *Die neue Loreley* (1878), a reworking of Heine's poem in which Loreley is credited for alerting the German "knights" to the attack of French soldiers with her songs.[19] The cover of the sheet music (fig. 8.3) offers a fair-haired and imperial Loreley in front of a German army, warding off a fleet of French soldiers crossing the Rhine. Siegmey's poem turned Heine's opening phrase, "I don't know what it means," into "Now I know what it means," and he went from there to proclaim the new Loreley as victorious, with the imperial crown on her golden locks.[20] At the beginning of World War I, the same poem—to be sung to Silcher's well-known melody—was distributed by Emil Freiherr von Mirbach as a morale-boosting song text to the German troops.[21]

It was the conflation of universal archetype and national, if not "Teutonic," icon that, combined with her dangerous sexual allure, turned Loreley into such a modern siren. Right from the outset, the Rhine Siren was trapped within the opposing tensions of German Romanticism, which tried to create a German national identity through a universalist, *allgemein menschliche* culture.[22] As Cecilia Hopkins Porter has put it: "The appearance of the Romantic Loreley image in the work of Brentano and the Heidelberg Romantics illustrated the process whereby a culture's need to rediscover its mythic past resulted in the formulation of a new mythology based on an object of nature's beauty and its surrogate symbols."[23]

The Music of a Siren

Once Brentano had given birth to the romantic Loreley, the Rhine Siren ignited the fantasy of poets and composers. Poets reveled in descriptions of the effects of her singing. Heinrich Heine, for example, called it "a weird refrain / that steeps in a deadly enchantment / the listener's ravished brain."[24] In his 1840 novella, *Irrungen der Liebe,* Carl Matzerath's retelling of Heine's "old fairy-tale of Lorelei, the siren of the Rhine" portrayed her music as that of "a ghost voice singing a song of magic euphony."[25] Karl Geib described her song as "wondrously beautiful," like "the sound of a flute in the evening gold."[26] And the romantic poet Wolfgang Müller von Königswinter tried over and over again to capture the siren's music in his poems, culminating in his *Rheinfahrt,* which only throws in her name at the opening and continues by describing the result:

> Die Lorelei!—Der Schiffer schaut und lauscht,
> der Fahrt vergessend. Weh, am Felsenriffe
> Zerschellt der Kahn! Die nasse Woge rauscht
> Verderbend ob dem Jüngling und dem Schiffe!—
>
> (The Lorelei!—the sailor looks and listens, / Forgetting the voyage. Woe! On the crags / The boat is wrecked! The wet wave rushes / Fatally over the youth and the ship!—)[27]

Composers, however, faced a mighty challenge, especially in dramatic settings that would take up Brentano's story line of a beautiful woman being transformed into a nymph or sorceress because she was betrayed by her beloved and then sold her soul for magic power. As with Orpheus, composers were confronted with musically representing a being whose expressive force lays within music itself, but not just any music. Loreley embodies the dangerous, seductive side of music, its sensual *jouissance,* its feminine part, its fatal attraction. In the nineteenth century—and based on it, in the twentieth—musical conventions offered composers a rich toolbox to represent feminine seduction and sensuality, which included lush instrumentation and chromaticism.[28] The musical representation of Loreley, however, needed more than just these musical signifiers in order to signal the difference between mere female guile and the magic attraction of a being both feminine and eternal. In dramatic compositions, another problem occurs as well: when do we hear Loreley simply communicate and when do we hear her siren's song? A look at some nineteenth-century compositions might help answer this question.

In 1854, Ferdinand Hiller—a well-respected German composer active in the middle of the nineteenth century—set out to compose his version of the Loreley legend in a dramatic cantata, a popular genre, in particular with amateur choruses. He collaborated on it with Wolfgang Müller von Königswinter. A letter that Hiller wrote to the poet at the outset of their project allows us a glimpse into his reasoning:

> [I]ch habe nachgedacht, warum man sie auf alle Weise in Musik gesetzt hat, nur nicht auf die *eigentlichste* — ich bin zu keinem andern Resultat gekommen als zu dem Entschluß, es selbst zu thun, wenn Sie mir dabei helfen wollen. Der Moment nämlich, wo die schöne Hexe durch ihren Gesang den Schiffer dem Untergang weiht, die eigentliche Quintessenz der Sage, ist nicht komponirt und doch eigentlich so musi-

kalisch, dass man höchstens ihm vorwerfen könnte, er sei es zu sehr. [emphasis Hiller]

(I have thought about the fact why so far, one has set [Loreley] to music in all sorts of ways, but never in the *truest*—I came to no other result than the resolution to do it myself if you would agree to help me with it. Namely the moment, in which the beautiful sorceress dooms the sailor through her singing, the real quintessence of the legend, has not been composed and is yet so musical that one could reproach it at best as being too musical.)[29]

After outlining the scene, Hiller continued:

Was Details anlangt, so würde es vielleicht gut sein, *vor* dem Gesang der Loreley nur *männliche* Geister auftreten zu lassen, um auch den Effekt der weiblichen Stimme der Hexe aufzubewahren. . . . Das Lied des Schiffers muss ein Strophenlied sein — wo hingegen der Gesang der Loreley eine gewisse ungebundene phantastische Wildheit bewahren müßte. [emphasis Hiller]

(In as far as details are concerned, it might be good to have only *male* spirits *before* the song of the Loreley in order to reserve the effect of the female voice for the sorceress. . . . The song of the sailor has to be strophic, whereas the singing of Loreley would need to retain a certain unbound fantastical wildness.)[30]

In the finished composition, Hiller kept to his plan to set the sailor's song strophically, but Loreley's is far from the "unbound fantastical wildness" to which he referred. Hiller represented the alluring song in a closed bipartite setting with a coda, with harp accompaniment and chromatic passages in the melodic line, while the general harmonic structure remained firmly grounded in a diatonic frame.[31] It appears that the harp accompaniment and the closed musical form were part of the sign system that composers used to represent Loreley's songs. Paul and Lucien Hillemacher, in their *Loreley* cantata from 1883 on a text by Eugène Adenis, employed similar means as Hiller to render the siren's music.[32] This cantata opens with Loreley's ballad set as a separate piece, like Silcher's setting in a barcarole rhythm, accompanied by the harp (ex. 8.2). The siren's song thus becomes diegetic music, a "song" performed by Loreley. But this song proves deadly to the sailors on the river. The scenic description that accompanies her ballad in 6/8 informs us about its effect:

Plusieurs navires descendent le fleuve . . . les voix se rapprochent . . . tout à coup, un chant triste s'élève: c'est la Ballade de Lore.

(Several ships descend on the river ... the voices approach ... all at once a sad song begins: it is the ballad of Lore.)

After the ballad:

Le fleuve s'entr'ouvre et les navires, entraînés vers le rocher de Lore, se brisent et disparaissent dans l'abîme... Peu à peu les eaux se referment et le calme reparaît.

(The river opens itself, and the ships, pulled toward Lore's rock, crash and disappear in the abyss... Slowly the waters close again, and the calm returns.)[33]

Both Hiller and the two Hillermachers use diegetic song as the element of seduction and the tool of destruction.[34] Hiller's Loreley tells the story of her pain and transformation as the source of her fatal power while destroying by way of her song the young man approaching on the river, collapsing narration and dramatic action into one theatrical moment. Even in its apparent simplicity, her song thus seems to fit into the characteristic topos of dramatic narration in nineteenth-century operas. As Carolyn Abbate has shown, such narrative song often represents reflexive instances within the dramaturgy of an opera.[35] It is usually reserved for a unique moment, whether as revelation of a person's history or through informing the characters and audience about events that take place outside the scene. But in Hiller's cantata, and in contrast to Abbate's view, Loreley's narration of her history becomes a never-changing performance "on demand" whose effect is already a foregone conclusion, turning the uniqueness of narration within a dramatic context into an absurdity: every time Loreley repeats her story a man drowns.[36] In the later cantata by Paul and Lucien Hillemacher, however, Loreley does not even narrate her life in her destructive song, but rather she alludes to a "sleeping past" and "dark silence" (ex. 8.2), yearning for eternal sleep "under roses." The absence of narration within a song designated as "narrative" through its generic title as a "ballad" creates tension between text and music. The sailor should hear the sad tale but the text offers only fragments and relies on the audience's memory of the Loreley myth. Thus both Loreley narrations differ from the habitual narrative song in operas such as Meyerbeer's *Robert le Diable* (1831) or Wagner's *Der fliegende Holländer* (1843) in that they take an operatic trope and mould it into a siren's song, where music rather than text becomes the dramatic agent. Neither Hiller's nor the Hillemachers' Loreley creates narration as a "composing singer" in the way Tannhäuser does in his Rome narrative, where "Tannhäuser in effect

261 RHEINSIRENEN

Example 8.2. Paul and Lucien Hillemacher, *Loreley, légende symphonique en trois parties*, text by Eugène Adonis. Paris: Tresse Editeur, 1883, 10, mm. 1–7.

begins to make music as a translation for the events that he narrates."[37] Instead the sirens are imprisoned in the act of performance, in an endless loop of repetition, performing music disguised as a narrative song, whose text is inconsequential in a plot whose quintessence, as Hiller's letter (cited above) indicated, was if anything only "too musical."

Indeed Loreley's act of seduction consists in the act of musical performance. What kind of music she performs will depend on the context of composition, but the seductive song needs to be different from other music in the piece, and the composer has to set a sign for the beginning of the magic song. In his opera *Loreley* (1890), Alfredo Catalani used, like Hiller and the Hillemachers, a change of instrumentation, especially the harp arpeggios, and the alluring call "come, come, come to my heart" to indicate the beginning of the siren's song, which he set as a closed musical form. The opening verses of Loreley's magic song allude even to another enchantress, Armida, with her:

Vieni! sul Reno, ho un' isola
tutta profumi e fior. . . .
(Come! On the Rhine, I have an island / all perfumed and flowering. . . .)[38]

However, unlike the representation of other sorceresses such as, for example, Massenet's Esclarmonde, it is not the virtuosic and alluring female vocalize that indicates Loreley's seductive singing in these nineteenth-century compositions, but a song accompanied by the harp. Indeed, the iconographic link of Loreley to her golden harp is so strong that composers make us listen to it even in a miniature such as Schumann's setting of Eichendorff's *Waldesgespräch* (1840), a dialogue between Loreley and a knight. The beginning of Loreley's seductive song is marked—as in dramatic settings—by a different harmony, melody, and "instrumentation": here the piano's contrasting arpeggios after the chordal first strophe clearly invoke the harp (ex. 8.3). The harmonic shift to C major in mes. 15 creates enough tonal distance to suggest another musical world, while Loreley's lilting and diatonic melody plays on musical signifiers of well-bred femininity.[39]

Example 8.3. Robert Schumann, *Waldesgespräch*, poem by Joseph von Eichendorff, mm. 11–20.

It is surprising that Loreley's magic music in nineteenth-century compositions lacks virtuosity, especially if compared to the prototype of all magic vocal music: Monteverdi's "Possente spirto," the lyre-playing Orfeo's showpiece.[40] It may reflect the siren's ancestry as a fisherman's daughter from the Rhine turned siren—therefore someone simple in her expression. She is not the highly trained male singer, the composing poet such as Orpheus or Tannhäuser. Loreley is just a woman with a sweet, bewitching voice that complements her beauty. Although, in literature and painting, we find her represented as a *femme fatale*, in music she sings almost like a bourgeois daughter in the parlor. The simplicity of her music might also reflect the overwhelming influence of Silcher's *Loreley* and of the folk-tone tradition that stems from it. But there may be more. It could well be the "grain" of her female voice that creates such fatal attraction, not the elaborate "science" of her musical art; thus what a composer makes us listen to in Loreley's diegetic songs is music whose simplicity allows us to admire without distraction "the grain, that is the body in the singing voice."[41]

Rhine Maidens

The centrality of the "grain" of the seducing female voice, and also the oedipal desire toward the alluring sound that stands at the beginning of consciousness, becomes more obvious in a different nineteenth-century incarnation of Loreley. Richard Wagner's version of the enchantress in the guise of three "mermaid Rhine Maidens"[42] in *Der Ring des Nibelungen* combines the sexual allure of Loreley plus her mermaid role as the protector of the river and its treasures with the Platonic concept of the sirens as figures that were part of the origins of the world.[43] The very first appearance of the Rhine Maidens in *Das Rheingold* (1869) offers a multiplicity of roles for these three creatures. The most obvious and traditional is that of three mermaid-guardians. Wagner's stage directions have them floating gracefully around the treasure that they are guarding, and the first performance in Bayreuth in 1876 tried to convey this visual impression with the means of the time, including "swimming cars" (*Schwimmwagen*). The barcarole rhythm in 6/8 and the periodic structure of Woglinde's "Weia! Waga! Woge du Welle!" ("Weia! Waga! Undulate you wave!"), with its arpeggiated accompaniment, takes up the familiar pattern of representing Loreley's diegetic song in nineteenth-century music, and Woglinde's is also a song containing the sexual allure that brings Alberich into the drama. We hear Woglinde over the *pianissimo* orchestra, the grain of her voice almost touchable in the simple triadic music whose onomatopoeic text does not distract from the sound (ex. 8.4).

But Woglinde's music is more than the short diegetic song of a Wagnerian Loreley. It is also a siren's contribution to the development of theories of music and language, in particular of the Wagnerian drama. In a famous passage in *Opera and Drama* from 1851, Wagner tried to describe his notions of music, language, and drama in gendered terms echoing contemporary theories of femininity and masculinity, such as the burning issues as to whether women did have a soul.[44] Wagner wrote:

Example 8.4. Richard Wagner, *Das Rheingold,* act 1, scene 1.

Die Musik ist die Gebärerin, der Dichter der Erzeuger. . . . *Die Musik ist ein Weib.* Die Natur des Weibes ist die *Liebe:* aber diese Liebe ist die *empfangende* und in der Empfängnis rückhaltlos *sich hingebende.* Das Weib erhält volle Individualität erst im Moment der Hingebung. Es ist das Wellenmädchen, das seelenlos durch die Wogen seines Elementes dahinrauscht, bis es durch die Liebe eines Mannes erst die Seele empfängt. [emphasis Wagner]

(Music is the child bearer, the poet, the procreator. . . . *Music is a woman.* Her nature is *love:* but this love is the *conceiving* kind, which in conceiving *gives itself* without restraint. Woman only receives full individuality at the moment of self-abandonment. She is the mermaid who swims, soulless, through the waves of her element, until she receives her soul through the love of a man.)[45]

The metaphor stands for the relationship of text and music in the generating of the drama. Wagner, as Reinhart Meyer-Kalkus puts it, composed in the song of the Rhine Maidens a myth of the genesis of language.[46] Woghilde's first words were derived by Wagner from the old German *Heilawac* ("holy water"). The procedure of forming Woghilde's verses, Wagner explained to Nietzsche, was similar to the way in which nursery rhymes such as "eia popeia" function.[47] But Wagner did not stop with the onomatopoeic derivations for the text. Woghilde's first utterance offers a—what one might call Wagnerian—"nursery rhyme" in musical terms, undulating up and down the triadic structure of an A flat major chord that floats over the E flat pedal like the mermaid in the water, while her nonsense sounds of "Weia waga" become words of invitation to the listener to approach the cradle: "Walle zur Wiege." These few bars encapsulate the moment when text emerges from music, when—to take on Wagner's metaphor—the drama is born. Thus the Rhine Maidens seem to represent a mythical but also human original state, the return both to the mother and a mythical past. They float in what Wagner called the "It"—the water—in dancing movement, communicating in an archaic sung language—a mythical *Ursprache*—where the "signified" has not yet been become alienated from the signifier.[48] Woglinge's *Stabreime* emerge out of the triadic sounds of the *Rheingold* prelude, shaping knowledge from the "mother element, the musical tone."[49] Therefore Wagner's multiple versions of Loreley in his Rhine Maidens turned the fisherman's daughter into the symbol of the power of music not only through their effect on the men present in the story (such as Alberich) but also through their alluring appeal to the listener today longing for an ideal state of being.

The mythical words that Woglinde evokes in her onomatopoeic lullaby "Weia! Waga!," however, belong not to a universal but to a particular language: German.[50] Thus the claim to universality of Wagner's myth is curbed by the specificity of its location within the heritage of German culture. If Brentano's and Heine's incarnations of Loreley, "the Rhine Siren," are embodiments of a landscape invested with national significance, Wagner's Rhine Maidens take this form of nationalizing a step further. The specificity of the landscape and her elementary spirits in the form of his Rhine Maidens nationalizes the myth of creation of humanity as culture. Indeed, by superseding the traditional Germanic landscape of the Teutonic forest—epitomized in Carl Maria von Weber's *Der Freischütz* (1821)—with the more universal water flowing down the Rhine, Wagner shifted, in one fell swoop, the location of national identity from the specific to the universal by invoking, in Wagner's words, the "lullaby of the world."[51] No other incarnation of Loreley took so far the romantic German-national notion of establishing national identity through universal cognition.[52]

But Loreley's modest ancestry as a fisherman's daughter and her fusion with the "Rheinromantik" seems to have triggered a further strand of reception in popular novels, tourist souvenirs, and other forms of trivialization.⁵³ They were as much part of the Loreley reception as were satire, irony, political reference, and music drama. Indeed, few sirens have been appropriated so widely as Loreley in the Western world of the nineteenth and twentieth centuries. She served not only as a social and artistic sign for the dangerous woman in all her colors but also as a political symbol both in creating a national myth and in identifying political danger. She developed from the simple fisherman's daughter to a first-rate *femme fatale,* and she still seems to continue her transformations according to the needs of our time. When surfing the Internet, I came across a variety of references, of which the most dire was probably the pornographic "Bedroom Bondage—Lorelei's Diary," in the tradition of Loreley's *femme fatale* image, and of which the most pathetic may well be the homepage of a student from the University of Oregon, "Lorelei's Love Page," where we learn that

> [Lorelei's] beauty was her undoing. Lorelei was not willfully seductive, but men could not resist her charms, and she could not resist their advances. She was bringing scandal and disgrace to the respectable town of Bacharach-on-the-Rhine.⁵⁴

The student has echoed the soppy kitsch of the popular nineteenth-century reception of the Loreley myth, particularly in trivial novels.⁵⁵ Indeed, the Mills & Boon list of romance novels bears witness to its ongoing popularity with books such as Lucy Gordon's *Song of the Lorelei* (1993). "Reading Loreley" has become a popular activity of which "singing Loreley" constitutes only a small part. It is the imaginary voice of the siren more than the actual sound that continues to seduce us. We do not even need to hear the sound of her voice—the simple reference to her best-known incarnation in Silcher's *Loreley*-setting might be enough to create a web of intertextual references, as for example in the installation *Autour de la Lorelei* by the Belgian symbolist Marcel Broodthaer, or in the poster for the Oberhausen Theater production of *Die Loreley* in 1984.⁵⁶ Nevertheless, we not only see or read, but we still hear Loreley sing, not only when we see Wagner's *Das Rheingold* in the opera house but also even in popular music such as the Pogues' Irish hit "Lorelei" or Eagle-Eye Cherry's song "When Mermaids Cry."

Whereas the musical means and materials changed during the twentieth century, the notion of creating musical difference when setting Loreley's siren song remained a constant factor as regards her sonic representation. In *Gentlemen Prefer Blondes,* Lorelei Lee has only one solo number. It is the piece which—according to Dorothy—shows the "true" Lorelei. It is a diegetic piece, a performed song aiming to seduce men both onstage and in the audience. As in the other compositions discussed earlier, the composer begins the piece with musical signs to alert us to the fact that this is the film's siren-song. Difference in a Broadway musical can mean the use of traditional operatic elements. In "Diamonds Are a Girl's Best Friend" we find as the opening sequence a ballet-style dance instead of a show number and operatic coloratura instead of the usual, straightforward text setting. The subsequent song presents us with a "composite" Loreley image: simple, witty lyrics in a strophic setting with refrains, but rendered by a sexually alluring blonde with a voice whose grain promises everything that a siren can offer: seduction, danger, and knowledge.

NOTES

I have presented versions of this text at scholarly meetings from Cambridge and Dublin to Malta, Zaragoza, and Chapel Hill. I am grateful for the fascinating contributions in discussions by colleagues and friends, of whom several were generous enough to offer me their time reading drafts. I wish to thank Juan José Carreras, Tim Carter, Jon Finson, and Anne MacNeil for their help and time.

1. *Gentlemen Prefer Blondes,* Twentieth Century Fox Film Corporation, 1953; directed by Howard Hawks; screenplay by Charles Lederer, based on Anita Loos's and Joseph Fields's successful Broadway version (1949) of Loos's novel (1925).

2. I do not agree with Lawrence Kramer's reading of the film, in particular with his understanding of both women as sirens. If anything, Dorothy is shown as an unsuccessful siren. Her song "Ain't There Anyone Here for Love"—what he calls a "poolside extravaganza" (174)—does not attract the attention of the Olympic team that she woos; they ignore her invitation for love. In the double numbers with Lorelei she serves as the background (her gesture urging Monroe to dance in "When Love Goes Wrong" plays on this difference). The closest Dorothy comes to being a siren is in her impersonation of Lorelei in the courtroom; but this scene reveals her as a cunning actress, not a seductive siren. See Lawrence Kramer, *After the Lovedeath: Sexual Violence and the Making of Culture* (Berkeley: University of California Press, 1997), 174–76.

3. The Internet advertisement informs us: "Marilyn Monroe's role of Lorelei Lee in the musical Gentlemen Prefer Blondes. Barbie wears a glittering sequin gown with a v-neck and high slit." See "Gentlemen prefer Blondes #1 Barbie." http://www.newbarbie.com/marilyntop.htm. Meyer's Toy World New Barbie Center: "Marilyn Monroe Barbie® Series," accessed July 2, 1998.

4. "[M]y family all wanted me to do something about my music. Because all my friends said I had talent and they all kept after me and kept after me about practising. But some way I never seemed to care much about practising. I mean I

simply could not sit for hours and hours at a time practising just for the sake of a career. So one day I got quite temperamental and threw the old mandolin clear across the room and I have really never touched it since." Anita Loos, *Gentlemen Prefer Blondes: The Illuminating Diary of a Professional Lady* (Harmondsworth, U.K.: Penguin Books, 1992), 20.

5. Daniel Chua and Henry Stobart, announcement for the international symposium "Knowledge, Seduction and Danger: Music and the Sirens," Cambridge, U.K., 1998.

6. See Elisabeth Frenzel, *Stoffe der Weltliteratur: Ein Lexikon dichtungsgeschichtlicher Längsschnitte,* 8th ed. (Stuttgart: Alfred Kröner Verlag, 1992), 467. For an excellent and concise overview of the development of the Loreley subject in the nineteenth century, see Heinrich Heine, *Historisch-kritische Gesamtausgabe der Werke,* 1:2. *Buch der Lieder: Apparat,* ed. and annotated by Pierre Grappin (Hamburg: Hoffmann und Campe Verlag, 1975), 878–86.

7. Cecilia Hopkins Porter, *The Rhine as Musical Metaphor: Cultural Identity in German Romantic Music* (Boston: Northeastern University Press, 1996), 112.

8. Heinrich Heine, *Historisch-kritische Gesamtausgabe der Werke,* 1:2, 881.

9. Ibid., 1:1. *Buch der Lieder: Text,* ed. Pierre Grappin (Hamburg: Hoffmann und Campe Verlag, 1975), 206: "Ein Mährchen aus alten Zeiten."

10. The song was published in many adaptations and translations all over the world. One early example for this is C. Everest's translation, published in Philadelphia in 1859, of which the first eight bars are reproduced in Hopkins Porter, *The Rhine as Musical Metaphor,* 127. Other publications include, for example, a song collection published in Boston in 1848, and a version from 1870, *That Fatal Lore Ley!* (London: Augener & Co., 1870).

11. Marcel Genevoix, *Lorelei* (Paris: Editions du Seuil, 1978). On Genevoix's ambiguous relation to Germany, see Klaus Heitmann, "Deutschland als Bezauberung und Bedrohung: Maurice Genevoix und sein Roman *Lorelei,*" *Zeitschrift für französische Sprache und Literatur* 92 (1982): 9–27.

12. " . . . le Romantisme? . . . c'est dangereux. Plus que l'éblouissante parure d'or et le chant de la Lorelei au-dessus des écueils du Rhin." Given in Heitmann, "Deutschland als Bezauberung," 20.

13. A. H. Bernard, *Legends of the Rhine,* trans. Fr. Arnold, 11th ed. (Wiesbaden: Gustav Quiel, 1900), 233.

14. Hans Pfitzner, *Meine Beziehungen zu Max Bruch* (Munich: Albert Langen/Georg Müller, 1938), 5–6. Bruch's opera was based on a libretto that Emmanuel Geibel had written in the mid-1840s for Felix Mendelssohn Bartholdy. It was the only operatic project Mendelssohn ever took beyond discussion toward actual composition, but only some fragments survive. See R. Larry Todd, "On Mendelssohn's Operatic Destiny: *Die Lorelei* Reconsidered," in *Felix Mendelssohn Bartholdy: Kongreß-Bericht Berlin 1994,* ed. Christian Martin Schmidt (Wiesbaden: Breitkopf & Härtel, 1997), 113–40.

15. Frederick Herendon and Edward Horan, *A Royal Exchange,* "a romantic

269 RHEINSIRENEN

musical play at His Majesty's Theatre" (London: Chappell & Co., 1935). The song entitled "Lorelei" starts with hummed broken chords and the lyrics: "I hear you call / From the clear blue, / And when I hear you, / I must be near you. / And when I'm near you / I fear you, / You're such a dear, / You mean more than all." George and Ira Gershwin's *Pardon My English* was first performed on January 20, 1933 at the Majestic Theatre, New York.

    16. Lawrence D. Stewart, "Words upon Music," in the booklet for *Ella Fitzgerald Sings the George and Ira Gershwin Song Books* (Verve 1998), 19–65, at 61.

    17. Charles Gilbert, *Mission Loreley en Lorraine occupée, 5 novembre–24 décembre 1944* (Les Sables d'Olonne: Cercle d'Or, 1985).

    18. Hopkins Porter, *The Rhine as Musical Metaphor*, 110.

    19. Leonard Emil Bach, *Die neue Loreley*, opus 28, text by Siegmey (Berlin: C. A. Challier & Cie, 1878).

    20. Bach, *Die neue Loreley*, 1: "Nun weiss ich, was soll es bedeuten." Inna Naroditskaya, in her contribution to this volume, shows that both the Russian Rusalka (in Dargomyzhsky's 1858 opera) and Hansler and Kauer's *Donauweibchen* (1798) are crowned sirens who serve as national emblems.

    21. Heinrich Lindlar, *Loreley-Report: Heinrich Heine und die Rheinliedromantik* (Cologne: Verlag Christoph Dohr, 1999), 135.

    22. See in this context Siegfried Oechsle, "Nationalidee und große Symphonie: Mit einem Exkurs zum 'Ton,'" in *Deutsche Meister—böse Geister? Nationale Selbstfindung in der Musik*, ed. Hermann Danuser and Herfried Münkler (Schliengen: Edition Argus, 2001), 166–84; Carl Dahlhaus, *Die Musik des 19. Jahrhunderts*, vol. 6: *Neues Handbuch der Musikwissenschaft* (Laaber: Laaber-Verlag, 1980), 29–34.

    23. Hopkins Porter, *The Rhine as Musical Metaphor*, 108.

    24. The translation cited is by Mark Twain [Samuel L. Clemens], *A Tramp Abroad*, 2 vols., Stormfield ed. (New York: Harper & Brothers, 1929), 126. Heine, *Historisch-kritische Gesamtausgabe*, 1:1, 208: "Und singt ein Lied dabei; / Das hat eine wundersame, / Gewaltige Melodei."

    25. Carl Matzerath, *Irrungen der Liebe* (1840), given in Heine, *Historisch-kritische Gesamtausgabe der Werke*, 1:2, 880: "Nun erhebt sie die Geisterstimme zu einem Liede zauberischen Wohllauts; sehnsuchtsatmend verschweben die Töne über Berg und Thal."

    26. "Wie Flötenklang im Abendgold / Durch Auen und den Hain / Tönt eine Stimme wunderhold / Von Lurleis Fels am Rhein," given in Gerhard Bürger, *Im Zauber der Loreley: Eine kleine Monographie* (St. Goarshausen: Loreley-Verlag, 1952), 39.

    27. Given in Dr. Nicolaus Hocker, *Rhein-Album* (Berlin: in Commission bei Mitscher & Röstell, 1873), n.p.

    28. The literature on musical representation of gendered voices has grown significantly over the past decade. One of the key texts is still Marcia J. Citron, *Gender and the Musical Canon* (Cambridge: Cambridge University Press, 1993).

29. Letter by Ferdinand Hiller to Wolfgang Müller from September 6, 1854, given in Helmut Loos, "Wolfgang Müller von Königswinter und die Musik," in *Musikalische Rheinromantik: Bericht der Jahrestagung 1985,* ed. Siegfried Kross, vol. 140, *Beiträge zur rheinischen Musikgeschichte* (Kassel: Merseberger, 1989), 113–24, letter on 115–16.

30. Ibid., 116.

31. Ferdinand Hiller, *Lorelei,* opus 70, poem by Wolfgang Müller von Königswinter (Leipzig: Fr. Kirstner, 1857). See also Reinhold Sietz: "Die musikalische Gestaltung der Loreleysage bei Max Bruch, Felix Mendelssohn und Ferdinand Hiller," in *Max Bruch-Studien,* ed. Dietrich Kämper, vol. 87, *Beiträge zur rheinischen Musikgeschichte* (Cologne: Arno Volk Verlag, 1970), 14–45, here 44–45.

32. Paul and Lucien Hillemacher, *Loreley. Légende symphonique en trois parties,* text by Eugène Adenis, "Ouvrage couronné au Concours Municipal de la Ville de Paris" (Paris: Tresse Editeur, 1883).

33. Hillemacher, *Loreley,* 1, 2.

34. See Carolyn Abbate, *Unsung Voices: Opera and Musical Narrative in the Nineteenth Century* (Princeton, N.J.: Princeton University Press, 1991), 62.

35. Abbate, *Unsung Voices,* 70.

36. The naiads demand "Komm herbei, Lorelei . . . O singe, süsse Lorelei," to which Lorelei responds: "Ach! sie fordern meine Lieder und des neuen Opfers Gaben!" See Hiller, *Lorelei,* passim.

37. Abbate, *Unsung Voices,* 117–18.

38. Alfredo Catalani, *Loreley,* text by Carlo D'Ormeville and Angelo Zanardini, piano-vocal score (Milan: Ricordi, n.d.), 198.

39. Opera criticism has shown how these musical signifiers have an almost standardized reception field within the context of European nineteenth-century music. An obvious example for such nineteenth-century use of signifiers could be the contrasting musical representation of Carmen and Micaëla in Georges Bizet's opera *Carmen* (1875).

40. See John Whenham, *Claudio Monteverdi: "Orfeo,"* Cambridge Opera Handbooks (Cambridge: Cambridge University Press, 1986), 68–69.

41. Roland Barthes, *L'obvie et l'obtus. Essais critiques III* (Paris: Editions du Seuil, 1982), 243: "Le 'grain', c'est le corps dans la voix qui chante, dans la main qui écrit, dans le membre qui exécute." For an interpretation of Barthes' notion of the "grain" of the voice, see Reinhart Meyer-Kalkus: "Das 'Korn der Stimme'—Sprachtheoretische Voraussetzungen der Kritik Roland Barthes am Liedsänger Dietrich Fischer-Diskau," *Germanisch-Romanische Monatsschrift,* n.s., 42 (1992): 326–40.

42. Hopkins Porter: *The Rhine as Musical Metaphor,* 108.

43. Plato, *[πόλιτεια] / Politeia,* ed. Dietrich Kurz, Greek text established by Emile Chambry, trans. Friedrich Schleiermacher (Darmstadt: Wissenschaftliche Buchgesellschaft, 1990), §617c, 862–63.

44. Silke Leopold, "Von der Allgewalt vollsten Hingebungseifers: Weibs-Bilder in Wagners 'Ring,' " in *Richard Wagner "Der Ring des Nibelungen": An-*

sichten des Mythos, ed. Udo Bermbach and Dieter Borchmeyer (Stuttgart: Metzler, 1995), 59–74.

45. Richard Wagner, *Oper und Drama,* ed. Klaus Kropfinger (Stuttgart: Reclam, 1984), 118.

46. Reinhart Meyer-Kalkus, "Richard Wagners Theorie der Wort-Tonsprache in 'Oper und Drama' und 'Der Ring des Nibelungen;' *Athenäum: Jahrbuch für Romantik* 6 (1996): 153–95, 187: "Wagner dichtet im Gesang der Rheintöchter einen Sprach-Entstehungsmythos."

47. Richard Wagner: "An Friedrich Nietzsche" (1872), quotation given in Meyer-Kalkus, "Richard Wagners Theorie der Wort-Tonsprache," 184–85: "Dem Studium J. Grimms entnahm ich einmal ein altdeutsches 'Heilawac', formte es mir, um für meine Zwecke es noch geschmeidiger zu machen, zu einem 'Weiawaga' (eine Form, welche wir heute noch in 'Weihwasser' wiedererkennen), leitete hiervon in den verwandten Sprachwurzeln 'wogen' und 'wiegen' endlich 'wellen' und 'wallen' über und bildete mir so, nach der Analogie des 'Eia popeia' unserer Kinderstubenlieder, eine wurzelhaft syllabische Melodie für meine Wassermädchen."

48. Dietrich Borchmeyer, "Wagners Mythos vom Anfang und Ende der Welt," in *Richard Wagner "Der Ring des Nibelungen,"* ed. Bermbach and Borchmeyer, 1–25, at 5.

49. Wagner, *Oper und Drama,* 288: "sein Mutterelement, den musikalischen Ton."

50. See Meri Lao, "Un feminile musicale possibile," in *Les Symbolistes et Richard Wagner—Die Symbolisten und Richard Wagner,* ed. Wolfgang Storch (Berlin: Edition Hentrich, 1991), 29–31, at 29: "Cantano parole farcite di onomatopeie e allitterazione, come se dovessero richiamare il linguaggio dei primordi, ma si tratta pur sempre di lingua tedesca."

51. Cosima Wagner, *Die Tagebücher,* ed. Martin Gregor-Dellin and Dietrich Mack, vol. 1, 1869–1872 (Munich: Piper, 1982), 129: "Von der Wellenbewegung im Rheingold sagt R., 'es sei gleichsam das Wiegenlied der Welt.'" The association of forest and German nationality dates back to Tacitus's *Germania.* See Simon Shama, *Landscape & Memory* (London: HarperCollins, 1995), 75–134.

52. Wagner's Rhine Maidens did, however, have another mermaid ancestress in addition to Loreley in the figure of Melusina as she was portrayed in Felix Mendelssohn's 1833 concert overture *Zum Märchen von der schönen Melusine,* op. 32, and Mendelssohn's static arpeggiated wave motif found its echo in the *Rheingold* opening. Melusina, the mermaid emerging from (and returning to) the waves, shares traits also with Loreley (in the Brentano version) in that her mermaid existence was tied to betrayal in love. I am grateful to Jon Finson for pointing me to this connection. See also Thomas Grey, "The Orchestral Music," in *The Mendelssohn Companion,* ed. Douglass Seaton (Westport, Conn.: Greenwood Press, 2001), 395–568, esp. 475–83.

53. For an example of nineteenth-century Loreley tourism, see the entries for July and August 1878 in *Mark Twain's Notebooks & Journals,* vol. 2 (1877–1883),

ed. Frederick Anderson, Lin Salamo, and Bernard Stein (Berkeley: University of California Press, 1975), esp. 116, 125, and 212; Mark Twain, *A Tramp Abroad*, "An Ancient Legend of the Rhine," 119–29.

54. http://gladstone.uoregon.edu/~cek/@.html, accessed June 12, 1998.

55. See Heine, *Historisch-kritische Gesamtausgabe der Werke*, vol. 1:2, 878–86.

56. Julia Schmidt, "Jetzt lockt die Sirene in den sicheren Hafen der Ehe," *Frankfurter Allgemeine Zeitung*, April 28, 1998, 45. I wish to thank Eva Rieger for sharing this article with me.

CHAPTER 10

Creating Madame Landowska

THE FAMOUS POLISH HARPSICHORDIST Wanda Landowska has recently been characterized as an "uncommon visionary" and an "epochal exception."[1] Such epithets recognize her as a singularly influential musician and, at the same time, mythologize her into a modern revolutionary who almost single-handedly initiated the worldwide harpsichord revival of the twentieth century by championing above all the "authentic" performance of Bach on the harpsichord. Over the past seventy years the legend of Wanda Landowska has become firmly enshrined in the histories and mythologies of the early music movement. This image stems from her successful and sustained international solo career—flourishing to her death in 1959—and from the worldwide impact of her midcareer recordings of the 1930s.[2] Wanda Landowska's story is one of struggle, controversy, and triumph in

---

1. See the PBS production *Uncommon Visionary: A Documentary on the Life and Art of Wanda Landowska* (1997), by Barbara Attie, Janet Goldwater, and Diane Pontius (Video Artists International DVD 4246). For her being an "epochale Ausnahmeerscheinung" see Martin Elste, *Meilensteine der Bach-Interpretation 1750–2000: Eine Werkgeschichte im Wandel* (Stuttgart: Metzler; Kassel: Bärenreiter, 2000), 337. For other castings of Landowska as the key figure in the twentieth-century harpsichord revival see, for example, Norbert Dufourcq, *Le clavecin* (Paris: Presses universitaires de France, 1949), 118–22; Howard Schott, "Wanda Landowska: A Centenary Appraisal," *Early Music* 7 (1979): 467–72; Harvey Sachs, *Virtuoso* (New York: Thames and Hudson,

1982), 153; Alice Hudnall Cash, "Wanda Landowska and the Revival of the Harpsichord," in *Music in the Theater, Church, and Villa: Essays in Honor of Robert Lamar Weaver and Norma Wright Weaver*, ed. Susan Parisi (Harmonie Park Press, 2000), 277–84.

2. In particular, her 1933 recording of Bach's *Goldberg Variations* as well as her versions of the *Chromatic Fantasy and Fugue* (1935) and several suites (1936–37) were the first recordings of these works on the harpsichord. See Elste, *Meilensteine der Bach-Interpretation*, 362–88.

which personal sacrifice engenders musical greatness while the performer becomes anointed as the true voice of the composer. Her visual and artistic self-representation and the aura of aristocratic mystique and inspiration turned her concerts into ritualized celebrations during which she appeared as a high priestess of the cult of Bach. From her clothing to her hairstyle, every element of her public appearances was deliberate and choreographed.[3] Landowska "would not have dreamt of beginning a recital without first establishing the proper atmosphere: the lighting on stage had to be very dim before she would glide, wraith-like, onto the platform, hands clasped as if in prayer and eyes cast heavenward."[4]

The roots of Landowska's self-representation as the "goddess of the harpsichord" and the myths associated with it reach back to the beginnings of her career in prewar Paris at the turn of the twentieth century.[5] The French capital provided the cultural context within which Landowska's career as performer, composer, and scholar was molded. As a young woman in her twenties she could draw on models of gendered performance tested by other female musicians in the French capital. Indeed, the strategies that she and her entourage developed in these early years created "Madame Landowska," as she was known, by instrumentalizing successful female career tactics in prewar Paris so as to forge her own unique artistic identity. Landowska's claim for artistic uniqueness, her increasing musical specialization as a harpsichordist, her (self-)representation as "musical daughter" of Bach, her emphasis on a special musical calling, the relentless rhetoric of exceptionality and artistic struggle not only characterize her (auto)biography since the 1940s but also reflect key elements of women's professional strategies in the Parisian musical world around 1900.[6] Her correspondence and other documents from these early years reveal that she was an active agent in the creation of her public persona while drawing on a support network that included her husband, Henri Lew, her impresario, Gabriel Astruc, and a host of wise if not always old men such as Charles Bordes and Leo Tolstoy.

Paris, Women, and Harpsichord Music

Women musicians in particular were attracted to fin de siècle Paris because it offered career opportunities that were scarce in other cities such as Vienna, Berlin, and London.[7] Paris had a cosmopolitan and financially well heeled audience, dozens of concert series, hundreds of salons and concert societies, many schools and conservatories—all spaces within which a young, ambitious musician could carve out a place for herself. What Walter Benjamin so famously called the capital of the nineteenth century represented not only a place full of career opportunities but also the cultural and musical center of a Europe that needed to be conquered for any major international career to flourish.[8] Paris presented thus an ideal milieu for the ambitious young pianist and

---

3. Her companion Denise Restout discusses Landowska's concert preparation in *Uncommon Visionary*.
4. Sachs, *Virtuoso*, 154.
5. Bernard Gavoty, *Wanda Landowska*, trans. F. E. Richardson, with illustrations by Roger Hauert (Geneva: René Kister, 1957), 6.
6. "[E]lle nous apparaît comme une fille musicale de ce Jean-Sébastien Bach" (Robert Brussel, "Wanda Landowska ou la renaissance du clavecin," *Musica* 4 [1905]: 7–8, 8). On women's career strategies in fin de siècle Paris see, for example, Annegret Fauser, "*La Guerre en dentelles*: Women and the *Prix de Rome* in French Cultural Politics," *Journal of the American Musicological Society* 51 (1998): 83–129, and "Zwischen Professionalismus und Salon: Französische Musikerinnen des *Fin de siècle*," in *Professionalismus in der Musik*, ed. Christian Kaden and Volker Kalisch (Essen: Blaue Eule, 1998), 261–74; Florence Launay, *Les compositrices françaises de 1789 à 1914*, Ph.D. dissertation, Université de Rennes II, 2004.

7. Sophie Fuller, "A Mount Everest in Music? Ethel Smyth and the Other Women Composers," paper given at the Symposium of the International Musicological Society, Melbourne, July 14, 2004. For women's career opportunities in late-nineteenth-century Britain see Paula Gillett, *Musical Women in England, 1870–1914: "Encroaching on All Man's Privileges"* (New York: St. Martin's Press, 2000).
8. That Paris was perceived as "the capital of the world" was not a new phenomenon around 1900; the myth of Paris reaches back to the ancien régime. See Patrice Higonnet, *Paris: Capital of the World*, trans. Arthur Goldhammer (Cambridge MA: Harvard University Press, 2002).

fledgling composer Wanda Landowska, who moved to the French capital in 1900 at the age of twenty-one to fulfill her "mad desire to be famous."[9]

What follows presents the story usually told: Landowska and her new husband, Henri Lew, arrived in Paris as unknown, impoverished Polish immigrants who struggled to survive. Rather than pursuing a lucrative career as a piano virtuoso, Landowska instead began her battle for the revival of the harpsichord as the true instrument of early keyboard music. Driven by her love for the music of Bach, she followed this dream even against the advice of her close friends. An oft-quoted letter dated July 31, 1903, from Landowska's friend Charles Bordes serves as evidence, since in it he suggested that Landowska should play early music *"but not on the harpsichord."*[10] Landowska persisted, however, and introduced unsuspecting Parisian audiences to the harpsichord in baby steps by programming one or two works played on the instrument in concerts otherwise performed on the piano.[11] "Imagine how I had to fight," she said in a 1953 interview, identifying pianists as the "enemy . . . against me."[12] But by 1908 she had arrived. She was, in her own words, "the most popular instrumentalist of this time."

As is the case with most such myths of artistic beginnings, Landowska's story is revealing particularly in what she and her entourage omitted in order to legitimize the claim of an exceptionality that set her apart from her contemporaries. That Landowska, from an early age, hoped to play works by the composers whose music she loved is not in question.[13] Contrary to common belief, however, Landowska was not the only woman harpsichordist in early-twentieth-century France. Nor was her choice of repertoire uncommon or particularly visionary when seen in the context of fin de siècle Paris. What set her apart, however, was the brilliant use she and her supporters made of the cultural field of Parisian musical life to establish her highly successful career within less than a decade.

The harpsichord was never entirely absent from French music making, but it regained wider interest during the Second Empire, especially within musicians' and salon circles, following the imperial court's interest in all things rococo. Thus in 1856 the Parisian piano maker Charles Fleury restored a Taskin harpsichord that was played by a Joséphine Martin in a concert on April 5, 1857, during which "the instrument, which has become quite rare, . . . produced a lively sensation and the success that it shared with the performer was complete."[14] Both the well-known pianist Amédée Méreaux and his even better-known female student, Charlotte de Malleville, performed Baroque repertoire sporadically on the harpsichord.[15] The highlight of an evening in April 1861 at the Rothschild

---

9. Wanda Landowska, diaries, cited in *Uncommon Visionary*.
10. Letter given in English translation in Denise Restout, ed., *Landowska on Music* (New York: Stein and Day, 1964), 10.
11. Restout, *Landowska on Music*, 12. That Bordes' admonition may have had more impact than Landowska later admitted may be reflected in the fact that she performed harpsichord music on the piano later in 1903.
12. This and the following remark come from the 1953 interview shown in *Uncommon Visionary*.
13. Not only do the documents reproduced in the documentary *Uncommon Visionary* corroborate this part of her story, but an early article published in *Musica* in 1905 also claims that her interest in Baroque music began before she came to Paris.
14. For information on the harpsichord see Edward L. Kottick, *A History of the Harpsichord* (Bloomington: Indiana University Press, 2003), 296. For a review of the concert see "Nouvelles," *Revue et Gazette Musicale de Paris*, April 5, 1857, 118: "A l'une des dernières réunions musicales de M. et Mlle Martin, cette dernière a fait entendre un clavecin construit en 1770 par Pascal Taskin. Cet instrument, devenu fort rare, a produit une vive sensation, et le succès tout nouveau qu'il a partagé avec l'exécutante a été complet."
15. Katharine Ellis, *Interpreting the Musical Past: Early Music in Nineteenth-Century France* (New York: Oxford University Press, 2005), 40, 50–52. I am grateful to Katharine Ellis for sharing the information about Mlle de Malleville. Already by April 28, 1844, Amédée Méreaux had organized a *grand concert historique* at the Salle Pleyel, where he performed on both the harpsichord and the piano (Malou Haine, "Concerts historiques dans la seconde moitié du 19e siècle," in *Musique et société: Hommages à Robert Wangermée*, ed. Henri Vanhulst and Malou Haine [Brussels: Editions de l'Université de Bruxelles, 1988], 121–42, 124).

salon was Georges Pfeiffer's harpsichord performance of works by Rameau, Grétry, Mozart, and Haydn; in the 1860s the Parisian piano virtuoso Louis Diémer started to include one or two pieces on the harpsichord in his piano recitals; and later, in the 1870s, Camille Saint-Saëns gave several lecture-recitals on the harpsichord for the Société des Compositeurs.[16] Though the harpsichord remained an antiquarian curiosity, it also held fascination as a sound object from the ancien régime. Indeed, by the 1860s the eighteenth century had been transformed into a time of past French glory, with Marie-Antoinette's harpsichord the most fetishized musical instrument from this past.[17] Even though harpsichords continued to be criticized for their tone quality and limited expressive range (in Bordes' later formulation reducing "superb and often large-scale works to the size of its tiny, spindly legs"), the growing fascination with "all things past" opened the path for the harpsichord revival of the fin de siècle.[18] In the Third Republic the harpsichord and its repertoire soon became musical signifiers of an aristocratic France that embodied national taste, grace, elegance, and finesse, celebrating courtly refinement in the performance especially of works by the French *clavecinistes*.[19]

This growing interest in the instrument led, in the mid-1880s, to the development of newly constructed harpsichords by three Paris piano manufacturers, Pleyel, Erard, and Tomasini.[20] They were presented to the public for the first time at the 1889 Exposition universelle in the Galerie Desaix, together with new pianos and harps. Marie-Antoinette's harpsichord, on the other hand, fascinated visitors in the retrospective of historical musical instruments, and Diémer's performances on his Taskin harpsichord charmed listeners at the Trocadéro, while visitors to the art exhibition could admire Horace de Callias' rendering of a salon concert with Diémer at the harpsichord.[21] Pleyel's, Erard's, and Tomasini's new harpsichords were celebrated as improved music machines, useful in particular for the revival of the glorious past of French music and to provide enjoyment for society women. Indeed, the discourse on the instrument was ambiguous, veering between nationalist fascination, on the one hand, and gendered mistrust, on the other. Thus in 1889 Saint-Saëns praised the "delicious" nature of the new Pleyel instruments but insisted that harpsichords were instruments of women's boudoirs, best suited to accompanying delicate song.[22] But

---

16. On Diémer see Kottick, *A History of the Harpsichord*, 400. I am grateful to Katharine Ellis for sharing the information about Camille Saint-Saëns. Pfeiffer's concert is reviewed in "Nouvelles," *Revue et Gazette Musicale de Paris*, April 7, 1861, 109.

Une séance curieuse au point de vue de l'art musical, a eu lieu la semaine dernière dans les salons du baron de Rothschild. M. Georges Pfeiffer y avait été appelé par le célèbre financier pour faire apprécier les qualités du fameux clavecin du XVIe siècle dont il s'est rendu acquéreur, et que possédait M. Pigeory, architecte de la ville de Paris, et fondateur de la *Revue des beaux-arts*. Le jeune artiste a fort intéressé l'auditoire, en faisant redire à cet instrument les airs de Rameau, Grétry, Mozart et Haydn, dont il avait mainte fois retenti sans doute à l'époque où florissaient les célèbres compositeurs.

17. Anecdotes about and references to the harpsichord of Marie-Antoinette abound in the press from the 1830s onward; see, for example, "Variétés: Le clavecin de Marie-Antoinette," *Le Pianiste*, July 1834, 132–35; its attribution to Taskin in "Nouvelles diverses," *Revue et Gazette Musicale de Paris*, July 7, 1867, 219.

---

18. For Bordes see Restout, *Landowska on Music*, 10. Discussing the modern harpsichord in 1889, Julien Tiersot attributed its development to the immense "engouement actuel pour tout ce qui touche aux choses du temps passé" ("Promenades à l'Exposition," *Le Ménestrel* 55 [1889]: 180).

19. Ellis, *Interpreting the Musical Past*, 90–96.

20. For an excellent discussion of these instruments see Martin Elste, "Nostalgische Musikmaschinen: Cembali im 20. Jahrhundert," in *Kielklaviere: Cembali, Spinette, Virginale*, ed. John Henry van der Meer, Martin Elste, and Günther Wagner (Berlin: Staatliches Institut für Musikforschung Preußischer Kulturbesitz, 1991), 239–77, esp. 245–47.

21. On the presence of harpsichords at the 1889 Paris World's Fair see Annegret Fauser, *Musical Encounters at the 1889 Paris World's Fair* (Rochester: Rochester University Press, 2005), 27–34.

22. "Et c'est délicieux! c'est bien l'instrument du boudoir, de la femme nerveuse et délicate, sur lequel on peut accompagner un chant discret, une mélodie murmurée dans l'oreille entre deux propos d'amour" (Camille Saint-Saëns, "Le 'Rappel' à l'Exposition: Les instruments de musique," *Le Rappel*, October 5, 1889/14 vendémiaire an 98, 1–2, 2).

in particular through Diémer and other pianists concertizing on the harpsichord the instrument was reintroduced into the salon circuits and elite concerts of Paris, keeping the repertoire alive in the circles of nobility and upper bourgeoisie.[23] Furthermore, concerts by ensembles such as the Société des Instruments Anciens—founded in 1895 by Louis van Waefelghem (viola d'amore) with Jules Delsart (viola da gamba), Laurent Grillet (hurdy-gurdy), and Louis Diémer (harpsichord)—started to bring into the more mainstream worlds of Parisian music a repertoire played on "authentic instruments," as they were called then and now.[24] The harpsichord also began to attract composers, including Francis Thomé (who wrote a rigadon for harpsichord in 1889), Armande de Polignac, and Marie Prestat.[25]

As Katharine Ellis has recently shown in her magisterial monograph on the revival of early music in nineteenth-century France, music from the past played an increasingly significant role in nineteenth-century Parisian concert life. By 1900 early music formed an unquestioned part of the repertoire, but not all early music carried the same weight. The gendered connotations of keyboard music had become rather complicated.[26] Baroque keyboard works associated with the harpsichord had become a staple of concert programs by female performers, and in 1898 and 1900, for example, Bach was assigned in the end-of-year competitions for female piano students at the Paris Conservatoire.[27] This contrasts with the far more masculine image associated with both Handel's and Bach's organ works as championed by Saint-Saëns, Charles-Marie Widor, and Alexandre Guilmant, among others.[28] Around 1900, however, we see shifts in repertoire, with more and more male pianists integrating Bach, Handel, and the French harpsichord composers into their concert programs, albeit mostly still on the piano.[29] Indeed, playing the works of the French *clavecinistes* became a form of local legitimization, as in the case of Joaquín Nin, whose 1904 debut concert in Paris included pieces by Chambonnières, Couperin, and Rameau.[30]

But Bach and his contemporaries also remained firmly in the domain of female pianists and harpsichordists. Most prominent among these was the young pianist Blanche Selva. Barely twenty years old, Selva presented Bach's complete keyboard works in 1904 in seventeen piano recitals at the Schola Cantorum, a feat that she then repeated in subsequent years. A review in 1906 designated her as "without doubt Bach's most worthy priestess."[31] Selva also played Bach

---

23. On the class-specific consumption of early music see Catrina Flint de Medicis, "Nationalism and Early Music at the French *fin de siècle*: Three Case Studies," *Nineteenth-Century Music Review* 1 (2004): 43–66. For example, the performance of Rameau's *Dardanus* at the Polignac salon featured a harpsichord that had belonged to the father of Prince Edmond de Polignac (Sylvia Kahan, *Music's Modern Muse: A Life of Winnaretta Singer Princesse de Polignac* [Rochester NY: Rochester University Press, 2003], 92). Prince Edmond de Polignac often "greeted visitors to his Parisian salon by playing his harpsichord" (Kottick, *A History of the Harpsichord*, 396).
24. The Société des Instruments Anciens started its public concert series in 1895 with a sequence of three concerts at the Salle Pleyel (Haine, "Concerts historiques," 134–35). The Société's repertoire consisted mainly of French early music.
25. On Thomé see Kottick, *A History of the Harpsichord*, 400, which gives a later date of 1892 for the piece. Armande de Polignac's unpublished "Petite suite pour clavecin" and Marie Prestat's three *Pièces dans le style ancien* (*Menuet Louis XIV*, *Passepied*, *La reine au petit lever*) are mentioned in Launay, *Les compositrices françaises*, 338. Neither piece is dated.
26. Critical discourse in France teemed with gendered approaches to musical repertoire and performance. See Annegret Fauser, "Gendering the Nations: The Ideologies of French Discourse on Music (1870–1914)," in *Musical Constructions of Nationalism: Essays on the History and Ideology of European Musical Culture, 1800–1945*, ed. Michael Murphy and Harry White (Cork: Cork University Press, 2001), 72–103.
27. Katharine Ellis, "Female Pianists and Their Male Critics in Nineteenth-Century Paris," *Journal of the American Musicological Society* 50 (1997): 353–85, esp. 363. As Ellis has shown, from 1897 through 1900 male pianists were assigned works by Beethoven, a composer never once given to women in the nineteenth century.
28. Ellis, *Interpreting the Musical Past*, 55, 85–87.
29. Ellis, *Interpreting the Musical Past*, 88.
30. Carola Hess, "Nin, Joaquín," in *Grove Music Online* (Oxford University Press), <http://www.grovemusic.com>.
31. "Le 16 janvier, Mlle Blanche Selva reprenait la série coutumière de ses hommages à Jean-Sébastien Bach, dont elle est sans contredit la plus digne prêtresse" ("Revue de la quinzaine," *S.I.M.* 2, no. 1 [1906]: 117).

on the harpsichord, albeit more rarely and with less success. Other female harpsichordists who performed in Paris during these years were Pauline Auclert, Marguerite Delcourt, Elodie Lelong, Régina Patorni-Casadesus, and Juliette Toutain.[32] Male harpsichord players included not just Louis Diémer but also a younger generation such as Alfred Casella, Jules Jemain, Joaquín Nin, and Ricardo Viñes. None of these female and male musicians was exclusively dedicated to the harpsichord, but they all counted among the growing circle of Paris's early music keyboard players. Their performances were complemented by their musical anthologies, lectures, and publications.[33] It is this Parisian context that shaped and enabled the career of Wanda Landowska.

The Parisian Beginnings of a Polish Composer-Pianist

After the young musician arrived in Paris she soon started to emerge in public as both a composer and a pianist. Indeed, within a year of her move Enoch & Cie, one of the major Parisian music publishers, had brought out several of her piano compositions, including the *étude caractéristique, En route*, op. 4; *Lied*, op. 5; *Rêverie d'automne*, op. 6; and *Danse polonaise*, op. 7.[34] The latter was dedicated to Clothilde de Kleeberg, one of the star pianists of the period.

Landowska herself performed another one of her own pieces, *Rapsodie orientale* for piano, in a concert in November 1901, during an evening concert at which fifteen performers presented works published by Enoch. A second concert that season, organized by the journal *Femina* on March 14, 1902, featured her playing three of her piano pieces and her variations for two pianos as well as accompanying four of her songs.[35]

Through Enoch, Landowska also seems to have gained links with the publisher Pierre Lafitte & Cie, which brought out two prestigious illustrated journals, *Femina* and *Musica*, both of which presented Landowska as a composer-pianist in those early years.[36] In 1902 she was featured alongside highly respected women composers such as Augusta Holmès and Cécile Chaminade in an article about women's admission to the Prix de Rome.[37] Landowska claimed, "I don't understand the puerile objections to this project, I see only the fear of competition among the men, and that is not a pretty sentiment."[38] Less than a year later, in February 1903, the same elegant but resolutely plain photograph that had accompanied the *Femina* write-up appeared as a full-page portrait in *Musica*, with a brief text that presented her as a charming pianist and a composer of brilliant piano music:

> The subscribers of the Concerts Lamoureux are still under the spell of the highly individual

---

32. Indeed, while Marguerite Delcourt was the main harpsichordist of the Société de Concerts d'Instruments Anciens in its early years, Régina Casadesus prepared herself to take over this role by studying the harpsichord with Louis Diémer (Régina Patorni-Casadesus, *Souvenirs d'une claveciniste: Ma famille Casadesus* [Paris: La Ruche Ouvrière, 1962], 54–55).

33. When Van Waefelghem's Société des Instruments Anciens gave its first concert series in March and April 1895 in the Salle Pleyel, the programs were introduced by *conference-causéries* (introductory remarks) (Haine, "Concerts historiques," 134–35). Lectures accompanying concerts became a regular, if not unexpected, feature in concerts of early music. Marie Mockel organized a series of five concerts featuring "une exposition complète du chant monodique," with lectures by Julien Tiersot (*Le Ménestrel* 71 [1905]: 157), while Magda le Goff's 1907 concerts, "Musique de XVIIe et XVIIIe siècles," were accompanied by a lecture by Henri Expert (*S.I.M.* 3 [1907]: 167–68). In 1906 Joaquín Nin presented a series of twelve lecture-recitals on musical form (*S.I.M.* 2 [1906]: 318–19).

34. Copies of these scores, stamped with the date of the "dépôt legal" (copyright deposit), are at the Bibliothèque nationale de France, Département de Musique.

35. Restout, *Landowska on Music*, 8–9. See also Max Rivière, "Nos musiciennes et le Prix de Rome," *Femina*, April 15, 1902, 115–16: "Mme Wanda Landowska est une physionomie curieuse et séduisante qu'ont pu apprécier les spectatrices du concert de *Femina* le 14 mars dernier" (116).

36. Around 1900 Enoch had close business links with Lafitte. See the documents in the private archives of Gabriel Astruc preserved in the Archives nationales, Papiers Astruc, 409AP/1.

37. On female self-representation and strategies and male resistance in the early years of women's competition for the Prix de Rome see Fauser, "La Guerre en dentelles."

38. "[J]e ne comprends pas les objections puériles faites à ce projet, je ne vois guère chez les hommes que la crainte de la concurrence et ce n'est pas un sentiment bien joli" (Rivière, "Nos musiciennes et le Prix de Rome," 116).

Fig. 1. "Wanda Landowska," *Musica* 2 (1903), 73 (Bibliothèque nationale de France)

talent with which she played a delicate Mozart concerto last year, and the worshipers at the Schola Cantorum consider her the dream interpreter of Bach. She is the author of brilliant piano compositions and of a number of songs that are animated by the powerful spirit of her Polish fatherland. Is she more composer than virtuoso or more virtuoso than composer? The future will pronounce: perhaps she is equally talented as either.[39]

In this short promotional text the comparison with Chopin, the great Polish composer-pianist, is all too obvious. Indeed, two months earlier a reviewer had already made the link explicitly by explaining to his readers that "Madame Wanda Landowska, who, if I am right, has only recently made her appearance in France, is a compatriot of Chopin, and she too [is] a pianist and composer."[40] As a Polish composer in the good company of the Romanian Georges Enesco and the Russian Vladimir Dyck, Landowska was celebrated as a prizewinner in *Musica*'s 1903–4 composition "tournament," where she shared first prize for an unspecified piano composition and won second prize for a song.[41] Thus her nationality added a special flavor of cosmopolitanism and artistic lineage to her artistic persona as a composer-pianist.

Her debut as a pianist in a major Parisian concert took place on February 16, 1902, at the Concerts Lamoureux, where she performed Mozart's Piano Concerto in E-flat Major, K. 271. In a lukewarm review the critic for *Le Ménestrel* attested to a "certain elegance" in her rendering of this "charming concerto."[42] Her first appearance in a concert associated with the Schola Cantorum occurred two months later, on April 26, 1902, in the context of a Bach cantata evening during which she played a prelude and fugue in F major by Bach and his second partita, both on the piano.[43] Most of her documented performances between April 1902 and June 1903 were connected with the Schola Cantorum, usually in the guise of a short

---

39. "Les abonnés des Concerts Lamoureux sont encore sous le charme du talent si personnel avec lequel elle joua l'an dernier un délicat concerto de Mozart et les fervents de la *Schola Cantorum* la considèrent comme l'interprète rêvée de Bach. Auteur de brillantes compositions pour piano et de quelques *lieder* qu'anime le souffle puissant de la patrie polonaise. Est-elle plus compositeur que virtuose ou plus virtuose que compositeur? L'avenir le dira:

peut-être est-elle les deux avec un égal talent" ("Wanda Landowska," *Musica* 2 [1903]: 73).

40. "Mme Wanda Landowska qui n'a fait que depuis peu de temps, si je ne me trompe, son apparition en France, est une compatriote de Chopin, pianiste et compositeur elle aussi" (review signed P.L., in *Le Courrier Musical*, December 15, 1902, 299). I am grateful to Catrina Flint de Medicis for sharing this review with me.

41. "La Russie est représentée par M. Vladimir Dyck, la Pologne par Mme Wanda Landowska, la Roumanie par M. Georges Enesco" (Bretigny, "Les lauréats du tournoi," *Musica* 3 [1904]: 244–48, 247).

42. "Il s'agit d'une séance agréable sans rien de précisément captivant. Mme Wanda Landowska s'est assurée un joli succès auprès d'une assistance sympathique; elle a joué avec une certaine élégance le charmant concerto pour piano en mi bémol de Mozart" (Alice Hudnall Cash, "Wanda Landowska and the Revival of the Harpsichord: A Reassessment," Ph.D. dissertation, University of Kentucky, 1990, 53 n. 18).

43. I am grateful to Catrina Flint de Medicis for sharing with me the program for the second concert in the second series of sacred Bach cantatas on April 26, 1902.

Fig. 2: Wanda Landowska, "Une leçon de piano," *Femina*, 15 February 1904, 54 (Collection of the Author)

appearance within the concert series dedicated to either Bach or Mozart. Save for her performance of an unspecified piano concerto by Mozart on November 27, 1902, she appeared not as a soloist but as a chamber music player in Mozart evenings.[44]

The years immediately after Landowska's arrival in Paris thus brought her moderate success as a Polish composer-pianist whose achievements were compared to those of Chopin and, to a lesser extent, Paderewski. While Landowska clearly tried to explore where this path might lead her, she tried other career tactics typical of women musicians in Paris. She established herself as a sought-after piano teacher and was featured in *Femina* in an article in which she promoted herself as such to the daughters of the journal's readership.[45] This not only gave her some economic stability but also played on the trope of female nurturing that pervaded discourse on teaching in Third Republic France.[46] The article in *Femina* is illustrated by pictures that emphasize the motherly quality of music teaching, while her text reproduces the by then familiar clichés of femininity in performance by contrasting male virtuosity with female elegance, especially by stressing the need for "the finest and most delicate hand" in order to play

---

44. During the 1902–3 season Landowska appeared as a chamber music player in all three concerts of the Mozart cycle on December 8, 1902, January 15, 1903, and February 13, 1903. I am grateful to Catrina Flint de Medicis for the information on these concerts.
45. Wanda Landowska, "Une leçon de piano," *Femina*, February 15, 1904, 54.
46. Teaching as a female profession was strongly encouraged by successive governments in Third Republic France. Discourse focused not only on women's pseudomaternal roles as teachers but also on gender-specific teachings that

perpetuated the ideal of "Republican motherhood." See, in particular, Françoise Mayeur, *L'éducation des filles en France au XIXe siècle* (Paris: Hachette, 1979); Linda L. Clark, *Schooling the Daughters of Marianne: Textbooks and the Socialization of Girls in Modern French Primary Schools* (Albany: State University of New York Press, 1984); Jo Burr Margadant, *Madame le Professeur: Women Educators in the Third Republic* (Princeton: Princeton University Press, 1990); Anne T. Quartararo, *Women Teachers and Popular Education in Nineteenth-Century France: Social Values and Corporate Identity at the Normal School Institution* (Newark: University of Delaware Press, 1995).

the feminine repertoire of Bach, Haydn, and Mozart.[47]

But while Landowska tapped into the career opportunities and rhetoric of teaching, she also sought out allies and supporters, whether in the context of Parisian journalism or through the institutions of the French capital. This was clearly her strategy in terms of her affiliation from 1902 onward with the Schola Cantorum (founded in 1894), which was known as a place hospitable to women and foreigners, in contrast to the Conservatoire, which was closed to foreigners and dominated by men.[48] Landowska's link to the institution seems to have been mainly through Charles Bordes, a composer trained by César Franck who, in the 1890s, became best known for his work on early music through the performances in particular of Renaissance polyphony with his chapel choir, the Chanteurs de Saint-Gervais. Bordes was the driving force behind the foundation of the Schola Cantorum and dominated its concert activities for the first decade.[49]

As a soloist Landowska's specialization in Baroque and Classical keyboard music not only associated her with a newly canonic repertoire traditionally associated with female performers but also enabled her, like numerous other female performers of the period, to style herself as a specialist, serving the music of great masters from the past. Bordes' letter to Landowska from July 1903, which is normally used to prove that he discouraged her from playing the harpsichord, offers insight into this strategy of specialization. After his sideswipe against the instrument, Bordes suggested that she should create a "splendid specialty" by playing the works of Bach, Couperin, Chambonnières, and Rameau, and he offered "to give a whole series of concerts with you this winter, at the Schola, to build up your name in this repertoire."[50] It seems that only one concert happened and that the rest of the series that Bordes planned for Landowska was cancelled after Bordes' stroke in the same month.

The first of these concerts, the "Concert of French Music of the Seventeenth and Eighteenth Centuries," took place at the Schola Cantorum on November 12, 1903. Masterminded by Bordes to celebrate the national heritage of France, the concert opened the winter season at the Schola with "the *flowers* of Rameau, Clérambault, du Mont, etc. . . . *nothing but French.*"[51] This multiartist concert featured Landowska playing, for the first time, French Baroque repertoire, with three dances each by Chambonnières, Louis Couperin, and François Couperin as well as Rameau's *Les tricotets*, *La poule*, and *L'Egyptienne*. It is clear that Landowska's choice of repertoire at this point relied on widely accessible editions, in particular by Diémer.[52] Although announced in the program as a harpsichordist, Landowska performed her selection of

---

47. "S'il est vrai qu'une certaine musique de pure virtuosité exige des mains de chef de claque, celle de Bach, de Haydn, de Mozart peut et même doit être jouée avec la main la plus fine et la plus délicate" (Landowska, "Une leçon de piano," 54). For the gendering of piano repertoire since the early nineteenth century see Ellis, "Female Pianists."

48. For substantive research on the Schola Cantorum and the complex economic and artistic shifts relating to the roles of Charles Bordes and Vincent d'Indy see Catrina Flint de Medicis, "The Schola Cantorum, Early Music, and French Cultural Politics," Ph.D. dissertation, McGill University, 2006.

49. Landowska credited Bordes as the key figure of the French early music revival in her 1909 book *Musique ancienne*. "En France, nous voyons à la tête du mouvement tous les plus grands musiciens: Saint-Saëns, D'Indy, Debussy, Dukas, et cet infatigable Bordes, auquel nous devons tant" (Wanda Landowska, avec la collaboration de M. Henri Lew-Landowski, *Musique ancienne* [repr., Paris: Editions Ivrea, 1996], 232).

50. Restout, *Landowska on Music*, 10.
51. Charles Bordes to Maurice Emmanuel, September 4, 1903, cited in Bernard Molla, "Charles Bordes: Pionnier du renouveau musical français entre 1890 et 1909," Ph.D. dissertation, Université de Lyon II, 1986, 3:289. In an earlier letter of August 1, 1903, to Emmanuel Bordes emphasized that his preoccupation "maintenant c'est *le triomphe de la musique française et le culte qu'on doit en avoir*" (288).

52. Several of the pieces (such as Rameau's *La poule* and *L'Egyptienne*) were published in the first edition of Diémer's *Les clavecinistes français du XVIIIe siècle. Couperin—Daquin—Rameau. 20 pièces choisies et transcrites par Louis Diémer* (Paris: Durand & Schœnewerk, 1887). It is unclear how much autonomy Landowska had in this concert as far as the choice of repertoire is concerned.

works on the piano, a decision that the reviewer of *Le Courrier Musical* criticized as stylistically problematic because "the abundant ornamentation, meant to compensate for the dryness of the harpsichord and to bring into relief the accents of the melodic line, becomes useless overfilling on the piano."[53] What this and other reviews indicate is an awareness in musical circles of performance issues regarding late-seventeenth- and early-eighteenth-century harpsichord music. These reviews also encourage rather than discourage attempts at historically informed performance practice on "authentic" instruments. This is a far cry from Landowska's later claims to being a pioneer, especially given that the review in *Le Courrier Musical* actually chastised her for playing on the piano.

When Bordes' stroke brought about his marginalization within the Schola and aided the rise of his colleague, the composer, teacher, and conductor Vincent d'Indy, Landowska lost this institution as a performance environment. Almost immediately after taking over d'Indy shifted the aesthetic priorities of the Schola Cantorum toward a more monumental conception of history, a change reflected in the concert programming of the school, where large-scale performances—starting with Monteverdi's *Orfeo*—took the place of the more eclectic approach of Bordes. D'Indy also clearly began to push his protégée, the young Bach interpreter Blanche Selva, at the expense of Landowska, who had been aligned with Bordes.[54] In January 1904, in the new spirit of the Schola of representing the monumental work, Selva started her first Bach cycle (on the piano), establishing her reputation as the unrivalled interpreter of Bach, a composer who had two Parisian societies dedicated to spreading his gospel: the Société des Concerts J. S. Bach and the Fondation J. S. Bach. Indeed, Selva was to dominate Bach performance at the Schola for years to come. "A star of the first order," she was praised as a commanding performer "who better than anyone else . . . knows how to trace the form of the god in powerful lines."[55] While Landowska began to establish herself in Paris as both a composer-pianist and a competent performer of early music, she could not rival the Schola-sanctioned reputation of Selva as Bach player during those years.

Consequently, in 1904 Landowska seemed no more visible in the Paris concert circuit than in 1902–3. After winning the *Musica* tournament in January 1904 she played in the salon of Madame Maurice Gallet in February.[56] Also in February 1904 Landowska seems to have given her first major solo recital, an all-Bach evening, in the Salle Erard. It included mostly Bach's so-called pianistic works—those on a smaller scale written for harpsichord and performed by female musicians for decades rather than his organ compositions—and some of his more "commanding" works, such as the *Chromatic Fantasy and Fugue*. This was the first occasion when Landowska played several pieces publicly on the harpsichord, following the concert model that Diémer had launched almost half a century before, when he began to include performances on the harpsichord in his piano recitals. An un-

---

53. See the review in *Le Courrier Musical*, December 1, 1903, 329:

> Mme Wanda Landowska nous a fait entendre un très beau choix de pièces de clavecin, les unes un peu frêles, de Chambonnières, d'autres, au contraire, d'une beauté singulièrement hardie et expressive, comme la "Passacaille" de François Couperin. Nous fûmes un peu surpris de les entendre au piano. L'ornementation très abondante, destinée à suppléer à la sécheresse du clavecin et à mettre en reliefs les accents de la phrase mélodique, devient au piano une surcharge inutile. . . . Mais louons sans réserve la compréhension et les qualités techniques fort remarquables dont Mme Landowska a fait preuve.

I am grateful to Catrina Flint de Medicis for communicating the program and the review to me.

54. The extent to which Landowska was absent from d'Indy's musical world can be seen in his published correspondence, in which Landowska is not mentioned once. See Vincent d'Indy, *Ma vie: Journal de jeunesse—correspondance familiale et intime, 1851–1931*, ed. Marie d'Indy (Paris: Editions Séguier, 2001).
55. "Revue de la quinzaine," *S.I.M.* 2 (1906): 117 ("une étoile de première grandeur"), 519 ("mieux que tout autre elle sait dessiner en lignes puissantes la figure du dieu").
56. On her performance in Gallet's salon see Myriam Chimènes, *Mécènes et musiciens: Du salon au concert à Paris sous la IIIe République* (Paris: Fayard, 2004), 184–85.

identified reviewer praised her as an "excellent interpreter" of Bach and lauded in particular her "very beautiful performance" of the *Chromatic Fantasy and Fugue* on the piano and her "extraordinarily colorful" rendition of the gigue from the Partita No. 1 in B-flat Major on a modern Erard harpsichord.[57] As a result, an article on eighteenth-century female harpsichord players, published in *Musica* in April 1904, refers in its introduction to Landowska, "the remarkable Bach interpreter who played various pieces by her favorite master on the harpsichord," while a sister harpsichordist, Elodie Lelong, had just ravished the musical world with a harpsichord recital on her own historic instruments.[58] But compared to other musicians such as Selva, Landowska made little headway in Parisian concert life during these months.

Career Shifts and Identity Slippages

Things changed dramatically, however, in September 1904, when Landowska signed up with the Société Musicale, the new concert agency established by the impresario and editor Gabriel Astruc.[59] In Astruc, Landowska found—at least at the outset—an experienced manager who believed in her and who helped her channel her desire for fame and fortune into a clear and highly successful strategy. A five-year contract guaranteed Landowska a minimum annual income of 6,000 francs. While its conditions were rather restrictive compared to those of Astruc with, for example, the opera stars Lucienne Bréval and Lina Cavalieri, it nevertheless seemed to boost Landowska's enthusiasm for and commitment to a career as an early music specialist.[60] After signing the contract Landowska must have felt that she was on her way to becoming for early music keyboard playing what Cavalieri was for opera: a glorious and glamorous star.[61] As he did with other musicians, Astruc saw success as a multistep campaign: an international tour came first, followed by the great presentation in Paris. From November 1904 to January 1905 Astruc sent Landowska on a European tour to Brussels, Berlin, Vienna, Budapest, Venice, and Brescia, about which she and her husband reported in almost daily telegrams, celebrating success after success.[62]

---

57. Cash wrongly cites a review for this concert, which she dates February 7, 1904, as published in *Le Ménestrel* on February 15, 1903:

> Mme Wanda Landowska s'est montrée excellente interprète des œuvres de Sébastien Bach dans un récital qu'elle a donné mercredi dernier, salle Erard. Son programme comprenait en majorité les compositions de caractère "pianistique"; exception faite toutefois pour la *Fantaisie chromatique*, œuvre d'une puissance extraordinaire, souveraine, dont l'exécution a été fort belle. Mme Landowska n'a pas commis la faute de séparer les deux parties; mais elle produit en quittant une à une toutes les notes de l'accord en ré mineur, pour commencer la fugue [*sic*]. Certaines œuvres ont été jouées sur le piano, d'autres sur un beau clavecin construit par la maison Erard. Parmi ces dernières, la *Gigue*, qui fait partie de la partita no. 1, en si bémol, a été bissée d'acclamation. Cette musique, grâce à la variété des jeux de pédales du clavecin, prend un coloris extraordinaire, éblouissant. ("Wanda Landowska," 57 n. 26)

This (clearly misquoted) review does not seem to have been published in *Le Ménestrel* either in 1903 or in 1904; nevertheless, it refers clearly to the concert mentioned in *Musica* in April 1904.

58. "Dans un récent concert donné dans la salle Erard, Mme Wanda Landowska, la remarquable interprète de Bach, a exécuté diverses pièces de son maître préféré sur le clavecin. Elle a trouvé auprès du public l'accueil le plus enthousiaste. D'autre part, Mme Elodie Lelong, qui possède une superbe collection de vieux instruments et de manuscrits musicaux des VXIIe et XVIIIe siècles et à qui nous devons plusieurs indications précieuses, a passionné le monde musical par l'audition de clavecin qu'elle vient de donner au Figaro" (Robert Brussel, "Les femmes clavecinistes," *Musica* 3 [1904]: 288–99, 289).

59. On the contract see Chimènes, *Mécènes et musiciens*, 396. The contract is preserved at the Archives nationales, Papiers Astruc, 409AP/23.

60. The contract apportioned Landowska between 50 and 60 percent of any honorarium, depending upon whether it was a private or public concert, and 40 percent of the gross income of any concert organized by Astruc. Lucienne Bréval, in contrast, kept 95 percent of her honoraria. See the contract of December 3, 1908, between Raoul Gunsbourg and Lucienne Bréval, preserved in her *dossier d'artiste* at the Bibliothèque de l'Opéra. See Lina Cavalieri's dossier in the Archives nationales, Papiers Astruc, 409AP/18.

61. In a bitter letter of December 30, 1905, Landowska reproached Astruc that while she was short-changed and badly treated, never being accompanied on travels in the way other artists were, she had kept to her side of the contract by going from success to success in the concert hall (Archives nationales, Papiers Astruc, 409AP/23).

62. The telegrams are preserved in Landowska's file, Archives nationales, Papiers Astruc, 409AP/23.

TABLE 1.
Landowska's Concerts, November 1904 to May 1906

1904		11 November	Brussels, Cercle Artistique
		19 November	Berlin
		23 November	Vienna
		26 November	Berlin: *Voltes & Valses*
		3 December	Vienna
		16 December	Budapest
1905		6 January	Venice
		7 January	Brescia
		31 January	Paris (Société Philharmonique)
		10 February	Paris (Salle Pleyel): *Voltes & Valses*
		17 February	Paris (La Trompette)
		18 February	Paris (Ecole Normale de Musique)
		20 February	Paris (Salle Pleyel): *Voltes & Valses*
		25 February	Paris (Bouffes Parisiens)
		26 February	Paris (Arts & Métiers)
		27 February	Paris (salon Mme Gallet)
		10 March	Paris (salon Mr. de Monier)
		11 March	Paris: inaugural concert of Société J. S. Bach
		12 March	Paris (Concert Polonais)
		3 April	Paris (Cours Européen—Matinée)
	11 & 15	April	London (Queen's Hall)
		24 May	London
		5 June	London (Bechstein Hall)
		15 November	Edinburgh: *Bach & ses contemporains*
	22 & 24	November	Madrid (Sociedad Filarmonica Madrileña)
		28 November	Berlin
		1 December	Vienna
		4 December	Leipzig
		6 December	Vienna (concert Spalding)
		18 December	Vienna (Secession)
1906		15 February	Paris (Ecole des Hautes Etudes Sociales)
		18 February	Paris (Concerts Colonne)
		23 February	Paris (Reinach)
		25 February	Paris (Princesse de Polignac): *Voltes & Valses*
		15 March	Paris (Ecole des Hautes Etudes Sociales)
		21 March	Paris (Société J. S. Bach)
		30 March	Paris (Salle Pleyel): *Musique pastorale*
		9 April	Florence: Mozart Piano Concerto
	18 & 19	May	Paris (Bibliothèque nationale): *French Miniatures*
		22 May	Paris (Ecole des Hautes Etudes Sociales)

Source: The table is based on information found at the Archives nationales, Papiers Astruc, 409AP/2 and 409AP/23, as well as Parisian periodicals. The list also incorporates notes in Landowska's calendars for these years, preserved at the Library of Congress.

In Berlin Landowska performed on both a "beautiful, sonorous" Pleyel grand piano and one of Pleyel's modern harpsichords. In addition to unspecified works by Bach, her program included Couperin's *Les folies françaises*, a sarabande by Mattheson, and the *Grobschmiedvariationen* by Handel.[63] Her Parisian debut as a dedicated early music keyboard soloist with a new programming strategy was scheduled for February 1905 and prepared via a press campaign, including a feature article in *Musica* (see below).

As we may infer from later letters, Astruc and Landowska seem in September and October 1904 to have carved out her new image as that of a passionate performer of early keyboard music on authentic instruments and their modern siblings, foregrounding the performance practice over the repertoire. Through dress, performance, and rhetoric Landowska and her manager started to emphasize her femininity and elegance in ways customary for press campaigns for divas. No longer promoting her professionalism as a Polish composer-pianist and piano teacher, her revamped artistic identity played on a gendered trope of female self-representation that was probably familiar to Astruc, whose emphasis as impresario rested on opera and who represented some of the best-known singers of the time.[64] Landowska's earlier concerts had focused on repertoire, as in her 1904 Bach evening or the Bordes concert of French keyboard music in November 1903. Now her programming strategy, in addition to highlighting her femininity and aristocratic mystique, shifted dramatically to emphasize her exceptionality and specificity as a performer of exquisite musical rarities on unusual instruments. Thus in February 1905, on her return to Paris, she presented two solo recitals at the Salle Pleyel that were advertised as "a piano, fortepiano, and harpsichord recital in which she invokes Bach and his contemporaries" and that presented a history of the waltz from Byrd's *La volta* to Chopin's *valses*.[65] She introduced the instruments to her audience through a short verbal commentary before playing the various pieces on their appropriate instruments: voltas by Byrd, Chambonnières, and Morley on the harpsichord, followed by Schubert's *Valses nobles* and *Valses sentimentales* on the fortepiano, and the *Valse des sylphes* (Berlioz/Liszt) and an unspecified waltz by Chopin on the piano.[66] The chronological organization of the program aligned several hundred years of keyboard music with the developments of the various instruments, crafting a symbiotic relationship between musical and technical shifts that allowed the audience to enjoy aurally and visually what Landowska four years later called "the *jouissance* of the sense of history."[67]

The program contained a novelty, an 1830 Pleyel forte-piano that was Landowska's discovery and at first hers to perform on. While other musicians rivaled her on the harpsichord (in 1905, most notably, Marguerite Delcourt), Landowska was the one to introduce the fortepiano to Parisian audiences. But someone else soon threatened her exclusive use of the instrument. Marked "very urgent," a letter to Astruc revealed the danger in a cry for help that reflects

---

63. "Die Pianistin bot nur Bach und seine Zeitgenossen und zwar zur Hälfte auf einem schönen, klangvollen Pleyelschen Flügel, zur Hälfte auf einem in derselben Fabrik hergestellten Clavecin" (M.St., "Konzerte," *Signale für die musikalische Welt* 62 [1904]: 1170).

64. Lyric artists represented the vast majority of his concert agency business. The artists' dossiers are part of the Astruc papers preserved at the Archives nationales, with those of singers filling seven boxes alone (409AP/16–22), compared to a single box (409AP/23) for all the pianists, organists, and harpists he represented, including Ferruccio Busoni, Alfred Cortot, Raoul Pugno, Arthur Rubinstein, and Ricardo Viñes.

65. "[U]n récital de piano, piano-forte et clavecin, où elle invoque J. S. Bach et ses contemporains" (*Je Sais Tout: Magasin Encyclopédique Illustré*, February 15, 1905, 186). The recitals took place on February 10 and 20, 1905. For the program see Jean Marnold, "Musique," *Mercure de France*, March 1, 1905, 133–38, 137. According to this review, the program contained numerous pieces that were also given on February 25, 1906, at the Polignac salon (Kahan, *Music's Modern Muse*, 380).

66. A draft of her notes on the fortepiano, with corrections in red ink in the hand of Astruc, can be found in Archives nationales, Papiers Astruc, 409AP/23. Landowska incorporated some of her notes on the fortepiano into the chapter "Le clavecin" in *Musique ancienne*, 177–91.

67. "[L]a jouissance du sens historique" (Landowska, *Musique ancienne*, 119).

the importance she invested in the instruments themselves for her new artistic identity:

> Yvette Guilbert wants to steal the *fortepiano* in order to plug it into her sessions (at the same time as the harpsichord). I need continuous use of it for concerts & for sessions that I give at home for the press. Y. Guilbert can very well do without it given that until now she only used the piano and harpsichord. It is I who have found this old box at Pleyel; nobody cared about it before my concert. Mademoiselle Delcourt has never studied this instrument. One cannot permit it to be vulgarized in a maladroit manner, especially since once it is in the hands of Schiller he will stuff it in all his sessions, and I will never have it again.
>
> I hope, dear friend, that you will explain this all to Lyon, who promised at the beginning that he would not let the harpsichords dragged around everywhere, remember? As far as the fortepiano is concerned, before I have had enough time to impose it on the press and the public, *someone who does not know how to play it* will compromise it! will steal it from me.[68]

But Landowska pleaded in vain. The fortepiano was to enter the new show of Yvette Guilbert, an unsuspected and at first glance unlikely rival in the Parisian world of early music.

After a long and successful tour through the United States and parts of Europe Yvette Guilbert had returned in 1905 to Paris to pres-

YVETTE GUILBERT
dans le costume qu'elle portait lors de sa récente interprétation des vieilles chansons françaises.

Fig. 3. Yvette Guilbert in eighteenth-century costume, March 1905. Photograph in "Yvette Guilbert, par Yvette Guilbert," *Musica* 7 (1 November 1908), 171 (Music Library, University of North Carolina at Chapel Hill)

ent her new artistic persona. Formerly a cabaret star of Montmartre, the famous singer had transformed herself into an early music performer who celebrated the French *chansons anciennes* in concerts. She wore eighteenth-century costumes in a series of semistaged works at the Bouffes parisiens between March 23 and April 14, 1905.[69]

Accompanied in her concerts by Casadesus' Société de Concerts d'Instruments Anciens, Guilbert presented herself to the public as a specialist in the repertoire and an informed, "hardworking

---

68. Gustave Lyon was then director of Pleyel; Maxime Schiller was Guilbert's husband and manager. Undated letter (probably end of March 1905) from Wanda Landowska to Gabriel Astruc, Archives nationales, 409AP/23:

> Yvette Guilbert veut nous enlever de *piano-forte* pour le fourrer dans ses séances (en même temps que le clavecin). J'en ai besoin sans cesse pour des soirées & pour des séances que je donne chez moi pour la presse. Y. Guilbert pourrait très bien s'en passer puisque jusqu'à maintenant elle se servait du piano & clavec. seulement. C'est moi qui a trouvé cette vieille boîte chez Pleyel; tout le monde s'en moquait avant mon concert. Mlle Delcourt n'a jamais étudié cet instrument. Il ne faut pas permettre à ce qu'on le vulgarise maladroitement, surtout qu'une fois dans les mains de Schiller il va le fourrer dans toutes ses séances et je ne l'aurai plus.

J'espère, cher ami, que vous expliquerez tout cela à Lyon, qui au commencement a promis qu'il ne laissera pas trop traîner les clavecins, vous en rappelez vous? Quant au pianoforte avant que j'ai eu assez de temps pour l'imposer à la Presse et au public, *quelqu'un qui ne sait pas jouer dessus* va le compromettre! va me l'enlever.

69. Noëlle Giret, ed., *Yvette Guilbert: Diseuse fin de siècle* (Paris: Bibliothèque nationale de France, 1995), 77. While Guilbert performed *chansons anciennes* already in 1901, she herself saw this concert series in historic costume as a marker in establishing her "second" career (Yvette Guilbert, *La chanson de ma vie* [Paris: Bernard Castel, 1927], 191–200).

scholar."[70] The show had already competed with Landowska's Concerts in Berlin in November and December 1904, where Guilbert and the Société de Concerts d'Instruments Anciens performed to both a sold-out Bechsteinsaal and, the week after, a full Beethovensaal.[71] In Paris journalists credited her with bringing to life this old repertoire: "the harpsichord, made fashionable again by the *chansons* of Yvette Guilbert and also thanks to the agile fingers and impeccable and charming technique of Mademoiselle Delcourt." Delcourt was hailed as the Parisian "queen of the harpsichord" in 1905.[72] But to add insult to injury for Landowska, Delcourt not only performed solo harpsichord music of Couperin and Lully in Guilbert's shows at the Bouffes Parisiens but also—as they evolved over the weeks—accompanied her on the 1830 fortepiano, supplied by Pleyel, in a series of four songs grouped under the title "CHANSON '1830.'"[73] The self-conscious illusion of historical authenticity could not have been pushed further.[74]

But in the spring of 1905 Guilbert and the Société de Concerts d'Instruments Anciens were not the only performers to contend with Landowska for preeminence in the vibrant Parisian concert life dedicated to early music. On March 27 Ricardo Viñes presented a "historic concert" on an "authentic harpsichord," while in May Reynaldo Hahn organized two concerts, one dedicated to Lully, the other to Rameau. Not only did the Société de Concerts d'Instruments Anciens perform at these occasions, but Diémer played three Rameau pieces on the harpsichord in between operatic numbers by the same composer.[75]

Competition for Landowska the harpsichordist and early keyboard specialist was therefore quite strong in 1905 Paris, and she needed to distinguish herself even more sharply from other musicians than in previous years. Her public persona differed from that of Delcourt, who performed in an ensemble under the paternal guidance of the venerable French composer Camille Saint-Saëns, the cofounder and president of the Société de Concerts d'Instruments Anciens; Delcourt's subservient place was far more fitting to traditional female roles. In the concerts with the Société de Concerts d'Instruments Anciens Delcourt played some solo repertoire, such as Couperin's *Carillon de Cythère*, but she mainly performed as a continuo player and accompanist, as she had already previously in several concerts with Bordes' Chanteurs de Saint-Gervais.[76]

In contrast, Landowska worked unremittingly on becoming a star performer and recognized soloist by throwing herself into the battle with,

---

70. "Chercheuse, travailleuse, elle est par conséquent renseignée" (G. Davenay, "Yvette Guilbert XVIIIe siècle: La Guimard de la chanson," *Le Figaro*, March 23, 1905, 4). "Depuis plusieurs années déjà, l'intelligente artiste s'était faite collectionneuse d'antiquailles inédites; il était juste qu'elle nous invitât à goûter les fruits de ses patientes et laborieuses recherches" (*Les Annales du Théâtre et de la Musique* 1906:418).
71. "Yvette Guilbert führte in dem bis zum letzten Platz besetzten Bechstein-Saal die Pariser *Société des Concerts d'instruments* in Deutschland ein"; "in dem bis auf den letzten Platz belegten Beethovensaal" ("Konzerte," *Signale für die musikalische Welt* 62 [1904]: 1202, 1234).
72. "Voilà le clavecin remis en vogue par les chansons d'Yvette Guilbert et aussi grâce aux doigts agiles et à la technique impeccable et charmante de Mlle Delcourt" (Davenay, "Yvette Guilbert," 4). See also *Les Annales du Théâtre et de la Musique*, 1906:419: "Mlle Marguerite Delcourt, reine du clavecin."
73. Program of the "Représentation de Yvette Guilbert dans les *Chansons anciennes* avec le concours de la Société de Concerts d'Instruments Anciens" for the season 1904–5 at the Bouffes Parisiens, Bibliothèque nationale de France, Arts du Spectacle, Fonds Rondel, Ro.16.087: "CHANSON '1830' / a. Les Husards de la Garde / b. La Rue d'Anjou et de Poitou / c. La Lisette / d. Tirez le Rideau / Mme Yvette Guilbert accompagnée au Pianoforte (1830) par Mlle Delcourt."
74. On nineteenth-century discussions about authenticity in performance of early music see Fauser, *Musical Encounters*, 39–42.
75. Hahn's concerts were advertised and reviewed in great detail and with comments about issues such as authenticity and performing practice in *Le Ménestrel* 71 (1905): 142, 159, 164, 173. On Viñes see "Théâtres et concerts," *La Revue Musicale* 5 (1905): 215: "Premier concert historique de M. R. Viñes. C'est sur un clavecin authentique que sont exécutées les œuvres anciennes." The program included, among others, Purcell, Chambonnières, Couperin, Rameau, and Bach.
76. See the programs at the Bibliothèque nationale de France, Arts du Spectacle, Fonds Rondel, Ro.16.087. For Delcourt's performances with the Chanteurs de Saint-Gervais see Flint de Medicis, "The Schola Cantorum."

as she wrote later, "all the energy of her youth . . . sustained by the inner self-confidence of her God-given genius."[77] While her fledgling specialization was that of the scholarly yet delicate virtuoso keyboard player, the composer to whom she turned for validation was Johann Sebastian Bach. Although her choice was not unusual for the time, it raised the stakes significantly. Her declared aim was to secure her place as the foremost keyboard player of her time who performed Bach in the most authentic way. More striking still and in an interesting twist, she instrumentalized her gender and her cosmopolitanism in the service of this cause.

In preparation for her "launch" in Paris, as Landowska's husband, Henri Lew, put it in January 1905, *Musica*—whose editor was now Astruc—published an article entitled "Wanda Landowska, or the Renaissance of the Harpsichord."[78] Lavishly illustrated with photographs that show Landowska at a modern Pleyel harpsichord, the two-page article served as a fascinating advertisement for "Wanda," Astruc's pet *claveciniste*.[79] The opening sentence revealed to the Parisian readership that Landowska had been on tour for those last months, triumphing as a harpsichordist in Brussels, Berlin, and Vienna by performing masterfully on modern Pleyel instruments, "harpsichords of such perfection that the instrument museum in Berlin acquired an example for its famous collection."[80] Thus before finding out about Landowska's role in the musical renaissance of the harpsichord, the readers of the article encounter her as a sales advertisement for Pleyel's instruments, an economic role often given to female performers.[81] What makes this article so intriguing is the fact that its text presents the tactical cornerstones of Landowska's newly launched career: her physical self-presentation, her musical specialization, her anointing as "noble servant" to the great master(s), and her programming strategies.[82]

Fig. 4. Wanda Landowska at the harpsichord. Robert Brussel, "Wanda Landowska ou la renaissance du clavecin," *Musica* 4 (1905): 7–8, at p. 7 (Bibliothèque nationale de France)

After an introduction on the illustrious history of the harpsichord, especially in France, the author, Robert Brussel, began by representing Landowska as the modern reincarnation of the "grandes dames clavecinistes" of the fifteenth to the eighteenth centuries. He had already made that connection a year earlier in the same journal

---

77. Restout, *Landowska on Music*, 11.
78. Brussel, "Wanda Landowska." For Landowska's "launch" see Henri Lew to Gabriel Astruc, Brescia, January 11, 1905, Archives nationales, Papiers Astruc, 409AP/23: "Les concerts de Paris sont au point de vue de lancement d'une importance capitale."
79. In the first year or so the staff at the Société Musicale as well as Astruc himself referred to her as Wanda rather than Wanda Landowska or Madame Landowska. See the notes on the correspondence preserved at the Archives nationales, Papiers Astruc, 409AP/23, and in the notebook about letters, "Départ télégrammes; liste d'adresses, 2 août 1905–sept 1907" (409AP/2).
80. "Le succès triomphal que vient remporter, à Bruxelles, à Berlin, à Vienne, Mme Wanda Landowska remet en honneur le clavecin. . . . Déjà, un maître dans la facture instrumentale, M. Gustave Lyon, a produit des clavecins d'une perfection telle que le Musée de Musique à Berlin vient d'en acquérir un modèle pour ses célèbres collections" (Brussel, "Wanda Landowska," 7).
81. While male performers from Liszt to Paderewski could appear in a similar guise, endorsing specific piano manufacturers in their performances, the blatant foregrounding of Landowska as an advertisement "model" echoes the ubiquitous use of women for selling commercial products, including musical ones. See Katharine Ellis, "The Fair Sax: Women, Brass-Playing and the Instrument Trade in 1860s Paris," *Journal of the Royal Musical Association* 124 (1999): 221–54.
82. The trope of the "noble servant" and high priestess has been explored for fin de siècle Paris by Jeanice Brooks in her article "*Noble et grande servante de la musique*: Telling the Story of Nadia Boulanger's Conducting Career," *Journal of Musicology* 14 (1996): 92–116.

in his richly illustrated article on female harpsichordists that associated the praise of the modern harpsichordists Landowska and Lelong with reproductions of engravings and paintings that showed women in historic costume seated at the harpsichord as well as a photograph of, once more, the harpsichord of Marie-Antoinette.[83] Aristocratic female musicianship at the harpsichord—which he described as appropriate for the "fine," "delicate," and "subtle" aspects of the instruments—was contrasted there with the musicological scholarship on early music by the "savants musicographes," on the one hand, and with the compositional response by male French musicians, on the other.[84] In this context of a journal sponsoring Landowska, the harpsichord and its ideal performer were unequivocally gendered feminine.

After setting this feminized ancien régime context for Landowska, Brussel then described her beauty as reminiscent of the fragile heroines of Maeterlinck and the Pre-Raphaelite virgins of Burne-Jones, her hands "the finest and most spiritual that could be dreamt of."[85] By locating Landowska's artistic persona in her physiognomy Brussel played on popular imagination: through countless artifacts—whether in popular novels or paintings—physical traits had become trivialized markers of human character and ability.[86] For Brussel, Landowska's body as much as her playing turned her into the "musical daughter of Johann Sebastian Bach," the "ideal interpreter of this music."[87] Indeed, he summed up her achievement by claiming that "Wanda Landowska is one of the rare women virtuosos who do not attempt to imitate the performance of men," thus fully embodying her gender in performance.[88] Her fragile and elegant femininity thus turned into a significant asset, one on which Landowska played throughout her career.[89] Just how quickly the popular trope entered critical discourse can be seen in a review of Landowska's February concerts (which took place just a month after this article appeared) in which Jean Marnold lauded "the entirely feminine grace" of her performance.[90]

But Brussel's article contains more clues: he showed Landowska as a diligent researcher who went beyond the presentation of easily accessible scores by unearthing hidden treasures. Her "piety" as a performer and servant to great masters was thus as much proven by her assiduous preparation—to the point of studying the dance steps appropriate for the pieces—as it was audible in her tasteful playing. Her programs, so Brussel claimed, were special and atmospheric, re-creating the period from which they emanated. Contrary to those of other musicians

---

83. Brussel, "Les femmes clavecinistes."
84. "Il est naturel que le clavecin avec ses delicates rangées de sautereaux, ses fines plumes, ses cordes ténues, ses pédales sensibles, ses registres subtils, ait répondu plus profondément peut-être à des mains moins vigoureuses"; "Si cette renaissance est due principalement à des femmes qui ont su retrouver le fil mystérieux qui les lie à leurs devancières du XVIIIe siècle, elle a été préparée par les travaux de savants musicographes" (Brussel, "Les femmes clavecinistes," 298, 299-300).
85. Brussel, "Wanda Landowska," 8. Fragility had become one of the celebrated assets of female beauty in a performer and artist, starting with iconic divas such as Maria Malibran. Like Landowska, the composer Lili Boulanger was repeatedly compared to the fragile heroines of Maeterlinck; see Annegret Fauser, "Lili Boulanger's *La Princesse Maleine*: A Composer and Her Heroine as Literary Icons," *Journal of the Royal Musical Association* 122 (1997): 68-108.
86. Anne-Marie Thiesse, *Le roman du quotidien: Lecteurs et lectures populaires à la Belle Epoque* (Paris: Le Chemin Vert, 1984). See also Tamar Garb, *Bodies of Modernity:*

Figure and Flesh in Fin de Siècle Paris (London: Thames and Hudson, 1998), especially her chapter "Powder and Paint: Framing the Feminine in Georges Seurat's *Young Woman Powdering Herself*" (115-43).
87. Brussel, "Wanda Landowska," 8. On the body as locus for critical discourse see Lena Hammergren, "Different Personas: A History of One's Own?" in *Choreographing History*, ed. Susan Leigh Foster (Bloomington: Indiana University Press, 1995), 185-92.
88. "[L]a tradition des grandes dames clavecinistes du XVe au XVIIIe siècles"; "les mains les plus fines et les plus spirituelles qui se puissent rêver"; "fille musicale de ce Jean-Sébastien Bach"; "interprète idéale de cette musique"; "Wanda Landowska est une des rares femmes virtuoses qui ne cherchent point à imiter le jeu des hommes" (Brussel, "Wanda Landowska," 8).
89. Restout comments on the self-conscious presentation of Landowska and her relentless and often quite personal comments on performers' physical appearance in *Uncommon Visionary*.
90. "[L]a grâce toute féminine" (Marnold, "Musique," 137).

who were satisfied with old routines (a barely disguised barb aimed at Diémer), "each of her programs has a unity, and a general idea governs its composition."[91]

Once femininity, elegance, and grace became the overarching point of reference for Landowska's artistic persona, her aspirations to stardom seemed less threatening.[92] Not only could such quality be put to the service of her artistic cause, especially in the context of the still broadly feminized music of the *clavecinistes*, but it allowed Landowska and her entourage to focus on the traditional feminine roles of muse (even after the fact) and servant, following a familiar and well-tried story line in women's artistic biographies in which the artwork takes the place of either a man or God/Christ, who is usually put at the center of a woman's life.[93] The religious imagery in the article—Landowska's piety and her resemblance to Pre-Raphaelite virgins—represented her more in the role of the beautiful vestal, however, than in that of the conquered lover. A few years later she reinforced this image of the vestal artist by posing with bearded old men of great renown, such as Leo Tolstoy (in 1907) and Auguste Rodin (in 1908). Landowska used these clichés for postcards and to illustrate articles, as, for example, on the title page of *Musica* in which she published her article "Tolstoï musicien."[94]

Landowska created this vestal image not only through her physical appearance and public behavior but also through the complete elimination of her husband from any public discourse. While the designation "Madame" gave her a certain timeless authority, she kept her maiden

Fig. 5. "Tolstoï musicien." Title page of *Musica*, June 1908 (Bibliothèque nationale de France)

name. And just as absent as Henri's patronymic "Lew" was the man himself. While *Musica* and other illustrated journals such as *La Vie Heureuse* ran numerous articles on the family life of artists such as Ernestine Schumann-Heink and Madame Colonne, Landowska had no private side to her artistic identity.[95] As with her emphasis on mystique and charm, her image here seems to have been modeled more on that of French opera stars such as Lucienne Bréval and Rose Caron than on fellow instrumentalists. That this was probably a conscious strategy ap-

---

91. "Chacun de ses programmes a une unité, et une idée générale en régit la composition" (Brussel, "Wanda Landowska," 8).

92. On image and self-representation of women artists in fin de siècle France see Fauser, "*La Guerre en dentelles*"; visual and rhetorical tropes of femininity in early-twentieth-century France are discussed in broader terms in Anne Martin-Fugier, *La bourgeoise: Femme au temps de Paul Bourget* (Paris: Grasset, 1983); Thiesse, *Le roman du quotidien*; and Michelle Perrot, *Femmes publiques* (Paris: Editions Textuels, 1997).

93. Carolyn G. Heilbrun, *Writing a Woman's Life* (New York: Ballentine Books, 1988), 25.

94. Wanda Landowska, "Tolstoï musicien," *Musica* 7 (1908): 95. Postcards can be found among the Astruc papers (Archives nationales, Papiers Astruc, 409AP/23) and in the archives of the Musée Rodin, Paris, where Olivia Mattis has discovered a cache of Landowska letters and photographs dating from 1908 to 1910.

95. On Madame Colonne see "Un ménage de musiciens: Monsieur et Madame Colonne," *La Vie Heureuse*, 1904:34–35. On Schumann-Heink see Thomas Salignac, "Musique et maternité," *Musica* 6 (1907): 14–15.

pears in a letter in which Henri Lew explained to Astruc that even though the Spanish crown princess had invited both of them to a soirée, "of course Wanda went alone."[96]

Madame Landowska, or Performing Bach as a Woman

On her way to early music stardom Landowska had to set herself apart from one other young female soloist in particular: Blanche Selva, with whom she competed in terms of both repertoire and audience. If the 1905 article in *Musica* was written for her by a writer in the pay of Astruc and advertised her femininity, grace, and uniqueness in preparation for her Parisian solo concerts, Landowska's own battle cry, her article on the interpretation of Bach in *Mercure de France*, followed in November of the same year. In it she distanced herself from the musical practices of the post-Bordes Schola in general and took direct aim at her greatest rival of the moment in particular. While never mentioning Selva by name, her target was obvious as a "femme virile" whose Bach performances on the piano "stuffed" her audience with all that is "bulky, fat, big, strong, and powerful, all that collection of monsters and wild beasts."[97] This was not even barely veiled, given that Selva's Bach performances on the piano were widely celebrated for their virility, while her full figure found its way easily into caricature. Thus Landowska disassociated both her own performance and her new core repertoire—the music of Bach—from the controversial figure of the professional "new woman" aspiring to enter male realms.[98]

The article in *Mercure* was Landowska's first

Fig. 6. "Mademoiselle Blanche Selva," caricature de Dalliès, 1908 (Bibliothèque nationale de France)

published foray into the debates about performing Bach, and in it she played on tropes of femininity already established for her own performance style and persona by emphasizing the grace, elegance, and even, at times, frivolity of Bach's harpsichord music by characterizing Bach as an "author of gallant pieces, of almost frivolous music."[99] With this rereading of Bach against the grain of the more prevalent masculinist views of the fin de siècle she reaffirmed the femininity that Brussel had associated with her artistic identity eight months previously. Her argument introduced gender as a key category in understanding and evaluating music and its performance. Thus Landowska argued that we should allow ourselves to be seduced by this feminized Bach; when we do, we encounter "a past so admirably distant, so marvelously differ-

---

96. "L'infante Isabelle nous a invité pour ce soir tous les deux par le Marquis de Meza de Asta. Wanda est évidemment allée toute seule" (Henri Lew to Gabriel Astruc, Madrid, November 24, 1905, Archives nationales, Papiers Astruc, 409AP/23).
97. Wanda Landowska, "Bach et ses interprètes: Sur l'interprétation des œuvres de clavecin de J.-S. Bach," *Mercure de France*, November 15, 1905, 214–30, 222, 230: "On nous a trop rengorgés de tout ce qui est gros, gras, grand, fort et puissant, de tout ce musée de monstres et de bêtes fauves." Landowska included sections of this article in her *Musique ancienne*, mainly in the chapter "Le style."

98. See Debora Silverman, "The 'New Woman,' Feminism, and the Decorative Arts in Fin-de-Siècle France," in *Eroticism and the Body Politic*, ed. Lynn Hunt (Baltimore: Johns Hopkins University Press, 1991), 144–63. On the trope of the "new women" applied to female musicians in fin de siècle Paris see Fauser, "*La Guerre en dentelles*" and *Musical Encounters*, 129–38.
99. "[L]eurs grandes qualités de grâce et d'élégance . . . Bach, auteur de pièces galantes, de la musique presque frivole" (Landowska, "Bach et ses interprètes," 226).

ent from all that surrounds us."[100] Landowska's emphasis on historical distance and the benefits of "authenticity" was not unusual for the time.[101] Far more radical, however, was the way in which she inverted earlier negative tropes of the harpsichord's femininity, turning them to the positive not only as performance but also as an aesthetic category. For Landowska, Bach was neither a Romantic nor a Classical composer *avant la lettre*, and he most definitely was not that "modernized Bach, arranged according to today's fashion." Rather, Bach took listeners back to a time when women set the standards of artistic beauty to the point that men underwent "painful sacrifices so that they could obtain the sweetness, clarity, and charm of a woman's voice."[102] For Landowska, the world of early music was one in which feminine grace triumphed over brutal masculine strength, harking back to a world of nobility and aristocracy. This difference was symbolized by the sonic and visual contrasts between the grand piano and the harpsichord—or, when transferred to the two Parisian female Bach performers (as implied by the rhetoric of the article), between Blanche Selva and Wanda Landowska.[103]

By the time the article appeared Landowska was back on tour, gaining triumph upon triumph in Spain, Austria, and Germany. Before that, in April 1905, she had conquered London. All seemed to be working out to perfection, although it became clear after her return in December that Astruc, with whom she had collaborated to put her career on such a stellar course a year earlier, had lost interest in her amid his large-scale projects, which encompassed the Beethoven-Berlioz Festival at the Châtelet and the Opéra in 1906, the Concerts Historiques Russes (with, among others, Chaliapin) and French premiere of *Salomé* in 1907, and the seasons of Diaghilev's Ballets russes from 1908 onward. Landowska's concerts—while successful in artistic terms—created a financial loss of almost 3,000 francs for Astruc, and he saw little prospect of improving the situation in 1906. Landowska herself was disheartened both by Astruc's accounting methods and his attitude toward her.[104] It is clear from her letters that she had expected better.

After a serious discussion in early January 1906 Astruc made a renewed effort to place Landowska in Parisian concerts.[105] She played on February 18, 1906, at the Concerts Colonne, again performing Mozart's Piano Concerto in E-flat Major, K. 271, with which she had appeared first at the Concerts Lamoureux in 1902.[106] Astruc also became involved in casting the performers for the Société des Concerts J. S. Bach. He placed Landowska in a concert on March 21, 1906, in which she performed Bach's *Italian Concerto* on the harpsichord and two of his suites on the piano. The spring of 1906 also brought a prestigious appearance in the salons of the princesse de Polignac, whose concerts Astruc managed during these years. At the re-

---

100. "[C]e contact vivifiant avec un passé si admirablement lointain, si merveilleusement différent de tout ce qui nous entoure" (Landowska, "Bach et ses interprètes," 229).
101. Fauser, *Musical Encounters*, 41.
102. "On nous donne un Bach modernisé, arrangé à la mode d'aujourd'hui"; "Il n'y a pas longtemps encore qu'on avait l'habitude, à la cour papale, de faire subir aux hommes des sacrifices douloureux pour leur faire obtenir la douceur, la clarté et le charme d'une voix de femme." See also "Les romantiques voient en Bach un volcan tout en feu et flammes; les classiques nous offrent un Bach en congélation" (Landowska, "Bach et ses interprètes," 217, 222, 228).
103. While Landowska made her case for performing Bach on the harpsichord the subject of an entire article, the argument is not new. See, for example, Saint-Saëns, "Le 'Rappel' à l'Exposition," 2: "La musique de Bach semble particulièrement chez elle quand on la confie au clavecin de M. Tomasini."
104. The accounts for 1904–5 are in Landowska's file (Archives nationales, Papiers Astruc, 409AP/23). Astruc's exact loss consisted of 2,933.85 francs. Furthermore, the accounts reveal that he paid out 1,237.85 francs too much in 1905, a sum that he planned to subtract from the 6,000 francs guaranteed for 1906. In a passionate letter dated December 30, 1905, Landowska characterizes his accounting as "très injuste."
105. This is reflected in his "Départ télégrammes."
106. Landowska was not playing in the German city of Cologne, as Cash ("Wanda Landowska," 58) reads the note in *Le Ménestrel*, but at the Concerts Colonne, where she performed at the same concert as the Romanian violinist Georges Enesco, who captivated the audience with his rendering of Bach's chaconne for solo violin; see *S.I.M.* 2, no. 1 (1906): 213.

quest of the princess, Landowska adapted her waltz program for the occasion: "In my Voltas & Waltzes program I do not play Bach. This is what I propose: I will begin each grouping with a work by Bach."[107] By framing her revised waltz program with a Bach suite on the harpsichord at the beginning and a Chopin waltz on the piano at the end, Landowska created a trajectory that led straight from the German master of the keyboard to the Polish one. She also put the musical aesthetics of the earlier years of the Schola Cantorum into practice by emphasizing, according to Vincent d'Indy's memorable formulation, a "spiral" of historical development rather than the linear models of progress often associated with nineteenth-century aesthetics.[108]

This salon appearance was followed by a series of four high-profile concerts with works by Bach and the French *clavecinistes*, reported in some detail in the musical press. Each of those concerts emphasized the solo keyboard player. Landowska also became one of the artists participating in the musicological events of the Ecole des Hautes Études Sociales, illustrating lectures for the music historians Henri Quittard, known for his research on French lute music, and Jules Ecorcheville, whose research in those years focused on Lully and Rameau.[109] To perform in these venues exposed Landowska to an elite audience, while her contribution certainly added visual and musical appeal to the lectures.[110]

By the summer of 1906 Landowska had unequivocally "arrived." No longer second to Marguerite Delcourt, the 1905 "queen of the harpsichord," or to Blanche Selva, Bach's "most worthy priestess," she had established herself as one of a kind, a musician with a mission recognized for her own special brand of musical interpretation characterized by feminine beauty and historical depth. Even though Landowska played Mozart, Schubert, and Chopin in her 1906 concerts, both her own and her reviewers' emphasis lay on the exquisite and unusual nature of the repertoire selections in her early music performances. And in contrast to Selva, who also premiered new music, Landowska exclusively played repertoire composed before the 1850s. Indeed, her selection of repertoire seems to avoid any pieces that French critics associated with masculine qualities, including the music of Beethoven.[111]

Reviews teem with descriptions that could equally well be used to describe music and culture of the ancien régime, conflating repertoire and performer in a world of the past: a "delicious harpsichordist who reveals to us the aristocratic beauty of lute music" in Ecorcheville's lecture at the Ecole des Hautes Études Sociales; an "exquisite" and "ideal interpreter" of the *clavecinistes* at a concert of pastoral music; playing "delight-

---

107. "Dans mon programme Voltes & Valses je ne joue pas de Bach; voilà ce que je vous propose: Je commencerai chaque numéro par une pièce de Bach" (Wanda Landowska to Gabriel Astruc, n.d., Archives nationales, Papiers Astruc, 409AP/23).

108. Jann Pasler discusses d'Indy's spiral concept of history in her essay "Paris: Conflicting Notions of Progress," in *Man and Music: The Late Romantic Era from the Mid-19th Century to World War I*, ed. Jim Samson (London: Macmillan, 1991), 389–416. Landowska's programming reflected one of the prevalent strategies of constructing music history, most prominently outlined in Vincent d'Indy's *Cours de composition musicale*, by focusing on interconnections across historical periods rather than espousing progress. With the withdrawal of Bordes from the Schola after his stroke, the Schola moved toward different aesthetic ideals. On Bordes' and d'Indy's competing views of early music see Flint de Medicis, "The Schola Cantorum." See also Annegret Fauser, "Archéologue malgré lui: Vincent d'Indy et les usages de l'histoire," in *Vincent d'Indy et son temps*, ed. Manuela Schwartz (Liège: Mardaga, 2006), 122–33.

109. On the musical lectures see Jane F. Fulcher, *French Cultural Politics & Music: From the Dreyfus Affair to the First World War* (New York: Oxford University Press, 1999), 59–63.

110. A letter by Charles Bordes to Maurice Emmanuel from August 1, 1903 (cited in Molla, "Charles Bordes," 288), shows that the presence of female performers counted as an asset in these lectures: "Je vous donnerai pour appuyer *votre conférence* ce demoiselles Louise et Blanche Mante et moi-même pour les musiques; on n'a jamais vu 2 femmes pour un conférencier, meme sarrazin, croiriez-vous."

111. On gendering repertoire in nineteenth-century France see Ellis, "Female Pianists"; Marcia Citron, *Gender and the Musical Canon* (Cambridge: Cambridge University Press, 1993); Katharine Ellis, "Berlioz, the Sublime, and the *Broderie* Problem," in *Hector Berlioz: Miscellaneous Studies*, ed. Fulvia Morabito and Michela Niccolai, Ad Parnassum Monographs 1 (Bologna: Ut Orpheus Edizioni, 2005), 29–59.

fully . . . and with excellent style" and "leaving the audience with an exquisite impression" after the concert that opened the exhibition of miniatures at the Bibliothèque nationale.[112] By crafting programs that called attention to her scholarly preparation, however, Landowska not only managed to escape the danger of being marginalized as beautiful frivolity, but she also continued to play on the trope of the female educator, a strategy appreciated by her critics and audience: "Composed with impeccable taste, her programs always contain a very important lesson in musical aesthetics. How many virtuosos can be praised in such a manner?"[113]

Such specialization was a strategy adopted mostly by Parisian women musicians, notably Clothilde de Kleeberg, who was celebrated first and foremost as a Beethoven interpreter. In contrast, more often than not male musicians such as, for example, Diémer, Risler, and Viñes seemed to emphasize an all-encompassing repertoire with some specialization as a mark of distinction, whether early music for Diémer, Beethoven for Risler, or contemporary music for Viñes.[114] But Landowska pushed this envelope farther than most other soloists by aligning repertoire, aesthetics, and musical interpretation with a celebration of aristocratic femininity that was staged to perfection. Her strategies reveal to what extent she was attuned both to the musical world of Paris and to its construction of gender. Her actions to this point and later on in her career show a seismographic sensitivity to her environment that reflects significant awareness for often unformulated horizons of expectation toward female performers in terms of repertoire, self-representation, and performance style. Indeed, both her own rhetoric—starting with the 1906 Bach article—and the texts written about her openly play on gendered interpretations of repertoire and performance practice. Landowska's awareness of discursive tropes reasserted itself throughout her career. Thus when her presentation in concerts might have led to the danger of becoming inconsequential because she and her music could have appeared too delicate and delightful, she started to maintain a sustained public presence as a Bach scholar in publications such as *Musica*, *S.I.M.*, *Mercure de France*, *Le Monde Musical*, and the *Bach Jahrbuch*; and her book *Musique ancienne* (1909) gave her scholarship even greater prominence.[115]

From the 1906–7 season onward Landowska also took increasingly greater control over her career. While she was still bound to Astruc through her five-year contract (and she appeared in his 1907 publicity as one of the pianists on his roster), she also seemed to gain a certain autonomy. Although it is highly likely that Astruc, with his strong ties to Russian music, was involved in setting up the Russian tour in 1907, it was Landowska who decided on its length and itinerary.[116] It is not clear when the contract between Astruc and Landowska was dissolved, but from a later advertisement of the Société Musicale it is obvious that they canceled the contract in mutual agreement well before it expired.[117] Landowska and Astruc remained on good terms, sharing Christmas cakes and visiting each other; but while her former mentor

---

112. "[D]élicieuse claveciniste nous révélait l'aristocratique beauté de la musique du luth" (Louis Laloy, "Revue de la quinzaine," *S.I.M.* 2 [1906]: 167); "interprète idéale d'une pareille musique" (C.C., "Revue de la quinzaine," *S.I.M.* 2 [1906]: 370); "délicieusement jouées et dans un style excellent," "laissait aux auditeurs une impression exquise" ("Soirées et concerts," *Le Ménestrel*, May 27, 1906, cited in Cash, "Wanda Landowska," 61 n. 32).
113. "Composés avec un goût impeccable, ses programmes comportent toujours un très grand enseignement d'esthétique musicale. A combien de virtuoses peut-on décerner un tel éloge?" (C.C., "Revue de la quinzaine," 370).
114. On Kleeberg see, for example, Charles Joly, "Les interprètes de Beethoven," *Femina* 5 (1905): 208.

115. A list of Landowska's writings compiled by Denise Restout is reproduced in Cash, "Wanda Landowska," 331–36.
116. The 1907 publicity is at the Archives nationales, Papiers Astruc, 409AP/2. A letter to Astruc by J. P[aul] Landowski (409AP/23) informed him that Landowska "se trouve depuis 3 mois en Russie et la tournée, qui devrait terminer en décembre, se prolonge au moins jusqu'à fin janvier par suite de très nombreux engagements dans la province Russe. Ma sœur ne sera donc de retour à Paris que dans les premiers jours de février prochain."
117. A note in Landowska's file related to the contract leads me to suspect that it was dissolved on August 26, 1907. The later advertisement is at the Archives nationales, Papiers Astruc, 409AP/2.

directed his energies toward the foundation of the Théâtre des Champs-Elysées, his protégée and her invisible husband put into practice what they had learned about career management, tour organization, press releases, public image, and program strategies during the two years when they worked with one of the most astute music managers of the twentieth century.[118]

The creation of "Madame Landowska" in the years between 1904 and 1906 by the performer and her entourage therefore took place within and reflects the cultural field of Paris in which women were able to forge careers by conforming to two tropes: the "noble servant" to male genius and the exceptional woman defined by difference.[119] Landowska also redefined a repertoire whose femininity, once a cause of marginalization, could be turned to far more positive ends. But the discourse of exceptionality demanded the removing from the record of all who might show Landowska to be just one of many, whether fellow harpsichordists such as Marguerite Delcourt, fellow musician-scholars such as Yvette Guilbert and Blanche Selva, or fellow early music performers such as the members of the Société de Concerts d'Instruments Anciens. Nor could exceptionality admit a long lineage of predecessors, whether women harpsichordists such as Joséphine Martin or Charlotte de Malleville or women scholars such as Henriette Fuchs and Michel Brenet. This exclusion of her predecessors remains today in the various Landowska myths about her single-handed championing of the harpsichord and her pioneering role in the early music revival. She was indeed an exceptional woman who made brilliant use of the cultural field of Paris to establish her career. But she did so within a context that needs careful analysis to show just how she became the "uncrowned queen of the harpsichord."[120]

Note

I am grateful to Tim Carter, Katharine Ellis, Catrina Flint de Medicis, Brent Wissick, and my two anonymous readers for their insightful and helpful comments and suggestions on earlier versions of this article. A shorter text was presented at the annual meeting of the American Musicological Society in Washington DC, October 26–30, 2005.

---

118. In a letter to his collaborator at the head of *Musica*, Georges Pioch, Astruc pointed out that art was also created by those who enabled it: "Dites-donc, avez-vous fini de m'engueuler? Vous êtes tout le temps à me faire sentir votre supériorité de poète. Vous ne savez donc pas, malheureux, que les poètes les plus superbes, les plus exaltés, les plus fulgurants sont les gens d'affaires qui créent des usines formidables d'art ou d'industrie, font vivre des millions d'êtres et se font récompenser les 3/4 du temps par une déraison précoce. Je suis aussi poète que vous et je vous prie de me foutre la paix, nom de dieu!" (Archives nationales, Papiers Astruc, 409/AP1).

119. For the rhetoric of the "exceptional woman" see in particular the introductory chapter in Mary Sheriff, *The Exceptional Woman: Elisabeth Vigée-Lebrun and the Cultural Politics of Art* (Chicago: University of Chicago Press, 1996). Landowska's rival, Yvette Guilbert, used the same strategy when she presented her so-called second career in her autobiography, *La chanson de ma vie* (191–200).

120. Elste, *Meilensteine der Bach Interpretation*, 337.

CHAPTER 11

La Guerre en dentelles: Women and the *Prix de Rome* in French Cultural Politics

... to show the world ... the vain error of men, who so much believe themselves to be the masters of the highest gifts of the intellect, that they think those gifts cannot be shared equally by women.
—Maddalena Casulana, 1568[1]

In March 1912, the influential critic Emile Vuillermoz warned French men "to beware that women were on the march."[2] In an article entitled "The Pink Peril," he cautioned that women were on the point of taking over French public life, and that their achievements in the world of music would incite them to even bolder efforts:

> The Conservatoire, where they already hold the majority, will end by becoming their personal property, and the classes that are called "mixed" will be those where the presence of two or three mustache wearers will be tolerated.... In the director's office, Gabriel Fauré will be chased from his position by Hélène Fleury or Nadia Boulanger.[3]

I wish to thank Jann Pasler and Lesley Wright for taking so great an interest in this article as to share their own research with me, offering vital information and material. I also wish to express my deep gratitude toward Tim Carter, Marcia J. Citron, Katharine Ellis, Jann Pasler, and Lesley Wright for many helpful suggestions and encouraging comments after reading drafts of this text. Karen Henson and Ingrid Sykes were kind enough to pass on two important pieces of information which they found during their various searches through the Parisian archives.

1. Cited and translated by Jane Bowers in "The Emergence of Women Composers in Italy, 1566–1700," in *Women Making Music: The Western Art Tradition, 1150–1950*, ed. Jane Bowers and Judith Tick (Urbana and Chicago: University of Illinois Press, 1986), 116–67, at 140.

2. Léonie Rosenstiel, *Nadia Boulanger: A Life in Music* (New York and London: W. W. Norton, 1982), 96. Rosenstiel cites the article (see note 3 below) without reference to the source.

3. Emile Vuillermoz, "Le Péril rose," *Musica* 11 (1912): 45: "Le Conservatoire, où elles ont déjà la majorité, finira par rester leur propriété personnelle et les classes que l'on appelera 'classes mixtes' seront celles où l'on tolérera la présence de deux ou trois porteurs de moustache.... Gabriel Fauré aura été chassé de son fauteuil par Hélène Fleury ou Nadia Boulanger."

For music itself this would mean that "female" modes of behavior would determine the genesis of the artwork: fashion would replace creation.[4] When, on 5 July 1913, Lili Boulanger became the first woman to win the French *Prix de Rome* in composition, Vuillermoz commented on this unsettling phenomenon in his article "Fighting in Frills," which began as follows:

> A few months ago, in these columns, I warned musicians of the imminence of the "pink peril": events have not been slow to prove me right. A young suffragette, Mademoiselle Lili Boulanger, has just triumphed in the last competition of the *Prix de Rome* over all her male competitors and has won on her first attempt the first *Premier Grand Prix*, with such authority, speed, and ease as to cause great anxiety to those candidates who have for long years sweated blood and tears in striving for this goal.[5]

The awarding of the prize to Lili Boulanger in 1913 brought to fruition what journalists had announced in 1903 as a "great victory of feminism,"[6] the admission of women to the *Prix de Rome* competition. In the ensuing decade, four women played key roles in the process: Juliette Toutain,[7] who entered but could not participate in the competition in 1903; Hélène Fleury, who in 1904 became the first woman to receive a prize, the *Deuxième Second Grand Prix*; Nadia Boulanger, who failed to win the *Premier Grand Prix* in 1908 and 1909, even though on both occasions she was generally acknowledged to have written the best cantata; and her sister Lili Boulanger, who won the first prize in 1913.[8] Telling the story of these four composers and their quest for the *Prix de Rome* sheds new light not only on strategies that women employed in order to succeed in the artistic world of *fin de siècle* Paris, but also on that era's dialectical interplay of male and

---

4. Although Vuillermoz sets this scenario with a certain irony, appropriate for a monthly column, the elucidation of the dangers occupies more than 90 percent of the text. Only in the last paragraph does he moderate the warning by disguising it as an account of conservative positions rather than his own opinion. Through this narrative strategy, Vuillermoz avoids allying himself too closely with the conservatives—as an "apache" he considers himself as part of the avant-garde—but the peroration is not used to unmask the previous discourse, and thus the text remains an anti-feminist pamphlet using aggressive and militaristic vocabulary.

5. Emile Vuillermoz, "La Guerre en dentelles," *Musica* 12 (1913): 153: "Il y a quelques mois, à cette même place, je dénonçais aux musiciens l'imminence du 'péril rose'; les événements n'ont pas tardé à me donner raison. Une jeune suffragette, Mlle Lili Boulanger, vient de triompher, au dernier concours de Rome, de tous ses concurrents masculins et a enlevé, dès la première épreuve, le premier premier-grand-prix, avec une autorité, une rapidité et une aisance propres à inquiéter sérieusement les candidats qui, depuis de longues années, suent sang et eau pour se rapprocher laborieusement de ce but."

6. "Paris et Départements," *Le Ménestrel* 69 (1903): 55.

7. I wish to thank Lesley Wright for having drawn my attention to this composer at the beginning of my investigations about women and the *Prix de Rome*.

8. For biographical details of the four composers, see the Appendix. The prizes distributed in the *Prix de Rome* competition were, in ascending order, *mention honorable*, *Deuxième Second Grand Prix*, *Premier Second Grand Prix*, and finally the *Premier Grand Prix*.

female, its public and private spheres, its aesthetic and artistic conceptions, and the complex mechanisms of its cultural politics. The four women had to challenge the Académie des Beaux-Arts, an institution dedicated to defending the values of French culture, whose members now felt threatened in a new world of changing social, cultural, and political structures. Socialism was among the perceived threats, for it was intimately associated with the emancipation of women.[9] Moreover, the discussion about women and the *Prix de Rome* was inextricably linked with the highly polarized discourse on the antagonistic relationship between France and Germany following the French defeat in 1870.[10] As Edward Berenson has aptly put it, the French concern with gender resulted in large part "from a perceived decline of French power that commentators related to moral decay and to changing relations between the sexes. If France was weak, writers commonly asserted, its weakness stemmed from a growing demographic deficit caused by the emancipation of women, the legalization of divorce, and the emasculation of men."[11] That the "pink peril" was regarded as a challenge not just to male privilege but to French culture itself is clear from the speech delivered by the painter and *académicien* Luc Olivier Merson (1846–1920), who denounced the admittance of women to the *Prix de Rome* in February 1903:

9. Karen Offen, "Depopulation, Nationalism, and Feminism in Fin-de-Siècle France," *American Historical Review* 89 (1984): 648–76, 660; Debora Silverman, "The 'New Woman,' Feminism, and the Decorative Arts in Fin-de-Siècle France," in *Eroticism and the Body Politic*, ed. Lynn Hunt (Baltimore and London: The Johns Hopkins University Press, 1991), 144–63, 148–49.

10. On the question of the interweaving of musical and political life in *fin de siècle* Paris, see Jann Pasler's chapter "Paris: Conflicting Notions of Progress," in *Man and Music: The Late Romantic Era. From the Mid-nineteenth Century to World War I*, ed. Jim Samson (London and Basingstoke: Macmillan, 1991), 389–416; and her "Concert Programs and Their Narratives as Emblems of Ideology," *International Journal of Musicology* 2 (1993): 249–308. See also Jane F. Fulcher's forthcoming book, *French Cultural Politics and Musical Aesthetics from the Dreyfus Affair to the First World War* (Oxford and New York: Oxford University Press, 1998). Fulcher further exemplifies the interference of politics in musical life in *fin de siècle* Paris with two case studies: "Charpentier's Operatic 'Roman Musical' as Read in the Wake of the Dreyfus Affair," *19th-Century Music* 16 (1992): 161–80; and "Wagner in the Cultural Politics of the French Right and Left Before World War I," in *Wagner, Frankreich und die Folgen: Der französische Wagnerismus zwischen 1861 und 1914*, ed. Annegret Fauser and Manuela Schwartz (forthcoming). For a different political reading of Charpentier's *Louise*, see Steven Huebner, "Between Anarchism and the Box Office: Gustave Charpentier's *Louise*," *19th-Century Music* 19 (1995): 136–60.

11. Edward Berenson, *The Trial of Madame Caillaux* (Berkeley, Los Angeles, and Oxford: University of California Press, 1992), 11. Debora Silverman mentions three factors that conservative opinion linked with the emancipation of French middle-class women: the socialist attack on the institution of the family, access to higher education and therefore "entry to the centers of prestigious male vocations," and the "decline of the birthrate and the stagnation of France's population relative to its European neighbors [= Germany]" as a result of women leaving the private sphere of the home; see Silverman, "The 'New Woman,'" 148–49.

I protest the innovation of Monsieur le Ministre, which I consider an attack on the moral dignity and, in consequence, the very existence of the Académie, wherein rest the strength and the honor of French Art. It is to the Académie that our members owe the beautiful organization of their works and the loftiness of their inspiration. The duty of the government should therefore be to consolidate the Académie de France by its powerful protection and to defend it against its many enemies.[12]

The Académie des Beaux-Arts, Women, and the *Prix de Rome*

The "many enemies" to which Merson alluded comprised not only the female interlopers in the competition but also the French government itself, which had forced the change upon the Académie des Beaux-Arts. In this respect, the conflict over the *Prix de Rome* reveals the delicate relationship between the Académie and its patron, the government. Since 1635, when it was founded by Cardinal Richelieu, the Académie had depended on the support and favor of its patron, as the statutes required. Not only would "no one be received at the Académie who is not agreeable to Monsieur le Protecteur,"[13] but as stipulated in another article of the statutes, "in the Académie, political and moral matters will be treated only in conformance with the authority of the Prince, the estate of the government, and the laws of the Kingdom."[14] This did not change when France became a republic, and at the time of the dispute over the *Prix de Rome*, new members of the Académie still had to be approved by a decree from the minister responsible.

In 1903, the relationship between the Académie—a rather conservative institution—and the radical, left-wing government of Emile Combes's *Bloc* was strained at best. On 8 February, Joseph Chaumié (1849–1919), minister of Public Instruction, announced at the annual banquet of republican journalists his decision that henceforth women would be allowed to com-

---

12. Minutes of the weekly session of the Académie des Beaux-Arts [*Procès verbaux*] from 28 February 1903, preserved in the Archives of the Académie des Beaux-Arts at the Institut de France, Paris [AABA], shelf-mark 2E21, p. 24: "Je proteste contre l'innovation de M. le Ministre, que je considère comme attentoire à la dignité morale et, par suite, à l'existence même de l'académie que reposent la force et l'honneur [de] l'art français. C'est à elle que nos articles doivent la belle tenue de leurs œuvres et la hauteur de leurs inspirations. Le devoir de l'administration serait donc de consolider l'Académie de France par sa puissante protection et de la défendre contre ses nombreux ennemis."
13. "Personne ne sera reçu à l'Académie, qui ne soit agréable à Monsieur le Protecteur." This remark actually begins the *Règlements et Statuts de l'Académie Française* (1635), reproduced in *Les Femmes et L'Académie Française*, ed. François Fleutot (Paris: Les Editions de l'Opale, 1981), 103.
14. Fleutot, ed., *Les Femmes et L'Académie Française*, 108: "Les matières politiques ou morales ne seront traitées dans l'Académie que conformément à l'autorité du Prince, à l'état du gouvernement et aux lois du Royaume."

pete for the *Prix de Rome*.[15] Thus it was through the press that the members of the Académie des Beaux-Arts first learned that the rules of "their" prize had changed. At first, they were incredulous. When the Académie met in the weekly session on 14 February, the painter Merson inquired whether this news was true; the Secrétaire perpétuel could only answer that he had not received any official information.[16] The minister's letter did not arrive until a week later. It was then read to the members of the Académie:

> Paris, 17 February 1903
> Monsieur le Secrétaire Perpétuel
>
> I have just decided that women artists, of French nationality and unmarried, more than fifteen years of age and less than thirty, can from now on take part in the competitions for the *Grand Prix de Rome*.
>
> I have the honor of requesting that you should be so good as to inform the Académie des Beaux-Arts, adding that instructions have been given to Messieurs the Directors of the Ecole Nationale des Beaux-Arts and of the Conservatoire National de Musique et de Déclamation that the secretariats of these establishments should accept and enroll in the same way as young men any requests from women artists who should happen to present themselves.[17]

The minutes of the meeting report a rather moderate initial reaction among the members of the Académie, although one central concern became obvious in Merson's arguments: that the minister had neglected to ask for the Académie's guidance regarding a question on which it should have been consulted, given that "the Académie, following the prerogatives which the

---

15. The news was reported in the daily press; in *Le Temps* for instance, one finds the account of the banquet under the column "News of the Day": "M. Chaumié, ministre de l'Instruction publique, a fait ensuite l'éloge de la presse républicaine, puis, portant la santé des sociétaires femmes de l'Association, il a annoncé qu'il avait signé aujourd'hui même, l'admission des femmes aux concours du prix de Rome" (*Le Temps*, 10 February 1903, p. 2). A more detailed account was given in the weekly music journal *Le Ménestrel* of 15 February 1903, p. 55.

16. *Procès verbaux* from 14 February 1903, AABA, shelf-mark 2E21, p. 18: "M. Merson demande ce qu'il y a de vrai dans l'annonce, par les journaux, de l'admission des femmes au concours pour les grands prix de Rome. M. Pascal, remplissant par interim, les fonctions de secrétaire perpétuel, répond que l'Académie n'a reçu encore aucune communication officielle à ce sujet." The Académie des Beaux-Arts met regularly on Saturdays in order to discuss issues relating to French art and to decide on matters such as the attribution of prizes.

17. *Procès verbaux* from 21 February 1903, AABA, shelf-mark 2E21, p. 20:

> Paris, le 17 février 1903
> Monsieur le Secrétaire Perpétuel
>
> Je viens de décider que les artistes femme, de nationalité française et célibataires, âgées de plus de 15 ans et de moins de 30, pourront désormais prendre part aux Concours pour les Grands Prix de Rome.
>
> J'ai l'honneur de vous prier de vouloir bien en informer l'Académie des Beaux-Arts, en ajoutant que les instructions ont été données à MM. les Directeurs de l'Ecole Nationale des Beaux-Arts et du Conservatoire National de Musique et de déclamation [*sic*] pour que les Secrétariats de ces Etablissements acceptent et inscrivent au même titre que celles des jeunes gens, les demandes d'artistes femme qui viendraient à se produire.

law assigned to it, must be conferred with in all questions touching the progress, teaching and perfecting of the different areas of the Arts."[18] A week later, however, tempers began to flare, and in the succeeding conflict over the admission of women to the *Prix de Rome*, two formerly separate questions became intertwined. On the one hand, there was the issue of the delicate balance of artistic independence and political control that defined the relationship between the government and the Académie which depended upon it financially. On the other, we find the question of the right of women to have access to the Académie des Beaux-Arts and its prizes.

The history of women and the Académie dates back to the *ancien régime*, when female artists such as Elisabeth Vigée Lebrun and Adelaide Labille were full members of the Académie Royale.[19] With the French Revolution and the *Code Napoléon* (1804), French women lost the limited civil rights that at least aristocratic women had previously enjoyed.[20] After 1793, French women of all classes lived totally under the legal tutelage of their fathers, husbands, brothers, or other male relatives. "Republican motherhood" became the sole reason for their existence, and their education consequently had but one goal: to enable them to bring up future French soldiers, workers, and citizens in the best way possible.[21] The Republic gendered the public sphere as masculine after "the fall of the absolutist public sphere" in which "masculinity in and of itself carried some but not vast privileges"; this "structural change of the public sphere" necessitated the creation of a counterpart in the form of a feminine private sphere, demanding "women's domesticity and the silencing of 'public' women, of the aristocratic and popular classes."[22] The home emphatically developed into the "royaume de la femme,"[23] in which art, and especially music, served to educate children, entertain husbands and guests, and fill women's other-

---

18. *Procès verbaux* from 21 February 1903, AABA, shelf-mark 2E21, p. 21: "L'Académie suivant les prérogatives que lui confère la loi, doit être consultée dans toutes les questions qui touchent au progrès, à l'enseignement et au perfectionnement des différentes parties des Beaux-Arts."

19. See Tamar Garb, *Sisters of the Brush: Women's Artistic Culture in Late Nineteenth-Century Paris* (New Haven and London: Yale University Press, 1994), 42–43.

20. For an excellent study of the development of the bourgeois concept of gendered spheres and "the constitutional denial of women's rights under bourgeois law" (p. 1) in France, see Joan B. Landes, *Women and the Public Sphere in the Age of the French Revolution* (Ithaca and London: Cornell University Press, 1988).

21. For a short but detailed account of women's rights in nineteenth-century France, see Berenson, *The Trial of Madame Caillaux*, 103–17.

22. Landes, *Women and the Public Sphere*, 170, 2. My use of "structural change of the public sphere" appropriates Habermas's beautifully coined title "Strukturwandel der Öffentlichkeit" in order to describe this phenomenon of gendering public and private spheres in the nineteenth century. See Jürgen Habermas, *Strukturwandel der Öffentlichkeit: Untersuchungen zu einer Kategorie der bürgerlichen Gesellschaft* (Frankfurt am Main: Suhrkamp, 1990).

23. Berenson, *The Trial of Madame Caillaux*, 126.

wise idle hours of leisure. Countless books of etiquette enumerated the benefits to women of dilettante musicianship, which if need be might even secure them socially acceptable employment as governesses or private piano teachers.[24] The Paris Conservatoire, founded in 1795, catered to such bourgeois girls by offering them a variety of programs: they could attend women's classes in solfège, harmony, piano, and piano accompaniment, duly chaperoned by their mothers or maidservants. But women musicians were not content with these restrictions: soon other Conservatoire classes opened to them, and they were allowed to join male students in classes such as counterpoint and fugue.[25]

Throughout the nineteenth century, women had to negotiate their space as creative artists within gendered public and private spheres. The Académie des Beaux-Arts, the pinnacle of French artistic life, was firmly located in the public sphere of French cultural politics, and it resisted the efforts of women to regain the position they had enjoyed in the Académie under the *ancien régime*. The first major controversy began in the 1830s: when the writer George Sand provocatively questioned the concept of an all-male Académie, it became a public affair.[26] Closer to the events of 1903 was the debate provoked by the then famous sculptor Madame Léon Bertaux when, on 17 June 1892, she applied for a vacant seat at the Académie.[27] Although she lost the election, the public discussion of her candidacy pushed women one step further on their ascent to this Olympus of official French art. The left-wing press in particular saw in Bertaux's demand "only the claim for women under the Republic [of] that which women had already enjoyed under the Ancien Régime."[28]

If membership in the Académie offered a supreme sign of achievement for a mature artist, the *Prix de Rome* conferred a similar official accolade on a young painter, sculptor, architect, engraver, or composer. The prize brought financial reward, funding for a period of residence at the Villa

---

24. Katharine Ellis discusses issues of women's professional musicianship in her "Female Pianists and Their Male Critics in Nineteenth-Century Paris," this **Journal** 50 (1997): 353–85. See also my forthcoming article "Zwischen Professionalismus und Salon: Französische Musikerinnen des *Fin de siècle*," in *Professionalismus in der Musik,* ed. Christian Kaden and Volker Kalisch, Musik-Kultur 5 (Essen: Blaue Eule, 1998).

25. In 1861, the year in which the first woman, Julie Daubié, successfully passed her *baccalauréat*, Charlotte Jacques gained a *Deuxième Accessit* in counterpoint, and from 1874 on, women were regularly successful in the composition classes, beginning with Marie Renaud's (1852–1928) *Deuxième Accessit* in 1874, *Premier Accessit* in 1875, and finally, *Premier Prix* in 1876.

26. For a reproduction of the central documents, see Fleutot, ed., *Les Femmes et L'Académie Française*.

27. For an account of Madame Léon Bertaux's candidacy, see Garb, *Sisters of the Brush*, 42–45.

28. Ibid., 42.

Medici in Rome,[29] public attention and exposure, and artistic honor. Although a cynical attitude toward the prize was *de rigueur*—Debussy's comments being only the most famous—its importance and prestige should not be underestimated.[30] Women made repeated attempts to gain access to what was, throughout the nineteenth century, forbidden territory, as in 1889, when the *Union des Femmes Peintres et Sculpteurs* began a campaign that combined a claim for women's entrance as *élèves* into the Ecole des Beaux-Arts with their quest for admission to the *Prix de Rome*. After years of struggle, women were finally permitted to enroll at the Ecole in 1896, but the *Prix de Rome* remained out of reach.[31] Well before the campaign of these artists, the young composer Maria Isambert (fl. 1873–1905) had sought admittance to the *Prix de Rome* in 1874.[32] In a letter to the Direction des Beaux-Arts, she pointed out that the official regulations did not explicitly exclude women from the competition:

> Allow me to address myself to Your Excellency to ask you if you would agree to authorize my participation in the *Prix de Rome* competition, of which the *épreuves préparatoires* are to begin on 16 May forthcoming. The Director of the Paris Conservatoire . . . has deemed it necessary—since no young woman has ever enrolled in this competition and because the law is silent in this respect—that I turn to Your Excellency to obtain this authorization. . . . Would you, Monsieur le Ministre, please deign to receive my request favorably, and in permitting me to participate in the *Prix de Rome* competition, thus grant me the honor of opening to other young women—who, like myself, will have pursued advanced studies in harmony and composition—a career from which no law in any way bans them, so I believe.[33]

---

29. The amount of time allocated to the winners of the *Prix de Rome* kept changing. At the period discussed in this article, musicians were sent to Rome for three years.

30. Claude Debussy, "Considérations sur le prix de Rome au point de vue musical," in Claude Debussy, *Monsieur Croche et autres écrits,* ed. François Lesure, 2d rev. ed. (Paris: Gallimard, 1987), 175–79. On the *Prix de Rome,* see Lesley Wright, "Bias, Influence, and Bizet's *Prix de Rome,*" *19th-Century Music* 15 (1992): 215–28; eadem, "Prix de Rome," forthcoming in *Die Musik in Geschichte und Gegenwart,* ed. Ludwig Finscher, 2d rev. ed., 25 vols. (Kassel, Basel, London, and New York: Metzler and Bärenreiter-Verlag, 1993–); and Eugene Bozza, "The History of the 'Prix de Rome,'" *Hinrichsen's Musical Yearbook* 7 (1952): 487–94 (including a list of the winners of the first prizes in music). Lesley Wright is currently preparing a book on the *Prix de Rome* as a central institution of French musical life.

31. For an account of this struggle, see Garb, *Sisters of the Brush,* 70–104.

32. I wish to thank Lesley Wright for this information.

33. Letter to the Direction des Beaux-Arts from 7 May 1874: "Permettez-moi de m'adresser à votre Excellence, pour la prier de vouloir bien m'autoriser à prendre part au concours pour le prix de Rome dont les épreuves préparatoires doivent commencer le 16 Mai prochain. Monsieur le Directeur du Conservatoire de Paris . . . a jugé nécessaire, comme aucune jeune fille ne s'est présentée à ce concours et que la loi ne se prononce pas à cet égard, que je m'adresse à votre Excellence pour obtenir cette autorisation. . . . Daignez, Monsieur le Ministre, accueillir favorablement ma demande et en me permettant de prendre part au concours pour le prix de Rome, m'accorder ainsi l'honneur d'ouvrir à d'autres jeunes personnes, qui comme moi auront fait des études approfondies d'harmonie et de composition, une carrière

The Directeur passed this letter on to the Académie des Beaux-Arts, which decided with little discussion that Isambert was not entitled to compete for the prize.[34]

Since the *Prix de Rome* was affiliated with the Académie and any changes in its constitution required governmental approval, the relationship between government and the Académie was crucial. Maria Isambert's fate shows how a strongly conservative institution such as the Académie might collude with a right-wing government to keep the *femme nouvelle* out of the public sphere of official art: the more public space ceded to women, ran the argument, the greater the likelihood that they would renounce their assigned role of "republican motherhood" and become sterile *hommesses*.[35] Yet in 1902, the rise to power of Combes's radical party changed the political climate. Three young women, the painter Mademoiselle Rondenay, the sculptor Mademoiselle Rozet,[36] and the composer Juliette Toutain, sought to participate in the 1903 *Prix de Rome*. Each played her cards carefully, writing to the minister in charge of the Académie, the radical politician Joseph Chaumié. Overlooking the historical fact of Maria Isambert's earlier attempt to become a contestant, Chaumié would later explain his actions to the Académie as follows:

> The reason why this authorization [to participate in the *Prix de Rome*] has not been granted earlier is the fact that no one has applied to the public authorities; but since he has recently received three demands, one from Mademoiselle Toutain of the Conservatoire de Musique, and two others from two *massières* in the name of the painting and sculpture ateliers of the Ecole des Beaux-Arts, the Minister had to make the necessary dispositions to accede to these demands.[37]

In pitting the radical minister against the conservative administration, the three women exploited the new political climate to their own ends. They succeeded for three reasons: the diverging political directions of the radical party and the Académie; the dependence of the Académie on the government; and the personal ambition of the then Directeur des Beaux-Arts, Henri Roujon (1853–1914).

à laquelle la loi ne leur interdit aucunement, je crois de prétendre." I wish to thank Lesley Wright for a copy of this letter.

34. *Procès verbaux* from 9 May 1874, AABA, shelf-mark 2E15, pp. 259–60.

35. See Silverman, "The 'New Woman,'" 149–50 and passim.

36. In the daily newspaper *Le Matin* from 1 April 1903, an interview with these two artists was published on the front page at the beginning of the *Prix de Rome* competition in painting and sculpture.

37. *Procès verbaux* from 21 March 1903, AABA, shelf-mark 2E21, p. 37: "Si cette autorisation n'a pas été accordée plus tôt, c'est qu'aucune demande n'avait été encore adressée aux pouvoirs publics; mais, que s'étant trouvé récemment en présence de trois demandes, l'une émanant de Mad[lle] Toutain du Conservatoire de Musique et les deux autres, de deux massières, au nom des ateliers de peinture et de sculpture de l'Ecole des Beaux-Arts, le Ministre a dû prendre les dispositions nécessaires pour accueillir ces demandes."

In nineteenth-century France, all artistic matters fell under the aegis of the Direction des Beaux-Arts, headed by the Directeur, an administrative, rather than a political, figure. While the ministers of the Third Republic normally changed at short intervals, the Directeur could stay in office for twenty years or more, until he retired either by reason of age or to take a better position. This system encouraged stagnation and conservative cultural politics, since all ministerial directives were filtered through the office of the Directeur. The relationship between the Académie and the Direction des Beaux-Arts, then, was not just excellent but virtually symbiotic; at the time of the *Prix de Rome* affair, the Directeur des Beaux-Arts, Henri Roujon, was also a member of the Académie (he was by no means the first). Nevertheless, in the matter of women's enrollment in the *Prix de Rome*, Roujon was not entirely straightforward with the Académie: indeed, he was responsible for the minister's disturbing failure to consult the Académie before announcing his decision to admit women to the competition. His justifications for his actions reflect his delicate maneuvering between the left-wing minister Chaumié and the Académie where his loyalty lay: "Finding myself faced on one side with the formal wish of the government [to authorize the participation of women in the *Prix de Rome*], and knowing on the other that the feelings of most of my colleagues were unfavorable toward the proposed measures, I wanted to avert the danger of the conflict about which I was speaking earlier."[38] Roujon tried to prevent an open clash between the Académie and the Chambre des Députés, which would have been unavoidable had the former been consulted beforehand. But his actions should also be interpreted in the light of the Académie's internal politics. Secrétaire perpétuel Louis Laroumet was close to death, and Roujon would be a serious candidate for his post, especially if he could be seen to help the Académie through an awkward situation. Despite his urging to accept the situation as a *fait accompli*, many *académiciens* expressed such outrage at the notion of women's participation in the *Prix de Rome* as to drown out moderate voices like that of the architect Henri Nénot (1853–1919). Eventually, they dispatched a delegation to the minister to protest "the painful surprise" sprung upon them. The minister's response made it clear, however, that any further resistance was useless and would incur financial retaliation.[39] At this point, the Académie backed down, and the registration of women candidates for the *Prix de Rome* went forward. As for Henri Roujon, he was elected the next permanent secretary on 24 October 1903.

---

38. *Procès verbaux* from 28 February 1903, AABA, shelf-mark 2E21, pp. 25–26: "Me trouvant donc en présence de la volonté formelle du Gouvernement, et connaissant, d'autre part, les sentiments de la plupart de mes confrères, défavorables à la mesure projetée, j'ai voulu conjurer le péril du conflit dont je parlais tout à l'heure."

39. *Procès verbaux* from 21 March 1903, AABA, shelf-mark 2E21, pp. 37–38.

Juliette Toutain: A *Bourgeoise*, the Conservatoire, and the World of Musical Professionalism

This did not end the resistance to women's participation in the competition. Whereas the *Prix de Rome* conflict remained an internal affair between the Académie and the government, the story of Juliette Toutain became a public scandal. Her case brings into sharp focus the question of the public appearance of women—the perception of them as well as their self-representation—and its importance for official recognition of women musicians. Toutain, a *bourgeoise* from a good Parisian family, sought public recognition as a composer. This was a contradiction in itself, and one that would be a recurring theme in the history of women and the *Prix de Rome*.[40] The social and cultural framework of bourgeois femininity provided a powerful and complex semiotic system of imaginary and legislative structures that created horizons of expectation regarding women's appearance in public. Strict rules of decorum governed the behavior of a woman of good reputation, especially a virtuous young lady of the *bourgeoisie*. In fact, the appearance of women musicians, from their demeanor to their dress—a seemingly mundane topic better suited to the popular press than to a serious musicological study—reveals itself as a key component in the understanding of women's musical careers, as Marcia Citron, Katharine Ellis, and Nancy Reich have recently suggested.[41] These issues certainly played a central role in the scandal surrounding Toutain; indeed, they made that scandal possible.

The *Prix de Rome* in the early twentieth century consisted of two rounds. In the first, preliminary part, the candidates had to compose "a fugue in four voices and four clefs, on a subject written by one of the jury members" and "a chorus [SATB] accompanied by orchestra, setting a poem chosen by the jury just before the competitors received it."[42] The competitors wrote

---

40. Much research has been done on the *bourgeoise* and the importance of this notion for the actual life of French women, and views of them, in the Third Republic. See, for example, Bonnie G. Smith, *Ladies of the Leisure Class: The Bourgeoise of Northern France in the Nineteenth Century* (Princeton: Princeton University Press, 1981); James McMillan, *Housewife or Harlot: The Place of Women in French Society, 1870–1940* (Brighton: Harvester Press, 1981); Anne Martin-Fugier, *La Bourgeoise* (Paris: Bernard Grasset, 1983); and Marieluise Christadler, "Zwischen Macht und Ohnmacht" and "Die Frauenbewegung in der Dritten Republik," in *Bewegte Jahre—Frankreichs Frauen*, ed. Marieluise Christadler and Florence Hervé (Düsseldorf: Zebulon Verlag, 1994), 37–52 and 53–71.

41. Marcia J. Citron, *Gender and the Musical Canon* (Cambridge: Cambridge University Press, 1993); Ellis, "Female Pianists"; and Nancy B. Reich, "Women as Musicians: A Question of Class," in *Musicology and Difference: Gender and Sexuality in Music Scholarship*, ed. Ruth A. Solie (Berkeley and Los Angeles: University of California Press, 1993), 125–46. For a most insightful analysis of these factors in the judgment of women's public perception, see Edward Berenson's analysis of the trial of Henriette Caillaux (*The Trial of Madame Caillaux*).

42. Wright, "Bias," 217.

these pieces while locked away in the Château de Compiègne, thereby precluding external help. Competitors had their own rooms—their *loges*—in which to work and sleep, and they shared their meals and recreation. A jury of specialists, consisting of the six musician-members of the Académie at that time and three adjunct jurors, usually well-known composers,[43] selected a maximum of six finalists after hearing their pieces performed.[44]

> Those six (or fewer) finalists selected by the music jury in the preliminary round were then given the opportunity to write a cantata on an original text that was chosen in another competition just before its poetry was dictated to the contestants. In the succeeding twenty-five days, each of the young composers had to write and orchestrate a prelude and several vocal numbers that normally included airs for soprano, tenor, and bass soloists, as well as a duet and a trio.[45]

After these twenty-five days of sequestration and the official deposition of their completed cantatas, the candidates had several weeks to prepare for the last stage of the competition: the semi-public presentation of the works at the Académie des Beaux-Arts. Each finalist was responsible for choosing the singers and pianist for his or her cantata, rehearsing them, and conducting the final performance. Thus women candidates in the music competition of the *Prix de Rome* were highly visible, much more so than those in any other branch of the contest. They were seen to conduct, which added to the general problem of judging women candidates the visual aspect of yet another artistic activity that was—and still is—a male domain.[46] The self-representation of the women during these performances therefore became an essential ingredient of their success.

On 2 May 1903, the candidates for the *concours d'essai*, the first round of the *Prix de Rome*, were sequestered *en loge* in the Château de Compiègne. Two women had enrolled: Juliette Toutain, a pupil of Fauré who, after finishing her studies at the Conservatoire in 1902, had campaigned for

---

43. To serve on such a jury was one of the first steps toward a seat in the Académie. For example, in 1914, Claude Debussy was asked to join the jury, at a period when his name began to be mentioned as a possible member of the Académie (*Procès verbaux*, AABA, shelf-mark 2E23, p. 141). In a letter to Claude Debussy from the summer of 1914, Charles-Marie Widor, the newly elected Secrétaire perpétuel, wrote: "Je serais très flatté de vous servir de parrain à l'Académie et vous avoir pour successeur—avec dispense de faire mon éloge—on vous accueillera à bras ouverts" (quoted in John Richard Near, "The Life and Work of Charles-Marie Widor" [Ph.D. diss., Boston University, 1984], 269).

44. The practice of hearing the fugues performed by the competitors goes back to 1850, when it was first mentioned in the minutes of the meetings. See Wright, "Bias," 217.

45. Ibid.

46. See, for example, Jeanice Brooks's case study of Nadia Boulanger's conducting career and her complex negotiation of traditional expectations, in her article "*Noble et grande servante de la musique:* Telling the Story of Nadia Boulanger's Conducting Career," *Journal of Musicology* 14 (1996): 92–116.

the admission of women to the *Prix de Rome* in composition;[47] and Hélène Fleury, a student of Charles-Marie Widor. But when Toutain failed to appear for the *entrée en loge,* the competition started without her. The following week, Toutain publicly accused Théodore Dubois, the director of the Conservatoire, of having forced her to withdraw because he neglected to ensure her good reputation by accommodating her demands. She denounced Dubois's behavior as a deliberate act of exclusion. What, then, had really happened?

Again, one of the players was Henri Roujon and his Direction des Beaux-Arts. The others involved were herself, her father Jules—a highly ranked civil servant in the Ministère de la Marine—as well as Théodore Dubois and his chef du secrétariat du Conservatoire, Emile Bourgeat. The accounts of these participants differ in some salient details. After Toutain's enrollment, her father went to see Théodore Dubois, seeking three provisions that would ensure his daughter could preserve her respectability while locked in a building together with nine young men: only a chambermaid (as opposed to the usually male servants at Compiègne) should enter Toutain's *loge* for cleaning; a chaperone should be present at all times; and the women's meals and recreation should be separate from the young men's. In the context of women's status in this period, it is perhaps only logical that Toutain's father should have taken such precautions. Dubois, however, was in Italy, so Jules Toutain met with his deputy, Emile Bourgeat. Here, the stories vary. Dubois and Bourgeat claimed that the first request had already been granted, but that Bourgeat had asked Monsieur Toutain to put his other two requests in writing. According to Bourgeat, Toutain failed to do so.

> Monsieur Bourgeat answered that the rules adopted up to now, which guarantee the legality of the competition, would not allow him to authorize any competitors to be separated from the others during the hours in which they were not locked in their rooms, and he added that, if Monsieur Toutain wanted to ask for these changes in long-established practice, he would need to express his wishes in writing in a letter addressed to the Minister of Public Instruction and the Fine Arts, or to the Director of the Conservatoire who

---

47. Fauré noted in his class reports, underlining every word, *"veut poursuivre le concours de Rome!!"* (Archives Nationales, Série AJ[37] 298, fol. 97r). Toutain's campaign consisted not only of letters to the respective authorities; it had a public side as well, owing to newspaper coverage. Thus the women's journal *Femina* ran a series of interviews with established artists who were invited to comment on female participation in the *Prix de Rome*. Augusta Holmès, for example, found the exclusion of women up to that time rather "arbitrary," and used the occasion to criticize the *Prix de Rome* in general. Compare the inquiry entitled "Mlle Augusta Holmès" in *Femina,* 15 April 1902. This interview is kept in the Collection Laruelle, vol. 155, Do53696, at the Bibliothèque Nationale de France. I wish to thank Karen Henson for sharing this finding with me.

would then, because he has no authority to decide this question by himself, refer it to the Minister and to the Académie des Beaux-Arts.[48]

There is no evidence to confirm whether Toutain's father actually wrote the letter or not. He did maintain, however, that Bourgeat had told him that he would send Toutain's written request to the Direction des Beaux-Arts, together with a recommendation for refusal.[49] Jules Toutain then went to meet Dubois a second time on 28 April. Surprised to hear his story, Dubois asked Toutain why he had not come earlier, and claimed that Bourgeat had neglected to inform him of the earlier visit. In the discussion that followed, Dubois appeared reluctant to grant Toutain's request for a chaperone, and here Roujon seems to have interfered: "Monsieur Bourgeat added [to his report] that Monsieur Roujon had instructed him not to accept, on account of the women, any modification of the practices followed in previous years."[50] The spirit of Minister Chaumié's original decision, in which he instructed the Académie to enroll women in the *Prix de Rome* in the same way as men, was deliberately misunderstood by the administration in order to inhibit women's involvement in the competition. In the end, Dubois refused in principle to give any special treatment to women, but agreed to grant the requests if the other competitors would accept a change of practice. Again, we find two differing accounts of the meeting on 28 April: Dubois states that he was cautious only during the discussion, but that he spent the next days arranging the matter; Toutain's father understood that Dubois had refused his request categorically. On 1 May, Toutain's father wrote a letter in which he announced his daughter's withdrawal:

> Monsieur le Directeur,
> Faced with the failure of my action in trying to obtain the measures of decency which, in my opinion, are implicit in the realization of the generous

---

48. Théodore Dubois's report to the Académie des Beaux-Arts, recorded in *Procès verbaux* from 9 May 1903, AABA, shelf-mark 2E21, pp. 54–55: "M. Bourgeat a répondu que les règlements adoptés jusqu'à présent pour assurer la loyauté du concours ne lui permettraient pas de prendre sur lui d'autoriser des concurrents à se séparer des autres aux heures où ils ne sont pas enfermés dans leur loges, et ajouta que, si M. Toutain voulait demander ce changement aux coutumes établies, il fallait qu'il fixât ses desiderata par écrit, dans une lettre adressée au Ministre de l'Instruction publique et des Beaux-Arts ou au Directeur du Conservatoire qui, n'ayant pas qualité de trancher à lui seul cette question, en réfèrerait au Ministre et à l'Académie des Beaux-Arts."

49. Maurice Leudet, "Le Cas de Mlle Toutain," *Le Figaro*, 10 May 1903, p. 4: "M. Bourgeat répondit . . . qu'il pourrait se charger de transmettre la demande écrite à l'Académie, mais qu'il la ferait suivre d'un avis défavorable."

50. *Le Petit Journal*, 7 May 1903, p. 3. Almost the same wording was used in the account given in *Le Temps*, 8 May 1903, p. 3: "M. Bourgeat ajouta que M. Roujon lui avait donné pour instruction de n'admettre, à cause des femmes, aucune modification à l'usage suivi les années précédentes."

decision of Monsieur le Ministre . . . , my daughter is renouncing her participation in the *concours d'essai* for which she has enrolled.[51]

On the morning of 2 May 1903, all the requests were granted, but because Toutain did not appear at the *mise en loge* (which began that day), it was too late. Clearly, Roujon and Dubois manipulated matters, whether because of their general antipathy to women or as a deliberate attempt to keep Toutain out of the competition: they knew, and could have anticipated, her scruples as a lady with social pretensions.[52] After all, not only had she actively campaigned for the admission of women to the *Prix de Rome* in the first place; she had also garnered a succession of first prizes at the Conservatoire, including that in fugue (the prize for composition) in 1902.

But there might be another reading of how the affair was handled: Toutain was at the point of transgressing the boundary between a *bourgeoise* and a professional composer. It is possible either that her father forbade her participation or that he exploited this conflict and misinformed her unconsciously—or even consciously—so as to keep her within both the limits of good behavior and the space of the salon, which was only semipublic. This space was already occupied by Toutain's mother, who organized a lesser-known salon attended by a number of musicians, including Massenet. Here, Toutain could show herself off in a safe social environment without exposure to the public sphere:

> At Madame Toutain's, presentation of works by Massenet. *La Marche de Szabady,* for two pianos four hands, arranged and performed by Madame L. Filliaux-Tiger and Mademoiselle Toutain, brilliantly opened the occasion. Mademoiselle Toutain, whose serious talent is already so well known, executed with dexterity the *Improvisations,* fragments of the delicious ballet from *Thaïs* and the famous *Toccata* which was a triumph for this very young artist.[53]

---

51. Paris, Archives Nationales, F[21] 5351 (1E): "Devant l'insuccès de mes démarches tendant à obtenir les mesures de convenance que me semblait comporter l'exécution de la décision liberale de M. le Ministre de l'Instruction publique et des Beaux-Arts, ma fille renonce à se présenter au Concours d'Essai pour lequel elle s'est fait inscrire."

52. In the realm of the Conservatoire, the "grand-bourgeois" attitude of Juliette Toutain and her family was notorious, as a letter from 8 April 1901 by Maurice Ravel to their common classmate Florent Schmitt reveals. Schmitt had left for Rome and tried to correspond with Juliette Toutain: "Il y a lieu de douter que vous receviez jamais une lettre de Mlle Toutain, une demoiselle ne devant pas correspondre avec un jeune homme. Cet argument, fourni par la mère de la jeune personne, m'a paru spécieux, ayant toujours considéré une femme faisant de la fugue comme quelque peu hermaphrodite." In Maurice Ravel, *Lettres, écrits, entretiens,* ed. Arbie Orenstein (Paris: Flammarion, 1989), 65.

53. *Le Ménestrel* 61 (1895): 215: "Chez Mme Toutain, audition d'œuvres de Massenet. *La Marche de Szabady,* à deux pianos à quatre mains, arrangée et jouée par Mme L. Filliaux-Tiger et Mlle Toutain, a brillamment ouvert la séance. Mlle Toutain, dont le sérieux talent est déjà si connu, a exécuté avec dextérité les *Improvisations,* des fragments du délicieux ballet de *Thaïs* et la célèbre *Toccata* qui a été un triomphe pour cette si jeune artiste."

Toutain also performed in concerts of the Société Nationale de Musique, another semi-public musical space whose programs were by invitation only, with talented socialites such as Henriette Fuchs appearing side by side with professional musicians.[54] Even the final "public" competitions of the Conservatoire were located in a respectable and controlled environment with restricted public access, and women had been taking part in them since the Conservatoire was founded. Toutain's activities prior to her enrollment in the *Prix de Rome* competition were still—if only just—appropriate for a "jeune fille rangée." But by 1903, twenty-five-year-old Toutain was no longer a young girl; if she had continued to compete for the *Prix de Rome,* she would have had to remain unmarried, since the rules demanded that the candidates—male or female—be single. But candidates very rarely won the *Premier Grand Prix de Rome* on their first attempt. Had Toutain chosen to continue her pursuit of the prize, her marriage might have been delayed until she was twenty-eight or twenty-nine years old. Her class and upbringing made such a deferral difficult to negotiate, since marriage and motherhood still defined the success of a *bourgeoise.*[55]

Whatever the reasons, Toutain's exclusion from the first round of the 1903 *Prix de Rome* competition turned into a public scandal when the Toutains received a letter from Théodore Dubois—*after* she had already withdrawn from the competition—in which her requests were granted:

> The Director of the Conservatoire consequently sent a recorded letter to Monsieur Toutain, which had the date of 3 May on the envelope and at the head of the letter the number 2, clearly written over the number 3. This alteration can be explained only if one remembers the date when the competition began in Compiègne, on the morning of [2] May.[56] In this letter, Monsieur Dubois announced that the Académie had agreed to all that Mon-

---

54. Juliette Toutain played the piano part in Florent Schmitt's *Chant du soir* for violin and piano in the Salle Erard on 4 February 1899. See Michel Duchesneau, *L'Avant-garde musicale à Paris de 1871 à 1939* (Liège: Mardaga, 1997), 259. I wish to thank Jann Pasler for this reference. Ricardo Viñes, who participated in the same concert, recorded his personal success in his diary and reported that he had turned pages for Juliette Toutain: "Chausson m'a félicité aussi, et Ravel, et Garban qui m'a tourné les pages et moi je les ai tournées pour Mademoiselle Toutain" (quoted in Nina Gubisch, "Le Journal inédit de Ricardo Viñes," *Revue Internationale de Musique Française* 1 [1980]: 154–248, 196). In 1902, Viñes mentioned Toutain's presence in the auditorium for the performance of Ravel's cantata *Semiramis* at the Conservatoire: "Toute la famille de Ravel était là, et aussi Fauré et Juliette Toutain et Février et Kœchlin, etc." (p. 199).

55. See Gabrielle Houbre, *La Discipline de l'amour: L'Education sentimentale des filles et des garçons à l'âge du Romantisme* (Paris: Plon, 1997), 244–54; Anne-Marie Sohn, *Femmes dans la vie privée (XIXe–XXe siècles),* 2 vols. (Paris: Publications de la Sorbonne, 1996), 69–73, 449–547; and Martin-Fugier, *La Bourgeoise,* 43–76.

56. The author of this text gives 3 May as the date for the *entrée en loge,* but the correct date is Saturday, 2 May 1903.

sieur Toutain had asked for. It was a bit late for Mademoiselle Toutain to go to Compiègne.⁵⁷

Toutain immediately wrote to the minister of Public Instruction, Joseph Chaumié, and asked that the competition, which was already under way, be annulled.⁵⁸ But Chaumié was away, and his deputy did not wish to take the decision upon himself. By the time the minister returned to Paris, the first round of the competition was over, and an annulment was ruled out. Outraged by this "abuse of power" by both the Conservatoire and the Académie, the Toutain family brought the incident to the attention of the Conseil d'Etat, and after the summer break, on 28 November 1903, it was even discussed in the Chambre des Députés. Such an affront to a highly placed state employee and his family provided moral grounds for their complaint and a guaranteed hearing. Both the Conservatoire and the Direction des Beaux-Arts were construed as guilty in the parliamentary debate: "You have rightly intended, Monsieur le Ministre, to open the *Prix de Rome* to young women. Everyone congratulates you on this good intention; however, good intentions of ministers are not enough if administrations forget them."⁵⁹ The incident had other consequences as well: at the end of June 1903, Dubois asked the Académie to relieve the Conservatoire administration of organizing the *Prix de Rome*; there had been too

---

57. Leudet, "Le Cas de Mlle Toutain," 4: "Le directeur du Conservatoire envoya alors une lettre recommandée à M. Toutain, portant sur l'enveloppe la date du 3 mai, et sur l'en-tête de lettre le chiffre 2, surchargeant visiblement le chiffre 3. Cette surcharge ne peut s'expliquer que si l'on se souvient de la date du commencement du concours à Compiègne, le [2] mai au matin. Dans cette lettre, M. Dubois annonçait que l'Académie avait accordé tout ce que M. Toutain avait demandé. Il était un peu tard pour que Mlle Toutain pût se rendre à Compiègne."

58. It was impossible for Toutain to join the competition belatedly on 3 May because the Catholic journal *La Croix* had prematurely made the poem public. This might be interpreted as further evidence that the incident was a willful attempt to keep specifically Toutain out of the competition.

59. "Séance du 28 Novembre 1903," in *Annales de la Chambre des Députés* (1904), 855: "Vous avez bien voulu, monsieur le ministre, ouvrir le concours de Rome aux jeunes filles. De cette bonne intention, tout le monde vous félicite; mais les bonnes intentions des ministres ne suffisent pas, quand les administrations les oublient." The sequence of events is presented unequivocally:

on n'a répondu que par un geste de refus et une fin de non-recevoir. Dans ces conditions, Mlle Toutain s'est vue obligée de retirer son inscription et le Conservatoire fut informé de sa détermination.

Or, quand on sut que la redoutable Mlle Toutain renonçait au concours, voici comment on opera: le matin même du 2 mai, à Compiègne, on fit savoir à Mlle Fleury, qui se présentait au concours, que l'on accordait à Mlle Fleury tout ce qu'on avait refusé à Mlle Toutain. Quant à M. Toutain, il ne fut averti de cette décision *in extremis* que par une lettre mise le lendemain, 3, à la poste.

I wish to thank Jann Pasler for a copy of the pages from the *Annales de la Chambre des Députés* that refer to the incident.

much trouble recently, "especially since the admittance of women."[60] As for Toutain, she never did participate in the *Prix de Rome*. She married in March 1904, and apart from occasional appearances as a pianist, her reputation was based mainly on her salon, where she received composers such as Saint-Saëns, Massenet, and her former teacher, Fauré.[61]

The official attention that this incident received was mirrored in its press coverage. For one week, such newspapers as *Le Temps, Le Figaro, Le Matin, Le Petit Journal,* and *Le Petit Parisien* published articles on the scandal and interviews with the parties involved. Toutain's portrait even appeared on the front pages, as in *Le Matin* on 10 May. The mystery-laden story contained enough newsworthy elements to pique the Third Republic readership's insatiable appetite for spicy *faits divers:* a young woman of good family had been wronged through the abuse of power by a "dark" government agency.[62] Now, for the first time, Toutain's own voice was heard in interviews and articles.

In her public appearances, Toutain sought to conform to the ideal image of a well-bred young lady. Journalists to whom she granted an interview described her as "amiable, elegant, with a svelte physiognomy and gestures full of grace."[63] A photograph in the fashionable music periodical *Musica* shows her surrounded by flowers, in a sumptuous evening dress, graciously leaning toward the piano in a self-consciously feminine pose, more the muse that she would eventually become than the composer she sought to be (Fig. 1). In his study of the murder trial of Henriette Caillaux, Edward Berenson has analyzed how essential the outward appearance of a woman was in determining public perception of her character.[64] Physical descriptions of a woman played a key role in newspaper reports, and the iconography of these portrayals was as accessible as that of pictures of saints,

---

60. *Procès verbaux* from 20 June 1903, AABA, shelf-mark 2E21, p. 82: "surtout depuis l'admission des femmes aux concours de Rome."

61. See the introduction of Jean Bureau for the exhibition catalogue *Rétrospective Jules Grün: 1868–1938,* Caen, Hôtel d'Escoville, 4–25 May 1975.

62. See Berenson, *The Trial of Madame Caillaux,* 210–35; Anne-Marie Thiesse, *Le Roman du quotidien: Lecteurs et lectures populaires à la Belle Epoque* (Paris: Le Chemin vert, 1984), 107–9; and Anne Cova, *Maternité et droits des femmes en France (XIXe–XXe siècles)* (Paris: Anthropos, 1997), 29–71.

63. *Le Petit Journal,* 10 May 1903, p. 1: "Aimable, élégante, la physionomie fine et le geste plein de grâce."

64. See Berenson, *The Trial of Madame Caillaux.* In this context, see also Anne Higonnet, "Frauenbilder," trans. Sylvia M. Schomburg-Scherff, in *19. Jahrhundert,* ed. Geneviève Fraisse and Michelle Perrot, vol. 4 of *Geschichte der Frauen,* ed. Georges Duby and Michelle Perrot (Frankfurt and New York: Campus Verlag, 1994), 313–65; Silverman, "The 'New Woman' "; and Virginia M. Allen, *The Femme Fatale: Erotic Icon* (Troy, N.Y.: Whitston Publishing Company, 1983).

Figure 1 Portrait of Juliette Toutain, by V. Michel. *Musica* 1 (1903): 141 (Bibliothèque Nationale de France, Cliché 94 B 138 804).

due to their relentless repetition in both press and popular novels.[65] These images were also a determining factor in the definition of a woman's public place. Toutain clearly set herself in the sphere of the elegant bourgeois salon through both her demeanor and her appearance, and the journalists translated this into code words that their readers would decipher without difficulty. Svelte grace, amiability, and elegance described the *bourgeoise* "grande dame" with aristocratic aspirations,[66] thus presenting Toutain's class, manners, and social role as those of a "lady of the leisure class."[67]

Toutain's own words echoed these images. In her article for *Musica* from that period, her rhetoric avoids all reference to women's professionalism in the guise of the *femme nouvelle*. Accompanied by such carefully chosen pictures as Figure 1, her reasoning presented her as a "true woman" of deep emotion. Being a "woman-artist," she claimed, corresponds to female nature in a much more essential way than any other—already practiced—form of study such as medicine because it takes advantage of the feminine leaning toward sentiment instead of favoring masculine intellect:[68] "I love these two hyphenated words [women-artists]. The receptive nature of the woman, her capacity to feel very deeply and very quickly the slightest things, her gifts of assimilation prove the woman as a being particularly able to seize and render the beauty of forms and sounds."[69] Women could

---

65. See Thiesse, *Le Roman du quotidien*, 144–45, 158–65.

66. When the fashionable periodical *La Grande Dame* was launched in 1893, the editorial policy statement defined elegance: "Ce qui s'appelle 'l'élégance' n'est pas simplement un art subtil de se vêtir et de se loger. Le mot caractérise aussi bien une certaine façon de sentir, de penser et de vivre. S'il y a une fantaisie tout extérieure, fille de la mode et du caprice, il y a, de même, une intime distinction, faite de raison malicieuse et de souriante dignité avec laquelle on naît et que l'éducation perfectionne. Une femme peut dédaigner la toilette, rester indifférente aux artifices luxueux de la coquetterie et, néanmoins, être un modèle de grace et de séduction. On est aristocrate,—et nous prenons le mot dans son acception la plus générale,—en sa conversation, en ses lectures, en ses ouvrages familiers, par la justesse aiguisée de ce qu'on pense et le tour de ce qu'on dit, par son attitude, enfin. Mais, sous ses formes diverses, le sens de l'exquis reste l'infaillible instrument de règne, bien plus puissant que la beauté et qui fait de la femme l'éternelle charmeresse" (*La Grande Dame: Revue de l'élégance et des arts* 1 [1893]: 2).

67. Smith, *Ladies of the Leisure Class*. Code words in the press were used with regard not only to women but to French society in general. See Eugen Weber, *France: Fin de Siècle* (Cambridge, Mass., and London: The Belknap Press of Harvard University Press, 1986), 44–45.

68. On the attribution of emotional and intellectual qualities to women in nineteenth-century France, see Christine Battersby, *Gender and Genius: Towards a Feminist Perspective* (Bloomington and Indianapolis: Indiana University Press, 1989); Citron, *Gender and the Musical Canon*, 44–54; and Berenson, *The Trial of Madame Caillaux*, 100–117. With respect to artistic creativity, see the arguments discussed in Garb, *Sisters of the Brush*, 105–17.

69. "Mlle Juliette Toutain & le concours de Rome . . . ," *Musica* 1 (1903): 140: "J'aime ces deux mots [femmes-artistes] accouplés. La nature impressionnable de la femme, ses facultés de ressentir très profondement et très rapidement les moindres choses, ses dons d'assimilation font de la femme un être particulièrement apte à saisir et à rendre la beauté des formes et des sons."

not be a threat to men, for whom music is a public profession, because "in music as in anything else, woman maintains such a different personality from man."[70] Toutain here taps into a well-established concept of "equality in difference," which tried to reconcile true republican womanhood with the emancipatory aspirations of women.[71] Her explicit statement that any competition between the sexes is but illusion reflects a discourse consciously employed by women to mitigate the perceived danger to the male establishment.[72] Indeed, this attitude is found consistently in the words of the women participants in the 1903 *Prix de Rome* competition. The painter Rondenay claimed that she participated only because the minister had opened up the possibility, neglecting to mention her earlier campaign to be admitted. Avoiding any display of ambition, she commented on passing the first round: "My success, as you call it, is of no great consequence. It just gives me the right to continue with the competition, but I have no hopes to figure among the last ten *logistes*.[73] That would certainly be pretentious on my part."[74] The sculptor Rozet and the second woman competitor for the composition prize, Hélène Fleury, expressed similar sentiments. Self-deprecation and the denial of a desire to win the prize were principal elements of a woman's rhetorical repertory. It was a strategy that would be used by the next female *Prix de Rome* competitors as well.[75]

Lesley Wright has recently shown that musical talent was only one of the factors in the competition's political game.[76] The influence of the teacher, the competitor's friends, and his—or her—own maneuvering among the jurors carried at least as much weight. For women, it was essential to find

70. Ibid.: "la femme, en musique comme en tout, conserve une personnalité tellement différente de celle de l'homme."
71. "[Ernest] Legouvé's slogan of 'equality in difference' became the leitmotif of the organized republican movement for women's rights, and the reform program he had outlined, their program during the early Third Republic" (Karin Offen, "Ernest Legouvé and the Doctrine of 'Equality in Difference' for Women: A Case Study of Male Feminism in Nineteenth-Century Thought," *Journal of Modern History* 58 [1986]: 452–84, 454). For a broader perspective on this issue, see Joan Wallach Scott, *Only Paradoxes to Offer: French Feminists and the Rights of Man* (Cambridge, Mass., and London: Harvard University Press, 1996).
72. In her article "*Noble et grande servante de la musique*," Jeanice Brooks shows how this form of discourse became an essential element in the strategy that Nadia Boulanger and her entourage used in order to make her career as female conductor possible.
73. The number of *logistes* for the final round was different in each of the five competitions (sculpture, painting, engraving, architecture, and music).
74. "Le Concours de Rome," *Le Matin,* 1 April 1903, p. 1: "Mon succès, comme vous dites, est sans grande conséquence. Il me confère simplement le droit de continuer le concours, mais je n'espère nullement figurer parmi les dix logistes définitifs. Ce serait de ma part vraiment de la prétention."
75. Recent research in women's biography and autobiography has shown that this form of rhetorical negotiation persists today. See, for example, Carolyn Heilbrun, *Writing a Woman's Life* (New York and London: W. W. Norton, 1988); Linda Wagner-Martin, *Telling Women's Lives: The New Biography* (New Brunswick, N.J.: Rutgers University Press, 1994).
76. Wright, "Bias."

a form of self-representation that would persuade the *Prix de Rome* jury to open the gates to official acknowledgment. Through her behavior, appearance, and language, Toutain personified the true daughter of a society lady and a highly ranked civil servant of the Third Republic, which made her both dangerous and vulnerable. Indeed, when this well-bred young woman crossed the boundary of the feminine sphere into the public domain of official art, she created a threatening dissonance between the horizon of expectation that her performance of a traditionally feminine persona evoked, and her professional aspirations. In contrast to the vicomtesse de Grandval, the baroness Willy de Rothschild, or Armande de Polignac, Toutain was not a privately trained aristocrat indulging herself with a musical career; nor did her family come from the white-collar or middle class, which—apart from musical families—was the most common background for female musicians.[77] She embodied the political and cultural power of the *grande bourgeoisie,* the social elite of the Third Republic. But this elevated social status also explains Toutain's vulnerability. She was trapped in a strict code of *bourgeois* behavior that would not forgive such transgressions as an unchaperoned sojourn in secluded premises with individuals of the opposite sex. Her own social performance offered the ideal means of keeping her out of the competition, and her exclusion was vital at this stage, because of all the candidates in the 1903 competition, she was the best prepared. Though she might not have won the final round, her recognized skills in counterpoint and fugue, as shown by her first prize at the Conservatoire in 1902, were superior to those of most of her co-competitors,[78] including—as will be seen—her classmate Maurice Ravel.

Hélène Fleury: Professionalism, *Camaraderie,* and Unobtrusiveness

Juliette Toutain was not the only female participant in the 1903 competition. As noted in *Le Ménestrel,* the very first woman to enroll for the *Prix de Rome* in composition was Hélène Fleury, a student of Charles-Marie Widor: "Well, and Mademoiselle Toutain? Does she let herself be overtaken? . . . Mademoiselle Hélène Fleury, student of Monsieur Widor, has just been enrolled for the next competition in musical composition. The name of Mademoiselle Hélène Fleury is thus the first female name to be

---

77. This observation is based on a survey of the *Registres d'inscription des élèves admis au Conservatoire,* Paris, Archives Nationales, Série AJ^{37} 391–96.

78. See her teachers' comments in the "Rapports des professeurs" of the Conservatoire, which without exception are glowing; terms such as "excellente élève," "élève de 1er ordre," and "élève très remarquable" recur regularly (Paris, Archives Nationales, Série AJ^{37} 293–98).

inscribed in the annals of the Rome competition."[79] These two contestants provided bemused male journalists with an ideal opportunity to stage their participation as a cat fight: on the one hand was the "mondaine" and "redoubtable" Mademoiselle Toutain, on the other Mademoiselle Fleury, "a very kind young woman, tall, with a most intelligent manner and a simplicity which does not exclude distinction."[80] Again, code words place the subject in a specific social context. Fleury emerges as a specimen of a relatively new female breed: the *femme nouvelle,* that is, the young, professional, middle-class woman who strives for social, economic, and political power. Her "intelligent manner" demonstrates her professional aspirations, and her "simplicity" her republican middle-class background.

Indeed, Fleury came from such a middle-class family. Her father's profession is given as "licencié en droit" in the transcription of her birth certificate, and he is later referred to as a provincial "fonctionnaire."[81] At the time of the 1903 *Prix de Rome,* twenty-six-year-old Fleury had begun to establish herself as an independent music teacher of middle- and upper-class girls.[82] She had published an organ composition and several piano pieces, among them her "valse de salon" *Espérance* (1897), and according to *Le Monde musical,* she had several pieces performed in concerts of the Société des Compositeurs de Musique and the Société de Musique Nouvelle.[83] Her training at the Conservatoire had only recently begun: she joined Charles-Marie Widor's composition class in 1899.[84] Unlike Toutain —and later Nadia Boulanger—Fleury did not collect the Conservatoire's end-of-year prizes. In 1899, her teacher found her "progressing but not mature enough for the competition (wait)."[85] In 1900, she participated in the fugue competition without success, and in 1901, she fell ill; finally, in 1902, Fleury left the Conservatoire without a prize. These awards were not trivial. They constituted official recognition of professional musical

---

79. *Le Ménestrel* 69 (1903): 111: "Eh bien, et Mlle Toutain? Elle se laisse donc dévancer? . . . Mlle Hélène Fleury, élève de M. Widor, vient de se faire inscrire pour le prochain concours de composition musicale. Le nom de Mlle Hélène Fleury est donc le premier nom féminin qui sera inscrit dans les annales du concours de Rome."

80. *Le Petit Journal,* 10 May 1903, p. 2: "C'est une jeune fille fort aimable, grande, l'air très intelligent, avec une simplicité qui n'exclut pas la distinction."

81. *Registres d'inscription des élèves admis au Conservatoire,* Paris, Archives Nationales, Série AJ³⁷ 395, p. 93; "La première candidate au prix de Rome," *L'Illustration,* 21 May 1904, p. 351.

82. Her advertisement in the *Annuaire des artistes et de l'enseignement musical* (Paris, 1903), 29, reads as follows: "Hélène Fleury / Compositeur-Pianiste / Professeur de Piano / Harmonie, Contrepoint / Cours d'Accompagnement / Leçons en Français, Allemand, Anglais / 43, Rue de Douai, 43 / Mercredi de 4 à 6 heures."

83. *Le Monde Musical* 15 (1903): 132.

84. Before Hélène Fleury joined the Conservatoire, she studied with H. Dallier.

85. "Rapports des professeurs," Paris, Archives Nationales, Série AJ³⁷ 296, entry from 13 June 1899: "En progrès mais peu mure pour le concours (attendre)."

standards, and, especially in the case of private music teachers, they could take on the role that the all-important "brevet de capacité" had had for lay women teachers since 1819.[86] Fleury had made her name in the Parisian musical world not through garnering Conservatoire prizes but through participating in the more avant-garde Parisian concert life. Nevertheless, the *Prix de Rome* could provide her with both official artistic recognition and, finally, a legitimizing prize.

Although the musical press considered Fleury a serious candidate when she entered the competition in 1903,[87] the general public became aware of her only after the Toutain scandal. Through her professional and unobtrusive demeanor, Fleury proved herself the ideal female candidate who could be held up as a model by those critical of Toutain. Théodore Dubois, for example, explicitly referred to Fleury's proper conduct on numerous occasions, such as in the letter that he wrote to Toutain's father after Juliette withdrew[88] and in his interviews with *Le Petit Parisien*, *Le Petit Journal*, and *Le Matin*.[89] Dubois pointed out that by presenting herself at Compiègne and thus implicitly trusting the patriarchal authority of the Conservatoire and the Académie, Fleury benefited from all the precautions taken to preserve the good reputation of women candidates. Indeed, correct behavior here consisted in placing faith in the state institutions to care for their "dependents" in the best possible way, rather than in challenging their sense of responsibility as had Toutain and her family. That Toutain might have been right not to rely on Roujon and Dubois was never acknowledged, and Fleury served as living proof of their unimpeachable behavior.

Once the Toutain scandal hit the newspapers, Fleury was trapped. She could either criticize the institutions and go down with Toutain, or she would have to show herself loyal to the Conservatoire and Académie by actively participating in the cat fight that both the press and the Conservatoire had staged. Although Fleury carefully avoided any direct reference to Toutain, she chose to align herself with the two institutions. It was the only strategy she could adopt if she wished to retain any chance of success

---

86. Jo Burr Margadant, *Madame le Professeur: Women Educators in the Third Republic* (Princeton: Princeton University Press, 1990), 19. On the corporate identity of French women teachers in the nineteenth century, see Anne T. Quartararo's highly informative study *Women Teachers and Popular Education in Nineteenth-Century France: Social Values and Corporate Identity at the Normal School Institution* (Newark: University of Delaware Press, 1995).

87. See, for example, the comparison between Toutain and Fleury in *Le Monde Musical* 15 (1903): 132.

88. The letter is quoted in the *Procès verbaux* of the Académie des Beaux-Arts, giving the date of 2 May 1903, with no reference to the dispute about its being sent on 3 May instead. Dubois writes: "Or ce matin j'ai obtenu tout ce que vous demandiez et dont profitera seule Mad[lle] Fleury, puisque Mad[lle] votre fille n'a pas jugé à propos de se présenter" (*Procès verbaux* for the meeting on 9 May 1903, AABA, shelf-mark 2E21, p. 57).

89. See *Le Petit Parisien*, 10 May 1903, p. 2; *Le Petit Journal*, 10 May 1903, pp. 1–2; and *Le Matin*, 10 May 1903, p. 1.

in future competitions: to alienate the Conservatoire through criticism would have been counterproductive. In an interview with *Le Petit Journal,* she described her sojourn in Compiègne: "I can only be delighted with everyone. The service of my *loge* was provided by a woman, and she also served my lonely meals. . . . During the first three days, I ate alone in this manner. Then my nine competitors of the stronger sex insisted that I dine at their table, and, what can I say, I capitulated."[90] The interview is interesting not only for its implicit criticism of Toutain—who insisted on taking meals and recreation apart from the men in obedience to good manners—but also for its rhetoric. In order to present herself as unthreatening and feminine, Fleury (or the journal's editor) used the traditional language of courtship in which a woman finally submits to the insistence of a man. In an interview in *Le Petit Parisien,* Fleury was even more critical of Toutain—although again without explicit mention of her—calling the precaution of separate dining and recreation space "exaggerated" and "unreasonable."[91] But the author of the article made sure he did not portray Fleury as an ill-bred young woman of loose morals. Before quoting her potentially inflammatory words, he characterized her as "all blonde and rosy, smiling, [and] as friendly as can be."[92] This description would have sounded familiar to the paper's readers, for it echoed that of the pure and good-natured heroine of popular novels often serialized in the press underneath the news of the day.[93]

Fleury's unobtrusiveness and professionalism became apparent again when she participated in the competition the following year. Although she seemed intent on keeping a low profile, her picture appeared in several papers after she was admitted to the final round. As in the case of Toutain, these photographs reflected the persona she tried to convey. In Figure 2, Fleury demurely poses at the edge of the group of competitors in front of the Château de Compiègne.[94] She looks confidently into the camera lens, her sober appearance congruent with countless pictures of other professional women, although the richness of her fur collar and hat identifies her as a lady of some means as opposed to a woman of lesser status such as a primary-school teacher. Nor would anyone mistake Fleury for a dilettante society-lady here. She creates an impression of well-calculated strictness; neither feathers nor frills draw the observer's attention to her femininity. A

---

90. *Le Petit Journal,* 10 May 1903, p. 2: "Je n'ai qu'à me féliciter de tout le monde. Le service de ma loge était fait par une femme et c'est elle qui me servait mes repas solitaires. . . . Pendant les trois premiers jours, j'ai mangé seule, de cette façon. Puis, mes neuf concurrents du sexe fort insistèrent pour que je vinsse à leur table et, ma foi, j'ai capitulé."
91. *Le Petit Parisien,* 10 May 1903, p. 2: "Mais les précautions exagérées qui consistent à vous faire déjeuner et dîner à part, promener à part, comme un petit fauve, n'ont rien de raisonnable. Les logistes de Compiègne sont des gens de bonne société, qu'on se le dise!"
92. Ibid.: "Toute blonde et rose, souriante, affable au possible."
93. See Thiesse, *Le Roman du quotidien,* 107–9.
94. Published on the front page of *Le Monde Musical* 16 (30 May 1904).

Figure 2 Portrait of the six candidates for the *Prix de Rome* in 1904, photographed in front of the Château de Compiègne on 21 May 1904. They are, from left to right, Paul Pierné, Philippe Gaubert, Raymond Pech, Victor Gallois, Raymond Saurat, and Hélène Fleury. Front page of *Le Monde Musical* 16 (1904) (Bibliothèque Nationale de France, Cliché 94 B 139 181).

second picture (Fig. 3) conveys a similar message: the seriousness of her artless hair and severe pose virtually contradict the frivolous "sea spray" effect of her elegant evening dress.[95] The semiotic impact of the portrait becomes all the stronger in the context of its publication in *L'Illustration*, which featured photographs of fashionable *bourgeoises* and aristocrats in each issue. As if to underline this reading of the photograph, the accompanying text refers to Fleury as "hard-working," "courageous," and "valiant."[96]

---

95. Published in *L'Illustration*, 21 May 1904, p. 351. On the issue of photographic message and rhetoric, see Roland Barthes's still fundamental essays "Le Message photographique" (1961) and "Rhétorique de l'image" (1964), published in Roland Barthes, *L'Obvie et l'obtus: Essais critiques III* (Paris: Seuil, 1982), 9–42.

96. *L'Illustration*, 21 May 1904, p. 351.

Figure 3 Portrait of Hélène Fleury. *L'Illustration*, 21 May 1904, p. 351. By permission of The British Library.

Such exemplary behavior merited reward, and in 1904 Fleury found herself with a *Deuxième Second Grand Prix* for a cantata with "expressive declamation" and "skillful instrumentation."[97] But she achieved her success —hailed as the inauguration of the "official triumphs of feminism in musical art"[98]—through not only her musical skill but also her self-representation as a good "republican" woman-professional obedient to the Académie and Conservatoire in both the 1903 and the 1904 competitions. When the prizes were awarded at the Conservatoire, Joseph Chaumié, still minister of Public Instruction, found reason to congratulate himself as he praised this first female winner in the *Prix de Rome*:

> You may remember that I decided two years ago that women would be allowed to participate in the competition for the *Prix de Rome*. This created quite a stir and caused much ink to flow. This measure, approved by some, was considered by others as a criminal concession to new tendencies that did not find approval in their eyes. They took comfort, however, in thinking that the minister's decision would remain a dead letter, that no woman would compete for a long time, and that, more or less, the inevitable failures would quickly cure them of such ambition. A student of the Conservatoire, Mademoiselle Fleury, student of Monsieur Widor, has wasted no time in giving these predictions a brilliant refutation. In this very year, she has received the second *Grand Prix*. With enthusiasm I applaud this fine success, which far exceeds the usual importance—as big as it otherwise may be—of this high reward. In effect, it is not just a prize that Mademoiselle Fleury has won; it is an act of possession that she has carried out over a domain from which an obsolete tradition wanted to keep women away. She has made a conquest.[99]

Hélène Fleury had indeed conquered a portion of art's public arena. But it would be seven more years before the first woman—sculptor Lucienne Heuvelmans—would win a *Premier Grand Prix*. Up to this point, Fleury's participation in the *Prix de Rome* followed the usual pattern of successful

---

97. *Procès verbaux* from 2 July 1904, AABA, shelf-mark 2E21, p. 261: "Mad^{lle} Fleury, déclamation expressive; instrumentation habile."

98. *Musica* 3 (1904): 368: "Mlle Fleury . . . inaugure ainsi les triomphes officiels du féminisme dans l'art musical."

99. *Le Ménestrel* 70 (1904): 251: "Il y a deux ans, vous vous en souvenez, je décidais que les femmes seraient admises à prendre part au concours pour le prix de Rome. Cela fit quelque bruit et verser pas mal d'encre. La mesure, approuvée par les uns, fut considérée par d'autres comme une concession condamnable à des tendances nouvelles qui ne trouvaient pas grâce à leurs yeux. Ceux-ci s'en consolaient cependant, en pensant que la décision du ministre resterait à l'état de lettre morte, qu'aucune femme ne concourrait de longtemps, et que, tout au moins, d'inévitables échecs les guériraient vite de pareille ambition. Une élève du Conservatoire, Mlle Fleury, élève de M. Widor, n'a pas tardé à donner à ces prévisions un éclatant démenti. Cette année même, elle a obtenu le second grand prix. J'applaudis des deux mains à ce beau succès qui dépasse la portée ordinaire, quelque grande qu'elle soit, de cette haute récompense. Ce n'est pas seulement un prix, en effet, que Mlle Fleury a obtenu, c'est la prise de possession qu'elle a effectuée, d'un domaine à l'écart duquel une tradition surannée voulait maintenir les femmes, c'est une conquête qu'elle a accomplie."

candidates, in which the crown of the first prize was approached gradually. Contestants would generally participate at least twice if not three or four times,[100] working their way up from admission to the final round, then to winning second prizes and—possibly—the *Grand Prix de Rome* itself. Fleury's next step might lead, for example, to the *Premier Second Grand Prix.*

Whereas in the seven years prior to her prize (1897–1904) Fleury had published only one piece for organ and six for piano, she now brought out seven compositions for various scorings within one year, most of them with Enoch & Cie. Her success encouraged women composers to participate in the *Prix de Rome,* and in the following year, she was joined by Marthe Grumbach, a student of Fauré, and Marguerite Audan, like Fleury a student of Widor. None of them, however, moved on to the final round. They were in good company: one of the male candidates who failed to reach the final stage was Maurice Ravel, who had won the *Deuxième Second Grand Prix* in 1901. Thus, two former prizewinners were excluded from the competition after the first round. This was unheard of, and suddenly Fleury found herself at the center of the next *Prix de Rome* scandal. As the press reported, "Since the foundation of the *Prix de Rome,* we have never seen permission to compete for the first prize withheld from the second *grands prix* of the previous year."[101]

The party responsible for this astounding breach of tradition was easily identified as Charles Lenepveu, one of the three composition teachers at the Conservatoire and the only Conservatoire teacher involved in the 1905 *Prix de Rome* jury because of his seat in the Académie. All six candidates admitted to the final round were in fact his students. Not a single student of either Widor or Fauré proceeded further in the competition. The focus of the scandal, however, soon shifted from the biased treatment of two candidates—Fleury and Ravel—to concentrate merely on Ravel, the hope of the young male avant-garde. Ravel's supporters kept him in the spotlight; they did not bother to extend their outrage to include Fleury's case.[102] Yet one element of Lenepveu's plot to eliminate all but his own

---

100. For example, Claude Delvincourt, who won the second available *Premier Prix* in 1913—the prize was not awarded in 1912 and was instead given in the following year—had competed five times before.

101. *Le Matin,* 21 May 1905, quoted in Gail Hilson Woldu, "Au-delà du scandale de 1905," *Revue de Musicologie* 82 (1996): 245–67, 248: "On n'a jamais vu, depuis la fondation du Prix de Rome, les seconds grands prix d'une année n'être pas admis à concourir pour le premier, l'année suivante."

102. Neither Arbie Orenstein nor Marcel Marnat mention Hélène Fleury in their account of the 1905 scandal or in the annotations to Ravel's letters. This biased coverage of the event turns the scandal into a personal vendetta of the conservative jury against a young avant-garde composer instead of taking into account the wider ramifications of the incident. See Arbie Orenstein, *Ravel: Man and Musician* (New York and London: Columbia University Press, 1975); Marcel Marnat, *Maurice Ravel* (Paris: Fayard, 1986); and Ravel, *Lettres, écrits, entretiens,* ed. Orenstein.

students might have been his desire to ensure that no woman candidate would proceed to the final round, and all three women were students of either Fauré or Widor.[103] It would be ironic indeed, if Ravel's exclusion was due—at least in part—to Lenepveu's well-known opposition to official recognition of women as composers. In fact, from the moment he stopped teaching the women's harmony class at the Conservatoire because of his accession to the late Ernest Guiraud's composition class in 1894, Lenepveu did not admit a single woman to his course. All his other colleagues (Massenet, Dubois, Fauré, and Widor) regularly had women composition students attending their classes. It appears almost as if Lenepveu wished to purge himself of having taught a female class for several years during the 1880s and 1890s. Preventing women from succeeding in the *Prix de Rome* would certainly have been one way of achieving that aim.

Hélène Fleury did not participate in the *Prix de Rome* competition again. The reasons are not clear, given that she had one more year in which she could compete before turning thirty on 21 June 1906. She did marry, but publications suggest that she did so after 1910. Most probably she lost confidence in the competition and recognized her second prize as the glass ceiling for female contestants. Fleury received at least some official acknowledgment after the scandal, though, when she was asked to compose the official end-of-year competition piece for the viola class of the Conservatoire, possibly a public gesture of support from the new director, Gabriel Fauré.[104]

Nadia Boulanger: Aristocratic Behavior and the Rules of the Competition

While Hélène Fleury continued her career as a piano teacher and composer after 1905, receiving less and less public attention, a new female star entered the arena of the *Prix de Rome* in the person of Nadia Boulanger. Already in 1904, Arthur Pougin had mentioned her name in the context of Fleury's success, asking, "Who knows if she will not triumph in the *Grand Prix de Rome* as once did her father?"[105] Sixteen-year-old Nadia had just won three important first prizes at the Conservatoire in a single year: fugue,

---

103. Jann Pasler is currently preparing a study on the politics of the Académie and Conservatoire, which includes a thorough examination of Lenepveu's undertakings and aims during that period.

104. *Fantaisie* for viola and piano, Op. 18, published in 1906 by Enoch & Cie with the note on the title page: "imposée au Concours du Conservatoire (Année 1906)."

105. *Le Ménestrel* 70 (1904): 251: "Qui sait si maintenant elle ne triomphera pas, comme autrefois son père, du grand prix de Rome." Ernest Boulanger won the *Prix de Rome* in 1835. He became a successful composer of *opéras-comiques* and a singing teacher at the Conservatoire.

organ, and piano accompaniment. And, indeed, her next goal was the *Prix de Rome*. After a year of intensive preparation, she entered the competition in 1906, but both women participants of that year—Marthe Grumbach tried her luck again—failed to proceed to the final round. In the next year, 1907, Boulanger was the only female participant among the fourteen candidates, and although she was one of the six to continue to the next stage, she did not receive a prize for her cantata. So far, she was following the usual path of candidates eventually successful in winning the *Prix de Rome*. Accordingly, her then composition tutor Charles-Marie Widor analyzed what had gone wrong with her 1907 submission and advised her on changes she should make in the following year:

> Pugno[106] will tell you what we said about your cantata: your technique is superior to that of all the competitors; unfortunately, the effect was much diminished in the great hall of the Institute; furthermore, the contrasting effects of full sound and "pp" (which we had tried to achieve the day before) were forgotten by your interpreters . . . thus some monotony. One of the reasons for Le Boucher's success was the colorings which Madame Mellot Jaubert was able to give to the solo scene, a very beautiful scene handled very dramatically besides. So, we are going to work on this external and decorative side of things in the coming year: as for the fundamentals, you have nothing more to learn. Be assured that I am very devoted to and interested in your success, to that which is due to you.[107]

This letter is interesting for several reasons. First, it shows that Boulanger had Widor's full support, based on his high opinion of the quality of her work. Second, it allows an insight into the preparations for the *Prix de Rome:* candidates went through their unsuccessful cantatas with their teachers, analyzing weak points that required further development. Thus, Boulanger, by now twenty years old, was well prepared for the next competition in 1908. Once again, she was the only woman to participate, together with nine male candidates, and this time she chose to distinguish herself by challenging the Académie. As already mentioned, candidates had to compose a four-part vocal fugue and a short chorus with orchestral

---

106. Raoul Pugno (1852–1914), a pianist and composer of high renown, was one of Nadia Boulanger's mentors and a friend of the family.

107. Letter from Charles-Marie Widor to Nadia Boulanger, 30 June 1907, Bibliothèque Nationale de France, Département de la Musique (hereafter *F-Pn*), n.l.a.69, nos. 181–82: "Pugno vous dira comment nous avons parlé de votre cantate: votre technique est supérieure à celle de tous les concurrents; malheureusement l'effet s'est trouvé très diminué dans la grande salle de l'Institut; de plus les effets d'opposition de son et de 'pp' (que nous avions cherchés l'avant-veille) ont été oubliés par vos interprètes . . . de là quelque monotonie. Une des raisons du succès de Le Boucher se trouve dans les colorations qu'a su donner Mme Mellot Jaubert à la scène solo, scène très dramatiquement traitée d'ailleurs, fort belle. Enfin, nous travaillerons le côté extérieur, décoratif des choses l'an prochain: quand au fond, vous n'avez rien à apprendre. Croyez-moi bien devoué et intéressé à votre succès, à celui qui vous est dû."

Example 1 Jules Massenet's fugue subject for the 1879 *Prix de Rome*. "Grands Prix de Rome: Sujets de fugue," Paris, Archives Nationales, F²¹ 5351.4E.

Example 2 Charles Gounod's fugue subject for the 1889 *Prix de Rome*. "Grands Prix de Rome: Sujets de fugue," Paris, Archives Nationales, F²¹ 5351.4E.

accompaniment. Boulanger's setting of the given text—Sully Prud'homme's poem *L'Hirondelle*[108]—acceded to these demands. Her fugue did not.

Each year, the fugue subject was invented by one of the composers of the Académie. Traditionally, the theme had a rather sedate character, such as Massenet's subject for the competition in 1879 and Gounod's in 1889 (Exx. 1 and 2). But from time to time, it would be more lively, as were two examples by Thomas and Gounod (Exx. 3 and 4). The subject dictated by Camille Saint-Saëns in 1908 (Ex. 5), which Nadia Boulanger had to develop in her fugue, fell into the latter category,[109] and its instrumental character inspired her to compose a string quartet instead of a vocal piece (Ex. 6). At least, this is what she claimed. According to Léonie Rosenstiel, Boulanger's inherent "rebelliousness" might also have partly accounted for this breach of practice.[110] Whatever her reasons, her action precipitated the next *Prix de Rome* scandal.[111]

When on 9 May 1908 Nadia Boulanger arrived with her musicians in the room in which her pieces were to be judged, one member of the jury— probably Saint-Saëns—objected that her fugue should not be allowed to

---

108. *F-Pn*, Ms. 3897; set for 2 flutes, 2 oboes, 2 clarinets, 2 bassoons, 4 horns, 2 harps, strings, mixed choir.

109. I have been unable to establish whether the subject that Saint-Saëns dictated to the *Prix de Rome* candidates in Compiègne had been composed by him or—as Lili Boulanger mentions in her diaries (see Lili Boulanger, *Agenda* for 1908, *F-Pn*, Rés.Vmf.ms.110, 2–7 May 1908)—by his friend Théodore Dubois. Usually the composer who dictated the subject was also the one who wrote it. Because of Saint-Saëns's reaction to Nadia Boulanger's fugue, however, I do assume that he was the author and felt insulted by the implicit criticism. But whatever the case, my following argument concerning Saint-Saëns's reaction would be the same, since both he and Dubois shared aesthetic values that were felt to be under attack by Nadia Boulanger's behavior.

110. Rosenstiel, *Nadia Boulanger*, 66.

111. For accounts of the 1908 events, see Rosenstiel, *Nadia Boulanger*, 65–73; Jérôme Spycket, *Nadia Boulanger* (Lausanne: Payot, 1987), 28–30; and Jeanice Brooks, "Noble et grande servante de la musique," 99.

Example 3 Ambroise Thomas's fugue subject for the 1885 *Prix de Rome*. "Grands Prix de Rome: Sujets de fugue," Paris, Archives Nationales, F²¹ 5351.4E.

Example 4 Charles Gounod's fugue subject for the 1892 *Prix de Rome*. "Grands Prix de Rome: Sujets de fugue," Paris, Archives Nationales, F²¹ 5351.4E.

Example 5 Camille Saint-Saëns's(?) fugue subject for the 1908 *Prix de Rome*, as given in Nadia Boulanger's submission. Paris, Bibliothèque Nationale de France, Ms. 3896.

be performed, since it did not adhere to the rules of the competition. The jury decided, however, to listen to Boulanger's pieces first and to settle the problematic issue of the string quartet later.[112] The outstanding musical quality of Boulanger's submissions finally outweighed her transgression of the rules. The jury allowed her to continue with the competition as one of the six finalists, given that the work of the remaining four was not of a sufficiently high standard to admit them to the *concours définitif* anyway.

> After all contestants had been heard, the jury proceeded to vote after a comparative scrutiny of the works. There also had to be examined again whether Mademoiselle Boulanger should not be removed from the competition for having substituted an instrumental fugue for a vocal one. While regretting that this contestant had not conformed strictly to the rules, the jury felt that exclusion might perhaps show excessive rigor toward an artist who had just given more than enough proof, as much by this otherwise satisfactory work as by her chorus with orchestra, of her compositional abilities. In admitting her to the final competition, the jury has used its prerogative of judgment for which it assumes full responsibility. What prompted it to give such a liberal interpretation to the rules was its awareness that the rights of the other contestants were not damaged. In fact, among the *ten* young composers whose

---

112. The jury consisted of the following composers: Théodore Dubois, Charles Lenepveu, Jules Massenet, Emile Paladhile, Ernest Reyer, Camille Saint-Saëns (members of the Académie) and the three supplementary annual judges Arthur Coquard, Paul Hillemacher, and André Wormser.

Example 6 Nadia Boulanger, *Fugue pour 2 Violons, Alto et Violoncelle*, mm. 1–11. Paris, Bibliothèque Nationale de France, Ms. 3896.

Note: The sixteenths on F in m. 3 (Alto) and m. 9 (1er Violon) were added in a different color.

merits had just been compared, only six by any reckoning had appeared worthy of admission [to the final competition].[113]

The judgment of the jury members was certainly informed by Nadia Boulanger's musicianship and family background, for most of them were friends of the Boulanger family. Other issues may have played some role, however, not least the recent scandal over Ravel's supposedly faulty fugue. Echoes of the public accusations of 1905—in which the jury failed to acknowledge the most important (male) avant-garde composer of the time—are found in the wording of their statement: they had avoided "excessive rigor toward an artist" who had shown "her compositional abilities." Another scandal so soon after the last two in 1903 and 1905 was certainly undesirable, but the jury's hope of preventing one was nevertheless destroyed, presumably by the insulted Saint-Saëns whose fugue subject was implicitly criticized, through Boulanger's composition, as inadequate to its purpose. The story of the instrumental fugue was skillfully leaked to journalists, and the "affaire fugue" made the front pages. Five years after the Toutain scandal, pictures of yet another woman candidate appeared in the press.[114] Even worse, when Gaston Doumergue, the minister of Public Instruction in 1908, received an anonymous complaint—probably from Saint-Saëns—about the jury's decision, he postponed the beginning of the final round for a week in order to give the Académie enough time to sort things out.[115] The Académie defended its decision, and Nadia Boulanger entered the second part of the contest with her co-competitors on 19 May 1908 (Fig. 4). Beforehand, she had tried to set matters right with Saint-Saëns, but in a bitter response he accused her of an ethically questionable act, saying that she had wanted only to "dazzle" the jury with her unusual fugue and was now laughing at their gullibility.[116]

---

113. *Procès verbaux* from 16 May 1908, AABA, shelf-mark 2E22, pp. 151–52: "Tous les concurrents ayant été entendus, le Jury a procédé au vote, après examen comparatif des ouvrages. Il y a eu à examiner à nouveau si, pour avoir substitué une fugue instrumentale à une fugue vocale, Mlle Boulanger ne devait pas être mise hors concours. Tout en regrettant que cette concurrente ne se fût pas conformée strictement à la lettre du règlement, le Jury a estimé que l'exclusion serait peut-être d'une rigueur excessive à l'égard d'une artiste qui venait de faire, tant par ce travail, d'ailleurs satisfaisant, que par son chœur avec orchestre, une preuve largement suffisante de ses aptitudes à la composition. En l'admettant au Concours final le Jury a usé d'un pouvoir d'appréciation dont il assume la responsabilité. Ce qui lui permettait de donner à la règle cette interprétation libérale, c'est qu'il avait conscience de ne léser, en l'espèce, les droits d'aucun des concurrents. En effet, sur le *dix* jeunes compositeurs dont il venait de comparer les mérites, six, seulement, en toute hypothèse, lui avaient paru mériter l'admissibilité."

114. The most detailed account of the press coverage is given in Rosenstiel, *Nadia Boulanger*, 66–67.

115. *Procès verbaux* from 16 May 1908, AABA, shelf-mark 2E22, p. 150.

116. The full letter and facsimiles of its first and last pages are reproduced in Spycket, *Nadia Boulanger*, 28–29: "Elève depuis plusieurs années d'une classe de composition, ayant

118 Journal of the American Musicological Society

Figure 4 Portrait of the six candidates for the *Prix de Rome* in 1908, photographed in front of the Château de Compiègne on 19 May 1908. Nadia Boulanger is surrounded by Marc Delmas, Edouard Flament, André Gailhard, Jules Mazellier, and Marcel Tournier. Photograph preserved in the Fondation Internationale Nadia et Lili Boulanger, Paris.

Under the eyes of a curious public, the six settings of the cantata *La Sirène* were judged on 14 July 1908. Henry Roujon, still the Secrétaire perpétuel, presided over both the specialist jury and the general assembly of the Académie. In the first round of voting by the specialist jury, the *Grand Prix de Rome* went to André Gailhard and thus once again to a student of Lenepveu.[117] For the *Premier Second Grand Prix*, four judges voted

---

déjà concouru, vous voulez faire croire que vous ignoriez les conditions du concours; il y en a qui vous croient et cela doit bien vous amuser. . . . Non, vous avez voulu éblouir. Pendant que vos camarades luttaient dans l'arène ingrate de la fugue d'école, vous avez évolué sur un autre terrain qui vous offrait de plus brillantes ressources; c'est une mauvaise action. . . . On aurait dû vous mettre hors concours."

117. Gailhard received his prize with five votes to four. This was hardly a resounding endorsement, but the five-vote majority on the first round suggests that Lenepveu manipulated matters in securing these votes in advance. On the relative power of teachers and mentors with respect to the *Prix de Rome*, see Wright, "Bias."

in favor of Boulanger's cantata and one for that of Edouard Flamant. Four abstained. In the second round, however, Boulanger retained only two votes, with seven judges abstaining. Their message was clear: only Boulanger's cantata was considered worthy of second place after Gailhard's, but under no circumstances would the daring contestant receive such a reward after the faux pas of her fugue. The prize was therefore not awarded. Next came the vote for the *Deuxième Second Grand Prix,* which Fleury had won in 1904. Again four judges—presumably the same as before—voted in Boulanger's favor; the other votes were split. Unusually, five more rounds of voting followed before a fifth judge joined the faithful four in their decision to award this prize to Nadia Boulanger.[118]

Whatever the quality of Boulanger's cantata, it was highly unlikely that she, a student of both Fauré and Widor, could have won the *Prix de Rome* when Lenepveu had two of his favorite students—André Gailhard and Jules Mazellier—in the competition. But that she did not receive the next lower prize probably had to do with both the "affaire fugue" and her sex. As a rule, the awarding of the *Premier Second Grand Prix* hailed the crown-prince(ss) of the following year, whereas the *Deuxième Second Grand Prix* merely acknowledged achievement without committing the Académie to future recognition. The lower second prize could thus be awarded to a woman since it did not represent a strong endorsement, particularly in such a high-profile case.

Nadia Boulanger's victory became the center of attention during the summer of 1908; celebrated as a *femme nouvelle* with the abilities necessary to achieve her goals in the male world of official art, she was tipped to win the 1909 *Prix de Rome.*[119] Even more than Fleury, Boulanger embodied the *femme nouvelle* of the musical world. So far, she had proven herself a very successful young professional woman, recognized by her peers and earning enough money to keep her family afloat. Not yet twenty years old, she held the piano accompaniment class at the private Conservatoire Femina-Musica, and she had an ever-growing circle of private pupils to whom she taught various theoretical and practical skills.[120] Her career as a concert pianist and organist was taking off, and her talent as a composer began to be recognized. Boulanger's background lay at the basis of her career, with

---

118. In the general election through the Académie, which included all members, from the painters to the architects, Boulanger received eleven votes of twenty-eight in the round for the *Premier Second Grand Prix,* and twenty in that for the *Deuxième Second Grand Prix* (*Procès verbaux* from 14 July 1908, AABA, shelf-mark 2E22, pp. 167–69). The awarding of a prize required the votes of at least half of those present.

119. Extracts from an article by Camille de Sainte-Croix (*La Petite République,* 22 July 1908) are given in English translation in Rosenstiel, *Nadia Boulanger,* 71–73.

120. Spycket reproduces a 1905 publicity announcement adorned with a stylish *art nouveau* engraving: "Mademoiselle Nadia BOULANGER reprendra le 15 Octobre ses leçons particulières de piano, orgue, harmonie, fugue et accompagnement, et recevra le Vendredi de 1 heure à 3 heures" (*Nadia Boulanger,* 26).

her father and his family well-known musicians and composers, and her mother a musical dilettante and Russian princess.[121] This combination of artistic and aristocratic lineage created a different context from the bourgeois surroundings in which Juliette Toutain and Hélène Fleury grew up. Self-expression that flouted convention was socially accepted if not expected in aristocratic circles,[122] and children, both male and female, in musical families traditionally had a better chance of a musical career.[123] Instead of interpreting Boulanger's gesture to compose an instrumental fugue as "rebellious," as Rosenstiel did, one might call it "aristocratic," an attitude that did not care for the opinion of the lesser—even if they were members of the Académie.

The public persona that Boulanger developed in these years expressed and emphasized the feminine success story of her recent career. Photographs of that time show an elegantly dressed young woman radiating self-confidence. A good example of this public image is a portrait from around 1910, in which she wears a classic tailored suit, as was most appropriate for a professionally active young woman; the soft pleats of her blouse and the appliqués on the sleeves add a discreet touch of femininity, however (Fig. 5).[124] Journalists who covered the story of her *Deuxième Second Grand Prix* commented upon her appearance, praising her beauty and modesty.[125] Boulanger, in gaining public acknowledgment of her musical achievements, had become a symbol for the *femme nouvelle*. Yet her self-confident and compelling embodiment of the new woman might have been one reason why the still conservative Académie refused to go along with the scenario that had been developed in the press during that summer of 1908: Nadia Boulanger did not become the first woman to win the *Prix de Rome*. In fact, in the 1909 competition she received no prize at all.

---

121. Rosenstiel doubts that Madame Boulanger—née Raïssa Myschetsky Shuvaliv—was a princess of the noble Tartar Myschetsky family and labels her an "adventuress" (Rosenstiel, *Nadia Boulanger*, 13–15). Whether or not she was of noble descent is of little consequence in this context, however, given that both her daughters believed firmly in their aristocratic lineage. See Spycket, *Nadia Boulanger*, 12.

122. See Weber, *France*, 27–40.

123. Reich, "Women as Musicians."

124. Rosenstiel's description of Nadia Boulanger as "ungainly and heavy-set" seems to be informed by an American fashion ideal of the 1970s and is far from corresponding to early twentieth-century concepts of femininity in France. And judging Boulanger as "exceptionally formal and reserved by Parisian standards" reveals Rosenstiel's complete lack of knowledge of French Third-Republic etiquette (Rosenstiel, *Nadia Boulanger*, 67). As Beatrix Borchard has observed, Rosenstiel seems to reproach Nadia Boulanger throughout her four-hundred-page biography for failing to correspond to her own ideal of fragile femininity, which Rosenstiel finds embodied in Lili Boulanger instead. See Beatrix Borchard, "Lili Boulanger—Eine Komponistin," in *Vom Schweigen befreit (3. Internationales Komponistinnen-Festival Kassel)—Lili Boulanger, 1893–1918*, ed. Roswitha Aulenkamp-Moeller and Christel Nies (Kassel: Internationales Forum "Vom Schweigen befreit" e.V., 1993), 28–37, 35.

125. Given in Rosenstiel, *Nadia Boulanger*, 69, 71.

Figure 5 Portrait of Nadia Boulanger, ca. 1910. Photograph preserved in the Fondation Internationale Nadia et Lili Boulanger, Paris.

It is interesting to see how the jury came to this conclusion. A *Prix de Rome* candidate could receive only a higher prize in successive competitions, never an equal or lower one. Thus Nadia Boulanger could only be awarded the *Premier Grand Prix* or the *Premier Second Grand Prix* in 1909.

When the jury of specialists cast their ballots on the first prize, Boulanger's cantata *Roussalka* received not a single vote. This can only have been a political decision, since no other candidate was judged to be sufficiently competent to receive the *Premier Grand Prix* in 1909. Consequently, the judges proposed that no first prize be awarded in that year: perhaps the time was not ripe for a female triumph in the competition. The next prize developed into a "duel" between two candidates: Lenepveu's student Jules Mazellier and Fauré's and Widor's student Nadia Boulanger. The jury of eight composers (not nine, for Jules Massenet, a declared Boulanger supporter, was not present) was equally divided for three rounds of voting, but decided in the end to give the prize to Mazellier.[126] This decision—a slap in the face for Boulanger—was political on two grounds: the sex of the candidates and the relative power of their teachers. Even more pronounced in its bias was the subsequent general decision by the Académie des Beaux-Arts as a whole, which decisively overthrew the recommendation of the jury of specialists. Mazellier was awarded the *Grand Prix de Rome,* and two other Lenepveu students—Jean Gallon and Marcel Tournier—received the second prizes. Whereas the specialist jury had demonstrated at least some artistic responsibility by not awarding the first prize at all, given that it could not go to the woman contestant who had deserved it, the Académie's vote was blatantly gender-biased and as misogynous as the opinions voiced in the Académie debates of 1903. Many musicians perceived Boulanger's well-performed cantata to be "the most expert and original composition,"[127] and "would have preferred to have seen the prize awarded to Mademoiselle Nadia Boulanger."[128] The *Deuxième Second Grand Prix,* it appears, continued to be the glass ceiling for a woman composer. In spite of public support in both the general and the musical press, Nadia Boulanger did not compete again for the *Prix de Rome.* Like Fleury, she had doubtless learned her lesson, as had the other female students of the Conservatoire. No woman competed for the prize in 1910 or 1911.

Lili Boulanger: Genius, Creativity, and the Icon of the *Femme fragile*

Only in 1912 did a woman again enter the competition for the *Prix de Rome* in composition. Lili Boulanger may have felt encouraged to take that step because a *Grand Prix de Rome* had at last been awarded to a woman,

---

126. *Procès verbaux* from 26 June 1909, AABA, shelf-mark 2E22, p. 172.
127. Critic in *Le Courrier musical,* given in Rosenstiel, *Nadia Boulanger,* 83.
128. Profile of Jules Mazellier in *Musica* (May 1909), given in Rosenstiel, *Nadia Boulanger,* 83.

the sculptor Lucienne Heuvelmans, the previous year.[129] Things had changed in the Académie with the death of Charles Lenepveu in August 1910. In the 1912 competition, Lili Boulanger was not promoted to the final round. One year later, however, she and four male candidates set Eugène Adenis's cantata *Faust et Hélène* to music, and she became the first female musician to win the *Premier Grand Prix de Rome*. From the specialist jury, she received five votes out of eight in the first round, and she obtained an overwhelming majority in the general Académie election with thirty-one votes to five. It was sensational by any standards that a nineteen-year-old candidate had won the *Prix de Rome* both with a first cantata and with an unusually large majority. Moreover, she was a young woman.[130]

Like Fleury, Lili Boulanger had enrolled in the Conservatoire for a brief period of time in order to study composition in an environment closer to the Académie and its *Prix de Rome*. But she did not compete for the Conservatoire's end-of-year prizes that her sister had collected so successfully. Because of constant illness,[131] the young and frail composer spent much time at home with private tutors, concentrating her limited energy on her priorities. Indeed, winning the *Prix de Rome* for the honor of the Boulanger family became almost an obsession for her,[132] especially after following closely her sister Nadia's vigorous but fruitless attempts to achieve this goal. Lili Boulanger recorded the "affaire fugue" of 1908 in detail in her diary: "Nadia wrote an instrumental fugue and a very pretty chorus—the instrumental fugue was not allowed to be judged in the Conservatoire—St.-Saëns did not want Nadia's work to be heard, but the jury disregarded this and admitted her nevertheless."[133] Lili Boulanger was very much aware

---

129. During their stay in Rome, Heuvelmans would make a terra-cotta bust of Lili Boulanger, which is now preserved at the Musée Marmottan.

130. For an exact protocol of the events, see *Procès verbaux* from 5 July 1913, AABA, shelf-mark 2E23, pp. 64–69. Léonie Rosenstiel reconstructs much of the competition in her biography of Lili Boulanger; see Léonie Rosenstiel, *The Life and Works of Lili Boulanger* (London and Rutherford, N.J.: Fairleigh Dickinson University Press, 1978), 54–82. For a more analytical approach with respect to Boulanger's cantata *Faust et Hélène*, see Manuela Schwartz, "Mehr als ein Gesellenstück: 'Faust et Hélène' von Lili Boulanger," in *Vom Schweigen befreit*, ed. Aulenkamp-Moeller and Nies, 64–71; Melanie Unseld, " 'alles, was man erwarten und wünschen kann'—Gedanken zu Lili Boulangers Kantate *Faust et Hélène*," *Vivavoce*, no. 41 (April–June 1997): 8–17.

131. Lili Boulanger "contracted a severe case of bronchial pneumonia" at age two (Rosenstiel, *Life and Works of Lili Boulanger*, 33). Her health remained very fragile, and during the last ten years of her life, she suffered from intestinal tuberculosis.

132. Ibid., 46–57.

133. Lili Boulanger, *Agenda* for 1908, F-Pn, Rés.Vmf.ms.110, 2–7 May 1908: "Nadia fait une fugue instrumentale et un chœur tout-à-fait joli—la fugue instrumentale n'est pas permise au jugement au Conservatoire—St.-Saëns ne veut pas qu'on entende l'œuvre de Nadia, mais le jury passe par dessus et l'admet quand même."

of every move her sister made to win the *Prix de Rome*,[134] and she saw the professional and highly competent Nadia fail because of a misogynous jury. Accordingly she developed—probably consciously—a different strategy to deal with the public sphere of professional musicianship. Portraits and descriptions of her reveal a public persona carefully chosen and cultivated, which her physical frailty undoubtedly enhanced: the divinely chosen genius in the fragile body of a beautiful child—the literary icon of the *femme fragile*.[135] In a series of photographs released at the time of the 1913 competition, she seems almost androgynous: in one (Fig. 6), she sits in front of the piano surrounded by flowers, but both her pose and her clothes evoke the familiar image, replicated a thousandfold in *bourgeois* family portraits, of a young adolescent boy in a sailor suit. Her gaze does not engage with the onlooker but is directed toward distant horizons of inspiration, much like the iconographic trope of the ecstatic saint. By using this androgynous imagery of the frail child-genius to separate herself from the icon of the mature woman professional—the *femme nouvelle*—Lili Boulanger also disassociated herself from the "pink peril"—in the guise of Hélène Fleury and Nadia Boulanger—invading public male space. An interview with Lili Boulanger and her mother in the aftermath of winning the *Prix de Rome* is revealing in this context. When asked if she could sleep after her success, she replied:

> "Oh yes, indeed. I dreamed that—didn't I, Mother?"
> "That what?"
> "Well, that I was a little child and was teaching my little doll to play the piano."
> "You see," said her mother, smiling, "she is still only a child."[136]

But Lili Boulanger's embodiment of the *femme fragile* constituted a carefully constructed role, in which she took on the unthreatening aspect of the eternal female who needed the support and help of the strong masculine sex. This portrayal of her can be found in the press reports of her

---

134. Rosenstiel, *Life and Works of Lili Boulanger*, 46–57.
135. On the *femme fragile*, see Ariane Thomalla, *Die "femme fragile": Ein literarischer Frauentypus der Jahrhundertwende* (Düsseldorf: Bertelsmann Universitätsverlag, 1972). On the issues of the perception of Lili Boulanger as *femme fragile*, see Annegret Fauser, "Lili Boulanger's *La Princesse Maleine*: A Composer and Her Heroine as Literary Icons," *Journal of the Royal Musical Association* 122 (1997): 68–108. Ellen Thormann draws parallels between the public perception of both Marie Bashkirtseff and Lili Boulanger as "femmes fragiles"; see her article "Lili Boulanger: Eine 'Funkelnde kleine Taube des (Heiligen) Geistes'?—Anmerkungen zur Rezeption einer Komponistin," in *Lili Boulanger-Tage 1993. Bremen. Zum 100. Geburtstag der Komponistin*, ed. Kathrin Mosler (Bremen: Callas/Zeichen und Spuren, 1993), 20–24.
136. "Young French Women Winning Honors," *The Musical Leader* 26 (1913). I wish to thank the Music Division of the New York Public Library for sending me a photocopy of this article.

Figure 6 Portrait of Lili Boulanger, May 1913. Photograph preserved in the Fondation Internationale Nadia et Lili Boulanger, Paris.

victory.[137] There is no doubt that she won her prize because of her musical achievement: her cantata is an outstanding contribution to the genre.[138] But she also received the *Premier Grand Prix* because she succeeded in conforming to a popular concept of femininity that appeared not only in "decadent" literature[139] but also—once more—in widely distributed popular novels. Evoking images of family happiness, Emile Vuillermoz's description of the candidate could well be found in any such novel: "The frail grace of Mademoiselle Lili Boulanger [moved] the audience, softened by the sight of the touching group formed by the contestant and her sister united at the piano in an attentive and affectionate collaboration."[140] Throughout the performance of her cantata, Lili Boulanger behaved passively and submissively in the manner of the ideal woman, avoiding any gesture that could be interpreted as directing or conducting her musicians: "Her modest and simple bearing, her gaze cast down on the score, her immobility during the performance, her absolute abandonment to the will of her excellent interpreters—she did not allow herself even once to beat time or indicate a nuance—all this contributed to her cause."[141] She did nothing that could be construed as aggressive, assertive, or arrogant. As in the 1913 photograph (Fig. 6), her performance here physically enacted the plot of a feminine vocation through Art itself, which Carolyn Heilbrun has likened to the story line of romantic love: the woman is conquered against all obstacles by the hero or—in a religious context—God or Christ.[142] Journalists could not resist the implicit parallel to Jeanne d'Arc, the national, and by then, the right-wing, Catholic symbol of France: "The suffragettes smash windows and burn houses. But a maiden of France has gained a better victory."[143] The powerful imagery of Boulanger's campaign to win the *Prix*

---

137. Lili Boulanger's diaries disclose that she had an iron will as well as determination to get what she wanted, even at the cost of her own health. Like any cunning young Parisian artist, she knew how to manipulate juries and the press, as her scheming to obtain the *Prix Lepaulle* in 1912 reveals. See Fauser, "Lili Boulanger's *La Princesse Maleine*," 107.

138. See Schwartz, "Mehr als ein Gesellenstück"; and Unseld, " 'alles, was man erwarten und wünschen kann.' "

139. On "decadence" in literature, see Erwin Koppen, *Dekadenter Wagnerismus: Studien zur europäischen Literatur des Fin de siècle* (Berlin and New York: Walter de Gruyter, 1973).

140. Vuillermoz, "La Guerre en dentelles," 153: "La frêle grâce de Mlle Lili Boulanger [a ému] les spectateurs, attendris au spectacle du groupe touchant que formaient la concurrente et sa sœur réunies au piano dans une collaboration attentive et affectueuse."

141. Ibid.: "Son maintien modeste et simple, ses yeux baissés sur la partition, son immobilité pendant l'exécution, son abandon absolu à la volonté de ses excellents interprètes à qui elle ne se permit pas une seule fois de battre la mesure ou d'indiquer une nuance, tout contribua à servir sa cause." An accompanying sketch by Dagnan-Bouveret conforms exactly to Vuillermoz's description.

142. Heilbrun, *Writing a Woman's Life*, 21.

143. *Le Matin*, 6 July 1913, p. 2: "Les suffragettes brisent les vitres et incendient les maisons. Mais une jeune fille de France a rapporté une meilleure victoire."

de Rome undoubtedly contributed to her overwhelming success. Were her cantata not of high quality, she would not have won the prize, but her sister Nadia's fate shows that musical talent alone was not sufficient.

The story of women and the *Prix de Rome* before the First World War was not just one of ongoing prejudice against women by the Académie. It was also the story of women's attempts to quell the anxieties of the *académiciens*. Although both Hélène Fleury and Nadia Boulanger were taken seriously, Juliette Toutain's self-representation as *salonnière* and *jeune fille rangée* supplied her adversaries with the weapons they needed to undermine her professional ambitions. Indeed, each of the four stories illustrates the precarious balance that female competitors had to achieve between the journalistic and literary images of the ideal Republican woman, loyal and submissive to the state and its institutions, and the self-confident and professional composer who must be taken seriously. Because it was necessary to conduct the performance of the cantata, the physical appearance of a female contestant assumed more importance in the musical competition than it did in other areas, in which artists such as sculptors or painters remained invisible behind the physical presence of their artifacts. Thus the persona of a woman composer became an integral part of her submission. Each of the four women tried to craft an image that could earn her a position in the public arena of French official art; the most successful strategy, however, proved to be that which yoked an excessive and frail femininity with images both religious and androgynous. Neither an aggressive socialite nor a "dangerous" *femme nouvelle*, the first female winner of the musical *Prix de Rome* was an artist who skillfully negotiated the concerns over women's emancipation pervading the cultural politics of pre-war French society through her unthreatening rendition of the child-genius.

Appendix

Marie-Juliette Toutain (b. Trouville, 22 July 1877; d. after 1939). French composer and pianist. Toutain entered the Conservatoire in 1891 to study piano. In 1896 she received the first prize in piano. She continued studying at the Conservatoire and participated in classes in piano accompaniment, harmony, and organ, all of which she finished with a first prize. In 1900 she was admitted to the composition class of Gabriel Fauré, which she successfully completed in 1902, again with a first prize. In the same year, she undertook a letter-writing campaign in order to get permission for women to participate in the *Prix de Rome*, which was granted in 1903. She enrolled for the competition in April 1903 but withdrew because the arrangements for women were unsatisfactory. In March 1904, she married Jules-Alexandre Grün, a painter and engraver. Toutain continued a low-key career as pianist, harpsichordist, and piano teacher in Paris, where she also held an artistic salon. In 1920, she undertook a concert tour to Argentina. She still appears in the registers of the Société des Artistes Musiciens in 1939, after which there is no trace of her.

Published works: *Rondel* (voice and piano, 1903; poem by Villehervé), *Chanson d'été* (voice and piano, 1907; Samain), *Heures douces* (voice and piano, 1907; Hettrich), *Mélancolie* (voice and piano, 1907; Samain), *L'Oiseau Bleu* (voice and piano, 1907; Hettrich), *Les Menottes. 10 Morceaux très faciles* (piano, 1908).

Hélène Fleury (b. Carlepoint, 21 June 1876; d. after 1917), French composer and pianist. Fleury studied with Planchet and Dallier before entering Widor's composition class at the Conservatoire in 1898. She left the Conservatoire in 1902 without any prize. In 1903, she participated without success in the *Prix de Rome*. One year later, in 1904, she won the *Deuxième Second Grand Prix*. She was the first woman to win a prize. Fleury participated in the competition again in 1905, but (together with Ravel) was not permitted to move into the final round. She continued to teach piano and later married, taking the name Hélène Fleury-Roy. No more biographical details are known, and after 1910, she stopped publishing.

Published works: *Espérance, Valse de salon* (piano, 1897), *Pensée* (piano, 1897), *Scherzo* (piano, 1898), *La Nuit* (piano, 1898), *Etude* (piano, 1899), *Offertoire* (organ, 1900), *Intermezzo-Valse*, Op. 10 (piano, 1902), *Soir de Bretagne* (voice and piano, 1904; poem by Bellessort), *Médora. Prélude. Cantate de Concours de Rome 1904* (piano, 1904), *Roussalka* (violoncello [violin] and piano, 1905), *Matutina* (voice and piano, 1905; A. Silvestre), *Arabesque*, Op. 12 (piano, 1905), *Brise de Soir*, Op. 13 (violin and piano, 1905), *Impromptu*, Op. 14 (piano, 1905), *Bourrée-Gavotte*, Op. 15 (piano, 1906), *Canzonetta*, Op. 16 (piano, 1906), *Fantaisie, imposée au Concours du Conservatoire (Année 1906)*, Op. 18 (viola [violin] and piano, 1906), *Minuetto*, Op. 19 (piano, 1906), *Fleurs des champs*, Op. 20 (piano, 1906), *En promenade*, Op. 21 (piano, 1906), *Joyeux départ*, Op. 22 (piano, 1906), *Rêverie* (violoncello and piano, 1906?), *Valse-Caprice*, Op. 17 (piano, 1907), *Les Sorcières*, Op. 23 (four-voice female chorus and piano, 1908; Guinand), *Trois pièces faciles* (violin and piano, 1910), *Cœur virginal* (voice and piano, 1910; Rochecantin).

Nadia Boulanger (b. Paris, 16 September 1887; d. Paris, 22 October 1979). French composer, composition teacher, and conductor. After highly successful studies at the Conservatoire, in 1906 she participated for the first time in the *Prix de Rome* and in 1907 advanced to the second round (the *concours définitif*). In 1908, she caused controversy with her submission of an instrumental fugue instead of a vocal piece, but was nevertheless awarded the *Deuxième Second Grand Prix* with her setting of *La Sirène*. In 1909, she reached the final round but did not receive any award. For her further biography (and a list of works) as composer, teacher, and performer, see Vivian Perlis and Léonie Rosenstiel, "Nadia Boulanger," in *The New Grove Dictionary of Women Composers*, ed. Julie-Anne Sadie and Rhian Samuel (London: Macmillan, 1994), 79–80.

Lili Boulanger (b. Paris, 21 August 1893; d. Mézy, 15 March 1918). French composer. After mostly private training in composition, she enrolled for the *Prix de Rome* in 1912 but did not reach the final round. In 1913, she won the *Premier Grand Prix de Rome* (the first woman to do so in music). Her illness and the outbreak of the First World War shortened her sojourn at the Villa Medici in Rome, and she died in 1918. For more biographical information and a list of works, see

Robert Orledge and Annegret Fauser, "Lili Boulanger," in *The New Grove Dictionary of Women Composers*, ed. Julie-Anne Sadie and Rhian Samuel (London: Macmillan, 1994), 77–79.

Abstract

In 1903, one hundred years after the *Prix de Rome* had been created in music composition, women were allowed to participate in the competition for the first time. In 1913, Lili Boulanger became the first woman to win the prize, crowning the efforts of three others—Juliette Toutain, Hélène Fleury, and Nadia Boulanger—to achieve this goal. Their stories are fascinating case studies of the strategies women employed to achieve success and public recognition within the complex framework of French cultural politics at the beginning of the twentieth century.

CHAPTER 12

Composing as a Catholic: Rereading Lili Boulanger's Vocal Music*

In 1990, I set out to discover the music behind the legend of Lili Boulanger (1893–1918). Ever since then, I have focused on Boulanger the composer of modern music, the contemporary of Milhaud, Poulenc, and Honegger.[1] My work aimed at deconstructing the public persona of the "femme fragile" and child genius that seemed to have permeated the literature on Boulanger both during her lifetime and for many decades afterwards. I also felt that far too many scholars fused Boulanger's religious beliefs with the images of the devout virgin and suffering child who found consolation in her faith and in her music.[2] Boulanger's angelic qualities were credited for the power and imagination of her works, and her early death justified such divine inspiration—or worse, actually became the price she had to pay. How else could a woman's creative achievement and innovative work be explained?[3] Given such rhetoric, it is perhaps understandable that I went in the opposite direction and ignored Boulanger's Catholicism in favor of a more secular, less sacrosanct approach to the composer.[4] But while I addressed Boulanger's social and artistic contexts, ranging from the Prix de Rome to Symbolist poetry, I left out a significant part of her personal history by ignoring the important role of her Catholic faith. The present essay represents a first attempt at redressing this imbalance and at answering the question of what it may have meant to compose as a Catholic in France in the early twentieth century.

For all the references to Boulanger's faith, we know precious little about it. Miki Piré, her close friend and confidante, stated that the two of them "had never really discussed religion

---

* This is the English original of "Composer en tant que catholique: une relecture de la musique vocale de Lili Boulanger," translated by Marie-Hélène Benoit-Otis, *Intersections: Canadian Journal of Music* 26 (2006): 114–23. In order to preserve the integrity of the text, I have not updated any of the footnotes or added further references, even though the issue of Catholic modernism as well as music and religion more broadly conceived have become a major strand in scholarship.

[1] Annegret Fauser, "Die Musik hinter der Legende. Lili Boulangers Liederzyklus *Clairières dans le Ciel*," *Neue Zeitschrift für Musik* 151/11 (November 1990): 9–14. For a notable exception, see Jacques Chailley, "L'Œuvre de Lili Boulanger," *La Revue musicale*, special issue: "Lili et Nadia Boulanger," 353–54 (1982): 15–44, where he emphasizes (19) that Boulanger's work needs to be understood in the context of her contemporaries born between 1890 and 1895, including Honegger, Milhaud, Ibert, and Hindemith.

[2] See in particular Camille Mauclair, "La vie et l'œuvre de Lili Boulanger," *La Revue musicale* 10 (1921): 147–55; Christiane Trieu-Colleney, "Lili Boulanger (1893–1918), ou Musique pour une éternité," *Jeunesse et Orgue* (1972), given in Birgit Stièvenard-Salomon, *Lili Boulanger: l'œuvre retrouvée* (Issy-les-Moulineaux: Municipalité d'Issy-les-Moulineaux, 1993), 88.

[3] Henri Barraud, "Regards sur la musique" (1968), given in Stièvenard-Salomon, *Lili Boulanger*, 53.

[4] Annegret Fauser, "Lili Boulanger's *La Princesse Maleine*: a Composer and Her Heroine as Literary Icons," *Journal of the Royal Musical Association* 122 (1997): 68–108; ead., "*La Guerre en dentelles*: Women and the *Prix de Rome* in French Cultural Politics," *Journal of the American Musicological Society* 51 (1998): 83–129.

together."[5] In her diaries, Boulanger refers to meetings with clerics, in particular Father Arthur Desprez, and she sometimes mentions their prayers or topics of conversation; thus she notes in her diary for 2 June 1916 that she had discussed theosophy with Father Arthur.[6] Attendance at Mass was a matter of course for both Boulanger and her family, and Lili's sister, Nadia, emphasized their Catholic upbringing as an essential part of their spiritual and moral education.[7] An early document has Lili Boulanger perform as an eight-year old at a musical Mass at Notre Dame de Trouville, together with Nadia and with Juliette Toutain.[8] Later, in 1916, an intriguing photograph shows the Boulanger family, with Lili all in white, leaving an audience with Pope Benedict V. This image may attest to Boulanger's standing, for not every twenty-two-year-old can just turn up for an audience with the Pope. Finally, the announcement of her funeral service states explicitly that she had died "fortified with the rites of the Church."[9]

What can be extrapolated from this slim evidence is that for Lili Boulanger, religion was both private and also a way of life. On the surface, she seems like a "jeune fille rangée," whose good bourgeois and Catholic upbringing would have satisfied such educational writers of the late nineteenth century as Monseigneur Dupanloup or Clarisse Bader.[10] That her last composition in 1918 was a *Pie Jesu*, dictated to Nadia when she was too weak even to hold a pen and write, would seem to support this view, were it not for the fact that the work itself is transgressive in its musical means. Its intertext is another, far more comforting setting of the same words by Gabriel Fauré, a family friend. Boulanger refuses the consolation offered by Fauré, pushing instead towards a disquieting, polytonal language that leaves open the question of whether or not the music will come to the eternal rest—*requiem aeternam*—that the words seek.[11] This presumably private setting of a liturgical text may even point towards a different version of the traditional story of Boulanger. Instead of the devout and frail adolescent, the work reveals a strong personality, someone who poses questions and may not accept given truths at face value.

This suggestion should, in fact, come as no surprise. The Boulanger household had ties with all kinds of intellectuals and artists, from architect William Bouwens van der Boijen and archaeologist Théophile Homolle to poets Gabriele D'Annunzio and Emile Verhaeren, orientalist Suzanne Karpelès, and Louise Gonet, who was a friend of Rabindranath Tagore.[12] Boulanger's diaries often refer to dinner parties with lively discussions, even if they leave us

---

[5] Leonie Rosenstiel, *The Life and Works of Lili Boulanger* (Rutherford, Madison, and Teaneck: Fairleigh Dickinson University Press, 1978), 133.

[6] "Je reste avec P. Arthur, avec qui parlons théosophie etc." Bibliothèque Nationale de France, Département de la Musique, Fonds Boulanger, Agenda 1916, entry for 2 June 1916.

[7] Bruno Monsaingeon, *Mademoiselle: Conversations with Nadia Boulanger* (Manchester: Carcanet, 1985), 82.

[8] Rosenstiel, *Lili Boulanger*, 36.

[9] Ibid., 133.

[10] See, for example, Clarisse Bader, *La femme française dans les temps modernes* (Paris: E. Perrin, 1883), and Mgr Dupanloup, Evêque d'Orléans, *Lettres sur l'éducation des filles et sur les études qui conviennent aux femmes dans le monde*, 2nd edn. (Paris: J. Gervais, 1879). The extent to which these ideas were still permeating women's education at the turn of the twentieth century has been shown in Anne Martin-Fugier, *La bourgeoise: femme au temps de Paul Bourget* (Paris: Bernard Grasset, 1983).

[11] Olivia Mattis, "Lili Boulanger: Polytoniste," in *Lili Boulanger Tage 1993, Bremen: Zum 100. Geburtstag der Komponistin*, edited by Kathrin Mosler (Bremen: Callas, 1993), 48–50.

[12] Rosenstiel, *Lili Boulanger*, 33–34.

wondering about the topics of conversation. But as Nadia Boulanger told Leonie Rosenstiel, these conversations were challenging and stimulating, and touched upon a wide range of issues, with Lili holding her own.[13] Thus her experience seems to reflect that of other Parisian artists and intellectuals—from Fauré to Jammes and later Messiaen—in that her religious education and practice as a devout Catholic served as a foil against which other faiths and ideas could be explored, judged, and appropriated.

This kind of integrative Catholicism, rather than an exclusive one, was one of the strands of French Catholicism in the late nineteenth and early twentieth centuries. The period between 1890 and 1914 was characterized not only by the well-known antagonistic relationship between Church and State which would lead to the anticlerical reforms and a formal separation in 1905. No less typical was an equally acrimonious debate within the Catholic Church itself between the modernists following Alfred Loisy and Maurice Blondel on the one hand, and the scholastic anti-modernists inspired by the newly elected reactionary Pope Pius X, on the other.[14] Catholic modernists wanted a historically responsible theology rather than the perpetuation of ultramontane ecclesiastical dogma as expressed in Pius X's 1906 encyclical *Pascendi*, which aimed at increasing the authority of the papacy, at opposing historical study of the Bible, at supporting neo-scholasticism, and at resisting any erosion of the Church's influence.[15] In France, the new form of conservative ultramontane piety was strongly encouraged by Rome and focused on intensified Marian devotion (most obviously in the case of Lourdes), the spread of Eucharist adoration in the cult of the Sacred Heart, and anti-intellectualism in religious teachings.[16]

Based on the few available documents, I would argue that in theological terms, Boulanger leaned towards Catholic modernism. Her religious practice was a far cry from the devotion to the Virgin and the Sacred Heart associated with anti-modern Catholicism, let alone the practice of Lourdes pilgrimages. On the contrary, her mind seemed open to other religious denominations, not the least because of her part-Russian background, with friends and servants practicing Russian Orthodoxy. I would further suggest that her intellectual interests might even have extended to theosophy, in particular because of her setting of the *Vieille prière bouddhique* which echoes theosophist concerns with Indian philosophy. An interest in theosophy is also reflected in Boulanger's fascination with number symbolism and her use of a psalter translated by Henri Lesêtre, who seems to have been involved with Catholic modernism at least at the margins and who later became a member of the theosophist fraternity of the "Polaires."[17]

---

[13] Ibid., 34.

[14] For a short outline of Catholic concerns at the turn of the twentieth century, see Jean-Baptiste Duroselle, *Le France de la "Belle Epoque"* (1972, repr. Paris: Presses de la Fondation Nationale des Sciences Politiques, 1992); on Loisy, see Charles J. T. Talar, "Innovation and Biblical Interpretation," in *Catholicism Contending with Modernism: Roman Catholic Modernism and Anti-Modernism in Historical Context*, edited by Darrell Jodock (Cambridge: Cambridge University Press, 2000), 191–211.

[15] Darrell Jodock, "Introduction II: The Modernists and the Anti-Modernists," in *Catholicism Contending with Modernism*, ed. Jodock, 20–27, at 25–26.

[16] Ralph Gibson, *A Social History of French Catholicism, 1789–1914* (London and New York: Routledge, 1989), 265.

[17] The Fondation Internationale Nadia et Lili Boulanger holds a copy of Henri Lesêtre, curé de Saint-Etienne du Mont, *Les Psaumes du bréviaire, traduits de l'hébreu* (Paris: P. Lethielleux, 1913). I am grateful to Alexandra Laederich for providing me with the information. On number symbolism and Boulanger, see Bonnie Jo Dopp, "Numerology and Cryptography in the Music of Lili Boulanger:

Boulanger's music, especially her vocal compositions, seems to support this interpretation of her as a moderate Catholic modernist. What is most revealing is the fact that she predominantly selected psalms as texts for her religious settings (Table 1). In Catholic liturgy, psalms had their place in the Office and not in the Mass.[18] Furthermore, since the sixteenth century, they had been associated in France with the individualism of Protestant piety as opposed to the more collective practice of Catholicism. A brief survey of the output of Boulanger's immediate predecessors and contemporaries shows that psalm-settings constituted a negligible portion of their works, even in the case of well-known Church composers such as Charles-Marie Widor (who set two psalms) and Louis Vierne (who set none).[19] But all of them set the Ordinary, the *Ave Maria*, or other liturgical texts fitting in the context either of the Mass or of personal Catholic piety in nineteenth- and early-twentieth-century France.

Table 1: Sacred Music Composed by Lili Boulanger

Psalms	Liturgical Works	Other
Surviving Compositions		
Ps. 129, "Ils m'ont assez opprimé" (1910–16)	*Pie Jesu* (1918)	*Pour les funérailles d'un soldat* (A. de Musset;1912–13)
Ps. 130, "Du fond de l'abîme" (1910–17)		*Vieille prière bouddhique* (after *Visuddhimagga*, trans.
Ps. 24, "La terre appartient à l'Eternel" (1915–16)		S. Karpelès; 1914–17)
Incomplete or Lost Works		
Ps. 131 (1907)	*Ave Maria* (1908)	*Apocalypse* (1909)
Ps. 137 (1907)		Setting of Corinthians 1:13 (1909)
Ps. 1 (1909)		
Ps. 119 (1909)		

The Hidden Program in *Clairières dans le ciel*," *Musical Quarterly* 78 (1994): 557–83. Boulanger's *Vieille prière bouddhique* is the subject of an unpublished thesis, Antje Ruhbaum, *Das "Vieille prière bouddhique" von Lili Boulanger: ein Beispiel für den Einfluß außereuropäischer Kulturen auf die französische Musik der Jahrhundertwende*, Hausarbeit zur künstlerlisch-wissenschaftlichen Staatsprüfung, Berlin, Hochschule der Künste, 1994.

[18] For the psalter in the Catholic liturgy, see John Harper, *The Forms and Orders of Western Liturgy from the Tenth to the Eighteenth Century: a Historical Introduction and Guide for Students and Musicians* (Oxford: Clarendon Press, 1991), 67–72. The subsequent chapter (73–108) addresses the Office in great detail.

[19] Vincent d'Indy, Camille Saint-Saëns, Florent Schmitt, Charles Tournemire, and Charles-Marie Widor each set two psalms; César Franck, Gabriel Fauré, and Albert Roussel each set one; and Louis Aubert, Charles Bordes, Nadia Boulanger, Alfred Bruneau, Gustave Charpentier, Claude Debussy, Maurice Delage, Augusta Holmès, Charles Koechlin, Jules Massenet, Francis Poulenc, Maurice Ravel, Jean Roger-Ducasse, and Louis Vierne set none.

Boulanger's selection of texts for her religious vocal music seems unique for her time in France. As texts, psalms present several distinct features to a composer: they are religious without necessarily being liturgical; they form part of an archaic body of texts, thus providing a "primitive" quality compared with the newer Christian literature; they possess an individual character because they were written from the position of the lyrical "I" of King David; and they have authority because they are part of the biblical canon. Few other texts might, in fact, be as powerful a tool for a composer whose diaries reveal that she saw her music as a humanitarian and political act.[20] When Boulanger searched for a subject for an opera in 1915, she looked for a libretto that would address the issues of war, and her three surviving psalm settings—together with her *Pour les funérailles d'un soldat* and her *Vieille prière bouddhique*—form a body of works that could be read as addressing humanitarian issues in the context of World War I.[21] In particular, her setting of Psalm 24—conceived in 1915 and finished in 1916—reminds her listeners that "the earth is the Lord's" (Example 1) and that it is He who owns the armies.

Example 1:   Lili Boulanger, *Psaume XXIV*, mes. 1–8

---

[20] See Fauser, "Lili Boulanger's *La Princesse Maleine*," 75. See also Eduard Reeser's description of a lost symphonic poem in which he found impressions of landscapes filled with "the sound of canons, the night, the casualties, the pain and solitude" [die de plat geschoten vlakten, de nacht, de gewonden, de smart en de eenzaamheid oproepen]; Eduard Reeser, "Lili Boulanger," *De Muziek* 7 (1932/33): 210–21, 264–71, at 269.

[21] Paul Gentien (Ricordi), letter to Lili Boulanger, 2 September 1915(?), Bibliothèque Nationale de France, Fonds Boulanger.

Boulanger's treatment of Psalm 24 might contain keys to several questions as to why she chose such texts for her large-scale choral works of the 1910s. Its music points to what might have been a crucial influence on her discovery of the psalms, Florent Schmitt's setting of Psalm 47, op. 38 ("O clap your hands, all ye people"). Schmitt's psalm setting had its première in France on 27 December 1906, with Nadia Boulanger at the organ. According to Nadia, her sister was entranced with Schmitt's work and did not miss a single rehearsal.[22] Indeed, Boulanger's setting of Psalm 24 could be read as an intertext to Schmitt's in terms of both music and content.

If we compare Schmitt's opening (Example 2) with Boulanger's war-time *Psaume XXIV*, the similarities are striking. Even the musical structure of both works is alike: each starts with a homophonic choral section, followed by a middle part for a soloist and concluded by another choral section. Boulanger's initial gesture in the brass is also remarkably similar to Schmitt's, as is the rhythm of the text-setting in the opening choral section.

Example 2:   Florent Schmitt, *Psaume XLVII*, mes. 1–8

---

[22]   Rosenstiel, *Lili Boulanger*, 47.

Schmitt's *Psaume XLVII* was well known in the early part of the twentieth century, and it had widespread musical influence. Boulanger started sketches for her very first psalm settings (of Psalms 131 and 137) immediately after hearing it, in early 1907, and she was not alone: Charles Tournemire began his large-scale setting of Psalm 57 for chorus and orchestra in 1908. Messiaen later acknowledged the influence of Schmitt's psalm on his *Trois petites liturgies de la présence divine* (composed 1943–44).[23] Thus it seems very likely that Schmitt provided Boulanger with an initial impulse towards the use of psalm texts for her music. His example also opened up for her a source of texts that would be religious without being liturgical. But in the case of her setting of Psalm 24, the intertextual relationship with Schmitt's *Psaume XLVII* also has other resonances. Psalm 47 celebrates the power and glory of God, whereas Psalm 24 is darker-hued, with its obvious wartime references to "l'Eternel fort et puissant dans les combats" (the Eternal, strong and powerful in battle).

What makes Boulanger's musical setting so striking, however, is the "primitive" and self-consciously archaic quality both of the psalm translation that she used and of her musical language. The same applies to her other two psalm settings. Boulanger chose Lesêtre's translation of Psalm 130, "Du fond de l'abîme" ("Out of the depths"), which uses the address of "Iahvé" and "Adonaï" rather than "Seigneur," giving the text a more archaic quality.[24] This psalm, whose link to Stravinsky's *Rite of Spring* and other works has often been observed, is even more strongly inscribed within musical modernism than Boulanger's *Psaume XXIV*. We know from her diaries that she worked through Stravinsky's music in 1916, at the same time that she composed one of her psalm settings (most likely *Psaume CXXX*): "Go to the piano—work a bit on the psalm—which I pick up again—then lie down—go after lunch to the piano—take *Le Rossignol*, by Stravinsky."[25] Her diaries for this period also reveal a preoccupation with mode and counterpoint. In November 1916, for example, she noted that a discussion of early modes with Nadia was followed by the singing of improvised counterpoint. Several months earlier she composed a fugue to pass the time, just to see what one could do with its (musical) subject.[26] *Psaume XXIV*—as well as the other two psalm settings—have long stretches that are modal, and in it, Boulanger then exploits a striking diatonicism to color the tenor solo when the text moves to the benediction of those who have clean hands and a pure heart, and who have not lifted up their souls to vanity or who will not swear deceitfully. The archaic tonal language of the beginning is also supported by the psalm's orchestration for brass, harp, organ, and timpani, as well as the initial performance indication for the chorus: "very rhythmical and hammered out,

---

[23] Marc Vignal, liner notes for the recording of Olivier Messiaen, *Trois petites liturgies de la présence divine* (Paris: Erato, 1989), 4.

[24] Lesêtre, *Les Psaumes du bréviaire*, 221–22. Although Boulanger used Lesêtre's translation as the principal text, she added exclamations and variations.

[25] "Vais au piano—travaille un peu au psaume—que je reprends—puis reste couchée—vais après déj. au piano—prends le *Rossignol*, de Stravinsky." Bibliothèque Nationale de France, Département de la Musique, Fonds Boulanger, Agenda 1916, entry for 27 May 1916.

[26] "Parlons modes anciens—chantons toutes deux contrepoints improvisés." Bibliothèque Nationale de France, Département de la Musique, Fonds Boulanger, Agenda 1916, entry for 20 November 1916. For the reference to the fugue composition, see the entry on 25 May 1916: "Fais de la fugue, au lit—sur le sujet de Fauré, de l'examen, afin de voir ce qu'on en pouvait tirer."

rough."[27] In *Psaume CXXX*, Boulanger uses an even more pronounced contrast to express the difference between the initial despair and the later invocation of clemency and deliverance, although at the end, she returns to the text and sonorities of the beginning.

Boulanger's three psalm settings are characterized by an interplay between modernist idioms, modal archaisms, rhythmic primitivism, and nostalgic moments of beauty. Archaism also characterizes Boulanger's choice of texts, whether for these psalms or for the *Vieille prière bouddhique*. Her music and its texts refer to origins in ways similar to other modernists in search of original yet archaic languages with the goal of reaching a truer and less mediated form of artistic expression: think, for example, of Milhaud's *La Création du monde* or Stravinsky's *Symphony of Psalms*. Boulanger's psalms address humanity and criticize humanity's mutual destruction in acts of wartime barbarism. Thus composing as a Catholic during World War I, for Boulanger, was not a retreat in the private world of devotional music, but involved the creation of large-scale works addressing a vast audience and not just God alone.

---

[27] "très rythmé et scandé, rude." Lili Boulanger, *Psaume XXIV: transcription pour chant et piano par l'auteur* (Paris: Durand, 1924), 1.

CHAPTER 13

Lili Boulanger's *La princesse Maleine*: A Composer and her Heroine as Literary Icons

ON 22 July 1917 Maurice Maeterlinck wrote to the composer Lili Boulanger:

> Dear Mademoiselle and Friend,
> All my thoughts are with you in your pain and your anxiety. But I have a confidence which comes to me from I don't know where and which I would like to share with you. I feel – I would nearly say, I know – that the child-genius who must give a voice to *La princesse Maleine* cannot pass away before having accomplished her work, which seems fused with her destiny.
>
> Maeterlinck[1]

This one letter, written to a fatally ill, 23-year-old woman, contains in essence the usual biographical reading of the story of Lili Boulanger's setting of Maeterlinck's play.[2] Boulanger was a real-life *femme fragile* born to give to a play which was a literary icon of symbolist drama its true voice, a voice which according to symbolist aesthetics could only be musical. As in the sphere of literature, the fragility and suffering of the heroine Lili Boulanger became a sign for her uniqueness; she was born a Pippa, a Mélisande, a Gabriele in order to breathe life into the

---

I wish to thank Mlle Cécile Armagnac (Fondation Internationale Nadia et Lili Boulanger, Paris) and the Archivio Storico Ricordi (Milan) for access to scores, letters and documents. I am also grateful to Jeanice Brooks, Tim Carter, Katharine Ellis, Anne MacNeil, Jann Pasler and Ruth Solie for critical and helpful comments on earlier drafts of this text. First versions of this essay were presented as papers at Franklin & Marshall College (Lancaster, PA, October 1995) and at the British Musicology Conference, King's College London, 18-21 April 1996. It is partly based on an earlier essay, '*Femme fragile*: Zu Lili Boulanger's Opernfragment *La princesse Maleine*', published in German in *Vom Schweigen befreit: 3. Internationales Komponistinnen-Festival Kassel 12.–16.5.1993: Lili Boulanger (1893–1918)*, ed. Christel Nies and Roswitha Aulenkamp-Moeller (Kassel, 1993), 72-6.

[1] 'Chère Mademoiselle et amie, Toutes mes pensées sont avec vous dans votre douleur et votre inquiétude. Mais j'ai une confiance qui me viens je ne sais d'où et que je voudrais vous faire partager. Je sens, je dirais presque, je sais que l'enfant de génie qui doit donner une voix à "la Princesse Maleine" ne peut pas s'en aller avant d'avoir accompli son œuvre qui semble se confondre avec son destin. Maeterlinck.' Paris, Bibliothèque Nationale de France (hereafter F-Pn), Département de la Musique, Fonds Boulanger. This letter is kept in a folder containing Maeterlinck's letters to Lili Boulanger, yet it is not entirely clear if it is written to Lili Boulanger herself or to her sister, Nadia. All translations – unless otherwise stated – are my own.

[2] See, for example, Camille Mauclair, 'La vie et l'œuvre de Lili Boulanger', *Revue musicale*, 2 (1921), 147-55; Paul Landormy, 'Lili Boulanger (1893–1918)', *Musical Quarterly*, 16 (1930), 510-15; René Dumesnil, *Portraits de musiciens français* (Paris, 1938), 11-23; Léonie Rosenstiel, *The Life and Works of Lili Boulanger* (Rutherford, etc., 1978), 117; Eva Weissweiler, 'Lili Boulanger: Eine Repräsentantin des musikalischen Impressionismus', ch. 12 of her *Komponistinnen aus 500 Jahren: Eine Kultur- und Wirkungsgeschichte in Biographien und Werkbeispielen* (Frankfurt am Main, 1981), 325-46; Sylvie Croguennoc, 'Les mélodies de Lili Boulanger', *Autour de la mélodie française: Actes du colloque*, ed. Michelle Biget (Rouen, 1987), 99-122.

literary model of the fragile woman and therefore of herself, *La princesse Maleine*.³ In this telling of Boulanger's story we not only discover a *fin-de-siècle* female version of the child-genius Mozart struggling with destiny when composing his Requiem, a romanticized reading of musical biography such as found successful revival in Peter Shaffer's famous play *Amadeus*; we are also confronted with a subtle yet completely effective form of silencing a woman's voice through representing her as mouthpiece and creature of a great writer.

Such identification of Boulanger with her operatic heroine corresponds to the main thread of a story-line common in women's biography: the art-work takes the place of either the man or God/Christ who is usually put in the centre of a woman's life as the agent of meaning.⁴ Furthermore, this 'only script insisted that work discover and pursue [the woman artist], like the conventional romantic lover'.⁵ This form of narrative structure achieves its ultimate fulfilment in Maeterlinck's reading of Boulanger as chosen by destiny to complete as an opera the play which portrayed the scenario of her own life before she was even born: life and work become one to the point that the work appears as the real version of a story acted out in Boulanger's life.

Although feminist scholars are now beginning to approach biographical issues in their discussion of women musicians,⁶ reflection upon the interaction of biography and work – a central issue in feminist literary criticism and art history – is only slowly emerging,⁷ mirroring a general uneasiness which the discipline of musicology has developed with respect to biography.⁸ In her introduction to *Feminine Endings*, Susan McClary provocatively asserts that we are afraid of too evocative a reading of music in the light of its social and political contexts.⁹ Yet these contexts would be incomplete without that of the individual constellation of biography. Although the shop-worn concept of the 'death of the author' has opened

---

³ These names stand here for the literary *femme fragile* as discussed in Ariane Thomalla, *Die 'Femme fragile': Ein literarischer Frauentypus der Jahrhundertwende* (Düsseldorf, 1972). They are characters in the following works: Gerhart Hauptmann, *Und Pippa tanzte* (1906), Maurice Maeterlinck, *Pelléas et Mélisande* (1892) and Thomas Mann, *Tristan* (1903).
⁴ Carolyn G. Heilbrun, *Writing a Woman's Life* (New York and London, 1988), 20-1.
⁵ *Ibid.*, 25.
⁶ See, for example, Ruth A. Solie, 'Changing the Subject', *Current Musicology*, 53 (1993), 55-65; Jeanice Brooks, 'Nadia Boulanger and the Salon of the Princesse de Polignac', *Journal of the American Musicological Society*, 46 (1993), 415-68; *eadem*, 'Noble et grande servante de la musique: Telling the Story of Nadia Boulanger's Conducting Career', *Journal of Musicology*, 14 (1996), 92-116; Katharine Ellis, 'Gender and Professionalism: Women Pianists in Nineteenth-Century Paris', paper read at the British Musicology Conference, King's College London, 18-21 April 1996 (publication forthcoming).
⁷ Cf. Suzanne Cusick, 'Of Women, Music, and Power: A Model from Seicento Florence', *Musicology and Difference: Gender and Sexuality in Music Scholarship*, ed. Ruth A. Solie (Berkeley and London, 1993), 281-304; Marcia J. Citron, *Gender and the Musical Canon* (Cambridge, 1993), ch. 4: 'Music as Gendered Discourse', 120-64.
⁸ Although biographies of composers and interpreters flourish more than ever, the theoretical discussion of the genre has barely progressed since Carl Dahlhaus's sceptical remarks on voluminous accounts of lives and works in *Grundlagen der Musikgeschichte* (Cologne, 1977), 40, 44-6. Biographical issues in musicology in recent years have been addressed mainly in the context of feminist and gay/lesbian scholarship, apart from Hans Lenneberg's historical study *Witnesses and Scholars: Studies in Musical Biography* (New York, 1988).
⁹ Susan McClary, *Feminine Endings: Music, Gender, and Sexuality* (Minnesota and Oxford, 1991), 3-26.

up important ways of reading music in a contextualized manner,[10] its implication for women's work has had disastrous consequences: excluded from the canon of Western music for nearly 2,000 years,[11] their work is now denied the discussion of 'authorship' that would embrace issues of the individual female biography.

Boulanger's lost setting of *La princesse Maleine* offers a case-study which demands a rethinking of the complex relationship between life and work: we could not argue for an autonomous existence for the composition even if the score had been preserved, because (auto)biographical elements played a decisive role in its creation as well as its reception. Nor should we fall into the trap of confusing an account of the genesis of the work with its analysis. Although Boulanger almost finished her setting of *La princesse Maleine*, only fragments of the opera survive: two versions of the libretto,[12] the short score of Act 1, scene ii, and a late sketchbook, which appears to be a sort of daybook of her corrections of the opera's complete short score.[13] At least three red-bound sketchbooks which contained the Particell of the opera are lost.[14] But together with other sources, such as the correspondence between the composer, poet and librettist, the remaining fragments of the opera allow a reading of Boulanger's *La princesse Maleine* which can deconstruct the myth of its creation without reducing its complex intertwining of composition, (auto)biography and reception history to unrelated fragments. Yet reading Boulanger's *La princesse Maleine* offers a double challenge, demanding as much a factual as an interpretative approach: it raises the issues not only of how to reconstruct a 'lost work' but also of the contextualizing and interpreting of fragments which can be understood only as signposts towards a result which was not only lost, but also unfinished. Without a 'work' as such at hand, our usual tools of interpretation have to be adjusted to an archaeological undertaking, reconstructing what it uncovers and reading its reconstruction simultaneously.

Already as a young composition student Boulanger showed interest in setting *La princesse Maleine* as an opera. When she first read Maeterlinck's play in 1911, she jotted down musical sketches for several scenes.[15]

---

[10] Carolyn Abbate discusses the feminist implications of contextualization as opposed to an author-centred approach in her fascinating reading of Richard Strauss's *Salome*. However, Abbate's writings, as much as those of other critics such as McClary, focus almost exclusively on the canon, thus reinforcing a traditional male-centred choice of important and 'great' works worthy of our attention in the light of today's latest critical approaches; see Carolyn Abbate, 'Opera; or, the Envoicing of Women', *Musicology and Difference*, ed. Solie, 225–58.

[11] On fundamental reasons for this exclusion, see Christine Battersby, *Gender and Genius: Towards a Feminist Aesthetics* (2nd edn, Bloomington and Indianapolis, 1989). Marcia Citron discusses the exclusion of women's musical works in her chapter 'Canonic Issues' in *Gender and the Musical Canon*, 15–43.

[12] One libretto is in F-Pn ThB.4928; the other is in the collection of the Fondation Internationale Nadia et Lili Boulanger at the Musée Marmottan. The F-Pn libretto is handwritten (by an unknown copyist, perhaps Miki Piré?), with annotations in Lili Boulanger's hand; the other consists of typed sheets with autograph annotations in the hands of Lili Boulanger, Maurice Maeterlinck and Tito Ricordi.

[13] F-Pn MSS 19469, 19470.

[14] Boulanger refers to these sketchbooks on several occasions in her late sketchbook (MS 19470), as, for example, on f. 31 ('IVe Acte - p. 30 cahier rouge'; 'Act 4 - p. 30 in the red book') and on f. 31^v ('Ve Acte - 2^e cahier rouge'; 'Act 5 - second red book').

[15] Rosenstiel, *The Life and Works of Lili Boulanger*, 146.

Although this did not lead any further at that stage, her early fascination with the text sowed the seed for her choice of subject when she later started composing the first opera for which she had received a contract.

In July 1913 Lili Boulanger won the Prix de Rome. She was the first woman to receive this highly prestigious composition prize. It caused a sensation, especially because the prize-winner was only 19 years old: a beautiful and fragile young woman who deliberately cultivated her public persona as child-genius, even in interviews.[16] One of the results of that success was an exclusive contract for Boulanger with the publishing house Ricordi, then as now one of the most important in the world. At this time Ricordi was aggressively expanding its business in Paris, competing with the long-established Parisian houses such as Durand or Rouart, Lerolle & Cie in order to contract promising young composers. The contract with Ricordi gave Boulanger a regular monthly income, enabling her to devote herself entirely to composition; it also guaranteed the regular publication of her works and all the publicity that a large publisher could provide. For any young composer, such a contract represented an important career goal – witness, for example, Giuseppe Verdi, Giacomo Puccini, Camille Saint-Saëns, Jules Massenet and Claude Debussy – but Lili Boulanger was probably the first woman to receive such an opportunity.[17] Among the conditions of her contract was the composition within eight years of 'two operas, each of them forming a complete stage-spectacle'.[18]

The correspondences between Boito and Verdi, Illica and Puccini, and Hofmannsthal and Strauss offer vivid examples of how intricate the procedures of finding a suitable opera subject could be, taking into account questions such as the composer's interest, the author's consent (if she or he was a contemporary writer), the permission of the music publisher and the plot's suitability for an operatic setting. Traditionally, the writing of a libretto consisted of constructing a balanced matrix in a specific literary form as the basis for a composition. The functioning of the plot and of the language were more important than literary quality: a skilled librettist would sacrifice a good turn of phrase for a clumsier version whose keywords were in the right place. Thus, to quote Jürgen Maehder, there is no significant difference in structure between 'a libretto by Scribe based on a play by Schiller and a libretto by Scribe of the author's own invention'.[19] By the turn of the twentieth century, however, the situation had changed in so far as the sources of texts for settings had become more varied. Now, with the acceptance of Wagner's operas and

[16] For example in an interview in the *Musical Leader* in 1913, cited in Annegret Fauser, '*La guerre en dentelles*: Four Women, the Prix de Rome and French Cultural Politics', paper read at the Sixty-First Annual Meeting of the American Musicological Society in New York, 2-5 November 1995 (publication forthcoming).

[17] As far as we know, none of the nineteenth-century French women composers, such as Louise Farrenc, Cécile Chaminade or Augusta Holmès, had ever been offered a similar contract; they usually had to negotiate the publication of each individual piece, even if they had a privileged relationship with a specific publisher.

[18] Letter from Tito Ricordi to Nadia Boulanger, 12 July 1913: 'deux opéras qui formeront chacun spectacle complet'. Milan, Archivio Storico Ricordi, *Copialettere 1913–14*, no. 337.

[19] Jürgen Maehder, 'The Origins of Italian *Literaturoper*: *Guglielmo Ratcliff*, *La figlia di Iorio*, *Parisina*, and *Francesca da Rimini*', *Reading Opera*, ed. Arthur Groos and Roger Parker (Princeton, 1988), 92-128 (p. 93).

his aesthetic theories, the setting of pre-existing plays without their being rewritten by a librettist became a new alternative to the traditional libretto. 'Musical prose', with its 'dismissal of a musical structure based on the cadential frame' in favour of text-setting following the tone of speech, directed the composer to prose texts instead of rhyming librettos.[20] Through such texts, composers tried to avoid the trap of the sometimes poor literary quality of an old-fashioned libretto.[21] *Literaturoper* became the accepted form of more avant-garde operas in France at the turn of the century in the light of French *Wagnérisme* and the discovery of Mussorgsky in the late 1880s.[22] Boulanger's decision to set a symbolist play by Maeterlinck places her directly in the context of French *Literaturoper* of the early twentieth century. Moreover, in choosing Maeterlinck as the poet, she put herself in the line of composers such as Debussy and Dukas.

The setting of *La princesse Maleine* represented a highly ambitious project. Claude Debussy's *Pelléas et Mélisande*, premièred in April 1902, had become something of a cult opera for modern French composers before the First World War. In 1907, Paul Dukas's successful *Ariane et Barbe-Bleue* – an opera for which Maeterlinck wrote the libretto – was premièred in Paris. Henry Février's composition of Maeterlinck's *Monna Vanna*, premièred in 1909, counted as a triumphant new opera, and in 1914 Albert Wolff, the musical director of the Paris Opéra Comique, was just about to finish his setting of Maeterlinck's *Sœur Béatrice*. Maeterlinck had become a *bête sacrée* of modern poetry and drama. But there was one play left – one surrounded by the legendary aura of being the first symbolist masterpiece for the theatre: *La princesse Maleine*. First published in 1889, it was celebrated by the Parisian intellectual élite, beginning with a rave review by Octave Mirbeau in *Le Figaro* (24 August 1890). Debussy was only one of the composers who then asked Maeterlinck for permission to set the play to music. Maeterlinck refused, and in a letter to Jean Huret in June 1891 he indicated that the only composer to whom he might have given his permission was Vincent d'Indy.[23] Another French composer

---

[20] Stefan Kunze describes thus the relationship between musical and textual prose in a short and excellent passage: 'Zu klären wäre, welcher Zusammenhang besteht zwischen dem Aufgeben des gliedernden und Dynamik freisetzenden Kadenzgerüsts sowie der harmonischen, vom Einzelakkord ausgehenden Spannungsbeziehungen und einer dem Sprechfall folgenden Sprachvertonung, die die Prosa zu ihrem Strukturprinzip erhob. Im strengen Sinn sind hier sprachliche und musikalische Prosa, die bereits früh im 19. Jahrhundert sich ankündigten, zur Deckung gebracht. Musikalische Prosa ist dabei als die Konsequenz eines Satzes zu verstehen, der mit der Verabschiedung einer auf dem Kadenzgerüst beruhenden Bauweise keine überschaubare Korrespondenzen mehr entstehen ließ und dadurch den Sprechton musikalisch nachzuvollziehen vermochte. Die dem Sprechen analoge Form der verfaßten Sprache ist jedoch die Prosa. Sobald die Musik sich am Sprechakt orientierte, wurde sie auf Prosatexte verwiesen.' 'Der Sprechgesang und das Unsagbare: Bemerkungen zu *Pelléas et Mélisande* von Debussy', *Analysen: Beiträge zu einer Problemgeschichte des Komponierens: Festschrift für Hans Heinrich Eggebrecht zum 65. Geburtstag*, ed. Werner Breig, Reinhold Brinkmann and Elmar Budde, Beihefte zum Archiv für Musikwissenschaft, 23 (Wiesbaden and Stuttgart, 1984), 338–60 (p. 342).

[21] On the resulting category of *Literaturoper*, see Carl Dahlhaus, 'Berg und Wedekind' and 'Zur Dramaturgie der Literaturoper', *Vom Musikdrama zur Literaturoper: Aufsätze zur neueren Operngeschichte* (rev. edn, Munich, 1989), 170–85, 294–312. On *Literaturoper* after 1945, see *Für und Wider die Literaturoper: Zur Situation nach 1945*, ed. Siegrid Wiesmann (Laaber, 1982).

[22] Dahlhaus, 'Zur Dramaturgie der Literaturoper', 302.

[23] See François Lesure, *Claude Debussy avant 'Pelléas' ou Les années symbolistes* (Paris, 1992), 105.

who showed an interest in the play was Erik Satie, while Pierre de Bréville composed a concert overture *La princesse Maleine* (1891) which was performed in concerts in Paris and Brussels.[24] To the end of the century and beyond, the play remained a point of reference as one of the most important symbolist plays; but it also acquired a reputation as a play which Maeterlinck would never allow to be set to music.

A second reason for Boulanger's choice of subject may have been more personal. Boulanger and her family and friends not only were avid readers, but also – in the best nineteenth-century tradition – copied texts or fragments of texts for each other. Thus Boulanger kept in the cover of her diary from 1915 a passage from Maeterlinck's *Le trésor des humbles* which her mother had copied for her.[25] Although Boulanger read a wide range of literature from Sophocles to Tolstoy, including Shakespeare and Racine, she most loved symbolist writers such as Francis Jammes, Paul Claudel and Maurice Maeterlinck. In fact, she set – or tried to set – texts by all three poets: her song cycle *Clairières dans le ciel* is based on Francis Jammes; she wrote two songs to poems by Maeterlinck (*Attente* and *Reflets*); and in a letter to Darius Milhaud, Paul Claudel mentions that Boulanger had asked his permission to set his *La jeune fille Violaine*, which 'of course' he refused.[26] *Clairières dans le ciel* is interesting in this context, since the poems form a lover's reminiscence of a mysterious young woman who has vanished. In the first song, the woman actually appears, and the more suggestive than descriptive allusions to her physique echo the literary topos of the *femme fragile*, the innocently suffering, beautiful, aristocratic and fragile counterpart to the more flamboyant and dangerous *femme fatale*.[27]

It is difficult to say how strongly Boulanger saw herself as one of the 'lost princesses' of these poets. In an interview with Léonie Rosenstiel, Boulanger's sister Nadia insisted that Lili 'identified herself with Maeterlinck's poor little heroine [Maleine] just as she had already felt a sense of union between herself and the young girl evoked by Francis Jammes in the *Clairières*'.[28] This view was never contradicted by Boulanger herself; rather she confirmed it through her public persona

---

[24] For a detailed account of the public history of Maeterlinck's *La princesse Maleine*, see Georges Hermans, *Les premières armes de Maurice Maeterlinck* (Ledeberg and Ghent, 1967), 95–103.

[25] F-Pn Rés. Vmf. MS 116.

[26] 'Naturellement j'ai refusé.' Paul Claudel, letters to Darius Milhaud, 18 March 1916 and 5 July 1916; cited in Rosenstiel, *The Life and Works of Lili Boulanger*, 118, 280 (notes 129-30).

[27] In Boulanger's case, the aristocratic element was particularly accentuated through the fact that her mother was a Russian princess. Although some authors such as Rosenstiel have doubts about the reality of the title, the important point is that both Nadia and Lili were convinced of their aristocratic lineage. Compare also Cella Delarrancea's reminiscences of Lili Boulanger: 'Zu dieser Zeit war sie herrlich schön, wie die Lilien, noch leuchtender am Abend, wenn ihr Parfum zum Wesentlichen ihres kurzen Blühens wird... Zurückhaltend, elegant, graziösaristokratisch in ihren Gesten, meist weißgekleidet, den forschenden Blick ihrer schwarzen Augen zielgerichtet – man könnte sagen, im Bewußtsein ihrer Unvergänglichkeit – so erscheint sie in meiner Erinnerung.' 'Lili Boulanger', *Vom Schweigen befreit*, ed. Nies and Aulenkamp-Moeller, 38–41 (p. 38).

[28] 'On eût dit qu'elle s'était identifiée à la pauvre petite héroïne de Maeterlinck [Maleine], comme il y avait déjà eu fusion entre la jeune fille évoquée par Francis Jammes et elle-même.' Interview on 8 June 1972, quoted in Rosenstiel, *The Life and Works of Lili Boulanger*, 117, 280 (n. 123). I have used Rosenstiel's translation here.

of the Prix de Rome period as child-genius in the fragile body of a beautiful woman. In the words of the violinist Albert Spalding: 'Lili, slight, fair and frail, looked like the lost princess of a Maeterlinck play next to Nadia's healthy vitality. It was evident even then that the flame of Lili's talent was likely to overtax her meager physical resources.'[29] Yet both reminiscences – Nadia Boulanger's and Albert Spalding's – were formed long after Boulanger's premature death. The composer had been ill throughout her life, and her fragile appearance was certainly caused by her constant illness, which culminated in intestinal tuberculosis. From the perspective of someone who knows how Boulanger's story ended, it is almost impossible not to blend the figures of the frail, ill composer and the frail, ill heroine Maleine. But the two forms of identification should be distinguished. On the one hand, Boulanger's self-identification with Maleine – a heroine trapped in a despairing situation through a cruel game of destiny in a similar way to the composer in her illness, both fighting fate and losing in the end – might well have been one of several reasons to choose Maeterlinck's play as the basis for her opera, but it was by no means Boulanger's only or major one. On the other, the identification of composer and heroine at the time and by later musicologists has had the effect of blinkers, narrowing the gaze exclusively to a single aspect of the composer.[30]

The combination of literary taste, ambition and the autobiographical implications of the subject form together a strong but not decisive set of reasons for Boulanger's choice of *La princesse Maleine* as the libretto for her new opera. She must have discussed the project with her unofficial 'impresario', her sister Nadia, who herself had recently composed *La ville morte*, an opera based on a symbolist play by Gabriele d'Annunzio.[31] Boulanger's editor, Tito Ricordi, who would soon become a friend of the family, was consulted in later 1914 in his role as music publisher in order to obtain Maeterlinck's permission to set *La princesse Maleine*,[32] and in the letter with his New Year greetings for 1915, Ricordi announced the good news:

> Monsieur Maeterlinck is all ready to entrust you with *La princesse Maleine*, and he doesn't oppose modifications, cuts, etc., etc. So it is for you to decide if you still want to set this poem to music: if the answer is *yes* – which I hope

---

[29] Albert Spalding, *Rise to Follow: An Autobiography* (New York, 1943), 160, quoted in Rosenstiel, *The Life and Works of Lili Boulanger*, 62.

[30] On the problematic reception history of Boulanger's *Clairières dans le ciel*, see Annegret Fauser, 'Die Musik hinter der Legende: Lili Boulangers Liederzyklus *Clairières dans le ciel*', *Neue Zeitschrift für Musik*, 151 (1990), 9–14.

[31] Léonie Rosenstiel, *Nadia Boulanger: A Life in Music* (New York and London, 1982), 91, 121, 125–6; Jérôme Spycket, *Nadia Boulanger* (Lausanne, 1987), 34. Part of the material of *La ville morte* is kept in F-Pn, including the autograph short score (MS 19624), the libretto (ThB.4929(1–3)) and parts of the full score (MSS 19675, 19676).

[32] At this stage of selecting an opera topic, it was usual to involve the publisher. He not only had to approve the choice in general but also had to sort out the legal and financial details involved in the setting of a contemporary text. In France particularly, authors had a strong notion of copyright, which was reflected, for example, in the pathbreaking creation of associations such as the Société des Auteurs et Compositeurs Dramatiques (SACD) in 1829 and the Société des Auteurs, Compositeurs et Editeurs de Musique (SACEM) in 1851. Unsatisfied French authors, such as Victor Hugo in the famous trial on *Rigoletto* in 1857, often took legal action. On the legal implications of opera composition in nineteenth-century Paris, see Christian Sprang, *Grand opéra vor Gericht*, Schriftenreihe des Archivs für Urheber-, Film-, Funk- und Theaterrecht, 105 (Baden-Baden, 1993).

– it would be very easy to arrange Maeterlinck's play as an opera libretto – and if you agree, I would do this task myself.³³

The surviving correspondence and other material do not offer any reason why Boulanger, after having asked Ricordi to seek Maeterlinck's permission, hesitated for such a long time – nearly a year – to agree on her side, and Paul Claudel's letters to Darius Milhaud suggest that she actually looked elsewhere for a subject. Furthermore, the outbreak of the First World War established new priorities for a good while. Together with other former members of the Conservatoire, Boulanger founded the Comité Franco-Américain du Conservatoire National de Musique et de Déclamation. This organization tried to provide moral and even material support to former students of the Conservatoire who were now fighting as soldiers. For Boulanger, war had no glory; it represented only human suffering and misery, as entries in her diaries show. On 3 June 1916 she noted: 'Naval battle in the North Sea between the English and the Germans – what horror! – without result other than innumerable atrocities, suffering – oh! it is too painful.'³⁴ Her preoccupation with the war was reflected in the texts of her compositions. Among other works in these years she composed the *Vieille prière bouddhique* – a prayer for peace for humanity – and she set Psalm 130, *Du fond de l'abîme*, the 'De profundis'.³⁵ Eduard Reeser mentions that in 1915–16 Boulanger composed a now lost *Poème symphonique* with a programme which 'makes one realize that she tried to put into music the impression evoked by plains devastated through battles: the night, the wounded, the colour and the solitude'.³⁶

In the summer of 1915 Boulanger was still discussing the subject of her future opera, this time with Paul Gentien, Ricordi's Paris representative, who had a week's leave from military service. Returning to duty, he continued their discussion in his letters:

> Yesterday, after leaving you, I thought again about your desire to write a work related to current events which would not be precisely that. This is excessively difficult to realize dramatically. Apparently, a play entitled *Attila*, which is the story of the current invasion, has been given in Paris this winter, and it had a certain success. I believe nevertheless that such a play, even set in the distant past of more than a thousand years ago, necessarily possesses the offensive and banal appearance of *faits divers*. Yet it is possible for a poet to

---

³³ 'Monsieur Maeterlinck est tout disposé à vous confier "La Princesse Maleine" et il ne s'oppose pas à ce qu'on y fasse des remaniements, des coupures, etc. etc. C'est donc à vous de décider si vous voulez encore mettre en musique ce poème: si c'est *oui* – ce que j'espère – il sera très facile d'arranger le drame de Maeterlinck en livret lyrique – et si vous me le permettez je ferai moi-même cette besogne.' Ricordi to Lili Boulanger, 4 January 1915 (F-Pn, Département de la Musique, Fonds Boulanger).

³⁴ 'Bataille navale d[an]s la mer du Nord, entre les Anglais et les Allemands – quelle horreur! – Sans résultat autre que abominations sans nombre, souffrance – oh! c'est trop pénible.' F-Pn Rés. Vmf. MS 116 (3 June 1916).

³⁵ On the influence of the First World War on Lili Boulanger, see the unpublished study of Meike Tiemeyer, 'Claude Debussy – Lili Boulanger: Auswirkungen des Ersten Weltkrieges auf Leben und Werk' (Hausarbeit im Rahmen der Ersten Staatsprüfung für das Lehramt am Gymnasium, Osnabrück University, 1994).

³⁶ 'Zooals de motto's aanduiden heeft zij getracht, de stemmingen, die de plat geschoten vlakten, de nacht, de gewonden, de smart en de eenzaamheid oproepen, in klanken te realiseeren.' Eduard Reeser, 'Lili Boulanger', *De muziek*, 7 (1932-3), 210-21 and 274-71 (p. 269).

circumvent this difficulty (but he would need a lot of talent, that's the problem); the solution would be to write a sort of very simple fairy-tale with only few protagonists, the general subject of which would be a war.[37]

The story of a war is in fact a central layer in Maeterlinck's play *La princesse Maleine*, and indeed this appears to have been the last and decisive factor in Boulanger's selection of it as a text for her opera. She must have contacted Tito Ricordi in late 1915 with her request to proceed with the libretto; again, Ricordi successfully negotiated with Maeterlinck. The poet and the composer met in Nice for the first time early in February 1916, when Boulanger was on her way to Rome for her second stay there, and they discussed the opera project.[38] On 16 February 1916 Maeterlinck wrote his first letter to Boulanger, in which he personally authorized her to compose *La princesse Maleine*. Two days later he announced in a second letter that she would receive the 'cleaned-up exemplar of *La princesse*'.[39] It is not entirely clear what this version consisted of, but it was certainly not the final adaptation of the drama as a libretto. Yet the passage reveals that Maeterlinck himself gave suggestions for reworking the play into an operatic text on the basis of his and Boulanger's discussions in February. This version seems to have been the foundation on which Ricordi built his adaptation of *La princesse Maleine*.

Extant documents do not specify exactly when the libretto was shaped out of the original play, but they justify the assumption that Boulanger had told Ricordi in early spring 1916 in Milan – before he undertook his work on the text – what she expected from his adaptation. Ricordi was actually due to see Maeterlinck in Nice in March, but a letter to Nadia Boulanger indicates that he was detained in Milan because of the serious illness of his mother.[40] Boulanger herself nevertheless started with the composition of the opera, as an entry in her diary on 5 May 1916 suggests:

---

[37] Letter from Paul Gentien to Lili Boulanger, 2 September 1916: 'J'ai repensé après vous avoir quitté à votre désir d'écrire une œuvre d'actualité qui n'en serait précisément pas une. C'est excessivement difficile à réaliser dramatiquement[.] On a paraît-il joué cet hiver à Paris une pièce intitulée "Attila" qui est l'histoire de l'invasion actuelle, et qui a eu un certain succès. Je crois pourtant qu'une telle pièce même avec le lointain recul de plus de mille ans doit avoir une tournure "Faits-divers" choquante et banale. Il y aurait peut-être une façon de tourner la difficulté pour un poète (mais il lui faudrait beaucoup de talent, voilà le hic); ce serait d'écrire un conte de fées très simple, à peu de personnages, ayant pour sujet général une guerre.' F-Pn, Département de la Musique, Fonds Boulanger. In his following letter (not dated), Gentien recommended Claudel's *L'annonce faite à Marie* as a suitable and patriotic opera subject.

[38] This earlier date is suggested by the copy of a telegram which Tito Ricordi sent to Lili Boulanger: 'Heureux [sic] conclusion. Maeterlinck vous attend vendredi.' Milan, Archivio Storico Ricordi, *Copialettere 1915–16*, viii, no. 438. Rosenstiel gives 20 February 1916 as the date of the first meeting between Maeterlinck and Boulanger: 'Maeterlinck sent Lili another letter on February 20, inviting her to visit him with Tito Ricordi the next day at four o'clock.' Rosenstiel, *The Life and Works of Lili Boulanger*, 118. The letter which Rosenstiel mentions is not among Maeterlinck's letters to Lili Boulanger in F-Pn. Yet Maeterlinck writes in his letter of 18 February 1916 that he had realized only after Boulanger's departure that he had forgotten to talk about financial details with her. Thus their meeting must have taken place earlier.

[39] Letter from Maurice Maeterlinck to Lili Boulanger, 18 February 1916: 'l'exemplaire expurgé de "La Princesse"'. F-Pn, Département de la Musique, Fonds Boulanger. The letter continues: 'Peut-être faudra-t-il, çà et là, retoucher ou rétablir un raccord négligé ou oublié. La musique le sentira mieux que moi et il va sans dire que je suis tout à vos ordres pour vous donner les textes nécessaires.'

[40] Letter from Tito Ricordi to Nadia Boulanger, 3 April 1916: 'Quant à mon voyage à Nice pour voir Maeterlinck je ne peux même y penser.' F-Pn n.l.a. Boulanger 99, 5/6.

'Perhaps I have Hjalmar's theme in what I did today.'[41] On 22 or 23 June 1916, Boulanger, Maeterlinck and Ricordi eventually met in Nice to discuss the final shape of the libretto, which found Maeterlinck's full approval: 'I find the adaptation very dextrous and very successful. Some cuts might still be necessary – I propose two or three minor changes to you.'[42] The subsequent correspondence over the libretto turned to more pragmatic points: the question of whether Tito Ricordi's name should appear on the libretto and score. Ricordi asked Boulanger to intervene with Maeterlinck, and the poet wrote to Boulanger: 'Since the adaptation or cuts were made by Ricordi, it is only just that his name should figure on the libretto and the score.'[43] For Ricordi, this must have been important, because he thanked Maeterlinck in terms which were even more effusive than those he normally used in his letters to the poet:

> Mademoiselle Lili Boulanger informs me that you have had the kindness to agree with my desire and that my modest name will figure on the libretto of *La princesse Maleine* next to your illustrious one. I am infinitely grateful to you for that.[44]

Thus it is absolutely clear that it was Tito Ricordi who did the actual work of shaping the play into a libretto for Boulanger's setting, and not the composer herself as has been assumed until now.[45]

When Boulanger started on the composition of *La princesse Maleine*, she had just heard that she had two years left to live. This opera was the *magnum opus* which she wanted to finish before her death – an ambition which reflects the fact that in the hierarchy of French music, even at that time, five-act operas held the highest position – and she focused almost all her creativity on it. In May 1916 she began the composition of *La princesse Maleine* seriously, although the final version of the libretto had not yet been established. In September 1916 Ricordi reported to

---

[41] 'J'aurai peut-être d[an]s ce que j'ai fait aujourd'hui, le thème de Hjalmar.' F-Pn Rés. Vmf. MS 116 (2 May 1916).

[42] Letter from Maurice Maeterlinck to Lili Boulanger, 24 June 1916: 'L'adaptation me paraît très habile et très heureuse. Peut-être faudra-t-il encore quelques coupures – je vous soumets deux ou trois retouches sans importance.' F-Pn, Département de la Musique, Fonds Boulanger.

[43] Letter from Maurice Maeterlinck to Lili Boulanger, 8 August 1916: 'Il est fort juste que l'adaptation ou les coupures ayant été faites par Ricordi, son nom figurera sur la brochure et la partition.' F-Pn, Département de la Musique, Fonds Boulanger.

[44] 'Mademoiselle Lili Boulanger m'informe que vous avez eu l'amabilité d'acquiescer à mon désir et que mon nom modeste figurera à côté du vôtre illustre sur le livret de *la Princesse Maleine*. Je vous en suis infiniment reconnaissant.' Milan, Archivio Storico Ricordi, *Copialettere 1916–17*, ii, no. 171. Maeterlinck clearly made his permission to print Ricordi's name on the title-page dependent upon receipt of belated contracts for the project. Ricordi's letter contained not only the contract but also a cheque for 5,000 francs.

[45] The fact that the libretto was adapted by Tito Ricordi has never been revealed in the writings about Lili Boulanger. Even Rosenstiel, who had access to the majority of Boulanger's letters, including those of Maeterlinck and Ricordi, does not mention that it was Ricordi and not Boulanger who shaped the libretto. Ricordi's adaptation of *La princesse Maleine* was not his first, for he had been involved in at least two other operas: in 1912–13 he shortened Gabriele d'Annunzio's play *Francesca da Rimini* for Riccardo Zandonai; and later, in 1918, he adapted *La nave* by the same author for Italo Montemezzi (see Maehder, 'The Origins of Italian Literaturoper', 110, 122–5). Mosco Carner mentions in his biography of Giacomo Puccini (*Puccini: A Critical Biography*, 3rd edn, London, 1992) that Ricordi apparently suggested changes for the libretto of *Tosca* (p. 114). He also gives a short biographical survey of Tito Ricordi's life and work (pp. 121–2, 221, 241) in which he emphasizes Ricordi's strong interest in the actual production of operas.

Maeterlinck: 'I have good news from Mademoiselle Lili Boulanger, and I know that she works with great enthusiasm on this piece, in which she will put all her soul and all her artist's heart.'[46] Maeterlinck and Boulanger stayed in contact about *La princesse Maleine*, while the composition progressed smoothly. In February 1917 Boulanger took up revisions of her composition, as the entries in a green-bound sketchbook suggest.[47] In March she revised the love duet from Act 2, and revisions continued through April and May. After her illness in summer 1917 she started work again in October, and the surviving fragment of the fair copy of Act 1, scene ii ('Une forêt') is dated 'copied: Saturday 27 to Monday 29 October 1917, Gargenville'.[48] By the end of the year the composition of the opera must have been far advanced: Boulanger was copying her opera into a clean Particell, and she had set herself a deadline: a desperate note bearing testimony to her conscious race against death – 'Copied in December 1917. Everything *must* be finished before 1 January. It *MUST!!!* Will I be able to do it?'[49] In February 1918, one month before her death, a last entry in the hand of her sister appears in the sketchbook: a musical fragment which is not related to the composition of the opera. Boulanger wanted her sister Nadia to finish *La princesse Maleine*, but in a letter to Eduard Reeser written in January 1932 Nadia confessed that she was unable to do so: 'Although my sister had wished that I should finish these works [a sonata and *La princesse Maleine*] – I did not succeed with it – Will I ever succeed? *Maleine* is far progressed, wonderful, and yet impossible to perform.'[50]

Maeterlinck's play *La princesse Maleine* was first published in 1889,[51] and the Paris élite welcomed it enthusiastically as 'the most brilliant work

---

[46] Letter by Tito Ricordi to Maurice Maeterlinck, 8 September 1916: 'J'ai de bonnes nouvelles de Mlle Lili Boulanger et je sais qu'elle travaille avec grand enthousiasme à cette œuvre où elle va mettre toute son âme et tout son cœur d'artiste.' Milan, Archivio Storico Ricordi, *Copialettere 1916–17*, ii, no. 408.

[47] F-Pn MS 19470.

[48] 'Copié: Samedi 27 au / L. 29 Octobre 1917 / Gargenville'. F-Pn MS 19469, p. 9.

[49] 'Copié en / déc. 1917 / il *faut* tout finir / avant le 1er Janv. / il *FAUT* !!! / Le pourrai-je?' F-Pn MS 19470, f. 37ʳ.

[50] 'Obwohl meine Schwester den Wunsch geäußert hatte, daß ich diese Werke [eine Sonate und *La princesse Maleine*] vollenden sollte – es ist mir nicht gelungen – wird es mir je gelingen? *Maleine* ist sehr weit gediehen, wunderbar, und dennoch unaufführbar.' German translation of a letter from Nadia Boulanger to Eduard Reeser, published as 'Ein Brief von Nadia Boulanger an Eduard Reeser', *Vom Schweigen befreit*, ed. Nies and Aulenkamp-Moeller, 88–91 (p. 91).

[51] *La princesse Maleine* is a five-act play set in unspecified (medieval) times in Holland. Marcellus and Hjalmar, kings of the two parts of Holland, decide to marry their children Maleine and Prince Hjalmar. During the engagement festivities in Harlingen, Maleine's home, a dispute erupts, instigated by Queen Anne of Jutland, who had left her husband for King Hjalmar (the Old King) and who plots to marry her daughter Uglyane to his son. After the dispute, King Hjalmar and his court leave, while Marcellus demands that Maleine should renounce Prince Hjalmar. When she refuses, he locks her in a tower. A war erupts between the two parts of Holland, devastating Harlingen. When Maleine and her nurse finally manage to break out of their prison, they find their home destroyed. Maleine eventually makes her way to Ysselmonde, King Hjalmar's residence. There she finds employment as chambermaid to Uglyane. Meanwhile, Queen Anne pushes forward Uglyane's and Prince Hjalmar's wedding, while poisoning the Old King and trying to seduce the prince herself at the same time. With a fake letter, in which she pretends to be Uglyane, Maleine asks Prince Hjalmar to meet her at the fountain in the garden. There she discloses her true identity to him and they reconfirm their engagement.
  Prince Hjalmar informs his father that Maleine is still alive and that they want to marry. The Old King tries to dissuade him out of fear for Queen Anne's reaction. But Maleine appears in public, and when the king does not refuse his son's marriage with Maleine instead of Uglyane, Anne starts to poison Maleine as well. Throughout the wedding preparations Maleine

of our time':⁵² 'From this moment, we have proof: there is indeed a symbolist theatre.'⁵³ *La princesse Maleine* became an emblem for the 'overcoming of naturalism', as Hermann Bahr declared in 1891:

> The common bluntness of things, the palpable real, the outdoor dress of truth is disdained, and the bottom of the deep soul's waves, mad desire, which does not know how to interpret itself, and the sultry swell of blind dreams, everything enigmatic and unarticulated is sought out. It is the return to the living man, away from the insolent tyranny of dead objects.⁵⁴

The play does not correspond to the structure of classic French tragedy – regardless of its division into five acts – nor is it a symbolist 'closet drama' (*Lesedrama*): its stage was not simply imaginary. The piece consists of a loose succession of scenes: 'What a distant tapestry is this *Princesse Maleine*, with an otherworldly wind in all its holes.'⁵⁵ Yet it is a symbolist play, and 'the symbol never tolerates the active presence of man'.⁵⁶ Human actors would give too much 'palpable reality' to a drama which emphasizes the hidden world of the human soul and which 'tries to make apparent the invisible forces at work in life',⁵⁷ thus creating the apparent paradox that the 'return to the living man' (Bahr) excludes the human on stage. When Jules Huret asked Maeterlinck about *La princesse Maleine*, he gave the slightly ironic answer: 'When I wrote *La princesse*

---

becomes paler and weaker, but her resistance keeps her alive. The wedding approaches, and Queen Anne locks Maleine in her room with her dog Pluto as her only company. Maleine is terrified. The door opens, and in come Queen Anne and the Old King. When King Hjalmar refuses to kill Maleine, Queen Anne throttles her with a noose. While the couple try to remove the traces of the crime, the court fool appears at the window. The king kills him with his sword while, outside, Maleine's nurse, Prince Hjalmar and little Allan (Anne's neglected son and now a friend of Maleine) start searching for her. When the corridor is clear, the king and queen depart hastily from the room, leaving Anne's red coat behind. In the cemetery, peasants discuss strange occurrences: a thunderbolt has struck the crucifix of the castle chapel, and it has fallen into the moat. In the castle, the courtiers try to understand what is happening. Finally Prince Hjalmar, Angus, the Old King and Queen Anne join them. When they start talking about Maleine, the king begins to give away that something has happened. Hjalmar and the nurse go to look for Maleine and they find her dead. The seven Beguines (nuns) enter, followed by the Old King and Anne. The king accuses Queen Anne of murdering Maleine, with the red coat proving his words. Prince Hjalmar stabs the murderess before killing himself. The king stays behind, mad.

⁵² 'L'œuvre la plus géniale de ce temps'. Octave Mirbeau's 1890 review of *La princesse Maleine*, quoted in Peter Szondi, *Das lyrische Drama des Fin de siècle*, ed. Henriette Beese (2nd edn, Frankfurt am Main, 1991), 353.

⁵³ 'Désormais, la preuve est faite: il y a un théâtre symboliste.' Retté, quoted in Marcel Postic, *Maeterlinck et le symbolisme* (Paris, 1970), 42.

⁵⁴ 'Die gemeine Deutlichkeit der Dinge, das handgreiflich Wirkliche, das Straßenkleid der Wahrheit wird verschmäht und der Grund der Wogen in der tiefen Seele, die irre Sehnsucht, die sich nicht zu deuten weiß, und der schwüle Schwall der blinden Träume, alles Rätselhafte und Unartikulierte wird aufgesucht. Es ist, von der frechen Despotie der toten Dinge weg, die Rückkehr zum lebendigen Menschen.' Hermann Bahr, *Die Überwindung des Naturalismus* (Dresden and Leipzig, 1891), 196, quoted in Erwin Koppen, *Dekadenter Wagnerismus: Studien zur europäischen Literatur des Fin de siècle* (Berlin and New York, 1973), 278.

⁵⁵ Letter from Maurice Maeterlinck to Octave Mirbeau, 1890: 'Quelle lointaine tapisserie que cette "Princesse Maleine" avec un vent d'au delà dans les trous.' Quoted in Szondi, *Das lyrische Drama des Fin de siècle*, 354.

⁵⁶ 'Le symbole ne supporte jamais la présence active de l'homme.' Maurice Maeterlinck, 'Menus propos, le théâtre', *La jeune Belgique*, 9 (1890), 334, quoted in Carole J. Lambert, *The Empty Cross: Medieval Hopes, Modern Futility in the Theater of Maurice Maeterlinck, Paul Claudel, August Strindberg, and Georg Kaiser* (New York and London, 1990), 46.

⁵⁷ Susan Youens, 'An Unseen Player: Destiny in *Pelléas et Mélisande*', *Reading Opera*, ed. Groos and Parker, 60–91 (p. 64).

Maleine, I told myself: "I will try to create a work in the manner of Shakespeare for a puppet-play." '[58] Maeterlinck's references to the 'distant tapestry' and to Shakespeare map two of the major influences on his early writing: medieval mysticism and the world of the Elizabethan stage. Other influences can be detected in Maeterlinck's allusions to Grimm's *Kinder- und Hausmärchen* no. 198 (*Jungfrau Maleen*), to Edgar Allen Poe and to the Romantic tradition.[59] Maeterlinck himself was aware of these influences, and he expressed his anxiety over them in a letter to Mirbeau soon after the latter's review of the play was published:

> I am deeply confused at the moment, and never have I been more profoundly in doubt about myself. I only see in my poor *Princesse* Shakespeare, Edgar Poe and the influence of my friend Van Lerberghe, and I can't recognize anything which is particular to me.[60]

Although the success of *La princesse Maleine* established Maeterlinck's reputation as one of the most important symbolist writers, the poet retained a very ambivalent attitude towards the play.[61] His uneasiness might have been one of the reasons why he was so reluctant to grant his permission to set it to music. However, when Lili Boulanger asked for Maeterlinck's authorization to compose *La princesse Maleine*, the play was already more than 25 years old, and Maeterlinck himself had acquired wide experience with the adaptation of his dramatic works for the needs of opera. Indeed, he might have seen a chance to revive this problem-child through its being reshaped into the more focused structure of an

---

[58] 'Quand j'ai écrit *La Princesse Maleine* je me suis dit: "Je vais tâcher de faire une pièce à la façon de Shakespeare pour un théâtre de marionnettes." ' Jules Huret, *Enquête sur l'évolution littéraire* (Paris, 1901), 129. Marionettes as non-human players held an important place in symbolist dramatic theory, but puppet-plays were also part of the French Wagner reception in the salon (e.g. of Judith Gautier). In 1888 Henri Signoret founded the Petit-Théâtre des Marionnettes in the Galérie Vivienne, which gave not only contemporary pieces by writers such as Maurice Bouchor or Anatole France but also adaptations of Shakespeare. In 1888, Bouchor's adaptation of Shakespeare's *The Tempest* was performed with music by Ernest Chausson. Since Maeterlinck had been in Paris when this theatre was founded, it is highly probable that he not only knew about it but actually went there.

[59] The following discussion is based upon several studies: Hermans, *Les premières armes de Maurice Maeterlinck*, 95-103; Szondi, *Das lyrische Drama des Fin de siècle*, 351-63; Postic, *Maeterlinck et le symbolisme*, 42-51; Lambert, *The Empty Cross*, esp. pp. 42-8; Hans Felten and Elke Pacholek, 'Überdetermination und Heterogenität im frühen Theater Maeterlincks', *Germanisch-Romanische Monatsschrift*, new ser., 36 (1986), 320-30; Paul Gorceix, *Les affinités allemandes dans l'œuvre de Maurice Maeterlinck* (Paris, 1975), 305-71; Stefan Gross, *Maurice Maeterlinck oder der symbolische Sadismus des Humors: Studie zum Frühwerk mit angehängten Materialien* (Frankfurt am Main, 1985).

[60] Letter from Maurice Maeterlinck to Octave Mirbeau, 1890: 'Je suis profondément troublé en ce moment et je n'ai jamais plus profondément douté de moi-même. Dans ma pauvre Princesse je ne vois que de Shakespeare, de l'Edgar Poe et l'influence de mon ami Van Lerberghe et je n'y distingue plus rien qui m'appartienne.' Quoted in Maurice Maeterlinck, *Serres chaudes, Quinze chansons, La princesse Maleine*, ed. Paul Gorceix (Paris, 1983), 289.

[61] Maeterlinck addressed this point in his preface to the 1901 edition of his collected plays: 'The texts of these short plays, which my publisher now collects in three volumes, have hardly been changed. It is not at all that they seem perfect to me - far from it. But one does not improve a poem by successive corrections. The best and the worst in it have entwined roots ... It would for example have been easy in *La princesse Maleine* to suppress many a risky naïvety, a few superfluous scenes and most of those astonished repetitions that make the characters seem like slightly deaf sleepwalkers constantly roused from painful dreams. I could have thus spared them some smiles, but the atmosphere and the very world in which they live would seem changed.' Trans. David Grayson, 'The Libretto of Debussy's *Pelléas et Mélisande*', *Music and Letters*, 66 (1985), 34-50 (p. 35).

operatic text. We have already seen that Maeterlinck actively participated in the rewriting through discussion, proposals and annotations. Even in the quasi-final version of the libretto, he gave advice which shows his pragmatic experience with the theatre.

Ricordi's adaptation of the play comprised extensive cuts of scenes, a reduction of the number of characters, and a restructuring of the action through shifts and fusions of scenes. Table 1, a synopsis of Maeterlinck's original play and Ricordi's adaptation, shows how far-reaching his cuts were even just in terms of the loss of text: he eliminated nine complete scenes and retained only parts of the remaining 15. Furthermore, he reversed the order of two scenes in Act 1 of the libretto, fused several together in Acts 2 and 4, and created a new five-act structure. Ricordi's comments in the typescript of the libretto clearly indicate that his first objective was to reduce the rather long play to a manageable amount of text for the composition of an opera: at the end of each act, he added up the lines in Italian, noting at the end of Act 3, for example:

```
linee lunghe  26                              52
   "  medie  31                              31
   "  corte  46                              ___
                                             83 medie
                                          +  46 corte
                                             ___
                                             129⁶²
```

On the last page, he marked down a total of 991 lines 'di cui linee medie 734 [e linee] corte 257'.[63]

The removal of more than half the text produced changes in the drama's substance. Out of the loose and associative series of scenes in Maeterlinck's play, which was far more complicated, Ricordi created a well-structured plot in which the different acts correspond to stages of the action's development:

Act 1   Maleine's journey to Ysselmonde.
Act 2   Maleine's arrival at Ysselmonde and her reunion with Hjalmar.
Act 3   Maleine's public appearance at Ysselmonde and her direct encounter with Queen Anne.
Act 4   The public banquet. Maleine's poisoning by Queen Anne.
Act 5   Maleine's murder by Queen Anne and its consequences.

Ricordi focused the action on Maleine and on her conflict with Queen Anne by eliminating all digressions and thoroughly pruning the scenes which concentrate on the Old King, Prince Hjalmar, Queen Anne and her daughter Uglyane, and on their complex interrelationships. This is especially apparent at the end, where the action is reduced to a dense sequence of deaths in Maleine's room, whereas in the play Maeterlinck had interpolated a scene at the cemetery and an extended gathering of the court in which the Old King publicly reveals his guilt,

---

[62] Libretto of *La princesse Maleine*, Musée Marmottan, p. 8.
[63] *Ibid.*, final page.

TABLE 1
LA PRINCESSE MALEINE: SCENE-BY-SCENE COMPARISON OF MAETERLINCK'S PLAY AND RICORDI'S LIBRETTO

Maurice Maeterlinck, *La princesse Maleine*[a]	Tito Ricordi, libretto adaptation[b]
ACTE PREMIER	ACTE 1°
~~Scène première~~	
~~Les jardins du château [de Hartingen]~~	
~~Scène II~~	
~~Un appartement du château~~	
Scène III	Scène 1°
Une forêt	Une chambre voûtée dans une tour
Scène IV	Scène 2°
Une chambre voûtée dans une tour	Une forêt
	Scène 3°
ACTE DEUXIÈME	
Scène première	
Une forêt	
Scène II	ACTE 2°
Une salle dans le château [d'Ysselmonde]	Scène 1°
Scène III	Une salle dans le château
Une rue du village	
~~Scène IV~~	
~~Un appartement du château~~	
Scène V	Scène 2°
Un corridor du château	Un corridor du château
Scène VI	Scène 3°
Un bois dans un parc	Un bois dans un parc
ACTE TROISIÈME	ACTE 3°
Scène première	Scène 1°
Un appartement du château	Une salle dans le château

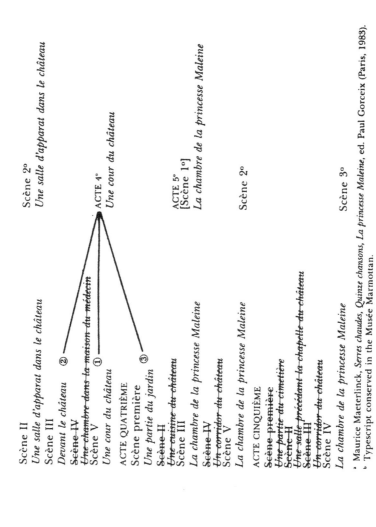

[a] Maurice Maeterlinck, *Serres chaudes, Quinze chansons, La princesse Maleine*, ed. Paul Gorceix (Paris, 1983).
[b] Typescript conserved in the Musée Marmottan.

scenes strongly modelled on Shakespeare's *Hamlet* and *King Lear* respectively.

Ricordi also reduced the number of characters: Maleine's complete family and environment, except for her wet-nurse, are removed. Through this, Maleine loses her history, origin and background, and the change reinforces her presentation as *Naturwesen*, a notion of womanhood which Maeterlinck developed in his *Trésor des humbles*.[64] Such a concept of the female draws upon the Romantic dialectic between male *logos* and female *physis*, between culture and nature, which can be resolved only in the synthesis of art created by the male genius.[65]

> [Women] are truly the closest relatives of the infinite which surrounds us, and only they know how to smile at it with the familiar grace of the child which is not afraid of its father. They preserve here on earth, like a celestial and functionless jewel, the pure salt of our souls.[66]

Women's and children's deficiency of intellect makes them ideal yet futile recipients of the eternal. Functionlessness counts as an essential quality in symbolist poetry; indeed, women's direct link to nature and eternity places them in close proximity to the symbol itself, a poetic sign with an affinity to the eternal, in contrast to male activity: 'There is an uninterrupted antagonism between the forces of the symbol and those of the man who is active. The symbol of the poem is an ardent centre whose rays stretch out to the eternal.'[67] Like the symbol in poetry, the female lack of consciousness puts woman closer to eternal truth and to God, in other words to the instinctive understanding of the object in its context. But, like an animal, she lacks the comprehension of her insight and therefore any subjectivity, given that she has 'less intelligence than man'. Through her direct contact with nature, woman experiences living in a symbiotic relationship with natural processes such as death, and instead of leading her life consciously she is driven through it:

> Woman is closer to God than man. Of all the beings we know, woman seems to be the closest to God ... Woman has more insight and less intelligence than man. She sees nothing in isolation. In every object, she seems to see, without knowing it, more the eternal relations of the object than the object itself ... There are unfathomable *sous-entendus* between woman and death, for example. She does not die as we do; she dies like animals or little children.[68]

---

[64] The chapter is entitled 'Sur les femmes', in Maurice Maeterlinck, *Le trésor des humbles* (3rd edn, Paris, 1896), 81–98.

[65] On the development of this essentialist dichotomy in Western culture since Greek antiquity, see Battersby, *Gender and Genius*.

[66] '[Les femmes] sont vraiment les plus proches parentes de l'infini qui nous entoure et, seules, savent encore lui sourire avec la grâce familière de l'enfant qui ne craint pas son père. Elles conservent ici-bas, comme un joyau céleste et inutile, le sel pur de notre âme.' Maeterlinck, *Le trésor des humbles*, quoted in Gorceix, *Les affinités allemandes dans l'œuvre de Maurice Maeterlinck*, 305.

[67] 'Il y a divergence ininterrompue entre les forces du symbole et celles de l'homme qui agite. Le symbole du poème est un centre dont les rayons divergent dans l'infini.' Maeterlinck, 'Menus propos, le théâtre', quoted in Lambert, *The Empty Cross*, 46.

[68] 'La femme est plus près de Dieu que l'homme. De tous les êtres que nous connaissons, la femme semble l'être le plus près de Dieu ... La femme a plus de raison et moins d'intelligence que l'homme. Elle ne voit rien isolément. En tout objet, elle semble voir, à son insu, les relations éternelles de l'objet, plus exactement que l'objet lui-même ... Il y a des *sous-entendus* introuvables entre la femme et la mort, par exemple. Elle ne meurt pas comme nous, elle meurt

With an almost ethnological viewpoint, Maeterlinck here describes woman as Other. Woman cannot be understood through intellect alone. Woman is foreign, elusive and therefore dangerous. Yet, as the inspired artist and knowledgeable man, Maeterlinck as symbolist poet is the explorer of human nature; from his authoritative standpoint, he explains this foreign being and savage to his male fellows. Instead of feminizing the Other, Maeterlinck describes the Other as feminine. In understanding woman as the essence of Otherness and nature, symbolism draws upon Romantic traditions of essentializing the 'eternal feminine', setting the contrast between individual male will and nature-bound female passivity.[69] If, therefore, Maeterlinck's symbolist dramas unfold in a 'quasi-Schopenhauerian determinism',[70] they could be read as the undoing of the 'eternal feminine' in the attempt of achieving their poetic purpose: 'to represent the unrepresentable and make known the unknowable'.[71]

Such a conception of the feminine is paramount to Maeterlinck's characterization of male and female figures in *La princesse Maleine*. Though all the protagonists in his plays are subjected to the intervention of destiny in their lives,[72] their reaction to it differs according to their sex: the men try to understand and analyse events, while the women act without reflection. Intellect and instinct are clearly gendered concepts, and their antagonistic relationship appears even more sharply in the adaptation of *La princesse Maleine* as a libretto. Here instinctive love drives Maleine to force her way out of the tower through the forest to Ysselmonde. Her actions are never the result of reflection, her answers never indicate any logical reason. In fact, against all logic, she remains in Ysselmonde and dies, weakened through poison, strangled by being dragged along the floor by Queen Anne with a noose around her neck. Maleine's death appears all the more animal-like as she spends her last moments in the company of Pluto, her black dog. It whimpers and howls in the face of the approaching danger, while Maleine utters incoherent phrases, expressing her fear in child-like exclamations.

But if Maleine represents the instinctively 'good' virgin of Marian passivity, Queen Anne represents the other elementary force of human nature, evil and cruelty. A fairy-tale witch with all the threats and power of such a *Naturwesen*, she spreads unintelligible terror.[73] Like Maleine,

---

comme les animaux et les petits enfants.' Maeterlinck, 'Menus propos' (1891), quoted in Gorceix, *Les affinités allemandes dans l'œuvre de Maurice Maeterlinck*, 305. The description of women and children as similar is a common phenomenon in Western history which can also be seen in the context of colonial attitudes towards the 'Other'; see J. J. Wilson, 'Carrington Revisited', *Between Women: Biographers, Novelists, Critics, Teachers and Artists Write about their Work on Women*, ed. Carol Asher, Louise DeSalvo and Sara Ruddick (2nd edn, New York and London, 1993), 327–41 (p. 329).

[69] For an interesting reading of the essentialist understanding of the 'eternal feminine' within the discussion in gendered categories of muse and poet, see Germaine Greer, *Slip-Shod Sibyls: Recognition, Rejection and the Woman Poet* (London, 1995), 1–35. See also 'The Queen's Looking Glass: Female Creativity, Male Images of Women, and the Metaphor of Literary Paternity', Sandra M. Gilbert and Susan Gubar, *The Madwoman in the Attic: The Woman Writer and the Nineteenth-Century Literary Imagination* (New Haven and London, 1984), 3–44.

[70] Youens, 'An Unseen Player', 63.

[71] Youens thus summarizes the purpose of drama according to Maeterlinck; *ibid.*, 65.

[72] The role of destiny in Maeterlinck's plays is discussed in almost all writings on him. With specific reference to *Pelléas et Mélisande*, see Youens, 'An Unseen Player'.

[73] Felten and Pacholek, 'Überdetermination und Heterogenität im frühen Theater Maeterlincks', 324.

she loses her history in the course of the play's adaptation as a libretto and, in the libretto even more than in the play, both women just are, embodying essential and opposite qualities of life. Maleine's nurse, on her side, is motivated by maternal instinct, another quality which – especially in the nineteenth century – is understood as essentially feminine.

For the men, culture is the driving force in their actions: all three – the Old King, Prince Hjalmar and his confidant Angus – try to understand in a rational way what happens to them in the course of their histories. The events of their lives are placed in a linear unfolding, leading to different forms of action. Ultimately, the Old King and Prince Hjalmar kill as well, but both their actions are motivated through intellect: the Old King silences a witness of the murder (the fool), and Hjalmar executes the murderer (Queen Anne). Their weapons are phallic and honourable – dagger and sword – as opposed to the more bestial methods of Queen Anne; yet essential powers orchestrated by Destiny have broken into the cultured structure of their lives, sweeping them along in the swirl of disaster.

Were the composer of this opera male, an interpretation similar to Ruth Solie's reading of Schumann's *Frauenliebe und -leben* would almost suggest itself.[74] The libretto could indeed be understood as the reworking of an already misogynist play by composer and librettist in order to emphasize the dichotomy of nature and culture as female and male. This could easily be further interpreted in the light of the passionate discussions of the *femme nouvelle* and of feminism in France at the beginning of the twentieth century: the 'new woman' was widely perceived as a threat to French society because her striving for a place in the public sphere would jeopardize traditional values of 'republican motherhood' and femininity.[75] But the composer of the opera was female, and she had strong influence on the shaping of this libretto. She met with Maeterlinck and Ricordi on several occasions in order to discuss the adaptation, and she also made changes to the resulting text: surviving letters and the two versions of the libretto indicate Boulanger's far-reaching involvement in the creation of the operatic text. Furthermore, she was obviously aware of feminist movements and concepts, even if it is unclear whether and how strongly she identified with them. Her victory in the Prix de Rome competition catapulted her into the ranks of successful women in the male public world of early twentieth-century France and, although she never became directly involved with feminist propaganda, she did not object to her name appearing in this context. Moreover, on several occasions during her lifetime, her works were performed in concerts which embraced the cause of propagating women's music, as for example on 15 November 1917 in Paris in the Festival de Musique Féminine.

[74] Ruth A. Solie, 'Whose Life? The Gendered Self in Schumann's *Frauenliebe* Songs', *Music and Text: Critical Inquiries*, ed. Steven Paul Scher (Cambridge, 1992), 219–40.
[75] On this discussion, see Karen Offen, 'Depopulation, Nationalism and Feminism in Fin-de-siècle France', *American Historical Review*, 89 (1984), 648–76; Debora Silverman, 'The "New Woman", Feminism, and the Decorative Arts in Fin-de-siècle France', *Eroticism and the Body Politic*, ed. Lynn Hunt (Baltimore and London, 1991), 144–63; Edward Berenson, *The Trial of Madame Caillaux*

But while the libretto's characterization of Maleine and Queen Anne could be read as a staged dispute between women in the sense of a cat-fight, observed by men, it can also be interpreted as a feminization of the opera's subject. The essential conflict of the drama is acted out between two women whose actions force the other characters – especially the Old King and Prince Hjalmar – to follow. Maleine could be seen as the 'lost princess', but she also appears as a driving force in the drama: she goes to Ysselmonde, she sets the meeting with Hjalmar, and she decides to stay and regain her place as future queen of Ysselmonde. Queen Anne, on the other hand, has all the traits of the wicked stepmother and witch, yet she is a dangerous political figure, calculating every step and using every means available to her. Although Maleine dies for her love like any traditional operatic heroine evoked by Catherine Clément,[76] she also dies for her political obstinacy and by the hand of another woman, a political opponent. This form of death is unusual for an opera heroine, and both elements become strongly emphasized in the libretto, whereas in the play the Old King is much more involved in Maleine's death, and the political aspect remains far in the background. Moreover, the libretto of *La princesse Maleine* shows strong evidence that despite her two male collaborators, Boulanger tried to create a woman's text about war and its horrors, leaving all glorious and militaristic aspects aside.[77]

Bearing in mind that Boulanger wanted to compose an opera 'related to current events' in the context of the war, the reworking of Maeterlinck's text can be interpreted as an attempt to write the 'sort of very simple fairy-tale with only few protagonists, the general subject of which would be a war' that she discussed with Paul Gentien in summer 1915. The libretto could be read as an allegory, with Maleine and Anne representing the essential forces that fight in war: good and evil, light and dark. The other protagonists are weak: although the three men are involved in the conflict, trying to understand and to act in threatening circumstances, they appear as instruments in the hands of the two women who are the real agents of the opera. Hjalmar's actions follow the demands first of Anne, then of Maleine. His killing of Anne is a consequence of

---

(Berkeley, Los Angeles and Oxford, 1992), esp. ch. 1, 3 and 4; Marieluise Christadler, 'Zwischen Macht und Ohnmacht: Die Musen der Republik' and 'Mondäner und rebellischer Feminismus: Die Frauenbewegung in der Dritten Republik', *Bewegte Jahre – Frankreichs Frauen*, ed. Marieluise Christadler and Florence Hervé (Düsseldorf, 1994), 37–52, 53–71.

[76] Clément's pathbreaking book on the undoing of women in opera focuses, as Mary Ann Smart puts it, on tragic operas, 'conveniently forgetting comic operas, in which no one dies and the girl usually gets what she wants' ('The Lost Voice of Rosine Stoltz', *Cambridge Opera Journal*, 6 (1994), 31–50, p. 33). Yet Smart does not seem to be aware of the fact that, although women do not die in comic operas, their role is still fenced by society's notion of femininity, creating a less obvious form of 'undoing', especially in role stereotypes such as the *komische Alte*. Heroines in comic operas usually get marriage as their reward, thus enacting the female 'success story' of the well-adjusted bourgeoise. Clément's discussion of Mélisande in Debussy's *Pelléas et Mélisande* draws upon the concept of the little witch, representing a *Naturwesen* similar to Maleine; see Catherine Clément, *L'opéra, ou la défaite des femmes* (Paris, 1979).

[77] Suzanne Cusick discusses a similar constellation of the reading of a libretto through a female composer as feminist act in her essay 'Of Women, Music, and Power'. Although the public situation is different, given that Francesca Caccini's *La liberazione di Ruggiero* was a commission from a female patron, the pattern of reinterpreting a male libretto in a female perspective corresponds with Boulanger's later effort in the case of *La princesse Maleine*.

Maleine's death, as is his suicide. Angus appears (like Kurwenal in *Tristan und Isolde*) as Hjalmar's second self, and his actions only prolong Hjalmar's responses to Anne and Maleine. Queen Anne, for her part, completely dominates the Old King: he is her weapon and her victim, and Maleine's approach to his court creates an inner conflict through which he ultimately loses his *logos* and therefore his masculinity. At the end, the king is left impotent, capable only of uttering the syllables 'Ha, ha, ha, ha', which, significantly, were added to the original libretto by Boulanger. This 'feminine ending' of the opera can be interpreted as the undoing of culture as the only result of war: none of the opponents survives the conflict, and the men impersonating culture either die (Prince Hjalmar) or lose exactly those differentiating agents that make them 'cultured' (the Old King).

Moreover, the adaptation of the play as libretto shows other characteristics of female writing, such as the 'images of enclosure and escape'[78] which are more dominant in the operatic text: in contrast with the celebrations that open the play, the libretto of *La princesse Maleine* begins in darkness and enclosure, as Maleine and her nurse are imprisoned in a tower without light. Because the first part of the play is cut, the spectators (and Maleine?) do not know why they are locked away: it is never explained. The imprisonment presents a mysterious starting-point as a basic female condition. The women escape after the nurse loosens the first stone of the wall, but only to end up in another trap. At the end, Maleine is locked into her room, waiting for death in the dark. This time, the other woman does not free her for life but for death, in an almost Schopenhauerian sense. Given that Boulanger had considerable input in the shaping of the libretto, such emphasis on feminine narrative strategies can be understood as a feminine reinterpretation of a man's text, not only with respect to its being an allegory of war, but also in so far as the libretto reflects both the female condition in French *fin-de-siècle* society and Boulanger's own experience of enclosure due to her illness.

Nevertheless, the libretto remains ambiguous. However, Boulanger's interpretation ought to become more visible in her setting of the text, and an analysis of the score could indicate whether she composed a work in the line of male composers such as Debussy, depicting a *femme fragile* and her undoing, or whether she ventured into a different, more feminine reading. But only fragments of the music survive. Again, the letters and diaries reveal themselves as important sources, even if they remain mute on this particular question: they certainly tell us more about the genesis of the opera, and the surviving sketches show various musical concerns on the part of the composer. For all the incompleteness of the surviving material, the sketches and documents do give some indication about the composition: to begin with, they present some of the opera's motivic material; they also suggest some of Boulanger's structural concepts; and, finally, the surviving scene allows us a look into her workshop. Moreover, some elements in this material do indeed support the contention that Boulanger tried to find a distinctly female voice in this opera.

[78] Gilbert and Gubar, *The Madwoman in the Attic*, xi.

As was usual for a *Literaturoper* of this period, the composition was structured through leitmotifs. Boulanger's diary entry from May 1916 mentions 'Hjalmar's theme', and in the green sketchbook she marked down three more: 'Maleine's theme', 'Queen Anne's theme' and 'Destiny'. Maleine's theme (see Example 1) begins with a minor second and a minor third, a combination of intervals which, in melodic and harmonic terms, is a characteristic feature of Boulanger's music.[79] The motive continues with a chromatic upward movement which contains the nucleus of the 'Tristan motive', widely used in French music as a musical sign of love and desire: Boulanger herself used it as basic material in her song *Si tout ceci n'est qu'un pauvre rêve* (see Example 2).[80] Twice more the second-third combination appears, building a descending sequence. The last five notes of the theme mirror its beginning, creating a decidedly circular structure. The central three notes form another second–third (minor-major) configuration.

Queen Anne's theme (see Example 3) is structured differently; at first sight it is not circular, but open, traversing almost two octaves in a dramatically falling gesture which develops out of the sequence at the beginning of the theme and accelerates in its fall. The motivic cell is constructed on the alternation of major and minor thirds (b). Falling major thirds (ß) are in fact the dominant interval of the theme, which could itself be read as nothing more than a chain of descending major thirds. The momentum of the sequence and the repetition of the thirds reveal Queen Anne's theme as having a much more circular character than its shape suggests. Both motives share an energetic dotted rhythm at the beginning.

The third theme outlined in the sketchbook, that of Destiny, is reminiscent of Puccini's use of the so-called 'Scarpia motive' in his opera *Tosca*: dissonant chords which sound 'like bells' (see Example 4). The bell-like oscillation of these chords forms a directional pattern which recurs frequently in the surviving sketches of *La princesse Maleine*. Like the second–third configuration, this sort of repetitive movement pervades Boulanger's compositions as a whole.

In the sketches, Maleine's theme appears at least twice. At the beginning of the duet between Maleine and Hjalmar in Act 2, scene iii (see Example 5), the sketches give Maleine's theme first in its original form, and then in a slightly embellished variation. The theme reappears at Maleine's entry: 'Où êtes-vous, Seigneur?' Given that these bars are a sketch for a reworking of this part of the duet, it is possible that Boulanger noted only essential changes, leaving the rest of the musical texture aside. But it is also possible that Maleine's entry does indeed begin with the theme unaccompanied, the pure melodic line set in contrast to the often dense harmonic texture of the score whose most intense expression can be seen in the motive of Destiny. This would correspond to the dramatic moment when Maleine meets Hjalmar for the first time since her escape,

---

[79] Birgit Stiévenard-Salomon, 'Zum Religiösen in der Musik Lili Boulangers', *Vom Schweigen befreit*, ed. Nies and Aulenkamp-Moeller, 77–83.
[80] On the *Clairières dans le ciel*, see Fauser, 'Die Musik hinter der Legende'; Sabine Giesebrecht-Schutte, 'Lili Boulanger: "Clairières dans le Ciel" – ästhetischer Ausdruck und musikalische Form', *Die Musikforschung*, 47 (1994), 384–402.

Example 1. Lili Boulanger, *La princesse Maleine*, sketches, F-Pn MS 19470, f. 37ᵛ.

Example 2. Lili Boulanger, *Clairières dans le ciel* (Paris, 1919), no. 6: *Si tout ceci n'est qu'un pauvre rêve*, bars 1–6.

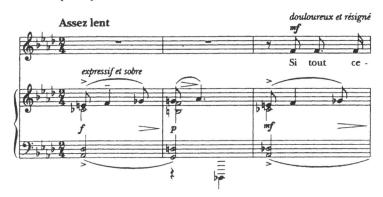

Example 3. Lili Boulanger, *La princesse Maleine*, sketches, F-Pn MS 19470, f. 37ᵛ.

Example 4. Lili Boulanger, *La princesse Maleine*, sketches, F-Pn MS 19470, f. 37ᵛ.

Example 5. Lili Boulanger, *La princesse Maleine*, sketches, F-Pn MS 19470, f. 19.

[*Samedi 14 Avril 1917*]

now revealing her true identity. The second sketch in which Boulanger used Maleine's theme shows a thematic transformation in order to develop the musical material of the three poor men in Act 1, scene iii (see Example 6).

Example 6. Lili Boulanger, *La princesse Maleine*, sketches, F-Pn MS 19470, f. 29ᵛ.

13 Oct. 1917

In so far as such scant musical material permits one to draw a conclusion, Boulanger seems to have developed and transformed Maleine's theme to create different threads of musical narrative. This form of leitmotif technique was introduced into French opera in the vogue of *Wagnérisme*,[81] especially through the reception of *Tristan und Isolde* and *Der Ring des Nibelungen*. No longer an avant-garde technique in the 1910s but firmly rooted in the musical vocabulary of opera composition, the use of leitmotifs enabled the composer to construct musical prose with a narrative quality. In the absence of the almost finished Particell, any interpretation of the present fragments is necessarily speculative. Yet this material suggests that Maleine's theme constitutes the central thematic cell of the opera, out of which further motivic structures are developed. Hence the heroine's musical signature would achieve an essential quality as a primary agent within the musical text.

Yet Maleine's theme is linked not only to the heroine of the opera but also to the composer herself. Boulanger was deeply interested in number symbolism: she generally used numeric signifiers in her music, one

---

[81] On the question of musical *Wagnérisme* in France, see Manuela Schwartz, 'Die Wagner-Rezeption und die Oper des Fin de siècle: Untersuchungen zu Vincent d'Indys Fervaal' (Ph.D. dissertation, Technische Universität, Berlin, 1995). In June 1995 an international conference in Berlin (organized jointly by the Centre Marc Bloch, the Musikwissenschaftliches Seminar der Humboldt-Universität and the Konzerthaus Berlin/Schauspielhaus am Gendarmenmarkt) on 'Der *Wagnérisme* in der französischen Musik und Musikkultur (1861–1914)' discussed different aspects of French *Wagnérisme* in new perspectives. The proceedings are being prepared for publication.

much discussed example being her self-identification with the number 13, the number of letters in her name.[82] Maleine's theme does indeed consist of 13 notes and could therefore be interpreted as Boulanger's musical signature. Such a reading of the theme would be consistent with similar findings in other works. In the opera, the link is strengthened through the combination, within the heroine's theme, of both musical signs linked to the composer's identity: the second–third structure and the number 13. It opens up two possible interpretations: the link of composer and heroine through Maleine's theme could be understood as an autobiographical statement, reflecting a 'secret programme', as, for example, in Berg's *Lyric Suite* or Violin Concerto. Indeed, the structure of Maleine's theme underlines the moment of self-identification already apparent in at least some of Boulanger's reasons for her choice of subject. But although autobiographical traits are certainly present in the work, another reading of this theme as an authorial gesture of a woman's work, and therefore as the inscribing of female creativity in the thematic material and its development, suggests itself in the context of the reworking of the play as opera.

In the surviving musical fragment of *La princesse Maleine* (Act 1, scene ii: 'Une forêt'), several of the points discussed above in the context of the play's adaptation and its setting become clearer. Table 2 presents the three versions of the text for this scene: Maeterlinck's play, Ricordi's/Boulanger's adaptation and the text that Boulanger finally set. In their adaptation of this scene, Ricordi and Boulanger reduced Maeterlinck's text by half. Through these cuts they achieved several things. Intrusive details, such as the Latin inscription on a ruined windmill in the forest (lines 41–56) – a different tower from the one in which Maleine was locked away – are avoided, thus removing a distracting allusion to other threads of the story. References to Maleine's personal history are eliminated: neither her mother's name (Godelive; line 14) nor the circumstances of the war following the severance of her engagement to Hjalmar are retained. Indeed, the remaining text does not indicate how the three persons mentioned by Hjalmar and Angus ('le vieux roi Marcellus', 'la vieille reine', 'la princesse Maleine') are interrelated, especially since the explanatory beginning of the play had been cut altogether. The war of the play was a battle between two Dutch kings in the late Middle Ages; in the libretto, war appears as a less specific and more universal condition. Similarly, all of Anne's history is lost in the adaptation. Lines 94–115, cut by Ricordi and Boulanger, inform the spectator that Anne is married to the King of Jutland, that she has left her husband whom she is fighting for his throne, and that she has incited Hjalmar's father against Marcellus, thus starting a war. But whereas the women's history has disappeared in this scene, Hjalmar's story is recreated through his answers to Angus's questions. Indeed, in the adaptation, Hjalmar's recollection of Maleine takes a central place in the scene: a faint memory of a gaze full of freshness, contrasting with the surrounding reality of death and misery caused

---

[82] See for example Rosenstiel, *The Life and Works of Lili Boulanger*, 173–4; Fauser, 'Die Musik hinter der Legende'; Bonnie Jo Dopp, 'Numerology and Cryptography in the Music of Lili Boulanger: The Hidden Program in *Clairières dans le ciel*', *Musical Quarterly*, 78 (1994), 557–83.

TABLE 2

LA PRINCESSE MALEINE: SYNOPSIS OF TEXTS FOR LIBRETTO, ACT 1, SCENE II

H = LE PRINCE HJALMAR
A = ANGUS

Maurice Maeterlinck play, Act 1, scene iii	Tito Ricordi / Lili Boulanger libretto, Act 1, scene ii *Note*: Boulanger's cuts are indicated by lining out, her additions by underlining.	Lili Boulanger opera sketch, Act 1, scene ii *Note*. Additions are underlined.
UNE FORÊT	UNE FORÊT	UNE FORÊT
Entrent le prince Hjalmar et Angus	(*Entrent le prince Hjalmar et Angus*)	– *Entrent le prince Hjalmar et Angus* –
H: J'étais malade; et l'odeur de tous ces morts! et l'odeur de tous ces morts! et maintenant c'est comme si cette nuit et cette forêt avaient versé un peu d'eau sur 5 mes yeux	H: J'étais malade; et l'odeur de tous ces morts! et maintenant c'est comme si cette nuit et cette forêt avaient versé un peu d'eau sur mes yeux	H: J'étais malade; et l'odeur de tous ces morts! (*avec mélancolie*) Et maintenant c'est comme si cette nuit et cette forêt avaient versé un peu d'eau sur mes yeux . . . .
A: Il ne reste plus que les arbres! H: Avez-vous vu mourir le vieux roi Marcellus?	A: Avez-vous vu mourir le vieux roi Marcellus?	(*avec une inquiétude subite*) Avez-vous vu mourir le vieux roi Marcellus?
10 A: Non, mais j'ai vu autre chose; hier au soir, pendant votre absence, ils ont mis le feu au	A: Non, mais j'ai vu autre chose; hier au soir ils ont mis le feu au château, et la vieille reine	A: (*sombre*) Non, mais j'ai vu autre chose; hier au soir, ils ont mis le feu au château, et la vieille

Table 2 (cont.)

15		château, et la vieille reine Godelive courait à travers les flammes avec les domestiques. Ils se sont jetés dans les fossés et je crois que tous y ont péri.		reine courait à travers les flammes avec les domestiques.
	H:	Et la princesse Maleine? Y était-elle?	H:	Et la princesse Maleine? Y était-elle?
20	A:	Je ne l'ai pas vue.	A:	Je ne l'ai pas vue.
	H:	Mais d'autres l'ont-ils vue?		
	A:	Personne ne l'a vue, on ne sait où elle est.		
25	H:	Elle est morte?	H:	Elle est morte?
	A:	On dit qu'elle est morte.	A:	On dit qu'elle est morte.
	H:	Mon père est terrible!		
	A:	Vous l'aimiez déjà?	H:	Vous l'aimiez déjà?
	H:	Qui?	A:	Qui?
30	A:	La princesse Maleine.	H:	La princesse Maleine.
	H:	Je ne l'ai vue qu'une seule fois ... elle avait cependant une manière de baisser les yeux; – et de croiser les mains; – ainsi – et des cils blancs étranges! – Et son regard! ... on était tout à coup comme dans un grand canal d'eau fraîche ... Je ne m'en souviens pas très bien; mais je voudrais revoir cet étrange regard ...		Je ne l'ai vue qu'une seule fois ... elle avait cependant une manière de baisser les yeux; – et de croiser les mains; – ainsi – Et son regard! ... on était tout à coup comme dans un grand canal d'eau fraîche ... Je ne m'en souviens pas très bien; mais je voudrais revoir cet étrange regard ...
35				
40				

Right column speaker annotations (additional):
- H: (avec émotion) Et la princesse Maleine? Y était-elle?
- A: (un peu indifférent) Je ne l'ai pas vue.
- H: Elle est morte?
- A: On dit qu'elle est morte.
- H: (doucement) Vous l'aimiez déjà?
- A: Qui?
- H: La princesse Maleine.
- A: (avec une grande émotion continue) Je ne l'ai vue qu'une seule fois ... elle avait cependant une manière de baisser les yeux; – et de croiser les mains; – ainsi – Et son regard! ... on était tout à coup comme dans un grand canal d'eau fraîche ... (songeur – avec mélancolie) Je ne m'en souviens pas très bien; mais je voudrais revoir cet étrange regard ...

A:	Quelle est cette tour sur cette bute?
H:	On dirait un vieux moulin à vent; il n'a pas de fenêtres.
45 A:	Il y a une inscription de ce côté.
H:	Une inscription?
A:	Oui, – en latin.
H:	Pouvez-vous lire?
A:	Oui, mais c'est très vieux. – Voyons:
50	Olim inclusa
	Anna ducissa
	anno..., etc.,
	il y a trop de mousse sur tout le reste.
55 H:	Asseyons-nous ici.
A:	*Ducissa Anna*, c'est le nom de la mère de votre fiancée.
H:	D'Uglyane? – Oui.
60 A:	Voilà un *oui* plus lent et plus froid que la neige!
H:	Mon Dieu, le temps des *oui* de flamme est assez loin de moi....
65 A:	Uglyane est jolie cependant.

A:	Et maintenant vous allez vous marier avec la fille de la reine Anne.
H:	Uglyane? – Oui.
A:	Voilà un *oui* plus lent et plus froid que la neige!
H:	Mon Dieu, le temps des *oui* de flamme est assez loin de moi....
A:	(*étonné*) Et maintenant vous allez vous marier avec la fille de la reine Anne.
H:	(*lointain*) Uglyane? – Oui.
A:	Voilà un *oui* plus lent et plus froid que la neige!
H:	(*avec une grande lassitude*) Mon Dieu, le temps des *oui* de flamme est assez loin de moi....

Table 2 (cont.)

Line		Version 1		Version 2		Version 3
	H:	J'en ai peur!	H:	J'en ai peur!		
	A:	Oh!				
	H:	Il y a une petite âme de cuisinière au fond de ses yeux verts.				
70						
	A:	Oh! oh! mais alors, pourquoi consentez-vous?	A:	Oh! oh! mais alors, pourquoi consentez-vous?	A:	(*inquiet*) Oh! oh! Oh! oh! mais alors, pourquoi consentez-vous?
75	H:	A quoi bon de ne pas consentir? Je suis malade à en mourir une de ces vingt mille nuits que nous avons à vivre, et je veux le repos! le repos! Et puis, elle ou une autre, qui me dira 'mon petit Hjalmar' au clair de lune en me pinçant le nez! Pouah! – Avez-vous remarqué les colères subites de mon père depuis que la reine Anne est arrivée à Ysselmonde? – Je ne sais ce qui se passe; mais il y a là quelque chose, et je commence à avoir d'étranges soupçons; j'ai peur de la reine!	H:	A quoi bon de ne pas consentir? Je suis malade à en mourir une de ces vingt mille nuits que nous avons à vivre, et je veux le repos! Avez-vous remarqué les colères subites de mon père depuis que la reine Anne est arrivée à Ysselmonde? – Je ne sais ce qui se passe; mais j'ai peur de la reine!	H:	(*d'un air détaché et résigné*) A quoi bon ne pas consentir? Je suis malade à en mourir une de ces vingt mille nuits que nous avons à vivre, et je veux le repos! le repos! (*comme dans un rêve*) le repos! (*comme confidentiel avec une certaine anxiété*) Avez-vous remarqué les colères subites de mon père depuis que la reine Anne est arrivée à Ysselmonde? – Je ne sais ce qui se passe; (*dramatique*) mais j'ai peur de la reine!
80						
85						
90	A:	Elle vous aime comme un fils cependant.	A:	Elle vous aime comme un fils cependant.	A:	(*simplement*) Elle vous aime cependant comme un fils.
95	H:	Comme un fils? – Je n'en sais rien, et j'ai d'étranges idées; elle est plus belle que sa fille, et voilà d'abord un grand mal. Elle travaille comme une taupe à je	H:	Comme un fils? – Je n'en sais rien, et j'ai d'étranges idées; elle est plus belle que sa fille, et voilà d'abord un grand mal.	H:	(*mystérieux*) Comme un fils? – Je n'en sais rien, et j'ai des étranges idées;

100	A:	ne sais quoi! elle a excité mon pauvre vieux père contre Marcellus et elle a déchaîné cette guerre; – il y a quelque chose là dessous!	~~ne sais quoi! il y a quelque chose là dessous!~~ Allons-nous-en!	
	A:	Il y a, qu'elle voudrait vous faire épouser Uglyane, ce n'est pas infernal.		
105	H:	Il y a encore autre chose.		
	A:	Oh! je sais bien! Une fois mariés, elle vous envoie en Jutland vous battre sur les glaçons pour son petit trône d'usurpatrice, et délivrer peut-être son pauvre mari, qui doit être bien inquiet en l'attendant; car une reine aussi belle, errant seule par le monde, il faut bien qu'il arrive des histoires....		
110				
115	H:	Il y a encore autre chose.		
	A:	Quoi?	A:	Quoi?	A:	(effrayé) Quoi?
	H:	Vous le saurez un jour; allons-nous-en.	H:	Vous le saurez un jour; allons-nous-en.	H:	(grave) Vous le saurez un jour; (désabusé) Allons-nous-en.
	A:	Vers la ville?	A:	Vers la ville?	A:	Vers la ville?
120	H:	Vers la ville? –Il n'y en a plus; il n'y a plus que des morts entre des murs écroulés!	H:	Vers la ville? – Il n'y en a plus; il n'y a plus que des morts entre des murs écroulés!	H:	(avec une ironie douloureuse) Vers la ville? – (las) Il n'y en a plus; il n'y a plus que des morts entre des murs écroulés!
						Ils sortent.

by Anne. Because Anne no longer has explicitly practical reasons for her behaviour, her power as an evil *Naturwesen* appears strengthened, as Hjalmar's now abrupt and isolated question shows: 'Have you noticed my father's sudden fits of rage since Queen Anne arrived at Ysselmonde? – I don't know what is going on; but I am afraid of the Queen!'[83] In the scene as set in the opera, Hjalmar possesses less power than in the play: he is at the mercy of Anne's machinations, his passive memories of Maleine a distant consolation. Indeed, in this scene in the opera, Hjalmar appears feminized in his passivity. He will regain 'male' activity only in the moment when Maleine reveals herself to him at Ysselmonde.

Boulanger composed the 'forest scene' in accordance with the declamation and grammatical structure of the text. In that respect, as well as in her use of leitmotifs, she follows the compositional tendencies of her time, closer to Dukas in her idiom than to Debussy.[84] Some points, however, are worth mentioning in this context. When Hjalmar and Angus enter, a motive, sharing musical material with Maleine's theme, sounds 'en dehors' in the upper system of the Particell (horn or cello?). From Boulanger's diaries we know that she had found 'Hjalmar's theme' in May 1916, and the location of this motive in the score suggests that Example 7 does indeed represent Hjalmar's leitmotif. Here, again, the circularity of the motive's structure and its reference to Maleine's theme (a second-third combination as a headmotif, diminishing to an oscillating second) mark this theme as a transformation of the latter. The biblical image of 'Adam's rib' could be used in reverse, given that the earlier Maleine's theme is the origin of Hjalmar's theme.[85] This finding confirms the centrality of Maleine's theme to the score as suggested above.

Example 7. Lili Boulanger, *La princesse Maleine*, Act 1, scene ii, bars 5–9 (F-Pn MS 19469).

[83] 'Avez-vous remarqué les colères subites de mon père depuis que la reine Anne est arrivée à Ysselmonde? – Je ne sais ce qui se passe; mais j'ai peur de la reine!'

[84] On Boulanger and Dukas, see Manuela Schwartz, 'Mehr als ein Gesellenstück – *Faust et Hélène* von Lili Boulanger', *Vom Schweigen befreit*, ed. Nies and Aulenkamp-Moeller, 64–71.

[85] As far as the surviving documents and Rosenstiel's account (*The Life and Works of Lili Boulanger*, 146) reveal, Boulanger found Maleine's theme early in her work on *La princesse Maleine* in 1911. But the loss of almost all the musical material necessarily leaves room for doubt over this chronology.

A second leitmotif appears prominently in the 'forest scene'. When Hjalmar asks Angus if he realizes that Anne's arrival in Ysselmonde has changed everything, Queen Anne's theme is heard in the orchestra (see Example 8). The appearance of Queen Anne's theme is all the more effective because the orchestra falls silent just before it is heard, evoking her menacing presence which is visible in every aspect of Hjalmar's reality. But whereas Queen Anne as an inescapable threat is musically present in this dialogue between Angus and Hjalmar, Maleine's music remains mute in this scene, even when the two friends talk about her and her destiny. She is a faint memory for her former fiancé, who remembers her only vaguely ('Je ne m'en souviens pas très bien'), and the second-third structure appears only in passing when Angus recalls her in the conversation (see Example 9). More than the words, the music expresses the oblivion into which Maleine has already fallen. However, although Maleine's theme remains silent in Hjalmar's recollection, the Particell allows the presumption that another essential aspect of Boulanger's music would have created a change of atmosphere at this point through an evocative use of orchestral colour, together with the suddenly regular off-beat rhythm in the bass and chords in the right hand which could well have been conceived for the harp (see Example 10). Through its texture, the central part – Maleine's – is clearly contrasted with the framing moments of misery related to Queen Anne. Therefore, in the first scene in which both women are represented musically, Boulanger characterizes them as opposite poles.

Feminist critics have begun to discuss the readings of a clearly aimed musical structure and harmonic development in Western tonal music as encoding 'masculinity', and circularity in harmonic and melodic sense as representing the 'feminine'.[86] Most obviously, this dichotomy appears in the aesthetic debate about sonata form in the second half of the nineteenth century, especially in Vincent d'Indy's elaborate metaphor in his *Cours de composition musicale*, where he defines the 'masculine' in music as 'force and energy, concision and clarity' and the 'feminine' through 'its verbosity and modulatory vagueness', spreading out 'progressively the curve of its ornamented melody'.[87] Feminine and masculine qualities in music were constantly discussed in French *fin-de-siècle* music criticism, these categories being attributed to different nations, genres, composers and musical elements.[88] All this is embedded in a broader controversy in Paris about nationalism and feminism which had its origins in France's defeat in the Franco-Prussian War of 1870-1. Fear of the

---

[86] See, for example, McClary, *Feminine Endings*; Solie, 'Whose Life?'; Citron, *Gender and the Musical Canon*, 120-64.

[87] Quoted in Citron, *Gender and the Musical Canon*, 136, 260.

[88] See, for example, Jann Pasler's analysis of the French perception of Russian music in her paper 'Making Alliances through Music: Russia as Embraced by the French', read at the International Conference on Nineteenth-Century Music, University of Surrey, 14-17 July 1994; and Jeffrey Kallberg, 'The Harmony of the Tea Table: Gender and Ideology in the Piano Nocturne', *Representations*, 39 (1992), 102-33. Debussy's ambivalent verdict on Massenet's music is grounded in his perception of the composer as someone 'searching in music for documents that would serve as a history of the feminine soul' ('à chercher dans la musique des documents pour servir à l'histoire de l'âme féminine'); see Claude Debussy, *Monsieur Croche et autres écrits*, ed. François Lesure (2nd edn, Paris, 1989), 59.

Example 8. Lili Boulanger, *La princesse Maleine*, Act 1, scene ii, bars 82–91 (F-Pn MS 19469).

nation's feminization became a public neurosis after the turn of the century.[89] Women's music did not escape this pattern of discourse; nor could a woman artist be ignorant of the discussion. Even women such as Augusta Holmès, whose large symphonic compositions were understood as 'masculine' in their musical means, were publicly unmasked as particularly feminine. According to Saint-Saëns, 'Women are strange when they seriously interfere with art; they seem to be preoccupied with making us forget that they are women and with showing an overflowing virility without realizing that it is just this preoccupation which betrays the

Example 9. Lili Boulanger, *La princesse Maleine*, Act 1, scene ii, bars 34–6 (F-Pn MS 19469).

[89] See n. 75 above.

Example 10. Lili Boulanger, *La princesse Maleine*, Act 1, scene ii, bars 37–41 (F-Pn MS 19469).

woman.'⁹⁰ Indeed, in whatever way gendered compositional qualities characterize the music of a female composer, women were perceived either as composing in a 'feminine' way – emphasizing softness and melody – or as putting on the mask of male composers, which marks them even more strongly as female in an essentialist understanding. A verdict such as Saint-Saëns's on Augusta Holmès is possible only in a context in which the 'feminine' and 'masculine' signifying of musical material is common understanding. No woman composer of that period could escape this horizon of meaning: her training confronted her with a gendered musical language, and her works were judged within this framework of signifiers.[91]

In the case of Boulanger and her sister, their at least passive involvement in feminist circles and their personal experience had sharpened this awareness, and so, too, had the comments of the musical press on their sex in relation to their music.[92] Lili Boulanger, no less than any other woman composer, had to work in this gendered musical field. Thus, if in her opera Boulanger used repeated harmonic and motivic cells together with circular motives and a highly chromatic and unresolved structure turning in on itself,[93] this could be interpreted, especially in the case of Maleine's theme, as a conscious application of musical material that in late nineteenth- and early twentieth-century France possessed a gendered meaning. Of course, none of these elements is absent from the compositions of Boulanger's male contemporaries: Stravinsky's *Rite of Spring* could be cited as the paradigmatic ostinato-based composition of that time; Debussy's *Pelléas et Mélisande* is a work where harmonic structures defy

[90] 'Les femmes sont curieuses quand elles se mêlent sérieusement d'art: elles semblent préoccupées avant tout de faire oublier qu'elles sont femmes et de montrer une virilité débordante, sans songer que c'est justement cette préoccupation qui décèle la femme.' Camille Saint-Saëns, 'Les Argonautes' (1881), *Harmonie et mélodie* (Paris, 1885), 225–39 (p. 228).

[91] Gilbert and Gubar explain woman's imprisonment in her cultural context by adapting Harold Bloom's concept of the anxiety of influence: 'Unlike her male counterpart, then, the female artist must first struggle against the effects of a socialization which makes conflict with the will of her (male) precursors seem inexpressibly absurd, futile, or even . . . self-annihilating. And just as the male artist's struggle against his precursor takes the form of what Bloom calls revisionary swerves, flights, misreadings, so the female writer's battle for self-creation involves her in a revisionary process. Her battle, however, is not against her (male) precursor's reading of the world but against his reading of *her*.' *The Madwoman in the Attic*, 49.

[92] From early encounters with male colleagues and the press onwards, the Boulanger sisters' sex had been the focus of attention. Saint-Saëns commented on Nadia's 'search for the effect' ('recherche de l'effet') when she presented an instrumental instead of a vocal fugue at the Prix de Rome competition of 1908 (see Spycket, *Nadia Boulanger*, 28). Nadia's sight-reading piece for the Conservatoire's final-year piano competition for women pianists in 1914 was judged as 'a long and unintelligible, and therefore very feminine page', revealing Nadia Boulanger as 'a criminal' who 'offered to the unfortunate female contestants a harmony bristling with harmonic difficulties' (Rosenstiel, *Nadia Boulanger*, 123), terms that remind one of Saint-Saëns's unmasking of Augusta Holmès as a woman overdoing the harmonic complexity of a piece because she does not understand and 'master' the 'masculine' side of music. In March 1912, when Lili enrolled for her first Prix de Rome competition, Emile Vuillermoz – citing Nadia Boulanger and Hélène Fleury, two women who so far had each received a second prize in the Prix de Rome competition – warned his readers against the danger that women were just about to take over French music, with dire results for its quality because fashion would replace creation. Emile Vuillermoz, 'Le péril rose', *Musica*, 11 (1912), 45.

[93] In the green sketchbook, as well as in sketches of other pieces (e.g. F-Pn MS 19438), Boulanger often used letters as abbreviations for different cells, which would then be noted as a sequence of A-B-A-B-A-B-A-B, etc. under a melodic line. This repetitive structure is one of the main characteristics of Boulanger's compositional style: it can be found in works such as the songs *Si tout ceci n'est qu'un pauvre rêve* and *Deux ancolies* from *Clairières dans le ciel*, or the *Vieille prière bouddhique*.

resolution; and circular motives have appeared in Western music since Gregorian chant. The reason why Boulanger's use of such musical vocabulary can be seen as a distinctly feminine solution to a compositional problem is twofold. First, if the thematic material of *La princesse Maleine* is based on Maleine's theme – and here the surviving sources can serve only as signposts to a virtual score – it relies indeed on circular, closed structures, presenting in its use a feminine reading of a potentially anti-feminine libretto, reinterpreting Maeterlinck's misogynist portrayal of his women characters as the story of two women and their interaction. At the same time, Boulanger uses a harmonic language which in its 'avant-garde' richness of polytonal ambiguity – especially in her late works such as *Pie Jesu* – disclaims 'feminine' musical language and self-restriction.[94] Thus the combinatory use of a progressive 'masculine' harmony and motivic material that is gendered 'feminine' could be interpreted as a – probably unconscious – attempt to create her own language as a woman composer in the early twentieth century. Thus she would neither remain in the cage of 'lady-like' composing nor try to escape by disguising herself as a composing man.

Second, there is a noteworthy absence of 'male strength' in the libretto, and also in the surviving musical fragments, which are exactly those moments where the representation of 'male strength' would be expected. Boulanger's music – such as her *Vieille prière bouddhique* or her orchestrations of the *Clairières dans le ciel* – uses a rich spectrum of sound, not only in the sense of harmonic colour but also in the sense of a highly differentiated orchestration. Even if the Particell of *La princesse Maleine* had survived as a whole, the orchestration would still be missing, but, judging from her other compositions with orchestra, the orchestral part would have been neither soft and small-scale nor merely 'noisy', overemphasizing 'masculine' signifiers such as the prominent use of brass, percussion and orchestral tuttis.[95] Boulanger's lavish and nuanced orchestration, using all registers of expression from the softest to the strongest,[96] could be understood as a very affirmative use of sound in its whole richness, a refusal to submit to well-behaved female silence. The musical fragments of *La princesse Maleine* let us hear only a whisper, but, seen in the context of Boulanger's other works, the feminine voices in this 'virtual' opera – Maleine, Anne and Lili Boulanger – create a distant but powerful echo.

With *La princesse Maleine*, Boulanger composed for the public sphere in its most exposed institution, the Paris Opéra. It was by no means a private work, some sort of musical diary of self-exploration, but was politically

---

[94] On Boulanger's musical language, see Olivia Mattis, 'Lili Boulanger – Polytoniste', *Lili Boulanger zum 100. Geburtstag: Bremer Lili Boulanger-Tage, 19.–22.8.1993*, ed. Kathrin Mosler (Bremen, 1993), 48–51. Mattis cites contemporary sources such as Charles Koechlin, who refers to Boulanger's harmonic progressiveness in discussing her works together with those of Georges Auric, Darius Milhaud, Igor Stravinsky and Béla Bartók.

[95] In his critique of Holmès's *Les Argonautes*, Saint-Saëns explicitly mentions harmonic complexity and powerful orchestration as signifying maleness in music; see Saint-Saëns, 'Les Argonautes', 229.

[96] On Boulanger's orchestration, see Annegret Fauser, 'Zur Orchestrierung der *Clairières dans le ciel*', *Vom Schweigen befreit*, ed. Nies and Aulenkamp-Moeller, 61.

and artistically ambitious through its choice of subject, author and form. Yet, from the beginning of its composition onward, the reception of *La princesse Maleine* has focused exclusively on biographical aspects, identifying Lili with Maleine and creating an ideal image of a fragile virgin sacrificing herself for her ideals and suffering all pain without resistance. In this interpretation, disturbing aspects have been faded out. The literary figure Maleine offered a looking-glass through which the successful woman composer Boulanger would appear less threatening. She was Lili, Nadia's saintly sister, whose life was never tainted by anything impure or ugly and who was ennobled through her suffering. For Maeterlinck, she was the pure and beautiful voice of music, born to give life to his creation: his whole discourse puts Boulanger in the position of a divinely inspired interpreter, not that of an equal creator in her own right. This becomes fully obvious in a photograph of Maeterlinck which she received on 15 February 1917 carrying the dedication: 'To my dear little collaborator Lili Boulanger, who has to give the awaited soul to the Princess Maleine, according to the will of the Gods of Music and of Destiny'.[97] Neither Boulanger's will nor her talent was perceived as lying at the origin of an artistic creation in its own right; Destiny (and Maeterlinck) chose her as an instrument in order to make audible the 'inexpressible' in his work. For Spalding and others, such as Mauclair and Delarrancea,[98] death and fragility were the price of and explanation for Boulanger's genius, and again the literary model allowed Boulanger's environment to shape her complex and difficult persona into the sweet girl Lili. Léonie Rosenstiel used Maeterlinck's play to interpret Lili's own perception of her enduring martyrdom as that of the enclosed princess in the tower.[99] Lili, saint and virgin martyr, became an icon, which was justified through the sacrifice of the last two years of her life in order to finish the composition of *La princesse Maleine*. Furthermore, the fact that this opera remains lost, and that even its fragmented remains are not easily accessible but could be presented here only after a laborious search, reinforces such a mythologizing reading.

This reading corresponds to one of the narrative models of traditional stories of women's lives which Ruth Solie has summarized as:

> ... 'happily ever after' or 'she came to a bad end'. Both of these stories focus tenaciously on the appropriateness of the heroine's behaviour – she is either rewarded for virtue (with marriage) or punished for transgression (with death); neither story is of the slightest use in explaining or evaluating a life whose very triumphs result from the refusal to behave in 'appropriate' ways.[100]

The interesting twist in this tale is the fact that in the Maleine–Lili story the transgression of the heroine is veiled. Through her highly ambitious

---

[97] 'A ma chère petite collaboratrice Lili Boulanger / qui doit donner à la Princesse Maleine, de par la volonté des dieux de la musique et du Destin, l'âme attendue'. Quoted in Rosenstiel, *The Life and Works of Lili Boulanger*, 281. In her diary from 1917, Boulanger notes on 15 February: 'Reçu: Photo dédicacée Maeterlinck – encadrée par la suite –'. F-Pn Rés. Vmf. MS 118.
[98] Delarrancea, 'Lili Boulanger', 38–41.
[99] Rosenstiel, *The Life and Works of Lili Boulanger*, 42–3.
[100] Solie, 'Changing the Subject', 56.

project, Boulanger had overstepped the limits of appropriate bourgeois female behaviour. This becomes evident not only in her winning the Prix de Rome, in her operatic project and in her exclusive contract with Ricordi, but also in cautiously hidden traces of her demeanour. The carefully constructed story of the pure and saintly child-genius Maleine–Lili was a way to dilute 'any threat a woman with power might have [through emphasizing] her moral goodness'.[101] Boulanger's daily life as an ambitious young composer, which led her to seek all possible assistance just like every other Parisian composer, was totally silenced. Yet some evidence survives which shows exactly this ambitious side of an up-and-coming young composer using the Parisian method of calling in favours:

> I don't often get on your nerves, admit it – so let me do it for once and ask you to do your utmost to oblige your old Lili. I will present at the exam one chorus and one vocal quartet – intervene with those members of the jury whom you particularly honour with your friendship in order to persuade them to have these two pieces performed, and ask them to award the Prix Lepaul to me if they find my work as good as people say, and to have my compositions played in the orchestra class.[102]

As Jeanice Brooks has shown in her article on Nadia Boulanger's conducting career,[103] Nadia herself, her associates and her critics used the same model of a saintly *vita* (the morally good and divinely chosen servant of music) in order to tell the story of her own public career, thus silencing any hint of her ambition. A similar strategy was used in Lili's case.

Given that *La princesse Maleine* 'died' with the composer,[104] it cannot contradict or qualify the myth regarding Boulanger. Thus, instead of being seen as an artistically and politically ambitious work which inscribed self-confidently a feminine authorship in its musical material, Boulanger's opera *La princesse Maleine* has been interpreted as Maeterlinck's 'lost princess' who had tragically lost her voice. Certainly, *La princesse Maleine* invokes a complex interaction of creation and reception, and, as we have seen, autobiography does have its part to play and should be taken into consideration just as in the case of other composers such as Berlioz (*Harold en Italie*), Schubert (*Winterreise*), Massenet (*Manon*), Brahms (*Ein deutsches*

---

[101] Linda Wagner-Martin, *Telling Women's Lives: The New Biography* (New Brunswick, NJ, 1994), 51. The question of feminine autobiography and biography has been discussed extensively in recent years in literary, sociological and historical disciplines.

[102] Letter to Fernand Bourgeat from 1912(?), sold at auction by Drouot (Paris) in June 1987: 'Je ne te rase pas souvent, avoue-le – laisse-toi donc faire pour une fois et mets-toi en quatre pour obliger ta vieille Lili. Je montre à l'examen 1 chœur et 1 quatuor vocal – interviens auprès de ceux membres du Jury que tu honores tout particulièrement de ton amitié afin qu'il fassent exécuter les deux choses et prie-les, s'il trouvent mon travail aussi bien qu'on le dit, de m'octroyer le Prix Lepaul et qu'on me joue à la classe d'orchestre.' F-Pn, Fichier des ventes aux enchères. Bourgeat had played a central role in the affair of the Prix de Rome in 1903 in his function as Chef de Secrétariat du Conservatoire (see Fauser, '*La guerre en dentelles*').

[103] Brooks, '*Noble et grande servante de la musique*'.

[104] The Particell has not been found, in spite of my intensive search for over three years. It might appear one day unexpectedly – like Berlioz's allegedly burnt *Messe solennelle*. It is highly unlikely that Nadia Boulanger destroyed any of Lili Boulanger's manuscripts (as she has sometimes been accused of doing), especially *La princesse Maleine*, given that other unfinished material survived. A more probable reason for the loss of several of Lili Boulanger's works can be found in the fact that during the period after Nadia Boulanger's death, when her estate was moved and catalogued, some pieces were allegedly misplaced.

(Requiem) or Berg (the *Lyric Suite* or the Violin Concerto). But in none of these cases does the biographical element explain exclusively the composer's choices or offer a pre-eminent reading of the subject and/or texts – even if in all of them the circumstances of the composer's life represent an essential factor in the interpretation of the work. Moreover, in most of them the autobiographical element remains a private rather than a public programme, and one not intended to overshadow the work's public life. This is precisely the boundary transgressed by contemporary and modern readings of Lili Boulanger as one with *La princesse Maleine*.

The close identification of the literary Maleine with the composer is a fate not uncommon for women creators. Many writers were identified with their heroines – Colette as Claudine is one of the most prominent examples – and Boulanger is not the only musician whose life was understood through a literary figure.[105] In all these cases, the use of diminishing images with regard to creative women – they can easily be contrasted with the potent idealization of Beethoven or Michelangelo as Titan – makes the stories of their lives conform to the traditional narratives of woman's biography. In Boulanger's case, its effect was that we see a *femme fragile* of French *fin-de-siècle* music instead of a potent young composer of the avant-garde, a composer of major modernist works.

City University, London

[105] Another example would be Isabella Andreini, whose 'divine madness' could explain her creative talent to her contemporaries, blending the mad character she played in the *commedia dell'arte* with her person; see Anne MacNeil, 'The Divine Madness of Isabella Andreini', *Journal of the Royal Musical Association*, 120 (1995), 195–215.

Index

Abbate, Carolyn, 6, 13, 44, 223
Adam, Adolphe
   Giselle, 8, 43
   Le Postillon de Longjumeau, 57, 68
Adenis, Eugène, 222
   Faust et Hélène, 301
Adler, Mortimer, 156
Adorno, Theodor W., 108
Agulhon, Maurice, 76
Albèra, Philippe, 113, 116
Alton, Robert, 198
American Federation of Musicians, 199–200
American Guild of Organists, 134
Americanism, xiv, xv, 121–51, 153, 157, 160, 165, 185–86, 190, 200
Anderson, Benedict
   Imagined Communities, 122
André, Naomi, 192
Antheil, George
   Ballet mécanique, 127
Anti-Semitism, 124, 126
Aristotle, 78, 202
   Politics, 76
   See also Drama, Aristotelian principles
Arnold, Billy, 128–29
Asch, Sholom
   The God of Vengeance, 168
Assmann, Aleida, 122
Astruc, Gabriel, xv, 238, 247, 249, 252, 255–56
Auber, Daniel François Esprit, 14, 24, 30, 32
   Fra Diavolo, 165
   Gustave III, 34
   La Muette de Portici, xiii, 34, 35
Auclert, Pauline, 242
Audan, Marguerite, 289
Autobiography
   See Biography
Azevedo, Alexis, 19, 21, 26, 29

Bach, Johann Sebastian, xv, 155, 237–39, 241, 243–47, 249, 252–53, 255–58

   Chromatic Fantasy and Fugue, 246–47
   Italian Concerto, 256
Bach, Leonard
   Die neue Loreley, 219
Bader, Clarisse, 310
Bahr, Hermann, 328
Baker, Josephine, 167
Balakirev, Mily
   Second Overture on Russian Themes, 116
Ballet, xii, xiii, 5, 13–14, 28, 31–53, 130, 192–95
Ballets Russes, 32, 112, 256
Ballets Suédois, 129
Balzac, Honoré de, 31
Barbier, Jules
   Jeanne d'Arc, 74
Barg, Lisa, 195
Barnes, Howard, 190
Barney, Natalie, 123
Bartók, Béla, 156
   The Miraculous Mandarin, 115
Bathori, Jane, 128
Baudelaire, Charles, 7, 20, 29, 111
Bauer, Henry, 62
Bauer, Marion, 137–39
Bay, Howard, 177, 183
Beaujoyeulx, Baltasar de
   Balet comique de la Royne, 33
Beecham, Sir Thomas, 199
Beethoven, Ludwig van, 5, 6, 73, 87–89, 155, 157, 160, 162, 256, 258, 357
   Fidelio, 185
Belafonte, Harry, 164
Belasco, David, 168
Bellaigue, Camille, 86
Bellini, Vincenzo, 24
Benedict V, Pope, 310
Benjamin, Walter, 238
Bennett, Robert Russell, 170, 178, 197–99
Bentley, Eric, 190
Berenson, Edward, 263, 278

Berg, Alban
  Lyric Suite, 342, 357
  Violin Concerto, 342, 357
  Wozzeck, 132
Berger, Richard, 170, 196
Berlin, Irving, 137
  This Is the Army, 190
Berlioz, Hector, 6, 9, 14, 21, 28, 32, 37, 249, 256
  Benvenuto Cellini, 37
  Harold en Italie, 356
  Le Troyens, xiii, 12, 37–40, 115
Bernard, Paul, 19, 20, 22, 24, 28
Bernstein, Leonard, 139
Bertaux, Madame Léon [Hélène], 267
Bertrand, Gustave, 71, 86
Bhabha, Homi K., xvii, 108
Biography, xii, xvi, 318–19, 323, 342, 355–57
Bismarck, Otto von, 66, 79
Bizet, Georges, 10, 11
  Arlesienne Suite, 199
  Carmen, xv, 163–67, 169–70, 178, 181, 184–85, 190–92, 196–99, 203
  La Jolie fille de Perth, 199
  Roma Suite, 194, 199
Blitzstein, Marc, 184
Bloch, Ernest
  Suite for Viola and Piano, 132
Blondel, Maurice, 311
Blues, xiv–xv, 130, 137, 153, 155, 158–62
Boieldieu, François-Adrien
  La Dame blanche, 83
Boito, Arrigo, 320
Bordes, Charles, 84, 238–40, 245–46, 249, 251, 255
Borodin, Alexander, 135
  In the Steppes of Central Asia, 113
Boulanger, Ernest, 290
Boulanger, Georges Ernest, General, 79
Boulanger, Lili, xii, xv, xvi, 109, 117, 123, 262, 300–07, 309–16, 317–57
  Attente, 322
  Clairières dans le ciel, xi, xvi, 109, 322, 354
  Faust et Hélène, xvi
  Pie Jesu, 310, 354
  Pour les funérailles d'un soldat, 312–13
  La Princesse Maleine, xii, xvi, 109, 317–57
  Psalm 24, 313–15
  Psalm 130, 315–16, 324
  Reflets, 322
  Si tout ceci n'est qu'un pauvre rêve, 338–39
  Vieille prière bouddhique, 311, 313, 316, 324, 354
Boulanger, Nadia, xii, xiv, xv, xvi, 121–51, 261–62, 283, 290–302, 305–07, 310–11, 315, 322–23, 325, 327, 353, 355
  La Ville morte, 323
Boulez, Pierre, 109
Bourgault-Ducoudray, Louis-Albert, 76–77, 84
  Esprit de la France, 77
Bourgeat, Emile, 273–74
Bouwens van der Boijen, William, 310
Bradford, Roark
  John Henry, 165
Brahms, Johannes, 73, 89
  Ein deutsches Requiem, 356
Brenet, Michel [Marie Bobillier], 259
Brentano, Clemens, 220
  Lorelei, 214–15, 221, 228
Bréval, Lucienne, 247, 254
Bréville, Pierre de, 322
Broodthaer, Marcel
  Autour de la Lorelei, 229
Brooks, Jeanice, 356
Brubaker, Rogers, 122, 125
Bruch, Max
  Die Loreley, 216–17
Bruneau, Alfred
  Messidor, 36
Brussel, Robert, 252–53, 255
Bryant, Glenn, 177
Buell, Lawrence, 160
Bumbry, Grace, 203
Burke, Peter, 105
Burke-Wadsworth Draft Bill, 181
Burley, Dan, 193, 194, 201
Burne-Jones, Edward, 253
Byrd, William
  La volta, 249

Caillaux, Henriette, 278
Callias, Horace de, 240
Calloway, Cab, 170, 172, 200
Carmen: a Hip Hopera, 203
Caron, Rose, 254
Carter, Tim, xvii
Casella, Alfredo, 134, 242
Casulana, Maddalena, 261
Catalani, Alfredo
  Loreley, 224
Catholicism, xvi, 73, 109, 309–16
Catullus, 85

Cavalieri, Lina, 247
Cavalli, Francesco
    Ercole amante, 33
Chadeuil, Gustave, 20, 27
Chaliapin, Feodor, 256
Challemel-Lacour, Paul, 19, 21
Cham [Amédée de Noé], 10–11, 15
Chambonnières, Jacques Champion de, 241, 245, 249
Chamillac, 63
Chaminade, Cécile, 63, 242
Champfleury, Jules, 7, 10, 29
Chanteurs de Saint-Gervais, 245, 251
Chaplin, Charlie, 130
Chapman, John, 196, 197, 202
Charles, Ray, 130
Chaumié, Joseph, 264, 269–70, 274, 277, 288
Chausson, Ernest
    Poème de l'amour et de la mer, 87
Chávez, Carlos, 140, 159
    Sinfonía india, 115
Chebroux, Ernest, 79
Cherubini, Luigi, 8
Chizzola, Charles, 56
Chopin, Frédéric, 73, 243–44, 249, 257
Choron, Alexandre-Etienne, 84
Citron, Marcia, 271
Clark, Robert L. A., 164
Claudel, Paul, 322, 324
    La Jeune fille Violaine, 322
Clemenceau, Georges, 124
Clément, Catherine, 336
Clérambault, Louis-Nicolas, 245
Cleveland, Grover, 217–18
Clurman, Harold, 121, 125–26, 130–31
Cole, Cozy, 191–92, 194–95, 199–200
Colette, Sidonie-Gabrielle, 357
Collin, Laure
    Histoire abrégée de la musique et des musiciens, 89
Collingwood, Robin George, 106
Colonne, Eugénie [Madame], 254
Combarieu, Jules, 77
Combes, Emile, 264, 269
Comettant, Oscar, 18–19, 21, 23, 25–26
Comité franco-américain du Conservatoire de Paris, 123, 132, 324
Comte, Auguste, 97
Connelly, Marc
    The Green Pastures, 186
Conrad, Joseph, xvii

Conservatoire Américain de Fontainebleau, 124
Cooper, Frederick, 122, 125
Copland, Aaron, xii, xiv, 121–51, 157
    Billy the Kid, 177
    El salón México, 140
    Grogh, 138
    Music for the Theatre, 126
    Rodeo, 115
Cosmopolitanism, 7, 72, 86, 238, 243, 252
Coulanges, Fustel de, 72
Couperin, François, 241, 245, 251
    Carillon de Cythère, 251
    Les Folies françaises, 248
Couperin, Louis, 245
Cousin, Victor, 82, 87
    Du vrai, du beau et du bien, 19
Cowell, Henry
    Antinomies, 115
    Piano Concerto, 115
Crawford, Cheryl, 165–66, 169, 176, 182
Crist, Elizabeth, 140–41
Criticism, xiii, 3–30
Cultural Transfer, xii, xvii–xviii, 13, 81, 89, 122–23, 156, 157–58, 164–66, 184, 190–91, 195–96, 198, 203

Dafora, Asadata, 175
Dahlhaus, Carl, 44, 103
Dalayrac, Nicolas
    Nina, 38
Dallier, Henri Edouard, 306
Damrosch, Walter, 124
Dance
    See Ballet
Dandridge, Dorothy, 164
D'Annunzio, Gabriele, 310, 323
Danuser, Hermann, 153, 155
    Die Musik des 20. Jahrhunderts, 160
David, Félicien, 28
Dawson, Mary Cardwell, 202
Debussy, Claude, 32, 88–89, 116, 320–21, 337
    Pelléas et Mélisande, 321, 353
    Prélude à l'Après-midi d'un faune, 110, 112
    Sirènes, 214
Dégas, Edgar, 31
Delacroix, Eugène, 35
Delcourt, Marguerite, 242, 249–51, 257, 259
Delarrancea, Cella, 355
Delmas, Marc, 296
Delsart, Jules, 241
Derrida, Jacques, 103

Deschamps, Emile
   Les Huguenots, 26
Despléchin, Edouard, 12
Desprez, Father Arthur, 310
Destouches, André Cardinal, 37
Diaghilev, Sergei, 256
Dickstein, Samuel
   'Alien Actors' Bill, 185
Diémer, Louis, 240–42, 245–46, 251, 254, 258
Dietsch, Pierre-Louis, 14
   Le Vaisseau fantôme, ou Le maudit des mers, 8
Donizetti, Gaetano, 13, 17, 24
   L'Ange de Nisida, 8
Dornford-May, Mark, 203
Dostoyevsky, Fyodor, 136
Doucet, Clément, 128
Doumergue, Gaston, 295
Downes, Olin, 185, 188, 192
Drama, Aristotelian principles, 23–24, 27, 33
Dreyfus Affair, 72
Du Bois, Raoul Pene, 203
Dubois, Théodore, 273–77, 284, 290
Du Bois, W. E. B., 173, 202
Duchamp, Marcel, 125–26, 127
Dukas, Paul, 321
   Ariane et Barbe-Bleue, 321
Duke, Vernon
   Cabin in the Sky, 165, 193, 201
Dumas, Alexandre, 202
Du Mont, Henry, 245
Dunbar, Laurence, 155
Duncan, Todd, 174
Dunham, Katherine, 171, 175
   Tropical Review, 165
Dupanloup, Monseigneur Félix, 310
Duparc, Henri, 86
Dvořák, Antonín, 135, 140
   Rusalka, 214
Dyck, Vladimir, 243

Eagle-Eye Cherry
   When Mermaids Cry, 229
Ecorcheville, Jules, 257
Eichendorff, Joseph Freiherr von, 224
Elie, Rudolph, 190
Ellington, Duke, 167, 169, 172, 174
   Black, Brown, and Beige, 195
Ellis, Katharine, xiii, xvii, 7, 241, 271
Elwell, G. Herbert, 139
Enesco, Georges, 243
Escudier, Léon, 9

Espagne, Michel, xvii, 89
Espiard, François Ignace d'
   Essais sur le génie et le caractère des nations, 81
Ethnomusicology, xii, xviii
Everist, Mark, xiii
Expert, Henry
   Les Maîtres musiciens de la Renaissance française, 84–85
Exposition Universelle (1889), xiii, 240

Fairchild, Blair, 123
Falla, Manuel de, 127
   Il retablo de maese Pedro, 115
Farrenc, Aristide
   Le Trésor des pianistes, 84
Farrenc, Louise, 63
Fauchery [Henry de Gramont], 65
Fauré, Gabriel, 84, 133, 261, 272, 278, 289–90, 297, 300, 305, 310–11
Favart, Charles-Simon
   Le Procès des ariettes et des vaudevilles, 55
Federal Theatre Project, 185, 187
   Swing Mikado, 165, 197
Femme fatale, 214, 226, 229, 322
Femme fragile, xvi, 109, 253, 302, 304, 309, 317, 322–23, 337, 355, 357
Femme nouvelle
   See New Woman
Ferry, Jules, 72
Fétis, François-Joseph, xiv, 8, 19, 65–66, 87
Février, Henry
   Monna Vanna, 321
Filliaux-Tiger, Louise, 275
Finkielkraut, Alain, 72
Fiorentino, Pier Angelo, 15, 19–20, 22, 25, 29
Flament, Edouard, 296–97
Fleury, Charles, 239
Fleury, Hélène, xvi, 261–62, 273, 281–90, 297–98, 300–02, 305–07
   Espérance, 283
Fordin, Hugh, 170, 174
Folk drama, 186–88, 190
Folk music and song, xiv, 69, 73, 79–84, 85, 116, 131, 135, 137, 139, 154, 155, 159
Forte, Allen, 116
Foucault, Michel, 117
   Archéologie du savoir, 107–08
France, Anatole, 40–41
Franck, César, 86, 88–89, 245

Franck-Marie [Franco Maria Pedorlini], 19–20, 23, 25, 27
Franco-Prussian War, xii, xiv, 66, 68, 71–72, 74–76, 78, 86–87, 89, 220, 263, 349
François I, King of France, 74, 81
Franzell, Carlotta, 174, 200
Freidenberg, Olga, 156
Friedman, Charles, 177, 203
Friese, Heidrun, 122
Fuchs, Henriette, 259, 276
Fukuyama, Francis, 108
Fulcher, Jane, 6

Gagliano, Marco da, 32
Gahan, Jerry, 190
Gail, Sophie, 86
Gailhard, André, 296–97
Gallet, Louis, 41
Gallois, Victor, 286
Gallon, Jean, 300
Garland, Robert, 188–89
Gasperini, Auguste de, 17, 29
Gatayes, Léon, 15
Gaubert, Philippe, 286
Gédalge, André, 129
Geib, Karl, 220
Genevoix, Maurice
    Lorelei, 215–16
Gentien, Paul, 324, 336
Gentlemen Prefer Blondes, 213, 229–30
Geoffroy, Julien-Louis, 80
Géricault, Jean-Louis André Théodore, 35
Gershwin, George, 198, 203
    Pardon My English, 217–20
    Porgy and Bess, 163–66, 169–71, 176, 178, 182, 188
    Rhapsody in Blue, 139
Gershwin, Ira, 169, 217
Giacomelli, Adolphe, 20
Gide, André, 121, 133, 136
Gilbert, Henry F., 139
Gilbert, William S., 165,
    The Mikado, 197
Gilroy, Paul, 165
Gjerdingen, Catherine, xvii
Glass, Philip, 109
Gluck, Christoph Willibald Ritter von, 10, 55
Goldberg, Louise, xvii
Gonet, Louise, 310
Gordon, Lucy
    Song of the Lorelei, 229

Gordon, Max, 171, 175
Gounod, Charles, 3, 6, 28, 292–93
    Jeanne d'Arc, 74–76
    La Reine de Saba, 12, 27, 36
Gramont, Henry de
    See Fauchery
Grandval, Marie Clémence Vicomtesse de, 63, 282
Green, Paul
    In Abraham's Bosom, 169
Grétry, André Ernest Modeste, 10, 240
Grétry, Lucile, 86
Grévy, Jules, 72
Grillet, Laurent, 241
Grimm, Jacob and Wilhelm
    Kinder- und Hausmärchen, 329
Grumbach, Marthe, 289, 291
Grün, Jules-Alexandre, 305
Gubar, Susan, 173
Gubbay, Raymond, 204
Guilbert, Yvette, 250–51, 259
Guilmant, Alexandre, 241
Guinon, Albert, 56, 62
Guiraud, Ernest, 290

Hába, Alois, 138
Hahn, Reynaldo, 251
Halévy, Fromental, 8, 14, 24, 30, 43
    La Juive, 26, 36
    Le Reine de Chypre, 26
Halévy, Ludovic, 171
Halle, Adam de la
    Jeu de Robin et de Marion, 68, 83
Hammerstein, Bill, 176, 178, 180, 183, 191
Hammerstein, Dorothy, 182
Hammerstein, Oscar, II
    Buddy on the Nightshift, 178
    Carmen Jones, xii, xv, 163–210
    Oklahoma!, 166, 174, 176–77, 182, 186, 189–90, 197, 198
    Show Boat, 169–70, 173–74, 178, 182, 189
    The Last Time I Saw Paris, 196
Hammond, John, Jr., 177
Handel, George Frideric, 241
    Grobschmiedvariationen, 248
Handy, William C., 154
    St. Louis Blues, 155–56
Hanson, Howard, 154–55
Harlem Renaissance, 157–58, 161–62, 192
Hart, Moss
    Winged Victory, 190
Hartmann, Paul and Gracie, 198

Hartog, François, 110
Hauptmann, Gerhart, 186
Hawkins, June, 200
Haydn, Joseph, 240, 245
Hayward, Dorothy and DuBose
   Porgy, 169
Heartz, Daniel, 79
Hegel, Georg Friedrich Wilhelm, 105–08
Heilbrun, Carolyn, 304
Heine, Heinrich, 8, 220
   Lorelei, 215, 220, 228
Herendon, Frederick
   A Royal Exchange, 217
Herodotus, 110
Hérold, Ferdinand
   Le Pré aux Clercs, 71
Heugel, Henri, 74
Heugel, Jacques Léopold, 20–21, 24, 28–29
Heuvelmans, Lucienne, 288, 301
Hillemacher, Paul and Lucien, 222–24
Hiller, Ferdinand, 221–24
Historiography, xiv, xvi–xvii, 32, 46–47, 73, 87–90, 103–08, 164, 309
Hitler, Adolf, 181
Hoffmann, Ernst Theodor Amadeus
   Undine, 214
Hofmannsthal, Hugo von, 320
Holiday, Billy, 189
Holland, Charles, 174
Hollywood Anti-Nazi League, 173
Holmès, Augusta, 63, 242, 351, 353
   La Montagne noire, 36–37
Holocaust, 215
Holt, Nora, 189, 192–94, 200
Homer
   Odyssey, 214
Homolle, Théophile, 310
Honegger, Arthur, 109, 309
   Le Roi David, 132
Hoover, Herbert, 157
Horace, 85
Hugo, Victor
   Hernani, 4
Huret, Jean-Etienne, 321
Huret, Jules, 328
Hurston, Zora Neale, 172
Hutchins, Robert, 156

Iggers, Georg, 106
Illica, Luigi, 320
Indy, Vincent d', 84, 87–89, 134, 246, 257, 321
   Cours de composition musicale, 249
International Composers' Guild, 154, 160
International Society for Contemporary Music, 136
Isambert, Maria, 268–69
Ives, Charles, 116, 162

Jackson, Jeffrey H., 127
Jammes, Francis, 311, 322
Jarry, Alfred
   Ubu Roi, 56
Jazz, xiv, 121, 123, 127–32, 134–41, 199–200
Jemain, Jules, 242
Jockey Club, 5, 6, 28, 31
Johnson, Hall, 170, 174
   Run, Little Chillun, 165, 193
Jones, Gavin, 186
Jouvin, Benoît, 17, 19–21, 25, 28
Joyce, James, 127

Karamu Dancers, 193, 195
Karpelès, Suzanne, 310, 312
Kelly, Jude, 204
Kern, Jerome, 198
   Show Boat, 169–70, 173–74, 178, 182, 189
   The Last Time I Saw Paris, 196
Kleeberg, Clothilde de, 242, 258
Knopf, Alfred, 127
Koechlin, Charles, 130, 134
Koselleck, Reinhart, 107
   Vergangene Zukunft, 106
Koussevitzky, Serge, 126–27
Kramer, Lawrence, 44, 107
Kraus, Karl, 186

Labarre, Théodore
   Graziosa, 14
Labille, Adelaide, 266
La Borde, Jean-Benjamin de
   Essai sur la musique ancienne et moderne, 87
Lalo, Pierre, 84
Lamoureux, Charles, 65–67
Landowska, Wanda, xii, xv, 237–59
Lapommeraye, Pierre de, 130
Laroumet, Louis, 270
Lavignac, Albert
   La Musique et les musiciens français, 85
Lavoix, Henri, 88
   La Musique française, 89
Le Boucher, Maurice, 291
Lebrun, Elisabeth Vigée, 266

Lederman, Minna, 121
Lee, Everett, 200
Lefèvre, Georges, 69
Lefort, Jules, 9
Lelong, Elodie, 242, 247, 253
Lenepveu, Charles, 289–90, 296–97, 300–01
Lerberghe, Charles van, 329
Leroy, Léon, 17, 20, 29
Lescaze, Mary, 140
Lesêtre, Henri, 311, 315
Le Sueur, Jean-François, 37
Lévi-Strauss, Claude, 103
Lew, Henri, xv, 238–39, 247, 252, 254–55, 259
Ligeti, György, 109
Liszt, Franz, 249
Literaturnoe Nasledstvo, 156
Literaturoper, 321, 338
Littau, Joseph, 200
Lloyd, Margaret, 194
Lobrot, Jean, 129
Locke, Alain, 159
Loisy, Alfred, 311
Lomax, John, 156
Loos, Anita
    Gentlemen Prefer Blondes, 214
Lorbac, Charles de, 14
Loreley, xv, 213–35
Loring, Eugene, 177, 193–95
Louis XIV, King of France, 33–34
Louis-Philippe, King of France, 82
Ludwig II, King of Bavaria, 3, 6
Lully, Jean-Baptiste, 33, 37, 55, 251, 257
Luther, Martin, 77
Lyotard, Jean-François, 103, 106

MacArthur, Charles
    Lulu Belle, 167–69
Macé-Montrouge, Marguerite, 56
Madeleine, Stéphen de la, 19, 21, 26, 27
Maehder, Jürgen, 320
Maeterlinck, Maurice, xvi, 253, 317–57
    Ariane et Barbe-Bleue, 321
    Monna Vanna, 321
    Pelléas et Mélisande, 321
    La Princesse Maleine, 317–57
    Sœur Béatrice, 321
    Le Trésor des humbles, 322, 333
Mahler, Gustav, 116
Maistre, Joseph de, 72
Malleville, Charlotte de, 239, 259
Maney, Richard, 177

Manning, Susan, 193
Marie-Antoinette, Queen of France, 240, 253
Marnold, Jean, 253
Marot, Clément, 85
Marrow, Macklin, 180
Martial, 85
Martin, Joséphine, 239, 259
Martin, Linton, 197
Masculinity, xiv, 34, 66, 71, 73–74, 79, 84, 86, 88, 90, 109, 190, 226–27, 256, 266
Mason, Evelyn, 168
Massenet, Jules, 6, 32, 37, 40, 57, 84, 275, 278, 290, 292, 300, 320
    Le Cid, 34
    Esclarmonde, 35, 45, 224
    Hérodiade, 36, 41–42
    Manon, 356
    Thaïs, xiii, 37, 40–43, 45–46, 275
Maswanganyi, Tsakane Valentine, 204
Mattheson, Johann, 248
Matzerath, Carl
    Irrungen der Liebe, 220
Mauclair, Camille, 355
Mauri, Rosita, 40
Mazellier, Jules, 296–97, 300
McClary, Susan, 107
    Feminine Endings, 318
Meeropol, Abel
    Strange Fruit, 189
Méhul, Etienne Nicolas, 6
    Chant du départ, 77
Meilhac, Henri, 171
Mellot-Joubert, Charlotte, 291
Mercier, Ernest, 124
Méreaux, Amédée, 239
Mérimée, Prosper, 181
Mermet, Auguste
    Jeanne d'Arc, 76
Merson, Luc Olivier, 263–65
Messiaen, Olivier, 109, 311
    Trois petites liturgies de la présence divine, 315
Metternich, Pauline von, 11
Métra, Olivier
    Quadrille des lanciers, 10, 56
Meyerbeer, Giacomo, 3, 8, 17, 24, 30, 43
    Les Huguenots, 26–27
    Robert le diable, 34–36, 40, 43, 223
Meyer-Kalkus, Reinhart, 227
Michelangelo [di Lodovico Buonarroti Simoni], 357

Michelet, Jules, 74
Milhaud, Darius, 109, 121, 127–28, 130, 135, 309, 322, 324
   Le Bœuf sur le toit, 128
   La Création du monde, 127, 129–30, 139, 316
   Sonata for flute, oboe, clarinet, and piano (op. 47), 128
Miller, Leta, 197
Mirbach, Emil Freiherr von, 220
Mirbeau, Octave, 321, 329
Mistral, Frédéric, 84
Modernism, xiv, 32, 46, 90, 103, 106, 108–17, 128, 136–39, 140–41, 153–54, 157–59, 162, 164, 170, 175, 182, 186–88, 190–91, 193, 195, 311–12, 315–16, 321, 357
Monnais, Edouard [Wilhelm], 18, 21, 25, 26
Monroe, Marilyn, 213–15
Monteverdi, Claudio, 133
   Orfeo, 225, 246
Montrouge [Louis Hesnard], 56
Morelli, Antonio, 12
Morley, Thomas, 249
Moseler, Günter, 161
Most, Andrea, 173
Mozart, Wolfgang Amadeus, 10, 240, 244–45, 257, 318
   Der Schauspieldirektor, 55
   Don Giovanni, 13
   Piano Concerto in E-flat Major (K. 271), 243, 256
Müller von Königswinter, Wolfgang, 220–21
   Rheinfahrt, 221
Murphy, Gerald, 130–31
Music of the Future, 10–11, 14–15, 21, 40, 56
Musicology, xiv, xvi–xviii
Musset, Alfred de
   Pour les funérailles d'un soldat, 312–13
Mussorgsky, Modest, 135

Nadaud, Gustave
   La Française, 74
Napoléon III, Emperor of France, 6, 11
National Negro Opera Company, 202
National Urban League, 174, 178
Nattiez, Jean-Jacques, 103–04
Nénot, Henri, 270
Nerval, Gérard de
   Chansons et légendes du Valois, 79
   Loreley, souvenirs d'Allemagne, 215

New Woman, 63–64, 269, 280, 283, 297–98, 302, 306, 335
Nicolodi, Fiamma, 84
Niemann, Albert, 12
Nietzsche, Friedrich, 73, 104, 191–92, 228
Nijinsky, Vaslav, 112
Nin, Joaquín, 241–42
Nisard, Charles, 79
Noé, Amédée de
   See Cham
Norton, Barbara, xvii
Nourrit, Adolphe, 13
Nuitter, Charles, 56, 62, 67

Offenbach, Jacques
   Le Carnaval des revues, 10, 15, 56
Office of War Information, 179, 180
Opera, 163, 184–85, 188, 190, 202, 320–21
   Grand opéra, xii, xiii, 8, 17, 23–24, 26, 28, 30, 31–53, 86
   Opéra comique, xiv, 57, 64, 68–69, 71, 83, 84, 86
Orpheus, 221, 225
Ortigue, Joseph d', 19, 21, 23, 29
Ovid, 85

Paderewski, Ignacy Jan, 244
Paris, Gaston, 82
   Chansons du XVe siècle, 80
Parody, 10, 55–56, 65
Patorni-Casadesus, Régina, 242
Pech, Raymond, 286
Péladin, Joséphin, 73
Perlis, Vivian, 128
Persuis, Louis-Luc
   Nina, 38
Petipa, Lucien, 12
Pfeiffer, Georges, 240
Pfitzner, Hans, 216
Philetas of Kos, 108
Piccinni, Niccolò, 55
Pierné, Paul, 286
Piré, Miki, 309
Pius X, Pope, 311
Planard, Eugène de
   Le Pré aux Clercs, 71
Planchet, Dominique Charles, 306
Plato, 78, 226
   Republic, 76
Pléïade, 83, 85
Poe, Edgar Allen, 329

Pogues, The
    Lorelei, 229
Polignac, Armande de, 241, 282
Polignac, Princesse de
    See Singer, Winnaretta, Princesse de
        Polignac
Poole, Mary Ellen, 79
Porter, Cecilia Hopkins, 220
Porter, Cole, 198
    Night and Day, 192
    Within the Quota, 129–31
Pougin, Arthur, 16, 19, 21, 29, 290
Poulenc, Francis, 309
Pound, Ezra, 127
Prestat, Marie, 241
Prix de Rome, xvi, 242, 261–307, 309, 320, 323, 335, 356
Prud'homme, Sully [René François Armand]
    L'Hirondelle, 292
Puccini, Giacomo, 184, 320
    Tosca, 338
Pugno, Raoul, 291

Quittard, Henri, 257

Rachmaninov, Sergei, 157
Racine, Jean, 322
Rahn, Muriel, 174
Rameau, Jean-Philippe, 37, 240–41, 245, 251, 257
Ranke, Leopold von, 104–07, 109–10, 117
    Geschichten der romanischen und germanischen Völker von 1494 bis 1514, 104–05
Rathenau, Walther, 136
Ravel, Maurice, 32, 135, 282, 289, 295, 306
    A la manière de Borodine, 113
Reed, Napoleon, 174
Reeser, Eduard, 324, 327
Reich, Nancy, 271
Renan, Ernest, 72, 76, 85
Reyer, Ernest, 10
    La Statue, 27–28
    Sigurd, 65
Richelieu, Cardinal [Armand Jean du Plessis], 264
Ricordi (publishing house), 320, 356
Ricordi, Tito, 323–26, 330, 333, 335, 342
Rimsky-Korsakov, Nikolai, 135
Risler, Edouard, 258
Rivueltas, Silvestre, 159
Robeson, Paul, 165, 174
Rodin, Auguste, 254

Roger, Victor
    Oscarine, xii, xiii, xiv, 55–70
Romberg, Siegmund, 198
Rondenay, Marcelle Andrée, 269, 281
Ropartz, Guy
    Quatre poèmes d'après l'"Intermezzo" d'Henri Heine, 87
Rose, Billy, 176–77, 182, 194, 196, 199–200, 203
Rosenstiel, Léonie, 292, 311, 322, 355
Rossini, Gioacchino, 6–7, 17–18, 30, 184
    Il barbiere di Siviglia, 185
    Guillaume Tell, 27, 34, 56
Rothschild, Mathilde de, 282
Roujon, Henri, 269–70, 273–75, 284, 296
Rousseau, Charles, 63
Rousseau, Jean-Jacques, 79–80, 85, 88
Roussel, Albert, 128
Rowden, Clair, 46
Royer, Alphonse, 5, 12–13
Rozet, Fanny, 269, 281
Rumbold, Ian, xvii
Russell, Jane, 213
Russell, Sylvester, 168

Said, Edward, xvii, 107
Saint-Etienne, Sylvain, 22
Saint-Georges, Jules-Henri Vernoy de
    Le Reine de Chypre, 26
Saint-Saëns, Camille, 37, 85–87, 240–41, 251, 278, 292–93, 295, 301, 351, 353
    La Fiancée du timbalier, 87
    Henry VIII, 34, 41
    Phryné, 86
Saint-Valry, Gaston de, 16, 22, 24, 30
Saint-Victor, Paul de, 20
Sallé, Marie, 33
Sand, George [Amantine-Lucile-Aurore Dupin], 267
Sanderson, Sibyl, 41
Sass, Marie, 12
Satie, Erik, 32, 128, 322
Saurat, Raymond, 286
Saxon, Luther, 177, 202
Sayn-Wittgenstein, Caroline Princess, 39
Schaeffner, André, 128
Schiller, Friedrich, 320
Schiller, Max, 250
Schloezer, Boris de, 127
Schloss, Edwin H., 203
Schmitt, Florent, 126
    Psalm 47, 314–15

Schneider, Louis, 84
Schoenberg, Arnold, 127
   Harmonielehre, 132
   Pierrot lunaire, 132
Schubert, Franz, 249, 257
   Die Winterreise, 356
Schumann, Robert, 6, 89
   Frauenliebe und -leben, 335
   Waldesgespräch, 224–25
Schumann-Heink, Ernestine, 254
Schuré, Edouard, 84
Schwartz, Manuela, 7
Schwerké, Irving, 158–60
Scott, George, 175
Scott, Sir Walter, 105
Scribe, Eugène, 320
   Les Huguenots, 26
   La Juive, 26
Scudo, Paul, 9, 19–21, 23, 29
Segregation, xiv, xv, 172–75, 178, 181–82, 189
Seldes, Gilbert, 129
Selva, Blanche, xv, 241–42, 246–47, 255–57, 259
Sept-Fontaines, Francis, 29
Serpette, Gaston
   Jeanne d'Arc, 74–75
Servières, Georges, 6
Sessions, Roger, 139
Shaffer, Peter
   Amadeus, 318
Shakespeare, William, 202, 322, 329
   Macbeth (FTP production), 165, 202
   Othello (Theatre Guild production), 174
Shaw, Artie, 154
Shaw, Elizabeth A., 171
Shaw, Robert, 203
Sheldon, Edward
   Lulu Belle, 167–69
Short, Hassard, 177, 183, 203
Siegmeister, Elie, 157
Siegmey
   Die neue Loreley, 219–20
Sieyès, Emmanuel-Joseph [Abbé], 72
Silcher, Friedrich, 219
   Lorelei, 215, 226, 229
Singer, Winnaretta, Princesse de Polignac, 123, 129, 256–57
Sloper, L.A., 192
Smetana, Bedřich
   Ma Vlást, 116
Smith, Marian, 34, 43, 45
Smith, Melville, 132

Smith, Muriel, 177, 200–02
Smith, Warren Storey, 190–91, 202
Société des Instruments Anciens, 241, 250–51, 259
Société Musicale Indépendante, 126
Solie, Ruth A., 335, 355
Sophocles, 322
Soubies, Albert, 88–89
Soullier, Charles, 34
Spalding, Albert, 323, 355
Spontini, Gaspare, 8
Spycket, Jérôme, 132
Staël, Germaine de
   De l'Allemagne, 72
Stage Door Canteen, 179
Stein, Gertrude, 121
   Four Saints in Three Acts, 164, 193
Stendhal [Marie-Henri Beyle], 89
   Vie de Rossini, 80
Stereotypes, xiii, xiv, 123, 126, 131, 140–41, 172, 187
Still, William Grant
   Africa, 192
   Afro-American Symphony, xii, xiv–xv, 153–62
Stokowski, Leopold, 154
Strauss, Johann, II
   Rosalinda (*Die Fledermaus*), 165–66
Strauss, Richard, 320
   Salome, 256
Stravinsky, Igor, 10, 32, 109, 127, 129, 135–36
   Petrushka, 136
   Le Rossignol, 315
   Le Sacre du printemps, 110–16, 129, 136, 315, 353
   Symphonie des psaumes, 316
Sullivan, Sir Arthur
   The Mikado, 197
Symphony, xv, 25–26, 87, 153–62

Tacitus, 82
   Annals, 81
Taglioni, Marie, 34
Tagore, Rabindranath, 310
Taine, Hippolyte, 80
Talmadge, Nora, 130
Taruskin, Richard, 115–16
Tarzan, 192
Taylor, Deems, 184, 196
Tchaikovsky, Pytor Ilyich, 197
Tedesco, Fortunata, 12

Terrasse, Claude
  Ubu Roi, 56
The Thrill of Brazil, 194
Theosophy, 311
Thiéry, Henri
  Il pleut, il pleut, bergère, 10, 56
Thomas, Ambroise, 57, 292–93
  Hamlet, 35
  Mignon, 83
Thomé, Francis, 241
Thomson, Virgil, 126–27, 135, 139, 184, 196
  Four Saints in Three Acts, 164, 193
  Symphony on a Hymn Tune, 162
Thuillier-Leloir, Madame, 56
Tibbett, Lawrence, 180
Tiersot, Julien, 88
  Histoire de la chanson populaire, 69, 79, 80–84
Todd, Mike
  The Hot Mikado, 197
Tolstoy, Leo, 134, 238, 254, 322
Tournemire, Charles, 315
Tournier, Marcel, 296, 300
Toutain, Jules, 273–77, 284
Toutain, Juliette, xvi, 242, 262, 269, 271–85, 298, 305–07, 310
Townsend, Robert, 203
Transfer culturel
  See Cultural Transfer
Translatio studii, 81, 85, 88
Treitler, Leo, 107
Turbow, Gerald, 6, 11
Tuskegee Airmen [99th Pursuit Squadron], 181

U-Carmen e-Kayelitsha, 203
Ugalde, Delphine, 56

Vale, Michael, 204
Varèse, Edgard, 154, 159
Verdi, Giuseppe, 17, 24, 184, 320
  Aida, 203
  Don Carlos, 14
  I Lombardi alla prima crociata [Jérusalem], 12–13
  Il trovatore, 13
  Les Vêpres siciliennes, 15
Verhaeren, Emile, 310
Véron, Louis, 33
Viardot, Pauline, 74
Vierne, Louis, 312

Vigoureux, Elise
  Manuel d'histoire générale de la musique à l'usage des classes de solfège, 89
Viñes, Ricardo, 242, 251, 258
Viollet-le-Duc, Eugène, 82
Virgil, 85
Vogt, Gustave, 38
Voltaire [François-Marie Arouet], 16
Vuillermoz, Emile, 261–62, 302

Waefelghem, Louis van, 241
Wagner, Richard, 36, 73, 76, 79, 82, 84, 88–89, 184, 192, 320
  Das Liebesverbot, 8
  Das Rheingold, 226–29
  Der fliegende Holländer, 8, 9, 223
  Der Ring des Nibelungen, 226
  Lohengrin, 9, 66
  Tannhäuser (Paris 1861), xii, xiii, 3–30, 31, 33, 56, 66
  Tannhäuser (opera), 223, 225
  Tristan und Isolde, 8–9, 111–13, 337, 341
  Die Walküre, 86, 219
  Theoretical writings, 8, 15, 19, 25–28, 30, 66–67, 83, 226–27
Wagnerism, xii, xiii, xiv, 40–43, 55–70, 83, 321, 341
Warren, Whitney, 123
Waxman, Abraham P., 163
Weber, Carl Maria von, 10, 13
  Der Freischütz, 35, 56, 228
  Euryanthe, 190
Weckerlin, Jean-Baptiste, 80, 82, 84
  La Chanson populaire, 69, 79
Weill, Kurt
  Buddy on the Nightshift, 178
  One Touch of Venus, 177
Weissmuller, Johnny, 192
Werner, Michael, xvii, 89
White, Walter, 202
Whiteman, Paul, 154
Whitney, Mrs. Cornelius Vanderbilt [Eleanor Searle], 170
Widdemer, Margaret, 157
Widor, Charles-Marie, 241, 273, 282–83, 288–91, 297, 300, 312
Wiéner, Jean, 128–29
  Concerto franco-américain, 129
Wilhelm
  See Monnais, Edouard
Wolff, Albert (music journalist), 17, 25

Wolff, Albert (composer and conductor)
    Sœur Béatrice, 321
Women musicians, xv, 55–70, 86, 237–59, 261–307, 351, 353
World War I, 123–24, 220, 313, 316, 324–25, 336
World War II, xv, 90, 163–64, 175, 178–85, 188, 190–91, 195, 202–04, 220
World's Fair
    Chicago (1893), 173
    See also Exposition Universelle

Wright, Lesley, 281
Wright, Richard, 187
Writers' War Board, 179
Wuiet, Caroline, 86

Yolanda and the Thief, 194

Zola, Emile, 31, 36
Zuck, Barbara, 133
Zukunftsmusik
    See Music of the Future